And Justice for All

Philosophy and Society

General Editor
MARSHALL COHEN

Also in this series:

RIGHTS
Theodore M. Benditt

ETHICS IN THE WORLD OF BUSINESS
David Braybrooke

MARX AND JUSTICE: The Radical Critique of
  Liberalism
Allen E. Buchanan

LUKÁCS, MARX AND THE SOURCES OF
  CRITICAL THEORY
Andrew Feenberg

THE REVERSE DISCRIMINATION
  CONTROVERSY
A Moral and Legal Analysis
Robert K. Fullinwider

THE MORAL FOUNDATIONS OF
  PROFESSIONAL ETHICS
Alan H. Goldman

THE LIBERTARIAN READER
Tibor R. Machan (ed.)

READING NOZICK
Jeffrey Paul (ed.)

EVOLUTIONARY EXPLANATION IN THE
  SOCIAL SCIENCES
An Emerging Paradigm
Philippe Van Parijs

And Justice for All

NEW INTRODUCTORY ESSAYS IN ETHICS AND PUBLIC POLICY

edited by
Tom Regan
and
Donald VanDeVeer

ROWMAN & ALLANHELD
Totowa, New Jersey

For
Bryan and Karen Regan
and
Evelyn VanDeVeer

Copyright © 1982 by Rowman and Littlefield

First published in the United States 1982 by
Rowman and Littlefield, 81 Adams Drive, Totowa, New Jersey 07512.

Reprinted 1983 by Rowman & Allanheld

Library of Congress Cataloging in Publication Data
Main entry under title:

And justice for all.

  (Philosophy and society)
  Bibliography: p.
  Includes index.
  Contents: Paternalism and restrictions on liberty/
Donald VanDeVeer—Homosexuality/Joseph Margolis—
Reverse discrimination/Louis I. Katzner—[etc.]
  1. Social ethics—Addresses, essays, lectures.
2. Science and ethics—Addresses, essays, lectures.
3. Social justice—Addresses, essays, lectures.
4. Decision-making (Ethics)—Addresses, essays,
lectures. 5. Social policy—Addresses, essays,
lectures. I. Regan, Tom. II. VanDeVeer, Donald,
1939-   . III. Series.
HM216.A447 1982   1970   81-23446
ISBN 0-8476-7059-7   AACR2
ISBN 0-8476-7060-0 (pbk.)

10 9 8 7 6 5 4 3 2

Printed in the United States of America

Contents

Preface vii

Introduction 1

I   Paternalism and Restrictions on Liberty,
Donald VanDeVeer 17

II   Homosexuality, *Joseph Margolis* 42

III   Reverse Discrimination, *Louis I. Katzner* 64

IV   Genetic Engineering: How Should Science Be
Controlled?, *Stephen P. Stich* 86

V   Nuclear Power—Some Ethical and Social
Dimensions, *Richard and Val Routley* 116

VI   Future Generations, *Mary Anne Warren* 139

VII   On the Ethics of the Use of Animals in Science,
Dale Jamieson and Tom Regan 169

VIII   Individual Rights, *Lawrence C. Becker* 197

IX   Utilitarianism, *Dan W. Brock* 217

X   Justice and Equality, *David A. J. Richards* 241

XI   Capitalism, Socialism and Justice,
Kai Nielsen 264

XII   International Human Rights,
Hugo Adam Bedau 287

About the Authors 309

Preface

Whether or not we personally choose to address them, important questions about how we should be treated and how we should treat others—indeed, the kind of society toward which we should strive—do not go away. And as the world changes, as new technological innovations occur, new policy alternatives arise which we can decide to pursue or not. Today we are confronted, as private persons and as citizens, with urgent issues of social policy, most of which demand answers to fundamental moral questions. On reflection it is clear that the period of the last decade or so has been one of great social change and intellectual ferment. As such, it is a challenging and exciting time. The studies in this volume aim at addressing and systematically analyzing a variety of the pressing social-policy questions which confront us. To achieve this aim we have invited leading philosophers to contribute fresh essays especially written for readers who are *not* assumed to have a background in philosophy or familiarity with the terminology or theories often presupposed in the professional literature. The resulting collection, we believe, provides an inviting and stimulating place to start exploring the important issues the authors address.

There is no single order in which the essays must be read, but something should be said here both about the essays themselves and why we have arranged them as we have. What public policies a given society does or should accept has immediate implications for the present generation of that society's citizens, especially in terms of the amount of liberty and opportunities (e.g., in employment) individuals will have if these policies are in place. Since no one has to be persuaded that restricting individual liberty or having a fair chance to secure a job are serious matters, it is natural to begin with three essays which explore these issues. The primary question investigated in the initial essay, "Paternalism and Restrictions on Liberty", is whether individuals or government may coercively interfere with the actions of

vii

competent adult persons for their own good, e.g., to prevent them from harming themselves. Such a question is relevant to the justification of consumer protection laws, legal prohibitions or restrictions on drug usage, prohibitions on consenting homosexuality, involuntary commitment of the psychologically disturbed, and prohibitions on suicide. The second essay, "Homosexuality", explores the currently controversial questions of whether there is good reason to judge homosexual acts to be immoral and, relatedly, whether there is a justification for discrimination against homosexuals, e.g., by means of criminal penalties for homosexual behavior. Homosexual activity between consenting adults is a legally punishable offense in virtually all state and local jurisdictions. Are there legitimate grounds for assuming that society has the right to limit the sexual freedom of some of its adult citizens by legally punishing those whose sexual behavior differs from that of the majority? If we are to think seriously about insuring justice for all, this is a question we cannot ignore, whether or not we are members of the minority community.

Society has, through custom and law, not only restricted the sexual behavior of its citizens. It has also allowed, and sometimes fostered, policies and institutions which discriminate against some of its members when it comes to such vital concerns as securing an education or finding gainful employment. That women, blacks, chicanos, and native americans have been and, in many places, continue to be victims of discrimination in these matters is abundantly clear. What is less clear is what steps, if any, society ought to take to rectify such injustices. In particular, does justice require that preferential treatment be given to the presently existing members of a group of citizens (e.g., blacks or females), in such matters as hiring practices and admissions to institutions of higher learning, on the grounds that these people belong to a class of individuals whose members have suffered in the past, or are currently suffering, from discriminatory hiring or admission policies? That is the central question explored in the third essay, "Reverse Discrimination."

Questions about the moral propriety of certain public policies may require that we take into account more than just the interests of the *presently* existing members of a given society. Whether we should build our future by relying on nuclear power raises this question in a particularly stark way, since the problems of storing nuclear wastes, for example, will have to be borne by *future* generations of human beings, not just those of us who presently exist. A similar problem exists in regard to the harmful consequences which could result if we allow further development of certain types of genetic research, since the knowledge gained from such research could allow us to "engineer" what future generations of human beings will be like. The next pair of essays, on "Nuclear Power" and "Genetic Engineering," thus serve the important purpose of expanding our moral horizons by forcing us to question whether, in addition to our own well being and that of other presently existing members of human society, justice for *all* includes future generations. Both raise important questions about what sorts of constraints society should place upon activities which, while aimed at beneficial results, generate serious risks to others— and, hence, questions about whether these risks are justly distributed across existing persons, as well as across current and future generations.

To speak of "obligations to future generations" raises some difficult problems in its own right. How can we have obligations to those who do not yet exist and who, should an unforeseen catastrophe occur (e.g., the nuclear destruction of the planet) will never come to exist? Moreover, even if the case can be made for our having such obligations, how stringent are they? What steps should we take to control population growth, and should elective abortion be one of them? These matters need to be explored with considerable care, if we are to reach informed assessments about the acceptability of developing nuclear power and the pursuit of genetic engineering.

They are examined at length in the sixth essay, "Obligations to Future Generations."

But those public policies a society does or should accept do not affect only the interests of human beings, even taking the interests of future generations of human beings into account. For example, *non-human animals* frequently are used, in publicly supported and approved ways, to further what are claimed to be the legitimate interests of human beings. Are there any significant moral questions to be raised about our using animals as we do? Does justice for all require interspecific justice as well? Or are all non-humans beyond the moral pale? These questions are investigated, with particular reference to the use of animals in science, in the essay, "On the Ethics of the Use of Animals in Science."

The reflective exploration of any particular moral question soon unearths the need to identify and apply relevant general moral principles. However, merely to identify and apply such principles is not the same as to defend them, and one of the distinctive tasks moral philosophers set for themselves, when they attempt to develop a moral theory, is to defend the reasonableness of one or a number of general moral principles. At the level of ethical theory, then, the objective is not so much to argue for a particular position regarding particular moral questions, including those involving public policy issues, as it is to argue for the rational propriety of approaching any and all moral questions from a particular vantagepoint. The next pair of essays, "Utilitarianism" and "Individual Rights", explore two such vantagepoints—ones provided by ethical theories which compete for our rational assent.

A further question about the moral dimensions of the relation between the individual and society, one which, viewed historically, is perhaps *the* central question, concerns the nature of a just society. The next pair of essays, "Justice and Equality" and "Capitalism, Socialism, and Justice", explore alternative conceptions of a just society, including the justice of some of those public policies these competing conceptions would allow. Though these two essays, like the earlier ones on utilitarianism and individual rights, are more theoretical in tone and substance, the practical implications of the theories defended therein will be self-evident.

Whichever conception of justice one might favor, it seems clear that justice knows no geographical boundaries. Especially at a time when the world at large can reasonably be viewed as "a global village," it would be arbitrary to think that questions of justice begin and end at our nation's geographical boundaries. The final essay, "International Human Rights", identifies and assesses some of the major questions which arise when we consider the varying and sometimes contradictory claims that have been made about "the rights of man". It is also germane to the contemporary dispute over whether members of one nation may legitimately intervene, in the name of "human rights," in "the domestic affairs" of another sovereign nation.

There are many questions in addition to those examined in these essays which involve the theme of "justice for all", e.g., the much discussed question of the ethics of punishment. While not all the issues which bear on this theme have found a place in the present collection, those which have are among the main ones. Our hope is that anyone who works through these essays carefully will acquire a familiarity and understanding of a) the leading ethical theories, b) their application to a number of pressing current disputes, and c) a sense of how such disputes are to be located within the broader frameworks of contemporary moral and political philosophy. And that, though it will not bring an end to investigation of disputes involving justice for all, is a fair place from which to begin.

To begin the journey through the thicket of questions, arguments, and counter arguments which must be traversed if we are to reach informed judgments about the theoretical and practical issues addressed in the several essays requires that we have some grasp of how one may rationally explore such recalcitrant issues—as well as some sense of the landscape of substantive ideas which will unfold before us. The "Introduction" attempts to supply the needed guidance, in the modest way an introduction can.

In addition to the practical significance of the issues discussed, we also note that there is something personally rewarding about exploring, and coming to understand, important ethical controversies, if not "completely," at least better than we did at the outset. At an appropriate stage in one's life, the process of inquiry can be intellectually stimulating and challenging—an opportunity for personal growth and maturation. It is our hope that the study of the essays in this volume will stimulate and challenge, and, as a result, that the reader will experience a bit of the drama that is inherent in intellectual challenge and response.

It is a pleasure to thank the contributors for their patience and cooperation with our editorial aims; our colleagues in philosophy at North Carolina State University for their suggestions and criticisms concerning the project in general and our personal contributions to it in particular; Jim Feather, of Rowman and Littlefield, for his support of the project; and last, but by no means least, Ruth Boone and Ann Rives for their exemplary skill and patience in preparing the manuscript for publication.

TOM REGAN
DONALD VANDEVEER
Raleigh, North Carolina
September 1981

Introduction

I. The Influence of Prevailing Ideas

The kinds of lives we may lead, the quantity and quality of our lives, are directly and strongly influenced by various sorts of contingent circumstances, for example, the availability of natural resources, the level of economic development of our society, climate, and accidents. While we may try to deliberately determine our destinies, much is simply given—a framework over which we have little or no control. In many respects we are pure recipients of such circumstances. At the same time, there is much we can control or affect. Human institutions—organizations, governments, laws, public policy—are, in principle, alterable. What sorts of institutions we have depends in an important way on "prevailing ideas," on the dominant consensus about what sorts of social institutions we should have. In certain times and places it was, and in some places it still is, thought permissible and desirable to allow the purchase and sale of human beings, to radically subordinate (legally and otherwise) persons who happen to be female, to treat children as property, to criminally punish consenting homosexuality, to capitally punish those who dissent from prevailing religious beliefs, or to extend suffrage only to property owners. There is nothing *inevitable* about such practices; they exist in some societies at some times but not in others. They exist, when they do, because the belief in their acceptability and desirability, happens to prevail in a given society. Some practices, e.g., slavery, may strike us as repugnant and the correlative belief, that slavery is acceptable, as indefensible. In contrast, some ideas, e.g., that homosexuality should be a crime or that parents should have the prerogative to raise their children in any way they please, may strike us as perfectly "natural." What "strikes us" as "natural", "normal", "inevitable" or "despicable" and "repugnant" often depends significantly on

1

the society into which we happen to be born and what happen to be the "prevailing conceptions" in that particular society. We often grow up and acquire assumptions about what is acceptable or not, desirable or not, without critically reflecting on such assumptions. It is often difficult to even *recognize* that we have such assumptions or that our social institutions are arranged accordingly. Such assumptions are often like lenses *through which* we see our world, our institutions, and our behavior. Small wonder that it is difficult to take the lenses off and examine them—difficult but not impossible. Those who do, for example, the early critics of slavery in the United States, were often "seen as" fanatics, extremists, or misguided do-gooders; the almost visceral, rejecting, unreflective attitude of those who shared the prevailing norms testifies to the intellectual and psychological difficulty of critically re-examining one's own (and society's) deeply *embedded assumptions* about the way things are supposed to be. At least in retrospect, it seems clear that many former social institutions and the prevailing ideas which lay behind them, are intolerable, arbitrary, and unjust. This simple point provides a compelling reason to "take ideas seriously", to seek to identify the assumptions underlying current practices, policies, and institutions, and subject them to critical examination. That there are serious obstacles to doing so is a point to which we shall return. A point deserving stress here is that aside from certain specific events which have a readily recognized impact on the kinds of lives we may lead (e.g., you are drafted, you are raped, your house burns down, your lover leaves you!) certain general ideas about the kind of society we should have, when they are dominant, determine the fundamental structure of the society in which we live, and, hence, the kinds of choices we may make—hence, the quality of lives we may lead.

A central task of philosophy, especially moral and political philosophy, is to render explicit and precise such "ruling ideas" and to assess them as far as it is rationally possible to do so. Such ideas or beliefs are seldom narrow or "concrete". They tend to determine the macrostructure of our lives and only indirectly the microstructure; nonetheless, the common fallacy is to underestimate their importance. A remark of the famous economist, J. M. Keynes is worth bearing in mind here:

> The ideas of economists and political philosophers, both when they are right and when they are wrong, are more powerful than is commonly understood. Indeed the world is ruled by little else. Practical men, who believe themselves to be quite exempt from any intellectual influences, are usually the slaves of some defunct economist. Madmen in authority, who hear voices in the air, are distilling their frenzy from some academic scribbler of a few years back. I am sure that the power of vested interests is vastly exaggerated compared with the gradual encroachment of ideas.[1]

II. *The Role of Ethical Assumptions*

In beginning to think about those packages of claims which constitute the prevailing ideas—the familiar "isms" of capitalism, socialism, liberalism, and so on—it is crucial to draw some fundamental distinctions. The sciences are primarily concerned with *empirical* questions, questions about what *was, is,* or *will be* the case. Empirical claims are contrasted with *normative* (sometimes called 'evaluative' or 'ethical') claims, claims about what *ought* or *ought not* to be done, or about what it is *permissible* or *impermissible* to do. The claim that dinosaurs are extinct is an empirical claim, but so is the claim that dinosaurs are *not* extinct. Hence, the distinction between *true* and *false* claims is different from the empirical versus normative distinction. The empirical claims whose assessment is the central concern of the sciences are typically of interest in order to arrive at correct *explanations, descriptions,* or *predictions* of events. The ultimate focus of moral philosophy or ethics is on different questions: primarily, how we are to determine what we ought to do, or what it is permissible to do. The latter concern is, then, with the *justification* of acts, practices, or policies. Such a concern differentiates moral philosophy from what is often labeled the "sociology of morals", an inquiry into *what* moral beliefs people have, *what* practices are thought to be permissible (or not), or *why* people have the moral beliefs they have; these latter are *empirical* questions "about morality". It is worth noting that even if we discover *what people believe* (e.g., slavery is all right), and *why* they believe that, we may still want to know whether the practice in question is *justifiable.* It appears that no correct answer to these empirical questions "about morality" will provide us with a basis for deciding what we ought to do or what kind of society we ought to have or work toward creating. In this regard it is worth reflecting on a famous remark of the eighteenth century Scottish philosopher. David Hume:

> In every system of morality which I have hitherto met with, I have always remark'd, that the author proceeds for some time in the ordinary way of reasoning, and establishes the being of a God, or makes observations concerning human affairs; when of a sudden I am surpriz'd to find, that instead of the usual copulations of propositions, *is,* and *is not,* I meet with no proposition that is not connected with an *ought,* or an *ought not.* This change is imperceptible; but is, however, of the last consequence. For as this *ought* or *ought not,* expresses some new relation or affirmation, 'tis necessary that it should be observ'd and explain'd; and at the same time that a reason should be given, for what seems altogether inconceivable, how this new relation can be a deduction from others, which are entirely different from it. But as authors do not commonly use this precaution, I shall presume to recommend it to the readers.[2]

Hume's point, as it is usually understood, is that no normative claim about what we ought or ought not to do logically follows from any set of purely empirical assumptions, i.e., about what was, is, or will be the case. If this is correct, it will follow that we cannot set out any valid argument (one where the conclusion necessarily follows from the premises) for a normative conclusion unless our argument has normative premises. Hence, any defense of a specific normative claim by a valid argument must appeal to normative premises. So, when someone claims, e.g., that abortion is wrong, punishing homosexuals is right, civil disobedience is wrong, capitalism is unjust, experimenting on people (or animals) is wrong, building nuclear power plants is unjustified, genetic engineering is all right, or prohibiting the sale of heroin is justified, such a person cannot base such claims on purely empirical assumptions, including scientific ones. Typically, when people defend such *specific* moral claims, in an attempt to show that they are justified or reasonable, they, respectively, may appeal to more *general* moral principles, e.g., killing innocent humans is wrong, we should prevent wrongdoing by law, society has a right to maintain order, vastly unequal distributions of income are unjustified, only consenting subjects should be used in risky experiments, and so on. Sometimes, the principles are even more general, e.g., it is always wrong to infringe rights, we should do whatever maximizes the balance of good over evil, or the Golden Rule. Specific recommendations about what laws, policies, or institutions we ought to have rest on influential moral assumptions, assumptions we can be oblivious to or ignore—or, on the other hand, attempt to *identify* and *assess.* Many, but not all, of the "ruling ideas" are ethical, in spite of a certain popular and academic reluctance to acknowledge as much.

III. The Reluctance to Explore Ethical Questions

There are reasons for such reluctance and they deserve some examination here, albeit a brief one. One popular view of ethics has it that "ethics" is only about sexual matters (e.g., the permissibility of pre-marital sex, adultery, or homosexuality) and, perhaps, lying or cheating. As may be clear by now, such a view is myopic. The range of questions about what we ought to do or what it is permissible to do is far broader and more important than the narrow view assumes. Another widely held view, one which engenders a reluctance to take ethical inquiry seriously, is, we believe, our common reluctance to be viewed as "moralists." A popular image of a "moralist" is that of a person who *moralizes* in the sense that he (or she) is inclined to be harshly and overly "judgmental" and "proper" and, indeed, quite eager to *impose* his moral judgments on others. e.g., support harsh penalties for those who produce, sell, or read "risque" novels. A common reaction, perhaps unconscious, seems to be "if that is the sort of person who takes ethical questions seriously, I shall not be among them!" But one who seeks to ascertain what is right need not believe that imposing moral beliefs is justifiable in all or any cases. A third reason for the frequent reluctance to give serious attention to ethical dilemmas is the widespread assumption that it is *not possible* to systematically and rationally examine such matters. After all, it is frequently held, there are *matters of fact* and *matters of opinion,* and *ethical* claims are a matter of opinion. This pair of claims, sometimes referred to as *moral* or *ethical subjectivism,* is like many other "deeply embedded assumptions," i.e., those who hold them are not always conscious of the fact that they hold them and/or have not given serious reflection to the question of whether there are any compelling reasons to do so. Again, the assumptions are not *seen as* assumptions, that is, as claims which require justification or defense just as other assumptions do. As suggested before, they function as lenses: one looks through them and what one intellectually "sees" is influenced by the lenses one happens to have. For example, owners of slaves tended to "see" savages and not oppressed human beings. If what we have called ethical subjectivism were true, that would have an important bearing on the question of whether we *can* rationally and systematically resolve ethical disputes. A careful discussion of the reasonableness of ethical subjectivism would take us far afield here; hence, we limit our remarks to a few. First, the view itself is unclear. What is meant by 'matter of fact' and 'matter of opinion'? On one interpretation to have an opinion is to have a belief, and beliefs, in general, may be true or false, reasonable or unreasonable. If one is "of the opinion" that one can fly out of tenth-story windows (after one's ninth gin and tonic), it is not preposterous to suggest that one has an unreasonable or unjustified opinion. The claim that "*I think* I can fly" is, nevertheless, *one's* opinion is, of course, true, but that is a trivial point. It does *not* follow that rational inquiry is unable to resolve the question of whether or not one can fly. A critic might say, as a reply, that "it is not because ethical opinions are *opinions* that they cannot be rationally examined and resolved but because they are *ethical* matters." To this claim any rational person must reply "perhaps that is true, but *why* think so?" If it is proposed that ethical questions cannot be resolved, that each person can only have, so to speak, his or her private opinion, we must be told *why* that is the correct view to take; to simply *assume* without reason that it is, is to "beg the question" (to arbitrarily assume an answer to a question without giving any reason to think that it is the correct answer).

The similarly posed claim that "values are subjective" is unfortunately ambiguous. In one sense of the word 'values', one often employed in the writings of economists, one's values are the same as one's preferences (Cf. David values leisure time). These "values" are indeed subjective *in the sense* that they will vary from subject to subject and are evidently influenced by fortuitous factors, e.g., the place of one's birth, cultural influences, and so on. However, none of this *shows* that there is nothing one *ought* to value or that there are no objective standards of moral judgment. One may not value (i.e. prefer) treating people fairly; it does not follow that there is no obligation to do so. It may be true that "Hitler valued killing Jews"; whether such a practice ought to be valued is another matter. What people *do* value (prefer) may well be, in one sense, subjective; this point is simply independent of the question of whether there are acts, policies, or states of affairs that all persons *ought* to value,

Our persistent critic (hardest of all is to be one's own) may insist that there is, nevertheless, a very *good reason* to assume, indeed to *conclude,* that ethical questions are not amenable to rational inquiry, namely, because *ethical disagreement has persisted* over thousands of years. On reflection this response, while true, is unpersuasive. Analogously, disagreement over the shape of the earth, the occurrence of evolution, and the existence of beings in outer space has also persisted. In brief, persistent, even widespread, disagreement over the answer to certain questions does not by itself show that such questions are incapable of resolution. What it *does* tend to show is that certain questions are difficult and that progress in answering them is slow. It is worth recalling here, for example, how tiny the period is during which human beings have had some understanding of the transmission of genetic information. Science commonly proceeds not so much by conclusively showing that some very general theory is unquestionably correct but by *excluding* certain theories as highly implausible and narrowing the range of plausible candidates for the title "most acceptable theory given the current data." One view deserving consideration, as one explores ethical questions and ethical theories, is whether progress in resolving ethical problems is like that in science, where the *exclusion* of certain views as unreasonable is by no means unimportant.

So far we have been concerned to clarify the notion of an ethical question, to suggest why such questions are important and eminently practical, to suggest why, nevertheless, certain conventional beliefs or "received opinions" tend to engender a reluctance to systematically and openly investigate questions of ethics.

IV. The Assessment of Ethical Claims

How *can* one go about assessing ethical claims? In *part,* the answer is: just as any rational and impartial person would attempt to assess any controversial claim. Confronted with such a claim (or asking ourselves whether one of our own beliefs is reasonable) we initially ask: *why accept it.* Usually some reason can be given and, hence, we have an *argument,* or the beginnings of one. Suppose someone claims that abortion is wrong. We ask why and it is said that abortion is wrong because all killings are wrong. More formally we have:

1. All killings are wrong.
2. Hence, abortion is wrong.

By 'argument' philosophers, and logicians, mean a set of statements where the proponent of the set puts forward one claim as his or her main contention and seeks to rationally *support* that claim by appeal to other claims, possibly thought to be less controversial. The supporting claims are called *premises* and the main contention the *conclusion.* If a claim is defended by one or more reasons we can, in principle, identify and formulate the argument. The task of carefully identifying or formulating arguments is often no easy one. Try to extract one or more explicitly formulated arguments from a typical editorial, and the problem may be evident. Advocates of a view sometimes make little effort to set forth their arguments in a desirably explicit way—possibly because they do not wish to call attention to a dubious assumption. It is often the assumptions "lurking in the background" which need to be dragged into the daylight and given thorough scrutiny.

There are two primary ways in which an argument may fail to do the job of providing a good reason to believe that the conclusion is true or reasonable. First, one or more of its premises may be false or unreasonable. Our argument on abortion seems to suffer in this respect for the premise, *as stated,* seems to have the absurd implication of condemning the mowing of grass or destroying harmful viruses. Or compare the argument that capital punishment should be employed for serious crimes because social scientists have shown it to have a significant, enduring deterrent effect. One problem with this argument is that the premise (following 'because') is false. Some premises are empirical ones and their assessment may be a quite technical matter, e.g., smoking marijuana is harmless or high stress in humans universally causes hormonal changes. Philosophers today do not pretend to be scientists or expert about empirical claims; that was not true in prior centuries—partly because some scientists were philosophers and partly because no clearcut distinction was made between "science" and "philosophy" (Sir Isaac Newton described himself as a "natural philosopher" or philosopher of nature). There is no way of making armchair assessments of difficult empirical claims, and, confronted with such a problem, one must locate the consensus of expert opinion—whether it can be provided by the sociologist, psychologist, economist, chemist, geneticist, physicist, or whoever. The search for truth requires us to do "whatever it takes" to rationally examine the claim in question.

A second way an argument may fail is this: *even though* its premises may be true or reasonable, they may *fail to support* the conclusion. This failure of support may be of two sorts. We clarify one type of failure here and the other at a later point. Consider the argument that women are intellectually inferior because none has ever been a great mathematician, musician, philosopher, or physicist. This argument has the logical property of being *invalid* (a technical term) because it is one where it is *possible* that it have *both* true premises and a false conclusion. Alternatively, it is said that the conclusion is *not entailed* by the premises or that the conclusion does *not necessarily follow* from the premises. In sharp contrast, with some arguments it is *not possible* that: the conclusion be false *and* the premises true; philosophers and logicians label these latter arguments *valid*. Validity is a desirable feature since if one's argument is valid, one has a kind of assurance, namely, that if one starts off well (with true premises) one is bound to end up well (with a true conclusion)—and not just, as can happen, by accident. The following is a valid argument:

> All and only humans have rights
> Dagwood is a human
> _____
> Dagwood has rights.

The first premise may be questioned (and is questioned in the essay by Jamieson and Regan) and the second may be false—if, for example, 'Dagwood' names my pet snake. But none of that would alter the fact that the argument is valid. In fact, valid arguments may have all false premises, e.g.,

> 2 is greater than 4
> 4 is greater than 6
> _____
> 2 is greater than 6.

In short, validity is *no guarantee* of the truth of the premises or the truth of the conclusion. Still, for reasons deserving reflection (and, perhaps, a course in logic), validity is a desirable feature in an argument. Indeed, if an argument has *another* feature along with validity, we can be certain its conclusion is *true*. The other feature is that the argument have all *true premises*. Philosophers define a *sound* argument as one which is *both* valid *and* has all true premises. Any sound argument has a true conclusion. So a decisive way of showing that a given claim is true is to provide a sound argument where the claim in question is the conclusion. We note, in passing, that if an argument is *unsound* (not sound) it *need* not have a false conclusion.

A more important upshot of these remarks is that in assessing the reasonableness of any philosophically interesting claim several important steps should be followed: 1) *identify* carefully and explicitly the relevant arguments for or against the claim, 2) attempt to ascertain the truth or falsity (the "truth-value") or reasonableness of the premises, and 3) attempt to ascertain the validity or invalidity of the argument. These steps are, more generally, appropriate for the rational assessment of any claim, be it "philosophical" or not. Thoroughly understanding the technical concepts introduced here is essential to philosophical inquiry and these concepts are frequently invoked, sometimes implicitly, in the essays in this volume.

The reader will recall that we said earlier that the premises of an argument may fail to *support its conclusion* in two ways. One kind of failure was identified, namely the sort labeled 'invalidity'. The other was not. We lead up to the second type of failure indirectly. Consider this argument:

No major nuclear catastrophe has occurred in the construction and maintenance of any existing nuclear power plant in the United States (as of 1981).

Hence, no major nuclear catastrophe will occur at such plants.

On reflection, it may be obvious that this argument is invalid. Is it, however, entirely "bad"? To answer that question we need explicit criteria for *what counts as* a bad argument. Note this, however. Even if an argument is one where it is *possible* that the conclusion is false even if the premises are true, we may query whether the truth of the conclusion is *rendered probable given the truth of the premises*. If so, it may be reasonable to rely on it. It is possible, for example, that a bomb has been rigged into your car such that when the ignition is turned the car will explode. Perhaps, we believe that it is reasonable to start the car as usual because on all previous occasions the car has not exploded when started. Such reasoning (the argument therein) is invalid. However, we may think that given the past it is *highly probable* that the car will not explode next time. One common label (though not a universal one) for invalid arguments where the conclusion is highly probable given the truth of the premises is: *strong* argument (and where the conclusion is not highly probable: a *weak* argument). Our central point here is that the best type of argument that we may be able to discover, for certain claims, will be a *strong* argument, and a strong argument may provide us with a good reason for accepting its conclusion. The latter may be belief-worthy even if not the conclusion of a valid argument. Now we have identified the two ways in which an argument may be one in which its conclusion is not adequately supported: it may be invalid, or worse yet, it may be weak. We leave it as an open question whether our argument about nuclear power plants is strong or is weak; if the latter, it does not merit our acceptance. There is no *short* answer to the questions: What is it reasonable to believe or how exacting should our standards be in the assessment of argument. The counsel of Aristotle is worth recalling (especially when we hear people glibly claim, in debate, "there is no proof that . . ."); he said, almost 2500 years ago that ". . . it is the mark of an educated man to look for precision in each class of things just so far as the nature of the subject admits."[3]

Having introduced, in a *most* succinct fashion, a few of the fundamental tools for assessing arguments (and, hence, for adjudicating competing claims) we draw attention to one further aspect of such assessment. We focus first on a trivial example. Suppose Ann claims "Raleigh (North Carolina) is a large town," and Ruth claims "Raleigh is not a large town." We have a disagreement; it appears to be an empirical disagreement. This might be verified if Ann adds "because Raleigh has 150,000 people" and Ruth adds "because Raleigh has 75,000 people." Suppose, however, that each *agrees* that Raleigh's population is 150,000, but, nevertheless disagree over the truth of "Raleigh is a large town." Why might such conflict arise? The explanation may be that each employs different *criteria for applying the term* 'a large town'—Ann counting as a large town only cities of, say, 100,000 or more and Ruth counting as a large town only cities of 50,000 or more (New Yorkers, of course, are likely to use different criteria!). If so, their disagreement is not *over the facts but over how to describe the facts*. Philosophers call such disagreement *conceptual disagreement*. We suggest that it would be unwise to describe such disagreement as "merely verbal" because such disagreement is genuine disagreement and may be a source of substantive conflict. Some policy disagreements and some ethical disputes may have their source in avoidable conceptual disagreement unbeknownst to the disputants. A case in point may be the argument over whether the United States, in recent years, has held *political prisoners*. If by 'political prisoner' one means 'a person imprisoned solely because of his or her political dissent' one may answer the question quite differently than if one means 'a person whose punishment was influenced by political considerations.' Hence, some, though probably not all, of that dispute may be traceable to a certain element of conceptual disagreement. In attempting to adjudicate such disputes it is worth scrutinizing the arguments for this source of disagreement. It is, then, often worth inquiring as to *what precisely is meant* by a key expression. Without pursuing this point here, certain important expressions or terms, *possibly* unclear or ambiguous, occur in the following essays: liberty, coercion, paternalism, rights, exploitation, discrimination, unnatural, abnormal, future generations, sexist, racist, speciesist, equality, proof, and so on. If we are not clear about the *meaning* of key terms in significant and disputed claims, we may be drawn into, or overlook, avoidable conceptual disagreement; relatedly, and perhaps worse, we will simply not know *what is being claimed,* and, if we do not know that, the attempt to determine what is true or rationally defensible is undermined at the outset. To note this is, at the same time, to suggest why philosophy in this century especially, has regarded questions about language and meaning as of crucial importance.

In addition to the task of critically examining the defenses of competing views on the controversial issues discussed in this volume—by engaging in the philosophical analysis we have briefly characterized—we note another aspect of such a task. We seldom approach most of the large questions later discussed from an entirely neutral point of view; typically, we already have beliefs and inclinations, perhaps deepseated ones, about what the right answers are or, perhaps, what some of the wrong answers are. A critical *re-assessment* of *our own* conceptions and convictions is *psychologically* more difficult than critically examining the beliefs or assertions of others. As noted, one reason for this is that we may never have consciously and carefully tried to identify our own views, our own empirical or ethical assumptions. Not being "visible" to us, it is unlikely that we will focus our critical tools on such assumptions. Further, even if we are clear about our own principles or beliefs, there is another factor which tends to make us reluctant to critically examine them. It is this: our beliefs are part of our identity or self-image; an attack on them often makes us "feel threatened". There is a very human inclination to want to *avoid* the conclusion that some long-held belief or "value" is arbitrary or a mere prejudice.

Hence, it is psychologically difficult for a person who has had an abortion to question its acceptability, for the scientists who experiment on animals to question its permissibility, for the soldier to question the morality of a war in which he fought, for the religious to question religious beliefs, for the heterosexual to question laws repressive toward gay persons, for the white person to impartially consider reverse discrimination, for the nuclear engineer to question the morality of generating nuclear risks, for males to recognize or acknowledge their own chauvinistic attitudes, for blacks to avoid *a priori* cynicism about police interventions, or for liberated women not to assume that patriarchal motives lie behind all male offers of assistance. Skill in logic will not automatically help us shed our prejudices but, in assessing different views and arguments, especially one's own, a useful rule of thumb is to *consider objections*—seriously, impartially as possible, thoroughly, and relentlessly.

V. Ethical Theories

If we recall Hume's observation, that in order to validly derive an 'ought' in the conclusion of an argument we need a normative premise, we can begin to get some sense of what an ethical theory is. Despite many areas of acknowledged moral disagreement, including, for example, the moral questions that can and do arise over reliance on nuclear power as a source of energy, there is widespread agreement that certain sorts of actions are normally right, and similar agreement that others are normally wrong. Acts regarded as normally wrong include stealing, cheating, killing, and violating a trust, while those regarded as normally right include assisting others in distress, respecting the property and liberty of others, keeping our promises, and being loyal to our friends or associates. One question that arises when we reflect on the variety of acts which are judged right or wrong concerns the *grounds* of their respective rightness or wrongness. When we raise this question, what we are asking for is some specification of the reasons acts are right or wrong, respectively; we want to know what are the "right-making" and "wrong-making" characteristics of actions. In the nature of the case, any specification of what these characteristics are will have to be rather general. For example, the view that all and only those acts which are right conform with God's will would seem to have the generality we would naturally expect to find in such a specification, whereas the view that all and only those acts which are right involve keeping one's promise lacks this generality, since there are obviously many other acts besides promise-keeping which are right. Now, the search for the correct specification of these right-making and wrong-making characteristics is the overarching goal of an *ethical theory,* and the specification of what these characteristics are is what is expressed by the fundamental, basic or supreme ethical principles identified by such a theory.

The *logical* indispensibility of having such a principle should be clear, once Hume's observation takes root. With such a principle we can argue *validly* to a given conclusion about a controversial moral issue, (for example, that it is wrong to hire a less qualified person from a minority race in preference to a more qualified person from the majority race) by being careful that our arguments have the following structure:

Any act (policy, institution, law, etc.) is wrong if it has a given characteristic—x.
Preferential hiring based on racial considerations has characteristic x.
Therefore, preferential hiring based on racial considerations is wrong.

Without such a principle, on the other hand, our arguments about the morality of particular acts, policies, laws or institutions are certain to be invalid or question begging. Small wonder, then, that in addition to attempting to clarify concepts that play major roles in moral controversies (concepts such as liberty, coercion, and individual rights) moral philosophers traditionally have also sought to identify the correct, the true, or the most reasonable fundamental ethical principles. Lacking such principles we would seem to be rationally barred from even approaching, let alone resolving, the controversial moral problems that arise in our own personal lives or in society at large.

CONSEQUENTIALIST AND NON-CONSEQUENTIALIST THEORIES

It is customary to distinguish between two kinds of ethical theory: (1) consequentialist theories and (2) non-consequentialist theories. Theories of the former kind all maintain that the rightness or wrongness of an act, or kind of action, depends on its consequences, on the effects or results which the performance of a given act, or an action of a given kind, brings about. Theories of the latter type (non-consequentialist theories) all hold that consequences do not alone determine an act's rightness or wrongness. Each type of theory, consequentialist and non-consequentialist, allows for a variety of alternative positions. An example of a consequentialist theory is *utilitarianism*. The supreme or basic moral principle, according to this view, is the principle of utility. This principle states, roughly, that any act is right which brings about consequences for those affected by its outcome that are at least as good as those that would have resulted if any other act had been performed in those circumstances; hence, a wrong act is any act that brings about consequences that are less good than these. Utilitarians sometimes disagree over what consequences are good or bad. Some maintain that pleasure and pleasure alone is good, and pain and pain alone is bad. Others maintain that the satisfaction of one's preferences is what is good, while their frustration is what is bad. Differ though they do on these matters, all utilitarians agree, by definition, that the rightness or wrongness of actions, or actions of a given kind, ultimately depends upon their consequences and *only* on their consequences.

Among non-consequentialist theories there are some that maintain that the rightness or wrongness of actions depends upon respecting the moral rights of persons. A right act, then, is one that displays such respect, while a wrong act is one that violates a person's rights. Whereas the utilitarian would locate the grounds of the wrongness of stealing or breaking a promise in the bad consequences that result from stealing or going back on one's promises, the rights theory, if we might use this designation to refer to the non-consequentialist theory just characterized (very roughly), locates the grounds of their wrongness in different considerations. According to the rights theory, what makes such acts wrong is not their bad consequences; it is that stealing from another or failing to keep one's word to another is a violation of that person's moral rights.

As these two examples of ethical theories suggest, there is no lack of alternatives from which to choose. The challenge is, rather, to choose the best one. That would be the theory which, more adequately than its competitors, meets the standards which a reasonable person would apply to such theories. The importance of having the best theory is twofold. First, it will enable us to argue *validly* to conclusions about controversial moral questions, and, second, it will make it possible to develop *sound* arguments in support of our answers to such questions. Before we can attempt to decide which theory is the best, however, we must first identify appropriate standards for evaluating ethical theories. There is widespread agreement on the appropriateness of some standards, including (1) consistency, (2) adequacy of scope, (3) precision, (4) simplicity, and (5) conformity with our intuitions. We discuss these in the order mentioned.

1. *Consistency.* A minimum requirement for any ethical theory is that it be consistent. Consistency concerns the *possible conjoint* truth of two or more statements. Any combination of two or more statements (let us refer to this as "any set of statements") is consistent if and only if it is possible that all the statements comprising the set can be true at the same time. Here is an example of a consistent set. (It is assumed that 'Jack' and 'Jill' each refers to the same individual, at the same time, in the same circumstances).

Set A(1): Jack is taller than Jill.
(2): Jill is shorter than Jack.

Here is an example of an inconsistent set.

Set B (3): Jack is taller than Jill.
(4): Jill is taller than Jack.

Set A is consistent because it is possible for both (1) and (2) to be true at the same time; there is, that is, nothing involved in 1's being true that automatically or necessarily makes 2 false, and vice versa, though neither 1 nor 2 must be true (for it might be that Jack and Jill are the same height). Set B is inconsistent, however, because if 3 were true, then 4 would have to be false, and if 4 were true, then 3 would have to be false; necessarily, that is, 3 and 4 cannot both be true.

Now, an adequate ethical theory must be consistent. This is true because such a theory aims at providing us with a principle by reference to which we may rationally decide which actions are right and which are wrong. If, however, a proposed theory turns out to be inconsistent, then its failure in this regard would undermine the very point of having an ethical theory in the first place—namely, to provide rational guidance in the determination of what is right and wrong.

One way of arguing that a proposed theory is inconsistent is to show that it implies that the very same act can be both right and wrong. One (but by no means not the only) interpretation of the view called ethical relativism has this implication. On this interpretation, an act is right or wrong whenever the majority in any given society approve or disapprove of it, respectively. It is important to be clear about what, on this interpretation, ethical relativism comes to. The claim is not that a given act is *thought* to be right in a given society if the majority approve of it; nor is it that the act of which a given society's majority approves is right *in that society;* rather, an act *is right,* according to the interpretation presently under review, whenever the majority of the members of any given society happen to approve of it. This way of viewing right and wrong does imply that the very same act can be both right and wrong. To make this clearer, suppose that the majority in one society happen to approve of killing and eating foreigners, while the majority in another society happen to disapprove of it. Then it follows, given the interpretation of ethical relativism we are discussing, that a) killing and eating foreigners is right, and b) it is not the case that killing and eating foreigners is right, are both true. However, since a) and b) are inconsistent, they cannot both be true. And that, as noted, shows that ethical relativism, as understood here, cannot be an adequate ethical theory.

2. *Adequacy of scope.* A further legitimate requirement is that an ethical theory have adequate scope. The reason for this should be clear when we recall that the principle(s) advanced by any given theory are intended to provide us with practical guidance in the determination of what is right and wrong. Since we find ourselves in a great variety of circumstances in which we have to make such determinations, a given theory will succeed in providing guidance to the extent that it can be applied in these circumstances, and this will depend on the theory's scope. Of the two theories mentioned earlier—utilitarianism and the rights theory—the former would seem to

have far broader scope than the latter. Since utilitarianism directs us to bring about the best consequences for all those whose preferences, pleasures or pains will be affected by the outcome of what we do, and since there is virtually nothing that we do that does not affect someone, even if only ourselves, then it follows that utilitarianism applies to virtually every act which any one performs in any circumstance. The rights theory, on the other hand, may have less scope than this. Much will depend on how the troublesome notion of a *person* is understood. If, in order to be a person, one must be a rational, self-directing individual, possessing a concept of one's own identity over time and having the capacity to make long range plans about one's future, then not only most non-human animals but also many humans, including infants and the mentally enfeebled, will not be persons, in which case how we may treat these individuals will not be determinable merely by appealing to the principle that we are to *respect the rights of persons.* Whether utilitarianism is indeed broader in scope than the rights theory is a question we leave open here.

3. *Precision.* What we want from an ethical theory is not just vague direction concerning a broad range of cases; we expect specific or determinate direction. Without this precision, a theory's usefulness will be seriously diminished. It is of little help to be told, for example, to "Love your neighbor" or "Do no harm" if we are not told, in a clear and helpful way, what "love" and "harm"—and "neighbor" for that matter!—are supposed to mean. If a theory is vague in what it requires, in a significant range of cases, we will be uncertain of what it requires; and to the extent we are thus uncertain, we will also be unsure about what we must do if we are to follow the theory's direction in the present or whether we have compiled with the theory by acting as we have in the past. A high degree of precision then is a legitimate requirement for any ethical theory.

Is utilitarianism or the rights theory the more precise? There is, at this stage, no quick and easy answer. To give a fair assessment would require a more detailed examination of each, one to be found in a number of the essays, including "Utilitarianism," "Rights" and "Justice and Equality." However, both theories may encounter serious problems when it comes to the question of their precision (or lack of it). If we are only told to "respect the rights of persons," for example, just what is it that we are being directed to do? Unless we are clear about the key notions involved—respect, rights, persons—the principle will be too vague to be of significant help. Utilitarianism also has its share of worries. To be directed to bring about "the best consequences" can only be as helpful as it is clear what "the best" consequences are. Is it better, for example, to bring about consequences where everyone gets an equal share of the good produced, or is the equality or inequality of how the good consequences are distributed irrelevant to determining what consequences are "the best"? And, in either case, what does it mean to talk about "equal shares of good consequences" or "equal distribution"? Until the principle of utility is supplemented with additional information in these respects, it, like the rights theory, will be found to be seriously lacking in precision, even granting, in compliance with the quote from Aristotle given earlier, that we should not expect precision from such a theory equal to the precision we find in, say, geometry or calculus.

4. *Simplicity.* Competing scientific theories sometimes explain the same range of facts with comparable precision. If one theory is also able to predict future occurrences better than the other, thus having what is termed greater predictive power, then its having greater predictive power is a reason for choosing it in preference to its competitor. It sometimes happens, however, that two competing theories are relevantly similar in terms of consistency, scope, precision and predictive power. When

this occurs it is customary to invoke another standard for evaluating the competing theories—namely, the principle of simplicity (also referred to as the principle of parsimony). Briefly put, this principle states that, other things being equal, the simpler theory should be chosen. Now, the simpler theory is the one which makes the fewest assumptions or which requires that we accept the fewest unproven, and perhaps unprovable, premises. The standard of simplicity seems eminently wise. After all, how can it be reasonable to make more assumptions—(in the case of science, assumptions about what exists)—when fewer will do? Why overpopulate the world with entities whose existence is demonstrably unneeded to explain what one wants to explain?

Both utilitarianism and the rights theory *appear* to be simple. Each advances what appears to be a single ethical principle. But appearances can be deceiving. In the case of the rights theory, for example, we should ask whether all the rights we are enjoined to respect are of equal importance. It is implausible to suppose that they are. An individual's right to life, for example, would seem to be of greater moral significance than the right to free speech or to emigrate to another country, assuming that all three are moral rights. But if all moral rights are not equal, then the rights theory will need to supply us with some basis for rationally ordering moral rights in terms of their respective weight or importance. And this will be to complicate what at first blush seemed to be a comparatively simple theory. Utilitarianism also may be less simple than it appears. On one interpretation of that theory we are enjoined to bring about those results which will result in maximizing the preferences of everyone affected by the outcome. However, unless we first consider all the preferences of those involved *and* count equal preferences equally, acting to bring about the best consequences might neglect or underevaluate some of the preferences of some of the individuals affected by that outcome. Thus, in addition to advocating that we act to bring about the best consequences for all affected, this version of utilitarianism also must direct us to take account of all the preferences involved and to count equal preferences equally. The problem, then, is whether, given this bit of direction, the apparent simplicity of utilitarianism has been compromised. Do we, that is, have just one principle—"Act to bring about the best consequences"—or two—that principle *and* the (different) principle, "Consult all the preferences of those involved and count equal interests equally"?

These two questions—the one about whether certain versions of utilitarianism turn out to have two principles, instead of one, and the other question about how the rights theory will or can rank rights in terms of their moral importance—will not be further pursued here. Each is explored in the essays referred to earlier. The remarks we have made should suffice to make the point that a theory which looks "simple," in the sense that it may appear to advance just a single basic principle, may turn out to be less simple than at first appeared.

5. *Conformity with our intuitions.* One final basis for evaluating competing ethical theories concerns whether they conform to our moral intuitions. The apparent strengths and possible weaknesses of this requirement will be clearer after we have sketched what it involves.

There are some acts which seem to be quite *obviously* wrong (or right). Murder, rape, genocide, and torture, at least in normal circumstances, are wrong, as is discriminating against persons on the basis of their race or sex, their religious beliefs or birthplace. It is natural, therefore, to require that any ethical theory conform with those moral beliefs regarding which, on reflection, we are most certain, and to reject any theory which fails to conform with them—one which implies, for example, that torture, except in the most extenuating circumstances, is perfectly all right. Such a theory, it is natural to suppose, could not be a satisfactory one on which to base decisions in our personal lives or to invoke in assessing the morality of our social, political and economic arrangements.

But this appeal to "what we think," to "our intuitions," is not free of problems. As was noted earlier, many people in the past did, and many still do, have moral beliefs that significantly differ from some of those sketched in the previous paragraph. Racist and sexist bases for discriminating against people, for example, have been, and in some places continue to be, generally approved. Given the significant disagreement over what people think about right and wrong, how can we reasonably appeal to *our* moral beliefs, *our* moral intuitions, as a basis for testing competing ethical theories? Would not an uncritical appeal of this kind simply show that we are guilty of what sociologists call ethnocentrism—the uncritical assumption that our beliefs, the beliefs of "our group" or "our society," are the only correct or reasonable ones? Indeed, might it not be more appropriate to test the reasonableness of our intuitions by asking how well *they* conform to an ethical theory that is satisfactory in other respects (i.e., in terms of scope, precision and the like) rather than using conformity with our intuitions as a further, independent test of ethical theories?

There is no easy answer to this question. Competent philosophers disagree about the answer, and little can be said in the brief compass of this Introduction to resolve the controversy once and for all. But it is worth noting that a distinction can be drawn between (1) what we believe *before* we have critically examined our beliefs (our "pre-theoretical convictions") and (2) what we believe *after* having critically examined them. To illustrate the difference, suppose that, because of socialization or custom, we believe that certain acts, such as homosexual activity, even between consenting adults, and rape are simply wrong and ought to be illegal. Suppose we begin to think critically about why we believe this. Suppose, further, that the primary reason we would give for thinking that rape is wrong is that it violates a woman's right to freely determine certain aspects of her conduct, especially as these relate to her determining with whom, and under what conditions, she will have sexual relations. Reasoning along these lines suggests that we would accept a quite general principle (let us call this "the liberty principle") concerning individual liberty, to the effect that it is in general wrong to interfere with a person's exercise of his or her liberty so long as that person is not harming others.

Now, the liberty principle stands in need of careful analysis. In particular, a good deal would need to be said about what 'liberty' or 'autonomy' mean, if this principle is to have the precision it is reasonable to expect from any moral principle. However, this principle seems to have considerable scope, applying, as it does, to a variety of cases, and in a way that unifies and illuminates, in a general and helpful way, what it is about these cases that serves as the ground for making rational judgments about them. It illuminates why, for example, it is wrong to make slaves of some individuals for the benefit of others, why it is wrong to force some persons to pursue particular careers even though they would prefer to pursue others, why it is wrong to deny persons the opportunity to speak their mind about the troubling political and social problems of the day, why it is wrong to require that certain people live in certain locales whether they want to or not, and why it is wrong to deny certain individuals the opportunity to vote in a democratic society because of the color of their skin, their place of national origin, their religious beliefs or their gender. The liberty principle provides us with a general and plausible basis on which to rest our moral judgments in such cases. What all these acts or policies arguably have in common, what makes each of them wrong, is that they involve a violation of that principle. Because the liberty principle applies to a broad range of cases, and because this principle identifies what appears to be the underlying morally relevant feature which serves as the basis for the judgments we make in these cases, we have a reasonable principle on which to rest our judgments about other cases, even cases about which we have never thought much.

Consider, once more, the belief that homosexual activity between consenting adults is wrong and ought to be illegal. To make such activity illegal would be to limit individual liberty by making those who engage in it punishable by law. Now, in some cases, such as that of rape, it is reasonable to limit individual liberty by the force of law. But the case of homosexual activity between consenting adults is importantly different from the case of rape. In the latter case, a person is forced by another to engage in sexual relations not of her own (autonomous) choosing. In the case of homosexual activity between consenting adults, however, the participants *themselves* choose to engage in it. This is what is meant by saying they "consent" to do so. Moreover, if these individuals are adults, it is difficult to see how one could sustain the argument, as one perhaps may in the case of young children, that "they don't know any better." As adults, it is reasonable to assume that they are competent to determine, on their own, what it is that they want and to act accordingly. To have and enforce laws which limit consenting adults from engaging in homosexual activity, therefore, seems to violate the liberty principle, and the belief that such activity is wrong and ought to be illegal thus seems to conflict with this principle.

What the preceding discussion is intended to illustrate is how, by beginning to think critically about some of our moral beliefs, we may first identify a general principle (e.g., the liberty principle) that unifies, by illuminating the grounds for, a large number of these beliefs. Having once identified such a principle, we may then come to see that a particular belief which we previously accepted, is (1) relevantly like the cases covered by the general principle we have identified but (2) conflicts with the general principle. In the case of homosexuality between consenting adults, it would seem that we should surrender the view that it ought to be made illegal if we accept the liberty principle.

There is, then, an important difference between (1) appealing to our moral beliefs *before* critically assessing them and (2) appealing to these beliefs after we have critically reflected on the grounds for holding them. If, when we "appeal to our intuitions," we are *merely* appealing to our unexamined moral beliefs, then this appeal is indistinguishable from naive appeals to prejudice or bias and has no built-in safeguard against elevating narrow-mindedness or ignorance to the lofty perch of being a test for the adequacy of competing normative ethical theories. No rational person could accept this. If, instead, the appeal to our intuitions allows for the dynamic interplay between our moral beliefs about particular cases and the general principles which underlie our beliefs (so that after having identified the relevant principles we may come to see that a particular belief which we had previously accepted uncritically is unreasonable), then there is a built-in safeguard against making unexamined prejudice a basis for assessing moral theories. When the "appeal to intuitions" is understood in this latter way, a way which permits and, indeed, encourages us to reflectively assess the credentials of our pre-reflective moral beliefs, the case for retaining such appeals to test the adequacy of competing ethical theories is considerably stronger than when such appeals are understood merely as an invitation to "say what we think" without having first critically reflected on the reasonableness of thinking it. Unless it can be shown that there is something inherently irrational or prejudicial about the appeal to intuitions, when properly understood, it, like the other standards outlined in the preceding, has a rightful role to play in the assessment of ethical theories.

VI. Confirming and Disconfirming Ethical Theories

It is one thing to disconfirm an ethical theory, and quite another to confirm it. To show that a given theory is inconsistent, such as was argued against the version of ethical relativism considered in Section V, is to show that it cannot have any claim on our rational assent. To show that a proposed theory has implications which fail to conform with a body of well considered intuitions or principles also constitutes a compelling reason against that theory. For example, consider a theory whose basic principle is "Do everything you can do to reduce the total amount of suffering in the world." That principle implies that we ought to set out murdering or rendering permanently comatose all those individuals who can suffer: To do *that* would be to do "something we can do to reduce the total amount of suffering in the world!" Less decisive perhaps, but still highly relevant, are the standards of scope, precision, and simplicity. To demonstrate that, other things being equal, one theory is considerably less extensive in scope, or considerably less precise, or considerably more complicated than its competitor, is to provide good reasons for choosing the latter in preference to the former. The patient assessment (and reassessment) of ethical theories by reference to the standards discussed in this Introduction will narrow the field of viable theories. By itself this may not determine which theory is the best. But to narrow the field, in this principled way, is no small accomplishment and, once again, has its counterpart in other human activities, including the natural sciences.

In addition there remains the possibility that some yet unformulated ethical theory, or revision of an existing theory, may, more than any currently discussed theory, better satisfy the standards of rational acceptability. If we are to avoid being mired in the theoretical status quo, we must remain alert to this possibility. Hence, even though some existing theory may seem to best satisfy the canons of rational thought, it seems wise to aim at that degree of critical detachment which will allow us to recognize and critically examine fresh candidates for the title "justified ethical theory." To do less would be to arbitrarily narrow our vision and to fall victim to what Immanuel Kant described as "dogmatic slumbers." The practical constraints of making choices, here and now, in our private and public lives, of course, forces us to act on the basis of our best current vision. But to passively content ourselves with that vision, or to let others do our thinking for us, is to be satisfied with something less than realizing our full potential as rational creatures who help to give moral shape to the world both by what we do and by what we fail to do.

Notes

1. J. M. Keynes, *The General Theory of Employment, Interest, and Money* (New York: Harcourt, Brace, & World, 1936), pp. 383-4.

2. David Hume, *A Treatise of Human Nature*, Book III, Section 1.

3. Aristotle, *Nicomachean Ethics*, 1094:25.

chapter one

Paternalism and Restrictions on Liberty

DONALD VANDEVEER

On reflection it is rather strange that many persons who have acquired the mathematical skills involved in calculus have not spent the equivalent of a full day in systematic investigation of another range of problems which are both perplexing and of great practical significance. As examples of the range of questions I have in mind, consider the following: whether abortion should be permitted, whether capital punishment is an acceptable means of punishment, whether the state has the right to coerce the young into military service, whether affluent societies have an obligation to relieve famine, whether it is permissible or obligatory to extend preferential treatment to members of ill-treated minority groups, and whether it is permissible for the current generation to impose certain risks on future generations (by, e.g., creating nuclear wastes). The way we answer these questions, explicitly-and-reflectively or inadvertently-and-tacitly, directly affects the kinds of lives we may lead. This latter fact provides a compelling reason to thoughtfully explore questions about what *we ought to do*—individually and as a society. Such questions are commonly labeled ethical questions.

In this essay our focus will be on one rather specific ethical question which, although specific, has wide-ranging implications. The question, quite generally, concerns our liberties and restrictions on our liberties. We tend to take for granted that it is all right to restrain people from engaging in certain forms of behavior, e.g., murder, but that other restraints are wrongful, e.g., forcing people to supply bodily organs for others. Why do we, at least in practice, condone some constraints and condemn others? To begin to reflect on such matters is to think about the different ways societies may be arranged or "designed." And as soon as we begin to consider alternative customs, laws, or public policies we can begin to reflect critically on the acceptability and desirability of our own social arrangements. We tend, often, to take them for granted—as if they were "engraved in stone" but they are not, and any reflective person may wonder whether the *existing* set of constraints on individual liberty is the most desirable or just. This question, very generally, is the focus of the intellectual expedition on which we now embark.

We shall explore three allegedly legitimate grounds for restricting the liberty of adults. In Section I we examine the view that it is legitimate to limit the liberties of such adults in order to prevent them from causing harm to others. In Section II we explore a second view, "legal moralism," that claims that it is permissible to limit liberty in order to prevent wrongful acts. In Section III and following we explore a third view, the position of paternalism which maintains, generally, that it is all right to interfere with others in order to prevent them from harming themselves. The paternalist view, an historically neglected one, is our central concern here and will receive our greatest attention. Its uniqueness and seductiveness will stand out more clearly after we examine the contrasting approaches noted.

I. Defense Against Harm

We shall gradually narrow our focus, but let us initially examine the very general question of whether it is *ever* permissible to restrict the liberty of others. What kinds of situations are there where this question might arise? An enormous number of diverse cases may come to mind. Suppose, for example, that you are caring for your senile mother and, while she believes that she is taking her arthritis medicine, she is in fact about to ingest rat poison. Is it permissible to forcefully remove it from her grasp? Our answer is surely affirmative. In another case suppose that your former spouse, having lost the custody battle for your children, attempts to strangle them, preferring that they not live at all than to live with you. May you forcefully restrict his or her liberty to prevent the children's coming to be harmed? Again, the answer is certainly an affirmative one. In short, it seems to be crystal clear that it is permissible *in some cases* to restrict the liberty of others. In contrast, may I kidnap Richman's children and hold them ransom in order to buy a sailboat? May I rape whom I please because it relieves my tensions? After all, some popular writers encourage us to "pull our own strings," "win through intimidation," or "look out for number one." Nonetheless, the acts mentioned seem evidently wrong. Under normal conditions it seems certain that there are *both* cases where some restriction on the liberty of others is permissible *and* other cases where it is not. To agree to that is to reject two possible principles: (A) That *any* restriction on the liberty of others is permissible, and (B) that *no* restrictions on the liberty of others are permissible. There is not only a consensus about the inadequacy of these two principles, there seem to be good *reasons* to reject these two views. They both conflict with deep, well-established convictions about how we ought to treat others, ones which will not be elaborated here. However, this agreement does not take us very far since it fails to provide a basis for deciding hard cases, cases where we need a specific, reasoned, and positive answer to the question "when is it permissible to limit the liberty of others and when not?" This question is one of the fundamental questions of moral philosophy and an answer to it, stated either as a (theoretical) principle or as embodied in our actual treatment of others (through private act, public policy, or the law) affects virtually every area of our lives.

What presuppositions lie behind our natural assumption that (A) is unacceptable, i.e., that it is at least sometimes wrong to restrict the liberty of others? Perhaps it is simply that people are generally, though not always, made worse off when we somehow restrict their liberty. Persons usually prefer to be able to act in ways unhindered by others, and their desire to so act is frustrated by interference. Hence, interference makes them worse off in at least one respect. It is this feature which supports the view that there is a *presumption against* restricting the liberty of others; to do so is to make another person worse off, at least in the absence of any compensating benefits for that person. It is for this reason that actions falling in the class of "restrictions on liberty" need to be *justified,* if they can be. Our concern here, then, is with the question "when can we *justifiably restrict* the liberty of others and when not?"

If we agree that restrictions on a person's liberty are *presumptively wrong* and are presumptively wrong because they generally render that person worse off in at least one respect, why do some restrictions, as we have noted, seem quite justified? For a start, one might claim that *it is permissible to restrict the liberty of someone when he (or she) is about to harm another.*[1] Let us call this the Principle of Other Defense (POD). Perhaps it is because of the correctness of POD that it is permissible to restrict the liberty of your former spouse to prevent him (or her) from strangling your children. Tempting as POD may be, there appear to be *counter-examples* to it, i.e., cases where it would not be right to follow this principle. Suppose that you are about to forcibly restrict the liberty of your former spouse by preventing him from strangling your children; hence, you are about to *harm* him. May a bystander, Busybody, observing the activities, restrict *your* liberty to so act? According to POD he may rightly do so (since you are about to harm another), but this implication of POD seems unacceptable. You may permissibly prevent the strangling, and it is wrong for Busybody to prevent you from so doing. Hence, *not all acts in defense of others* are permissible. Hence, POD is not acceptable; while it may sanction some permissible acts it sanctions those which are impermissible as well. But perhaps there is no *more* plausible view than POD. Perhaps, but if so this should be the conclusion of a careful investigation and not a hasty conclusion drawn at this stage. After all there are other views to consider.

As an alternative, suppose we revise POD by adding a qualification to it and formulate the following (different) view: it is permissible to restrict the liberty of another when he (or she) is about to harm an *innocent* other. Let us call *this* principle the Principle of Defense of Other Innocents (PDOI). Since it is indeed *permissible* for you to protect your innocent children (PDOI implies that it is), then your restriction of your former spouse's liberty is not one imposing a wrongful harm on another even if imposing a harm on another. May Busybody justifiably prevent you from so acting? Not according to PDOI, for your former spouse is intent on acting impermissibly— by harming an innocent person. For Busybody to restrict *your* liberty in order to protect your ex-spouse would *not* be a case of protecting the liberty of an innocent other. This failure of PDOI to sanction Busybody's interference lends some credibility to PDOI since if it had sanctioned such an act, we would rightly dismiss it as a patently unreasonable principle.

So far we have identified, at least roughly, what appears to be one *legitimate ground* for restricting the liberty of others: restrictions are permissible to prevent persons from harming others who are behaving innocently (i.e., not engaged in causing wrongful harm to others). Further reflection suggests, however, that PDOI is insufficiently comprehensive in that we may believe there are other cases, ones not sanctioned by PDOI, where it is permissible to restrict another's liberty. Consider this case. You are simply out for an evening stroll and you are threatened with bodily harm by a gang unless you hand over your money. May you restrict their liberty by fighting back? While it may not be prudent to do so, it certainly seems permissible. In brief it seems plausible that it is permissible to restrict the liberty of individuals when it will prevent them from wrongfully harming *others* or prevent them from wrongfully harming *oneself*. Let us call this principle the Principle of Defense of Innocents (PDI). PDI is, evidently, a more comprehensive principle than PDOI and, in addition, a more satisfactory one.

However, PDI is not entirely satisfactory. There are acts which PDI would sanction as permissible which may well strike us as impermissible. A tired insurance salesman, for example, insists on a bit of your attention in order to sell his wares. Although you, standing in your driveway, vaguely agree to listen to his pitch for a few minutes while you are involved in removing stains from an old jacket with lye, your inattentiveness offends him. Words are exchanged and he picks up your broom in a threatening manner. May you at this point, in self-defense, hurl lye into his eyes—with the likely result that he will be permanently blind? It is reasonable to think that this act would be wrong and that, even if substantial blame attaches to the salesman, one may *not* employ such extremely harmful means to defend oneself against a non-lethal threat. Indeed it is worth observing that in virtually all jurisdictions the law does *not* permit one to do just *anything* in self-defense. One may be legally required to retreat in the face of a threat or to employ only the least violent although effective method of warding off the threat. Some such qualifications might be added as a proviso to our formulation of PDI. The result would be a more plausible version.

Let us take note of a further complication, one which would have to be considered before one could arrive at a fully satisfactory view of when it is permissible to restrict the liberties of those who threaten others. While PDI sanctions restrictions on the liberty of others who are not innocent (those who are bent on wrongfully harming others), PDI, as it is formulated, also implies the permissibility of restricting the liberty of blameless individuals under certain conditions (individuals who though they may be about to cause a wrongful harm to others are not themselves to blame). An example will make this point clearer. Suppose that you, your neighbor and his three year old daughter are at the firing range. While your neighbor has gone for refreshments his daughter picks up a loaded pistol and points it at your forehead and begins to squeeze the trigger. Not a likely event, to be sure, but we may assume that your liberty will be eliminated or considerably reduced if she fires the weapon. You are "threatened" even if not deliberately. The child is "innocent" in the sense of not being to blame for her prospective act. To excuse *her* of blame is not, however, to say that her *act* ("shooting an innocent person") would be permissible. In this case the prospective act is wrong even though the agent is innocent. If the only way to eliminate the threat is to shoot the child, may you do it? In general is it permissible to restrict the liberties of blameless persons (e.g., the child) in order to prevent them from significantly harming other innocent individuals? PDI implies an affirmative answer. Notice that our formulation of PDI does not sanction defensive acts only against "threateners" who have malicious intentions or, more broadly, only against those who foresee the harmful consequences of their acts. The claim that it is all right to shoot the child is not *obviously* correct. Indeed this is a *hard case* to decide. I shall not offer any proposals here, but it is instructive to note that a *fully adequate* revision of PDI would have to take into account the two complications we have observed: 1) the question of the extremity of the means employed in defense of innocents, and 2) the question of the permissibility of restricting the liberties of "threatening" though blameless parties in order to protect other innocent parties (why should harm accrue to one innocent person rather than another?).

It is appropriate to review briefly where our inquiry has led. Unlike some acts which may be purely beneficial to others, acts which restrict the liberty of them make others worse off in at least one important respect. As such, liberty-limiting acts are *presumptively* wrong. In the absence of an adequate justification for such an act, it is wrong to limit the liberty of others. Nevertheless, there seem to be a range of cases where there is an adequate justification. We have roughly identified such a range of cases, namely, *cases where someone* (or some group or some institution) *is about to inflict a wrongful harm on another party, oneself or others*. The Principle of Defense of Innocents asserts the permissibility of restricting the liberty of the threatening party in such cases. We have also noted that such a principle may well need further qualifications given the two sorts of complications we have noted: one having to do with the means one may employ to restrict another's liberty and the other focusing on the somewhat unusual case where the "threatening" party is blameless (possibly lacking any intention to impose a harm). Examples falling in the latter category may include our gun-wielding three year old, psychopathic killers, a fetus (Homo sapien) which is a threat to the mother's carrying out her life plan, persons carrying serious contagious diseases, or a fat man stuck in the doorway of the only exit of a theatre where a fire has started. As the reader may have noticed, even these cases may involve relevant differences. The fat man stuck in the doorway is not "doing something" as is our gun-wielding three year old; further, he may not be stuck due to any negligent or reckless act of his own. Relatedly, the fetus is also not performing any *act* whose effects will render another worse off. Given the limitations of a single essay, we shall set aside the complications and fascinations of such hard cases.[2] It is worth observing, however, that the ground of defense of innocents against threats seems to be a plausible justification for imposing limits on the liberty of others. A great deal of our law, especially the criminal law, can be defended as a justifiable attempt to limit the liberties interfering with the decisions and/or actions of others. Even if we agree that the prevention of wrongful harm to others or oneself is a legitimate ground for intervention, we may inquire whether there are *other* legitimate grounds for restrictions on liberty. Two kinds of proposals shall be considered: 1) Legal Moralism, and 2) paternalistic principles. As noted earlier, our most thorough examination will focus on paternalistic grounds for restricting liberty. At this stage we shall turn to an investigation of Legal Moralism.

II. Legal Moralism

Our approach to the position of the legal moralist will be indirect. Let us initially reflect on the relation of *wrongful acts* to those classifiable as *harmful acts*. Many acts which seem to be paradigm (perfectly clear) examples of *wrongful* acts are also acts which cause *harm* to their "recipients." Consider, for example, rape or child-abuse. If by the not-so-easy-to-analyze term 'harmed' we understand 'made worse off,' one who is raped or a child who is beaten (compare the euphemisms 'spanked,' 'taught a lesson to') is, rather straightforwardly, harmed, i.e., he or she is physically and/or psychologically worse off. Hence, it is tempting to believe that *all wrongful acts are harmful acts*. It is also tempting to believe that the (logically) *distinct* (or different) claim that *all harmful acts are wrongful acts*. On reflection, the latter claim is doubtful. If the "special other" in your life, against your fondest wishes, decides to marry Mr. (Ms.) Wonderful, you will probably be worse off (substantially, but perhaps only for the short run); in that sense you are harmed. Is her/his act wrongful? Does not the other person have a right to so act? Barring extraordinary promises, such an act does not seem *wrong* even if it is unquestionably harmful. Therefore, it seems false that all harmful acts are wrongful. Let us turn our attention to the other claim, noted before, that *all wrongful acts are harmful*. It seems that *many* wrongful acts are harmful; again, consider rape, child-abuse, or murder. This fact, however, does not show that *all* wrongful acts are harmful. Can we think of any acts which are clearly wrong-but-not-harmful? Before considering a proposal or two, note that if we can agree that there are *any* such acts we will, if we are to have *logically consistent beliefs* (beliefs which *could* all be true), have to reject the claim that an act is wrong only if it is harmful. Some people certainly believe that even if reading pornography, engaging in consenting incest, cursing God, or for that matter, lying causes no harm to others such acts are nevertheless wrong—indeed, obviously wrong. Such alleg-edly wrongful acts are frequently labeled "*intrinsically* wrong." They are thought to be wrong independently of the occurrence of any harmful effect (including "risk of harm") on others. Now we are in a better position to understand legal moralism. *Legal Moralism* is commonly defined as a pair of claims whose import will now be clearer:

> 1) The "moralist" part: some acts are intrinsically wrong
> and 2) The "legal" part: wrongful acts should be illegal.

Let us recall the obvious. To employ the power of the law, the resources and coercive power of the "criminal justice system" in particular, is to *restrict the liberties* of those who choose (or desire) to perform legally prohibited acts. For our purposes here it must be noted that the Legal Moralist position maintains that in addition to the aim of protecting persons from wrongful *harms* which may arise from the acts of others (the "threateners"), there is *another legitimate ground* for restricting liberty, namely, the fact that an act is wrong even if it is harmless to others. In due course we will briefly look at some critical objections to both of the defining assumptions of this view.

Prior to doing so, it is worth digressing to note that the current and continuing controversy over "victimless crimes" can be traced to the fact that some people believe, on the one hand, that restrictions on the liberty (at least of adults), including legal restrictions, are justified if *and only if* they serve to protect innocents against wrongful *harms* and, on the other hand, others (Legal Moralists) believe that restrictions on liberty, including legal ones, are justified if they serve to prevent any wrongful act (*even if harmless* to others). To *label* an act as a "victimless crime" is often *not* the uncontroversial step it may appear to be. Are prostitution, consenting incest, consenting adultery, smoking pot, snorting cocaine, injecting heroin, or consenting homosexual acts "victimless crimes"? In virtually all jurisdictions in the United States they are, indeed, crimes. One question is whether they are victimless. One may be said to have been "victimized" by an activity in two different senses. In one sense a person is victimized if he is subjected to serious harm, e.g., an earth-quake victim. Note that in this use of 'victimized' there need be no human agent who is a "victimizer," i.e., one who causes another to be a victim. Alternatively, one may be a victim in another sense, namely, one who is subjected to a wrongful harm, e.g., a rape victim. A user of heroin may be a victim in the former sense without being a victim in the latter sense. Those who favor the elimination of "victimless crimes" (by legalizing the activity in question) generally do not deny that the activities in question (or, at any rate, many of them) may involve victims in the sense that participants may suffer harm. Their main point, in claiming that activities like those mentioned, are victimless *is* that if participants voluntarily choose to be involved no wrongful harm is imposed by others. However, acts which cause wrongful *harm to others*, directly or indirectly, are not only not victimless; there is a defense of their continued "criminalization" (legal prohibition) which need *not* appeal to Legal Moralism, one which may, instead, appeal to the widely accepted and plausible Principle of Defense of Innocents. One source of dispute, then, is whether or not such acts are properly classifiable as victimless (in the second sense noted above); the dispute is, to an extent, an *empirical* one, i.e., do such acts actually cause effects which count as wrongful harms to others. If usage of a certain drug did not harm the user, or if it did but that were not a good reason to intervene, then a key question would be whether the user causes wrongful harm to others. It is often pointed out that many heroin users, for example, spend several hundred dollars a day to support their habit. While this may be no obstacle for the wealthy, many users steal to raise the desired funds; hence, others are wrongfully harmed. As some economists and libertarians are fond of pointing out, the high cost of heroin is due in part to its being legally prohibited, a factor which increases costs to suppliers. "Legalize heroin and it will be readily affordable" is the proposed solution; the "necessity" of stealing will be circumvented. There is some truth in the proposal, but other questions arise as to whether increased usage (or current usage) results in wrongful harms other than theft. For example, to what extent is child or spouse abuse, or reckless driving, traceable to drug usage? But it is beyond my purpose to fully explore that issue here; it is worth observing, however, that this is one place, among many, where arriving at a specific, reasoned ethical position depends on a careful assessment of *both moral principles* (e.g., *Legal Moralism) and relevant empirical claims*.

Suppose, however, that certain currently criminal activities are indeed victimless in the sense of not violating PDI. For the sake of discussion we might specifically suppose that consenting prostitution does not victimize others. A defender of Legal Moralism need make only one further assumption, aside from the pair of assumptions which defines the position, to have a set of premises from which it logically follows that it is permissible, indeed obligatory, to restrict (by law) the liberties of prostitutes and their prospective customers, namely, that prostitution is an *intrinsically wrongful* act. So even if prostitution is a victimless activity (involves no wrongful harm to others), the frequently espoused argument of the Legal Moralist may be presented to defend its coercively enforced prohibition.

Since it is always possible to be right for the wrong reasons, the reasons which the Legal Moralist offers for restricting the liberty of others, e.g., a prostitute, warrant examination *even if* the conclusion that prostitution should be prohibited is the right view (I do *not* here assume that it is). We will briefly consider a number of objections to the Legal Moralist position.

One objection is that the Legal Moralist proposes to "enforce morality" and that either cannot be done or ought not to be done. The objection, on analysis, turns out to be capable of various interpretations, not all of which are equally plausible. It may be claimed that it is impossible to "legislate morality" in the sense of "making people moral" or virtuous by the use of the coercive power of the law. If a virtuous person is one who has certain sorts of desires, intentions, or "responsible" attitudes, then there is truth in the claim that the use of legal threats and penalties is unlikely to transform character, at least not directly or in the short run. However, Legal Moralists may simply concede this point and claim that their main contention is only that it is right and proper to minimize, prevent, and punish wrongful behavior by using the coercive power of the law; such use of legal powers may not make saints but, so it is insisted, it may and ought to be used to prevent wrongful acts.

A second objection to the Legal Moralist position stresses that the question of what laws we should have should be decided quite independently of moral considerations; hence, people should be left alone to decide what they wish to do—at least so long as they are not harming anyone else. The Legal Moralist may rightly point out, by way of response to this objection, that *any* claim about what laws we *ought* to have is itself a moral claim; indeed the claim that people ought to be left alone to do what they wish so long as their acts are harmless to others is itself a moral claim, and anyone who advocates such a principle is committed to the view that there is an acceptable moral principle to guide the determination of what laws are acceptable. Hence, anyone who believes that murder, for example, ought to be a crime may be asked "why" and if the answer is "because it is a serious wrong," such a person is committed to the view that *in one sense* it *is* appropriate to "legislate morality." The first two objections mentioned, then, fail to rebut Legal Moralism, and also fail to get at the heart of the disagreement between the Legal Moralist position and that of its critics.

More serious difficulties confront the Legal Moralist, however. Consider the "legal" part of the position defined, the claim that wrongful acts should be illegal. One objection to this blanket assumption focuses on the effects of legally proscribing an activity, especially in the case where it may be agreed that it is an harmless one. Concisely, the objection is that the cure may be worse than the disease. No one (well, almost no one) would accept the view that legal prohibition along with the penal sanction of capital punishment or long-term imprisonment is an appropriate means of dealing with acts which, we may agree, ought not to be committed, e.g., pointlessly issuing serious insults to others. It is not at all credible, then, that serious restrictions on the liberty of others are justifiable for *all* acts which are wrongful. However, the Legal Moralist may reply that from his assumption that wrongful acts should be illegal, it does not follow that extreme criminal penalties must be attached to "lesser wrongs." Perhaps a small fine would do. The point is well-taken; however, the general question remains as to whether *all* wrongs, even lesser ones, should be criminalized—especially in the case where the wrong, unlike our example of insulting, results in no harm to others. The degree of intervention, the magnitude of invasions of privacy, is likely to be substantial even if the aim is only to exact "fitting" or proportional penalties for wrong-doing. An interesting, analogous example which I shall only mention here (it is explored more fully in the essay by Joseph Margolis) is whether we should continue to seriously restrict, by law, the liberties of homosexuals *even if* it is assumed (and I do *not* assume it here) that homosexual behavior is intrinsically wrong. It has been the case, and in most states continues to be the case, that serious penalties are attached to even consenting adult homosexual behavior, historically ranging from capital punishment, life imprisonment, prison sentences up to ten years (as in North Carolina) to lesser penalties, as well as discrimination in housing or employment.

The Legal Moralist may be troubled by the objections mentioned and, on reflection, may be reluctant to maintain his strong assumption that *all* wrongful acts should be crimes, even if only minor crimes. If so, he may weaken his position and espouse a variant on the position noted. For example, he may claim that the wrongness of an act is only a *good reason* for criminalizing the act, but not by itself a sufficient one.[3] Hence, on this view, the wrongness of an act is relevant, along with other considerations, in deciding whether to criminalize the act. But both the original and the revised version confront a further difficulty to which we now turn.

This difficulty concerns the assumption that certain acts are *intrinsically* wrong even if harmless to others. In spite of the popularity of the view *about* moral judgments that each person must "decide for himself" or herself what is right or wrong, we generally do not, in practice, regard all moral judgments as equally reasonable. Indeed it is worth noting that we expect people to be able to give *reasons* for their judgments. Consider, for example, two possible events. Smith walks in and solemnly claims that capital punishment is wrong. Next Jones enters and solemnly proclaims that growing daffodils is also a serious wrong. We ask both Jones and Smith *why* they believe what they do. Smith states that in spite of some socially beneficial effects of the institution of capital punishment, all procedures for identifying those who commit heinous crimes (e.g., torture, rape, and murder of six year olds) are fallible. Hence, the administration of capital punishment contains the possibility of committing a serious judicial error, namely, killing an innocent person. An irreversible loss is imposed on such a person and no compensation can be made should the mistake be recognized belatedly. We may or may not think that this *argument* against capital punishment is *decisive*. However, it is clearly *relevant*. It is clearly a reasonable one. It deserves consideration. Note that it proposes that a certain act is wrong *because* it risks imposing an undeserved and serious harm on a person. Now consider the case of Jones. Perhaps we expect Jones to surprise us by, e.g., reporting a discovery that growing daffodils promotes the spread of a virus which causes cancer. But Jones does no such thing. Suppose Jones states "I just know it's wrong to grow daffodils," or "I dreamt that it is wrong," or "A Wise Man told me it is so." In this case our reaction is, I believe, that no serious defense of the moral judgment is made; we have not been given any good reasons to accept the claim; it has not been made belief-worthy. In particular, and in contrast to Smith's defense, no attempt has been made to show that performing the type of act in question will have a significantly *harmful* effect on any living creature. The fact that an act causes harm (to sentient creatures, in particular) creates a *presumption* (although an overridable one) that the act is wrongful. To merely assert that a certain type of act is wrong, intrinsically wrong, and to make no effort to link the claim or wrongfulness to the question of harmful effects is to make a puzzling assertion. Why is such-and-such a type of act judged to be wrong if it is not a harmful one? We see that at least there are some intelligible reasons to accept Smith's judgment, but it is not clear that there are intelligible reasons for accepting Jones' judgment. In short, the burden would seem to be on the Legal Moralist (or anyone who accepts such an assumption) to give us a reason why we should assume that certain types of acts are wrong when no plausible claim can be made that the act produces significant and undeserved harm to others. Reflection on this critical objection to Legal Moralism leads one to explore more fully a (perhaps, "the") fundamental question of moral philosophy: what are the legitimate *grounds* of moral judgment. This foundational issue is explored further in subsequent essays (especially by Lawrence Becker in his essay "Rights" and in the essay by Dan Brock on "Utilitarianism"); it will serve our purposes here to note that the claim that certain acts are *intrinsically wrong though harmless to others* leaves much unexplained. If there are such acts, how are we to distinguish, *within* the category of acts-harmless-to-others, which acts are wrong and which are permissible?

The careful reader may have noticed that in characterizing the "moralist" part of Legal Moralism we have only identified the assumption that "some acts are intrinsically wrong." We have implicitly equated 'intrinsically wrong' with 'not extrinsically wrong' or 'not wrong because the act harms innocent others.' There is, however, a view about the basis of right and wrong which, while it denies (as does Legal Moralism) that all wrongful acts are harmful to other sentient creatures, proposes another ground for the wrongfulness of an act, a ground which does not focus, so it seems, on features of "the act itself" *or* whether the act has harmful consequences for other creatures. Rather it is claimed that certain specific acts or types of acts are wrong *because* (and only because) God forbids them. Such a view is often called the Divine Command Theory. As one possible example, it is frequently held that even consenting adult homosexuality is wrong *because* God forbids it. Such a view commonly presumes the defensibility of the following argument:

(a) There is a God
(b) Whatever God forbids is wrong
(c) The Bible condemns homosexuality
(d) The Bible reliably indicates what God forbids
(e) So, homosexuality is wrong.

There are numerous variations of the above argument. The reader may reflect on how this type of argument is often invoked regarding other acts (cf. premarital sex, adultery, murder, lying, capital punishment, civil disobedience, or even abortion). There is, then, what we might not too misleadingly describe as a religious or theological version of the Legal Moralist view. It results from invoking the crucial general assumptions of the Divine Command Theory, namely (a) and (b) with further premises [e.g., (c) and (d)] to infer that some specific type of act is wrong, "intrinsically wrong" at least *in the sense* that the wrongness of the act-type is alleged not to derive from the causation of wrongful harm to humans (nor to God who, it is usually claimed, cannot be harmed); if the "legal" part of Legal Moralism is added we have, then, a religious version of the Legal Moralist argument. Some religious believers may well accept all but the "legal" part; it seems clear, however, that some believers accept the argument in its entirety and, hence, advocate various sorts of legal restrictions on the liberty of competent adults to engage in harmless-to-others behavior. The recently fashionable view of the "Moral Majority" in the United States seems a case in point.

It should be noted that the argument identified, (a) through (e), is *valid*, i.e., if its premises are true, its conclusion necessarily follows. The crucial questions to be raised about such a view, then, concern whether it is reasonable to accept *all* its premises; if any is false the argument is unsound. We shall note three types of questions which arise here, but will not here attempt to explore fully the perplexities with regard to each.

Most obvious are the array of questions concerning (a). Are there good reasons to believe in the existence of a being who is omnipotent, omniscient, and omnipresent? Is the evidence in favor of an affirmative answer sufficient to persuade a reasonable person? That such a being exists does not seem self-evident. For those who claim to have "directly encountered" God—and conceding the fact that some people seem to have "mystical" or "peak" experiences, why interpret such psychologically unusual events as "encounters with God"? For those who have had no such experience, is it reasonable for them to assume that reports of such encounters are veridical? We shall let these questions stand since a careful assessment of competing answers would require explorations beyond the aim of this essay.

A second type of difficulty arises regarding (b). Suppose, for the sake of discussion, that there exists a God who conforms, roughly, to the conception in the Judeo-Christian tradition. A puzzle about (b), one noted long ago, is whether an act is wrong just because God forbids it *or* whether God forbids an act because it is wrong. If the former is correct then even the most seemingly innocent act, e.g., nurturing a baby, *might* be wrong—so long as God forbids it. The reply that surely God would never forbid such an act is in tension with another widely held religious belief, i.e., that the ways of God are mysterious and the proper role for humans is "not to reason why." If the alternative that God forbids an act because it is wrong is the correct view, then it seems possible that the basis of an act's being wrong is *independent* of God's commands. If that is true, perhaps a reasonable ethic is one which identifies that ground and it need not include any reference to God's commands. This perplexity, which we only note here, is independent of the two problems of defending belief in the existence of God and ascertaining what God commands.

A final set of problems concerns this latter point. If the prior obstacles could be circumvented is there any reliable way of ascertaining God's will? In particular, are claims like (c) and (d) belief-worthy? Two problems may be recorded here. One concerns seemingly *inconsistent* ethical prescriptions in the scriptures. Certain scriptural passages advocate, so it appears, that we love our neighbors as ourselves; others seem to condone slavery (Deut. 15:12–13, Exodus 21:2, Ephesians 6:5). The second commandment states "Thou shalt not kill;" elsewhere it is said that "Whoever curses his father or mother shall be put to death." (Exodus 21:17) Some passages advocate forgiving your enemies; others condone making war and taking women and children as "booty for yourselves" (Deut. 20:10–14). Some advocate strict retributive punishment (Exodus 21:23–24), others the opposite (Romans 12:17). Aside from contrary prescriptions, others are in radical conflict with widely accepted views. For example, it is said that women should be silent in churches and be subordinate to their husbands (I Cor. 14:34–35); further, one should not collect interest from those who owe debts (Exodus 22:25). In short, there is a host of problems confronting the assumption that one consistent, intuitively plausible ethic can be found in the writings held sacred in the Judeo-Christian tradition.

A frequent response to such perplexities is the assertion that certain things have to be taken "on faith" and that it is "overly rationalistic" to do otherwise. But even if this were true there is a problem for any thinking person: *which* claims should be so taken? Why accept those of the Christian over those of a Jew, a Buddhist, an agnostic, an atheist, or Whirling Dervish (or conversely)? The necessity of rational reflection seems unavoidable, unless it matters not at all in which direction one takes a "leap of faith"—but that it matters not is not at all obvious.

We have explored Legal Moralism, it will be recalled, because such a view proposes to provide us with a basis for concluding that certain restrictions on the liberty of persons is permissible, a basis distinct from that contained in the Principle of Defense of Innocents, or a suitably refined version of the latter principle. However, there seem to be compelling reasons for rejecting Legal Moralism since 1) we have found reasons for *not* accepting the assumption that we should legally prohibit all that may be morally wrong, and 2) there is no obvious reason to accept the claim that certain types of acts are intrinsically wrong even though harmless to others. Now that we have considered, at some length, the question of why there is a serious problem about attempting to justify proposed restrictions on liberty and explored two major (alleged) grounds for such restrictions (PDI and Legal Moralism) we are in a better position to explore a third type of proposal, one which is the central concern of this essay.

III. Paternalism

As we have observed, people may give quite *different* sorts of reasons for proposing the acceptability of restrictions on liberty. So even when there may be a consensus that, for example, recreational use of heroin should be legally prohibited, the reasons which lie behind this consensus may be quite diverse. To carefully assess, or reconsider, the justifiability of such a policy we need to ask whether there are good reasons, indeed compelling reasons, in favor of such a policy. If acceptance of Legal Moralism is in fact the reason why many people advocate such a policy but Legal Moralism is a view which rational persons ought not accept, we must search elsewhere for a justification of such a liberty-limiting policy. If none can be found, then we must conclude that the policy is (at least presumptively) unjustified and it ought to be terminated. To consider the heroin example further, it is evident that one widely held view is that heroin usage is rightly prohibited because it is harmful *to the user*.

The last three words are very important. Implicit in this last judgment is the view that, *quite aside* from questions of whether there are intrinsically wrongful acts *or* whether heroin usage wrongfully harms non-users, *it is permissible to restrict the liberties of a person in order to prevent that person's causing significant harm to himself (or herself).*[4] Let us label this latter moral principle: The Paternalist View.[5] Defenders of this general view suppose that, to reiterate a point, there is a compelling reason or justification for restricting the liberty of persons which is distinct from the other proposals we have considered. It should be observed that the Paternalist View, like the Principle of Defense of Innocents, and unlike Legal Moralism, is a "harm-based" moral principle in that it supposes that prevention-of-harm (in this case "self-caused") is a morally relevant consideration (a consideration relevant to deciding the moral acceptability of an act). Unlike PDI, however, the Paternalist View asserts, to put the point in the language of "defense," that it is all right to defend people *from themselves,* from the risks generated by their own decisions or behavior.

The natural first recourse in an attempt to prevent someone from harming herself is to try to *persuade* that person to refrain from the act in question. To use the term 'persuade' here is to suggest the provision of *reasons* to the other person as to why she *should agree* that she ought not to carry out some activity. However, the Paternalist View sanctions the *restriction of liberty* even when persuasion, as is frequently the case, is unsuccessful.

What are the ways by which we can restrict another's liberty? I shall simply assume, without argument, that when we sincerely attempt to give good reasons to another (of a non-threatening type) as to why she *should decide* to refrain from, or discontinue, an activity (i.e., to persuade) we do not, thereby, restrict her liberty. She may, on reflection, disagree and forge ahead. While there are some subtleties which arise and which I largely ignore here, there seem to be three main ways in which we may restrict or interfere with another's liberty: 1) by use of force, 2) by use of coercion, and 3) by deceit.[6] Suppose you, at age sixteen, are about to fly to Berkeley to join a religious cult which I shall call the "Loonies." Your parents believe that you will suffer great harm (mainly, psychological damage) if you carry out this act. Having failed to dissuade you, they might 1) lock you indefinitely in your room, 2) coercively threaten you (if you go, we shall disown you), or 3) have a fake newspaper printed reporting that the Berkeley Loonies have suddenly disbanded and vanished. The three strategies are examples of 1) the use of force (cf. a more direct use: they put you in a straightjacket in spite of your resistance), 2) the use of coercive threat (this typically has the form: if you do x, I will impose a certain harm on you; if you comply with my demand, I will not), and 3) deceit (which may involve positive falsehoods, misleading claims, or omission of the truth). The term 'coercion' is sometimes loosely used to cover 1), 2), and 3), but the above distinctions seem worth making. There are different ways of *controlling* a person's behavior, each of which involves a limitation on liberty by placing a barrier between the person and his aims. Since people typically *resent* being forced or threatened (and may retaliate), it is not surprising that deception is so popular. After all, you may not learn of the deception and will not, thereby, be conscious of grounds for resentment. The attaching of enforceable penalties to certain activities by the criminal law is, in contrast, a clear use of coercive threat to control behavior.

Having identified the Paternalist View and the sorts of restrictions on liberty which it may sanction, let us consider some of the acts or policies which, *it is often claimed, are justified, partly or solely, on paternalistic grounds,* i.e., by virtue of the fact that they will prevent an agent from harming himself (or will be even better off as a result of the intervention). The range of such acts, policies, and laws is, on reflection, surprisingly broad. Here are some: required blood transfusions even when contrary to the convictions and wishes of the recipients, required waiting periods before divorce is permitted, restrictions on obtaining a wide variety of drugs, required contributions to Social Security or retirement accounts, required university courses, prohibitions on riding motorcycles without helmets, prohibitions on gambling, prohibitions on dueling, prohibitions on suicide, and prohibitions on selling oneself into slavery. One might add: civil commitment of the psychologically disturbed, involuntary sterilization, required vaccinations, restraints on obtaining certain products or services from unlicensed persons, requirements that welfare distributions be made in kind (e.g., food stamps) and not in cash, and restraints on advertising professional services by physicians, lawyers, dentists, or opticians. In this last regard, it is claimed, somewhat ironically in a land of "free enterprise," that competition would lead to lower quality of service or product, and, hence, it is "for our own good" that such restrictions are instituted. We briefly note here that some paternalistically motivated policies may restrict not only the party to be protected but others as well. Quite aside from examples drawn from law or official policy, it is worth considering other paternalistically motivated acts which occur with a certain regularity among friends or within families. One example, reported to me by a colleague, involved a physician who was ignorant of the fact that he, the physician, had cancer. In spite of his suspicion that this was so, he was repeatedly deceived on this point by both his medical associates and his immediate family even after he directly and repeatedly inquired whether he had cancer. Such practices are, of course, not uncommon.

In this last regard, it is especially noteworthy that paternalistically motivated acts differ from many other morally suspect acts in that they are, in one sense, *altruistic* in motivation. The person who paternalistically interferes with the activity of another considers himself to be conferring a "benefit" on that other, at least by way of preventing the other from harming himself or, possibly, by way of making the other party even better off. The familiar cliché about the road to hell being paved with good intentions is, of course, worth keeping in mind here. In recent years a case was reported where a mother roasted her young son in an oven for a few hours "in order to drive the devil out of him." However much one might be willing to concede the sincerity or kindness of her intention to benefit her child, reservations may linger about the moral acceptability of her act.

Let us begin to focus more directly on the question of whether it is permissible to *interfere* (by means of force, coercive threat, or deceit), for paternalistic reasons, with another's freedom to choose or act. Brief reflection on the last mentioned case, one where the young child is roasted with non-culinary but not malicious intentions, strongly suggests that interference for paternalistic reasons is sometimes wrong. In short, the view that *any* sort of interference for paternalistic reasons is permissible is wildly in conflict with our rather deeply embedded moral convictions. By way of contrast, consider another case. Suppose you are driving down a dark road to an area where, unknown to you, the bridge is out. You fail to see the detour sign. The only way I can stop you, as I walk along the road, is to shoot your tires. May I do that? If I do, I certainly impose a certain harm on you (by damaging your property) and do so without having obtained your consent. Further, it is presumptively wrong to so damage another's property. However, in such a situation it would seem right to so interfere; indeed, it seems permissible precisely in order to prevent you from causing significant harm to yourself. I am suggesting simply that this is an instance of justified paternalistic interference (barring other extraordinary and relevant considerations, e.g., you are on your way to bomb the Children's Hospital). The prior examples strongly support the view that *some* forms of paternalistic interference are justified and *some* are not. If that much is right, an important question comes into view. We need some reasoned basis, some statable criterion, for distinguishing as best we can (*even if* some residual hard cases remain) when interference on paternalistic grounds is justified and when not. The difficult task is just that. A reasonable person would, at this point, attempt to identify the tempting and at least *initially* plausible candidates which may be proposed to answer the question: under what conditions is paternalistic interference justified. Progress in this inquiry may be of *two* sorts: 1) ruling out certain answers as unreasonable, and 2) establishing a compelling case in favor of an affirmative answer. To achieve the second requires doing the first, though not conversely. We shall begin by examining a series of more-or-less tempting views. In the end one approach will be defended, at least as much as can be reasonably done here; however, our inquiry raises some deep questions of ethical theory, ones whose full exploration must go beyond the limits of a single essay.

The case of the roasted child is the only case mentioned so far as an obviously *unacceptable* piece of paternalistic interference, and someone may say "Oh, but the treatment of children is after all quite special." More commonly, this complaint would be made in response to the claim that paternalistic interference with children is quite *acceptable* (unlike the interference in the example). In fact, it does seem permissible to *interfere with children for their own good* in ways that would consti- tute unacceptable interference with adults.[7] I may permissibly force my very young child to receive a penicillin injection to halt her pneumonia; I do not seem to have any right at all to force a normal adult stranger to undergo painful surgery solely because I believe (rightly *or* wrongly) that it is "for her own good." It would be instructive, at some point, to ask why we commonly believe that more pervasive and, often, more invasive forms of paternalistic interference are acceptable toward children as op- posed to normal adults—and also to ask, if that is the view we *should* have, just what justifies that sort of frequent "discrimination" (different treatment). In order to deal with one issue at a time I propose that we ignore, temporarily, almost a billion people in the world—by setting aside the question of whether paternalistic interference with children is justifiable (and, if so, under what conditions). This proposal does not arise because of any W. C. Fields-like view of children (Fields is reported to have said, when asked whether he liked children, "yes, parboiled"). If it is correct that some forms of paternalistic interference towards children are permissible which are not permissible toward adults, that may be because there is a *stronger presumption* against employing force, coercive threat, or deception against adults, to restrict their liberty, than there is against children. If so, it is very important to try to determine *whether there is* a justification for the great array of liberty-limiting policies which violate this presumption, policies which are often paternalistically *motivated* (again, cases where people interfere out of a *desire* to prevent another's making himself worse off) and defended by appealing to paternalistic considerations (it is permissi- ble to interfere with Jones because the interference is "for his own good"). Hence, in what follows, we shall focus almost solely on the problematic question of when paternalist interference toward adults is acceptable and when not.

IV. The Appeals to Prior and Subsequent Consent

Sometimes reflection on what we *would* say (think) about a particular kind of example suggests a principle (although identifying and stating the principle is usually much harder than is commonly thought). Consider this example. You are wise enough to recognize your own weakness of will; for example, you are aware of your habit of consuming alcoholic beverages beyond a point which is prudent. So, you ask an acquaintance, Max, at a party to take away your car keys (or otherwise inhibit you) if you get roaring drunk. You do and Max does. In your drunken state you resist; in *some* sense, Max is interfering with you. It is *tempting* to think that this is a case of justified paternalistic interference on Max's part. Indeed, it is tempting to generalize from this case and infer that

A's paternalistic interference with B is justified if B has given *prior consent* to A's interference.

I have no objection to, and would indeed agree to, the claim that Max's interference was permissible. However this "principle of Prior Consent" fails, I believe, to show that a certain kind of *paternalistic* interference is justified. My reason is that the interference in question is dubiously labeled 'paternalistic interference'. This claim requires elaboration. First, as a minor point, it could be that Max agreed to take away your keys because and only because you will pay him for the service rendered. Hence, his motivation for so acting may not be paternalistic at all; he could not care less about your welfare. But suppose this is not true; suppose his behavior is paternalistically motivated. The second point is: is it really *interference?* Interference with what? If your settled preference is that you wish such a restriction on your momentary desire to drive, then his restriction is not an interference with your settled, and expressed, desire. His control of your behavior is, then, not a use of force *against your will* (in one important sense, and stands in sharp contrast to other cases where one "is forced" to act against one's will). Indeed, Max acts *in order to implement* your settled decision, not to override or disregard it. It seems at least misleading then to classify this case as one of "interference" and, hence, of "paternalistic interference." One might contrast this case with that of the motorcyclist who, all things considered, seriously objects to wearing a helmet, yet the law requires him to do so. Such a restriction is not an attempt by another to *implement* the cyclist's desire; it is, rather, a clear case of *interference*. What we should conclude about the Principle of Prior Consent can be put more cautiously. Either it does not show that genuine interference is justified (and, if so, then it does not show that some form of paternalistic interference is justified), or, if one insists that it does serve to justify a certain type of "interference" we must suggest that it fails to go any significant way toward justifying almost all the interesting cases of paternalistic interference, cases where force, coercive threat, or deception are employed *without the prior consent* of the subject of the interference. Whichever we say, the Principle of Prior Consent fails to significantly help in ascertaining when such tactics are acceptable.[8]

However, the presence of voluntary, informed consent (or its absence) does seem to be a morally significant factor. Consider the following. Imagine two clips of film each showing a closeup of someone getting cut by a scalpel. Is either act permissible? Neither? When we later learn that in the one case we are seeing surgery to which a patient has consented and that in the other film we are seeing part of a procedure to sterilize a young woman who has not consented to such an act (she came to have her baby delivered), we may agree that one cutting is permissible and the other not. If so, this difference in judgments may reflect our belief in the moral significance of (informed, unpressured) consent. It is for this reason that some attempts to justify a variety of paternalistic restrictions on liberty have sought to "locate" consent on the part of the subject (of restrictions). A second attempt to do so appeals not to prior but to *subsequent consent*. Let us explore it by means of an example.

If we force our young child to receive the penicillin shot to halt her pneumonia we may believe that she will, when older and wiser, come to approve our act, that is, will "subsequently consent" to our overriding her earlier, firm resolve not to have that needle stuck in her arm. How often we hear "when you get older you'll realize. . . ." Since we were to focus on adults, and not children, we might consider a case involving an adult. Suppose that you receive third degree burns over most of your body from an explosion. It is so painful that you wish to be allowed to die (or helped to die). Still, the medical personnel continue to treat you against your will. Even your relatives conspire to see to it that you are unable to talk with your lawyer. The defense is offered, once more, that you *will later* be glad that your liberty to choose your fate was restricted; hence, it is alleged, the interference is justified. The operative principle here, one which deserves our critical reflection, is

A's paternalistic interference with B is justified if B will subsequently consent to A's interference.

Let us call this the Principle of Subsequent Consent (PSC).

There are several difficulties with PSC. One obvious problem is that A, aiming to act on this principle, may well be in an epistemologically problematic position, i.e., there will frequently be difficulties in A's ascertaining whether it is certain, or at all probable, that B will subsequently consent to A's interference. Relatedly it is a still too ignored fact that persons who interfere with others are all too likely to assume, glibly, that their own view about what is prudent *for another* reflects their estimation of what they would like done to themselves in similar circumstances *given their own current preferences, beliefs, and goals,* ones which may be quite different from those of the subject interfered with—not only at the time of the interference but even when the subject is at a later stage in life. A similar consideration was no doubt behind George Bernard Shaw's reported reservation about (and rejection of) the Golden Rule. Shaw is said to have remarked that we should *not* "do unto others as we would have them do unto us" since, after all, their tastes may be different. (Imagine, for example, a sado-masochist who attempts to act according to the Golden Rule.) And one might add, "not only their tastes now but forever more." The risk of self-deception here, on the part of the interferer, runs deep. Relatedly, even if A has good reasons to believe that subsequent consent is likely, it may not in fact ever occur because of entirely fortuitous factors. If B, by chance, is struck by lightning, no subsequent consent will occur. At the least, betting on actual subsequent consent is a risky matter. Indeed, the notion that the moral permissibility of interference rests on future natural contingencies (e.g., will lightning strike?) is a suspect idea. A third difficulty with PSC is worth noting. Suppose, as in our example where you are badly burned, you, five years later, are pleased that your liberties were restricted earlier. Two questions arise. Does this mean that you, five years later, *consent* to the earlier interference? Does this mean that the earlier limitation on your liberty was permissible because you, as the subject, consented to it? It is not at all obvious that we should answer affirmatively. First, I may be pleased, in some sense, that I was knocked into unconsciousness by a gang of terrorists earlier in my life since, it is now clear, had I not been unconscious they would have realized I was alive and tortured and killed me. Rendering me unconscious turned out to be "for my own good" in the long run, but it does not follow that the act was, therefore, morally permissible. Even my belated positive view of that act does not support the view that it was permissible. Analogously, even if you are now "pleased" that, while suffering from third-degree burns you were treated against your will, it does not seem to follow that the earlier severe deprivation of your liberty was justified. Let us pursue this matter of "belated approval" (for want of a better expression) a bit further to see if it is properly labeled "consent." One way of understanding why we believe that unpressured, informed consent (to another's doing something to us that is presumptively wrong) is morally relevant (and which, indeed, may render the act permissible) is that when we so consent we *give permission* to another to do what is otherwise wrongful to do. In the language of rights, we *waive our right not* to be treated in a certain fashion. Hence, it is presumptively wrong to take vegetables from your neighbor's garden but, if she has consented, matters are entirely different. What is most puzzling about PSC is the idea that the subject's "belated approval" of a presumptively wrong act somehow, retroactively, renders that act rightful, as if one who did *not* consent at an earlier time, t, to interference at t really gave permission to the interference at t simply because of the occurrence of "belated approval" at a later time, t + n. What is clear in this case is that *no* permission was given at t and there was *no* waiving of rights at t. There is no basis, in *that* regard, for saying that the presumptively wrongful interference was, after all, permissible. "Belated approval" is hardly a giving of permission to another to perform now an act which calls for some justification. For this reason the expression 'subsequent consent' is misleading. Belated approval seems only to be, rather, a later judgment about the overall beneficial effect of some earlier wrongful act and, perhaps, in certain cases a *forgiving* of the one who earlier committed the wrong.

I cannot resist adding one further example before we leave our examination of PSC. Suppose (what may be true) that you are a woman who was raped when you were eighteen. The experience was devastating and the next few years an enormous struggle, psychologically and otherwise. Seventeen years later, at thirty-five, you judge that, in some sense, it was "good" that the rape occurred. This last remark strikes one as incredible. What could be meant? Suppose that, in spite of a difficult life, there is something that has made your life one of deep happiness for over a decade, namely, the loving and joyous relationship which you have experienced with the two daughters born of the trauma at eighteen. You might be able to say that your life is much happier than it would have been if numerous other sequences had occurred; in that sense and in that sense *only* you have a positive attitude toward the *set* of prior events. But none of this supports the view that the rape was consented to, permissible, or not a heinous wrong. Perhaps there is some way of revising PSC to discover a more acceptable principle. For the reasons given, I conclude that it fails to provide an acceptable basis for restricting the liberty of adult persons.

V. The Appeal to Hypothetical Consent

Another attempt to justify paternalistic interference is suggested by a natural reaction both to our prior example of preventing one's mother from ingesting poison and to the example of preventing you from driving onto a bridge which is out. In both of these cases the subject is about to act in a way most harmful to his or her welfare; further, there is a presumption that the subjects are unaware of the likely consequences of their action, and, if they were, they would voluntarily refrain from or halt the activity in question. Relatedly, it is reasonable to think that *if the subjects were fully aware of the relevant circumstances and were fully rational* each *would consent* to efforts to prevent them from coming to a catastrophic end. Hence, a tempting principle as to when paternalistic interference is permissible stresses this consideration of hypothetical rational consent. We may formualte it as follows

A's paternalistic interference with B is justified if B would consent to A's act were B both fully rational and aware of the relevant circumstances.

Let us call this the Principle of Hypothetical Rational Consent (PHRC). To understand and assess this principle it is useful, at this point, to recognize a distinction, one which in our final assessment seems of no little importance. Just how the distinction relates to PHRC is a question to which we shall return. Among cases of paternalistic interference where one party restricts the liberty of a subject with the aim of promoting the latter's own good, there are a range of cases where the *agent's* conception of what is for the good of the subject is different from that of the *subject*.

In contrast there are cases where the agent's conception of what is for the good of the subject is the same as that of the subject. Again, keeping examples before us will help us retain what the famous British philosopher, Bertrand Russell labeled, in another context, a "robust sense of reality." In the case where you are about to drive onto the fractured bridge, we may reasonably suppose that you do not intend to harm yourself. Hence, if I interfere to stop you I only promote one of your own goals, namely, self-preservation. Such a case stands in sharp contrast with others. While legislators, in passing a law requiring that cyclists wear helmets, might reason that they only promote the cyclist's *own* goal of self-preservation and, hence, are not "imposing foreign values" on the cyclist, we may entertain doubts about such reasoning. In contrast to the bridge-crossing case where you are entirely ignorant of the risks involved in driving ahead, the cyclist may be fully aware of the risks of not wearing a helmet. However, the cyclist may prefer the alternative of cycling with-no-helmet-and-greater-risks to the alternative of cycling with-a-helmet-and-lower-risks. If so, the legal requirement to wear a helmet does *not* promote the subject's own good *as the subject conceives it*. It will be useful to try to state our distinction more succinctly. Some cases of paternalistically motivated interference attempt to promote the good of the subject as the subject would conceive it if he were aware of the relevant circumstances (compare the bridge-crossing case). In other cases of paternalistically motivated interference the attempt is to promote the good of the subject according to some conception of the subject's good different from that of the subject, *even if* the subject were aware of the relevant circumstances. The latter type of interference merits the slippery label "imposing one's values on others" in a way that the former type of interference does not. Indeed, the restriction on our imagined cyclist seems to be, to put it abstractly, a case of A's imposing A's values on B; my interference to prevent you from crossing the bridge seems to be a case of A's imposing B's values on B. If we regard persons as having a right to decide for themselves what their goals shall be or what risks they wish to assume (at least if the goals do not involve impermissible acts, e.g., ordinary homicide or rape), we must conclude that there is a significant difference between the two types of paternalistic interference which we have just distinguished. For when A imposes his own ("foreign") values on B, even with paternalistic motivation, it would seem that such interference is far more destructive of B's *autonomy* (roughly, capacity to direct his or her own life) than in the case where A interferes with B to implement certain general goals which B has. In short, the presumption against interference of the former type seems far stronger than the presumption against interference of the latter type. If this is correct, any theory purporting to formulate a plausible view of which sorts of paternalistic interference are permissible must take it into account.

Let us, then, return to our consideration of our last formulated principle, the Principle of Hypothetical Rational Consent: A's paternalistic interference with B is justified if B would consent to A's act were B both fully rational and aware of the relevant circumstances. In our bridge-crossing example it seems likely that, if you were fully rational and aware of the relevant circumstances, you would consent to my interference. Assuming that the latter is a permissible bit of paternalism on my part, then PHRC gives us the "right result" for it would sanction the interference. A point in favor of PHRC. However, PHRC insists on the importance of another consideration, namely, *full rationality*. This insistence gives rise to certain difficulties with PHRC. The most obvious one concerns the problem of formulating explicit criteria for determining when a person, or his decision, belief, or goal is "fully rational." We might readily agree, intuitively, that a fully rational individual would consent to interference if he valued his self-preservation and he was ignorant of the fact that he was about to do something radically self-destructive. But other cases arise where it is not obvious what a fully rational individual would choose to do (*or* would consent to having done to him). Consider once more the cyclist example. A legislator, attempting to act according to PHRC, might claim that a cyclist's opposition to the helmet requirement when the cyclist is aware of the relevant risks of not wearing a helmet is *not* fully rational; further if cyclists were not only relevantly informed but *fully rational,* they would consent to the restriction. Hence, it is inferred, the restriction, assuming PHRC, is a perfectly permissible bit of paternalism. Now the last inference in the argument is not obviously a valid one, not at least if we take seriously the idea that ordinary persons (who probably fall short of being "fully rational" on many interpretations of that problematic expression) should be allowed to arrange their own lives and make their own choices (so long as they are not bent on wrongfully treating other persons). That is, if we believe that there is a strong *presumption in favor of respecting the autonomy of ordinary persons* (I set aside here those whose capacity for autonomous choice may be radically defective or undeveloped, e.g., the retarded, the senile, the brain-damaged, and young children), then we must doubt that paternalistic interference is permissible in *all* those cases where it is true that a *fully rational* person, aware of the relevant circumstances, would consent to it. More or less competent, but not necessarily fully rational, persons not only have goals; they value having the prerogative of deciding for themselves, as best they can, what they shall do—even if, on some criterion, their choice of action or their opposition to interference fails to count as being fully rational. What I am suggesting is that the Principle of Paternalism with Hypothetical Rational Consent allows a greater degree of invasive interference than might first appear and, indeed, that it is unacceptable since it would fail to adequately respect the autonomy of ordinary, generally competent persons.

Consider another example. As a generally competent adult one could play a chess match as best one could or, alternatively, be hooked up to the P-machine, the P-machine being a paternalistically-minded computer which prevents one from making any move which is not "fully rational" with respect to the goal of winning the match. So long as one is generally competent I presume one would want to *decide for oneself* whether an alternative move is prudent, i.e., to "play one's own hand." That is, one would not want the imposition by the P-machine of a "forced" avoidance of the consequences of one's own (possibly) less than fully rational decisions *even if* the result of such interference would be more prudent. One's goal in such a circumstance is not just to win the match but to *play* it. Perhaps it is now clearer how interference in accord with PHRC would be seriously invasive. We need not be committed to the view that individuals in all cases ought to be left alone to make their own decisions and carry them out, however irrational, when we take the view that people ought to be left alone with regard to certain decisions even though they would not be made by fully rational individuals. The prerogative to choose for oneself, if not of unlimited value, is a distinct value to be weighed against, for example, the desirability of imposing all those restraints acceptable to a fully rational individual. A precocious child might say: it is valuable to "do it myself" even if the *results* of so doing are not optimal. As Gerald Dworkin, a contemporary American philosopher, has observed, "to be able to choose is a good that is independent of the wisdom of what is chosen."[9] My point is that PHRC, in allowing all "those restrictions which would be permissible to fully rational individuals," fails to give due weight to that good.

It is also worth noting here that the appeal to the hypothetical consent of a fully rational individual is very different from another sort of appeal to "hypothetical consent." Sometimes it is reasonable to infer hypothetical consent on the part of another, e.g., if you knew that the bridge was unsafe and if you were sober, you would consent to my not allowing you to continue to drive. This type of hypothetical consent can be reasonably assumed or inferred only on the basis of empirical data *about you* (your beliefs and preferences). It is another thing altogether to judge what some hypothetical "fully rational" person would find acceptable if he were "in your place" (but exercising his full rationality). Indeed, talk of the hypothetical *consent* of a fully rational person is misleading for even if there is a fully rational person who would agree to the restriction imposed on you such a person has no authority to *give permission* to an interference with *your* behavior. In the latter case we have, at best, the hypothetical consent of a hypothetical individual; in the former we have, perhaps, grounds for determining what some *actual* individual, you, would consent to under non-actual circumstances. On the face of it, imposing on you a restraint which you would accept, given your conception of your own good, seems less difficult to justify than imposing on you a restraint which you, even functioning at your rational best and fully informed, would not accept.

VI. Weak Paternalism and Autonomy Respecting Paternalism

Joel Feinberg, a philosopher at the University of Arizona, in an important recent essay, has defended a type of limited paternalism which substantially avoids many of the difficulties previously discussed.[10] After distinguishing between acts where one directly harms oneself and those which create a risk of harm, he draws an important distinction between *fully and not fully voluntary assumptions of risk;* on this matter it is worth quoting Feinberg. With a "fully voluntary assumption of risk"

> . . . one shoulders it while fully informed of all relevant facts and contingencies, with one's eyes wide open, so to speak, and in the absence of all coercive pressure of compulsion. There must be calmness and deliberation, no distracting and unsettling emotions, no neurotic compulsion, no misunderstanding. To whatever extent there is impetuousness, clouded judgment (as e.g., from alcohol), or immature or defective facilities of reasoning, to that extent the choice falls short of voluntariness. Voluntariness is then a matter of degree.[11]

If someone is about to do that which it is doubtful a person in his right mind would do, then, in Feinberg's view, it is permissible to interfere ". . . not to evaluate the wisdom or worthiness of a person's choice, but rather to determine whether the choice is really his." Feinberg's position is more fully clarified, then, by his distinction between two versions of paternalism:

> According to the strong version of legal paternalism, the state is justified in protecting a person, against his will, from the harmful consequences of even his fully voluntary choices and undertakings. . . . weak paternalism would permit us to protect him from "nonvoluntary choices," which, being the choices of no one at all, are no less foreign to him.[12]

I leave aside the question of whether all of the items Feinberg includes under the category of 'nonvoluntary choices' merit the label 'choices'. The principle that Feinberg finds acceptable, weak paternalism, is not explicitly couched in terms of hypothetical consent. However, it seems possible to do so. For example, weak paternalism seems equivalent to the view that paternalistic interference is permissible, and only permissible, if the subject would consent to the interference if he were making a fully voluntary choice. More importantly here, Feinberg does *not* propose the permissibility of restrictions on liberty in just those cases where they would be acceptable to a *fully rational* person.

Weak paternalism sanctions only those interferences with Jones' activity where Jones is functioning at something less than *his* (or *her*) rational best. Weak paternalism, at least implicitly, rejects interferences with the fully voluntary acts of generally competent individuals, and it is clear that a fully voluntary act need not be a fully rational act. Its "let alone" prescription for fully voluntary acts, then, seems to *avoid* sanctioning an overriding of the autonomy of individuals in the way that, as I have argued, Paternalism with Hypothetical Rational Consent sanctions.

Another way of seeing the difference between PHRC and Feinberg's weak paternalism is the following. While, in a particular case, it may not be plausible to claim that it is in an individual's overall interest to perform an act he decides to perform, it is generally in one's interest to not be prevented from carrying out decisions which one *believes* to be in one's (other) interests—even if one is mistaken in this belief. An omnipotent, omniscient paternalist acting on Paternalism with Hypothetical Rational Consent would intervene with one whose fully voluntary acts were imprudent, and a fully rational individual would consent to such interference. It does not seem unlikely that this procedure would result in an intuitively unacceptable, serious diminishing of one's liberty to make choices, to make one's own way in life according to *one's own* lights. As noted before, for less than fully rational beings there is something of considerable value in having the effective prerogative to decide for themselves and effectively act on their own choices, even though imprudent results are not always avoided. Life is not in *all* respects unlike a game where there is something valuable, translatable perhaps in terms of self-respect, in *playing one's own hand* as best one knows how, rather than being "helped" to avoid mistakes by "benevolent" and controlling fellow persons. Any reasonable principle permitting paternalistic interference must, I think, give strong weight to this consideration.

Feinberg's weak paternalism substantially succeeds in this latter respect. Although Feinberg rightly regards voluntariness as a matter of degree, one may have qualms about the stringency of the conditions which must be satisfied, on his account, before a decision may count as being fully voluntary. In his view the decision must be one that is made a) where an individual is "fully informed of all relevant facts," b) "in the absence of all coercive pressure," c) "no distracting and unsettling emotions," d) "no misunderstanding," e) "no neurotic compulsion," and so on (see prior quotation). One might ask whether one has *ever* made a decision satisfying all these conditions. Perhaps Feinberg has overstated his case, although we should note that elsewhere he insists that a decision or act must be "substantially nonvoluntary" in order for interference to be permissible.

The worry, perhaps not a substantial one, is that weak paternalism seems, as Feinberg explicates it, not so weak after all. Why? It is not difficult to imagine many types of decisions which are unlikely to satisfy anything remotely like the mentioned conditions for being fully voluntary. For example, consider decisions to become a nun, to go to college, to renounce one's citizenship, to marry, to divorce, to engage in civil disobedience, to purchase nuclear accident insurance, to heavily gamble at a casino, to be sterilized, to have a child, to become a living kidney donor, or to consent to psychosurgery. Weak paternalism seems correct in prohibiting interference with fully voluntary acts. My reservation is that it may be overly interventionist in allowing excessive interference with acts which are *less* than fully voluntary—for many important decisions which persons commonly make are not fully voluntary. To follow a policy of interference based on "weak paternalism" may call for quite invasive intrusions into the decisions of ordinary folk who are acting, more or less, at their rational best under more or less ordinary circumstances. On certain occasions where we disapprove of another's decision, believing it to be most imprudent, "it's your life" may not only express our disapproval; it may identify a strong (if not always decisive) reason for letting alone when we also believe that the person is doing *his* (her) rational best. The alternative principle I am proposing then, is that (when interference cannot be justified by the Principle of Defense of Innocents) paternalistic interference with generally competent adults is permissible if and only if it respects the *substantially* voluntary acts and choices of such persons (where it is presupposed that such an act or choice may or may not be chosen by a fully rational individual). The principle defended here might be labeled the Principle of Autonomy Respecting Paternalism. The latter may be equivalent in its implications to a suitably weakened version of Feinberg's weak paternalism.

One possible example where the Principle of Autonomy Respecting Paternalism diverges from PHRC is the current ban on treatment with Laetrile for terminally ill cancer patients. If all the facts were in, it might well be the case that no fully rational person would decide in favor of such treatment; it may be totally ineffective. There is a certain concensus, even when not "all" the facts are in, that it is ineffective. If it is correct that a fully rational person would consent to its prohibition, the ban, on the Principle of Paternalism with Hypothetical Rational Consent, is an acceptable piece of paternalistic interference. However, if generally competent adults should be allowed to "play their own hand" and if the choice for Laetrile treatment is a substantially voluntary one, then such a ban is an unacceptable paternalistic act.

I am suggesting that there is an area, one difficult to define, where an adult person ought to be left alone to form his own opinions, make decisions, and act on them *even if* he does so with something less than complete rationality and even if his decisions and acts may make him significantly worse off. Consider one further example. Suppose Clancy decides to become a nun and live a life of enormous self-deprivation, but with the hope of enjoying bliss in the unending hereafter (though this is allegedly not earned, but a matter of "grace"). Suppose further that there is no life after death or, more weakly, that it is irrational to believe so. Ought Clancy be coercively prevented from so harming herself—sacrificing her well-being for an illusion? If Clancy's choice is substantially voluntary, then any attempt to compel her to act more rationally runs the risk of subscribing to what J. S. Mill described as the "logic of persecutors," i.e., that interference with others is permissible because *we* are right and *they* are wrong.

VII. A Hard Case

The argument so far has sought to establish a basis for discriminating, *within* the category of acts of paternalistic interference toward generally competent adults, those cases of permissible interference from those which are impermissible. The proposed criterion maintains that there is a strong presumption in favor of respecting the autonomy of such adults. We have set aside, as a matter for further investigation, the questions of what sort of paternalistic interferences are permissible toward children, the retarded, and generally *incompetent* adults (e.g., those who are seriously psychologically disturbed). The Principle of Autonomy Respecting Paternalism supposes that having the effective opportunity to live one's life *according to one's own lights* is a value for reasoning agents, one more important than actually making only the "right choices." Even if the principle defended is acceptable, a large task remains, namely, determining which sorts of interference, in a specific situation, would fail to respect a subject's autonomy and those which would respect it. The suggestion has already been put forward that interference with a subject which *in fact* promotes the subject's basic, autonomously chosen goals (as he or she conceives them) succeeds in respecting the subject's autonomy. Hence, interfering to prevent you from driving over the defective bridge when you falsely believe that it is intact does not undermine your dignity as an independent reasoning being. In contrast, imposing medical treatment on a seriously burned person who is reasonable, not seriously psychologically impaired, and who has a realistic picture of his future prospects would fail to respect the autonomous capacities of such a person. Still, hard cases remain, cases where the implications of our principle are not crystal clear.

By way of suggesting the need for further inquiry and the need for further elaboration of the view sketched here, I shall mention and also leave unresolved one such problematic type of case. It involves a subject who is about to perform a certain imprudent act where his decision to do so is based on a false belief; in *this* respect it is like our bridge-crossing example. Suppose that a friend, Christopher, as a result of being systematically indoctrinated at an early age, believes that one path to everlasting life is to prove his faith in God by allowing poisonous snakes to crawl over his body for many hours. The religious sect to which he belongs, the Venomites, have long held this belief because of a passage in a document which they believe to have been authored by an original disciple of God's Chosen Deliverer. Suppose further that the most respected scholars of sacred scriptures agree that there is decisive evidence showing that this document was written six hundred years later than the Venomites believe it to be. Hence, we may agree that Christopher is about to take serious risks with his life on the basis of a, let us say, dubious and almost certainly false belief, one which he has not critically questioned (as children initially do not question the veracity of the Santa Claus story). May we intervene for his own good? This case is difficult. *Given* his beliefs, Christopher may *autonomously* decide that the risk is worthwhile. Yet we are sure that some of those beliefs are false—as in our bridge-crossing case. Still, it does not seem that it is permissible to paternalistically interfere *whenever* some generally competent adult is about to act imprudently (from our perspective) on the basis of an unreasonable belief; if it were, far more prohibitive laws on gambling, the purchase of stocks, or marriage would be justifiable. It seems reasonable to regard people as *responsible* for some of their beliefs and their consequent choices, e.g., people can and ought to assess the advantages and disadvantages of alternate investment strategies, career choices, and so on. But Christopher does not seem morally responsible for his belief in the efficacy of cuddling up to snakes. Indeed we may believe that it was *unfair* that this belief was engendered in him when he had no real capacity to question it or rationally assess it. Is his capacity for autonomous choice impaired because of this? If so, may we interfere on the ground that doing so would not fail to respect his autonomy? Or must we refrain from interference and only, at most, seek to *persuade* him of the irrationality of his decision? Yet it also seems clear that persons who are thoroughly "brainwashed" are often immune to rational persuasion. I shall not attempt to offer a solution for this type of dilemma; it certainly seems to be a "hard case." Any principled-resolution of it would have important implications for other important questions we face, e.g., questions about the permissibility of paternalistic interference toward those who act on false beliefs, toward those who act on unreasonable-but-not-necessarily-false beliefs, and about the inculcation of beliefs in children and others who are "intellectually and emotionally vulnerable." For reasons that I have tried to make clear throughout, the ways that we answer these questions in our private lives and socially, through legislation or judicial decisions, will affect the quality of the lives that we may lead. Hence they deserve our careful assessment; in this respect questions about what we ought to do or what it is permissible to do are no different than many of the other perplexities which confront us.

VIII. Addendum

In closing, I should like to call attention to a consideration left almost entirely implicit in our discussion of paternalism. Although the following point has not gone unnoticed in discussions of paternalism, many examples of "paternalistic interference," while they may be acts or policies which are paternalistically *motivated* or paternalistic in *result, may* be *justifiable* solely by appeal to non-paternalistic considerations. As possible examples, consider laws prohibiting suicide or gambling, laws requiring the use of motorcycle helmets or seat belts, or laws (actual or possible) prohibiting or delimiting the use of certain drugs (cf. alcohol). In such cases permissive policies *not only* allow people to engage in activities risky to themselves, but *sometimes* result in harms (direct and indirect) *to others*. For example, consider not only injuries to others produced in part by alcohol induced automobile accidents but other less obvious costs imposed on others, e.g., the diverting of private and public resources to prevent and remedy the resulting catastrophies. Hospital beds are filled, medical personnel are preoccupied, research funds are diverted, children are neglected, and so on. Since the true costs of the practices mentioned are seldom, if ever, fully absorbed by the parties participating in the risky practices, others are often significantly harmed by taxes imposed and opportunities involuntarily foregone. Hence, in any case where an act of intervention is paternalistically motivated and/or paternalistic in result it is important to determine whether the act is justifiable by appeal to a less controversial principle like that of the Principle of Defense of Innocents. When the act cannot be, we must wrestle with the difficulties involved in sorting out permissible and impermissible paternalistic restrictions on the liberties of others.

We have grappled with such difficulties. Perhaps it is clear that the issues are fundamental ones and that identifying the outlines of a plausible theory is no simple task. Given the historical neglect of the difficulty of formulating a reasonable view about which sorts of paternalistic interferences are acceptable, it is not unlikely that some of the claims posed here are not quite right or demand refinement. Hence, there is a need to question the views sketched here, to explore further, and, indeed, to "locate" a plausible theory of paternalism within the context of a more comprehensive ethical theory.[13]

Notes

1. Much of the discussion here and throughout this essay is related to the central focus of the classic, and readable, treatise by John Stuart Mill, *On Liberty*.

2. Those interested in pursuing the question of when it is all right to employ violent tactics in self-defense should see the important discussions found in a) Robert Nozick, *Anarchy, State, and Utopia* (New York: Basic Books, 1974) and b) Judith Thomson, "Self-Defense and Rights" (The Lindley Lecture, University of Kansas, 1976).

3. On this point see Carl Cranor, "Legal Moralism Reconsidered" *Ethics,* Vol. 89, No. 2 (June, 1979), 147–164.

4. Constraining others "for their own good" is ambiguous between constraining others to prevent harm and doing so in order to benefit the person in question; in general, our focus is on the former, more common, type of case.

5. Our primary concern is whether it is *permissible* to interfere, on paternalistic grounds, with others. Deciding this matter is relevant to assessing the stronger claim that we sometimes have a *duty* to interfere on paternalistic grounds. On the latter see the essay by Amy Gutmann listed in the Suggested Readings.

6. On whether seduction may be a form of coercion, see my "Coercion, Seduction, and Rights" *The Personalist* (now: *Pacific Philosophical Quarterly*), 58, No. 4 (Fall, 1977), 374–380.

7. On these matters see the essay (cited in note 5) by Amy Gutmann; also Howard Cohen, *Equal Rights for Children* (Totowa, New Jersey: Littlefield & Adams, 1980), and William Aiken and Hugh LaFollette, *Whose Child?* (Totowa, New Jersey: Rowman and Littlefield, 1980).

8. On this issue see the essay by Rosemary Carter and my essay "Paternalism and Subsequent Consent", both listed in the Suggested Readings.

9. See the seminal essay by Gerald Dworkin, "Paternalism" cited in the Suggested Readings; one strain in Dworkin's position seems to rely on what I have called the "Principle of Hypothetical Rational Consent".

10. See Joel Feinberg's instructive essay, "Legal Paternalism" in his *Rights, Justice, and the Bounds of Liberty* (Princeton, New Jersey: Princeton University Press, 1980).

11. *Ibid.*, 115–116.

12. *Ibid.*, 129.

13. I am indebted to W. R. Carter, Tom Regan, Mark Richard, and Barbara Levenbook for their helpful comments on prior versions of this essay.

Suggested Readings

Richard Arneson, "Mill versus Paternalism", *Ethics* Vol. 90, No. 4 (July, 1980), 470–489.

Michael Bayles, "Catch-22 Paternalism and Mandatory Genetic Screening" in *Medical Responsibility* edited by Wade L. Robison and Michael S. Pritchard (Clifton, New Jersey: The HUMANA Press, 1979), p. 29–42.

——, "Criminal Paternalism" in J. R. Pennock and J. W. Chapman, eds., *The Limits of Law, Nomos XV* (Chicago: Atherton, 1974).

——, *Principles of Legislation* (Detroit: Wayne State University Press, 1978).

Allen Buchanan, "Medical Paternalism" *Philosophy and Public Affairs* Vol. 7, no. 4, (Summer, 1978).

Rosemary Carter, "Justifying Paternalism" *Canadian Journal of Philosophy* Vol. VII, no. 1 (March, 1977).

James Childress, "Paternalism and Health Care" in *Medical Responsibility, op. cit.*, p. 15–28.

Patrick Devlin, "The Enforcement of Morals" (London: Oxford Univ. Press, 1965).

Gerald Dworkin, "Paternalism" in *Morality and the Law*, edited by Richard Wasserstrom (Belmont, California: Wadsworth Publishing, 1971).

Joel Feinberg, "Legal Paternalism" *Canadian Journal of Philosophy* Vol. 1 (1971).

——, *Social Philosophy* (Englewood Cliffs, New Jersey: Prentice-Hall, 1973).

——, "The Child's Right to an Open Future" in *Whose Child? Children's Rights, Parental Authority, and State Power*, edited by W. Aiken and H. LaFollette (Totowa, New Jersey: Rowman and Littlefield, 1980).

N. Fotion, "Paternalism" *Ethics* Vol. 89, no. 2 (January, 1979).

Bernard Gert and Charles Culver, "The Justification of Paternalism" *Ethics* Vol. 89, no. 2 (January, 1979).

——, "Paternalistic Behavior" *Philosophy and Public Affairs* Vol. 6, no. 1 (Fall, 1976).

Amy Gutmann, "Children, Paternalism, and Education" *Philosophy and Public Affairs* Vol. IX, no. 4 (Summer, 1980).

H. L. A. Hart, *Law, Liberty, and Morality* (New York: Random House, 1963).

Douglas Husak, "Paternalism and Autonomy" *Philosophy and Public Affairs* Vol. X, no. 1 (Winter, 1981).

J. S. Mill, *On Liberty* (New York: The Liberal Arts Press, 1956).

Jeffrey Murphy, "Incompetence and Paternalism" *Archiv Fur Rechts und Social-Philosophic* Vol. 60 (1974).

Donald Regan, "Justifications for Paternalism" in *The Limits of Law, op. cit.*

C. L. Ten, "Paternalism and Morality" *Ratio* Vol. XIII, no. 1 (June, 1971).

Judith Thomson, "Some Ruminations on Rights" *Arizona Law Review*, Vol. 19, no. 1 (1978).

Donald VanDeVeer, "Intrusions on Moral Autonomy" *The Personalist*, Vol. 57, no. 3 (Summer, 1976).

——, "Paternalism and Subsequent Consent" *Canadian Journal of Philosophy* (forthcoming in Vol. X, no. 1).

——, "The Contractual Argument for Withholding Medical Information" *Philosophy and Public Affairs* Vol. 9, no. 2 (Winter, 1980).

——, "Autonomy-Respecting Paternalism" *Social Theory and Practice* (July, 1980).

chapter two

Homosexuality

JOSEPH MARGOLIS

I. Sex: The Private and Public Parts

What makes masturbation morally suspect in the minds of some is the secrecy and ease of gratification with which a single practitioner may maximize his or her pleasure again and again, without invoking or being bound by any explicit social bond. So the charges, largely raised by a kind of policing futility, cry (i) "unnatural," "immature," "arrested," "perverted"; (ii) "irrational," "self-indulgent," "gratuitous," "irresponsible," "uncontrolled," "orgiastic"; (iii) "unhealthy," "wasteful," "functionless," "meaningless," "dangerous," "harmful," "self-exploitative," "self-destructive"; (iv) "illicit," "evil," "forbidden," "indecent," "corrupting." What is so unconvincing about these familiar global charges raised in the name, respectively of (i) what is natural, (ii) what is rational, (iii) what is healthy, and (iv) what is moral—is at least their failure to come to terms with the subtlety and infinite detail of sexual life. One can imagine the kindness of introducing an inexperienced and somewhat frigid young woman to the first pleasures of masturbation in order to facilitate her grasp both of the possibilities of sexual relations with another and of the permanent importance of developing her sexual imagination and fantasy as a talent crucial to the success of such relations. Or, one can imagine the touching isolation of those insufficiently attractive to others who, out of timidity or a kind of rational economy or both, enliven their daily connection with the world by a grateful retreat to the interior satisfactions of masturbation. One can even imagine putting oneself to sleep, or quieting an anxiety, or reducing the likelihood of prostrate troubles, by the use of this modest skill—normally modest at least, though apparently raised to a substantial art by Jean Genet, in order to serve as the source of inspiration for his remarkable novels.

Charges similar to those posed against masturbation are brought against homosexuality, of course, with full recognition of the important difference that homosexual behavior (as opposed to fantasy) is fully interpersonal even if it is private or secret. Consequently, charges against homosexuality are complicated by considerations of what is acceptable or tolerable in affecting or influencing others as well as in the use of one's own body and life.

These two lines of thought converge because both direct us to appraise behavior in terms of some model (or models) of the right sort of life—of the four sorts previously noted. They are different, nevertheless, because to sit in judgment of what homosexuals "do" to themselves supposes that we have a defensible or correct model of how human beings should develop and control themselves, taken singly; whereas it is not unreasonable, in judging interpersonal relations, to appraise behavior in terms of its compliance with socially countenanced practices (including legal practices) and its consequences for society generally, independently of views about whether what homosexuals "do" to themselves in private accords with some model of how humans should develop and control themselves as individuals. Thus, for example, while one cannot hold that homosexual behavior is "unnatural," without a suitable theory of what *natural* sexual behavior is like, one *can* hold that homosexual intercourse is *socially* inadmissible (or admissible), without explicit regard to its fitting or failing to fit such a theory of natural behavior. Nevertheless, when the *mores* of a society are in transition, or when there are a variety of competing or opposing sexual practices clearly well supported by substantial communities, or when relevant legal and social reforms are being seriously considered, disputes of the second sort can no longer be assessed independently of those of the first sort. The present essay seeks to illuminate these interrelated arguments.

Recall the four types of appraisals brought against homosexuality. The first type (i) relies on *laws of nature* which allegedly enable us to distinguish between when human beings behave in accordance with their "essential nature" and when their behavior falls short of this, i.e., when it is "unnatural." Appraisals of the second type (ii) rest on some *rule of reason* which, we are to suppose, permanently requires that the pursuit of pleasure or gratification be subordinated to "higher" objectives. A third type of appraisal (iii) involves a *model of health,* a model of the functional well-being of a human life, from which we are supposed to be able to identify which activities are signs or symptoms of disease, ill-health, or dysfunction, and which healthy. Finally, there are (iv) *moral rules or laws* which require, permit, or condemn certain forms of behavior as right, wrong, etc. Our principal interest in the present essay lies in determining the adequacy of representative arguments which seek to show that homosexuality is unnatural, self-indulgent, a disease, or morally wrong. Some of these arguments are offered in defense of several judgments—for example, that homosexuality is both self-destructive (unhealthy) and self-indulgent. Others are more limited. We shall try to keep these matters straight, as best we can, beginning, in section II, with arguments which focus primarily on what kinds of sexual behavior are natural. In section III we consider the question of whether homosexuality is a disease or, if not a disease as such, at least a "psychological dysfunction." These two sections are largely critical. In section IV a positive account of human sexuality is sketched, and in the final section the justifiability of treating homosexual behavior as a criminal offense is examined.

II. Natural Sex

A good deal of the debate over homosexuality concerns whether it is or is not "natural." But how shall we determine what is "natural" in this context, and what, if any, moral conclusions would follow from this determination if we had it?

In one obvious sense what is unnatural is simply what is statistically unusual. But if we assume that what is unnatural is wrong and construe "unnatural" in this manner, it will turn out that skydiving or raising mushrooms is immoral. Not a promising appeal to what is "unnatural." Let us consider another appeal to what is natural (or not).

The sociobiologist Edward Wilson reminds us, pursuing his own rather cranky account of human sexuality, that Pope Paul VI condemned all "genital acts" outside the framework of heterosexual marriage (*Humanae Vitae,* 1964)—including both masturbation and homosexuality—as "intrinsically and seriously disordered."[1] *He* (Wilson) declares the Roman Catholic Church's natural law thesis "in error"; but his reason is that "the laws it addresses" were not actually writ by God on human nature, but were "written by natural selection" instead.[2] His intention is to be permissive, but his argument line is naive: for it confuses claims about the facts of the matter (claims about the biological function of homosexuality) with an attempt to justify homosexuality morally. Wilson does offer the provocative—hardly confirmed—suggestion that, viewed as a form of social bonding, homosexuality *may* have an important biological function. "Homosexuals [he says] may be the genetic carriers of some of mankind's rare altruistic impulses."[3] Lacking a special parental role, homosexuals may have played (through evolutionary history) various specialist roles supporting the families of their close relatives, so that "homosexual genes" may have been favored "by higher survival and reproduction rates . . . through collateral lines of descent, even if . . . homosexuals themselves do not have children."[4] Interesting theory. If heterosexuality is to be defended primarily in terms of the survival and reproduction of the species (in the spirit of the Pope's remarks), then, perhaps, homosexuality, considered in terms of its genetic function, might *itself* be defended on the Pope's terms. Wilson's thesis also suggests that, even where a highminded model of interpersonal conduct (not merely of self-development) is advanced, it is altogether too easy to ignore potentially relevant biological factors bearing on the viability of the population expected to conform to that model. Morality simply cannot (or cannot, in any rational and worldly way) override the conditions of existence and viability, whatever they may be.

Nevertheless, there is something preposterous about Wilson's proposed basis for moral tolerance, even if his factual claims are correct. For Wilson seems to imply that, if the biological facts were otherwise, there might not be a proper basis for defending homosexuality morally. Homosexuality, we are to suppose, may just *happen* to be all right, because, as a general practice, it *is* a factor which contributes to survival and reproduction *and* contributing thus (and only thus) is precisely why it *ought* to be morally favored. (The shift in the copula—from "is" to "ought"—is normally not taken to be conceptually important among those committed to so-called evolutionary ethics; that is, they assume that, if the evolutionary facts are what they are alleged to be, then they also are as they ought to be—there are no other morally relevant considerations than those of contributing to survival.[5]) But this is a mad view, for at least much the same reason Bernard Williams cleverly supplies in noting that there is something very odd in supposing that, in a moral dilemma case in which a man can save either his wife or a stranger but not both, he can, treating both persons impartially, still justify saving his wife on the grounds not that it was, after all, his wife but "that it was his wife and that in situations of this kind it is permissible to save one's wife." Considerations about the *personal* relationships we have with *particular* people are morally relevant considerations, not just how well or ill our reasons for acting conform with general, impartial rules.[6] For example, it seems preposterous to suppose that the moral defensibility of a routine homosexual act should depend on whether it does or does not contribute to maximizing the happiness of all (utilitarianism), or on whether it can or would be personally favored by impartial rational agents (Kantianism).

Related to the claim that homosexual behavior is unnatural is the cognate assertion that it is perverted. An important question here concerns the criteria for classification as "perverted." In a much-discussed paper Thomas Nagel tries to separate the question of sexual perversion, including, in his view, such practices as shoe fetishism, bestiality, sadism at least, possibly masturbation, homosexuality, and oral-genital sex, both from the issue of the biological or physiological function of sexual relations (reproduction, in particular) and the issue of social disapprobation or custom.[7] In this regard, Nagel avoids both *Humanae Vitae* and sociobiology. But he does offer a psychological account of sexual perversion, which, as he says, presupposes "unnatural sexual *inclinations* rather than just unnatural practices adopted not from inclination but for other reasons." and which "must reveal itself in conduct that expresses an unnatural *sexual* preference."[8] That is, he offers his own norms regarding what is natural in sexual behavior, and he does so in a way that unmistakably commits him to supposing that he is speaking primarily about the requirements of individual, personal development (the "private parts" of sex) more than about the way in which one person's behavior may affect another (the "public parts"). He is careful not to treat sexual desire merely as an appetite (though "being an appetite [he says] is no bar to admitting of perversions"); and he is careful not to construe "all our evaluations of persons and their activities [prominently, evaluations of sexual behavior] as moral evaluations."[9] Still, his argument cannot be very different in purpose from Pope Paul's or Wilson's, in that all three may be fairly construed as attempting to provide a theory about what makes some kinds of sexual behavior unnatural. This can be seen in the following claim:

> The object of sexual attraction is a particular individual, who transcends the properties that make him attractive . . . We approach the sexual attitude toward the person through the features that we find attractive, but these features are not the objects of that attitude. This is very different from the case of an omelet. Various people may desire it for different reasons . . .; yet we do not enshrine the transcendental omelet as the true common object of their affections. Instead we might say that several desires have accidentally converged on the same object. . . . The importance of this point will emerge when we see how complex a psychological interchange constitutes the natural development of sexual attraction. This would be incomprehensible if its object were not a particular person, but rather a person of a certain kind.[10]

Here, Nagel has prepared the ground for holding: (a) that it is, or is relatively or distinctly liable to be, unnatural to be inclined to desire sexually certain *kinds* of persons rather than *particular* (individual) *persons* and, (b) that sexual perversion may well involve (when it involves interpersonal relations) exploiting in a certain way particular persons as mere instances of certain kinds of persons (or even as mere "objects").

There are difficulties here. For one thing, desiring sexual relations with certain persons *because* of the kinds of properties they have is neither incompatible with desiring "those very persons" (whatever that may be made to mean—of which more in a moment) nor, in any obvious sense, monstrous or unnatural in itself. In fact, it is psychologically very unlikely that anyone *could* be interested in a sustained way in another person solely because that person has this or that property (e.g., is tall, or has a luscious mouth, or talks quickly); and it is equally unlikely that one could be interested in another person without any interest in certain properties possessed by that person. Indeed, it may be that a sexual interest in gratification linked to properties possessed by certain kinds of persons may actually facilitate sexual or other interest in a particular individual. For instance, it seems quite usual that one is initially attracted to certain forms of beauty, charm, force, and style, and that one gradually develops an interest in particular persons who exhibit such traits—not necessarily to the exclusion of a continued interest in those traits themselves. A man may be sexually attracted to a *particular* woman because he is attracted to a certain sort of voluptuousness, and she is voluptuous in that way. There is no clear reason why sexual interest should invariably, essentially, predominantly, or characteristically be directed to what Nagel terms the "transcendental" person (whatever that may mean)—the person only, or the person "as such."

There is a widespread view about the morality of interpersonal relations, idealized in Immanuel Kant's well-known injunction, that we must treat persons as "ends in themselves," never "as means only." Deviations from this norm might then be viewed as "perversions." But the injunction is either utterly vacuous (too easy to satisfy) or the expression of a particular prejudice or bias (not possible to justify): it is vacuous, if it is satisfied *merely* by one's being aware, or seriously considering, that one *is* using another person "as a means" to some further end—there is, after all, no way to avoid exploiting people in this sense; and it is a partisan view, if the restrictions imposed cannot be shown to be required objectively or on independent grounds. For example, even sadism and sodomy need *not* be perversions if pursued, say, by *consenting persons*; for then the Kantian injunction (which Nagel has in mind) is easily satisfied. In fact, these practices, far from being cases where another is used "merely as a means," may even come to signify an unusually generous and loving sort of interpersonal relation—in which the narrowly sexual may indeed function only instrumentally. Imagine, for instance, that one's mate reluctantly but with tact and affection (and even misgiving) learns to apply the whips (with a gradually enhanced appetite) in order initially to cater to the beloved's sexual demands. Or, a chance understanding or agreement or even contract between a sadist and a masochist may (trivially) combine treating one another "as ends" and exploiting one another ("as means") for particular kinds of satisfaction. If there are "transcendental" persons, then there certainly are such "persons" in sado-masochistic contracts. It is also not in the least clear that heterosexual relations (which, of course, may well include sado-masochism, fetishism, and the like) are likely to be more respectful of persons "as ends" as opposed to "means" than homosexual relations.[11] Charlotte Wolff's psychoanalytic material, drawn from the diary of a prostitute (Ingrid), compellingly shows various obvious respects in which even the bare need for sexual gratification forms a common bond—often rather remotely or indirectly linked to love—in which mutual exploitation may actually constitute a rather high form of human respect.[12] In a word, it is well-nigh impossible to admit that human beings *recognize* that they are dealing with other persons *and* to hold that there are no "transcendental" persons involved in such dealings (if there are such involved in any dealings), or that the persons involved are not, in some sense, being treated as "ends." Even murderers and thieves and rapists may not be able to be excluded. Nagel's constraint, therefore, is much too weak. Nagel appreciates this and moves on to a much more complicated formula of sexually appropriate respect; still, he has dropped more than a strong hint of disapprobation about those who (somehow) are attracted to a person as "a person of a certain *kind*." But the charge is entirely unsupported and tendentious, and the intended improvement brings us back to the difficulties of arguments involving (i)-(iv) (above).

Nagel clearly thinks that sex has a "structure," involving interpersonal relations, which is both natural and normative.[13] He actually says that "if humans will tend to develop some version of reciprocal interpersonal sexual awareness unless prevented, then cases of blockage can be called unnatural or perverted."[14] The operative words are "tend" and "prevented." They cannot be construed *statistically* if Nagel is to have his way. For example, imagine that the Marquis de Sade had actually managed to organize a substantial portion of French society to practice in accord with his sadistic games. Would that mean that the required "tendency" would already be effectively manifested because enough people exhibited it by their sexual practices and because those who deviated from the statistical norm suffered from a "blockage"? No, there can hardly be any question that Nagel advances a *non*-statistical *norm* for deciding what is natural or what perverted, in interpersonal sexual awareness and behavior. *His* principal concern is to argue that such a conception cannot by itself preclude homosexuality. Fair enough. But what he fails to realize is that it cannot be shown to preclude much else besides sadism, bestiality, voyeurism, fetishism, or masturbation. Moreover, Nagel nowhere explains why we should regard his own version of the "proper" interpersonal relationship as *objectively* appropriate; and the briefest scanning of his requirement shows that it is readily open to objection.

Though Nagel sketches his view quite informally, it has been rather clearly formulated by Sara Ruddick—who stresses the idiosyncrasy of Nagel's view as well as difficulties in applying it in a convincing way. Ruddick attempts to sort "three characteristics that distinguish better from inferior sex acts—greater pleasure, completeness, and naturalness."[15] The first characteristic (greater pleasure) would not directly affect the question of perversion and must, in any case, vary with sexual taste. The second (completeness) Ruddick says, obtains "if each partner (1) allows himself to be 'taken over' by desire, which (2) is desire not merely for the other's body but also for *his* desire, and (3) where each desire is occasioned by a response to the partner's desire."[16] The third characteristic (naturalness of function) Nagel himself rejects, though he uses the term "natural" more or less as equivalent to (Ruddick's construction of) the "complete."[17] According to Ruddick, Nagel's distinctive contribution is feature (3) of the completeness characteristic. But completeness and (biological) naturalness need not be coextensive (as in anal intercourse, for instance, or in imperfect heterosexual coitus); also, pleasure need not be closely correlated with either. But it seems decidedly counterintuitive (as Ruddick remarks) that perversion should be so closely linked with incompleteness: there is, in fact, no reason to deny that complete sexual satisfaction may be "unnatural" (homosexuality, on familiar views) *and*, conceivably, also perverted (if there is any reasonably straightforward sense of "perversion," which there may well not be). In any event, it appears difficult, if not impossible, to disengage the perverted from the (biologically) unnatural; and Nagel's feature (3) seems increasingly arbitrary, idiosyncratic, excessively constraining, and hardly objectively indicated by the data themselves. The point is that, *since* Nagel separates the question of perversion from considerations of putative biological function ("naturalness") and social approbation (what may be termed moral taste or other forms of prevailing taste), *he is obliged, in order to provide an objective ground for identifying bona fide instances of perversion, to champion some notion of normative personal relations with respect to which the would-be perverted may be seen to be defective.* But the sense of defect is itself an artifact of the theory. *Either* the standard of "complete" sex must be thought to capture an objective moral constraint on human relations *or* to express a certain "proper" or "essential" form of "natural" human taste with respect to the sexual. But there is absolutely no reason why it should be preferred in either regard, and there is no reason that Nagel actually provides. It is certainly not clear *how* to show that "complete" sex would rule out homosexuality as *morally* inadmissible, if empirical evidence were at all relevant; and it is equally not clear *how* to sort actual sexual taste as "natural" and "unnatural," without merely affirming one's own tastes. This is why Nagel's account reads very much like a form of Pope Paul's natural law doctrine, except that it explicitly does not invoke a moral law or a theological foundation and is (here) intended to identify only the essential form of interpersonal sexual respect. In rather different ways, then, Pope Paul VI, Edward Wilson, and Thomas Nagel all sort sexual practices as natural and unnatural in accord with appraisals of type (i). Pope Paul's account is additionally complicated, of course, by references to "the wise institution of the Creator to realize in mankind His design of love." He insists on "the unitive and procreative" functions of marriage and its being the exclusively licit context of sexual relations.[18] But all three alternatives belong to the same genus and raise precisely the same conceptual difficulties regarding validation. It takes very little to anticipate that analogues of the difficulties confronting theories of type (i) are bound to confront theories of types (ii)-(iv) as well.

III. *"Sick Sex"*

Probably the most influential of the secular views bearing on (i)-(iii) is the psychiatric and psychoanalytically informed medical characterization of homosexuality as a mental disease or disorder or illness. There is evidence of considerable disarray and radical divergence of opinion in the psychiatric community regarding the medical status of homosexuality. The American Psychiatric Association's Board of Trustees in 1973 deleted homosexuality as a medical disorder from the (APA's) *Diagnostic and Statistical Manual for Mental Disorders (DSM-II)*, a decision which still stands.[19] But the adjustment is unsatisfactory for a number of reasons. For one, in the *DSM-III*, although it is specifically stated that "homosexuality itself is not considered a mental disorder," "ego-dystonic homosexuality" (302.00) *is* specifically identified as a psychosexual disorder. It is essentially characterized as involving "a desire to acquire or increase heterosexual arousal, so that heterosexual relationships can be initiated or maintained, and a sustained pattern of overt homosexual arousal that the individual explicitly states has been *unwanted and a persistent source of distress.*"[20] Interestingly, there is no entry for "ego-dystonic heterosexuality," which, on logical grounds alone, would seem to be required. In fact, the *Manual* suggests that the homosexual "disorder" may subside in the "presence of a supportive homosexual subculture"; one might well argue that the corresponding heterosexual "disorder" might be overcome (by a homosexual avowal) in the presence of the same subculture. Furthermore, the "predisposing factors" seem to be primarily "those negative societal attitudes toward homosexuality that have been internalized"; also, "having children and socially sanctioned family life" may, it is surmised, be incompatible with "a homosexual arousal pattern." It is, on this view, very difficult to avoid concluding that homosexuality is construed as *somehow defective,* relative to "normal" sexual development, but defective in a way that falls substantially short of psychosexual disorder as such. However, there is not the slightest reason to suppose that homosexual inclinations *or* behavior is incompatible with having children and a socially sanctioned family life: that may be more of a social engineering problem than anything else. In fact, it is reasonably clear that there are usually legal sanctions against homosexuals as suitable "role-models" for children,[21] a tendency further abetted by adverse judgments regarding their allegedly "unnatural" or "diseased" behavior.

Secondly, although it classifies a very large array of mental disorders, the *Manual* concedes that "there is no satisfactory definition that specifies precise boundaries for the concept 'mental disorder' (also true for such concepts as physical disorder and mental and physical health)."[22] The concession is justified; but it wrongly suggests that the principal difficulty concerns *precision*, whereas the truth is that—as the *Manual* entry regarding homosexuality makes clear—the difficulty concerns the intrusion of ideological conviction about what is "healthy" or "natural." It would be out of place, here, to attempt to demonstrate the ideological dimension of health and disease in general, or of mental health and disease in particular.[23] But those opposed to the partially liberalized conception of *DSM-III* are strongly inclined to construe homosexuality as a distinct disorder in the course of psychosexual development or as the (disordered) consequence of a primary disorder in the course of psychosexual development.[24] The trouble is that, without a reasoned conception of "mental disorder," without in fact a reasoned conception of "normal" or "normal development" (utterly lacking in *DSM-III*), it is quite impossible to justify these would-be medical classifications. So seen, Wilson's speculations suggest a strong sense in which homosexuality may be (and may have to be) construed as falling within the range of (sociobiological) normality;[25] and Nagel's idealization suggests a sense (as the empirical evidence and the *DSM-III* sympathetically attest) in which homosexuality need not be construed to involve a disorder in psychosocial development. This is *not* to say that homosexuals are never ill, or ill as a result of complications due to their sexual orientation; it is to say only that there is no clear basis on which to maintain that homosexuality *as such* is a clinically significant disorder—any more than heterosexuality. The important point remains that the *DSM-III* fails to provide a concept or criterion of mental and sexual health and normality—and positively resists the idea that a satisfactory definition could be provided—in terms of which the alleged "disorder" of homosexuality could be specified. Furthermore, the conceptual difficulties involved in supposing that we might just *discover* the norms of mental and sexual health—as we might, say, discover the melting point of gold—are so overwhelming that it is impossible to pretend that any application of science would support such a claim as a neutral and objective discovery.[26]

The psychiatrist Judd Marmor cites approvingly the famous "Letter to an American Mother," in which Freud writes: "Homosexuality is assuredly no advantage, but it is nothing to be ashamed of, no vice, no degradation, it cannot be classified as an illness."[27] But Marmor also cites Freud's opinion to the effect that homosexuality is a "deviation from the normal," involves "a perverse orientation," though it need not otherwise impair an individual (and, again, does not constitute an illness or disease).[28] (In the Letter, Freud refers to "normal heterosexuality," in contrast to homosexuality.) Freud's view seems (to some extent) to have gained the upper hand in *DSM-III*.

Marmor himself is disarming, for he opposes would-be "scientific" arguments alleged to demonstrate the abnormality of homosexuality—on the premises: "(1) that homosexual behavior is a disorder of sexual development resulting from disturbed family relationships, (2) that it represents an obvious deviation from the biological norm, and (3) that when homosexuals are studied psychodynamically they are found to be emotionally disturbed and unhappy people."[29] There is, apparently, some evidence that there may be a genetic predisposition to homosexuality, in some homosexuals,[30] which, under the circumstances, would considerably complicate medical claims regarding biological deviation. There is, of course, a great deal of evidence regarding cultural variations in social attitudes toward homosexuals.[31] The fact is that Marmor lets stand Freud's view,[32] has himself nothing to say about normality, but ventures the explicit (entirely unexplained) judgment "that there are very few individuals indeed, heterosexual, or homosexual, in whom deep psychoanalytic probing would not elicit *some* evidences of deviance from ideal normality."[33] The truth is that the very notion of "ideal normality" is never explained and would be ideologically colored and tendentious in any case. There may well be minimal biological constraints on the viability of a species which could hardly be ignored in any account of what may fairly be termed "disease," "disorder," "illness," "developmental deviance," or the like; but there is no convincing conceptual basis on which either the ideally normal *could* be objectively specified, or on which homosexual behavior plausibly could be classified in any of these ways. It is simply unconvincing or paradoxical to make the normal depend only on *statistical regularities;* for then, one would not be able to speak of statistically prevalent disorders, or one would be obliged to concede that what at one time was a disorder (or normal) was, for purely statistical reasons, no longer such.[34] On the other hand, there is no generally recognized sense in which the norms of mental or sexual health can simply be discovered.

A final curious and significant fact is that *DSM-III* makes no reference to *bisexuality* at all. This is not to subscribe to Freud's theory of bisexual *development*, on the basis of which a homoerotic phase may normally be expected to manifest itself or else to be specifically repressed (the period of so-called homosexual dormancy). Apparently, that theory is not empirically confirmed—is even in conflict with the biology of sexual development.[35] But bisexuality, as a relatively balanced attraction and interest in sexual relations with both males and females (even mixed groups)—which may (but need not) be distinctly homosexual or heterosexual by turns—is an oddly neglected, yet reasonably well attested phenomenon.[36]

There is also good reason to suppose that anyone who does not practice in an exclusively heterosexual manner is dubbed homosexual (much as those who are not of exclusively white parentage are said, in the United States, to be black); and yet, on the evidence, a great many of these may actually be bisexual or bisexually disposed.[37] Masters and Johnson seem to have happened on such a population in recruiting for their homosexual studies. They assign such subjects a Kinsey preference rating of 3 (which is to say, individuals "with a history of approximately equal homosexual and heterosexual experience"). But they also note that, in addition to such bisexuals, provision must be made for the "ambisexual," that is, "a man or woman who unreservedly enjoys, solicits, or responds to overt sexual opportunity with equal ease and interest regardless of the sex of the partners, and who, as a sexually mature individual, has never evidenced interest in a continuing relationship."[38] They are rather dubious about bisexuality as a distinct category, though Charlotte Wolff's biographical materials suggest its importance.[39]

One of the interesting (purely argumentative) features of successful bisexual and ambisexual life is that it is as consonant with any supposed norm regarding reproduction as the heterosexual; and (on Marmor's account) it is bound to be contingently subject to the prevailing societal mores, in the ideologically relevant respect, no more and no less than are heterosexuality and homosexuality. Also, it is entirely possible that, with imagination and personal loyalty among such mates, a form of family life involving the rearing of children may be viable. This, of course, goes directly counter to Pope Paul's judgment, for the Pope characterizes conjugal love as "fully *human*, that is to say, of the senses and of the spirit at the same time" . . . [;] *total,* that is to say, it is a very special form of personal friendship, in which husband

and wife generously share everything . . . [;] *faithful* and *exclusive* until death . . . [;] and *fecund*, for it is not exhausted by the communion between husband and wife, but is destined to continue, raising up new lives."[40] But the realities of contemporary marriage and sexual behavior (and resistance within the Roman Catholic community) hardly support this characterization in terms of *any* plausible idealization of the patterns of actual practice (without intruding the claims of revelation); and any reasonable deviation from such strictures cannot fail to make room for the possibilities envisaged by homosexuality, ambisexuality, non-marital and extra-marital sex, and the so-called perversions.

Marmor's account is additionally instructive because it unwittingly betrays— through its own scruples—how similar are the arguments that treat homosexuality as perverted or unnatural ((i) above) *and* as unhealthy, abnormal, or functionless in a medical or quasi-medical sense ((iii) above). Even if it could be maintained with some plausibility that the functions of various organs and parts of the body can be identified in a value-neutral way, in terms of the homeostatic processes of the system and some indisputable, minimally reasonable account of the entire trajectory of human development, it is obvious that one can hardly claim such neutrality in speaking (not, say, of the contribution of sexual functioning to the tone of the body or the contribution of sexual relations to the genetics of populations) of the acceptability of forms of sexual conduct among responsible persons. Here, talk about health gradually slides into talk about happiness, "self-realization," "fulfilment," and the like—which can hardly be separated from partisan conviction, taste, ideology, and personal commitment.[41] Once the bare reproductive function is *distributed* among an entire *species*, the tendentious use of the medical model in Freud's, Marmor's, and the *DSM—III*'s treatment of homosexuals is plain enough. If (as seems entirely reasonable) sexual activity facilitates the smooth functioning of other bodily processes, then it is very likely that the body is "indifferent" as to whether such activity is heterosexual or homosexual—or even "bestial." The genetic and reproductive requirements of the *species* (whatever they may be) can hardly be convincingly assigned, by division, as constraints on isolated, single interpersonal relations. The confusion of arguments of types (i) and (iii) is natural enough. But even the concept of diseases of the body cannot be entirely freed from the historically and technologically shifting interests and the socially routinized purposes of actual human communities. What are counted as diseases of aging, for example, are clearly a function of the expectations of a given society at its own level of technical competence in actually prolonging life.[42]

IV. Sex for Persons

Thus far, our argument has been largely reactive. Still, we have provided a defense of a set of strategically important claims: (1) sexual activities serve a great variety of functions, hardly restricted to reproduction, including contingent, even idiosyncratic, functions of personal and social importance; (2) restrictive, defective, deviant, exploitative, and perverted sexual practices (so judged on any familiar grounds) are not incompatible with a reasonable measure of interpersonal respect and regard and personal pleasure and satisfaction; (3) there is no demonstrably objective basis for identifying the uniformly normal, appropriate, or best species-specific form of sexual relationship in terms of the putative functions of human nature, the conditions of human health and well-being, or the conditions of mutual affection and regard; the restrictive proposals considered are all ideologicaly colored; (4) the importance of the role, in the total life of human beings, of sexual activity of almost every sort tends to be exaggerated, distorted, oversimplified, and misleadingly raised to the level of a decisive criterion of personal well-being, health, functional and moral adequacy, reflexive and interpersonal respect, or maturity, by such conventionally global characterizations of persons as homosexuals, heterosexuals, sadists, and the like.

The rise of the Gay Liberation movement attests to the near irresistibility of invoking the doctrine of human rights wherever social and political discrimination is sensed: so we are confronted by Animal Lib, Women's Lib, Children's Lib, Prisoners' Lib, Patients' Lib, Plant Lib, Senior Citizen Lib, Chicano Lib, Black Lib, Nature Lib. These movements tend to be equivocal: on the one hand, they press for the recognition and relief of a distinct sub-population; on the other, for the uniform and equable extension of a measure of acceptable treatment to a more inclusive population than is currently favored, in which distinctions demarcating certain disadvantaged sub-groups will eventually become otiose. Herein lies a clue to a more satisfactory assessment of the puzzles regarding homosexuality. On any reasonable view, the nature and attributes of a *person,* relevantly specified for appraisals of health, well-being, morality, maturity, happiness, and the like cannot be exhaustively or even primarily characterized in terms of overt sexual practices or tendencies linked to such practices. The seemingly humane and fairminded question, whether homosexuals are (in Nagel's terms) capable of a Kantian-like regard for themselves and other persons, or (in Marmor's terms) capable of a suitable measure of normality, *suggests* both that we possess a reasonably good model of the normative development of persons and that heterosexuality holds a distinct edge over homosexuality with regard, merely as such, to the likelihood of a favorable quality of life. Here, several distinctions cannot fail to be decisive, undermining as they must, all such pretensions.

First of all, we must distinguish between *Homo sapiens* and *human persons.* Persons (not, necessarily, exclusively human) are, essentially, culturally emergent and culturally developed beings capable of using language, beings capable of exhibiting various skills that presuppose or entail linguistic ability—in particular, genuine conduct and freedom—beings groomed in accord with the historically favored practices of a particular society.[43] They are not merely specimens of a biological species, and their relationship to such specimens is open to dispute.[44] At any rate, one cannot *function* as a person without a suitably developed linguistic and cultural capacity. The thesis does not prejudice in the least questions regarding the treatment of fetuses, neonates, the comatose, and the like. But it is perfectly clear that favorable and unfavorable judgments about the behavior of homosexuals presuppose their capacity to function fully as persons; and their being able to do so depends essentially (as with all of us) on the variable cultural grooming that distinguishes one society from another.

If, then, persons are culturally emergent, it is *conceptually impossible:* (a) that moral norms in particular can be directly derived merely from an examination of the nature of *Homo sapiens;* (b) that norms thought to govern persons—regarding health, maturity, functional adequacy, mutual respect, happiness—can be satisfactorily derived merely from the conditions of life of *Homo sapiens,* even if minimal constraints on such norms (whatever they may be supposed to be) may be so derived; (c) that persons can be thought to have an essentially fixed nature or a nature objectively assignable independently of, or contrary to, the actual, historically variable and contingently prevailing features of viable societies. In short, distinguishing conceptually between *human persons* and *human animals* entails radical—even revolutionary—possibilities. One sees at once the strenuous presumptions on which Pope Paul's injunctions regarding marriage and sexual love depend, as well as the extraordinary narrowness with which sociobiology expects to be able to appraise the achievements of human culture. Also, we can now appreciate as well the

inevitably ideological dimension of a medicine addressed to the social and technological contingencies of historical societies; hence, of the tendentiousness of the *DSM-
III*, which actually concedes the *medical* bearing of the *mores* of particular societies.
Further, what is thought perverted is, perhaps, best understood in terms of sponta-
neous tendencies of disgust, horror, strong disapproval and distaste that prevail in a
given society. It is, in this sense, the reflection of the aesthetic and moral sensibilities
of a community: the perverted tends, then, to be the extreme along a possible
continuum, one liable to be viewed as less offensive at another time as human
societies legitimize the forbidden.[45] The condemnation of the sensibilities of one age
(*Humanae Vitae*, for example) cannot be taken to be automatically valid for another.

It should be remembered that the distinction between persons and members of
Homo sapiens has a double force: for one thing, it supports a presumption against the
mere discovery, from an examination of *Homo sapiens*, of "natural norms" governing persons. For a second, it places the onus of proof on those who claim to have
made such a discovery. This helps to explain, for example, how Kant manages to
insinuate his own moral bias regarding sexual relations in attempting to speak,
neutrally, of the universal requirements of treating persons "as ends." He claims, for
instance, that, essentially, sexuality does not involve a desire for another person or
for another particular person but rather (in effect, in opposition to Nagel's rather
Kantian-like argument) "for the sex of another"; to that extent, humanity cannot but
be "degraded," "subordinated," "sacrificed."[46] Even worse, Kant believes, are
"crimes" such as homosexuality and bestiality, since these go contrary to "the ends
of humanity"—that is to say, "to preserve the species without debasing the person."[47] It is reasonably clear, therefore, that Kant offers as a *moral* argument
(category (iv) above) substantially what (as we have seen) is offered in terms of
biological or developmental (category (i)) or medical (category (iii)) "norms." There
is no reason to expect that his moral argument can prove more decisive than the
others considered earlier. In fact Kant actually offers no other reason than the
"homogeneity of sex" against the compatibility of homosexuality and respect for
persons. But if the interests or desires of persons cannot be confined to the biological
requirements of *Homo sapiens* (whatever those may be supposed to be), then it is
hopeless to attempt to derive moral obligations regarding sexual respect from such
alleged requirements. In fact, Kant himself is obliged to show (perhaps gymnasti-
cally) how it is that respect for persons can be insured even in heterosexual encounters, in which (on his own view) sexuality tends to reduce persons to mere exploited
objects. In any case, *if* moral responsibility is ascribed only to persons, then there
cannot be any moral obligations that derive solely from human biology, just as there
can be no moral issues raised solely at the animal level; and *if* certain moral
obligations are said to be derived from the *relationship* between persons and their
bodies (just as, from another point of view, it may be claimed that obligations
regarding animals, plants, inanimate nature derive from the relationship between
persons and such entities and phenomena)[48] then it is quite impossible to attempt to
make the case out (whatever its prospects) without developing an adequate theory of
persons. The *non sequitur* of Kant's claim, therefore, is patent: from the *biological
fact* that reproduction of the species requires heterosexual mating (or at least the
union of sperm and egg) it hardly follows that homosexual activity entails a debasing
of *personal relations*. Ronald Atkinson, for instance, cites approvingly the opinion
advanced in a Quaker pamphlet: "we see no reason why the physical nature of a
sexual act should be the criterion by which the question whether it is moral should be
decided."[49] Not only should it not be so decided; it cannot reasonably be so decided.

Now, the distinction between persons and *Homo sapiens* entails *a* form of relativism regarding norms. But it is important to understand *what* form of relativism this is.

If human persons have an historical existence and nature,[50] then their "nature" cannot be restricted or reduced to whatever may be counted as the nature of *Homo sapiens,* and their "nature" is bound to vary with the emergent contingencies of human history. Human culture has a biological foundation, just as human persons "manifest" themselves in human organisms. Hence, it is not unreasonable to theorize that whatever may be advanced as the proper norms and constraints of distinctly human existence must be minimally conformable with the characteristic interests of *Homo sapiens* and the conditions of social viability—for example, the usual but quite general concerns of survival, avoidance of pain, gratification of desire, gregariousness, security, a measure of material power, and the like—so-called prudential interests.[51] Given such "rational minima"[52] *and* given the historically contingent circumstances of the life of particular human societies, relativism need be neither radical nor arbitrary: it can and must take a moderate or "robust" form,[53] allowing, as we shall see shortly, for the possibility of *rational* disagreement. And yet it must undermine the pretensions of the timeless canons and principles of human morality—Kantianism, for example.[54]

A moderate relativism has the following features. First, since it allows that two persons may be equally justified in believing what they do despite the fact that the one affirms what the other denies, it precludes our viewing *what* each person believes as either (simply) true or (simply) false. If, say, homosexuality may be justifiably condemned and approved (on different grounds, by different advocates), then the joint propositions condemning and approving homosexuality cannot be straightforwardly true—on pain of contradiction. But *if* those judgments are construed as genuinely and validly defensible, then truth-values of some sort, or suitable analogues of truth-values, must be assignable to them. For example, the relevant judgments may be said to be "plausible" or "reasonable" or "fair" or "responsible" or "justified" or the like. Secondly, since what is believed isn't to be viewed as (simply) true or false, a moderate relativism will deny our capacity "to discover" what is right and wrong, or true and false, regarding the practices in question: in such cases there must be an *ineliminable* conventional or ideological or appreciative or taste-determined element affecting the relevant range of judgments and practices. Justifying reasons may, therefore, be elicited, appraised, even confirmed relative to the condemnation or approval of homosexuality; opposed advocates are not thereby defeated but are required to muster comparable support. In effect, the justification of one's condemnation or approval of homosexuality is inescapably partisan, but not for that reason either arbitrary or irresponsible in terms of acceptable practices of reasoned defense. In a word, it is entirely possible that you may condemn homosexuality and I may defend it; that both our arguments be internally coherent, reasonably drawn from the traditions of the same society, and entirely opposed to one another; and *that neither of our views be strictly right or wrong about the matter or logically capable of precluding the defensibility of the other.* There may not be anything to be merely right or wrong about, though assuredly there will be grounds on which your argument and mine can be shown to be responsible or irresponsible, reasonable or unreasonable, conservative or radical, conventional or extreme, or the like. Thirdly, in relativizing the defense of a certain range of judgments (and practices), one need not, and indeed, logically cannot relativize *all* judgments: *radical* relativism (e.g., "what is true for one person may not be true for another") *is* incoherent, in the perfectly straightforward sense that some set of judgments would then have to be construed as both true and false; in contrast, the moderate relativism proposed here concedes that a two-valued system of truth-values ("true" and "false") *does* have application and, in fact, has application in some domain on which the application of the relativized judgments itself depends. So, for example, the very practice of defending and attacking homosexuality, for *reasons,* presupposes a domain of bio-logical, psychological, medical, and related facts relative to which that practice itself obtains. But these *facts* will be neutral as between conflicting appraisals. If, for instance, there is a genetic predisposition toward homosexuality, that fact may be interpreted to support a policy of social tolerance regarding sexual preference, or it may be interpreted to support a judgment of genetic disorder without regard to sexual policies, or it may be interpreted in some other way: the admission of a range of putative facts does not, in itself, entail any particular moral judgment. Finally, if relativized judgments may (on a model of truth and falsity) be logically incompatible, and if (as rational alternatives) such judgments can and must be defensible or indefensible, then such judgments presuppose (what may be termed) a three-valued system of truth-values or, alternatively, a system of values in which ascriptions of truth and falsity obtain asymmetrically. That is, in spite of the fact that contrary relativized judgments (and practices) cannot be shown to be true (or correct)—on pain of contradiction—such judgments (and practices) *can* be shown to be false (or incorrect), or at least incompatible with what may be judged to be true. The "plausi-ble" is, in this regard, opposed to both the true and the false. Hence, moderate relativism permits the falsification, or at least the indefensibility, of particular judg-ments and practices, without thereby conceding that *some* (relativized) judgments (or practices) are simply true (or correct). For instance, the argument purporting to show that homosexuality is a serious medical disorder may be demonstrably without force, without permitting us to conclude, as a matter of demonstrable fact, that it is not a medical disorder. We must be careful in assessing the play of relativized judgments.

Seen from this vantage point, Pope Paul's injunction—apart from the question of revelation or an alleged "essence" of human nature—commits the *fallacy of divi-sion:* even if the *species* ought to be "fecund," there is no plausible reason why every *single* sexual relationship (at this moment of dangerously increasing population, in the midst of widespread starvation and nearly exhausted hydrocarbon resources) ought to "raise up new lives" as well. Similarly, from the medical point of view, once it is admitted (as, according to *DSM-III*) that the clinical disorders of homosexuals (implicitly, of other sexual practitioners as well) may be a *result* of the inhospitable *mores* of a given society, medically informed advice would seem to require an increasingly tolerant and generous fellow-feeling among humans knowledgeable about the variety of sexual tastes and practices and the conditions of well-being.

What is, in fact, most noticeable about sympathetic views of homosexual life is their persistent sense of what can only be called *the joy of life and the search, whether furtive or public, for a congenial setting in which personal and sexual interests may be reliably and gracefully gratified.*[55] There's no doubt that every reasonably large category of sexual interest and behavior can be found to exhibit the entire continuum from the exalted to the depraved (on any familiar criteria). In our own period, homosexual practice has had to struggle against the authority, distaste, and power of the heterosexual community. The heterosexual objections have been rationalized in terms of biology, medicine, personal respect, and the like, but the ultimate inconclu-siveness of the theoretical arguments on which they rest has gradually been exposed.

It would be a mistake to infer from the inconclusiveness of these arguments that homosexual practices have been *shown* to be "normal," "healthy," "rational," etc. Acceptance of moderate relativism does not, itself, establish such brash claims. The most one can say—and to be in a position to say this is as much as one can reasonably hope for in the present case—is that the call for greater moral and legal toleration of homosexual activity is a plausible, reasonable, and responsible position to take. Not only do the arguments against the propriety of homosexual practices fail, for the reasons given in the preceding; to persist in discriminating against homosexuals, whether the discrimination be moral or legal, is strongly at odds with the importance Western culture places on the rights of privacy, personal freedom, and informed consent. Certainly there is something counterintuitive about the following: that human society should try to improve and increase the social and technological means for satisfying *the needs and desires* of people, should find it impossible to discover or confirm norms or rules of conduct forbidding or stigmatizing homosexuality, and should, nevertheless, insist on social and legal penalties against known homosexual inclination and behavior. A more reasonable position, given the perspective of moderate relativism, is one that calls for the legal protection of homosexuals and the abandonment of undefended and repressive personal prejudices. To that extent at least the arguments of the previous pages are in harmony with, and are supportive of, the spirit behind "gay liberation."

V. Legal Sex

The call for *legal* protection of homosexuals must face certain complications, ones which arise not primarily because of the details of homosexual behavior itself but because of the nature of the law. Two considerations are particularly salient: (a) effective enforcement of statutes; and (b) the conceptual relation between the law and the *mores* of a community. It is reasonably clear that legislation against having certain thoughts, feelings, inclinations, wishes, fantasies and the like cannot be effectively enforced; the law can act only against or to control or permit particular overt acts.[56] *What* will count as a determinate and pertinent act is, of course, open to extraordinarily elastic interpretation: greeting a stranger in a public men's room, for instance, may well count as a homosexual advance. But apart from the interpretive question, the most important disputes have concerned the enlargement of the "space" of private life, or privacy, which legal statutes are not permitted to invade (that is, which duly enacted statutes are, "by law," disallowed from controlling) and the enlargement of the public rights of homosexuals and/or others whose overt conduct deviates from socially prevalent or dominant (in effect, legally protected) forms of conduct.

On the first of these two matters, the most celebrated recommendation is the one proposed in the so-called Wolfenden report, in Great Britain: "that homosexual behavior between consenting adults in private should no longer be a criminal offense."[57] Clearly, the operative expression is "consenting adults in private." Apart from the residual cautions, doubts, and prejudices of the Wolfenden Committee itself, the point of protecting "privacy"—that is, the specification of "legal privacy"—is to permit overt acts, *at least as far as the law is concerned,* that, in principle, *could* be controlled by statute. Since, within any such private space (however restricted), the law is to remain officially blind or ignorant, the protection of privacy must be formulated in a suitably general way. It is quite unconvincing—yet logically possible—to protect the privacy of heterosexual sodomy, for instance, without protecting the privacy of homosexual sodomy. The issue is obviously a tricky one, because there *can* be public information about a putatively private (legally private) activity *and* that information may well betray a public, actionable feature of what would otherwise be a private matter. For example, imagine that, "in private," a sado-masochistic episode results in harming one of the participants: on the theory, the sexual aspects of the episode will not specify anything actionable, but the element of bodily harm would. The history of the legal treatment of homosexuality, of course, demonstrates that what would easily appear to fall within a reasonable interpretation of "in private" in fact has regularly triggered formally defensible police and legal action.[58] The British journalist Jeffrey Weeks notes, for instance, that, in the Sexual Offences Act (Britain, 1967), which decriminalized male homosexual activities in private for adults over the age of twenty-one, the meaning of "private" was "absurdly restricted," so that " 'public' was defined as meaning not only a public lavatory but anywhere where a third person was likely to be present."[59] There are and can be no purely logical grounds on which to demonstrate that such restrictions are inadmissible. Nevertheless, it is more plausible to believe that sexual behavior, undifferentiated within some private space, ought as such to be legally ignored than to believe that *only* heterosexual behavior should be protected. Realistically considered, it is difficult to imagine how, if homosexual practices are to be disallowed, one could possibly safeguard the entire range of heterosexual practice; to pick and choose among the latter is, effectively, to reject the very idea of sexual privacy.

Both with respect to privacy and rights, even where the obvious intent of legal reform is to make specific provision for homosexuals, the relevant formulations aspire to a measure of generality that explicitly avoids singling out the homosexual: thus, sexual privacy is to be safeguarded, without reference, as is said, to sexual preference; similarly, the public rights of citizens, normally undifferentiated with respect to sex, religion, ethnic origin, race, political creed, and the like (not always consistently defended), is to be extended to sexual preference as well and in the same spirit. (Sexual privacy itself may be claimed as the right to sexual privacy.) So the strategy of legal reform is primarily directed to the elimination of distinctions thought to be arbitrary, discriminatory, unnecessarily restrictive, or basically unfair to *persons* or *citizens*.

This also is a quarrelsome matter. In the first place, the theory of "human," "inherent," or "inalienable" rights—rights invested in persons *sans phrase*—has, historically, always been supported at the same time that effective deprivations of such rights are legally allowed. For example, the "inalienable" right of life is apparently quite compatible with capital punishment; the right of liberty, with life imprisonment; and the right of property, with eminent domain and taxation.[60] So the mere inclusion of the right of sexual privacy as a human or inalienable right would afford little protection, considered apart from an actual tradition or effective social practice; and the thrust of such tradition or practice could hardly be predicted from a society's nominal adherence to the "human" rights allegedly involved. Secondly, the effective rights (the positive rights) of the members of any community are always sorted in terms of some function or relationship more restrictive than the mere condition of qualifying as a human person; for example, voting rights accorded to citizens but not to resident aliens; or educational rights accorded to children but not perhaps to adults. Here, what is required is a measure of convergence between the proposed extension of recognized rights into a disputed area and a favorable consensus within the society in which it is to be promoted. In the United States, the fate of the Equal Rights Amendment bears witness to the complexity of every such effort, even where the effective change is normally thought to be already entailed in the operative rights of citizens. To speak of a right to sexual privacy or of a right to have one's sexual preferences legally ignored in all contexts in which equality of opportunity is legally protected is to propose that one's society interpret the relationship between its *legal* and *moral* concerns in a certain favorable way.

Ultimately, the justification for a given system of legal statutes—including the protection of personal rights and the preservation of privacy (whether construed as a right or not)—depends on a society's perception of the moral status of its own *mores*. It depends on more, of course: for instance, on the possibility of effective public enforcement and on the possibility of being applied to those affected by means of fair and just procedures. Inevitably, these become problematic in their own way. Certainly, it is difficult, *wherever* distinctions among persons regarding function, relationship, or status are involved and wherever distinctions regarding treatment or shares are involved, to separate the merely procedural and substantive aspects of legal and political justice.[61] But apart from that, there is no reasonable way to speak of the *justification* of a set of legal practices except in terms of its congruence with the larger practices and convictions of the society in which they obtain. Here, theory may be "positivistic" in the sense that such congruity alone is taken to be sufficient and relevant to the task; or it may be fully "normative" in the sense that a society's larger practices and convictions are themselves judged to embody in some ascertainable way a measure of the "proper" moral norms.[62] In either case, the legal is thought to be governed by reference to moral norms (that is, to underlying *mores* or independently applied rules of conduct). For instance, it is entirely possible that homosexuality not be approved on moral grounds but that its control within the space of legal privacy be impractical or even counterproductive. On the other hand, the actual provision of the right to sexual privacy or the right to have one's sexual preferences legally ignored probably depends on much more than mere procedural constraints. In this sense, there is no question that the so-called conservative view of the contemporary British judge, Patrick Devlin (Lord Devlin), is correct, that is, that "Society cannot live without morals . . . those standards of conduct of which the reasonable man approves" *and* that law is "the enforcement of morals."[63] This is not to endorse Devlin's own *application* of the principle—for instance, the enforcement of "Christian morals," without which (as Devlin believes) "the law will fail"[64]—or his sanguine view about what the reasonable man would approve. Still, it is to concede that the justification for installing or preserving or changing these or those statutes within the practice of a living society depends on claims regarding their congruity with, or derivability from, moral norms. In this sense, there is no possible way in which to appeal to the *legal* tradition of citizens' rights in order, say, to justify the inclusion or exclusion of sexual privacy without at the same time invoking the enveloping moral tradition within which the legal is itself sanctioned.

How intimately legal and moral debate ought to be linked is controversial. In fact, it is bound to be affected by what are perceived to be potential dangers to the underlying morality on which the legal depends and which, in principle, it is to serve. The important point is that it is hopeless to speculate about the extension or restriction of the rules of legal justice separated from a close examination of the actual historical practices of a society, practices that cannot themselves be confined to merely legal concerns and which must provide the justifying grounds for any intended such extension or restriction. There may be a demarcation between moral and legal procedures, but there cannot be a comparably clear distinction between moral and legal justification.

The British philosopher of law, H. L. A. Hart, objects to Devlin's view favoring "the legal enforcement of morality."[65] He states that the criminal law in England and America "still contains rules which can only be explained as attempts to enforce morality as such: to suppress practices condemned as immoral by positive morality though they involve nothing that would ordinarily be thought of as harm to other persons." Here, he mentions laws against homosexual behavior, sodomy, bestiality, living on the earnings of prostitution, and the like.[66] We may find our sympathies in accord with Hart's. But Hart does not recognize that, since homosexuality involves interpersonal *relations,* as does prostitution, we cannot logically preclude the (legal and moral) relevance (and possible force) of arguments holding that harm to another may be inherently entailed in homosexual activity. For example, both the heterosexual and homosexual molestation of children may be legally forbidden. Here, then,

Hart seems to follow the eighteenth-century English philosopher, Jeremy Bentham, who advocated decriminalizing sodomy on the grounds that, however perverted, it gave pleasure to both consenting parties.

The reason Devlin's claim (that it is legally permissible to "enforce morality," even in cases where acts involve no *immediate* injury) *may* be discounted lies elsewhere—for example, in the fact that the putative harm to another does not (normally) depend just on the immediate effects of the relationship but on the *long term* consequences which, it may be alleged, adversely affect the "normal" or "natural" development of each party. If so, then legal objections to homosexuality may have to depend on subscribing to "the right" view about the proper development or maturation of individual persons—whether in accord with moral, medical, biological, religious, or related convictions. We have already seen how difficult it is to confirm such convictions on rational grounds.

In *this* sense, the enforcement of morality may be a distinctly doubtful undertaking—and Devlin's view, a dubious one of how the law is to be morally informed and managed. But it is one thing to hold: (1) that one cannot convincingly support the thesis that the adequate function of the law is to defend and enforce "the actual institutions of any society, including its positive morality," because they "are open to criticism" (against Devlin),[67] and (2) that the law ought not to enforce morality in any way that is tantamount only to enforcing a particular doctrine of personal maturity, self-development, self-realization, natural or normal growth (along the lines already criticized); it is quite another to hold: (3) that the justification of a legal system ought to be free of *all* moral entanglements and, therefore, that legal systems ought not function so as to defend or enforce morality at all. Even Hart's criticism of Devlin implicitly concedes that (3) is an impossible view.

Hart asks "whether the [legal] enforcement of morality is morally justified."[68] He answers by distinguishing between "positive morality" ("the morality actually accepted and shared by a given social group") and "critical morality" ("the general moral principles used in the criticism of actual social institutions including positive morality").[69] Hence, in objecting to Devlin's views, Hart concedes that the law must be examined with a view to justification in terms of "critical morality." The trouble remains, however, that, first of all, Devlin himself (as Hart admits) rests his case largely on the general *principle* that a society is morally justified in preserving (as by law) its own distinctive form of existence; and that, secondly, it is difficult, in practice, to separate positive morality from critical morality, since any reasonably developed society will have incorporated within the former, convictions and doctrines characteristic of the latter.

In spite of these difficulties a defense of the view that homosexual behavior ought to be publicly tolerated *is* possible. There is a presumption that homosexuals, as persons, ought not to be victimized by legal or social discrimination unless it can be shown that there are nonarbitrary reasons to do so. Unless the latter can be supplied the general principles requiring just treatment of, and respect for, all persons take precedence. The same point applies to the critical reassessment of other traditional practices, e.g., slavery, ethnic and racial discrimination, sexual inequality, and the like. What is clear, as has been argued here, is that the standard defenses of discriminatory treatment toward homosexuals (as unnatural, as irrational, as unhealthy, as immoral) are unfounded. That may seem like a modest conclusion. But the truth is that, within our own time, it has taken an enormous effort to free the issue of how to regard homosexuals from unsupported medical, legal, and moral judgment (or in related ways) from prejudicial traditions, doctrines, and convictions which, cloaked in the mantle of positive morality, have in the past not been recognized as the prejudices they are. To show how very thin the standard objections to homosexuality are *is* to have shown prima facie that the continued exclusion of homosexuals from the range of application of general practices and rules of justice, fairness, respect for persons, and similar legal and moral concerns is only an expression of a continuing and undefended prejudice.

Notes

1. Edward O. Wilson, *On Human Nature* (Cambridge: Harvard University, 1978), pp. 141–142.
2. *Loc. cit.*
3. *Ibid.*, p. 143.
4. *Ibid.*, p. 145.
5. Cf. A.G.N. Flew, *Evolutionary Ethics* (London: Macmillan, 1967), particularly Ch. 4.
6. Bernard Williams, "Persons, Character and Morality," in Amelie Oksenberg Rorty (ed.), The *Identities of Persons* (Berkeley: University of California Press, 1976, pp. 214–215.
7. Thomas Nagel, "Sexual Perversion," reprinted in *Mortal Questions* (Cambridge: Cambridge University Press, 1979); appeared originally in *Journal of Philosophy*, LXVI (1969). References are to its appearance in *Mortal Questions*, pp. 39–40.
8. *Ibid.*, p. 39.
9. *Ibid.*, pp. 42, 51.
10. *Ibid.*, pp. 42–43.
11. Cf. Letitia Anne Peplau, "What Homosexuals Want in Relationships," *Psychology Today*, XV (1981), 28–34, 37–38.
12. Charlotte Wolff, *Bisexuality. A Study*, rev. and exp. ed. (London: Quartet Books, 1977), Ch. 8.
13. *Op. cit.*, p. 47.
14. *Ibid.*, p. 49.
15. Sara Ruddick, "On Sexual Morality," in James Rachels (ed.), *Moral Problems* (New York: Harper and Row, 1971); reprinted, *Moral Problems*, 2nd ed. (New York: Harper and Row, 1975), p. 18. Page references are to the 2nd ed.
16. *Ibid.*, p. 20.
17. For a closer discussion of Nagel and Ruddick, on aspects of the account, see Joseph Margolis, "Perversion," in *Negativities. The Limits of Life* (Columbus: Charles Merrill, 1975).
18. The relevant passages of *Humanae Vitae* are conveniently excerpted in Richard Wasserstrom (ed.), *Today's Moral Problems* (New York: Macmillan, 1975); the text is given in Robert Baker and Frederick Elliston (eds.), *Philosophy and Sex* (Buffalo: Prometheus Books, 1975).
19. The issue is canvassed in Joseph Margolis, "The Question of Homosexuality," in Baker and Elliston, *Philosophy and Sex;* cf. also, Judd Marmor, "Epilogue: Homosexuality and the Issue of Mental Illness," in Judd Marmor (ed.), *Homosexual Behavior. A Modern Reappraisal* (New York Basic Books, 1980).
20. *Diagnostic and Statistical Manual of Mental Disorders*, 3rd ed. *(DSM-III)* (Washington: American Psychiatric Association, 1980), pp. 281–282. The whole of the entry is confined to these two pages; further references to the *DSM-III* are to these pages, therefore, unless otherwise indicated.
21. Cf. G. G. Gibson, *By Her Own Admission* (Garden City: Doubleday, 1977).
22. *Ibid.*, pp. 5–6.
23. See Joseph Margolis, "The Concept of Disease," *Journal of Medicine and Philosophy*, I (1976), 238–255; "The Concept of Mental Illness: A Philosophical Examination," in Baruch Brody and H. Tristram Engelhardt, Jr. (eds.), *Philosophy and Medicine*, Vol. V (Dordrecht: D. Reidel, 1980); also, *Psychotherapy and Morality* (New York Random House, 1966). There is a forthcoming book by Michael Ruse, that addresses the issue also: *Homosexuality: A Philosophical Perspective* (Berkeley: University of California).
24. Cf. Irving Bieber, "Clinical Aspects of Male Homosexuality," in Marmor, *op. cit.*, pp 248–267; and "Homosexuality—An Adaptive Consequence of Disorder in Psychosexual Development," in (Symposium) "Should homosexuality be in the APA nomenclature?" *American Journal of Psychiatry*, XXX 1973), 1209–1211. Also, Charles Socarides, "Homosexuality and Medicine," *Journal of the American Medical Association*, CCXII (1970), 1199–1202; and "Homosexuality: Findings Derived from 15 Years of Clinical Research," in (Symposium)

"Should homosexuality be in the APA nomenclature?" *American Journal of Psychiatry,* CXXX (1973), 1212–1213.

25. Cf. Theodosius I. Dobzhansky, *Mankind Evolving* (New Haven: Yale University Press, 1962), Ch. 11.

26. See Joseph Margolis, *Psychotherapy and Morality.*

27. Sigmund Freud, "Letter to an American Mother," *American Journal of Psychiatry,* CVII (1951), 786–787.

28. Marmor, *op. cit.,* p. 394. The references are to *Three Essays on the Theory of Sexuality,* in John Strachey (ed.), *The Standard Edition of the Complete Psychological Works of Sigmund Freud,* Vol. 7 (London: Hogarth Press, 1905); and an interview in *Die Zeit,* Vienna, October 27, 1903, p. 5.

29. Marmor, *op. cit.,* pp. 395ff.; also, "Overview: The Multiple Roots of Homosexual Behavior" and "Clinical Aspects of Male Homosexuality," in Marmor, *Homosexual Behavior. A Modern Reappraisal.*

30. John Money, "Genetic and Chromosomal Aspects of Homosexual Etiology," in Marmor, *Homosexual Behavior. A Modern Reappraisal;* G. Dörner *et al,* "A Neuroendocrine Predisposition for Homosexuality in Men," *Archives of Sexual Behavior,* IV (1975), 1–8.

31. K. J. Dover, *Greek Homosexuality* (New York: Random House, 1978); C. S. Ford and F. A. Beach, *Patterns of Sexual Behavior* (New York: Harper, 1951), Ch. 7; A. C. Kinsey, W. B. Pomeroy, and C. E. Martin, *Sexual Behavior in the Human Male* (Philadelphia: W. B. Saunders, 1948); A. C. Kinsey *et al. Sexual Behavior in the Human Female* (Philadelphia: W. B. Saunders (1953); C. A. Tripp, *The Homosexual Matrix* (New York: McGraw-Hill, 1975).

32. Cf. Marmor, "Overview," *op. cit.,* p. 3.

33. Marmor, "Epilogue," *Ibid.,* p. 399.

34. Cf. Joseph Margolis, "The Concept of Mental Illness: A Philosophical Examination."

35. For an overview, cf. Leon Salzman, "Latent Homosexuality," in Marmor, *Homosexual Behavior. A Modern Reappraisal;* also, M. J. Sherfey, "The Evolution and Nature of Female Sexuality in Relation to Psychoanalytic Theory," *American Psychoanalytic Association Journal,* XIV (1966), 28–128.

36. Possibly the most sympathetic account is offered in Charlotte Wolff, *loc. cit.* It is somewhat rhapsodic about the creative implications of bisexuality. But it offers a variety of authentic cases; shows its distinction from homosexuality, heterosexuality, and androgyny; and, perhaps most important, suggests a basis on which both homosexuality and heterosexuality may be construed (from the bisexual viewpoint) as defective or incomplete (in Nagel's sense).

37. This has been anecdotally confirmed, to me, in private communications with a number of psychiatrists. There seems to be practically no literature on the issue.

38. William H. Masters and Virginia E. Johnson, *Homosexuality in Perspective* (Boston: Little, Brown, 1979), pp. 145–146, 8.

39. *Loc. cit.*

40. *Loc. cit.*

41. See Margolis, *Psychotherapy and Morality;* "The Concept of Mental Illness: A Philosophical Examination." Perhaps the most sustained effort to construe disease in general and its manifestations in terms of so-called mental health in value-neutral terms has been made by Christopher Boorse, "On the Distinction between Disease and Illness," *Philosophy and Public Affairs,* V (1975), 49–68; "What a Theory of Mental Health Should Be," *Journal for the Theory of Social Behavior,* VI (1976), 61–84. There is a sustained examination of the inherent unconvincingness of the thesis in Ruse, *loc. cit.*

42. Cf. Margolis, "The Concept of Disease."

43. The full theory of the nature of persons appears in Joseph Margolis, *Persons and Minds* (Dordrecht: D. Reidel, 1978), Chs. 1, 6. 12.

44. The argument that the relationship is not one of identity or composition, does not entail Cartesian dualism, and is best captured by a *sui generis* distinction ("embodiment") is developed in *Persons and Minds.* The essential clue is that the linguistic ability of persons is psychologically real and yet not reducible in physicalistic terms.

45. Cf. *Negativities,* Ch. 9.

46. Immanuel Kant, *Lectures on Ethics,* trans. L. Infield (New York: Harper and Row, 1963).

47. *Ibid.*

62   Joseph Margolis

48. Cf., for instance, Peter Singer, *Animal Liberation* (New York: New York Review, 1975); Stanley and Roslind Godlovitch and John Harris (eds.), *Animals, Men and Morals* (New York: Grove Press, 1971).

49. Ronald Atkinson, *Sexual Morality* (New York: Harcourt Brace Jovanovich, 1965); excerpted in Richard Wasserstrom, *loc. cit.*

50. The theme is essential, in the Continental tradition, to the influential work of Heidegger; see Martin Heidegger, *Being and Time,* trans. John Macquarrie and Edward Robinson (New York: Harper and Row, 1962); cf. also, Hans-Georg Gadamer, *Truth and Method,* trans. from the 2nd ed. Garrett Barden and John Cumming (New York: Seabury Press, 1975).

51. Cf. *Negativities;* also, "The Prospects of an Objective Morality," *Social Research,* XLVI (1979), 744–765.

52. These will have to be in some ideologically detailed manner. Cf. Joseph Margolis, "The Rights of Man," *Social Theory and Practice,* IV (1978), 423–444.

53. I have sketched a coherent form of robust relativism for aesthetic judgments: in "Robust Relativism," *Journal of Aesthetics and Art Criticism,* XXX (1976), 37–46,; incorporated, with adjustments, in *Art and Philosophy* (Atlantic Highlands and Hassocks: Humanities Press and Harvester Press, 1980), Ch. 7. The application in other areas, the moral for instance, is quite straightforward.

54. This, as I understand it, is close to the sense in which Alasdair MacIntyre opposes the characteristic emphasis, in Anglo-American moral philosophy, on the adequacy of universal, timeless moral principles. See his *After Virtue* (Scranton, Pa.: Harper & Row, 1981).

55. See, for instance, Dennis Altman, *Homosexual. Oppression and Liberation* (New York: Avon Book, 1973); Jonathan Katz, *Gay American History* (New York: Thomas Y. Crowell, 1976); Evelyn Hooker, "The Homosexual Community," in John H. Gagnon and William Simon (eds.), *Sexual Deviance* (New York: Harper and Row, 1967).

56. See, H. L. A. Hart, *The Concept of Law* (Oxford: Clarendon, 1961).

57. J. Wolfenden, *The Wolfenden Report: Report of the Committee on Homosexual Offenses and Prostitution* (New York: Stein and Day, 1963).

58. Cf. Jeffrey Weeks, *Coming Out* (London: Quartet Books, 1977); Vern L. Bullough, *Sexual Variance in Society and History* (Chicago: University of Chicago Press, 1976).

59. Weeks, *op. cit.,* p. 176.

60. Cf. Joseph Margolis, "The Rights of Man."

61. Cf. Joseph Margolis, "Political Equality and Political Justice," *Social Research,* XLIV (1977), 308–329.

62. See, Carl Joachim Friedrich, *The Philosophy of Law in Historical Perspective,* 2nd ed. rev. & enl. (Chicago: University of Chicago Press, 1963); Hans Kelsen, *What is Justice?* (Berkeley: University of California, 1957).

63. Patrick Devlin, *The Enforcement of Morals* (Oxford: Clarendon, 1965).

64. For a sustained criticism of Lord Devlin's view, cf. H. L. A. Hart, *Law, Liberty and Morality* (Oxford: Clarendon, 1963).

65. Hart, *op. cit.,* p. 21.

66. *Ibid.,* p. 25.

67. *Ibid.,* p. 82.

68. *Ibid.,* p. 17.

69. *Ibid.,* p. 20.

Suggested Readings

Bullough, Vern L. *Sexual Variance in Society and History* (Chicago: University of Chicago Press, 1976)

Devlin, Patrick. *The Enforcement of Morals* (Oxford: Clarendon, 1965)

Diagnostic and Statistical Manual of Mental Disorders, 3rd ed. *(DSM-III)* (Washington: American Psychiatric Association, 1980)

Dover, K. J. *Greek Homosexuality* (New York: Random House, 1978)

Gagnon, John H. and William Simon (eds.). *Sexual Deviance* (New York: Harper and Row, 1967)

Hart, H. L. A. *Law, Liberty and Morality* (Oxford: Clarendon, 1963)

Kinsey, A. C. *et al. Sexual Behavior in the Human Male* (Philadelphia: W. B. Saunders, 1948)

Kinsey, A. C. *et al. Sexual Behavior in the Human Female* (Philadelphia: W. B. Saunders, 1953)

Margolis, Joseph. *Psychotherapy and Morality* (New York: Oxford University Press, 1966)

Marmor, Judd (ed.). *Homosexual Behavior. A Modern Reappraisal* (New York: Basic Books, 1980)

Masters, William H. and Virginia E. Johnson. *Homosexuality in Perspective* (Boston: Little, Brown, 1979)

Money, John and A. A. Ehrhardt. *Man and Woman; Boy and Girl* (Baltimore: John Hopkins University Press)

Ruse, Michael. *Homosexuality: A Philosophical Perspective* (Berkeley: University of California Press, forthcoming)

Wilson, Edward O. *On Human Nature* (Cambridge: Harvard University Press, 1978)

Wolfenden, J. *The Wolfenden Report: Report of the Committee on Homosexual Offenses and Prostitution* (New York: Stein and Day, 1963)

Wolff, Charlotte. *Bisexuality. A Study,* rev. and exp. ed. (London: Quartet Books, 1977) *chapter three*

Reverse Discrimination

LOUIS I. KATZNER

I. Introduction

Our topic is reverse discrimination. It will help if we begin by developing a general feeling for the issue. In order to do this, consider the following situation.

During the 1960's there was an astronomy professor at the University of Michigan who gained considerable fame because of her reputed grading system: A for athletes, B for boys and C for coeds (*Time*, February 22, 1963, p. 38). Suppose that midway through the term your instructor for this class announced the adoption of this grading system. What would your reaction be? The first thing you would probably think about is how the policy affects you. If you were an athlete who was not doing particularly well in the class, you would feel relieved. If you were a woman who was doing well, you would be upset. And so on. But these kinds of self-centered concerns (philosophers call them egoistic or self-interested) do not take us very far. From the standpoint of self-interest, those who are advantaged by the policy will favor it, while those who are disadvantaged will disapprove. And aside from a discussion of whether or not one is really (dis)advantaged by it, in the long run as well as the short term, there is nothing more to be said.

But a moment's reflection reveals that there is more to say than this. In addition to concerns about how you are affected by the policy, questions of justice or fairness also arise. And these take two forms. The first are procedural, and are akin to questions of due process in the law. The idea is that it is not just or fair to change the rules in the middle of a game. Unusual grading practices should be announced at the beginning of the term, when students still have a chance to change their schedules. If someone takes a class knowing what the grading practices are, then he or she has no complaint on this score. If, on the other hand, this unorthodox system is sprung on an unsuspecting class half way through the term, students have every right to insist that they are being treated unfairly.

But focusing on *procedural justice* has its limitations. If the only considerations of justice or fairness that we entertain are those of a procedural nature, we may find ourselves forced to condone terrible, unjust acts, as long as they are done through acceptable procedures. Capital punishment, abortion and other such controversial questions do raise procedural questions. But we should not say that, as long as such practices are enforced in a procedurally fair way, they are just. This is because there is also a *substantive* dimension to such issues that must be considered.

In our particular case, we can question the justice of giving an A to athletes, B to boys and C to coeds even if we assume that this grading system is implemented in a procedurally fair way. On this substantive level, the issue is one of *desert* rather than procedure. Grades should be distributed on the basis of what students have *earned or deserve compared to the performance of others*. Although there may well be some disagreement as to what should serve as the basis of this comparison (e.g., Should grades be based upon performance, how hard a student tries, or a combination of the two?), there is general agreement that athletic ability and sex are not relevant to the fair distribution of grades.

Those who have been victimized by the grading system we are considering are the victims of discrimination. This does not mean simply that they have been treated differently than other people. It means rather that they have been treated in an *undeservedly different way that adversely affects them*. Their treatment is undeserved because athletic ability and sex are not relevant to grades. And they are adversely affected because of the way grade point averages are used by hiring agents and admissions officers. Given that individuals who have been victimized by this grading system may well be denied future opportunities which should be theirs, what should be done?

The most obvious answer is that all unfair grading practices should be stopped immediately. And although there are few people who would disagree with this in principle, it just is not going to happen. For one thing, teachers are individuals who suffer from the same shortcomings and hang-ups that beset everyone else. As a result, personal preferences are bound to continue to play a role in the assigning of grades—if not on the large-scale represented by our example, at least on a smaller one. More importantly, even if all discriminatory grading practices were stopped immediately, what about those individuals who have already been adversely affected by these practices? What about the young woman who just misses the cut for medical school, and who would have made it were it not for her undeserved C in philosophy? And what about the young man who got an undeserved B (he should have had an A) and was just barely denied a job in favor of an athlete who got an undeserved A in that same course? Although the cessation of discriminatory grading practices is a step forward, it neither restores to these individuals the grades they deserve, nor prevents future harms from befalling them as a consequence of previous acts of discrimination. The issue is: What is the just or fair thing to do in this situation? *Do individuals who have been discriminated against deserve special treatment designed to rectify the injustice that has been done to them?* And if so, might this rectification involve discrimination against other individuals? (You should spend some time thinking about these questions in the situation I have described. What do you think should be done? And why is that course of action the appropriate one?)

If you are like many of us, the more you think about these questions, the more confused you get. Everytime you think you have *the* answer, you come to see that there are problems with it. Every possible answer seems to generate new questions, and each new question requires that you consider a whole new range of ideas. Before long you do not have any idea what you think, and you begin to feel that there is no point in worrying about such questions because you are never going to be able to answer them.

Unfortunately, however, such resignation is no solution either. Not worrying about these questions is to bow to the status quo, and hence at least tacitly to accept whatever policy is in effect at the time. Thus not worrying about the questions lends support to one side or another. The trick is to try to bring some order to the myriad of thoughts that are going through your mind. Much progress can be made by looking at the issue systematically, distinguishing the real problems from the pseudo ones, and then focusing upon the former. Thus our first task is to develop a framework that will enable us to approach the issue in a systematic way.

II. *Sorting Things Out*

We are concerned with the justice or fairness of reverse discrimination. The first thing to notice is that statements about justice or fairness are *normative*. That is, they are value judgments: They place a value on things by reference to a norm or standard. Thus, just as when we say that "John is a good man," we are evaluating John positively by reference to the goodness-badness continuum, so when we say that a given practice or policy is just we are evaluating it favorably by reference to the justice-injustice norm or standard. What is involved in this kind of evaluation?

Many assume that normative statements are like judgments of taste. On this view, "This policy is just" is like "I like vanilla ice cream." When asked why one likes vanilla ice cream, the answer is, "Because it tastes good to me." And to the question, "Why does it taste good to you?" there is no answer; it simply does. If all normative statements are like those of taste, several important consequences follow. For one thing, normative statements (e.g. "Reverse discrimination is unjust") would be simply matters of personal preference. When asked why you think reverse discrimination is wrong, the only response that could be given would be, "I just do!" It would also follow that normative disagreements (e.g., "Reverse discrimination is wrong." "No, I think it is right!") are simply expressions of differing tastes. This would mean that the two parties to the dispute are not really contradicting each other. Contradictions occur when the same statement is both denied and asserted ("It is raining." "No it is not!" or "I like vanilla ice cream." "No *you* do not!") In contrast, statements of taste, although they may differ (Person A: "I like vanilla ice cream." Person B: "I like chocolate."), do not contradict each other.

In other words, statements of taste are self-referenced. This means they are about the speaker. They describe his or her attitudes or likes rather than the objects of these feelings. "I like applie pie" is a statement about me, not apple pie. On the other hand, "The apple pie is in the freezer" is not self-referenced. It is about the location of a particular pie, not the person who is making the statement. And it is because statements of taste are self-referenced that, when uttered by different individuals, they are about different things (each speaker's feelings) and do not contradict each other. Contradictions can only arise when conflicting statements are made *about the same thing*.

Although you may normally think of normative statements as being like statements of taste, this is not the only view. Many believe that normative claims are not self-referenced statements and can contradict each other. On this view, when I say "Reverse discrimination is just," I am saying something about reverse discrimination rather than expressing my likes and dislikes. And when you say "Reverse discrimination is unjust," you are saying something that contradicts what I have said. If we were only talking about our *own* feelings towards reverse discrimination, no conflicting claims would be made. But since we are both making claims about the *policy* of reverse discrimination, one attributing justice to it, the other injustice, we cannot both be right. Our statements are contradictory. And the way to resolve this contradiction (if indeed it can be resolved) is for each of us to offer the reasons for our beliefs and to examine these reasons critically in an attempt to determine which view is supported by the best reasons.

Which of these two understandings of the nature of normative statements is correct is a difficult philosophical issue. Rather than address it here, something which, if done adequately, would prevent us from ever getting to a discussion of reverse discrimination, I shall simply assume that normative claims are *not* self-referenced. For one thing, it does not make much sense to discuss the *arguments* that can be given for and against reverse discrimination unless one takes this view. Secondly, although not arguing for this view, it is my hope that our discussion of reverse discrimination will demonstrate the viability of viewing normative claims as statements which can contradict each other and need to be supported by reasons. I hope to show that normative disputes are not completely intractable; that progress can be made, and many disagreements eliminated, if the issues are approached in a careful and systematic way.

The key to this kind of approach is clarifying what is really at issue. Unclear issues lead to unclear thinking and unproductive discussion. You can see this yourself very easily. The next time you are party to a rap session, in which many individuals are expressing their feelings, but no progress is being made on the issue at hand, sit back for a moment and listen carefully to what is going on. Chances are that you will notice two things. First, most of the people who enter the conversation present their own ideas, without responding to those of others. Even when a speaker offers reasons for his or her view, those who disagree merely present their ideas. They do not explain *why* they reject the view of the previous speaker (i.e., they do not show what is unacceptable about the reasons that have been presented). A second thing you will probably notice is that many of the parties to the dispute are talking right past each other; almost as if they are discussing different topics. And quite often they are. Each understands the issue at hand in different terms, and thus has different things to say about it. If everyone were talking about the same thing, there would probably be considerably more agreement. Not that this is guaranteed. But what is certain is that as long as the parties are talking about different things, genuine agreement will never be reached.

Thus our first task is to clarify our central question: "Is reverse discrimination just or unjust?" We have already made some progress in this regard. We have indicated that this is a normative question which must be answered in a way that is not self-referenced. In other words, we are not asking whether or not reverse discrimination *is actually* practiced, but whether it *should* be. And we are not asking about what a particular individual feels, or even what the majority feel, but rather about the relationships that exist between the concepts of reverse discrimination and justice.

Although "reverse discrimination" and "justice" are commonly used terms, they are seldom clearly defined. Hence it is imperative that we explain their meanings.

Developing such analyses may well be as difficult and controversial as determining whether or not reverse discrimination is just. But any answer one gives to this question presupposes such analyses. Hence the only way we can make clear exactly what question we are answering, and the significance of the answer we are giving, is to provide them.

Once we know what we are asking (i.e. what reverse discrimination and justice are), we then have to identify what might be called the scope of the question. There are three possibilities. The question "Is reverse discrimination just?" might be asking (1) Is it *always* just?, (2) Is it *sometimes* just?, or (3) Is it just *in the particular situation* we are discussing? These are clearly different questions. If a policy is always just (or unjust) then it is so in every situation, including the particular one we are concerned with. If it is sometimes just, then it may or may not be so in the particular case at issue. And if it is just in the particular case we are concerned with, this in no way guarantees that it is always so.

In light of this, it might seem that we should direct our energies to the question: "Is reverse discrimination *always* just (or unjust)?" For once this question is answered, we know whether it is just or unjust for 20th century American society. Unfortunately, however, things are not this simple. Few social policies are *always* just or unjust; and, as we shall see, this is especially true of reverse discrimination. Hence our energies shall be better spent addressing the question: "Is reverse discrimination just (or unjust) in a particular situation (20th century American society)?" And given this focus on a particular situation, our discussion must be informed by an understanding of *the facts* of that situation. For it is the facts (what has happened in the past and what is happening now) that distinguishes one situation from another, and, in part, renders reverse discrimination either just or unjust in each particular case.

Another way of putting this point is as follows. We are concerned about a normative question: the justice of reverse discrimination. But we are concerned about its justice as a social policy for a particular society at a particular time. Thus our examination will consider both normative claims about the justice of reverse discrimination, and factual claims about the structure of our society, the way individuals have been and continue to be treated, and so on. And because the discussion will contain a mixture of normative and factual claims, care must be taken not to confuse the two. At every point in the argument, you should ask yourself, Is this a factual claim or a normative one? Because it is only if you know the answer to this question that you will be clear on (1) what is being claimed, (2) how it relates to other claims and (3) what kinds of critical questions it is appropriate to ask about this claim. Factual claims must be adequately supported by empirical evidence; normative claims by reasons.

Even if we fully explicate the concepts of reverse discrimination and justice, determine the scope of our question, and carefully distinguish the normative from factual components of the issue, there is still one additional pitfall to avoid. The question of reverse discrimination, like all questions of social policy, has both legal and moral dimensions. The question, "Is reverse discrimination legally permitted, prohibited or required?" is a question about laws that have been enacted and judicial decisions that have been made.

But our concern is not merely with what our laws or policies *are*, but rather with what they *should* be. Some people maintain that the sole determinant of what our law should be (i.e., the appropriate norm or standard) is the U.S. Constitution. On this view the question of the legality of reverse discrimination becomes entirely one of constitutional interpretation. This so-called strict constructionist view may or may not be correct. If it is not, then some other norm or standard must come into play in the interpretation of the constitution. But *even if* the strict constructionist view is correct, there is still room to ask, What *should* the constitution say? Indeed, one must raise this most fundamental moral question in order to determine whether or not amendments to the constitution are morally in order. So, regardless of whether or not one accepts the strict constructionist view, there is a need to identify a nonconstitutional standard or norm of justice. And this shall be our ultimate goal, although we shall not ignore the legal and constitutional issues on our way to it.

III. Discrimination and Justice

Our inquiry concerns the relationship between reverse discrimination and justice. As we have seen, this inquiry can only make progress if we examine and clarify these concepts. Hence we must explain exactly what the terms "reverse discrimination" and "justice" mean. And since reverse discrimination is *one form* of discrimination, we must begin by exploring the notion of discrimination.

To discriminate is to differentiate or distinguish between things. Although most of us have difficulty distinguishing domestic from imported wines, connoisseurs do it with ease. During the early stages of life, infants learn to distinguish their parents from other individuals. And herpetologists are trained to distinguish between different kinds of snakes. Discrimination is the act of drawing distinctions such as these.

Discrimination may or may not be associated with action. When I walk down the street I see different houses. If I am going to visit someone, my ability to discriminate will enable me to pick out my destination and go there. If I am just walking, I will still see all the different houses, although my ability to discriminate in this way will not affect what I do. Notice that the three examples of discrimination cited above are all of the sort which are likely to lead to action. Wine connoisseurs drink those wines which their refined sense of taste leads them to prefer. Once infants learn to distinguish their parents from others they "go to" them more readily. And the herpetologist's discriminatory powers are normally used to determine which snakes may be played with and which should be avoided (or at least handled carefully). But at least for the wine taster and the herpetologist, this connection is not essential. One can discriminate between wines "just for the heck of it"—i.e., with no intention of drinking wine oneself or influencing the wine-drinking habits of others. And one may confine one's snake differentiating abilities to looking at pictures in books or gazing at snakes through protective glass in a reptile house.

We shall focus upon those instances of discrimination that are intimately connected with action (i.e., discriminatory acts), for it is here that the question of justice arises. A discriminatory act may be based upon an unfair or unjust distinction. Thus we must now ask, What is it that makes acting on the basis of some distinctions just, and acting on the basis of other distinctions unjust? In other words, What is justice? This is not a question about the law. Rather, it is a question about the way our acts affect others; the way in which our acts *distribute benefits and burdens* among others.

As we saw in the earlier example about grade distribution, the root idea of justice is *comparative desert*—i.e., what one deserves compared to what others deserve. Philosophers have offered numerous analyses of this notion. What all of these have in common is the abstract or formal requirement that *equals be treated equally*. But what does this mean? What it does *not* require is that we treat everyone or everything in exactly the same way. It makes no sense to say that a doctor should treat someone with a head cold in the same way he treats someone with a broken leg. Nor does it make sense to say that our courts should treat those who are found innocent in the same way it treats those who are found guilty. Part of the idea of comparative desert is that entities should be treated on the basis of the characteristics or features they possess. Those that are similar in these respects should be treated the same, while those that are different in these respects should be treated differently (and in direct proportion to these differences).

But virtually all entities are equal in *some* respects (e.g. being composed of matter) and different in others (occupying different space). Thus we cannot *simply* speak of treating those who are equal the same (and those who are unequal differently). Rather, those who are equal *in certain respects* are to be treated the same. But what are these respects? Most simply, they are the respects that are *relevant* to the action in question. And although there are some cases in which what counts as a relevant similarity (or difference) is problematic, there are numerous clearcut examples which will serve to illustrate this notion.

When you go into a store looking for shoes, the clerk asks you about the size of your feet, not your head. When deciding how much food to prepare for a party, you consider the number of guests and the sizes of their appetites, not the color of their hair and the makes of the cars they drive. In assigning grades one looks to the quality of work done, not the area of the country a student comes from. And so on. In each case it is the former that is relevant to the activity in question, not the latter.

Thus the main problem of justice is determining what is relevant in deciding how things ought to be treated. Once this is determined, those that are equal in this regard are to be treated the same and those that are different are to be treated in direct proportion to the differences between them. Understood in this way, there are two components to the concept of justice. First, the (formal) requirement of equal treatment: Treat those entities that are equal in the relevant respects the same, and treat those that are unequal in the relevant respects differently (and in direct proportion to the differences between them). Second, the (substantive) specification of which respects are relevant. Without such specification, the former is a formula which does not tell us what to do in particular cases. Hence it is called the formal principal of justice. The specification of *which respects are relevant,* on the other hand, renders this formal principle applicable to particular situations. This task involves the formulation of what are called material or substantive principles of justice.

Before relating what we have been saying about justice to the notion of discrimination, some additional points must be clarified. In order to determine the *scope* of the principle of justice we must identify to *which entities* and *what acts* it applies. The former concerns what or who is affected by our actions; the latter the kinds of acts we perform. In other words, Are all types of acts directed at all things covered by the principle of justice? The answer to this question is clearly "no." For example, inanimate objects are not covered. When in a fit of anger I pick up a clod of earth and hurl it to the ground, smashing it into little pieces, it simply does not make sense to ask the question, Did the clod of earth *deserve* that kind of treatment? Clods of earth are not the kinds of things that can be said to deserve anything. Those things which intelligibly can be said to be deserving we shall call *moral entities;* those which cannot properly be said to be deserving, non-moral entities.

Just as there are some entities that are not covered by the principle of justice, so there are some *acts* which are not covered. If I give $10 to one of my children and nothing to another, it certainly is appropriate to ask whether or not they were treated fairly (got what they deserved). But when I give different color sweaters to them the question seems inappropriate. The difference is that questions about desert or just distribution are appropriate only when some kind of *benefit* or *harm* is involved.

These two qualifications of the principle of justice can be summarized in the following way:

Type of act	Type of entity affected by the act	
	Moral entity	Non-moral entity
Involves harm or benefit	Questions of justice arise	Do not arise
Does not involve harm or benefit	Do not arise	Do not arise

There is much more that can be said about these qualifications. Although it is clear that clods of earth are not moral entites, and human beings are, what about non-human forms of animal life? The answer to this question is clearly problematic. Yet it is not a problem to which we must attend here. For all parties to the reverse discrimination dispute limit their concern to human beings, and agree that human beings are moral entities. If our task were to decide whether or not experimentation upon non-human forms of animal life is legitimate (see the essay "On the Ethics of the Use of Animals in Science"), we would have to determine if any or all of these life forms are moral entities. Were we considering the claim that there should be reverse discrimination for at least some non-human forms of life, we would also have to resolve this issue. But given the scope of our concern, reverse discrimination for certain groups of human beings, we need go no farther than pointing out that human beings are moral entities.

The same kind of point applies to the second qualification as well. Where do we draw the line between what counts as a harm or benefit and what does not? Although looking at someone normally does not, and killing them clearly does, what about all the difficult cases that lie in between? A discussion of paternalism must address this question (see the essay "Paternalism and Restrictions on Liberty"). We do not. This is because all of the parties to the discrimination dispute agree that the actions in question involve harm to some and benefit to others. Thus it is clear that the acts we are concerned with raise questions of justice regardless of how we may end up fine-tuning the definitions of harm and benefit.

With these qualifications in hand, and the explication of the notion of justice before us, we are now in a position to articulate the concept of discrimination more fully. Discriminatory acts involve treating things differently. When the objects of such acts are non-moral entities (such as clods of earth), or the acts neither harm nor benefit their objects, then they have no moral significance, and questions of justice do not arise. On the other hand, when the objects of discriminatory acts are moral beings, *and* the acts produce either harm or benefit for those beings, the acts do have moral significance, and questions of justice do arise. For the remainder of our discussion 'discrimination' shall refer exclusively to this latter category of discriminatory acts.

Thus, *discrimination occurs whenever human beings are harmed (or benefited) by the failure to get what they deserve.* In other words, *whenever undeserved harm or benefit results from the failure to treat those human beings who are equal in the relevant respects the same and those who are unequal in the relevant respects differently (and in direct proportion to the differences between them) the result is discrimination.* This formal principle is as much as can be said about "discrimination in general". We cannot apply it until we specify which respects are relevant to the way individuals should be treated (i.e., supply substantive principles). And which respects are relevant depends upon the specific activity in question—performance (and perhaps ability) in the case of grading, symptoms or disease in the case of doctoring, being one's child in the case of parenting, and so on. In order to make progress, then, we must look at specific areas of discrimination. Only in this way can we specify which respects are relevant, and thus determine when discrimination occurs and when it does not.

We shall focus upon discrimination in education and vocational (job) opportunities. This means we shall not consider discrimination in housing, social clubs, credit and the like. This is not because discrimination in these areas is unimportant. Clearly it is. But we cannot discuss everything. Given this limitation, it makes sense to focus upon those areas which are most central to one's well-being. And in our society, one's education and job have great impact upon his or her life prospects (and those of his or her children).

Thus our focus is now on the question: What respects are relevant to the way individuals should be treated with regard to educational and job opportunities? In other words, what *criteria* should be used in determining admission of individuals to colleges and to post-graduate schools? And what *criteria* should be used in determining who should be hired? Once we identify these criteria, we will be able to determine whether or not discrimination is occurring. When the criteria are followed there is no discrimination (even though people are being treated differently). When the criteria are not followed, there is discrimination because people are being treated unjustly.

In our society, there is general agreement that the appropriate criteria for both of these activities is *merit*—i.e., demonstrated potential for success. And this makes a lot of sense. If not everyone can be admitted to college, it would seem reasonable to admit those who, based upon their past records, have the greatest chance for success. When hiring someone, it seems equally reasonable to hire that individual who is likely to do the best job.

This view can be defended in two different ways. On the one hand, considerations of *efficiency* can be offered. Given that the primary goal of colleges is to graduate the best (most educated) students they can, it follows that they should admit those students who are most likely to benefit educationally from a college experience. Similarly, given that the primary goal of a business is to make a profit, and profit is to a large extent a function of the quality of work done by a company's employees, it follows that a company should hire those people who are likely to do the best job.

On the other hand, one can look at the situation from the point of view of *desert*. From this perspective, the question is what is relevant to the task in question, rather than efficiency. Nevertheless, the argument yields the same conclusion. What is relevant to doing a job is the *capacity* to do it. Hence one should hire those most likely to do it well, and admit to college those most likely to learn. But how does one determine this? In other words, what is involved in the judgment that someone has the capacity to do something?

Most obviously, possession of the capacity to do something involves the *native ability* to do it. Some have the ability to play the piano well; others do not. Some have facility with numbers; others find them a mystery. Some have athletic ability that others lack. And so on. The parameters of performance (i.e., the range within which one can perform if he or she pursues a particular field) are determined by native ability.

But within the limitations set by these parameters (i.e., one's potential) actual performance also depends upon how dedicated he or she is to the task. Some individuals never achieve their full potential because they lack the *motivation* and drive to develop and use their abilities; others seem to exceed their potential because they milk their abilities for all they are worth. Thus the mere fact that two individuals have the same native ability does not ensure that they will perform equally well. Indeed, there are many instances in which individuals with less ability, because of their dedication and drive, outperform those who are more talented.

We are now in a position to explain more clearly discrimination in vocational and job opportunities. Discrimination occurs whenever someone is harmed or benefited by the failure to get what he or she deserved *compared* to what others are getting. *Comparative desert requires that we treat those who are equal in the relevant respects the same and those who are unequal in the relevant respects differently* (and in direct proportion to the differences between them). Relevant to vocational and educational opportunities is the capacity to do the work in question, and this is a function of native ability and the extent to which one is motivated to develop and utilize it. One major indicator of these attributes is past performance. Thus admissions and hiring officers should look primarily to past performance, treating those who are equal in this regard the same, and giving preference to those who have performed more effectively than others. Discrimination occurs whenever this is not done—whenever a less qualified applicant is offered a position instead of a more qualified one.

IV. Reverse Discrimination

There is no doubt that discrimination has been an important feature of "the American way of life." Racial and sexual quotas have existed at many colleges and universities. Women and blacks have been systematically excluded from many jobs, and frequently have been passed over for promotions in favor of a less qualified colleague. To whatever extent such practices still go on, they were accepted practice until quite recently. And they must bear much of the responsibility for the bleak employment picture which confronts women and blacks today.

According to *U.S. News and World Report* (December 8, 1980, pp. 50–54) in 1979 (1) the median full-time earnings of women is only 60% that of men, (2) women fill only 17% of the top positions at companies with 100 or more employees, and (3) private surveys of the top 50 U.S. corporations reveal just 400 women with jobs paying $40,000 a year or more, with none of these firms having a female chief executive officer. The equally bleak situation for blacks is perhaps most dramatically highlighted by the fact that unemployment among black youths is almost double that of their white counterparts.[1]

Beyond a handful of American Nazis, Klu Klux Klanners and other sexists and racists, everyone agrees that the discriminatory practices which have played a central role in creating this situation are wrong. We have shown why they are wrong. They violate the principle of comparative desert. (In this regard, it is instructive to ask yourself the following questions: How would people who favor discrimination respond to the argument that has been given so far? Would they claim that there is nothing wrong with discrimination? Or would they argue that the treatment they propose for blacks, women, etc. is not discriminatory?)

Given, then, both our argument that discrimination is unjust, and the fact that it has occurred, and on a lesser (though not insignificant) scale continues to occur, *What should be done about it now?* Some maintain that we should continue, albeit with a renewed effort, what we have been doing—viz. working to *eradicate discrimination* entirely. But this is as far as we should go because any attempt to compensate the victims of discrimination will create far more injustice that it will alleviate. A second view is that while the elimination of all discrimination is an important goal, it is not adequate. *Failure to compensate* the victims of discrimination will leave them forever handicapped by the results of previous discriminatory practices. Thus something more must be done. One version of the second view advocates reparations—i.e. monetary payments to the victims of discrimination to compensate them for their unfair treatment. Another version insists on reverse discrimination as the appropriate means of rectification. We shall begin by focusing on this latter view.

Reverse discrimination is first and foremost discrimination. It involves passing over the most qualified application for a position in favor of a less qualified one on the grounds that the weaker applicant has been victimized by discrimination. In other words, it is discrimination which goes in the reverse direction of previous acts of discrimination as a way of rectifying the unfair handicaps and advantages that prior discrimination produced. For these reasons reverse discrimination is a highly sensitive issue and is a policy which stands in need of justification. Such justification will be difficult to construct in light of the fact that *what needs to be justified is an apparently unjust mode of behavior.*

I have argued elsewhere[2] that reverse discrimination *is* justified if and only if four conditions are met. These conditions are:

1. It must be rectifying an initial act of discrimination.
2. The person who will benefit from the proposed reverse discrimination must have been handicapped by the initial act.
3. The person who will be victimized by the proposed reverse discrimination must have benefited from previous acts of discrimination.
4. The harm produced by discrimination will be passed on to future generations even if all discrimination is ended immediately. Let us examine these conditions carefully.

That there must have been an initial act of discrimination that the reverse discrimination is going to rectify follows from the meaning of "reverse discrimination". If there is no previous act of discrimination that is being offset, then we simply have an instance of discrimination, not *reverse* discrimination. Further, discrimination only occurs when a harm or benefit results. Thus if there is no resultant harm or benefit then there is no opportunity for *reverse* discrimination—there is nothing to reverse or rectify. But harms and benefits do result from acting on illicit distinctions in vocational and educational opportunities. And they are harms of a very significant kind, for they directly affect the nature and quality of one's life.

One's career directly affects his or her self-concept, life-style and career prospects. A deserving individual who is denied a career as a doctor because of discrimination will end up perceiving himself or herself differently and leading a very different life than if he or she had not been discriminated against. First, the feeling of failure that comes from not achieving one's goals is bound to arise, even (and perhaps most acutely) when the cause of failure is discrimination. Secondly, the image of oneself that emerges from being a physician is very different from that associated with many other lines of work (or unemployment). A physician is engaged in challenging work, and gains the satisfaction that comes from making a difference in the lives of others. He or she is also a highly respected member of society, one who reaps the benefits of high socio-economic standing.

By the same token, the education one receives directly affects his or her career. If you do not get into medical school, you cannot be a doctor. If you are denied access to the more prestigious colleges, your entry-level job prospects are affected. If you are denied access to college altogether, such prospects are diminished even more. Moreover those who start with better entry-level positions have a better chance for advancement, even if there is no discrimination in hiring and promotion. When there is, as clearly there has been and continues to be, its victims are obviously harmed.

It is also important to realize that the effects of discrimination are not necessarily limited to those who are *directly* victimized by it. The self-concept, life-style and careers of parents have a tremendous impact upon their children. Such factors greatly influence the home environment and, in turn, play a significant role in shaping a child's interests and motivation. Also, the financial, intellectual and social resources accumulated by parents play a large role in determining the opportunities their children get. Just consider the difference between the opportunities available to the offspring of middle-class suburbanites and those available to the children of unemployed slumdwellers. These differences range from diet (deficiencies can retard both mental and physical growth), to housing, to medical care, to social and cultural enrichment. Some view these disparities as an indictment of our socio-economic system. But the important point for our purposes is that they do exist. And because they do, the offspring of victims of discrimination can be severely handicapped, while the offspring of its beneficiaries can be highly benefited.

To see this even more clearly, imagine a society similar to ours with one exception—equality in educational and vocational opportunities is the reality, not a mere ideal. Then one day it is decided that redheaded people are to be discriminated against. Less qualified individuals with hair that is not red are to be given preference over those with red hair. Although there are some exceptions, this becomes the general practice of the land.

To see that the effects of discrimination can be cumulative, ask yourself: What would the effects of this practice be after one generation? Two? Five? As time passes, two things will happen. On the one hand, redheads will learn, first generation redheads from their own experiences, subsequent generations from the teachings and attitudes of their parents (followed by confirming experiences), that there is no point in trying to get ahead. They will lose their motivation to succeed as they come to view themselves as second-class citizens. At the same time, the educational, economic and social status of redheads will deteriorate rapidly. Each generation will be discriminated against on all fronts. And to the extent that redheads form a distinct group whose members tend to marry each other, the educational, economic and social effects of discrimination will be passed on to children by their parents.

With regard to these cumulative effects of discrimination there is an important disparity between the situation of racial minorities (e.g. blacks) and (white) women. Because blacks constitute a distinct group whose members tend to marry each other, they have experienced both the motivational *and* the educational/economic/social cumulative effects of discrimination. (White) women, on the other hand, have for the most part only experienced the former. This does not mean that the cumulative effects of discrimination are any less real for women than they are for blacks. But it does suggest that the cumulative effects have had a more devastating impact upon the latter than the former.

Everything that has been said about the harms inflicted on those who are victimized by discrimination also applies to those who benefit from it. Every time a qualified applicant is denied admission to a school, or a promotion, in favor of a less qualified applicant, the benefits that accrue to the successful candidate are undeserved. And for the same reasons that the debilitating effects of discrimination can be passed on to future generations, so can the undeserved benefits that result.

Given, then, that the harms and benefits which result from discrimination are frequently passed from generation to generation, it follows that an individual who has never been directly victimized by discrimination may indirectly suffer its debilitating effects. Thus we must allow for the rectification of the effects of discrimination not only for those who are its immediate victims, but for those who are indirectly debilitated by it as well. Similar points apply to the beneficiaries of discrimination; but in this case there is an additional complication.

The beneficiaries of discrimination are not necessarily its perpetrators. This point is most clear when the benefits of discrimination are passed on to one's children and grandchildren. But it is also true of most initial acts of discrimination as well. The individuals who set restrictive school admission policies are not the students who directly benefit from such policies; and the individuals who benefit from the exclusion of others in the hiring and promotion process are not those who do the hiring and promoting. This means that reverse discrimination aims at individuals who have benefited from discrimination, even though they are not normally the perpetrators of that discrimination. And this is bound to leave one uneasy. If the individuals who are going to be discriminated against under a policy of reverse discrimination were evil people who also benefited from their own acts of discrimination against others, I think few would oppose reverse discrimination. But such is not the case. They are often the innocent beneficiaries who have worked hard to capitalize upon (or are trying to capitalize on) the break they have received. All of this serves to reiterate that reverse discrimination is a serious business that must not be taken lightly. It usually involves imposing a cost on blameless persons, and hence must be shown to be justifiable.

It is because of considerations such as these that if all discrimination were ended immediately *and* its effects would not extend beyond those who have been directly victimized, reverse discrimination could not be justified. This conclusion will be of little comfort to those who have been victimized. After all, the wrong they have been done will not be rectified. But this view does acknowledge the fact that those who have benefited from discrimination are for the most part blameless, and have often made much of the break they have received. To penalize them clearly involves an element of injustice, and hence should be avoided if at all possible.

Thus, we are dealing with a situation in which we have to choose between two evils. Simply ending discrimination will leave many individuals handicapped. These handicaps will prevent them from enjoying their fair share of the goods and opportunities our country has to offer. The handicaps will also have deleterious effects upon their offspring. On the other hand, a policy of reverse discrimination will work against those who, although they have benefited from discrimination, are not its perpetrators. Moreover, as noted, these individuals may have worked hard and hence deserve the fruits of their labors, even though they do not deserve the break that made that labor possible.

This is the heart of the problem of reverse discrimination, and it is one which does not admit of simple solutions. Those who argue that reverse discrimination is justified simply because discrimination has produced an injustice which must be rectified are ignoring the fact that reverse discrimination itself involves an element of injustice. By the same token, those who argue simply that reverse discrimination is unjustified because it is a form of discrimination are ignoring the fact that discrimination often produces an enduring injustice that needs to be rectified. Thus any argument to the effect that reverse discrimination is justified must have two elements. It must show both that reverse discrimination is the preferred way of rectifying the injustice of discrimination (either because it is the most effective, the least unjust, or both), and that the injustice produced by reverse discrimination is less than the injustice that exists as a result of discrimination. We shall consider each of these elements in turn.

The argument that reverse discrimination is the preferred way of rectifying the injustice of discrimination must be a tentative one. To be decisive the argument would have to show that reverse discrimination is better than any other alternative. But since the number of possible alternatives is very great, we will have to focus on the limited but not insignificant claim that reverse discrimination is preferable to the most plausible of the currently considered alternatives.

One might maintain that we can accomplish the rectificatory goal of reverse discrimination without the associated cost by continuing and enhancing the numerous social programs that have been introduced over the past 40 to 50 years. In other words, social programs for the less advantaged work to offset the undesirable consequences suffered by the victims of discrimination, while programs aimed at enhancing the quality of education (e.g., bussing, teacher training, curriculum development) work to offset the debilitating effect of discrimination by equalizing the educational base from which all individuals begin.

But there is little reason to accept this argument. For one thing, social programs, even if effective, are designed to provide each individual with a minimal standard of living. Although this is a step in the right direction, there is far more to the good life than this. Just ask yourself: Would I rather be a gainfully employed suburbanite or an unemployed slumdweller? Secondly, these programs have proven to be terribly expensive. Indeed many argue that the primary beneficiaries of these programs are the educated individuals who have been hired to fill the bureaucratic structures that have been created to deliver the services, rather than the individuals for whom these services are targeted. The least that can be said is that there is no comparison between the quality of life of a government bureaucrat and that of a welfare recipient. Thus even though welfare programs undoubtedly improve the quality of life of many of their clients, they clearly do not sufficiently offset the debilitating effects of discrimination upon those who need the programs because of either direct or indirect discrimination.

On the educational end, there is little evidence that the programs that have been set up are doing much to offset the generations of discrimination and neglect that have led to the current situation. The improvement of inner city schools, cross district bussing, etc., policies designed to provide equal educational opportunity, have yet to bear fruit. Perhaps it is too early to tell, but there seems to be little hope that such programs can offset the massive cumulative effects of generations of discrimination. To admit as much is *not* to say that they should be abandoned. Improving our schools and the quality of education they provide to all youngsters should be a continuing goal of our society. However, improving our schools is one thing: offsetting the effects of discrimination is another.

If social programs are no substitute for reverse discrimination, perhaps reparations are. In other words, perhaps in addition to ending discrimination, we should rectify the harm done by discrimination by financially compensating its victims for their misfortune. There are two problems with this suggestion. The first is that, although it has clear precedent in the law, there must be grave doubts about the wisdom of translating the kind of harm that results from discrimination into monetary terms. To the extent that this harm is only a reduction in earning power, I see no problem. But there is more to the harm produced by discrimination than this. One's self-concept, motivation, and quality of life are also affected, and I see no reason to think that reparations can offset these kinds of effects. Secondly, reparations are only viable if they will prevent the passing on of the effects of discrimination to future generations. This result might be achieved if the cash payments were large enough and they were wisely used to improve the recipient's economic and vocational situation and the educational opportunities of his or her offspring. But given the current economic, social and educational situation of those who would receive payments, there is little reason to think that this would occur. Hence we must conclude that reparations are not an adequate substitute for reverse discrimination either.

Having argued that the most plausible alternatives to reverse discrimination are unacceptable, we must now determine whether the injustice associated with reverse discrimination is more or less than that which has resulted (and continues to result) from discrimination. And here two points seem to be most relevant.

We have already observed the extent to which discrimination pervades our society. In many families generation after generation has been discriminated against in both educational and job opportunities. When the cumulative nature of the effects of discrimination is added to this, it is clear that the harmful impact of discrimination is deep and pervasive. Thus it would be incorrect to think of the effects of discrimination as some minor evil which, because of the costs involved in removing it, will just have to be tolerated.

By contrast, the harm that results from reverse discrimination is not as great because those who have benefited from discrimination tend to be better off educationally, economically and socially than those who have been victimized by it. In our society one of the main advantages of being "better off" is the additional opportunities (the "margin of safety") it provides. Indeed, part of what is involved in being better off is being aware of business, professional and educational opportunities, knowing well-placed individuals who can provide an "inside track" to these opportunities, and having the economic resources to pursue them effectively. Thus a better off individual who is a victim of reverse discrimination (e.g. is denied admission to medical school in favor of a less qualified applicant who has been handicapped by discrimination) is in a better position to pursue satisfying alternative careers than is the less well off individual who has been victimized by discrimination and would not get into medical school without reverse discrimination.

The point is that the effects of individual instances of reverse discrimination on its victims will not erase all or even most of the benefits which have accrued from the systematic, comprehensive and extensive discrimination that has occurrred. The only way in which the benefits which have resulted from this could be totally offset is through an equally far-reaching policy of reverse discrimination. Yet such a comprehensive policy of reverse discrimination is not what is being proposed. It has been acknowledged that those who have made something from the "break" they received as the result of discriminatory practices against others deserve what they have achieved, even though they did not deserve the break. Thus the goal of reverse discrimination is *not* to return those who have benefited from discrimination to ground zero. Rather it is to offset some of the advantages beneficiaries have received by giving preferential treatment to individuals who are less qualified by virtue of the fact that they have been victimized by discrimination.

Thus it seems reasonable to conclude that the injustice involved in not rectifying the harm which has resulted from discrimination outweighs whatever injustice may be done to the victims of reverse discrimination. It follows that reverse discrimination (at least within the reasonable limits sketched) is justified. But now we must forge this conclusion into a workable social policy. This may well be the most difficult task of all.

V. Social Policy

There are a number of social policies which can be or have been enacted that will help those who have been discriminated against. Some of these involve reverse discrimination while others do not. For example, just because a college or university begins admitting more members of a previously discriminated against group does not necessarily mean that it has adopted a policy of reverse discrimination. The new procedure may be based upon the view that traditional admission criteria (grade point average, aptitude and achievement test scores, and letters of recommendation) are poor indicators of past accomplishment and future success because they have biases built into them. What is involved in this case is a *redefinition of what it means to be most qualified,* rather than accepting those who are less qualified over those who are more so.

Alternatively, the new policy may be based on the view that having a diversified student body is an essential ingredient in the learning process (both socially and academically); hence, achieving this mixture takes precedence over the criterion of merit. In this case, what is relevant to college admission is being redefined independently of considerations of prior discrimination; thus there is no reverse discrimination either.

On the other hand, the increase in the admission of members of previously discriminated against groups may involve giving preference to less qualified applicants on the grounds that they have been victimized by discrimination. Such a procedure does involve reverse discrimination. The best known example is the admission procedure used by the Medical School of the University of California at Davis. This procedure was the subject of the Bakke decision, in which the United States Supreme Court upheld the California State Supreme Court ruling that the policy was unconstitutional.

The Medical School of the University of California at Davis had set aside 16 of the 100 positions in each entering class for members of disadvantaged groups. Students indicated on their applications whether or not they wanted to be considered for one of these positions, and those so indicating were screened to determine whether or not they qualified. Those who did had their applications considered by a special committee. Minimum qualifications required for all other applicants were waived, and the students were only in competition with others applying for the special 16 positions. The result of this procedure was that some of the applicants in the special group who were admitted were less qualified than some of the applicants in the main group who were not. This is a paradigm case of reverse discrimination.

It was precisely this point that served as the basis of Allan Bakke's suit. Bakke had been denied admission to the medical school. He argued that if the sixteen positions had not been set aside for a special class of applicants, and had a different set of criteria not been used to evaluate the applicants for those positions, he would have been admitted. In other words, he was more qualified than many of the students admitted under the medical school's special admissions program. Hence denying him admission constituted reverse discrimination.

Supreme Court decisions are usually complicated. There are nine justices, and even when they all agree on a matter, they do so for a variety of different reasons. In the Bakke case two specific issues were decided. The court ruled on the constitutionality of (1) the medical school's admission procedure and (2) the issue of whether or not it is ever permissible to take race into account in admission procedures. Both decisions were decided on 5–4 votes, with Justice Powell being the swing vote. In other words, four justices (Burger, Rhenquist, Stevens and Stewart) argued that the Davis policy is unconstitutional *because* it is never legitimate to take race into account in admission procedures. Four other justices (Blackmun, Brennan, Marshall and White) argued that neither the Davis procedure nor sometimes taking race into account in admission procedures are unconstitutional. Justice Powell, however, split his vote. He argued that (1) the Davis policy is unconstitutional but (2) it is not always illegitimate to employ race as a factor in admission procedures. Hence the Davis policy was overturned and Bakke was admitted to the medical school: yet not all admission policies which take race into account are illegitimate.

The justices' arguments focused upon the Equal Protection Clause of the Fourteenth Amendment ("No state shall . . . deny to any person within its jurisdiction the equal protection of the laws") and Title VI of the 1964 Civil Rights Act. Those who approved of both the Davis procedure and the policy of sometimes taking race into account in making admissions decisions believe that this is permissible when seeking to offset the effects of previous acts of discrimination. Those disapproving of both maintain that it is *never* permissible to take race into account—neither to discriminate nor to discriminate in reverse. Justice Powell, on the other hand, maintained that no one could be *excluded* from consideration on the basis of race as the Davis admissions procedure required. Yet he also insisted that considerations of racial and ethnic diversity can be relevant to the admission process. This may seem inconsistent, but it is not. Powell fully rejects reverse discrimination, but he believes that cultural diversity can be a relevant consideration in the admission process; something to be considered along with merit. Thus he believes that the notion of "most qualified applicant" is not necessarily synonymous with "most meritorious." If one disagrees with Powell on this point, the disagreement is over what is relevant to the way applicants should be evaluated, rather than whether or not reverse discrimination is justified.

The Bakke decision raises a variety of difficult constitutional issues that cannot be addressed here. For one thing, these issues are far too extensive to be treated in the limited space available to us. For another, they require the talents of a legal scholar, something which I am not. However, there is an important issue raised by the Bakke case, but not addressed by the justices, which we must consider; for it is an issue which underlies the question of the appropriateness of reverse discrimination as a public policy.

We have argued that, within limits, the victims of past discrimination should be given preference over its beneficiaries whenever the debilitating effects of discrimination would survive the cessation of these unjust practices. Yet as our discussion has proceeded it has subtly changed from talk about *individuals* to *classes*, and we have begun to speak about the class of individuals who have been harmed by or benefited from discrimination. As long as this class is simply composed of all those individuals who have either benefited or been harmed, there is no problem. But this is not what happened in the Bakke case. To be eligible for the Davis special admissions program, one did not need to show that he or she was a victim of discrimination; all one needed to show is that *one belonged to a racial or ethnic group many members of which have been harmed by it*. Similarly, to be passed over in favor of a less qualified applicant one simply had to be a caucasian.

Interestingly, this was not an issue in the Bakke case. Yet it is crucial for the argument we have presented. In order to be operable, social policies must be formulated in terms of general classes or categories. It would be unworkable to require, for each proposed act of reverse discrimination, that evidence be presented which shows that the person who will benefit from it has been harmed by discrimination, and that the person who will be harmed by the reverse discrimination has benefited from discrimination. This requirement would be unworkable for two reasons.

For one thing, the bureaucracy that would be required to verify and evaluate claims would dwarf the huge government bureaucracy that already exists. The funds that would be siphoned off of an already hard-pressed economy to facilitate the policy would be enormous. In short, this cure would hurt everyone; and to many it would seem far worse than the disease. Of course this only shows that the cost of exacting justice would be very high. Someone who believes in justice *at any cost* will not be moved by it.

But suppose we set up such a bureaucracy. How could someone verify the claims that a person has been harmed by discrimination and someone else has benefited from it? The problem here is two-fold. It is necessary to determine (1) whether or not discrimination has occurred and (2) if it has, what harms or benefits have resulted. Each of these tasks has unique problems associated with it.

Once we resolve the sticky conceptual problem of what discrimination is, the determination of whether or not it has occurred would seem to be a straight-forward factual matter. One simply needs to look at what actually happened to determine whether or not discrimination was involved. Unfortunately, however, it is seldom this simple. Investigators are often confronted with conflicting accounts of what the facts are as well as conflicting interpretations of those facts. In other words, discrimination cases usually reveal conflicting accounts of what the prevailing standards of merit are and which individuals best meet these standards. Thus, what might seem to be a straight-forward factual matter is usually a very cloudy one.

An additional problem is that we are concerned as much with past acts of discrimination as with current ones. Because the cumulative effects of discrimination can accrue over generations, we are as concerned with discrimination that occurred 50 and 100 years ago as we are with that which is still happening today. But many of these "facts" are lost forever. Thus to require that an individual *show* that discrimination has occurred in his or her remote (ancestral) past is to ensure that few if any acts of discrimination will be rectified.

The problem is even more acute when it comes to showing that a specific individual has been either harmed or benefited by an act of discrimination. We are concerned with *actual* harms or benefits. If someone *would have* flunked out of medical school anyway, then in respect to becoming a doctor, he or she would have failed to achieve this goal even without discrimination. This does not imply that excluding such individuals on irrelevant grounds is legitimate. Such acts are still unjust. But because no harm has accrued, there is nothing to rectify.

Thus the legitimacy of claims for reverse discrimination depend upon the adequacy of *counterfactual* claims (what would have happened if . . .). In order to show that reverse discrimination is in order it must be shown both that its beneficiary would be better situated had it not been for some act(s) of discrimination in his or her past, and that the proposed victim of the reverse discrimination would be worse off were it not for some act of discrimination in his or her past. This simply cannot be done—at least in most cases. Thus to focus on individual cases (rather than classes) is to ensure that very few if any acts of discrimination will be rectified.

Some would undoubtedly applaud this conclusion. But we have tried to show that discrimination is a serious matter that should not be ignored. When one considers how pervasive it has been in our country over tens of decades, one cannot escape the conclusion that most members of most minority groups (and women) have been harmed by it. And this is true in spite of the fact that we cannot demonstrate the particulars of most cases.

By the same token, all members of the male (caucasian) majority must have benefited to some extent by the discrimination that has kept others out of the mainstream of American life. Some have benefited directly through acts of discrimination against others. Some have benefited indirectly by receiving advantages that have accrued to them as a result of acts of discrimination which have benefited their parents or grandparents. But all have benefited from the way in which the cumulative effects of discrimination has limited the pool of qualified applicants. In other words, as the cumulative effects of discrimination have built up over the years, both the motivation and qualifications of its victims have been reduced, and thus all members of the white male majority have had a better shot at the positions for which they have applied.

Thus all white males have benefited from the discrimination against minorities and women, although some have no doubt benefited more than others. The fairest thing to do would be to make those who have benefited the most the targets of reverse discrimination. But for the same reasons that it is not feasible to base a policy of reverse discrimination on the demonstration that specific individuals have been harmed by discrimination, it is infeasible to base it on showing that specific individuals have benefited from discrimination more than others. Thus there may be some individuals who would be harmed by a policy of reverse discrimination who benefited less from discrimination than others who would not be harmed. But because (1) all white males have benefited from discrimination, (2) it is not feasible to demonstrate how much *individuals* have benefited and (3) the harm done by reverse discrimination is considerably less than that done by discrimination, reverse discrimination based upon class membership rather than individual harms and benefits is justified.

This conclusion is at odds with the Supreme Court's rejection of reverse discrimination in Bakke. Because the Court has ruled reverse discrimination unconstitutional, it could only become public policy through a constitutional amendment or a change of mind by the Court. Since neither of these possibilities seem likely at the moment, it behooves us to consider other possibilities. Are there any policies which do not involve reverse discrimination, and hence might be acceptable to the Supreme Court, which could accomplish at least some of the objectives of reverse discrimination?

One possibility is simply a program of aggressive recruitment of members of previously discriminated against groups. The idea is to make these people aware of the opportunities that exist, and to encourage them to apply, while at the same time offering positions to the most qualified applicants. This policy recognizes and seeks to offset the motivational problems created by generations of discrimination. However it stops short of reverse discrimination because the selection process gives the available positions to the most qualified candidates.

To the extent that the handicaps created by discrimination are only motivational, aggressive recruitment may be an acceptable substitute for reverse discrimination (this would depend upon how great the motivational problems are and whether or not aggressive recruitment would be sufficient to offset them). On the other hand, to the extent that discrimination has also resulted in a diminution in the qualifications of its victims, aggressive recruitment is not sufficient because those who have been discriminated against will be disadvantaged in the final selection process. It was argued in Part IV (see p. 75) that although reverse discrimination has primarily affected the motivation of women, it has affected the motivation *and* qualifications of blacks. It follows that although aggressive recruitment *may* be sufficient to offset the effects of discrimination upon (white) women, it is definitely *in*sufficient in the case of blacks.

A second possible alternative to reverse discrimination designed to offset the debilitating effects of discrimination would be to define the minimum qualifications for positions, aggressively recruit members of discriminated against groups to apply for these positions, and then give preference to those victims of previous discrimination who meet (or surpass) the minimum requirements. It is important to realize that minimum qualifications are not necessarily low standards. What the minimum standards are would depend upon the activity involved. For example, the minimum standards for a surgeon, lawyer or accountant would undoubtedly be quite high.

Whether or not this alternative constitutes reverse discrimination is an interesting question. Because it replaces the idea that some are more qualified than others with the notion that a person is either qualified or not (i.e. no distinctions are drawn among those who qualify—one either qualifies or does not), it does not involve giving preference to the less qualified over those who are more qualified. But it does involve giving preference among those who are qualified to those who have been victims of discrimination. Thus individuals who lose out through this kind of process can not claim that they were passed over in favor of a less qualified applicant. On the other hand, they can claim that the selection process from among those who are qualified is unfair. In other words, they could argue that the fair thing to do would be to select from those who are qualified on a random basis (i.e. a lottery), rather than giving preference to those who have been discriminated against in the past.

Thus we see that this policy is like reverse discrimination in one respect (individuals who have been discriminated against are given preference over those who have not been) and unlike it in another (the less qualified are *not* given preference over the more qualified). Whether or not this warrants calling it "reverse discrimination" is not really the crucial issue. *Whatever we call it,* it is a less extreme measure than the kind of reverse discrimination we have been talking about.

The important thing to note about this alternative is that it brings the issue of what it is to be qualified for a position to the fore. In other words, the policy rests upon the determination of minimum qualifications. Hence we must try to make some sense out of this notion.

Perhaps the best thing to do is to begin with the notion of being the most qualified. Most firms seek to hire, and most colleges seek to admit, those who will do the best work. Hence they rank people in order of their qualifications, and take the most qualified first. Notice, however, that not everyone who is given the opportunity succeeds, and many who do not qualify for one position do quite well when given an opportunity at an identical or similar position. This fact suggests that our ability to determine who is *most* qualified for a position is far from perfect. There are a number of reasons for this.

For one thing, criteria may be established that are simply not relevant. For example a degree (high school, college or graduate) may be required for a position which has nothing to do with that degree (consider the difference between requiring a bachelors degree for janitorial work and requiring it for a teaching position). Or criteria that are relevant may simply be ignored—as in the case of hiring people for teaching positions without considering their teaching ability. We tend to think of hiring and admission criteria as identifying in a clearcut way those who are the most qualified individuals. But this is assuming far greater precision than is warranted.

Possession of a college degree has been thought to indicate that an individual has certain skills (reading, writing, problem solving, etc.) and knowledge (the content of one's major). But many college graduates do not possess them, and those who do do so in widely varying degrees. Thus a college degree is at most a rough indicator that an individual is likely to possess certain skills and knowledge.

In addition to these supposedly objective criteria are the subjective aspects of attitude and personality. Knowledge and skills are at most necessary for a job, but they do not guarantee that the individual will do it well. Motivation, ability to work with others, emotional well-being and the like all have a direct and significant impact upon an individual's performance. Even the fact that an individual has performed well in the past gives no guarantee that he or she will continue to do so in the future. Given a new job, and working with different individuals at a different stage in one's life, there is considerable room for failure.

None of this is meant to suggest that past performance is no indicator whatsoever of future behavior. It is merely to point out that the idea that there is one individual who is *the most qualified* for a given position is to presume a degree of precision that is simply unwarranted. In light of this, the cost involved in setting minimum qualifications (from the perspectives of both efficiency and justice) would seem to be minimal. If we were to do this carefully, and give preference to those who meet these conditions and are members of discriminated against groups, we may find that we can rectify past acts of discrimination without resorting to what is most odious about reverse discrimination—viz., favoring the less qualified over the more qualified.

Whether or not such a policy would adequately rectify past injustices will depend upon what the minimum qualifications turn out to be, and how many members of discriminated against groups meet them. It would indeed be interesting to see the details of such a policy worked out, as well as some projections of its impact upon those who have been victimized by discrimination.

VI. Conclusion

The argument has been presented that justice requires us to take steps designed to offset the debilitating effects of generations of discrimination in the United States. It may be that, in the case of white women, aggressive recruitment (which does not involve reverse discrimination) would be sufficient. But in the case of blacks (and other minorities) this policy definitely does not go far enough. Because of the way in which the effects of discrimination have accrued over generations, the situation of blacks requires either a policy of awarding positions to black applicants who are less qualified than their white counterparts, or a policy of setting minimum standards for positions, and giving preference to the blacks who meet these standards.

In the development of this argument we considered the obvious ways in which individuals would be affected by such a policy—educational, social and economic opportunities would be enhanced for some (the beneficiaries) and limited for others (the victims). But we have yet to consider the more subtle psychological impact that the policy would have upon those who are affected by it. In particular, how would this policy affect *your* state of mind if you were one of its beneficiaries? Or one of its victims? Although the answer to these questions will in no way alter the conclusion that justice requires taking action to offset the debilitating effects of generations of discrimination, they will shed some light on the responses that will likely be generated by this policy, and put us in a position to evaluate the appropriateness of these responses.

First, imagine that you have been offered a position, for which you are not the most qualified applicant, under the aegis of a program designed to offset the effects of generations of discrimination against your racial group. What would your reaction be? Initially, it would probably be one of elation. Afterall, you have the position! Hence, with regard to both present benefits and future opportunities you are better off than you were before.

Upon reflection, however, some doubts may start to creep in. After all, you were *not* the most qualified applicant. What about the more qualified applicants who were passed over? Perhaps you received something that you do not really deserve? Will your self-respect suffer as a result of your good fortune? It may. But the argument that has been presented indicates that it should not!

For one thing, the argument indicates you are getting what you deserve under this policy. You have been offered the position because when qualifications are considered *along with* the undeserved handicaps and advantages possessed by the applicants, you are the most deserving. Secondly, there is more to success than getting "a break." As we have seen, some capitalize on their breaks. Others do not. And to the extent that you recognize that your break is deserved, and that it is up to you either to utilize or squander the opportunities presented by it, there should be no diminution in self-respect.

On the other hand, imagine that you are one of the victims of the policy. You have been passed over for the position in favor of someone whose credentials are inferior to yours simply because that person is a member of a discriminated against group. In this case, your initial reaction will probably be one of disappointment and resentment. Losing out on something you wanted is bound to generate disappointment.

And the fact that the person who gained the position is someone with inferior credentials may well turn the disappointment into resentment.

As long as you focus upon your own well being (i.e., look at the situation from an egoistic or self-centered point of view) these feelings are bound to persist. But to the extent that you are able to assume a more detached outlook, viewing the situation from the perspective of justice or fairness, they are likely to subside.

For one thing, you will see that your superior credentials are in part a result of previous acts of discrimination. For another you will realize that the reverse discrimination of which you have been a victim only partially offsets the advantages you have received. And finally, you will recognize that belaboring your setback will make the effects of the reverse discrimination upon you worse than they need to be. This is because there are other opportunities available to you. And to the extent that focusing upon your setbacks gets in the way of pursuing them, you will be losing far more than is necessary. In other words, resentment is both counterproductive and, as far as justice is concerned, unwarranted.

Notes

1. See Morris J. Newman, "The Labor Market Experience of Black Youth, 1954–78," *Monthly Labor Review*, October, 1979, pp. 19–27.

2. See Louis I. Katzner, "Is The Favoring of Women and Blacks in Employment and Educational Opportunities Justified?", in Feinberg and Gross, *Philosophy of Law*, 2nd ed. (Belmont, Calif.: Wadsworth Publishing Co., 1980), pp. 356–361.

Suggested Readings

Boxill, Bernard R. "The Morality of Reparation." *Social Theory and Practice,* Vol. 2, No. 1 (1972), pp. 113–122.

Cohen, Marshall, and Thomas Nagel and Thomas Scanlon, eds. *Equality and Preferential Treatment*. Princeton, New Jersey: Princeton University Press, 1977.

Feinberg, Joel. *Social Philosophy*. Englewood Cliffs, New Jersey: Prentice-Hall, 1973, Ch. 7.

Fullinwider, Robert K. *The Reverse Discrimination Controversy*. Totowa, New Jersey: Rowman and Littlefield, 1980.

Katzner, Louis. "Is the Favoring of Women and Blacks in Employment and Educational Opportunities Justified?" *Philosophy of Law*, 2nd ed. Eds. Joel Feinberg and Hyman Gross. Belmont, California: Wadsworth Publishing Company, 1980, pp. 356–361.

Katzner, Louis. *Man in Conflict*. Encino, California: Dickenson Publishing Company, 1975, Chs. 1 & 5.

Mill, John Stuart. *The Subjection of Women*. London: Longmans, 1869.

Newton, Lisa H. "Reverse Discrimination as Unjustified." *Ethics*, Vol. 83, No. 4 (1973), pp. 308–312.

Thalberg, Irving. "Visceral Racism." *The Monist*, Vol. 56, No. 4 (1972), pp. 43–63.

"Women's Liberation: Ethical, Social and Political Issues." *The Monist*, Vol. 57, No. 1 (1973).

chapter four

Genetic Engineering: How Should Science Be Controlled?

STEPHEN P. STICH

I. Introduction

Genetic engineering has been with us for a long time. Since before the advent of recorded history people have attempted to alter the hereditary properties of animals, plants, and people to better suit their needs. Cows have been bred for greater milk production, horses for strength or speed, and dogs for all manner of odd characteristics. During the last decade, however, a new technology has been developed which opens vast new possibilities for manipulating the genetic endowment of living systems. This new technology has also generated an enormous amount of controversy. For, though it promises great benefits, it suggests mind numbing dangers as well. The new genetic engineering technology thus raises in a particularly acute and pressing way what may turn out to be the most fundamental normative question confronting modern societies in the closing decades of the twentieth century: *How should science and technology be controlled?*

In this essay we shall look at a number of issues that must be confronted before we can reach a reasonable view on the regulation of genetic engineering research and technology. Though our focus will be on genetic engineering, most of the issues we consider arise, perhaps in a slightly different form, in decisions about the proper regulation of other technologies. Before we can address the genetic engineering question seriously, two preliminary chores need attention. First, we must review some science—enough to understand what is involved in the new genetic engineering technology, and to see the range of its benefits and the dangers it may harbor. Second, we must think a bit about the structure of moral argument and moral reasoning. The question we ultimately hope to answer is, after all, a moral question: What *ought* to be done to control this new science? And, as we shall see, a distressing proportion of the controversy surrounding genetic engineering can be traced to carelessness (or ignorance!) about what makes for a reasonable defense of a moral position.

II. Scientific Background

A. THE NEW GENETIC ENGINEERING

Let me begin with a brief refresher on some very basic biology. *Genes* are the carriers of hereditary information. The genes of most organisms are arrayed along *chromosomes*, sub-cellular structures which can be seen with a microscope under favorable circumstances. In the 1940's it was demonstrated by Avery and others that genes are composed of the complex molecule deoxyribonucleic acid (DNA). It is now known that DNA is one of the universal constituents of living systems. The genetic information of all living things, animals, plants, bacteria and even most viruses, is encoded within their DNA. In 1952 Watson and Crick discovered that the DNA molecule has the celebrated double helix structure: it consists of two coiled strands wound around each other. During cell division these strands separate, each daughter cell receiving one strand. The single strands then serve as templates guiding the reconstruction of the missing partner. Thus ultimately both daughter cells end up with DNA identical to the DNA in the parent cell. In the years since Watson and Crick's discovery a great deal has been learned about the genetic code and the way in which DNA molecules direct the development of new cells and organisms. But there is still much that remains unknown about the mechanisms that translate the genetic message into observable features of organisms.

The breakthrough that sparked the current controversy over genetic engineering occurred in the early 1970's. Though the details are quite complex, the basic idea is very simple. Techniques were developed that enabled scientists to take small amounts of DNA derived from just about any source and splice it into circular strands of bacterial DNA called *plasmids*. These plasmids could then be reintroduced into bacteria where they would duplicate each time the bacterial cell divided. Each time the plasmid duplicated, the bit of foreign DNA that had been spliced in duplicated as well. Since the technique involved recombining strands of DNA derived from various sources, it was given the formidable label recombinant DNA technology. The basic steps in this technology are illustrated in Figure 1.

B. APPLICATIONS OF THE NEW TECHNOLOGY

Now that we know what recombinant DNA technology is, the next obvious question is: Why should anyone want to do it? What can the technology be used for? The answer is that the applications of recombinant DNA technology are only beginning to be explored, but the possibilities are dazzling, and of enormous importance. A few illustrations will serve to make the point.

The application of recombinant DNA technology that was of most interest to the scientists who developed it is as a tool in pure research. Since higher animals have so

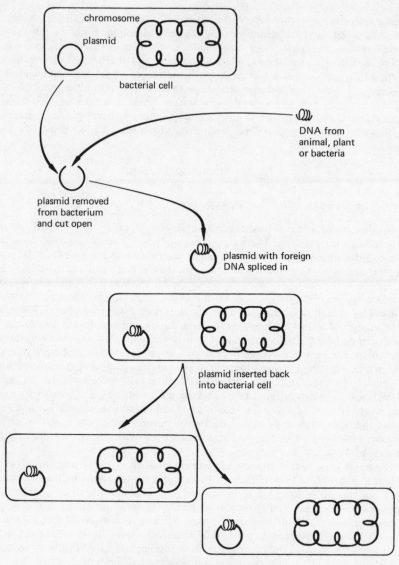

chromosome

plasmid

bacterial cell

DNA from animal, plant or bacteria

plasmid removed from bacterium and cut open

plasmid with foreign DNA spliced in

plasmid inserted back into bacterial cell

bacterium divides, duplicating plasmid and foreign DNA

Figure 1:
Basic Steps of Recombinant
DNA Technology

much DNA (enough for three to four million genes is the going estimate for man) it is enormously difficult and expensive, using standard chemical techniques, to isolate a single animal gene in quantities large enough for study. However, if the gene a researcher wishes to study can be spliced into a bacterial plasmid, the gene will duplicate each time the bacterial cell divides. Under optimal conditions *E. coli* bacteria, the kind commonly used in recombinant DNA work, divide about once every 20 minutes. So in 10 hours a single animal gene spliced into a bacterial plasmid could make 2^{30} copies of itself—that's 1,073,741,824 copies!—for the cost of a few pennies. The ability to isolate substantial amounts of a given animal gene quickly and inexpensively has enormously enhanced scientists' capacity to study the functioning of animal genes. Investigations using recombinant DNA technology have already made significant contributions to our understanding of basic biological processes, and there is certain to be a rich harvest of knowledge still to come. Moreover, the knowledge researchers hope to gain about the ways genes function promises to be of considerable practical importance. In many diseases, including cancer, genes appear to malfunction and fail to regulate growth and development properly. An understanding of the normal functioning of genes is likely to be a pre-requisite to finding the cause and cure for these diseases.

To understand the second application of recombinant DNA technology on my list, we need a bit more basic biological background. One of the ways in which genes determine what goes on in cells and organisms, indeed probably the principal way, is to direct the synthesis of proteins and other biologically important molecules. In a number of cases the gene responsible for the synthesis of a biologically active substance has already been isolated. It turns out that when these genes are spliced into bacterial plasmids they sometimes succeed in doing in their new bacterial home just what they originally did in the animal cell from which they were isolated. Thus, by using recombinant DNA technology, bacteria can be turned into microscopic factories which quickly and inexpensively produce substances that are otherwise obtainable only at considerable expense. It has already been demonstrated that this technique can be used to produce insulin and interferon. Insulin is the hormone required in the treatment of diabetes. Interferon is a substance which occurs in minute amounts in human blood. Until the advent of recombinant DNA technology it has been so rare and difficult to obtain that all the interferon ever purified from human blood would fit comfortably in a coffee cup. Since it is so rare, its properties have not been extensively studied. However, it appears to act as a broad spectrum anti-viral agent, aiding the body to fight off infection from a broad range of viruses. There is also some indication that interferon may be effective in combating certain forms of cancer. Several laboratories have succeeded in producing interferon in bacteria, and by the time this essay appears, extensive clinical testing of interferon will be underway. Other human proteins which have already been produced in bacteria by using recombinant DNA technology include growth hormone (used to treat dwarfism), somatostatin (a regulatory hormone), a thymosin (a stimulator of the immune system), and urokinase (used to break down blood clots).

Recombinant DNA technology also has many potential applications in industries other than the pharmaceutical industry. A single example will suggest the range of possibilities. Oil spills which befoul beaches, killing fish and wildlife, are one of the scourges of our modern petroleum dependent society. Wouldn't it be nice if there were a type of bacteria which would eat oil spills, turning the oil into harmless by-products of bacterial digestion like water and CO_2? Well, as it happens, there are types of bacteria that will eat oil, though none do a very efficient job. The thought occurs that we might transplant the genes which give various bacteria the capacity to metabolize oil in different ways into a single strain of bacteria, preferably one which thrives in salt water. This is just what has been done by a research team at General Electric Corporation. Interestingly, the G.E. team did not use recombinant DNA technology, but other, older techniques of genetic engineering. They succeeded in producing a "bug" (i.e., a bacterial strain) which, they hope, will prove useful in cleaning up oil spills before they can do much damage. G.E. and the researchers then applied for a patent on their "invention." The patent application raised a unique legal question: Is a living organism patentable? In 1980 the U.S. Supreme Court decided that question in the affirmative, thus making widespread commercial development of recombinant DNA technology economically possible!

All of the applications of genetic engineering technology that we have surveyed so far are within, or just beyond, the current state of the art. A number of scientists have speculated about future applications of genetic engineering, applications which are not possible with currently available technology. Most of these speculative applications involve modifying the genetic material in higher plants and animals, and the possibilities that have been envisioned are breathtaking. Some of the most welcome would be agricultural applications. For example, there are some species of agricultural plants, including soy beans and other legumes, which make their own nitrogen fertilizer from nitrogen in the air. Other crops, like wheat and corn, cannot make their own nitrogen fertilizer, and must be fertilized by the farmer. The cost of this fertilizer has increased sharply during the last decade—so sharply in fact, that many farmers in poorer third world countries simply cannot afford it. But suppose that by the use of genetic engineering technology we could modify currently existing strains of corn or wheat giving them the capacity to make their own nitrogen fertilizer. The result might be substantially increased food production in the third world, and significantly less starvation. This scenario is one of the dreams of some genetic engineers, though most concede that if it can be fulfilled at all, it will be some decades in the future.

C. SOME DANGERS

The potential uses of recombinant DNA technology are so numerous and striking that some observers have predicted they will lead to social changes as profound as those brought on by the industrial revolution. But from the beginning scientists and others have been concerned that this new technology would not be an unmixed blessing. The dangers that have been conjured may be divided into three categories: those arising from accidents or unexpected outcomes, those arising from intentional misuse, and those posed by the acquisition of knowledge we might be unable to handle.

Concern about accidental or unexpected consequences was first aroused by one of the earliest experiments proposing to use the new recombinant DNA technology. The plan was to insert DNA derived from the SV40 virus into *E. coli* bacteria. What was alarming is that SV40 virus is known to cause cancer in monkeys; it will also transform human cells in tissue culture into cells which resemble cancer cells. To add to the concern, certain strains of *E. coli* bacteria, including the distant ancestor of the strain that was to be used, are natural inhabitants of the human intestines. Might the SV40 DNA transplanted into *E. coli* ultimately find its way into the intestines of a laboratory worker and there cause cancer? Much more frightening was the possibility that the newly created strain of *E. coli* containing SV40 DNA might thrive outside the laboratory, causing an epidemic of contagious cancer. Though the scenario seemed unlikely, the researchers who were to do the experiments decided to postpone them until the issue of safety could be more widely discussed. Those discussions led to the call for a voluntary moratorium on certain sorts of experiments. The ensuing controversy quickly spilled over into meetings of university governing boards, city council chambers, and ultimately into the halls of Congress.

As the controversy heated up, it became clear that the scenario involving SV40 and contagious cancer was only one of many frightening accidents that might be imagined. Consider the idea of constructing a bacterial strain that produces insulin. Suppose these insulin producing bacteria were to escape from the laboratory and set up housekeeping in our intestines. Normal people have all the insulin they need, and the unwelcome additional dose might well prove fatal. Another worrisome possibility was suggested by the fact that scientists sometimes use genes conferring resistance to antibiotics as markers in genetic engineering experiments. If a scientist begins with a bacterial strain that is killed by an antibiotic, say streptomycin, and attempts to transfer a gene conferring streptomycin resistance, there will be an easy test for success. If he ends up with bacteria that will grow in the presence of streptomycin, the gene conferring resistance must have been transferred successfully. All this is harmless enough if the bacteria in question is harmless, or if streptomycin resistance is already common in the bacteria as they occur in nature. But suppose the gene for streptomycin resistance is accidentally introduced into a pathogenic organism, or worse a pathogenic organism against which streptomycin is our best available weapon. The result would be pathogenic bacteria which could no longer be controlled by what had previously been the best drug available.

Some of the accident scenarios that were conjured when the debate over recombinant DNA was at its irrational peak had a touch of black humor. We earlier described a bacterial strain designed to eat oil spills, turning them into harmless by-products. But what would happen, it was asked, if the "bug" should get loose and begin gorging itself in our gas tanks? Might the Israelis retaliate against Arab hostility by sprinkling oil eating bacteria over Arab oil fields? This particular threat is not one that oil sheiks should lose sleep over. For to do their work the oil eating bacteria need both water and oxygen, and neither is in abundant supply in oil wells or gas tanks.

Some of the scenarios for inadvertent disaster might also, with slight variation, be included on our list of intentional misuses. For example, a group of scientifically sophisticated terrorists, or a nation bent on pursuing biological warfare, might actually set out to build a pathogen resistant to antiobiotics. Recombinant DNA technology also opens possibilities for the biological warrior that could hardly happen by accident. Botulism bacteria (*Clostridium botulinum*) is one of the deadliest organisms in nature. Tiny amounts of the toxin it produces are fatal if swallowed. If the gene responsible for the synthesis of this botulinus toxin were introduced into *E. coli* which normally live in the human intestine, the consequence would be catastrophic. They would also be just about impossible for a military commander to control. For this reason most knowledgeable observers have concluded that new pathogens created using recombinant DNA technology are not likely to be of interest to the military. Even terrorists, who might be less concerned about controlling the pestilence they create, are not likely to be attracted to genetic engineering technology. Here the reason is simply that nature herself has provided the terrorist with pestilence aplenty, if he chooses to use them. Bacteria causing anthrax, bubonic plague and other ghastly diseases are readily available in nature. It is hard to imagine that the terrorist could manufacture anything much worse, and hard to see why he would waste his time trying.

The final category of dangers that genetic engineering may harbor is vaguer and less imminent, though in the long run it may prove to be most important. In addition to producing useful (or perhaps dangerous) organisms, research employing recombinant DNA technology also produces *knowledge*—knowledge about how genes work, knowledge about the genetic code, knowledge about the fundamental mechanisms of life. And knowledge of how nature works often brings with it knowledge of how to modify natural processes. Scientists already know how to make minor modifications in the genetic makeup of certain bacteria. We are still many years away from a technology that will enable scientists to build a virus or bacterium from scratch. And we are further still from a technology which will enable us to make substantial modifications in the genetic endowment of higher animals or man. Informed guesses vary widely on the question of how long it will be before we can make major modifications in the human genome. Some scientists believe it will be possible in a few decades, while others think a century or two is a more realistic guess. But whatever the time frame, it is clear that the capacity to engineer the human genome poses unprecedented challenges and unprecedented dangers for mankind. A number of writers, reflecting on the imperfect wisdom with which our species has applied other powerful technologies, have wondered whether the knowledge of how to modify our own genetic nature might not be knowledge we are better off without.

III. Moral Argument and Moral Reasoning

Our second preliminary chore, it will be recalled, is to take a look at what is involved in defending or attacking a moral view *rationally*. A good place to begin is with the distinction between *particular moral judgements* and *general moral principles*. The former heading covers claims about what should be done by a specific person or group of persons in a specific historical situation. By contrast, general moral principles make more general claims about what should be done in every case of a certain sort or by everyone in a certain sort of situation. The claim "The National Institutes of Health should now adopt more stringent guidelines on research involving recombinant DNA techniques," is an example of a particular moral judgement. Traditional moral codes, like the Ten Commandments, provide many examples of general moral principles. But not all general moral principles need be that global in their scope.

Using the distinction between particular moral judgements and general moral principles, we can isolate a feature of defensible moral views that proves central in the process of rationally supporting or attacking a moral position. The feature is this: If a particular moral judgement is defensible, it must be *supportable* by a defensible general moral principle. A general moral principle *supports* a particular moral judgement if the principle, perhaps supplemented by some true factual claims, logically entails the particular moral judgement. Stated abstractly, the idea sounds complex and difficult; but in fact the sort of support described is commonplace in the discussion of moral questions. An example far removed from genetic engineering will serve to make the point. Many states still have laws which make homosexual acts between consenting adults illegal. In arguing that these laws should be repealed (a particular moral judgement) some advocates of Gay Liberation invoke what might be called the Libertarian Principle. This general moral principle asserts that there should be no laws prohibiting actions which affect only the people voluntarily engaging in the action. The Libertarian Principle, along with the factual claim that homosexual activity affects only those engaging in it, logically entails that voluntary homosexual activity should not be illegal. If a person accepts the Libertarian Principle (and the factual claim), then he cannot reject the particular moral judgement, *on pain of contradiction*. The interrelations among general moral principle, factual claim and particular moral judgement are illustrated in Figure 2.

There is widespread agreement among philosophers (including many who agree on little else!) that a defensible particular moral judgement must be supported by a general moral principle. There is less agreement on exactly *why* particular moral judgements must be supportable in this way. Perhaps the most common view, and by

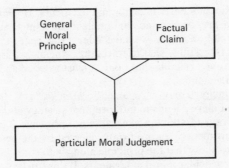

Figure 2:
Interrelations Among General Moral Principle,
Factual Claim, and Particular Moral Judgement

my lights the most plausible, is that this requirement is woven into the conceptual fabric of our moral concepts. If a person insists that he is a bachelor, then introduces us to his wife, proudly proclaiming they have been happily married for 20 years (and if he is neither joking nor insane), we would conclude that he simply did not use the words "bachelor" and "wife" the way we do. Analogously, if a person recognizes no need to support his particular moral judgement by appeal to general moral principles (and if he is neither joking nor insane) we should probably conclude that he uses moral terms like "ought," "should," "right," etc. with a meaning decidedly different from ours. He does not understand how our moral concepts are used; he is playing a different "language game."

Moral argument and moral reasoning can be complex and varied; often it is highly eliptical, leaving necessary premises implicit. However, a good deal of what goes on in rational moral argument can be interpreted in terms of the structure illustrated in Figure 2. Frequently the proponent of a particular moral judgement will defend his view by citing a general moral principle and some facts which together entail the particular moral judgement he is advocating. When this happens, the discussion may take a number of turns. If both the parties to the dispute are agreed in their support of the general moral principle, then debate will likely focus on the factual claims. Since the factual claims needed to complete the pattern of support are often difficult to evaluate, a great deal of the effort in a rational ethical discussion may be devoted to getting straight on matters of empirical fact. This is particularly true when the issue involves the hard to predict consequences of a new technology, as in the debate over nuclear energy or genetic engineering.

A moral argument may take quite a different turn if one party to the dispute rejects the general moral principle that the other uses to support his particular moral judgement. When this occurs, the debate may focus on whether the general moral principle is itself defensible. One way to defend a general moral principle that has been challenged is to appeal to a still more general principle. What we must do is find a more general principle which (perhaps together with some facts) entails the less general principle in dispute. And, of course, the more general principle must be one that our opponent accepts. Quite a different idea for supporting a general moral principle is to show that the principle, along with relevant facts, entails a significant number of particular moral judgements that our opponent accepts. In effect we are urging our opponent to accept our principle because it supports so many of his own particular moral judgements. This sort of argument is not an absolutely conclusive one, since there may be some quite different principle that does as well or better at supporting our opponent's particular moral judgements. However, if we can show our opponent that a proposed principle entails a substantial number of particular moral judgements that he accepts, we have at least succeeded in shifting the burden of argument to him. If he still wishes to reject the principle we are defending, he had best have an alternative principle that does at least as good a job in supporting his particular moral judgements.

General moral principles may, of course, be *attacked* as well as defended. Here too, the structure in Figure 2 helps to interpret that strategy of the argument. One of the most common ways to attack a general moral principle is to find one or more particular moral judgements that are firmly rejected by the person advocating the principle, and then to show that the principle along with some factual claims entails these unacceptable particular moral judgements. If this can be done, the defender of the principle is left with the choice of either abandoning it or changing his view about the particular moral judgements that the principle has been shown to support. This is the strategy invoked in the section that follows.

There is, of course, much more that might be said about the anatomy of rational moral argument. However, this brief introduction ought to give us enough background to venture a dissection of some of the arguments concerning genetic engineering. In trying to decide what constraints, if any, ought to be imposed on recombinant DNA research and technology, a central step is the search for relevant and defensible moral principles. Unfortunately, the public debate about genetic engineering has been marred by the recurrent appearance of arguments invoking patently unacceptable principles. Let us begin by taking a look at three of these principles, and seeing just why it is that the arguments invoking them fare so poorly.

IV. Three Implausible Principles

The first principle on my list might be labeled the Freedom of Inquiry Principle. It maintains that scientists ought to have full and unqualified freedom to pursue whatever inquiries they may choose. Defenders of the principle often invoke the specter of Galileo, the greatest scientist of his age, whose work was halted by the Church, to its enduring shame. The Freedom of Inquiry Principle is the central premise in an argument whose conclusion is the particular moral judgement that researchers using recombinant DNA technology ought to be free to pursue their research as they see fit. However, we need only consider a few examples to see that this blanket Freedom of Inquiry Principle is utterly indefensible. No matter how anxious a researcher may be to investigate the effects of massive doses of bomb-grade plutonium on preschool children, it is hard to imagine that anyone thinks he should be allowed to do so. No matter how sincere a researcher's interest may be in studying the dynamics of an artifically induced bubonic plague epidemic, no one thinks he should be allowed to release a cloud of plague bacteria in downtown San Francisco. Yet the Freedom of Inquiry Principle entails the moral acceptability of both of these projects and countless other Dr. Strangelove projects as well. Plainly, the simplistic Freedom of Inquiry Principle is unacceptable. But of course it would be a mistake to conclude that *no* principle protecting the freedom of scientific inquiry is defensible. A better conclusion would be that the right of free inquiry is a qualified right which must sometimes yield to conflicting rights and to the demands of conflicting moral principles. The task of formulating a suitably qualified principle of free scientific inquiry is a subtle and challenging one. Though we cannot pursue the topic further here, the reader is urged to try his or her own hand at setting out a defensible version of the principle.

The second argument I want to examine aims at establishing just the opposite conclusion from the first. The particular moral judgement being defended is that there should be a total ban on recombinant DNA research. The argument begins with the observation that even in those experiments which are likely to be the least dangerous—for example, those in which DNA obtained *from E. coli* is spliced back into *E. coli*—there is still at least a *possibility* of catastrophic consequences. The point here is not that the likelihood of catastrophe is great; it may be vanishingly small. But there can be no absolute guarantee that even an apparently safe experiment will not lead to disaster. We are, after all, dealing with a relatively new and unexplored technology. Thus it is at least possible that a bacterial culture whose genetic makeup has been altered in the course of a recombinant DNA experiment may exhibit completely unexpected pathogenic characteristics. Indeed, it is not impossible that we could find ourselves confronted with a killer strain of *E. coli*, and worse a strain against which humans can marshall no natural defense. Now if this is possible, if we cannot say with assurance that the probability of its happening is zero, then, the argument continues, all recombinant DNA research should be halted. For the negative utility of the imagined catastrophe is so enormous, resulting as it would in the destruction of our society and perhaps of our species, that no research which could possibly lead to this result would be worth the risk.

The argument just sketched, which might be called the "doomsday scenario" argument, begins with a premise that no informed person would be inclined to deny. It is indeed *possible* that even a low-risk recombinant DNA experiment might lead to totally catastrophic results. No ironclad guarantee can be offered that this will not happen. And while the probability of such an unanticipated catastrophe is surely not large, there is no serious argument that the probability is zero. Still, I think the argument is a sophistry. The moral principle needed to go from the undeniable premise that recombinant DNA research might *possibly* result in unthinkable catastrophe to the conclusion that such research should be banned is that *all* endeavours that might possibly result in such a catastrophe should be prohibited. Once the principle has been stated, it is hard to believe that anyone would take it at all seriously. For the principle entails not only that recombinant DNA research should be prohibited, but also that almost all scientific research should be prohibited, along with many other commonplace activities having little to do with science. It is, after all, at least logically possible that the next new compound synthesized in an ongoing chemical research program will turn out to be an uncontainable carcinogen many orders of magnitude more dangerous than aerosol plutonium. And, to vary the example, there is a nonzero probability that experiments in artificial pollination will produce a weed that will, a decade from now, ruin the world's food grain harvests.

I cannot resist noting that the principle invoked in the doomsday scenario argument is not new. Pascal used an entirely parallel argument to show that it is in our own best interests to believe in God. For though the probability of God's existence may be very low, if He nonetheless should exist, the disutility that would accrue to the disbeliever would be catastrophic—an eternity in Hell. But, as introductory philosophy students should all know, Pascal's argument looks persuasive only if we take our options to be just two: Christianity or atheism. A third possibility is belief in a jealous non-Christian God who will see to our damnation if and only if we *are* Christians. The probability of such a deity's existing is again very small, but nonzero. So it looks as if Pascal's argument is of no help in deciding whether or not to accept Christianity. For we may be damned if we do, and damned if we don't.

I mention Pascal's difficulty because there is a direct parallel in the doomsday scenario argument against recombinant DNA research. Just as there is a nonzero probability that unforeseen consequences of recombinant DNA research will lead to disaster, so there is a nonzero probability that unforeseen consequences of *failing* to pursue the research will lead to disaster. There may, for example, come a time when, because of natural or man-induced climactic change, the capacity to alter quickly the genetic composition of agricultural plants will be necessary to forestall catastrophic famine. And if we fail to pursue recombinant DNA research now, our lack of knowledge in the future may have consequences as dire as any foreseen in the doomsday scenario argument.

The third argument I want to consider provides a striking illustration of how important it is, in normative thinking, to make clear the moral *principles* being invoked. The argument I have in mind begins with a factual claim about recombinant DNA research, and it concludes that stringent restrictions, perhaps even a moratorium, should be imposed. However, advocates of the argument are generally silent on the normative principle(s) linking premise and conclusion. The gap thus created can be filled in a variety of ways, resulting in very different arguments.

The empirical observation that gets the argument started is that the new genetic engineering technology enables scientists to move genes back and forth across what had hitherto been natural barriers. In nature there is no way for frog genes or human genes to find their way into bacteria. Frogs mate only with other frogs of the same species, and bacteria, when they mate at all, do so only with other bacteria. By transporting genes across this natural barrier we create new sorts of organisms, bacteria which could not have been created by natural processes. Moreover, our interference with nature may well be a permanent one, since the new strains of bacteria we produce can then go on to reproduce themselves. Because recombinant DNA technology enables scientists to ignore natural barriers, it is urged that severe restrictions on the use of the technology is in order. Clearly, there is a central premise missing in this argument, viz. the moral principle. What sort of principle is being tacitly assumed?

The moral principle that comes first to mind is simply that natural barriers should not be breached, or perhaps that new sorts of organisms should not be created. The principle has an almost theological ring to it, and perhaps there are some people who would be prepared to defend it on theological grounds. But short of a theological argument, it is hard to see why anyone would hold the view that breaching natural barriers or creating new organisms is *intrinsically* wrong. For if a person were to advocate such a principle, he would have to condemn the creation of new bacterial strains capable of, say, synthesizing human clotting factor or insulin, *even if* creating the new organism generated *no unwelcome side effects*.

There is quite a different way of unpacking the "natural barriers" argument that avoids appeal to the dubious principles just mentioned. This second reading ties premise to conclusion with a second factual claim and a quite different normative premise. The added factual claim is that at present our knowledge of the consequences of creating new forms of life is severely limited, and thus we cannot know with any assurance that the probability of disastrous consequences is very low. The moral principle needed to mesh with the two factual premises would be something like the following:

> If we do not know with considerable assurance that the probability of an activity's leading to disastrous consequences is very low, then we should not allow the activity to continue.

Now this principle, unlike those marshalled in the first interpretation of the natural barriers argument, is not lightly dismissed. It is, to be sure, quite a conservative principle, and it has the odd feature of focusing entirely on the dangers an activity poses while ignoring its potential benefits. Still, the principle may have a certain attraction in light of recent history, which has increasingly been marked by catastrophes attributable to technology's unanticipated side effects.

I will not attempt a full-scale evaluation of this principle just now. For the principle raises, albeit in a rather extreme way, the question of how risks and benefits are to be weighted against each other. By my lights, that is the really crucial moral question raised by the new genetic engineering technology, and by new technologies in other areas as well. It is a question that bristles with problems. In the section that follows I will take a look at some of these problems and take a few tentative steps toward some solutions. While picking our way through the problems we will have another opportunity to examine the principle just cited.

V. Weighing the Risks and Benefits

A. THE MECHANICS OF RISK-BENEFIT ANALYSIS

At first glance it might be thought that the assessment of risks and benefits is quite straightforward, at least in principle. What we want to know is whether the potential benefits that may be produced by one or another application of recombinant DNA technology justify the risks involved. To find out, it might be thought, we need only determine the magnitude of the risks and benefits. This may require that we determine a substantial number of empirical facts; and that, in turn, may involve considerable ingenuity, effort and expense. But, this line of thought continues, while the assessment of risks and benefits may pose scientific or technological problems, it does not confront us with any normative or conceptual problems. Once the facts are in, we shall know whether the potential benefits justify the risk. There is plenty of work for the scientist or the technician to do in risk assessment but none for the philosopher or the moral theorist. Unfortunately, this view will not survive much more than a first glance. A closer look at the task of balancing risks and benefits reveals a quagmire of sticky conceptual problems and painful moral dilemmas. In this section I will catalogue and comment on some of these difficulties. I wish I could also promise to solve them all, but that would be blatant false advertising. It will prove useful to begin with a simplified step by step sketch of what is involved in a full dress "risk-benefit analysis." We can then pinpoint the step at which each of the problems we discuss arises.

Step 1: Enumerating alternative policies. The aim of a risk-benefit analysis is to evaluate *policies* or courses of action. The strategy is to assign a *number* to each policy being considered, which will reflect its relative desirability vis-a-vis all the other policies being considered. So to begin a risk-benefit analysis we must set down a list of policies that we are considering. In the case of research employing recombinant DNA technology, one of the policies that must be evaluated is what might be called the "laissez-faire policy" which would impose on recombinant DNA research *no* restrictions over and above those normally imposed on all research activities. Another on our list of potential recombinant DNA policies would be a complete ban on all experiments using recombinant DNA techniques. Between these two polls there will also be a range of more moderate policies that we want to consider and evaluate. Let us call the laissez-faire policy 'POLICY$_1$', the complete ban 'POLICY$_n$', and the various intermediate possibilities that we are considering 'POLICY$_2$', 'POLICY$_3$' . . . 'POLICY$_{n-1}$'.

Step 2: Partial outcomes and total outcomes. The next step in the analysis is to determine a set of outcomes that might result from the adoption of one or another of the policies on the list. Some of these outcomes will be desirable, while others will not. Thus, in the recombinant DNA example, our list of outcomes would have to include such contingencies as causing a cancer epidemic, spreading a strain of pathogenic bacteria which is resistant to antibiotic therapy, spreading bacteria which produce unneeded insulin in the human intestine, etc. The list would also have to include such possible outcomes as speeding up by a decade the discovery of the cause and cure for cancer, engineering bacteria capable of inexpensively synthesizing medically useful substances such as clotting factor and interferon, and developing strains of wheat and rice capable of making their own fertilizer. Actually, from the standpoint of risk-benefit analysis the possible outcomes I have been enumerating might best be called *partial outcomes*. The point of the label is to stress the fact that a given policy may produce several different partial outcomes. Adopting the laissez-faire policy, for example, might conceivably bring about *all* of the partial outcomes on our list. *Each possible combination of partial outcomes* will constitute what we shall call a *total outcome*. So if we have located n possible partial outcomes, there will in general be 2^n possible total outcomes. As an illustration, suppose we restrict our attention to four possible partial outcomes of recombinant DNA policies:

1) cancer epidemic
2) spreading an antibiotic resistant pathogen
3) speeding the cure for cancer by 10 years
4) creation of a strain of nitrogen fixing rice

The 16 $(=2^4)$ total outcomes that need be considered are then given by Figure 3.

Step 3: Assigning values to total outcomes. Once we have an enumeration of total outcomes, our next task is to assess the value or moral desirability of each of these total outcomes. Sometimes it will be possible to estimate the value of a total outcome by estimating the value of each partial outcome in isolation and simply adding up the appropriate partial outcome values. But often this strategy will not work. The negative value assigned to causing a cancer epidemic, for example, will surely be of a somewhat smaller magnitude if a cure for cancer is also at hand. If $TO_1, TO_2, \ldots, TO_k$ is our list of total outcomes, then we can denote the numerical measure of the moral desirability of each as $\text{Val}(TO_1), \text{Val}(TO_2), \ldots, \text{Val}(TO_k)$. (Read simply as "value of total outcome one," "value of total outcome 2," etc.)

Step 4: Determining probabilities. If we knew with certainty which total outcome would be produced by any given policy, our job of policy evaluation would be considerably simplified. Having assigned a value to each total outcome, we could then just select the policy which leads to the most highly valued outcome. Unfortunately, however, we almost never know what the total outcome of selecting a given policy will be. But neither are we totally ignorant about which policies will lead to which outcomes. We often know that a given outcome is *probable* if we adopt a given policy, while another outcome is considerably less probable, on that policy. Risk-benefit analysis attempts to exploit this probabilistic information in making our policy decisions. The basic idea is very simple. If we know that a given policy, say Policy$_2$, has a 90% chance of leading to a total outcome valued at $+100$ and a 10% chance of leading to a total outcome valued at $+20$, then if we adopt this policy we have a .9 chance of getting $+100$ on our value scale, and a .1 chance of getting only $+20$. Our "expected utility" for Policy$_2$ may then be set at $(.9 \times 100) + (.1 \times 20) = 90 + 2 = 92$. If another policy, say Policy$_3$, has a 50% chance of leading to $+10$, its "expected utility" would be $(.5 \times 100) + (.5 \times 10) = 55$. The expected utility numbers reflect the intuitive fact that we would prefer Policy$_2$ to Policy$_3$.

In order to apply this idea systematically, of course, we must determine for *each* policy on our list how likely it is to lead to *each* total outcome. Let us abbreviate 'the probability that Total Outcome$_i$ will result if we adopt Policy$_j$' as 'Pr(TO$_i$/POLICY$_j$)'.

Partial Outcomes

Total Outcomes

Partial Outcomes	TO_1	TO_2	TO_3	TO_4	TO_5	TO_6	TO_7	TO_8	TO_9	TO_{10}	TO_{11}	TO_{12}	TO_{13}	TO_{14}	TO_{15}	TO_{16}
cancer epidemic	yes	yes	yes	yes	yes	yes	yes	yes	no	no	no	no	no	no	no	no
antibiotic resistant pathogen	yes	yes	yes	yes	no	no	no	no	yes	yes	yes	yes	no	no	no	no
cancer cure	yes	yes	no	no	yes	yes	no	no	yes	yes	no	no	yes	yes	no	no
nitrogen fixing rice	yes	no	yes	no	yes	no	yes	no	yes	no	yes	no	yes	no	yes	no

Figure 3:
Constructing Total Outcomes From Partial Outcomes

Step 5: Calculating expected utilities. Once we have determined the required probabilities and assessed the values of each total outcome, we can proceed to calculate the *expected utility* of each policy. The expected utility of Policy$_1$, for example, is determined by multiplying the probability that Policy$_1$ will lead to Total Outcome$_1$ by the value of Total Outcome$_1$, then multiplying the probability that Policy$_1$ will lead to Total Outcome$_2$ by the value of that outcome, etc., and finally adding the numbers obtained. Using the notation we have adopted, the expected utility of Policy$_1$ in our simplified recombinant DNA example would be:

$$Pr(TO_1/Policy_1) \times Val(TO_1)$$
$$+$$
$$Pr(TO_2/Policy_1) \times (Val(TO_2)$$
$$+$$
$$Pr(TO_3/Policy_1) \times Val(TO_3)$$
$$+$$
$$\ldots$$
$$+$$
$$Pr(TO_{16}/Policy_1) \times Val(TO_{16}).$$

Step 6: Selecting a policy. The final step in a risk-benefit analysis is to actually select a policy from among those being evaluated. It might appear that this is the easiest step—so easy that it hardly counts as a step at all. For once we have succeeded in computing the expected utility of each policy under consideration we can simply scan the list and select the policy with the highest expected utility. But, as we shall soon see, even this apparently obvious step raises deep difficulties.

B. SOME PROBLEMS WITH USING RISK-BENEFIT ANALYSIS IN DETERMINING POLICY ON SCIENCE AND TECHNOLOGY

1. Problems with probabilities. It is obvious that determining the probabilities required in Step 4 of a risk-benefit analysis would be an arduous business. By carefully collecting data and using familiar experimental techniques some of the required probabilities can no doubt be assessed with considerable accuracy. Suppose, for example, that we are concerned about experiments proposing to splice SV40 DNA into *E. coli*. One policy that might be proposed is to allow such experiments only when a specially weakened (or "enfeebled") strain of *E. coli* is used, a strain which has great difficulty surviving outside of the controlled laboratory environment. (The tactic of using enfeebled bacterial hosts is called *biological containment*.) In evaluating this policy we shall want to know how likely it is that enfeebled *E. coli* cells might escape from the laboratory after being accidentally swallowed by a laboratory worker. To make its escape in this way the microbe would have to survive passage through the digestive system. And carefully controlled experiments with volunteer human subjects can tell us with some accuracy what the probability of survival is. But there are other outcomes whose probabilities cannot be easily assessed by experiment. Let me sketch a few examples. Suppose a new disease causing organism is accidentally produced in the course of an experiment using recombinant DNA technology, and suppose that this new pathogen somehow escapes from the laboratory. The situation is a potentially nasty one. But just how nasty will depend on whether the organism competes successfully and finds a niche for itself in nature. If it does not, then at worst it may infect a handful of people before dying out. On the other hand, if it does compete successfully in nature, we will have an epidemic to deal with, not simply an outbreak. But it is hard to think of an experiment which would tell us the probability that a newly synthesized pathogen will compete successfully in nature, and even harder to think of one we would seriously think of doing.

There are other cases in which the probabilities that are required for a risk-benefit analysis appear to be simply impossible to estimate by an experimental means. We would like to know just how likely it is that recombinant DNA research will lead to the development of corn or rice strains that will make their own nitrogen fertilizer. And we would like to know the probability that recombinant DNA research will lead to cures for various types of cancer. Yet no experiment we can perform nor any data we can gather will enable us to *empirically* estimate these probabilities. Nor are these the most problematic probabilities we may want to know. A possibility that weighs heavily on the minds of many is that recombinant DNA research may lead to negative consequences for human health or for the environment *that have not yet even been thought of*. The recent history of DDT and flourocarbon propellants surely demonstrates that this is not a foolish concern. Yet here again there would appear to be no data we can gather that would help much in estimating the probability of such potential outcomes.

It is important to see that the problems noted in the previous paragraph do not merely indicate that a risk-benefit analysis requires knowledge of probabilities that we do not now have. Rather, what is troublesome in all of these cases is that there seems to be *no objective experimental way* of determining the probabilities we need in order to assess the risks and benefits. The apparent impossibility of experimentally determining the required probabilities has led some writers to conclude that risk-benefit analysis is simply not applicable to genetic engineering and other new technologies. However, for two very different reasons, I am inclined to think that this quick dismissal of risk-benefit analysis is a mistake.

First, it is often possible to sidestep the problem that some of the needed probabilities are unknown. An example will serve to illustrate the point. Suppose we are concerned about the chance that a new bacterial strain created in a recombinant DNA experiment will cause a serious epidemic. For this to happen, the following four events must occur:

1) a new pathogen must be created
2) it must escape the laboratory
3) it must be able to live outside the laboratory
4) it must compete successfully with other microorganism (themselves the product of intense natural selections)

Now, the probability of a sequence of independent events all occurring is the product of the probabilities of the individual events. (E.g., the probability of flipping three heads in a row is $1/2 - 1/2 - 1/2 = 1/8$.) So the probability of all four events on our list occurring is the product of the probabilities of each individual event. And there are at least two items on our list, events 2 and 3, whose probabilities *can* be assessed empirically. The product of these two probabilities places an upper bound on the probability of an epidemic. For the remaining two, we can use the *highest* (and thus most pessimistic) guess of any responsible authority. This will enable us to make a "worst case" estimate of the probability of an epidemic. If, when using this worst case estimate, our risk-benefit assessment yields the result that benefits outweigh risks, then lower (i.e., less pessimistic) estimates of the same probabilities will yield the same conclusion. We thus will have sidestepped the awkward fact that some of the required probabilities are not known.

My second reason for resisting the quick dismissal of risk-benefit analysis is one which raises much deeper issues. The problem, recall, is that risk-benefit analysis often requires probabilities which cannot be experimentally determined. But it is far from clear that experimentally determined probabilities are the only ones that ought to be used in a risk-benefit analysis. We can and do often make *subjective probability* estimates concerning all sorts of contingencies, even though an experimental test of these estimates is, for one reason or another, quite out of the question. So why should we not use subjective probability estimates in our risk-benefit analysis?

One answer that has surfaced from time to time in the recombinant DNA debate is that subjective probabilities are guesses, pure and simple, and guesses have no proper place in a serious moral deliberation. This view, which I will call *generalized skepticism* about subjective probabilities, may be construed as making a pair of claims:

1) Subjective probability estimates are mere conjectures, "manufactured numbers" which have no rational foundation.
2) Because subjective probability estimates are without rational foundation it would be morally irresponsible to rely on them in deciding how to act.

On my view, both tenets of this generalized skepticism are mistaken.

To undermine the skeptic's first claim, it may suffice to point out how large a part of scientific thinking rests on subjective probability estimates. Consider an example. A palentologist uncovers the fossilized remains of an animal and, after studying them, draws conclusions about the likely appearance, diet and habitat of the species to which the animal belonged. Some of these may well be couched in explicitly probabilistic terms; our palentologist may conclude the probability that the animal was omnivorous is about .9. The inference underlying the palentologist's conclusion rests on a wealth of background knowledge which he himself may be able to articulate only partially. It bears little prima facie similarity to an inference about the efficacy of a new vaccine, based on controlled experimental trials. This latter sort of inference is the skeptic's paradigm of an "objectively determined" probability. Nonetheless, it would be simply perverse to suggest that the palentologist's subjective probability is without rational foundation. Inferences like the one in question are prototypical examples of rational inferences, and any explication of the notion of rational inference or rational conclusion must classify the bulk of such prototypical examples as rational.

A similar argument can be used to dispatch the skeptic's claim that it is morally objectionable to use subjective probability estimates in deciding how we shall act. Consider the example of a radiologist examining the X-rays of an accident victim. After studying them carefully he concludes that there is probably some foreign object lodged dangerously close to the patient's heart. If he is right, the emergency surgery is called for. But the radiologist says he cannot be sure. His subjective probability that the shadow on the X-rays is caused by a foreign object is only about .8. As in the previous case, the radiologist's probability assessment is not in any obvious sense experimentally determined. Indeed, we know relatively little about the mechanisms underlying complex clinical assessments of this sort. On the skeptic's view it would be morally unacceptable to use this subjective probability in deciding how to act. So a surgeon who relies on the radiologist's opinion when he decides to operate would be acting wrongly. Once the consequences of the skeptic's view have been drawn out in this way, however, it is hard to take his position seriously. Surely we all believe that the surgeon has a positive obligation to take account of the radiologist's opinion in deciding how to act, and *failing* to do so would be a prime example of morally irresponsible behavior.

My argument so far has been directed against the critic who urges a *generalized skepticism* about the rationality of subjective probability estimates. But having dispatched that windmill, a more formidable problem looms. I have argued that *some* subjective probability estimates are paradigmatically rational, and their use in moral deliberations is sometimes morally obligatory. But it is plain that not all subjective probability estimates are rational. People sometimes have foolish subjective probabilities just as they sometimes have foolish beliefs. This fact, lamentable as it is obvious, poses serious problems for risk-benefit analyses on public policy questions. For the policy making body must decide *whose* subjective probabilities to utilize in its computation of risks and benefits.

At first blush it might seem that there is a simple and obvious answer to this question. The subjective probabilities that should be used are those of the *experts*, the people who are best informed and most knowledgeable about the contingency whose probability is being sought. It is my view that this answer is, in spirit at least, the right one. However, it takes only a bit of reflection to see that the prescription to rely on expert opinion is neither simple nor obvious. It gives rise to a pair of questions which are vexing for both the policy maker and the philosopher:

> Who *are* the experts on a given question?

and

> Why *should* we accept their opinion?

There is a clear sense in which the second question presupposes an answer to the first. For the second question asks for a justification of a certain policy, *viz.*, the policy of utilizing the subjective probability of experts in social risk-benefit analyses, and until the first question has been answered, we have not really said just what that policy amounts to. So let us begin by asking what the hallmarks are of an "expert opinion" worthy of being incorporated into a decision about public policy.

I will start with a bit of history. In 1975, when the controversy over recombinant DNA research first began to attract a wide audience, the scientific community was profoundly divided over the probabilities of various gloomy scenarios that had been conjured. Some biologists thought the probability of these contingencies was infinitesimally small, and that concern about them was quixotic. Others thought the probabilities were high enough to merit serious concern and action. Nobel Laureate James Watson, for one, thought the risks so serious that he threatened to seek a court injunction to prevent workers in his labs from doing certain kinds of experiments. Today, however, there is widespread agreement in the scientific community that the earlier fears of some were unwarranted. This consensus is by no means unanimous, of course. Still, many scientists who were initially quite worried about recombinant DNA research have significantly lowered their subjective probabilities of various untoward contingencies. And their new lower probability estimates are shared by many who were not involved with the question earlier on. Watson, ever outspoken, now considers his earlier assessment "the biggest damn fool mistake I ever made." Fully as interesting as the changes that have taken place since 1975 are the events that led to them. Contrary to what might be expected, relatively little *new* data relevant to the safety issue has been accumulated. Rather, what has happened, for the most part, is that experts have discussed and debated the issue with each other and with experts in related disciplines. In this discussion the participants were reminded of (or informed about) bits and pieces of previously established knowledge from various disciplines which were relevant to assessing the probabilities of various scenarios. Stimulated by the public controversy, the scientific community set about assembling knowledge that bore on the issue at hand. The facts and theoretical arguments which were brought to the fore led many to lower their subjective probabilities.

I am inclined to think that the consensus reached in the community of biologists about the likelihood of various frightening recombinant DNA scenarios provides a paradigmatic example of the sort of expert subjective probabilities that *should* be utilized in risk-benefit analyses. If this is right, then we can use the case as a model in attempting to specify when expert subjective probabilities should be used. So let me list the features of this case that I take to be important.

i. Social sanction of expertise. Who are the experts? The answer, of course, is that different people are experts on different questions. On questions of physical containment of micro-organisms, the experts are biological safety officers and people experienced in handling pathogens in containment laboratories. In assessing the probability that recombinant DNA techniques will speed up our discovery of the causes and cures of cancers, the experts are the leading cancer researchers at the major universities and research institutes or that subset of them who are familiar with the potential of recombinant DNA methodology. On other questions, still other groups count as experts. Buy why these people? Why not the members of the Society of Automotive Engineers, the mayors of moderate sized cities, or the people who failed out of university molecular biology programs during the last decade? The answer, I think, is that the experts on a given question are the people who make a *socially sanctioned* claim to expertise on that question. This answer is a vague one, of course, since I have not said what this notion of *social sanction* comes to. Though in most cases it will be intuitively clear whose claims to expertise are socially sanctioned and whose are not. Thus, if the question concerns the probability that the pylons on a DC-10 will fail, the socially sanctioned experts are the safety officials of the FAA, not the passengers who offer their views to television interviewers on the evening news. And if the question is the likelihood that laetrile will aid a cancer patient, the socially sanctioned experts are professors of oncology at the leading medical schools, not the people who run laetrile clinics, or health food stores. The socially sanctioned experts on a given issue cannot, in general, be determined simply by polling the members of the society. The names of experts on various questions are generally unknown to the public, nor would most people have much of an idea about the governmental agency, research establishment, academic department, etc., with which appropriate experts will be affiliated. To determine who the socially sanctioned experts are, we would have to work our way up a hierarchy of socially recognized cognitive authority. So, for example, few people could name the experts on arthritis, or say where they could be found. But if asked how to find out who the experts are, most people would suggest that we ask their family doctor, the head of the local clinic, or perhaps the neighborhood pharmacist. These people, in turn, will not be likely to know who the experts on arthritis are, but they will suggest that we ask a professor at the nearby medical school. These professors will refer us to their colleagues in the appropriate departments. And their colleagues will likely know the names or institutional affiliations of people knowledgeable in the field. But even at this level we have not determined who the socially sanctioned experts are. To do that, we should have to poll the knowledgeable people about whom *they* consider to be experts. We can summarize the process briefly, if a bit paradoxically, by saying that the experts are the people whom the experts take to be experts.

To allay possible misunderstanding, let me stress that I am *not* claiming that a subjective probability ought to be used in a social risk-benefit analysis merely because it reflects the consensus of the socially sanctioned experts. Several additional conditions must be met as well.

ii. Political freedom and the expert selection process. Our understanding of how and why a given group of people come to acquire social sanction for their claims to expertise is very limited indeed. There is, however, a salient feature of the process in the recombinant DNA case that deserves comment. Whatever the social mechanisms may be by which leading professors of microbiology became regognized as experts, they did *not* involve explicit politically imposed requirements. No group outside the expert community decreed that certain views were unacceptable and others mandatory. The social dynamics by which people became recognized as experts evolved freely without externally imposed political constraints. The situation stands in stark contrast to other cases of socially sanctioned expertise. During the Lysenko period in the Soviet Union, for example, only those who cleaved to the externally imposed party line could hope to gain recognition as an expert in genetics. We should be under no illusions about the difficulties involved in deciding whether (or to what extent) a process leading to social recognition as an expert has evolved freely without external political interference. But these difficulties should not blind us to a distinction which is real and important.

iii. Absence of self-interest among the experts. A certain number of the scientists who have participated in the recombinant DNA debate had a deep personal stake in its outcome. Some of these people had plans to do experiments involving recombinant DNA methods and had invested much time and effort in planning the experiments, writing grant proposals, etc. Others had a substantial financial stake in companies established to commercially exploit recombinant DNA technology. If the technology were to be judged too risky, these people would be negatively effected in a clear and specifiable way. However, one of the striking facts about the recombinant DNA case is that many experts involved, on both sides of the debate, had no large personal stake in the outcome. They were people whose own research did not involve recombinant DNA techniques, and would not do so in the foreseeable future. Nor did they have any financial stake in the outcome of the debate. Some of these people were involved in the debate from early on, and in a number of cases their subjective probabilities about untoward contingencies have significantly declined. (I know of no major figure in the controversy whose assessment of the risks grew gloomier as the debate went on.) Of course, self-interest comes in degrees and, like political freedom, it is sometimes hard to assess. Still, in many cases it can be (and was) abundantly clear that the experts offering their views had little personally to gain or lose.

iv. Consensus after an ample dialogue. There are some questions on which most of the socially sanctioned experts share the same view without any sustained discussion, and there are some questions on which the experts fail to approach a rough consensus even after an ample dialogue. But neither of these was the case in the recombinant DNA controversy. There, a rough consensus was reached after a very visible debate in which experts from many different disciplines participated.

Now the thesis I want to urge is this: *If the socially sanctioned experts have reached a rough consensus about the probability of a given contingency, if that rough consensus obtains after an ample dialogue involving experts from a variety of disciplines, if the process of expert selection is relatively free of external political control, and if the community of experts includes a significant number of people who are free of conspicuous self interest, then the probability in question ought to be used in social risk-benefit analyses.* Note that I claim to be offering only a sufficient condition for the acceptability of a subjective probability assessment, and not a necessary condition. If the complex condition is met, then I would claim that a subjective probability assessment is sure to be an acceptable one. However, I do not claim that *all* acceptable subjective probability assessments must satisfy this condition. I suspect there are other subjective probabilities that also ought to be used in risk-benefit analyses, though I am not at all clear just which ones they are. There is a sense in which the view I am advocating is quite a weak one, since the complex condition I have specified applies to relatively few cases, and I say nothing about the cases to which it does not apply. Indeed, I once thought my thesis was so weak that it would be utterly uncontroversial. But in this I was clearly wrong. For despite all the hedging, my view is clearly an "elistist" view at odds with the populism currently fashionable in some circles. When the conditions specified have been met, I claim that we ought to accept the consensus of the experts about probabilities, and if the "man in the street" has any views of the issue, we should ignore them. Plainly this is a view which requires some defense. So let us now ask why we should, under the conditions specified, accept the subjective probabilities of the experts.

I suppose the nicest defense of the policy of accepting expert opinion would be one which showed that when the conditions I have specified have been fulfilled the experts generally have gotten the right answer. If we could establish this, or even the weaker claim that the experts have been right more often, on the average, than any other identifiable group, then we might try the following argument: Since the experts have been right more often than anyone else in the past, this is reason to think they will continue to be right more often than anyone else in the future. Unfortunately, however, I am unable to make any serious case for the basic premise of this argument. If there are data showing that expert subjective probabilities have been more accurate than those of other groups, I certainly do not know of them. I confess to being rather skeptical that *anyone* has such data. Indeed, on second thought, it is not at all clear that such data would do much to justify our reliance on expert opinion, or that data to the contrary would in the least undermine this reliance. For consider the following imaginary experiment. Suppose we set out to test the hypothesis that experts have been right more often than any other group. We randomly select a large number of issues where we are very confident that the right answer is now known. We then randomly select historical periods to pair with each issue, taking care that there were socially sanctioned experts on the issue in the historical period with which it is paired. We then set a team of historians to work comparing the track records of the experts with those of other identifiable groups. I think we all suspect that the experts would win hands down. But suppose that, much to our surprise, they did not. Suppose that our team of historians turned up a sect of mystics in Jerusalem which, for the last two millenia, has been taking heterodox stands on all sorts of empirical issues of the day. And while both the mystics and the experts have made their share of mistakes, the track record of the mystics is distinctly better. Would evidence like this be a good reason for no longer accepting expert opinion, or for relying on the mystics instead? I think the answer to both questions is clearly no. If this is right, then our justification for relying on experts has little to do with their past success. But if we cannot justify relying on expert opinion by citing their previous successes, why should we bet on the experts?

I am inclined to think that this question is a close cousin of a very venerable philosophical problem, the problem of induction. In its most general form, the problem of induction asks what reason or justification we have for placing our trust in patterns of inference which are not sanctioned by deductive logic. Much of the work that has been done on the problem of induction focuses on inferences from particular cases to generalizations. So, for example, it might be asked what justification we have in inferring from the fact that all pieces of copper hitherto examined have conducted electricity to the conclusion that *all* pieces of copper conduct electricity. Or we might inquire about the justification of the more modest inference from

All pieces of copper hitherto examined have conducted electricity

to the conclusion

The next piece of copper we examine will conduct electricity.

Now in both of these cases, the beginnings of the right answer are easy enough. We accept these inferences because they exhibit a pattern of reasoning which, after suitable reflection, we are inclined to endorse as rational. It remains to explain what justification we have for relying on rules or inferential principles which strike us as rational.

When the problem of induction is cast in this way, our problem about expert subjective probability is not merely a relative of the problem of induction, it is a special case of it. For one of the principles of non-deductive inference that I believe many of us are inclined to endorse as rational after suitable reflection is the principle of accepting expert subjective probabilities when the additional conditions I have specified are met. If I am right, then it should not be at all surprising that the past success of experts does not justify our reliance on them, for notoriously, past success is of no use in justifying more familiar inductive principles. For example, as Hume pointed out long ago, the past success of the principle:

Infer that future cases will be like past cases

gives us no justification for relying on the principle in the future, unless we presuppose the very principle we are trying to justify. The imagined historical "experiment" cited earlier also has an illuminating parallel in the case of more standard inductive rules. Suppose we set out to test the historical track record of the canons of induction we take to be rational, and discovered that, while their record was pretty good, there is a quite different set of inferential rules which would have done even better. Would such a discovery count as a good reason to abandon our standard inductive rules? The answer had better be no, since in this case we know a priori that, since the standard rules do not always get the right answer, there is bound to be an alternative set (perhaps quite ad hoc) with a better track record.

Here the argument over accepting expert subjective probability can take one of two paths, both of them short. First, an opponent may simply deny that after suitable reflection *he* is inclined to accept this principle as rational. For such an opponent I would have no persuasive reply. He is, I suggest, analogous to the person who uses terms like Goodman's celebrated 'grue' to describe the world and make predictions about it. An object is *grue* if it has been examined prior to now and found to be green, or if it has not been examined and is blue. Presumably all emeralds hitherto examined have been green, and this is the reason we believe the next one will be. But all emeralds hitherto examined have also been grue, and the person we are imagining infers from this evidence that the next emerald will be grue as well. Prior to unearthing the next emerald, there is no rational way of changing his mind. Of course, we are all inclined to think that a person who consistently invoked terms like 'grue' in his inductions would not be a good risk for a life insurance policy. I think much the same is true for the person or the society which rejects expert authority in favor of some more democratic way of determining probabilities.

The second path for the argument to take is for the critic to agree that accepting expert subjective probabilities (under the conditions specified) is rational, then go on to demand some reason why we should do it. His analog in the case of more familiar inductive principles is the person who concedes that a given inductive canon is rational, then demands some further reason why we should use it. The only response, I think, is the Wittgensteinian observation that justifications have come to an end.

Before leaving the topic of subjective probability and expertise, let me forestall a possible misunderstanding. The view I have been urging is that, under certain conditions we ought to accept the consensus of experts about probabilities. *But this is not to say that we should accept the consensus of experts on whether a risk is worth taking or even on whether the expected utility of a given policy is greater than the expected utility of another policy.* For to answer *these* questions we must know *more* than the probabilities that various policies will lead to various outcomes. We must *also* know how these outcomes are to be *valued*. And on that question the views of people who are experts in one field or another carry no special weight.

2. Problems in assigning values to outcomes: the value of life. In the outline of risk-benefit analysis presented earlier, the question of how outcomes are to be valued arises in Step 3. It will surely come as no surprise that this step bristles with difficulties. In the present essay I want to focus on just one of these, though a central one. Once again, the problem can be illustrated in the context of the recombinant DNA dispute. Some of the desirable partial outcomes that may result from a policy of encouraging recombinant DNA research would involve a very substantial economic gain for certain individuals and corporations. So, for example, one of the proposed applications of recombinant DNA techniques is the construction of a bacterial strain that would selectively absorb and retain valuable metals like platinum which are left in very low concentrations in certain industrial waste products. If such a bug could be constructed, it would be economically feasible to recover this platinum. However, the research leading to this pleasing outcome is not totally free of risk. There is some chance of inadvertently creating and releasing into the environment bacteria which will do substantial ecological damage, or even cause illness and death to humans. Now in deciding how we shall rank our outcomes, the total outcome including the platinum concentrating bacteria and, say, a dozen deaths caused by the research, will surely be ranked lower than the total outcome with the platinum eating bug and no deaths. But how much lower? Without an answer, our risk-benefit analysis simply cannot be run. But to give an answer is, in effect, to assign a monetary value to human lives. And what could that value possibly be?

Some writers have urged that since risk-benefit analyses on policies involving life and death generally require that we assign some economic value to human lives, it is morally repugnant to use risk-benefit analyses in making these policy decisions. On their view, the value of a human life simply cannot be reckoned in economic terms, and the attempt to do so reflects a callous disregard for the fundamental principle of the sacredness of human life. However, I think that a bit of reflection will convince us that this generalized refusal to assign an economic value to human lives is not a tenable moral stand. It forces us either to make absurd moral decisions, or to assume the posture of a moral ostrich and refuse to consider difficult moral questions at all. To see this, consider the example of automobile safety requirements. It would be easy enough to build vehicles which could withstand head-on crashes at their maximum speed without causing serious injury to their passengers. I would guess that most military tanks are examples of such vehicles. It is beyond dispute that if we required all the vehicles on our public roads to be built like tanks, thousands of lives would be saved each year. Yet no one seriously urges that we should require passenger cars to be built like tanks. The reason is obvious enough: to do so would be prohibitively expensive. We are simply not willing to spend *that* much money to save those lives. Now for those critics who find it morally unacceptable to assign any economic value to lives there appear to be only two choices. They can advocate building cars like tanks no matter what the cost, in effect assigning lives an infinite value, or they can wring their hands and refuse to say when a proposed safety regulation would cost too much. Neither alternative has much appeal.

I have been arguing that it is not morally objectionable to ask how human lives are to be weighed against economic considerations. But even if this point is granted, we have made no progress with our original question: How much is human life worth? How are we to find out?

Lest I raise false expectations, let me say now that I have no numerical answer to offer. I will not even *try* to say what a life is worth in dollars or Swiss Francs or ounces of gold. What I shall offer are a few reflections on why the question *seems* so hopelessly difficult, and how to make it easier. In brief, what I will urge is that the value of life question appears intractable because it is the conflation of many morally different questions. There is no single economic value to be assigned to a human life, but many different economic values depending on the details of the case in which the question arises. On first hearing, many people are inclined to accept a naive principle of equality which holds that when life and death are at stake, all people are to be counted equally under all circumstances. Thus if dollars must be balanced against lives, all lives must be valued the same. It is my view that this unsubtle egalitarianism will not endure scrutiny. There are many differences among persons and circumstances which *morally* justify valuing lives differently. To make the case let me list three of the differences that I think are most compelling.

(1) The quality and quantity of life saved. Suppose we are policy makers considering a pair of additions to our national health service. The first program is aimed at improving prenatal care, and the consensus of the experts is that the program will save the lives of a thousand infants a year, infants who without the program would die in early childhood. The second program proposes to treat a disease of the aged, and expert opinion holds that the program will save the lives of a thousand pensioners a year who would otherwise succumb. How much would we be willing to spend on each of these programs? The naive egalitarian holds that the answer must be the same in both cases. But most of us, I suspect, are inclined to think that the prenatal program merits a significantly greater expenditure. Analogously, a program which *cures* people of an otherwise fatal disease merits a much greater expenditure than one which keeps them alive but leaves them incapacitated by intense and enduring pain. In each of these cases, it is easy enough to say what the morally relevant difference is between the hypothetical health care programs. In the first it is the *quantity* of life that has been saved, measured in days or years, and in the second it is the *quality* of the life that has been preserved. It is, I would urge, morally defensible to take account of both factors in weighing the economic value of a life, and under some circumstances it is morally indefensible to ignore them.

(2) Known victims vs unknown victims. It is often noted with considerable irony that our society is willing to spend much more money to save the life of a person whose identity is known than to save the life of a person whose identity is unknown. Thus, for example, we consider it appropriate to spend millions of dollars to rescue a handful of coal miners trapped after a mine explosion, but we are reluctant to spend an equal amount of money on mine safety, even though expert opinion assures us that such an expenditure would, over the course of a decade, save substantially more lives than are saved by our rescue operation. For a naive egalitarian, such decisions are morally unacceptable; we should not value one coal miner higher than another simply because we know his name. On my view, however, there are morally significant differences between these cases, differences which may well justify spending more on the known victim than on the unknown.

It is a psychological fact of considerable importance that a decision which harms or helps a specific person whose identity is known to us is often substantially more traumatic or gratifying than a decision which will harm or help unknown persons. Thus it is no accident that the charities which help children in underdeveloped countries often pair off a donor with a needy child, arranging for the child to correspond with the donor and send him a picture. The personal relationship thus established provides strong motivation for the donor to continue his contributions. Donors find it a much more enriching experience when they know who is being helped by their contribution and how. On the other side of the coin, it can be a psychologically devastating experience to make a decision which condemns another person to death when we know the identity of the person. And this anguish must be taken account of in reckoning the moral costs of deciding that a life shall not be saved. When the decision is a public one the anguish may be multiplied many times over, since many of those in whose name the decision has been made will feel a sense of responsibility for the act, and will share some of the decision maker's trauma.

It is not only those who feel responsible for a life or death decision who react differently when the identity of the victim is known. The victim's friends and relatives react differently as well. In mine disasters, for example, it would not be unusual for the family of a man who was killed in an explosion to feel considerable hostility toward the mine operators and safety inspectors. However, we would anticipate much more intense and potentially explosive hostility if trapped miners were allowed to die because a rescue operation would be too costly.

Now the defender of the naive egalitarian principle may urge that the psychological differences we have noted are in some way irrational, and that people ought not to react as they do. (Actually, I am very skeptical indeed that any case can be made for this view.) But even if the egalitarian is right, the fact remains that people do react differently when the identity of the victim is known to the decision makers, and there is little hope of persuading them to react otherwise. Thus in our moral deliberations, the death of a victim whose identity was known in advance ought to be counted as a greater calamity than the death of a victim whose identity was not known (other things being equal), because the former death brings with it a greater burden of anguish to the decision makers and hostility to the bereaved.

(3) Voluntary risks and involuntary risks. People often choose to engage in a risky activity knowing full well that the choice may lead to their own death. Hazardous sports like mountain climbing and parachute jumping are good examples of such activities. However, not all of the risks we are subjected to are undertaken voluntarily. In many parts of the world the very act of breathing the air carries with it the risk of contracting cancer, emphysema and a variety of other diseases. Those who would avoid the risks of mountain climbing can simply stay on level ground. But there is no comparably simple way to avoid the risks of breathing.

Now suppose that a pair of public policies have been proposed, one to make mountain climbing safer, the other to make breathing safer by reducing pollution. Suppose further that the relevant experts agree that each policy can be expected to save about the same number of lives each year. How much would we be willing to spend on implementing each policy? The naive egalitarian holds that whatever the sum, it must be equal in each case. But most people are inclined to think that the pollution control project merits a significantly greater expenditure. More generally, I think we are inclined to discount the cost of a death to the extent that the person freely and knowingly undertook to endure the risk which led to his death. This principle raises some intriguing questions about how the degree of freedom of a decision is to be assessed. Are employment related risks, for example, undertaken freely? Intuitively I am inclined to say that the Hollywood stunt man's decision to accept the risks of his profession is considerably freer than the coal miner's decision to accept the risks of his. Building a theory which will capture such intuitions is a formidable task which I must leave to others.

I think it would be possible to add quite a number of items to my list. But the three I have already mentioned should suffice to establish the point I am arguing. That point, recall, is that the naive egalitarian is mistaken. We need not assign a single value to all human lives in all risk-benefit analyses. There are morally respectable reasons for assigning different values to different lives, and for assigning different values to the same lives under differing circumstances. Thus the task of assigning an economic value to a human life in a risk-benefit analysis is actually many different tasks, *all of them difficult*. It is not, as some have feared, a single task which is prima facie *impossible*.

Before leaving the topic of assigning economic values to lives, let me make note of a confusion that has, of late, had profoundly unhappy consequences. There are many contexts quite removed from risk-benefit analyses where it is necessary or appropriate to assign an economic value to a human life. One of these situations is in a court of law when one person is found at fault for the death of another, and the question to be settled is how much compensation should be paid to the family of the deceased. In deciding what just compensation would be, many issues of social policy come into play. However, contrary to what a naive egalitarian might urge, there is no reason to insist that the sum which would be a just compensation for the family would also be the appropriate sum to use in a risk-benefit analysis. It appears that the Ford Motor Company made the naive egalitarian's mistake in calculating whether it was worthwhile to redesign the gas tank on the ill fated Pinto. After estimating (with some accuracy) how many deaths would be avoided by moving the gas tank, and how much such a move would add to the cost of building the car, they calculated that the cost per life saved would be greater than the average compensation for a death awarded by the courts in recent years. Thus, they decided not to move the gas tank. Public outrage over Pintos which burst into flames after rear-end collisions ultimately convinced Ford that it had used the wrong number.

3. Problems about principles: how shall the results of risk-benefit analysis be used? Suppose, for a cheerful moment, that we have made our peace with the problems recounted in the previous two sections; we have both probability estimates and value assignments that we find satisfactory. It then requires no more than a bit of careful arithmetic to complete Step 5 in the risk-benefit analysis, the calculation of the expected utility of each policy. What shall we do with these numbers? As we saw earlier, the obvious suggestion is that we should select the policy with the greatest expected utility. But as I hinted, there are deep difficulties lurking in this "obvious" suggestion.

Let us call the principle that we should adopt the policy with the highest expected utility the *utilitarian principle*. The following example should make it clear that, far from being trivial or tautological, the utilitarian principle is a substantive and controversial moral principle. Suppose that the decision which confronts us is whether or not to adopt policy A. What is more, suppose we know there is a probability close to 1 that 100,000 lives will be saved if we adopt A. However, we also know that there is a probability close to 1 that 1,000 will die as a direct result of our adopting policy A, and these people would survive if we did not adopt A. Finally, suppose that the other possible consequences of adopting A are relatively inconsequential and can be ignored. (For concreteness, we might take A to be the establishment of a mass vaccination program, using a relatively risky vaccine.) Now plainly if we take the moral desirability of saving a life to be exactly offset by the moral undesirability of causing a death, then the utilitarian principle dictates that we adopt policy A. But many people feel uncomfortable with this result, the discomfort increasing with the number of deaths that would result from A. If, to change the example, the choice that confronts us is saving 100,000 lives while causing the deaths of 50,000 others, a significant number of people are inclined to think that the morally right thing to do is to refrain from doing A, and "let nature take its course."

If we reject policy A, the likely reason is that we also reject the utilitarian principle.

Perhaps the most plausible reason for rejecting the utilitarian principle is the view that our obligation to *avoid doing harm* is stronger than our obligation to do good. There are many examples, some considerably more compelling than the one we have been discussing, which seem to illustrate that in a broad range of cases we do feel that our obligation to avoid doing harm is greater than our obligation to do good. Suppose, to take but one example, that my neighbor requests my help in paying off his gambling debts. He owes $5,000 to a certain bookmaker with underworld connections. Unless the neighbor pays the debt immediately, he will be shot. Here, I think we are all inclined to say, I have no strong obligation to give my neighbor the money he needs, and if I were to do so it would be a supererogatory gesture. By contrast, suppose a representative of my neighbor's bookmaker approaches me and requests that I shoot my neighbor. If I refuse, he will see to it that my new car, which cost $5,000, will be destroyed by a bomb while it sits unattended at the curb. In this case, surely, I have a strong obligation not to harm my neighbor, although not shooting him will cost me $5,000.

Suppose that this example and others convince us that we cannot adopt the utilitarian principle, at least not in its most general form, where it purports to be applicable to all moral decisions. What are the alternatives? One cluster of alternative principles would urge that in some or all cases we weigh the harm a contemplated action will cause more heavily than we weigh the good it will do. The extreme form of such a principle would dictate that we ignore the benefits entirely and opt for the action or policy that produces the *least* expected harm. (It is this principle, or a close relation, which emerged in the second reading of the "natural barriers" argument at the end of Section IV.) A more plausible variant would allow us to count both benefits and harms in our deliberations, but would specify how much more heavily harms were to count.

On my view, some moderate version of a "harm-weighted" principle is preferable to the utilitarian principle in a considerable range of cases. *However, the recombinant DNA issue is not one of these cases.* Indeed, when we try to apply a harm-weighted principle to the recombinant DNA case we run head-on into a conceptual problem of considerable difficulty. The distinction between doing good and doing harm presupposes a notion of the normal or expectable course of events. Roughly, if my action causes you to be worse off than you would have been in the normal course of events, then I have harmed you; if my action causes you to be better off than in the normal course of events, then I have done you some good; and if my action leaves you just as you would be in the normal course of events, then I have done neither. In many cases, the normal course of events is intuitively quite obvious. Thus in the case of the neighbor and the bookmaker, in the expected course of events I would neither shoot my neighbor nor give him $5,000 to pay off his debts. Thus I am doing good if I give him the money and I am doing harm if I shoot him. But in other cases, including the recombinant DNA case, it is not at all obvious what constitutes the "expected course of events," and thus it is not at all obvious what to count as a harm. To see this, suppose that as a matter of fact many more deaths and illnesses will be prevented as a result of pursuing recombinant DNA research than will be caused by pursuing it. But suppose that there *will* be at least some people who become ill or die as a result of recombinant DNA research being pursued. If these are the facts, then who would be harmed by imposing a ban on recombinant DNA research? That depends on what we take to be the "normal course of events." Presumably, if we do not impose a ban, then the research will continue and the lives will be saved. If this is the normal course of events, then if we impose a ban we have *harmed* those people who would have been saved. But it is equally natural to take as the normal course of events the situation in which recombinant DNA research is not pursued. And if *that* is the normal course of events, then those who would have been saved are not harmed by a ban, for they are no worse off than they would be in the normal course of events. However, on this reading of "the normal course of events," if we *fail* to impose a ban, then we have harmed those people who will ultimately become ill or die as a result of recombinant DNA research, since as a result of not imposing a ban they are worse off than they would have been in the normal course of events. I conclude that, in the absence of a theory detailing how we are to recognize the normal course of events, harm-weighted principles have no clear application to the case of recombinant DNA research.

Harm-weighted principles are not the only alternatives to the utilitarian principle. There is another cluster of alternatives that take off in quite a different direction. These principles urge that in deciding which policy to pursue there is a strong presumption in favor of policies that adhere to certain formal moral principles (that is, principles which do not deal with the *consequences* of our policies). Thus, to take the example most directly relevant to the recombinant DNA case, it might be urged that there is a strong presumption in favor of a policy which preserves freedom of scientific inquiry. In its extreme form, this principle would protect freedom of inquiry *no matter what the consequences;* and as we saw in the first part of Section IV, this extreme position is exceptionally implausible. A much more plausible principle would urge that freedom of inquiry be protected until the balance of negative over positive consequences reaches a certain specified amount, at which point we would revert to the utilitarian principle. On such a view, if the expected utility of banning recombinant DNA research is a bit higher than the expected utility of allowing it to continue, then we would nonetheless allow it to continue. But if the expected utility of a ban is enormously higher than the expected utility of continuation, banning is the policy to be preferred.

VI. Dangerous Knowledge

Thus far in our discussion of risks and benefits, the risks that have occupied us have been what might be termed "short-term" risks, such as the release of a new pathogen. The negative effects of these events, though they might be long-lasting indeed, would be upon us relatively quickly. However, some of those who are concerned about recombinant DNA research think there are longer-term dangers that are at least as worrisome. The dangers they have in mind stem not from the accidental release of harmful substances in the course of recombinant DNA research, but rather from the unwise use of the *knowledge* we will likely gain in pursuing the research. The scenarios most often proposed are nightmarish variations on the theme of human genetic engineering. With the knowledge we acquire, it is conjectured, some future tyrant may have people built to order, perhaps creating a whole class of people who willingly and cheaply do the society's dirty or dangerous work, as in Huxley's *Brave New World*. Though the proposed scenarios clearly are science fiction, they are not to be lightly dismissed. For if the technology they conjure is not demonstrably achievable, neither is it demonstrably impossible. And if only a bit of the science fiction turns to fact, the dangers could be beyond reckoning.

Granting that potential misuse of the knowledge gained in recombinant DNA research is a legitimate topic of concern, how ought we to guard ourselves against this misuse? One common proposal is to try to prevent the acquisition of such knowledge by banning or curtailing recombinant DNA research now. Let us cast this proposal in the form of an explicit moral argument. The conclusion is that recombinant DNA research should be curtailed, and the reason given for the conclusion is that such research could possibly produce knowledge which might be misused with disastrous consequences. To complete the argument we need a moral principle, and the one which seems to be needed is something such as this:

If a line of research can lead to the discovery of knowledge which might be disastrously misused, then that line of research should be curtailed.

Once it has been made explicit, I think relatively few people would be willing to endorse this principle. For recombinant DNA research is hardly alone in potentially leading to knowledge that might be disastrously abused. Indeed, it is hard to think of *any* area of scientific research that could *not* lead to the discovery of potentially dangerous knowledge. So if the principle is accepted it would entail that almost all scientific research should be curtailed or abandoned.

It might be thought that we could avoid the extreme consequences just cited by retreating to a more moderate moral principle. The moderate principle would urge only that we should curtail those areas of research where the probability of producing dangerous knowledge is comparatively high. Unfortunately, this more moderate principle is of little help in avoiding the unwelcome consequences of the stronger principle. The problem is that the history of science is simply too unpredictable to enable us to say with any assurance which lines of research will produce which sorts of knowledge or technology. There is a convenient illustration of the point in the recent history of molecular genetics. The idea of recombining DNA molecules is one which has been around for some time. However, early efforts proved unsuccessful. As it happened, the crucial step in making recombinant DNA technology possible was provided by research on restriction enzymes, research that was undertaken with no thought of recombinant DNA technology. Indeed, until it was realized that restriction enzymes provided the key to recombining DNA molecules, the research on restriction enzymes was regarded as a rather unexciting (and certainly uncontroversial) scientific backwater. In an entirely analogous way, crucial pieces of information that may one day enable us to manipulate the human genome may come from just about any branch of molecular biology. To guard against the discovery of that knowledge we should have to curtail not only recombinant DNA research but all of molecular biology.

Before concluding, we would do well to note that there is profound pessimism reflected in the attitude of those who would stop recombinant DNA research because it might lead to knowledge that could be abused. It is, after all, granted on all sides that the knowledge resulting from recombinant DNA research will have both good and evil potential uses. So it would seem the sensible strategy would be to try to prevent the improper uses of this knowledge rather than trying to prevent the knowledge from ever being uncovered. Those who would take the more extreme step of trying to stop the knowledge from being uncovered presumably feel that its improper use is all but inevitable, that our political and social institutions are incapable of preventing morally abhorrent applications of the knowledge while encouraging beneficial applications. On my view, this pessimism is unwarranted; indeed, it is all but inconsistent. The historical record gives us no reason to believe that what is technologically possible will be done, no matter what the moral price. Indeed, in the area of human genetic manipulation, the record points in quite the *opposite* direction. We have long known that the same techniques that work so successfully in animal breeding can be applied to humans as well. Yet there is no evidence of a "technological imperative" impelling our society to breed people as we breed dairy cattle, simply because we know that it can be done. Finally, it is odd that those who express no confidence in the ability of our institutions to forestall such monstrous applications of technology are not equally pessimistic about the ability of the same institutions to impose an effective ban on the uncovering of dangerous knowledge. If our institutions are incapable of restraining the application of technology when those applications would be plainly morally abhorrent, one would think they would be even more impotent in attempting to restrain a line of research which promises major gains in human welfare.

VII. Conclusion

Convention dictates that at the end of an essay we should find the *Conclusion*. But this is not the sort of essay which accords comfortably with that convention. The problem of genetic engineering and what should be done about it has not been resolved in these pages; it is still very much with us. What is worse, we have discovered a host of new problems and puzzles which must be dealt with before we can comfortably conclude that the problem has been resolved. Yet it would be a mistake to conclude that we have made no progress. For we have sharpened our focus on the complexity of the issues involved, and on the ways they interlock with one another. Making the right decisions about the control of science and technology will require the work of many minds and the perspectives of many disciplines. It is an effort our society cannot afford to ignore.

Suggested Readings

1. David A. Jackson & Stephen P. Stich, eds., *The Recombinant DNA Debate* (Englewood Cliffs, NJ: Prentice-Hall) 1979.
2. Carl Cohen, "When May Research Be Stopped?" in Jackson & Stich.
3. Carl Cohen, "On the Dangers of Inquiry and the Burden of Proof," in Jackson & Stich.
4. Robert L. Sinsheimer, "Two Lectures on Recombinant DNA," in Jackson & Stich.
5. George Wald, "The Case Against Genetic Engineering," in Jackson & Stich.
6. Bernard B. Davis, "Evolution, Epidemiology, and Recombinant DNA," in Jackson & Stich.
7. Michael Rogers, *Biohazard* (New York: Alfred A. Knopf) 1977.
8. National Academy of Sciences, *Research with Recombinant DNA* (Washington, D.C.: National Academy of Sciences) 1977.
9. Amitai Etzioni, *Genetic Fix* (New York: Harper & Row) 1975.

chapter five

Nuclear Power—Some Ethical and Social Dimensions

RICHARD AND VAL ROUTLEY[1]

One hardly needs initiation into the dark mysteries of nuclear physics to contribute usefully to the debate now widely raging over nuclear power. While many important empirical questions are still unresolved, these do not really lie at the centre of the controversy. Instead, it is a debate about values . . . many of the questions which arise are social and ethical ones.[2]

I. The Train Parable and the Nuclear Waste Problem

A long distance country train has just pulled out. The train which is crowded carries both passengers and freight. At an early stop in the journey someone consigns as freight, to a far distant destination, a package which contains a highly toxic and explosive gas. This is packed in a very thin container which, as the consigner is aware, may well not contain the gas for the full distance for which it is consigned, and certainly will not do so if the train should strike any real trouble, for example, if the train should be derailed or involved in a collision, or if some passenger should interfere inadvertently or deliberately with the freight, perhaps trying to steal some of it. All of these sorts of things have happened on some previous journeys. If the container should break the resulting disaster would probably kill at least some of the people on the train in adjacent carriages, while others could be maimed or poisoned or sooner or later incur serious diseases.

Most of us would roundly condemn such an action. What might the consigner of the parcel say to try to justify it? He might say that it is *not certain* that the gas will escape, or that the world needs his product and it is his duty to supply it, or that in any case he is not responsible for the train or the people on it. These sorts of excuses, however, would normally be seen as ludicrous when set in this context. Unfortunately, similar excuses are often not so seen when the consigner, again a (responsible) businessman, puts his workers' health or other peoples' welfare at risk.

Suppose he says that it is his own and others' pressing needs which justify his action. The company he controls, which produces the material as a by-product, is in bad financial straits, and could not afford to produce a better container even if it knew how to make one. If the company fails, he and his family will suffer, his employees will lose their jobs and have to look for others, and the whole company town, through loss of spending, will be worse off. The poor and unemployed of the town, whom he would otherwise have been able to help, will suffer especially. Few people would accept such grounds as justification. Even where there are serious risks and costs to oneself or some group for whom one is concerned one is usually considered not to be entitled to simply transfer the heavy burden of those risks and costs onto other uninvolved parties, especially where they arise from one's own, or one's group's chosen life-style.

The matter of nuclear waste has many moral features which resemble the train case. How fitting the analogy is will become apparent as the argument progresses. There is no known proven safe way to package the highly toxic wastes generated by the nuclear plants that will be spread around the world as large-scale nuclear development goes ahead. The waste problem will be much more serious than that generated by the 50 or so reactors in use at present, with each one of the 2000 or so reactors envisaged by the end of the century producing, on average, annual wastes containing 1000 times the radioactivity of the Hiroshima bomb. Much of this waste is extremely toxic. For example, a millionth of a gramme of plutonium is enough to induce a lung cancer. A leak of even a part of the waste material could involve much loss of life, widespread disease and genetic damage, and contamination of immense areas of land. Wastes will include the reactors themselves, which will have to be abandoned after their expected life times of perhaps 40 years, and which, some have estimated, may require 1½ million years to reach safe levels of radioactivity.

Nuclear wastes must be kept suitably isolated from the environment for their entire active lifetime. For fission products the required storage period averages a thousand years or so, and for transuranic elements, which include plutonium, there is a half million to a million year storage problem. Serious problems have arisen with both short-term and proposed long-term methods of storage, even with the comparatively small quantities of waste produced over the last twenty years. Short-term methods of storage require continued human intervention, while proposed longer term methods are subject to both human interference and risk of leakage through non-human factors.

No one with even a slight knowledge of the geological and climatic history of the earth over the last million years, a period whose fluctuations in climate we are only just beginning to guage and which has seen four Ice Ages, could be confident that a rigorous guarantee of safe storage could be provided for the vast period of time involved. Nor does the history of human affairs over the last 3000 years give ground for confidence in safe storage by methods requiring human intervention over perhaps a million years. Proposed long-term storage methods such as storage in granite formations or in salt mines, are largely speculative and relatively untested, and have already proved to involve difficulties with attempts made to put them into practice. Even as regards expensive recent proposals for first embedding concentrated wastes in glass and encapsulating the result in multilayered metal containers before rock deposit, simulation models reveal that radioactive material may not remain suitably isolated from human environments. In short, the best present storage proposals carry very real possibilities of irradiating future people and damaging their environment.[3]

Given the heavy costs which could be involved for the future, and given the known limits of technology, it is methodologically unsound to bet, as nuclear nations have, on the discovery of safe procedures for storage of wastes. Any new procedures (required before 2000) will probably be but variations on present proposals, and subject to the same inadequacies. For instance, not only have none of the proposed methods for safe storage been properly tested, but they may well prove to involve unforeseen difficulties and risks when an attempt is made to put them into practice on a *commercial scale*. Only a method that could provide a rigorous guarantee of safety over the storage period, that placed safety beyond reasonable doubt, would be acceptable. It is difficult to see how such rigorous guarantees could be given concerning either the geological or future human factors. But even if an economically viable, rigorously safe long term storage method *could* be devised, there is the problem of guaranteeing that it would be universally and invariably *used*. The assumption that it would be (especially if, as appears likely, such a method proved expensive economically and politically) seems to presuppose a level of efficiency, perfection, and concern for the future which has not previously been encountered in human affairs, and has certainly not been conspicuous in the nuclear industry.

The risks imposed on the future by proceeding with nuclear development are, then, *significant*. Perhaps 40,000 generations of future people could be forced to bear significant risks resulting from the provision of the (extravagant) energy use of only a small proportion of the people of 10 generations.

Nor is the risk of direct harm from the escape or misuse of radioactive materials the only burden the nuclear solution imposes on the future. Because the energy provided by nuclear fission is merely a stop gap, it seems probable that in due course the same problem, that of making a transition to renewable sources of energy, will have to be faced again by a future population which will probably, again as a result of our actions, be very much worse placed to cope with it. Their world will most likely be a world which is seriously depleted of non-renewable resources, and in which such renewable resources as forests and soils as remain, resources which inevitably form an important part of the basis of life, are run-down or destroyed. Such points tell against the idea that future people must be, if not direct beneficiaries of energy from nuclear fission, at least indirect beneficiaries.

The "solution" then is to buy time for contemporary society at a price which not only creates serious problems for future people but which reduces their ability to cope with these problems. Like the consigner in the train parable, contemporary industrial society proposes, in order to get itself out of a mess arising from its own life-style—the creation of economies dependent on an abundance of non-renewable energy, which is limited in supply—to pass on costs and risks of serious harm to others who will obtain no corresponding benefits. The "solution" may enable the avoidance of some uncomfortable changes in the lifetime of those now living and their immediate descendants, just as the consigner's action avoids uncomfortable changes for him and those in his immediate surroundings, but at the expense of passing heavy burdens to other uninvolved parties whose opportunity to lead decent lives may be seriously jeopardised.

If we apply to the nuclear situation the standards of behaviour and moral principles generally acknowledged (in principle, if not so often in fact) in the contemporary world, it is not easy to avoid the conclusion that nuclear development involves *injustice with respect to the future* on a grand scale. There appear to be only two plausible ways of trying to avoid such a conclusion. First, it might be argued that the moral principles and obligations which we acknowledge for the contemporary world and perhaps the immediate future do not apply to those in the non-immediate future. Secondly, an attempt might be made to appeal to overriding circumstances; for to reject the consigner's action in the circumstances outlined is not to imply that there are *no* circumstances in which such an action might be justifiable. As in the case of the consigner of the package there is a need to consider what these justifying circumstances might be, and whether they apply in the present case. We consider these possible escape routes for the proponent of nuclear development in turn.

II. Obligations to the (Distant) Future

The especially problematic area is that of the distant (i.e. non-immediate) future, the future with which people alive today will have no direct contact; by comparison, the immediate future gives fewer problems for most ethical theories. In fact the question of obligations to future people presents tests which a number of ethical theories fail to pass, and also has serious repercussions in political philosophy as regards the adequacy of accepted (democratic and other) institutions which do not take due account of the interests of future creatures.

Moral philosophers have, predictably, differed on questions of obligations to distant future creatures. A good many of the philosophers who have explicitly considered the question have come down in favour of the same consideration being given to the rights and interests of future people as to those of contemporary or immediately future people. Others fall into three catagories: those who acknowledge obligations to the future but who do not take them seriously or who assign them a lesser weight, those who deny, or who are committed by their general moral position to denying, that there are moral obligations beyond the immediate future, and those who come down, with admirable philosophical caution, on both sides of the issue, but with the weight of the argument favouring the view underlying prevailing economic and political institutions, that there are no moral obligations to the future beyond those perhaps to the next generation.

According to the most extreme of these positions against moral obligations to the future, our behaviour with respect to the future is morally unconstrained; there are no moral restrictions on acting or failing to act deriving from the effect of our actions on future people. Of those philosophers who say, or whose views imply that we do not have obligations to the (non-immediate) future, many have based this view on accounts of moral obligation which are built on relations which presuppose some degree of temporal or spatial contiguity. Thus, moral obligation is seen as presupposing various relations which could not hold between people widely separated in time (or sometimes in space). Let us call the position that we have no obligations to (distant) future people the *No-constraints position*.

Among suggested bases or grounds of moral obligation for the position, which would rule out obligations to the non-immediate future, are these. Firstly, there are those accounts which require that someone to whom a moral obligation is held be able to *claim* his rights or entitlement. People in the distant future will not be able to claim rights and entitlements against us, and of course they can do nothing to enforce any claims they might have against us. Secondly, there are those accounts which base moral obligations on social or legal *convention*, for example a convention which would require punishment of offenders or at least some kind of social enforcement. But plainly these and other conventions will not be invariant over change in society and amendment of legal conventions; hence they will not be invariant over time. Also future people have no way of enforcing their interests or punishing offending predecessors.

The No-constraints view is a very difficult one to sustain. Consider, for example, a scientific group which, for no particular reason other than to test a particular piece of technology, places in orbit a cobalt bomb set off by a triggering device designed to go off several hundred years from the time of its despatch. No presently living person and none of their immediate descendants would be affected, but the population of the earth in the distant future would be wiped out as a direct and predictable result of the action. The No-constraints position clearly implies that this is an acceptable moral enterprise, that whatever else we might legitimately criticize in the scientists' experiment (perhaps its being over-expensive or badly designed) we cannot lodge a moral protest about the damage it will do to future people. The no-constraints position also endorses as morally acceptable the following sorts of policy: A firm discovers it can make a handsome profit from mining, processing and manufacturing a new type of material which, although it causes no problem for present people or their immediate descendants, will over a period of hundreds of years decay into a substance which will cause an enormous epidemic of cancer among the inhabitants of the earth at that time. According to the No-constraints view the firm is free to act in its own interests, without any consideration for the harm it does remote future people.

Such counterexamples to the No-constraints position, which are easily varied and multiplied, might seem childlishly obvious. Yet this view is far from being a straw man; not only have several philosophers endorsed this position, but it is a clear implication of many currently popular views of the basis of moral obligation, as well as of prevailing economic theory. It seems that those who opt for the No-constraints position have not considered such examples, despite their being clearly implied by their position. We suspect that (we certainly hope that) when it is brought out that their position admits such counterexamples, that without any constraints we are free to cause pointless harm for example, most of those who opted for this position would want to assert that it was not what they intended. What many of those who have put forward the No-constraints position *seem* to have had in mind (in denying moral obligation) is rather that future people can look after themselves, that we are not responsible for their lives. The popular view that the future can take care of itself also seems to assume a future causally independent of the present. But it is not. It is not as if, in the counterexample cases or in the nuclear case, the future is simply being left *alone* to take care of itself. Present people are *influencing* it, and in doing so thereby acquire many of the same sorts of moral responsibilities as they do in causally affecting the present and immediate future, most notably the obligation to take account in what they do of people affected and their interests, to be careful in their actions, to take account of the genuine probability of their actions causing harm, and to see that they do not act so as to rob future people of the chance of a good life.

Furthermore, to say that we are *not responsible* for the lives of future people does not amount to the same thing as saying that we are free to do as we like with respect to them. In just the same way, the fact that one does not have or has not acquired an obligation to some stranger with whom one has never been involved does not imply that one is free to do what one likes with respect to him, for example to rob him or to seriously harm him when this could be avoided.

These difficulties for the No-constraints position result in part because of a failure to make an important distinction. Some of our obligations to others arise because we have voluntarily entered into some agreement with them—for example, we have made a promise. Other obligations, however, such as our duty not to damage or harm someone, do not assume that an agreement has been struck between us. Let us call obligations of the former kind *acquired obligations* and those of the latter *unacquired obligations*. There is a considerable difference in the type of responsibility associated with each. In the case of acquired obligations responsibility arises because one should do something which one can fail to do, e.g. keep a promise. In the case of unacquired duties responsibility arises as a result of being a causal agent who is aware of the consequences or probable consequences of his action, a responsibility that is not dependent on one's having performed some act in the past (e.g., made a promise). Our obligations to future people clearly are unacquired, not acquired, obligations, a fact the No-constraints position simply fails to take into account. These obligations arise as a result of our ability to produce causal effects of a reasonably predictable nature, whether on our contemporaries *or* on those in the distant future. Thus, to return to the train parable, the consigner cannot argue in justification of his action that he has, for example, never assumed or acquired responsibility for the passengers, that he does not know them and therefore has no love or sympathy for them and that they are not part of his moral community; in short, that he has acquired no obligation, and has no special obligations to help them. All that one needs to argue concerning the train, and in the nuclear case, is that there are moral obligations against imposing harm which are not specially acquired. Nor can this claim be rebutted by the pretence that all obligations to the distant future involve heroic self sacrifice, something "above and beyond" what is normally required. One is no more engaging in heroic self sacrifice by not forcing future people into an unviable life position or by refraining from causing them direct harm than the consigner is resorting to heroic self sacrifice in refraining from shipping the dangerous package on the train.

III. Attempts to Reduce Obligations to the Future

In evading these difficulties the No-constraints position may be qualified rather than wholly abandoned. According to the *Qualified position* we are not entirely unconstrained with respect to the distant future. There are obligations, even to distant future people, but these are not so important as those to the present, and the interests of distant future people cannot weigh very much in the scale against those of the present and immediate future. The interests of future people then, except in unusual cases, count for very much less than the interests of present people. Hence such things as nuclear development and various exploitative activities which benefit present people should proceed, even if people of the distant future are (somewhat) disadvantaged by them.

The Qualified position appears to be widely held and is implicit in prevailing economic theories, where the position of a decrease in weight of future costs and benefits (and so of future interests) is obtained by application over time of a discount rate, so discounting costs and risks to future people. The attempt to apply economics as a moral theory, an approach that is becoming increasingly common, can lead then to the Qualified position. What is objectionable in such an approach is that economics must operate within the bounds of acknowledged non-acquired moral constraints, just as in practice it operates within legal constraints. What economics cannot legitimately do is determine what these constraints are. There are, moreover, alternative economic theories and simply to adopt, without further ado, one which discounts the future, giving much less importance to the interests of future people, is to beg all the questions at issue.

Among the arguments that economists offer for generally discounting the future, the most threadbare is based on the *Rosy-future assumption,* that future generations will be better off than present ones (and so better placed to handle the waste problem). Since there is mounting evidence that future generations may well *not* be better off than present ones, especially in things that matter, no argument for discounting the interests of future generations on this basis can carry much weight. For the waste problem to be handed down to the future generations, it would have to be shown, what recent economic progress hardly justifies, that future generations will be not just better off but so much better off that they can (easily) carry and control the nuclear freight.

A more plausible argument for discounting, the *Opportunity-cost argument,* builds directly on the notion of opportunity cost. It is argued from the fact that a dollar gained now is worth much more than a dollar received in the nonimmediate future (because the first dollar could meanwhile be invested at compound interest), that discounting is required to obtain equivalent monetary values. This same line of reasoning is then applied to the allocation of resources. Thus, compensation—which is what the waste problem is taken to come to economically—costs much less now than later, e.g. a few pennies set aside (e.g. in a trust fund) for the future, if need be, will suffice to compensate eventually for any victims of remote radioactive waste leakage. Two problems beset this approach.[4] First, there are, presently at least, insurmountable practical difficulties about applying such discounting. We simply do not know how to determine appropriate future discount rates. A more serious objection is that the argument depends on a false assumption. It is not true that value, or damages, can always be converted into monetary equivalents. There is no clear "monetary compensation" for a variety of damages, including cancer, loss of life, a lost species.

The discounting theme, however argued for, is inadequate, because it leads back in practice to the No-constraints position. The reason is that discounting imposes an "economic horizon" beyond which nothing need be considered, since any costs or benefits which might arise are, when discounted back to the present, negligible.

A different argument for the Qualified position, the *Probabilities argument,* avoids the objections from cases of certain damage through appeal to *probability consider-ations.* The distant future, it is argued, is much more uncertain than the present and immediate future, so that probabilities are consequently lower, perhaps even ap-proaching or coinciding with zero for any hypothesis concerning the distant future. Thus, the argument continues, the interests of future people must (apart from exceptional cases where there is an unusually high degree of certainty) count for (very much) less than those of present and neighbouring people where (much) higher probabilities are attached. So in the case of conflict between the present and the future, where it is a question of weighing certain benefits to the people of the present and the immediate future against a much lower probability of indeterminate costs to an indeterminate number of distant future people, the issue would normally be decided in favour of the present assuming anything like similar costs and benefits were involved. The argument is, however, badly flawed. Firstly, probabilities involv-ing distant future situations are not always less than those concerning the immediate future in the way the argument supposes. Though we do not know what kind of cars the denizens of earth will drive in the twenty-second century, for example, or even if they will drive cars, we do know that they will have a need for food, clothing, and shelter. Moreover, the outcomes of some moral problems often do not depend on a high level of probability. In many cases it is enough, as the train parable reveals, that a significant risk is created; such cases do not depend critically on high probability assignments. Nor, of course, can it be assumed that anything like similarly weighted costs and benefits are involved in the nuclear case, especially if it is a question of risking poisoning some of the earth for half a million or so years, with consequent risk of serious harm to thousands of generations of future people, in order to obtain quite doubtful, or even trivial, benefits for some present people in the shape of the opportunity to continue (unnecessarily) high energy use. And *even if* the costs and benefits were comparable or evenly weighted, such an argument would be defective, since an analogous argument would show that the consigner's action in the train parable, is acceptable provided the benefit (e.g. the profit the company stood to gain from imposing significant risks on other people) was sufficiently large.

Such a cost-benefit approach to moral and decision problems, with or without the probability frills, is quite inadequate when different parties are involved or when cases of conflict of interest involving moral obligations are at issue.[5] For example, such a cost-benefit approach would imply that it is *permissible* for a company to injure, or very likely injure, some innocent party provided only that the company stands to make a sufficiently large gain from it, that costs to some group are more than morally compensated for by larger benefits to another group. But costs or benefits are not legitimately transferred in any simple way from one group to another. The often appealed to maxim "If you (or your group) want the benefits you have to accept the costs" is one thing, but the maxim "If I (or my group) want the benefits then *you* have to accept the costs (or some of them at least)" is another and very different thing. It is a widely accepted moral principle that one is not, in general, entitled to simply transfer costs of a significant kind arising from an activity which benefits oneself onto other parties who are not involved in the activity and are not beneficiaries.[6] This *Transfer-limiting principle* is especially clear in cases where the significant costs include an effect on life or health or a risk thereof, and where the benefit to the benefitting party is of a noncrucial or dispensable nature—e.g., the manufacture and sale of thalidomide. The principle is of fundamental importance in the nuclear debate, and appears again and again: it applies not merely to the waste problem but also to several other liabilities of nuclear development, e.g. the risk of nuclear war, the matter of reactor meltdown. In particular, the principle invalidates the comparison, heavily relied on in building a case for the acceptability of the nuclear risks, between nuclear risks and those from such activities as airplane travel or cigarette smoking. In the latter case those who supposedly benefit from the activity are also, to an overwhelming extent, those who bear the serious health costs and risks involved. In contrast the users and supposed beneficiaries of nuclear energy will be risking not only, or even primarily, *their own* lives and health, but also that of others who may not be beneficiaries at all—who may be just the opposite!

More generally, the distribution of costs and damage in such a fashion, i.e. on to non-beneficiaries, is a characteristic of certain serious forms of pollution, and is among its morally objectionable features. Large-scale energy production, from nuclear or fossil fuel sources, can cause or lead to serious pollution. Thus from the Transfer-limiting principle emerges an important necessary condition for energy options: *To be morally acceptable an energy option should not involve the transfer of significant costs or risks of harm onto parties who are not involved, who do not use or do not benefit correspondingly from the energy source.* Included in the scope of this condition, which nuclear development violates, are future people, i.e. not merely people living at the present time but also future generations (those of the next towns). A further corollary of the principle is the *Transmission Principle,* that we should not hand the world we have so exploited on to our successors in substantially worse shape than we "received" it. For if we did then that would be a significant transfer of costs.

The Transfer-limiting principle can be derived from certain ethical theories (e.g. those of a deontic cast such as Kant's and Rawls') and from common precepts (such as the Golden Rule), where one seriously considers putting oneself in another's position. But the principle is perhaps best defended, on a broader basis, inductively, by way of examples. Suppose, to embroider the train parable, the company town decides to solve its disposal problem by shipping its noxious waste to another town down the line, which (like future towns) lacks the means to ship it back or to register due protest. The inhabitants of this town are then forced to face the problem either of undertaking the expensive and difficult disposal process or of sustaining risks to their own lives and health. Most of us would regard this kind of transfer of costs as morally unacceptable, however much the consigner's company town flourishes.

IV. Uncertainty and Indeterminacy Arguments for
Reduced Responsibility

Many of the arguments designed to show that we cannot be expected to take too much account of the effects of our actions on the distant future appeal to uncertainty. There are two main components to the General Uncertainty argument, capable of separation, but frequently tangled up. Both arguments are mistaken, the first, an argument from ignorance, on *a priori* grounds, the second on *a posteriori* grounds. The *Argument from ignorance* concerned runs as follows: In contrast to the exact information we can obtain about the present, the information we can obtain about the effects of our actions on the distant future is unreliable, woolly and highly speculative. But we cannot base assessments of how we should act on information of this kind, especially when accurate information is obtainable about the present which would indicate different action. Therefore we must regretfully ignore the uncertain effects of our actions on the distant future. A striking example of the argument from ignorance at work is afforded by official US analyses favouring nuclear development, which ignore (the extensive) costs of waste control on the grounds of uncertainty.[7] More formally and crudely the argument concerned is this: One only has obligations to the future if these obligations are based on reliable information. There is no reliable information at present as regards the distant future. Therefore one has no obligations to the distant future.

This argument is essentially a variant on a sceptical argument concerning our knowledge of the future (formally, replace 'obligations' by 'knowledge' in the crude statement of the argument above). The main ploy is to considerably overestimate and overstate the degree of certainty available with respect to the present and immediate future, and the degree of certainty which is *required* as the basis for moral consideration both with respect to the present and with respect to the future. Associated with this is the attempt to suggest a sharp division as regards certainty between the present and immediate future on the one hand and the distant future on the other. We shall not find, we suggest, that there is any such sharp or simple division between the distant future and the adjacent future and the present, at least with respect to those things in the present which are normally subject to moral constraints. We can and constantly do act on the basis of such "unreliable" information, which the sceptic as regards the future conveniently labels "uncertain". In moral situations in the present, assessments of what to do often take account of risk and probability, even quite low probabilities. Consider again the train parable. We do not need to know for certain that the container will break and the lethal gas escape. In fact it does not even have to be probable, in the relevant sense of more probable than not, in order for us to condemn the consigner's action. *It is enough that there is a significant risk of harm* in this sort of case. It does not matter if the decreased well-being of the consigner is certain and that the prospects of the passengers quite uncertain. It is wrong to ship the gas. But if we do not require certainty of action to apply moral constraints in contemporary affairs, why should we require a much higher standard of certainty in the future? The unwarranted insistence on certainty as a necessary condition before moral consideration can be given to the distant future, then, amounts to a flagrant double standard.

According to the second argument, the *Practical-uncertainty* argument, even if *in theory* we have obligations to the future, we cannot *in practice* take the interests of future people into account because uncertainty about the distant future is so gross that we cannot determine what the likely consequences of actions on it will be. Therefore, however good our intentions to the people of the distant future are, in practice we have no choice but to ignore their interests. Given that moral principles are characteristically of universal implicational form, e.g. of forms such as "if x has character h then x is wrong, for every (action) x", the argument may be stated more sharply thus: We can never obtain the information about future actions which would enable us to affirm the antecedent of the implication (x has character h). Therefore, even if in theory moral principles do extend to future people, in practice they cannot be applied to obtain clear conclusions.

It is true that if the distant future really were so grossly uncertain that in every case it was impossible to determine in any way better than chance what the effects of present action would be, and whether any given action would help or hinder future people, then moral principles, although applicable in theory to the future, would not in practice yield any clear conclusions about how to act. In this event the distant future would impose no practical moral constraints on action. However, the argument is factually incorrect in assuming that the future always is so grossly uncertain or indeterminate. Admittedly there is often a high degree of uncertainty concerning the distant future, but as a matter of (contingent) fact it is not always so gross or sweeping as the argument has to assume. There are some areas where uncertainty is not so great as to exclude constraints on action. For example, we may have little idea what the fashions will be in a hundred years or, to take another morally-irrelevant factor, what brands of ice cream people will be eating, if any, but we do have excellent reason to believe, especially if we consider 3000 years of history, that what people there are in a hundred years are likely to have material and psychic needs not entirely unlike our own, that they will need a healthy biosphere for a good life; that like us they will not be immune to radiation; that their welfare will not be enhanced by a high incidence of cancer or genetic defects, by the destruction of resources, or the elimination from the face of the earth of that wonderful variety of non-human life which at present makes it such a rich and interesting place. The case of nuclear waste storage, and of uncertainty of the effects of it on future people, is one area where uncertainty in morally relevant respects is not so great as to preclude moral constraints on action. For this sort of reason, the Practical uncertainty argument should be rejected.

Through the defects of the preceding arguments, we can see the defects in a number of widely employed uncertainty arguments used to write off probable harm to future people as outside the scope of proper consideration. Most of these popular moves employ both of the uncertainty arguments as suits the case, switching from one to the other. For example, we may be told that we cannot really take account of future people because we cannot be sure that they will exist or that their tastes and wants will not be completely different from our own, to the point where they will not suffer from our exhaustion of resources or from the things that would affect us. But this is to insist upon complete certainty of a sort beyond what is required for the present and immediate future, where there is also commonly no guarantee that some disaster will not overtake those to whom we are morally committed. Again we may be told that there is no guarantee that future people will be worthy of any efforts on our part, because they may be morons or forever plugged into machines for their enjoyment. Even if one is prepared to accept the elitist approach presupposed—according to which only those who meet certain properly civilized or intellectual standards are eligible for moral consideration—what we are being handed in such arguments is again a mere outside possibility. Neither the contemporary nor the historical situation gives any positive reason for supposing that a lapse into universal moronity or universal-pleasure-machine escapism is a serious possibility. We can contrast with these mere logical possibilities the very real historically supportable risks of escape of nuclear waste or decline of a civilisation through destruction of its resource base.

Closely related to uncertainty arguments are arguments premissed on the indeterminacy of the future. For example, according to the *Indeterminacy argument*, the indeterminacy of the number and exact character of people at future times will prevent the interest of future people being taken into account where there is a conflict with the present. Since their numbers are indeterminate and their interests unknown how, it is asked, can we weigh their competing claims against those of the present and immediate future, where this information is available in a more or less accurate form? The question is raised particularly by problems of sharing fixed quantities of resources among present and future people, for example oil, when the numbers of the latter are indeterminate. Such problems are indeed difficult, but they are not resolved by *ignoring* the claims of the future. Nor are distributional problems involving non-renewable resources as large and representative a class of moral problems concerning the future as the tendency to focus on them would suggest. It can be freely admitted, that there will be cases where the indeterminacy of aspects of the future will make conflicts very difficult to resolve or indeed irresoluble—no realistic ethical theory can give a precise answer to *every* ethical question. But, as the train parable again illustrates, there are cases where such difficulties do not hinder resolution, and cases of conflict which are not properly approached by weighing numbers, numbers of interests, or whatever, cases for which one needs to know only the most general probable characteristics of future people. The case of nuclear power is like that.

The failure of these various arguments reveals, what can be independently argued from the universalisability features of moral principles,[8] that their placement does not disqualify future people from full moral consideration or reduce their claims below the claims of present people. That is, *we have the same general unacquired obligations to future people as to the present;* thus there is the same obligation to take account of them and their interests in what we do, to be careful in our actions, to take account of the probability (and not just the certainty) of our actions causing harm or damage, and to see, other things being equal, that we do not act so as to rob them of what is necessary for the chance of a good life. Uncertainty and indeterminacy do not relieve us of these obligations.

V. Problems of Safe Nuclear Operation: Reactor Emissions and Core Meltdown

The ethical problems with nuclear power are by no means confined to waste storage and future creatures. Just as remoteness in time does not erode obligations or entitlement to just treatment, neither does location in space, or a particular geographical position. Hence several further problems arise, to which principles and arguments like those already arrived at in considering the waste problem apply. For example, if one group (social unit, or state) decides to dump its radioactive wastes in the territory or region of another group, or not to prevent its (radioactive) pollution entering the territory of another group, then it imposes risks and costs on presently existing people of the second group, in much the way that present nuclear developments impose costs and risks on future people. There are differences however: spatially distant people cannot be discounted in quite the way that future people can be, though the interests and objectives of the former often get ignored or overridden.

People living in the vicinity of a nuclear reactor are subject to special costs and risks. One is radioactive pollution, because reactors routinely discharge radioactive materials into the air and water near the plant: hence the *Emission problem.* Such "normal" emission during plant operation of low level radiation carries carcinogenic and mutagenic costs. While there are undoubtedly costs, the number of cancers and the precise extent of genetic damage induced by exposure to such radiation are both uncertain. If our ethical principles permitted free transfer of costs and risks from one person to another, the ethical issue directly raised by nuclear emissions would be: what extent of cancer and genetic damage, if any, is permissibly traded for the advantages of nuclear power, and under what conditions? Since, however, risks and benefits are NOT (morally) transferable in this way—recall the Transfer-limiting principle—such a cost-benefit approach to the risks nuclear emission poses for those who live near a reactor cannot with justice be approached in this fashion. And these risks *are* real! In the USA, people who live within 50 miles of a nuclear power plant bear a risk of cancer and genetic damage as much as 50 times that borne by the population at large. And children living in this region are even more vulnerable, since they are several times more likely to contract cancer through exposure than normal adults. The serious costs to these people cannot be justified by the alleged benefits for others, especially when these benefits could be obtained without these costs. Thus it is not just complacent to say 'It's a pity about Aunt Ethel dying of cancer, but the new airconditioners make life comfortable'. For such benefits to some as airconditioners provide, benefits which can be alternatively obtained, for example by modification of buildings, can in no way compensate for what *others* suffer.

Among the other strategies used in trying to persuade us that the imposition of radiation on those who live close to nuclear plants—most of whom have no genuine voice in the location of reactors in their environment and cannot move away without serious losses—is really quite allright is the *Doubling argument.* According to the US Atomic Energy Commission, it is permissible to double, through nuclear technology, the level of (natural) radiation that a population has received with apparently negligible consequences, the argument being that the additional amount (being *equivalent* to the "natural" level) is also likely to have negligible consequences. The increased amounts of radiation—with their large man-made component—are then accounted *normal,* and, it is claimed, what is normal is morally acceptable. This argument is not sound. Drinking one bottle of wine a day may have no ill-effects, whereas drinking two a day certainly may affect a person's well-being; and while the smaller intake may have become normal for the person, the larger one will, under such conditions, not be. Finally, what is or has become normal, e.g. two murders or twenty cancers a day in a given city, may be far from acceptable.

In fact, even the USA, which has very strict standards by comparison with most other countries with planned nuclear reactors, permits radiation emissions very substantially in excess of the standards laid down; so the emission situation is much worse than what consideration of the standards would disclose. Furthermore, the monitoring of the standards "imposed" is entrusted to the nuclear operators themselves, scarcely disinterested parties. Thus public policy is determined not so as to guarantee public health, but rather to serve as a "public pacifier" while publicly-subsidized private nuclear operations proceed relatively unhampered.[9]

While radioactive emissions are an ordinary feature of reactor operation, reactor breakdown is, hopefully, not: official reports even try to make an accident of magnitude, as a matter of *definition*, an 'extraordinary nuclear occurrence'. But "definitions" notwithstanding, such accidents can happen, and almost have on several occasions (the most notorious being Three Mile Island): hence the *Core-meltdown problem*.

If the cooling and emergency core cooling systems fail in American (light water) reactors, then the core melts and 'containment failure' is likely, with the result that an area of 40,000 square miles could be radioactively contaminated.[10] In the event of the worst type of accident in a very small reactor, a steam explosion in the reactor vessel, about 45,000 people would be killed instantly and at least 100,000 would die as a result of the accident, property damages would exceed $17 billion and an area the size of Pennsylvania would be destroyed. Modern nuclear reactors are about five times the size of the reactor for which these conservative US figures (still the best available from official sources) are given[11]: the consequences of a similar accident with a modern reactor would accordingly be much greater.

The consigner who risks the lives and well-being of passengers on the train acts inadmissibly. A government or government-endorsed utility appears to act in a way that does not differ in morally significant respects in siting a nuclear reactor in a community, in planting such a dangerous package on the "community train". More directly, the location of a nuclear reactor in a community, even if it should happen to receive a favourable benefit-cost analysis and other economic appraisal, would violate such ethical requirements as the Transfer-limiting principle.

The advocates of nuclear power have, in effect, endeavoured to avoid questions of cost-transfer and equity, by shifting the dispute out of the ethical arena and into a technological dispute about the extraordinary improbability of reactor malfunction. They have argued, in particular, what contrasts with the train parable, that there is no real possibility of a catastrophic nuclear accident. Indeed in the influential Rassmussen report—which was extensively used to support public confidence in US nuclear fission technology—an even stronger, an incredibly strong, improbability claim was stated: namely, the likelihood of a catastrophic nuclear accident is so remote as to be (almost) impossible. However, the mathematical models relied upon in this report, variously called "fault tree analysis" and "reliability estimating techniques", are unsound, because, among other things, they exclude as "not credible" possibilities that may well happen in the real world. It is not surprising, then, that the methodology and data of the report have been soundly and decisively criticised, or that official support for the report has now been withdrawn.[12] Moreover, use of alternative methods and data indicates that there is a real possibility, a non-negligible probability of a serious accident.

In response it is contended that, even if there is a non-negligible probability of a reactor accident, still that is acceptable, being of no greater order than risks of accidents that are already socially accepted. Here we encounter again that insidious engineering approach to morality built into decision models of an economic cast, e.g. benefit-cost balance sheets, risk-assessment models, etc. *Risk assessment*, a sophistication of transaction or trade-off models, purports to provide a comparison between the relative risks attached to different options, e.g. energy options, which settles their ethical status. The following assumptions are encountered in risk assessment as applied to energy options:

Ai. If option A imposes (comparable) costs on fewer people than option B then option A is preferable to option B;

Aii. Option A involves a total net cost in terms of cost to people (e.g. deaths, injuries, etc.) which is less than that of option B, which is already accepted; therefore option A is acceptable.[13]

These assumptions are then applied as follows. Since the number likely to be killed by nuclear power station catastrophe is less than the likely number eventually killed by cigarette smoking, and since the risks of cigarette smoking are accepted; it follows that the risks of nuclear power are acceptable. A little reflection reveals that this sort of risk assessment argument grossly violates the Transfer-limiting principle. In order to obtain a proper ethical assessment we need a much fuller picture, and we need to know at least these things: Do the costs and benefits go to the same parties; and is the person who *voluntarily undertakes* the risks also the person who primarily receives the benefits, as in driving or cigarette smoking, or are the costs *imposed* on other parties who do not benefit? It is only if the parties are the same in the case of the options compared, and there are no distributional problems, that this sort of a comparison would be soundly based. This is rarely the case, and it is not so in the case of risk assessments of energy options.

VI. Other Social and Environmental Risks and Costs of Nuclear Development, Especially Nuclear War

The problems already discussed by no means exhaust the environmental, health and safety risks and costs in, or arising from, the nuclear fuel cycle. The full fuel cycle includes many stages both before and after reactor operation, apart from waste disposal, namely, mining, milling, conversion, enrichment and preparation, reprocessing spent fuel, and transportation of materials. Several of these stages involve hazards. *Unlike the special risks in the nuclear cycle*—of sabotage of plants, of theft of fissionable material, and of the further proliferation of nuclear armaments—*these* hazards have parallels, if not exact equivalents, in other highly polluting methods of generating power, e.g. 'workers in the uranium mining industry sustain "the same risk" of fatal and nonfatal injury as workers in the coal industry.'[14] The problems are not unique to nuclear development.

Other social and environmental problems—though endemic where dangerous large-scale industry operates in societies that are highly inegalitarian and include sectors that are far from affluent—are more intimately linked with the nuclear power cycle. Though pollution is a common and generally undesirable component of large-scale industrial operation, radioactive pollution, such as uranium mining for instance produces, is especially a legacy of nuclear development, and a specially undesirable one, as rectification costs for dead radioactive lands and waterways reveal. Though sabotage is a threat to many large industries, sabotage of a nuclear reactor can have dire consequences, of a different order of magnitude from most industrial sabotage (where core meltdown is not a possibility). Though theft of material from more dubious enterprises such as munitions works can pose threats to populations at large and can assist terrorism, no thefts for allegedly peaceful enterprises pose problems of the same order as theft of fissionable material. No other industry produces materials which so readily permit fabrication into such massive explosives. No other industry is, to sum it up, so vulnerable on so many fronts.

In part to reduce its vulnerability, in part because of its long and continuing association with military activities, the nuclear industry is subject to, and encourages, several practices which (given their scale) run counter to basic features of free and open societies, crucial features such as personal liberty, freedom of association and of expression, and free access to information. These practices include secrecy, restriction of information, formation of special police and guard forces, espionage, curtailment of civil liberties.

> Already operators of nuclear installations are given extraordinary powers, in vetting employees, to investigate the background and activities not only of employees but also of their families and sometimes even of their friends. The installations themselves become armed camps, which especially offends British sensibilities. The U.K. Atomic Energy (Special Constables) Act of 1976 created a special armed force to guard nuclear installations and made it answerable . . . to the U.K. Atomic Energy Authority.[15]

These developments, and worse ones in West Germany and elsewhere, presage along with nuclear development increasingly authoritarian and anti-democratic societies. That nuclear development appears to force such political consequences tells heavily against it. Nuclear development is further indicated politically by the direct connection of nuclear power with nuclear war. It is true that ethical questions concerning nuclear war—for example, whether a nuclear war is justified, or just, under any circumstances, and if so what circumstances—are distinguishable from those concerning nuclear power. Undoubtedly, however, the spread of nuclear power is substantially increasing the technical means for engaging in nuclear war and so, to that extent, the opportunity for, and chances of, nuclear engagement. Since nuclear wars are never accounted positive goods, but are at best the lesser of major evils, nuclear wars are always highly ethically undesirable. The spread of nuclear power accordingly expands the opportunity for, and chances of, highly undesirable consequences. Therefore, what leads to it—nuclear development—is undesirable. This is, in outline, *the argument from nuclear war against large-scale nuclear development.*[16]

VII. Beneath Conflict Arguments:
The Ideological Bases of Nuclear Development

Much as with nuclear war, so given the cumulative case against nuclear development, only one justificatory route remains open, that of appeal to overriding circumstances. That appeal, to be ethically acceptable, must go beyond merely economic considerations. For, as observed, the consigner's action, in the train parable, cannot be justified by purely economistic arguments, such as that his profits would rise, the company or the town would be more prosperous, or by appealing to the fact that some possibly uncomfortable changes would otherwise be needed. So it is also in the nuclear case: the Transfer-limiting principle applies. But suppose now the consigner argues that his action is justified because unless it is taken the town will die. It is by no means clear that even such a justification as this would be sufficient, especially where the risks to the passengers is high, since the case still amounts to one of transfer of costs and risks onto others. But such a conflict situation, where a given course of action, though normally undesirable, is alleged to be the lesser of two evils in a given case, is morally more problematical than cases where the Transfer-limiting principle is clearly violated. Nuclear development is often defended in this way, through *Conflict arguments,* to the effect that even though nuclear development does have undesirable features, nevertheless the alternatives are worse.

Some of the arguments advanced to demonstrate conflict are based on competing commitments to present people, and others on competing obligations to future people, both of which are taken to override the obligations not to impose on the future significant risk of serious harm. The success of such conflict arguments requires the presentation of a genuine and exhaustive set of alternatives (or at least practical alternatives) and showing that the only alternatives to admittedly morally undesirable actions are even more undesirable ones. If some practical alternative which is not morally worse than the action to be justified is overlooked, suppressed, or neglected in the argument (for example, if in the train parable it turns out that the town has another option to starving or to shipping the parcel, namely earning a living in some other way), then the argument is defective and cannot readily be patched. Just such a suppression of practicable alternatives, we shall argue, has occurred in the argument designed to show that the alternatives to the nuclear option are even worse than the option itself.

A first argument, the *Poverty argument,* is that there is an overriding obligation to the poor, both the poor of the third world and the poor of industrialised countries. Failure to develop nuclear energy, it is often claimed, would amount to denying them the opportunity to reach the standard of affluence we currently enjoy and would create unemployment and poverty in the industrialised nations. And this would be worse—a greater evil—than such things as violating the Transfer-limiting principle through nuclear development.

The Poverty argument does not stand up to examination, either for the poor of the industrial countries or for those of the third world. There is good evidence that large-scale nuclear energy will help *increase unemployment and poverty* in the industrial world, through the diversion of very much available capital into an industry which is not only an exceptionally poor provider of direct employment, but also tends to reduce available jobs through encouraging substitution of energy use for labour use. The argument that nuclear energy is needed for the third world is even less convincing. Nuclear energy is both politically and economically inappropriate for the third world, since it requires massive amounts of capital, requires numbers of imported scientists and engineers, creates negligible local employment, and depends for its feasibility upon largely non-existent utility systems—e.g. established electricity transmission systems and back-up facilities, and sufficient electrical appliances to plug into the system. Politically it increases foreign dependence, adds to centralised entrenched power and reduces the chance for change in the oppressive political structures which are a large part of the problem. The fact that nuclear energy is not in the interests of the people of the third world does not of course mean that it is not in the interests of, and wanted (often for military purposes) by, their rulers, the westernised and often military elites in whose interests the economies of these countries are usually organised. But that does not make the poverty argument anything other than what it is: a fraud. There are well-known energy-conserving alternatives and the practical option of developing further alternative energy sources, alternatives some of which offer far better prospects for helping the poor, both in the third world and in industrial countries: coal and other fossil fuels, geothermal, and a range of solar options (including as well as narrowly solar sources, wind, water and tidal power).

Another major argument advanced to show conflict, the *Lights-going-out argument,* appeals to a set of supposedly overriding and competing obligations to future people. We have, it is said, a duty to pass on the immensely valuable things and institutions which our culture has developed. Unless our high-technology, high-energy industrial society is continued and fostered, our valuable institutions and traditions will fall into decay or be swept away. The argument is essentially that without nuclear power, without the continued level of material wealth it alone is assumed to make possible, the lights of our civilization will go out. Future people will be the losers.

The argument does raise important questions about what is valuable in our society and what characteristics are necessary for a good society. But for the most part these large questions can be by-passed. The reason is that the argument adopts an extremely uncritical attitude to present high-technology societies, apparently assuming that they are uniformly and uniquely valuable. It assumes that technological society is unmodifiable, that it cannot be changed in the direction of energy conservation or alternative (perhaps high technology) energy sources without collapse.

These assumptions are all hard to accept. The assumption that technological society's energy patterns are unmodifiable is especially so; after all, it has survived events such as world wars which required major social and technological restructuring and consumption modification. If western society's demands for energy were (contrary to the evidence) totally unmodifiable without collapse, not only would it be committed to a program of increasing destruction, but much of its culture would be of dubious value to future people, who would very likely, as a consequence of this destruction, lack the resource base which the argument assumes to be essential in the case of contemporary society.

The uniformity assumption should certainly be challenged. Since high-technology societies appear not to be uniformly valuable, the central question is, what is necessary to maintain what is *valuable* in such a society? While it may be easy to argue that high energy consumption centrally controlled is necessary to maintain the political and economic status quo of such a society, it is not so easy to argue that it is essential to maintain what is valuable, and it is what is valuable, presumably, that we have a duty to pass on to the future.

The evidence from history is that no very high level of material affluence or energy consumption is needed to maintain what is valuable. There is good reason in fact to believe that a society with much lower energy and resource consumption would better foster what is valuable than our own. But even if a radical change in these directions is independently desirable, it is unnecessary to presuppose such a change in order to see that the assumptions of the Lights-going-out argument are wrong. The consumption of less energy than at present need involve no reduction of well-being: and certainly a large increase over present levels of consumption assumed in the usual economic case for nuclear energy, is quite unnecessary. What the nuclear strategy is really designed to do then is not to prevent the lights going out in western civilisation, but to enable the lights to go on burning all the time—to maintain and even increase the wattage output of the Energy Extravaganza.

In fact there is good reason to think that, far from a high energy consumption society fostering what is valuable, it will, especially if energy is obtained by means of nuclear fission, be positively inimical to it. A society which has become heavily dependent upon a highly centralised, controlled and garrisoned, capital- and expertise-intensive energy source, must be one which is highly susceptible to entrenchment of power, and one in which the forces which control this energy source, whether capitalist or bureaucratic, can exert enormous power over the political system and over people's lives, even more then they do at present. Such a society would almost inevitably tend to become authoritatian and increasingly anti-democratic, as an outcome, among other things, of its response to the threat posed by dissident groups in the nuclear situation.

Nuclear development may thus help in passing on to future generations some of the *worst* aspects of our society—the consumerism, alienation, destruction of nature, and latent authoritarianism—while many valuable aspects, such as the degree of political freedom and those opportunities for personal and collective autonomy which exist, would be lost or diminished: political freedom for example, is a high price to pay for consumerism and energy extravagence.

Again, as in the case of the poverty arguments, clear alternatives, alternative social and political choices, which do not involve such unacceptable consequences, are available. The alternative to the high technology-nuclear option is not a return to the cave, the loss of all that is valuable, but either the adoption of an available alternative such as coal for power or, better, the development of alternative technologies and lifestyles which offer far greater scope for the maintenance and further development of what is valuable in our society than the highly centralised nuclear option. The Lights-going-out argument, as a moral conflict argument, accordingly fails.

Thus this remaining escape route, the appeal to conflict, is, like the appeal to futurity, closed. If we apply, as we have argued we should, the same moral standards to the future that we ought to acknowledge for the present, the conclusion that large-scale nuclear development is a crime against the future is inevitable. Closed also, in the much same way, are the escape routes to other arguments (from reactor meltdown, radiation emissions, etc.) for concluding that nuclear development is unacceptable. In sum, nuclear development is morally unacceptable on *several* grounds.

VIII. Social Options: Shallow and Deep Alternatives

The future energy option that is most often contrasted with nuclear power, namely coal power, while no doubt preferable to nuclear power, is hardly acceptable. For it carries with it the likelihood of serious (air) pollution, and associated phenomena such as acid rain and atmospheric heating, not to mention the despoliation caused by extensive strip mining, all of which will result from its use in meeting very high projected consumption figures. Such an option would, moreover, also violate the Transfer-limiting principle: for it would impose widespread costs on nonbeneficiaries for some concentrated benefits to some profit takers and to some users who do not pay the full costs of production and replacement.

To these main conventional options a third is often added which emphasizes softer and more benign technologies, such as those of solar energy and hydroelectricity. Such softer options—if suitably combined with energy conservation measures (for there are solar ways, as well as nuclear ways, of energy extravagance and of producing unnecessary trivia which answer to no genuine needs)—can avoid the ethical objections to nuclear power. The deeper choice is not however technological, nor merely an individual matter, but social, and involves the restructuring of production away from energy intensive uses and, at a more basic level, a change to nonconsumeristic, less consumptive life-styles and social arrangements.[17] These more fundamental choices between social alternatives, tend to be observed by conventional technologically-oriented discussion of energy options. It is not just a matter of deciding in which way to meet the unexamined goals nuclear development aspires to meet, but also a matter of examining the goals themselves. That is, we are not merely faced with the question of comparing different technologies for meeting some fixed or given demand or level of consumption, and of trying to see how best to meet these; we are also faced, and primarily, with the matter of examining those alleged needs and the cost of a society that creates them.

It is doubtful that any technology, however benign in principle, will be likely to leave a tolerable world for the future if it is expected to meet unbounded and uncontrolled energy consumption and demands. Even more benign technologies may well be used in a way which creates costs for future people and which are likely to result in a deteriorated world being handed on to them. In short, even more benign technologies may lead to violation of the Transmission requirement. Consider, to illustrate, the effect on the world's forests, commonly counted as a solar resource, should they be extensively used for production of methanol or of electricity by woodchipping. While few would object to the use of genuine waste material for energy production, the unrestricted exploitation of forests—whether it goes under the name of "solar energy" or not—to meet ever increasing energy demands could well be the final indignity for the world's already hard-pressed natural forests.

The effects of such additional demands on the maintenance of the forests are often dismissed by the simple expedient of waving around the label "renewable resources". Many forests are in principle renewable, it is true, given a certain (low) rate and kind of exploitation, but in fact there are now very few forestry operations anywhere in the world where the forests are treated as completely renewable in the sense of the renewal of all their values. In many regions too the rate of exploitation which would enable renewal has already been exceeded, so that a total decline is widely thought to be imminent. It certainly has begun in many regions, and many forest types, especially rain-forest types, are now, and rapidly, being lost for the future.[18] The addition of a major further and not readily limitable demand pressure for energy *on top of* the present demands is one which anyone with both a realistic appreciation of the conduct of forestry operations and a concern for the long-term conservation of the forests and remaining natural communities must regard with alarm. The result of massive deforestation for energy purposes, resembling the deforestation of much of Europe at the beginning of the Industrial Revolution, again for energy purposes, could be extensive and devastating erosion in steeper lands and tropical areas, desertification in more arid regions, possible climatic change, and massive impoverishment of natural ecosystems, including enormous loss of natural species. Some of us do not want to pass on, and by the Transmission principles we are not entitled to pass on, a deforested world to the future, any more than we want to pass on one poisoned by nuclear products or polluted by coal products. In short, as the forest situation illustrates, a mere switch to more benign technologies—important though this is—without any more basic structural and social change, is inadequate.

The deeper social option involves challenging and beginning to alter a social structure which promotes consumerism, consumption far beyond genuine needs and an economic structure which encourages increasing use of highly energy-intensive modes of production. The *social change option* tends to be obscured in most discussions of energy options and of how to meet energy needs, in part because it does question underlying values of current social arrangements. The conventional discussion proceeds by taking alleged demand (often conflated with reasonable wants or needs) as unchallengeable, and the issue to be one of which technology can be most profitably employed to meet them. This effectively presents a false choice, and is the result of taking needs and demand as lacking a *social context,* so that the social structure which produces the needs is similarly taken as unchallengeable and unchangeable. The point is readily illustrated. It is commonly argued by representatives of such industries as transportation and petroleum, as for example by Mc-Growth of the XS Consumption Co., that people want deep freezers, air conditioners, power gadgets, ... It would be authoritarian to prevent them from satisfying these wants. Such an *argument from created wants* conveniently ignores the social framework in which such needs and wants arise or are produced. To point to the determination of many such wants at the framework level is *not* however to assume that they are entirely determined at the framework level (e.g. by industrial organisation) or that there is no such thing as individual choice or determination at all. It is to see the social framework as a major factor in determining certain kinds of choices [such as those for jet set travel] and kinds of infrastructure [the priority given to highway construction over mass transit], and to see apparently individual choices made in such matters as being *channelled and directed by a social framework determined largely in the interests of corporate and private profit and advantage*.

The social change option is a hard option, insofar as it will be difficult to implement politically; but it is ultimately the only way of avoiding the passing on of serious costs to future people. And there are other sorts of reasons than *such* ethical ones for taking it: it is the main, indeed the only sort of option, open to those who adopt what is now called a *deep ecological* perspective, as contrasted with a *shallow ecological* outlook which regards the natural world and its nonhuman denizens as not worthwhile in themselves but only of value in as much as they answer back to human interests. The deep ecological perspective is an integral part of the *Alternative Ecological Paradigm* and is incompatible with central theses of the *Dominant Social Paradigm* (which is essentially the ideology of classical and neoclassical economics) and its variants (roughly, what are called State Socialism, and Democratic Socialism).[19] It is incompatible with viewing the natural environment as having value only as a resource, as by and large hostile and wild, calling for humans to tame, control, and manage it, and with the other human-domination-over-nature themes which characterize the Dominant Paradigm and its variants.

The conflict between Alternative and Dominant Paradigms, which is fast increasing, extends of course far beyond attitudes to the natural world, since core values of the Dominant Paradigm such as the merits of unimpeded economic growth and material progress are at stake; the conflict involves fundamental differences over the whole front of economical, political and social arrangements. The conflict underlies much of the nuclear debate, insofar as it is not specifically limited to questions of technological fixes, but takes up the basic ethical issues and the social questions to which they lead.[20] The ethical requirements already defended and applied bring us out, when followed through, on the Alternative side of the paradigm conflict, and accordingly lead to the difficult social change option.

The social changes that the deep alternative requires will be strongly resisted because they mean changes in current social organisation and power structure. To the extent that the option represents some kind of threat to parts of present political and economic arrangements, it is not surprising that official energy option discussion proceeds by misrepresenting and often obscuring it. But difficult as it is to suitably alter "the system," especially one with such far-reaching effects on the prevailing power structure, it is imperative to try: we are all on the nuclear train.

Notes

1. This paper is a condensation of an early version of our 'Nuclear power—ethical, social, and political dimensions' (ESP for short, available from the authors), which in turn grew out of Routley (i.e. the work so referred to in the reference list). For help with the condensation we are very considerably indebted to the editors.

In the condensation, we simplify the structure of the argument and suppress underlying political and ideological dimensions (for example, the large measure of responsiblity of the USA for spreading nuclear reactors around the world, and thereby in enhancing the chances of nuclear disasters, including nuclear war). We also considerably reduce a heavy load of footnotes and references designed and needed to help make good many of our claims. Further, in order to contain references to a modest length, reference to primary sources has often been replaced by reference through secondary sources. Little difficulty should be encountered however in tracing fuller references through secondary sources or in filling out much important background material from work cited herein. For example, virtually all the data cited in sections I and VII is referenced in Routley. At worst ESP can always be consulted.

2. All but the last line of the quote is drawn from Goodin, p. 417; the last line is from the Fox Report, p. 6.

While it is unnecessary to know much about the nuclear fuel cycle in order to consider ethical and social dimensions of nuclear power, it helps to know a little. The basics are presented in many texts, e.g. Nader & Abbotts, Gyorgy. Of course in order to assess fully reports as to such important background and stage-setting matters as the likelihood of a core meltdown of (lightwater) reactors, much more information is required. For many assessment purposes however, some knowledge of economic fallacies and decision theory is at least as important as knowledge of nuclear technology.

3. Naturally the effect on humans is not the only factor that has to be taken into account in arriving at moral assessments. Nuclear radiation, unlike most ethical theories, does not confine its scope to human life and welfare. But since the harm nuclear development may afflict on nonhuman life, for example, can hardly *improve* its case, it suffices if the case against it can be made out solely in terms of its effects on human life in the conventional way.

For reference to and a brief discussion of (human-oriented) simulation models see Goodin, p. 428.

4. The Opportunity-cost argument is also defective in other respects. It presupposes not merely the (mistaken) reductions involved in the contraction of the ethical domain to the economic; it also presupposes that the proper methods for decision which affect the future, such as that of energy choice, apply discounting. But, as Goodin argues, more appropriate decision rules do not allow discounting.

5. This is *one* of the reasons why expected utility theory, roughly cost-benefit analysis with probability frills, is inadequate as a decision method in such contexts.

6. Apparent exceptions to the principle such as taxation (and redistribution of income generally) vanish when wealth is construed (as it has to be if taxation is to be properly justified) as at least partly a social asset unfairly monopolised by a minority of the population. Examples such as that of motoring dangerously do not constitute counterexamples to the principle; for one is not morally entitled to so motor.

7. For details, and as to how the official analyses become arguments against nuclear development when some attempt is made to take the ignored costs into account, see Shrader-Frechette, p. 55 ff.

8. See Routley, p. 160.

9. For much further discussion of the points of the preceding two paragraphs, see Shrader-Frechette, p. 35 ff.; and also Nader & Abbotts.

10. Most of the reactors in the world are of this type; see Gyorgy.

11. See Shrader-Frechette, chapter 4.

12. See Shrader-Frechette. A worthwhile initial view of the shortcomings of the Rassmussen report may be reached by combining the critique in Shrader-Frechette with that in Nader & Abbotts.

13. There are variations on Ai and Aii which multiply costs against numbers such as probabilities. In this way risks, construed as probable costs, can be taken into account in the assessment. (Alternatively, risks may be assessed through such familiar methods as insurance).

A principle varying Aii, and formulated as follows:

Aii'. A is ethically acceptable if (for some B) a includes no more risks than b and b is socially accepted,

was the basic ethical principle in terms of which the Cluff Lake Board of Inquiry recently decided that nuclear power development in Saskatchewan is ethically acceptable: see *Cluff Lake Board of Inquiry Final Report,* Department of Environment, Government of Saskatchewan, 1978, p. 305 and p. 288. In this report, A is nuclear power and B is other activities clearly accepted by society as alternative power sources. In other applications B has been taken as cigarette smoking, motoring, mining and even the Vietnam war (!).

The points made in the text do not exhaust the objections to principles Ai—Aii'. The principles are certainly ethically substantive, since an *ethical* consequence cannot be deduced from nonethical premisses, but they have an inadmissible *conventional* character. For look at the origin of B : B may be socially accepted though it is no longer socially acceptable, or though its social acceptibility is no longer so clearcut and it would not have been socially accepted if as much as is now known had been known when it was introduced. What is required in Aii', for instance, for the argument to begin to look convincing is that B is 'ethically accepta*ble*' rather than 'socially accept*ed*'. But even with the amendments the principles are invalid, for the reasons given in the text, and others.

It is not disconcerting that principles of this type do not work. It would be sad to see yet another area lost to the experts, ethics to actuaries.

14. See Shrader-Frechette, p. 15.

15. Goodin p. 433.

16. The argument is elaborated in ESP.

17. For some of the more philosophically important material on alternative nonconsumeristic social arrangements and lifestyles, see work cited in V. and R. Routley, 'Social theories, self management and environmental problems' in Mannison et al, where a beginning is made on working out *one* set of alternatives, those of a pluralistic anarchism.

18. The imperilled situation of the world's tropical rainforests is explained in Barney and Myers, though the real reasons for this elude them; the reasons are untangled in R. and V. Routley 'World rainforest destruction—the social causes' (available from the authors). See also G. O. Barney, The Global 2000 Report to the President of the U.S. Entering the 21st Century. Volume I and Volume II (New York: Pergamon Press, 1980).

19. For a fuller account of the Dominant Social Paradigm and its rival, the Alternative Environmental Paradigm, see Cotgrove and Duff, especially the table on p. 341 which encapsulates the main assumptions of the respective paradigms; compare also Catton and Dunlap, especially p. 33. Contemporary variants on the Dominant Social Paradigm are considered in ESP.

The shallow/deep contrast as applied to ecological positions, which is an important component of the paradigm conflict, was introduced by Naess. For further explanation of the contrast and of the larger array of ecological positions into which it fits, see R. and V. Routley, 'Human chauvinism and environmental ethics' in Mannison et al, and the references there cited, especially to Rodman's work.

20. The more elaborate argument of ESP sets the nuclear debate in the context of paradigm conflict. But it is also argues that, even within assumptions framework of the Dominant Social Paradigm and its variants, (1) Nuclear development is not the rational choice among energy options. The main argument put up for nuclear development within the framework of the dominant paradigm is an *Economic growth argument*. It is the following version of the Lights-going-out argument (with economic growth duly standing in for material wealth, and for what is valuable!):— Nuclear power is necessary to sustain economic growth. Economic growth is desirable (for all the usual reasons, e.g. to increase the size of the pie, to postpone redistribution problems, etc.). Therefore nuclear power is desirable. The first premiss is part of US energy policy (see Shrader-Frechette, p. 111), and the second premiss is supplied by standard economics textbooks. But both premisses are defective, the second because what is valuable in economic growth can be achieved by (not without growth but) *selective* economic growth, which jettisons the heavy social and environmental costs carried by unqualified economic growth. More to the point, since the second premiss is an assumption of the Dominant Paradigm, the first premiss (or rather an appropriate and less vulnerable restatement of it) fails even by Dominant Paradigm standards. For of course nuclear power is not *necessary* given that there are other, perhaps costlier alternatives. The premiss usually defended is some elaboration of the premiss: Nuclear power is the economically best way to sustain economic growth, 'economically best' being filled out as 'most efficient', 'cheapest', 'having the most favourable benefit-cost ratio', etc. Unfortunately for the argument, and for nuclear development schemes, nuclear power is none of these things *decisively* (unless a good deal of economic cheating—easy to do—is done).

(2) On proper Dominant Paradigm accounting, nuclear choices should generally be rejected, both as private utility investments and as public choices.

Nuclear development is not economically viable but has been kept going, not by clear economic viability, but by massive subsidization of several types (discussed in Shrader-Flechette, Gyorgy and Nader & Abbotts).

Even on variants of the Dominant Paradigm, nuclear development is not justified, as consideration of decision theory methods will reveal:

(3) Whatever reasonable decision rule is adopted, the nuclear choice is rejected, as the arguments of Goodin on alternative decision rules help to show.

What sustains the nuclear juggernaut is not the Dominant Paradigm or its variants, but contemporary corporate capitalism (or its state enterprise image) and associated third world imperialism, as the historical details of nuclear development both in developed countries and in less developed countries makes plain (for main details, see Gyorgy p. 307 ff.). And the practices of contemporary corporate capitalism and associated imperialism are not acceptable by the standards of either of the Paradigms or their variants: they are certainly not ethically acceptable.

Suggested Readings

Works especially useful for further investigation of the ethical issues raised by nuclear development are indicated with an asterisk (*).

S. Cotgrove and A. Duff, "Environmentalism, middle-class radicalism and politics', *Sociological Review* 28(2) (1980), 333–51.

W. R. Catton, Jr., and R. E. Dunlap, 'A new ecological paradigm for post exuberant sociology' *American Behavioral Scientist* 24 (1980). 15–47.

Fox Report: *Ranger Uranium Environmental Inquiry First Report,* Australian Government Publishing Service, Canberra, 1977.

*R. E. Goodin, "No moral nukes', *Ethics* 90 (1980), 417–49.

*A. Gyorgy and friends, *No Nukes: everyone's guide to nuclear power,* South End Press, Boston, Mass., 1979.

*D. Mannison, M. McRobbie and R. Routley (editors), *Enironmental Philosophy,* RSSS, Australian National University, 1980.

N. Myers, *The Sinking Ark,* Pergamon Press, Oxford, 1979.

R. Nader and J. Abbotts, *The Menace of Atomic Energy,* Outback Press, Melbourne, 1977.

*K. S. Shrader-Frechette, *Nuclear Power and Public Policy,* Reidel, Dordrecht, 1980.

R. and V. Routley, 'Nuclear energy and obligations to the future', *Inquiry* 21 (1978), 133–79.

chapter six

Future Generations

MARY ANNE WARREN

Most moral problems concern the rights and obligations of presently existing persons. Our most important moral concepts, such as justice, equality and respect for human rights, have developed primarily in this context. It is therefore not surprising that conceptual problems arise when we attempt to extend those notions in order to determine our moral obligations towards human beings who do not yet exist. Nevertheless, most reflective people do believe that we have moral obligations to future people, i.e. those who *will* be conceived and born.

As individuals, it appears that we have obligations to whatever children we may have in the future. In our society, parents are legally obligated to provide for the material and emotional well-being of their offspring; and most would agree that there is a moral obligation upon potential parents not to have children under circumstances which would predictably prevent the latter from enjoying an at least minimally satisfactory human existence. While the obligation not to procreate under such circumstances cannot be construed as an obligation *to a particular future person*— since the fulfillment of the obligation would prevent the existence of that future person—nevertheless the commonsense and humanitarian view is that there *is* such a moral obligation; and we would normally say that it is an obligation to future generations.

Common sense and humanitarian intuition also seem to indicate that we *as a society* have moral obligations to the unborn generations of human beings in both the near and distant future, assuming of course that there will be such future generations. These presumably include the obligation not to either pollute the land and water or exhaust the nonrenewable resources of the planet to the extent that the quality of life is badly eroded in the future. Indeed even a *slight* erosion of the average quality of life for future generations might be held to be morally unacceptable, given that there are already hundreds of millions of people who exist in a condition of chronic and extreme deprivation.

In what follows, I will examine the moral case for limiting population growth through birth control, and argue that we ought to limit our own birth rate, not just for our own good (though that is *another* valid reason in many cases), but also out of concern for the well-being of future generations of human beings. I will also argue that the encouragement of *voluntary* means of birth limitations is generally (and perhaps always) preferable to the use of *coercive* means. I will consider the basis for the claim that we can, without logical contradiction, have moral obligations with respect to future persons; and I will examine some of the arguments of philosophers who believe that although we do have obligations to future potential persons, these are such as to morally *preclude*, rather than *require*, limiting our birth rate. Finally I will examine some of the objections to contraception and abortion as methods of birth control. I will argue that these objections do not suffice to show that either contraception or abortion is generally immoral, or that legal and other barriers to voluntary access to contraception and abortion are justified.

1. *The Moral Case for Birth Control*

As I have suggested, it seems only reasonable to believe that we have a moral obligation not to leave our successors a severely impoverished world, one with exhausted resources, poisoned lands and waters, and no escape from poverty for huge numbers of people. But if we believe this, then we must also believe that we ought to limit our own fertility; for if we do not, we are almost certain to produce a world of just this sort.

There are, as the contemporary Canadian philosopher Jan Narveson points out, two distinct questions here: *What do we owe to the members of future generations, however many of them there may be?* and *How many people ought there ideally to be in the future?[1]* Both questions are fraught with empirical and conceptual difficulties, and the interaction between the two questions increases the difficulty. Any answer to the first implies a corresponding answer to the second, and vice versa. Thus, if we were to deny that we have any obligations at all to future generations, then we would have no reason to adopt a birth limitation policy on moral grounds, unless it proved necessary to protect the rights of presently existing persons. On the other hand, if we believe that we owe it to future generations at least to try to leave them an unspoiled world, then it is difficult to avoid the conclusion that we ought to strive at least for zero population growth, and probably for a *reduction* of population in many parts of the world.

Nevertheless, this conclusion is vigorously resisted in many quarters. Socialists frequently argue that there is no worldwide population problem, but only a problem of the *unjust distribution* of resources; and that if the world's resources were equitably shared between nations and classes they could actually support a much larger world population. Third-world and minority groups often perceive birth-control programs—even those which are wholly noncoercive—as aimed particularly at *them*, and hence "genocidal." And, given that underprivileged groups typically do have a higher birth rate than privileged ones, as well as a real or perceived interest in maintaining it, their concern is understandable. There are also religious and political groups, notably Roman Catholics and "pro-life" groups, who object not to population limitation per se, but to some of the *means* which appear pragmatically necessary to achieve it, e.g., contraception and abortion.[2] Finally, there are those who object to population limitation on the grounds that increasing the number of human beings who exist (at an at least minimally satisfactory level of happiness) is good in itself, indeed obligatory, and that to limit the number of individuals who are born is in some way to wrong *those who might have been born,* in the absence of those limitations.[3]

For all of these reasons, talk about population limitation through increased birth control is politically unpopular. The need for conservation and avoiding environmental pollution is relatively uncontroversial—though many still feel free to ignore it where economic considerations are involved. Further, the need to limit population growth, in order that future generations not inherit a depleted world, is often subordinated to the supposedly inalienable right of individuals or couples to determine the size of their own families.[4]

Taken to extremes, this last attitude amounts to an invidious bias against the interests of future generations, in favor of (some of) those now living. I would argue that, while it may sometimes be in the real or apparent interests of women or couples to have (a large number of) children, their right to do so is sometimes overridden by (1) the severe and predictable bad effects of population increase on present and future persons other than the projected (extra) children, or (2) the predictable misery of the children themselves, should they be born under such adverse circumstances. Insofar as these conditions obtain today—as they do, throughout most of the world, even in the most privileged classes and societies—those who are alive now have a moral obligation to be more restrained in their exercise of the right to reproduce than they might otherwise wish to be. To deny this is to ignore one of the most crucial factors which will, inevitably, affect the well-being of future generations.

Of course, those who deny that the present generation has a moral obligation to restrict its fertility do not necessarily renounce *all* concern for the rights and well-being of future generations. It might be argued that some environmental issues can be dealt with entirely in terms of Narveson's first question, i.e. What do we owe to the members of future generations, however many of them there may be? Take, for instance, the issue of nuclear power. Even if most of *us,* those who are alive now, were willing to run the risks to health and environment posed by the use of nuclear power, we would still have to ask whether it is fair to future generations to inflict these risks upon *them.* Nuclear-power plants increase the radiation exposure of all those who live and work in or around them, thus increasing the risk of genetic abnormality for all of their descendants. They also generate radioactive waste products, which will remain toxic for hundreds of thousands of years; and there are no assurances that any currently feasible method of disposing of those wastes will render them harmless for anything like that long.

Can we say, therefore, that we owe it to future generations *not* to go on using nuclear power, regardless of whether or not effective population control measures are implemented? Perhaps. On the other hand, if we must assume a steady escalation of world population, then we must also assume a steadily increasing demand for energy; otherwise a satisfactory quality of life will neither be achieved where it is lacking, nor maintained where it exists at present. If energy usage is to be increased, then the only apparent alternative to the expanded use of nuclear power is the continued exploitation of fossil fuels. Not even the most optimistic experts believe that the earth's supply of petroleum will last longer than another generation or two, at the present rate of use; and coal, though more abundant, is more environmentally damaging both in its use and in its extraction, and will at any rate be exhausted within a century or two after the end of the petroleum supply is reached. So it seems that an *expanding* future population can be spared either the risk of nuclear contamination or the exhaustion of fossil fuels, but not both.

No doubt some would argue that these two unattractive alternatives do not really exhaust our choices. It is conceivable that an all-out push toward the use of solar power, synthetic fuels, energy conservation, recycling, and, on the political level, a more equitable system of distribution, could enable us to support a growing population, worldwide, without *either* accelerated nuclear development or the rapid depletion of fossil fuels. But it is doubtful that such heroic efforts could succeed in the long run, even if they could be achieved in the short run. Indeed, even to maintain a minimally adequate standard of life for *as many people as presently exist* may well prove impossible for future generations. At present there are estimated to be over eight hundred million people who exist in what Robert McNamara, then President of the World Bank, described as "absolute poverty." The absolute poor suffer chronic—and sometimes acute—malnutrition, a staggeringly high infant mortality rate, and a greatly lowered life expectancy. In McNamara's words, they struggle to survive "in a set of squalid and degraded circumstances almost beyond the power of our sophisticated imaginations and privileged circumstances to conceive."[5]

It may be argued that in spite of these facts the present worldwide level of food production is not really inadequate. If the *distribution* of food between rich and poor nations were somehow equalized, and if all the food which is suitable for human consumption were in fact consumed by humans (rather than being fed to meat-producing animals or to pets, for instance), malnutrition could probably be eliminated with no reduction in population size.[6]

We must remember, however, that the worldwide level of food production may be lowered in the future by a number of actual or possible developments, including global climatic changes, the increasing cost of petroleum-based fertilizers, and the degradation or destruction of agricultural land through improper use. (For instance, the U.S. Department of Agriculture reports that already one-third of this country's arable topsoil has been lost to wind and water erosion due to cultivation, and that the rate of loss is increasing.[7]) Improved agricultural methods *may* suffice to offset such losses, for a while, if we are lucky, thus enabling us to maintain the present worldwide level of food production. It would, however, be irrationally optimistic to hold that food production will be able to keep pace with a *continuously expanding* world population, for any extended period of time.

If this is true, then it follows that even the most just and efficient worldwide system of food production and distribution (were such a system miraculously to be established) *could* not provide all of the members of future generations with even a minimally satisfactory standard of life, *if rapid population growth were to continue*. Thus, if we owe it to them to do what we can to ensure them a reasonable chance for a reasonably good life, as opposed to one of absolute poverty for many or most of them, then we owe it to them to limit our own fertility to the extent necessary to make this possible. We should do this responsibly, voluntarily, and with due respect for the procreative rights of existing individuals, but we should do it. Birth limitation is no substitute for economic justice, but neither is the struggle for economic justice a substitute for birth limitation; both are essential, if we are to fulfill our obligations to future generations.

2. *Voluntary vs. Coercive Means of Limiting Population Growth*

If the case for population limitations is as powerful as I have made it sound, then why is there so much opposition to it? I have mentioned some of the political and religious sources of pronatalist (i.e. anti-birth-limitation) sentiment. The most basic reason, however, is probably just that most people continue to *want* to have children; and often they want to have more than the one, or possibly two, which we could each afford to have without necessarily contributing to overpopulation. This desire may be economic in origin (e.g., support in old age); or it may be based on the anticipation of personal satisfaction or social status resulting from parenthood. Some would argue that this desire for (more than one's "fair share" of) children is so strong, in so many people, and so certain to remain that way, that nothing short of coercive birth control—i.e., legally imposed restrictions on childbearing—will be sufficient to bring the birth rate down to an appropriate level.[8] But this conclusion is premature; there is ample reason to doubt the existence of a natural and uncontrollable human desire for *many* offspring, such as would necessitate coercive population-control programs.

Among the evidences that people can and perhaps will fundamentally change their attitudes toward having (more than just a few) children are two frequently noted facts. First, there is a rather general negative correlation between birth rate and economic status; in other words, poor people tend to have more children than rich ones. Second, birth rates tend to fall to the degree that women are liberated from the patriarchal family—that is, from the social system which defines the bearing and rearing of children as their primary social role, while assigning the role of provider, protector and "head of the family" to the father.

These two facts about birth rates are closely related. Women who have many children do not do so because of some blind maternal instinct. More often, the reasons include the poverty which makes children essential for economic security; the lack of access to contraception or abortion; or social roles and attitudes which, in the words of the nineteenth-century English feminist Harriet Taylor Mill, "make imperative on women that they shall be either mothers or nothing."[9]

On the other hand, women of the privileged economic classes, and more generally speaking women who have a significant social role apart from marriage and mother-hood, have usually found ways to free themselves from the burdens of too-frequent motherhood. In preliterate societies, offspring often are more or less deliberately spaced at four-or-five-year intervals, by means of taboos on marital intercourse (e.g. during the lactation period), polygamous sexual arrangements, or the use of contra-ceptives, abortion, or infanticide. The People's Republic of China has greatly low-ered its birth rate, through the full integration of women into the public labor force, improved access to contraception, and an ethic which favors late marriage and a good deal of sexual abstinence both before and within marriage.[10] A birth rate which is kept voluntarily low is almost always an indication that women have significant social roles and sources of status apart from motherhood, and therefore can neither afford nor effectively be forced to submit to incessant childbearing.

It would seem to follow, then, that where birth rates are high they may be expected to decline in proportion to two factors: (1) the improvement of material conditions and material security for the impoverished segments of society; and (2) the integra-tion of women into all aspects of economic, social and political life. Since these two goals are themselves necessary, on independent moral grounds (such as simple justice), there should be little objection to pursuing them in the belief that they will *also* result in a voluntarily lowered birth rate. Obviously, the general availability of contraception (and probably also of abortion) is a necessary condition for significant birth-rate reduction—at least short of a revolution in sexual mores in which hetero-sexuality is replaced, as the social norm, by homosexuality, sexual abstinence, or autoeroticism. We will presently consider some of the moral objections to making contraception and abortion available to all; but I would argue that this too is a goal which is both necessary on independent moral grounds, and instrumentally valuable as a means of lowering the birth rate.

Thus, there are a number of ways of facilitating the wholly voluntary reduction of birth rates, ways which do not involve any legal limitation upon the individual right to reproduce. Such means should certainly be preferred to those which involve legal or other kinds of coercion. The forms of compulsory birth control which have been (more or less surreptitiously) practiced by some members of the medical profession in this country, notably the involuntary or semivoluntary sterilization of poor women, are arguably unjust. It might be thought that laws could be framed which would place only *just and universal* restrictions upon the right to reproduce, ones which would be administered in a nonsexist, nonracist and nonclassist fashion. But I think that a little reflection will show that any legally enforced limitation on reproduction would inevitably be sexist, classist, and—in this country at least—racist, in its implications.

The racist and classist implications of a mandatory birth-limitation policy arise not only from the very real danger that the policy-makers might operate under overtly racist and/or classist assumptions (e.g. that large families should be encouraged among the white and prosperous, but discouraged among the nonwhite and the economically disadvantaged), but also from the fact that even a class- and race-blind program of mandatory birth control would have its harshest impact upon those groups which generally have the highest birth rate to begin with—the poor and the non-white. If the higher fertility rate of these groups were merely a sign of moral irresponsibility, as some people tend to assume, then perhaps authoritarian intervention could be justified. But if it is a conscious and not clearly irrational response to poverty and oppression—as it certainly is, at least to some extent—then there may be inherent injustice in imposing upon low-income or minority groups fertility limitations which will be felt as only a slight burden by the mostly-white-middle-class majority, but which will be a severe and bitterly resented burden for them.

The sexist implications of mandatory birth control should also be apparent. Any legal limitation on reproduction would have to be directed primarily towards women, rather than towards men, or couples. If any *couple* could legally have two children, then any *individual* could have as many as s/he wanted, simply by changing partners. And it would be extremely difficult to enforce a limitation on the number of offspring a *man* could have, since it is often difficult to determine just how many children a man *does* have. Men's reproductive rights therefore could not be effectively limited without limiting women's as well. But consider the practical implications for women of being legally limited to, for instance, two children. Will they be involuntarily sterilized after their second birth? Will third pregnancies be subject to compulsory termination?[11] Will women who are suspected of being pregnant when they have already had their quota of children be arrested and forcibly subjected to medical examination? Will all women be subjected to contraceptive chemicals, with the antidote to restore fertility available only from the state?

Unless such grossly coercive methods were used, compulsory birth limitation would probably not be effective. But would it be just to subject women to such *further* invasions of their privacy and autonomy, in the context of a sexist society which already tends in many ways to deprive women of the control of their own bodies? The continued prevalence of rape and other forms of violence against women, and the glorification of the rape mentality in sadistic pornography and certain popular horror films (in which crazed killers, usually male, pursue terrified victims, usually female) are just one index of the degree to which sexist attitudes towards women continue to dominate our own culture. Another is the persistence of paternalistic and invidiously stereotyped attitudes towards women among medical professionals, a group which would presumably be directly involved in the implementation of mandatory restrictions upon motherhood.[12] In such a context it is unlikely that mandatory birth control would be carried out in a manner consistent with women's moral and constitutional rights, e.g. their rights to privacy, autonomy, and bodily integrity.

Furthermore, even if nonracist, nonsexist and nonclassist mandatory birth-control laws could somehow be enacted, they would be apt to prove ineffective. Such laws might only drive the reproductive process underground; pregnancy, birth and even childbearing would become frequently-clandestine activities, conducted (like illegal abortion) in an atmosphere of fear, intimidation, and extortion; and often at the cost of the lives and health of the women and children who would be deprived of proper medical care as a result of such laws. The uniformly dismal results of the legal prohibition of the use of alcohol and other recreational drugs, and of prostitution, homosexuality, and abortion, ought to have taught us that the state is highly ineffective in preventing people from doing certain things which they (1) deeply want or need to do; (2) have traditionally done; (3) believe—with a considerable degree of reason and justice—that it is their *right* to do; and (4) can continue to do, more or less clandestinely. Of course, reproduction would not be forbidden *altogether* under the kind of mandatory birth control which we are considering, as was, say, the use and sale of alcoholic beverages under Prohibition. But neither will it merely be regulated and taxed as alcohol is now. *"Excessive"* procreation *will* be legally prohibited, on this option. This new prohibition might prove to be no more successful than any of the others have been; and it might have even worse consequences.

But, it might be pointed out, there is a difference between prohibiting excessive reproduction and prohibiting the enjoyment of certain drugs or forms of sexual behavior. In the latter case, so it can be argued, there is no serious violation of moral rights inherent in the activity to be prohibited. Voluntary drug use, or homosexual acts between consenting individuals, or the contact between a prostitute and his or her customer, cannot readily be shown to violate anyone's moral rights. Thus, they are unlike, say, shoplifting, traffic-light running, burglary, or other hard-to-eradicate crimes which *do* (always or sometimes) have clearly identifiable victims. Nonparticipants may *disapprove* of so-called "victimless crimes" such as these, but they are not as a rule *harmed* by these activities, in any manner which would justify their claiming to be legally protected from the behavior of the participants. (Where they *are* so harmed, e.g. when an influx of prostitutes into a business neighborhood drives away the customers of *other* business, then of course they have the right to complain; but what they should complain of is not the *existence* of prostitution, but rather the place and manner of its performance. After all, the customers of the other businesses might be equally alienated by a crowd of aggressive religious proselytizers in the area, or a persistent but inept street musician.)

Excessive reproduction, on the other hand, in the context of an already overpopulated or soon-to-be-overpopulated world, is an activity which is *unavoidably* harmful to others, to both one's own and future generations. Might not the imperative need to reduce the birth rate, in societies where this is crucial to maintaining a minimally decent standard of living, override the practical difficulties and hardships that would result from compulsory birth limitation? Might it not also override the apparent injustice of the fact that the impact of such compulsion would fall most heavily on women and the poor? These are difficult questions, ones which have no simple answers. Two points must be stressed, however.

In the first place, the United States is certainly very far from a situation in which a decent life for present and future citizens cannot be maintained except through compulsory birth control. Our birth rate has been declining for some time, and may well be brought to or below the zero population growth level *without* legal coercion—provided that access to contraception and abortion is expanded rather than limited, and provided that continued progress is made towards sexual equality and economic security for the least well-off. So when we speak of hypothetical cases in which disaster could be avoided only by involuntary birth control, we must remember that our own case is not of this kind—yet.

In the second place, we must remember that those parts of the world which presently appear to be suffering from overpopulation (e.g., India, Bangladesh) are precisely those in which the three crucial conditions for voluntary birth-rate reduction—i.e. a reasonable degree of economic security for all, the liberation of women, and adequate access to birth control and abortion—have not been met. Thus, we cannot say that voluntary reduction of the birth rate is impossible in these societies, but only that the social, economic, political, or religious obstacles to it remain great. Indeed, these same factors—e.g., extreme economic need, the domestic role of women, and the lack of adequate access to birth control and abortion—would also make the implementation of *compulsory* birth-control programs extremely difficult. So, here too, it would seem best to promote a lowered birth rate through the types of social reforms which have been shown to lead to *voluntary* birth-rate reductions. I am certainly not suggesting that this will be *easy,* or even pragmatically *possible* in every case—only that it is a preferable first step to the use of legal coercion.

3. The Use of Economic Incentives

The two alternatives we have thus far considered are not exhaustive of the means which societies may use to limit population growth. Governments may also offer positive or negative economic incentives to women or couples to have fewer children, or remove current economic or other incentives for having (more) children. For instance taxation, social security and other legal arrangements could be redesigned to give greater benefits to persons with no or few children, and/or to penalize those who have more than a certain number of children.[13] There are two moral objections to economic-incentive programs of this type, each of which is serious but neither of which is necessarily fatal.

The first problem is that any program of economic incentives to limit family size would be apt to place hardships on the children of large families, as well as on their parents. Unless the state itself takes over the economic support of all children, there can be no sharp distinction between economic benefits offered or denied to *parents,* and economic benefits offered or denied to their *children.* Thus, any economic penalties or disincentives which are inflicted on too-prolific parents will also tend to have an adverse effect on their children; and it seems clearly unjust to penalize children for their parents' decision to have (too many of) them. Any program of economic or other incentives to family limitation, to be morally acceptable, would have to avoid such consequences; and it is difficult to see how such consequences *could* be avoided unless the incentives were too small to have much effect anyway.

Perhaps a carefully designed economic-incentive program could avoid this first problem. But it would still have to face the charge that any use of economic incentives to encourage population control, in a class society characterized by great economic inequality, discriminates against the poor. In effect, it exploits their poverty in order to limit their reproductive freedom, in a way in which that freedom of the rich could not similarly be limited. There is an analogy between such a policy and the current policy of the federal government which refuses to pay the medical costs of so-called "elective" abortions (i.e., all those that involve pregnancies which do not directly threaten the woman's life, and which are not the result of *immediately reported* incest or rape). This means that many women will be denied access to medically safe, legal abortions, because they are too poor to pay for them. The lawmakers may deny that there is any *intention* of discriminating unjustly against poor women; but, as with the proverbial law which forbids both paupers and rich people from sleeping under bridges, the injustice lies in the obvious *effects,* rather than the explicit *intent* of the law.[14]

Again, it may be argued that it is possible to design incentive programs to promote population limitation which will avoid this particular type of injustice. It is possible that the right combination of progressive tax penalties for the wealthy, and welfare incentives for the poor, could distribute the burdens and benefits of population control in a way that is fair to both. Yet such a program would still be apt to unjustly penalize the children of large families.·

It is very hard to imagine a program of economic incentives which would not be unjust in at least one of these two ways. Consequently, I think that population-control programs of this sort, like the direct legal prohibition of e.g. third or fourth children, should be contemplated only as a last resort, when it is perfectly clear that strictly voluntary reductions in the birth rate will be impossible, or inadequate to preserve a decent life for present and future generations. And I have argued that this is not yet the case, even in those parts of the world which are apparently already overpopulated.

4. *Future Persons and Moral Rights*

There is, then, a powerful moral case for population control, though not for the coercive prevention of births. Tragically, there are also powerful social, economic, political and religious forces which mitigate against voluntary reductions in the birth rate. But it is time to consider the moral and philosophical objections to population limitation. Opposition to population control is often based on philosophical convictions which cast doubt on the basic claim which I am making, i.e. that we have a moral obligation not to reproduce at a rate which will result in overpopulation and misery for future generations.

Perhaps the most basic philosophical objection to this claim is that it appears to be in some way incoherent or logically peculiar to hold that we have moral obligations *towards persons who do not yet exist.* And even if it is admitted that we have *some* obligations towards future persons, it might still be thought that the claim that we owe it to them to *limit their numbers* is incoherent, or just false.

Those who doubt that we have *any* moral obligations with respect to future generations may doubt this because they are troubled by a number of peculiar features about the relationship between ourselves and not-yet-existent people. First, there is the fact that future people (by definition) do not exist *now.* It may seem odd to claim that we have moral obligations to *presently non-existent people.* Second, the very existence (in the future) of future generations is in doubt. Not only do we not know whether or not there will be human beings one hundred or one thousand years from now, or how many of them there will be, but the existence or nonexistence of future persons, as well as *which particular individuals* will exist in the future, is to some extent contingent upon our own actions. Either the *contingency* of future generations or our *ignorance* about them might be thought to defeat any claim that we have specific moral obligations regarding them. I would argue, on the contrary, that, as important as these facts are, they do not show that we lack moral obligations with respect to future generations.

That future persons do not exist *yet* constitutes what the contemporary American philosopher Gregory Kavka calls the "futurity problem."[15] Future persons do not exist *now* and therefore cannot (now) have any obligations to *us,* a fact which causes problems for those who hold that all moral obligations are ultimately contractual in origin, i.e., that they are based on some sort of actual or implicit agreement amongst the interested parties, an agreement which recognizes and protects their common interests. For we cannot negotiate mutually advantageous contracts with future generations; and we may not find it to be in our interest to protect *their* interests. Thus, on at least some versions of the contract theory it would follow that we owe them nothing. I will leave aside the question of whether the contract theory can be modified so as to cover what I think are our obligations to future people, and propose instead another way of understanding the basis for those obligations.

I would suggest that the source of our moral obligations to future generations is the simple fact that *we are in a position to materially affect their well-being.* Indeed, whatever we do, in reproducing or not, in saving or consuming resources, etc., our actions will have an impact on the interests of those who exist after us. Intuitively, there would seem to be no valid excuse for refusing to take into account, in our moral deliberation, the predictable and significant deleterious effects of our actions on the lives of future persons—even though we do not know *who* those future victims will be. As Kavka points out,

> Location in space is not a morally relevant feature of a person, determining his worthiness for consideration or aid. Why should location in time be any different?[16]

Why, for instance, should it be considered morally less culpable to cause the *foreseeable* death or injury of persons not yet born—e.g. through the culpably negligent disposal of nuclear wastes—than it is to do the same thing to persons who are alive now? In either case the question of moral responsibility turns on the *predictability* (and avoidability) of the fatal result, not on when, where or to whom it occurs. Anyone who acts in the knowledge that someday some innocent person or persons will probably be severely and unnecessarily harmed as a result of that action may be held to be morally responsible for those harms.

Suppose, for instance, that a nineteenth-century terrorist had planted a time bomb in the heart of Manhattan, setting it to explode in the year 2000. If it does so, killing many people, will we be apt to exonerate the terrorist of moral responsibility on the grounds that she knew that the action would harm no one who was alive at the time of the action? Obviously not. The terrorist would be just as guilty of deliberate and wrongful killing (i.e. murder) as if she had set the bomb to explode in ten years, or ten minutes. Nor does the fact that the terrorist, like the nuclear pollutor, cannot know the particular victims of her actions in any way exonerate her. So long as she knew that her action was likely to cause the death or injury of innocent people, she can be held morally responsible. It is true that placing such a very long fuse on the time bomb introduces some additional elements of uncertainty. The terrorist could not know with absolute certainty that there will be people in Manhattan (or even on the planet) in the year 2000; neither can we, for that matter. But she could certainly know that it is quite *probable* that there will be; and this is enough to establish her moral responsibility.

To support this claim at more than an intuitive level will require a brief excursion into certain metaethical questions, that is questions about the proper nature and scope of morality. In claiming that we owe something to persons who do not exist *yet,* I am advocating what has been called a timeless or four-dimensional view of morality. The view is roughly that morality requires us to be concerned with the effects of our actions upon the interests and well-being of other persons—and sometimes those of sentient beings which are not persons. The view does not necessarily imply a utilitarian ethical system, though many of its defenders are utilitarians.[17] For it is not necessary to claim that *all* moral rules or obligations can be derived from calculations of the effects of particular actions (or types of action) on human or other persons. The claim is simply that whenever we can reasonably predict that our actions will have a significant impact upon the interests of others, then we should take due account of that impact. The rights and interests of those who are affected by our actions may sometimes be rightly overridden by our own, but they are never without moral significance. Conversely, actions which have absolutely no predictable impact on the welfare of sentient beings, other, perhaps than the agent(s), do *not* generally have much moral significance, though it is conceivable that they might in some cases. Some philosophers have called this view of the scope of moral responsibility the *person-affecting* principle, and the term is a useful one, though it should not be taken to imply that sentient beings which are not persons have no moral rights at all.

This view is *timeless* in the sense that it offers no basis for ignoring the predictable effects of our actions on future persons just because the latter do not exist *now*. On the other hand, we don't, as a rule, pay much attention to the rights or interests of *past* persons—i.e., those now dead; but that is only because we are not generally in a position to affect their interests one way or another. In cases where it can be argued that we *may* adversely affect the interests of persons now dead, e.g. by spreading slander about them or breaking deathbed promises to them, the timeless view of morality would imply that we should give this fact some weight in our moral deliberations. And certainly if some new invention, such as time travel, were to make it possible to alter past events, we would be obligated, on the view which I am defending, to take account of the effects—e.g., the pain and pleasure—which these alterations would be apt to produce in the lives of people in the past.

Underlying this view—or perhaps an alternative statement of it—is what the contemporary American philosopher Joel Feinberg has called the *interest principle*. The interest principle presents what I think is a necessary and sufficient condition for the possession of moral rights—though not necessarily of *full* moral rights, as we shall see. It says "that the sorts of being who can have rights are precisely those who have (or can have) interests."[18] Feinberg argues for this principle on the following grounds:

> (1) because a right holder must be capable of being represented and it is impossible to represent a being that has no interests, and (2) because a right holder must be capable of being a beneficiary in his own person, and a being without interests is a being that is incapable of being harmed or benefitted, having no good or "sake" of its own. Thus, a being without interests has no "behalf" to act in and no "sake" of its own.[19]

What does it mean to say that a being has *interests,* that it has a "good" or a "sake" of its own? To have an interest is, minimally, to prefer, and/or to have sound (though perhaps unrecognized) reasons for preferring one set of events to another. Now it is only conscious, or sentient beings, entities which are capable of having experiences which can have preferences—or *reasons* for preferring some events to others. Entities which are not capable of feeling pleasure or pain (or anything else) cannot have interests, and neither can they be said to have rights, except in a secondary sense. Trees, mountains, works of art, and the like, may be *valued* by humans or other sentient beings, and thus may be said to have rights in a *derivative* sense; but such "rights" are conferred in recognition of the interests of the beings which do the valuing, not those of the nonsentient entities, since *they* do not have interests of their own.

But why, it might be wondered, should having interests be analyzed in terms only of having *preferences* (or reasons for having preferences)? Why should it not be understood in terms of some broader criterion, such as having *needs,* or being capable of being harmed or benefitted? Nonsentient entities, which lack preferences, may nevertheless be said to have *needs,* meaning that in the absence of certain conditions they will die, degenerate, or be destroyed. Thus, trees may be said to *need* water, sunlight, and unpolluted air if they are to thrive. Why can't such needs be a basis for the ascription of moral rights?

The answer is that a tree which *needs* water, like a car which *needs* oil, or a knife which *needs* sharpening, will not *suffer* without it, i.e., will not undergo pain, discomfort, frustration, disappointment, or loss of pleasure. Such talk about the *needs* of nonsentient entities ultimately reflects the interests not of cars, knives or trees, but of those persons who *care* about them, who have an interest in keeping the car running, the knife sharp, or the tree healthy. (Notice that we are much more apt to say of a rose than of a ragweed plant that it *needs* water, though both may die or fail to thrive without it.)

Of course, trees, unlike cars, are alive, and will die if their needs are not met. But a dying Douglas fir suffers no more than a rusting Chevrolet; nor does it have desires, plans or hopes which will be frustrated by its death. We may rightly regret the death of a tree, e.g. for aesthetic or ecological reasons. But from the *tree's* point of view, its demise is no more tragic than that of a dandelion or a drop of rain. Strictly speaking, such nonsentient entities do not *have* a point of view, and that is exactly my point. Because they are not *subjects,* because they lack even such elementary experiences as pleasure and pain, they not only cannot prefer one state of affairs to another, they cannot even be sensibly said to have a *reason* for doing so; for they have nothing to *gain* from continuing to live or to function mechanically, and nothing to *lose* by dying or suffering mechanical breakdown. I conclude, therefore, that it is only sentient beings which can be said to have interests, or, if the interest principle is correct, to be the subjects of moral rights.

It follows from the interest principle that human beings are the sorts of entities which can have moral rights, and so are other of the "higher" animals, i.e. those which are clearly sentient. It does not follow, however, that humans and nonhuman animals must have the *same* moral rights. Common-sense morality views the rights of humans as not only more *complex* than those of nonhumans, but also of comparatively greater moral significance, in that when, for instance, an animal's right to life conflicts with that of a human, it is generally the human's right which should prevail. There is something to be said for this common-sense viewpoint, however anthropomorphic it may appear to be. For at least most of the nonhuman animals with which we share the earth are indeed different from ourselves in ways which we ought to take account of in determining the relationships between their moral rights and our own.

On the other hand, not all nonhuman animals are alike; language-using chimpanzees and large-brained sea mammals may well have interests and moral rights which differ from those of chickens or mice. And a race of nonhuman but intelligent alien beings would be a different matter altogether; there might be no grounds at all for claiming that the aliens' rights were any different from our own. Indeed, it would probably be a mistake—as well as an insult—to refer to such aliens as (mere) animals, even if they looked, say, exactly like horses.

If we are to explain the difference between our own moral rights and those of (most) nonhuman animals, or the differences between the rights of different kinds of nonhuman animals, we must supplement the interest principle with another, which I will call the *personhood principle.* It says that *all and only persons have full and equal moral rights*. Persons are beings (not necessarily human) who are not only sentient, and therefore possessed of interests (and thus such minimal moral rights as the right not to be subject to pointlessly cruel treatment); they are also capable of (a fairly high level of) reason, self-awareness, individually motivated behavior, and, typically though not always, the use of language.[20] These are not arbitrarily selected peculiarities of mature human beings, chosen only to rationalize the refusal of most people to accord nonhuman animals or human fetuses the same moral status as adult human beings. On the contrary, this refusal is justified by the significant differences between the interests of persons and those of sentient but nonpersonal beings.

Most animals have fairly simple interests. So long as their biological needs are not denied and their instinctual drives are not severely thwarted, they or their human advocates have little grounds for complaint. It is different with persons, whose interests include the fulfillment of their own complex, unique, and individually determined desires, hopes, ambitions and personal projects. Self-awareness and reason, augmented by the use of language, give persons the capacity to have, indeed make it impossible for them *not* to have, interests of sorts which nonpersons cannot possibly have. It is in recognition of this fact that moral rights are accorded to persons which could not meaningfully be ascribed to nonpersons, e.g. the rights to liberty, equality under the law, and equality of opportunity.

The contemporary American philosopher Michael Tooley has argued that it is only persons who possess a *serious* right to life. He defines a person as an *organism* which "possesses the concept of a self as a continuing subject of experiences and other mental states, and believes that it itself is such a continuing entity."[21] On this definition, most nonhuman animals are not people, and neither are human fetuses or very young infants. I think that the *spirit* of this definition is right, though I prefer my own, because it does not rule out self-aware *machines* (which are at least a logical possibility), or human beings who may not happen to believe that they are, or possess, selves of this kind.[22]

On the other hand, I see no grounds for denying that entities which are not persons—especially those which do appear to have some degree of rationality and self-awareness (though not enough to qualify as persons)—may have a *significant* right to life. Various nonhuman animals, and perhaps, very young human infants, may fall into this category. The point is rather that they do not have the *same* right to life as persons do. The reason for this is that death is not the same kind of evil for them that it is for one of us, even though it is still arguably an evil of *some* kind for them, and not to be inflicted without good reason. It is not the same kind of evil for them because they lack the specific, individual, future-oriented desires and interests which make death the kind of evil that it is for us.

At the same time, however, we must recognize that when we are dealing with psychologically complex and imperfectly understood entities which are by all accounts rather *close* to the threshold of personhood, such as the seemingly intelligent dolphins, or a human infant, it is extremely difficult for us to know just what their experiences, cognitions, desires, etc., are, or even to *imagine* what they might be. Consequently the question of whether such "borderline" entities should be regarded as persons in the fullest sense, i.e. as self-aware beings with full moral rights, remains profoundly obscure. In view of our ignorance, I think that it behooves us to treat such "near-persons" with great respect, and perhaps even to confer upon them the status of full personhood, in order to be on the morally safe side in our dealings with them.

Now let's return at last to the question of whether we have any moral obligations with respect to future generations. The timeless view of morality, together with the interest principle and the personhood principle, implies that we do, because (1) they are, in the timeless sense, persons, like ourselves, with needs and interests of a kind essentially similar to our own; and (2) we are in a position to materially affect their future well-being by our present actions.

Furthermore, the proposed view implies that, insofar as the population policies adopted by those now alive will have predictable and significant effects on the well-being of future generations, we are morally obligated to adopt policies which will, so far as possible, protect rather than jeopardize their interests; and in practice, as we have seen, we can do this only if we limit our own reproduction.

5. Some Objections to the Person-Affecting View

While these conclusions seem to follow in a rather straightforward way from the general ethical perspective which I have outlined, a number of philosophers have argued that the latter cannot, for logical reasons, be used to provide a moral argument for population control. Their objections turn upon the *contingency* of future persons. I have argued that neither the temporal location of future generations nor our relative ignorance concerning them justifies a disregard for their interests. But additional logical puzzles arise when we consider the fact that the very *existence* of future persons—whether there will be *any at all, which* ones there will be, and how *many*—is contingent upon the actions of persons alive now. The problem is especially acute in cases in which an action must be morally evaluated on the basis of the interests of future persons whose existence or nonexistence is contingent upon *that very action*.

The American political scientist Thomas Schwartz has argued that the contingency of the *particular identities* of future persons upon whatever population policy the present generation adopts eliminates any obligation on our part to limit population growth. We have, he says, "no obligation to our distant descendants severely to limit population growth . . . even granting that uncontrolled procreation would beget a drop in the quality of life."[23] This is because—he says—any population policy or method of birth control which we adopt will inevitably result in *different individual persons* being born, to us and in succeeding generations. Any birth control alters, at the very least, the *timing of many* conceptions, and therefore the genotype, and the individual identity, of the persons conceived. In any given generation which practices birth control, some conceptions will occur just as they would have in the absence of birth control; but *these* people will (*tend* to) meet and procreate with different partners, and at different times, than would have been the case had there been no population control policy in their own or earlier times. Thus, any given population policy will have the result that within a few generations (Schwartz says six at most[4]), no one will exist who would have existed had a different population policy, or no population policy, been adopted.

From this, Schwartz concludes that we cannot possibly owe it *to our distant descendants* to practice population limitation; for if we do limit it, then the future people to whom the debt is supposedly owed, i.e. those who would exist and suffer if we don't, *will not exist*. Schwartz describes this problem as that of the "disappearing beneficiaries."[25] The problem is that there is no possible set of future persons, say in the year 2100, who would be better off if we adopt some particular policy for population limitation, than they—*the same set of individuals*—would have been if we had not adopted that policy. For *whatever* policy we adopt, the result will be the existence of an entirely different set of individuals from those who would have otherwise existed. So it seems that we cannot coherently say that we owe it to any particular set of distantly future people, actual or possible, to adopt a policy of population limitation. Any possible future person either (1) will not exist if the proposed policy is adopted, and hence not be benefitted by its adoption;[26] or (2) will exist but will not be better-off than they would have been had it not been adopted (since in that case they would *not* have existed). In neither case, it seems, can we intelligibly be said to owe it *to that possible future person* to adopt that policy.

The contemporary British philosopher Derek Parfit has called attention to a similar problem, which arises with respect to certain individual procreative choices. He considers a case in which a woman who intends to become pregnant learns that she has an illness which would cause any child she conceives now to have a certain serious handicap. If she waits a few months, however, the illness will have passed and she will be able to conceive a normal child. Intuitively, it seems clear that she ought to wait and conceive a normal rather than an impaired child.[27] But Parfit argues that, on the general moral view that I have sketched above, and which has been defended by Narveson and others, such a conclusion cannot be defended. On this view we are obligated to take account of the effects of our actions on persons who *will exist,* given those actions; we owe nothing, however, to the future persons who *might have existed,* had we acted differently. It seems, therefore, that we cannot say that the woman owes it to *any* of her possible children to delay her pregnancy until she can conceive a normal child. If she conceives immediately and has an abnormal child, she won't thereby have failed to benefit *it,* since had she waited she would have had a different child; and she owes nothing to the (indefinitely many) possible normal children which she *might* have conceived had she waited.

Paradoxes of the sort which Schwartz and Parfit describe seem to appear whenever we are faced with decisions regarding the creation of new persons. In both cases the apparent paradox arises from the necessity of evaluating one possible action, A, by comparing the effects A would have on certain possible future people—those who would exist if A were performed—to the effects that some other possible action, B, would have on a *different* set of possible future people—those who would exist if we did B rather than A. It is this kind of comparison which has seemed to these philosophers to be either impossible or morally irrelevant, even on the timeless view of morality. The problem is not simply that we cannot now *know* the particular identities of those who will exist in the future. It is rather that, given that *which* people will exist in the future, as well as how *many,* depends in part on our own actions, there is not and cannot be any particular, determinate set of possible future persons whose interests may be used to guide our actions, in preference to the interests of *other* possible future persons.

Fortunately, however, there is a way of understanding our moral obligations towards future persons which can avoid the apparent paradoxes which Schwartz and Parfit describe. The first point which must be stressed here is that all of our moral obligations towards *particular* future persons are contingent upon the latter's actual future existence. This means that no particular possible-but-as-yet-unconceived future person can meaningfully be said to have a *right* to be conceived and born—or a right *not* to be. I have argued that we have moral obligations towards future people, those who *will* be born; but I think it is self-evidently absurd to suggest that we could owe it to *particular* as-yet-merely-possible future persons to bring it about that *they* are conceived and born.

Schwartz is right, therefore, to point out that we do not owe it to any particular set of possible future people to adopt just that policy towards procreation which will cause *them* to exist. So too, Parfit is right to deny that the woman in his example can be said to owe it to one of her possible normal children to have it, rather than one of the possible abnormal ones. However, it does not follow from the first point that societies have no obligation to adopt policies designed to limit population growth; nor does it follow from the second that Prafit's prospective mother has no obligation to wait and try to have a normal child rather than an impaired one. What follows is rather that if such obligations exist, they cannot be construed as duties owed to particular *possible* future people.

How, then, can these obligations be explained, on the person-affecting view of morality? My suggestion is that a concern for the effects of our actions upon the interests and well-being of future persons—those who *will* exist, either because or regardless of what we do—requires us to recognize certain *minimal requirements of moral responsibility,* both in the making of individual procreative choices and in the shaping of social policies affecting population growth. Such concern is required by the timeless view of morality; and it in turn requires that in choosing whatever, when, and under what circumstances we should bring new persons into existence, we should always prefer (other things being equal) to bring into being persons with a good chance for happiness, rather than persons with a poorer chance. It also requires that we should make every reasonable effort to avoid bringing into being persons (or entire generations) who will have no reasonable opportunity of leading satisfactory human lives. It is irresponsible, and contemptuous of the welfare of future persons, to deliberately bring into being persons who will almost certainly be unhappy. It is wrong because it results in unnecessary suffering in the future, suffering on the part of individuals who in the timeless perspective are no less real than we are.

On these grounds, the woman in Parfit's example has a clear moral obligation to try to avoid becoming pregnant until her chances of having a normal child have improved, and, furthermore, not to have a child at all if she never becomes capable of having a normal one (assuming, of course, that the defect is a very severe one).

By the same reasoning, it is wrong, other things being equal, to deliberately have a child with a prospect of a miserable or an only minimally satisfactory life when one could have one with a prospect of a much happier life. (Hence the woman in Parfit's case probably ought to delay her pregnancy even if the impairment of a child conceived immediately would *not* be an extremely serious one.) Narveson points out that if we deliberately produce a miserable person when we could have produced a happy one, then

> it is true that we cannot say that we have done the miserable one a disservice, in the sense that *he* would have been happier had we done something else. On the other hand, however, we can say that the person there is if we produce the miserable one is worse off *than the person there would have been had we produced the other one.*[28]

This fact, it seems to me, is an adequate basis for the moral intuition that we ought not to deliberately bring into existence persons who will have a poorer chance for happiness, in preference to those who will have a better chance. Parfit, however, considers it a "cheat" to interpret the person-regarding principle in this way, since to do this, he says, is to treat "a whole group of possible people as if it were a single ('honorary') person."[29] In other words, it seems to require us to treat all of the indefinitely many children which the woman *might* have, depending on when (and with whom) she conceives, as if they were a *single* possible child, and to tell her to do her best for *that* possible child. If so, Parfit argues, the problems become even more severe when we consider the question of how *many* children one ought to have, or how numerous future generations ought to be. Are there to be "honorary persons" with varying numbers of members?

It is not, however, necessary to create "honorary persons" out of sets of possible ones in order to explain our moral obligations in such cases. It is only necessary to admit, as Narveson does, that we are making comparative judgments about the value of different possible human lives—or rather, different *types* of human life, since we cannot (usually) identify the *particular* possible future persons about whose quality of life we are concerned. In other words, we ought to try to bring into existence persons with a good chance for happiness in preference to persons who will probably lead miserable lives, because the former's existence will be of greater value *to them*. To accept this claim we need not believe that there are certain possible people "waiting in the wings" who have a right to be made actual, or certain others who have a right *not* to; we need only believe that it would be better for there to be people with a good chance for happiness in the future than for there to be those with less of a chance. And if we did not believe *that*, then I don't see how we could claim to have any concern at all for the interests or well-being of future persons.

So much for the reasons why we ought to try to bring into existence people who will have a good chance for happiness rather than people who will probably be miserable. We have not, however, resolved the question of how *many* people there ought (ideally) to be. To do this we will need to turn to another issue concerning our obligations to future persons.

6. Total vs. Average Happiness

Utilitarians have usually agreed that there is a moral obligation to consider the results of our actions upon the well-being of future as well as present persons; and I have argued that even those who are not, strictly speaking, utilitarians, have reason to accept this premise. There is, however, little agreement among utilitarians as to how this obligation is to be interpreted in the case of future persons. Should we, for instance, seek to maximize the *total amount of* happiness (the sum of the happiness of all) in the future, or should we try to make the happiness of the *average* person in the future as great as possible? Or is neither view correct?

With respect to presently existing persons the total and average views yield identical results, since the average is obtained by dividing the total amount by a fixed number of individuals; but with respect to future generations, whose numbers are as yet unknown, the two views may yield extremely different results. The total view appears to yield what Parfit has called the *repugnant conclusion:* that we ought to create as many people as possible, so long as the happiness of each is enough above the zero point to increase the total amount, and so long as they don't subtract from the well-being of presently existing persons *enough to cancel out the net gain*. On the total view, then, we may be forced to endorse a future in which vast numbers of human beings exist at a barely-better-than-death level of happiness.

A defender of the total-happiness view might reply that we need not seek to maximize total happiness in this particularly repugnant way. It might be that a much smaller population size would prove optimal on the total happiness view, because each individual would be many times happier than any of those in the more populous world. But whether this would prove true or not is at least in part an empirical issue, and an enormously difficult one. It would be better not to rest our dislike of the future world endorsed by the repugnant conclusion on such a debatable hypothesis.

The fundamental problem with the total happiness view, however, is that it forces us to neglect the individual well-being of future persons in favor of the abstract ideal of the "total amount" of happiness. As the contemporary American philosopher Jonathan Bennett points out,

> the mere notion of an *amount* lets philosophers introduce a surrogate for the proper notion of utility—it gives them utilities which are not *someone's,* in the form of quanta of happiness which nobody has but which somebody could have. As well as deploring the situations where a person lacks happiness, these

philosophers also deplore the situation where some happiness lacks a person . . .[30]

Like Bennett, I believe that it is a mistake to be concerned with *how many* people will exist to be (at least minimally) happy in the future, rather than with *how happy* people will be in the future. I would therefore favor something closer to the average than to the total view.

The average view, however, also appears to yield some counterintuitive results. For one thing, it seems to imply that it is always prima facie wrong to bring into existence a person or group of persons who will be less happy than the average individual will be. In a fortunate world in which the average person was extremely happy, it would not seem to be morally wrong to add additional persons who would probably be *quite* happy, though less so than the average.

I think that it is true that this would not necessarily be wrong—though it *might* be less than morally optimal. We do not, therefore, have an absolute obligation always to act so as to maximize the average happiness of future persons. We do, however, have an obligation to do what we *reasonably can* to promote the well-being of future persons, without demanding excessively severe sacrifices of ourselves, or adopting unrealistically high standards for them. To refrain from having a much desired child on the grounds that though the child would probably be *quite* happy, it would be less happy than the (very high) *average,* would be an excessive sacrifice, and one which would arguably not produce any significant improvement in human happiness—only a minute and strictly statistical one. Not having the child will not (we may assume) make any actual person happier, and having the child will not make anyone *unhappy* (certainly not the child); so it is surely permissible to have it.

Conversely, it would be a mistake to argue, on the basis of the average-happiness principle, that a person who is capable of bearing or begetting a child that would probably be *more* happy than the average person, has a moral obligation to do so. The point is not merely that if there is such a prima facie obligation it can (sometimes) be overridden by the potential procreator's own right, if he or she wishes, to pursue a life which does not include parenthood (or *additional* parenthood). It is rather that the fact that someone could probably produce a happy child does not *in the least* tend to show that it would be either virtuous or obligatory to do so. It shows only that *one* important precondition for morally responsible procreation has been met, i.e. that one possible moral *objection* to having a child does not apply. It does not in itself provide a positive moral reason for having the child. For that, as Narveson says,

> we need to turn to such facts as that his parents want children, or that his addition would add to the happiness of the existing community, or that people just like the idea of having more people around.[31]

The contemporary Canadian philosopher Richard Sikora raises another objection to the view that there is no moral obligation to create more people just because the new people would be happy. He argues that,

> In actual practice, it would never be justifiable *per se* to add any large group of people to the world unless there is at least some intrinsic moral worth in adding happy people to the world. The reason for this is that one can be virtually certain that at least *some* members of any large group that might be added to the world will, for one reason or another, have wretched lives, which of course counts negatively; so, unless adding happy people is to count *positively,* no matter by how much the happy outnumber the wretched and no matter how

happy they are, it would be as wrong to add the whole group, happy members included, as it would be if it contained only its most wretched members.[32]

One possible response to this argument is that in practice, given the happiness many people derive from having children, the misery of a few future people would be outweighed by the good effects of the existence of the entire set of new people on already existing people. But Sikora imagines a case in which such a reply would not be possible.[33] Suppose that the sole human survivor of a global disaster is a man named Jones. Jones has the means at hand (say a large "test-tube baby" factory) for producing many millions of new people, most of whom, predictably, would be very happy, but a few of whom would be wretched. Suppose, further, that he himself has no desire to create any new people, and would in fact be much happier if he did not. Should Jones repopulate the world, in spite of his own preferences? Sikora claims that he should because there is a moral obligation to create happy people, sometimes even at great cost to oneself. The average-happiness principle, however, would seem to imply that Jones has no such obligation, especially if his own individual happiness, if he lived out his life alone, would be higher than the average among the test-tube people.

It is not necessary, however, to adopt the total-happiness principle in order to explain the intuition which most people seem to have about this case, i.e. that it would be *good*—if not morally obligatory—if Jones were to choose to repopulate the world rather than to pursue his own solitary happiness. I have argued that he cannot be said to owe it to *possible future persons* to make some of them actual, or that if he did he would thereby be providing a benefit to *them*. The seductive but mistaken notion that he would be doing *them* a favor in creating them is one source of the conviction that he ought to do so. Another source, however, is the fact that *we*, though we would no longer exist when Sikora's scenario takes place, would nevertheless have a stake in the outcome of Jones' decision.

This is because most of us have a powerful, if unanalyzed, desire that the human race should survive, even after our own deaths, and indeed for as long as possible. Bennet describes this desire, in his own case, as "a strong, personal, unprincipled preference." It would, he says,

> be a great shame—a pity, *too bad*—if this great biological and spiritual adventure didn't continue: it has a marvellous past and I hate the thought of its not having an exciting future.[34]

If most people feel this way about the survival of humanity, and if they furthermore consider this good important enough that they and others should be willing to make large sacrifices to ensure it, then surely this fact is one which Jones ought to take account of in making his choice. The moral significance of people's interests and desires does not entirely cease with their deaths. That it does not is the moral presumption behind the legal institution of the will (whereby the wishes of individuals regarding the disposition of their property are protected after their deaths), and the general assumption that promises made to dying persons are (sometimes) morally binding. Indeed, if we were to assume that the frustration of a person's interests and desires is impossible or morally irrelevant once the person is dead, we would have difficulty explaining why *painless and unexpected* death is an evil.

For us, because we are conscious, self-aware beings with individual interests (desires, plans, hopes, etc.) with respect to the future, death is an evil because it frustrates so many of these interests at a single blow. The fact that, afterwards, a murder victim is not here to *suffer* from the frustration of her interests in no way shows that killing her was wrong. Neither does it show that there is nothing *further* that can be done to damage her interests. Some of her interests may be presumed to extend beyond her own death, and thus she may still be harmed, or her moral rights violated, e.g. by the destruction or misrepresentation of her work.

So too, I think that Jones would be damaging *our* interests, and those of past generations as well, if he were to choose not to try to perpetuate the human race. Whether he would be violating our *rights,* however, is another matter. It would be *heroic* of him to respect our interests at the cost of his own misery, and he should certainly be prepared to make *some* efforts to prevent their final frustration. But it isn't obvious that he owes it to us or to anyone else, to perpetuate humanity *regardless* of the cost to himself. After all, in his case *the further course of his life,* its relative happiness or misery—in short the satisfaction or frustration of virtually *all* of his interests—may be at stake; and this is not true of either those who existed in the past but are now dead, or of the millions of possible persons whom Jones might later cause to exist.

But is it even morally *permissible,* if we reject the total-happiness view, for Jones to bring new people into existence, given that some of them (a small proportion, but a large absolute number) will be miserable? If it isn't an intrinsic good to create happy people, then what can offset the evil of creating the unhappy ones? Is respect for the interests of past generations enough to outweigh the suffering and unhappiness of these future people? I think that this is the wrong question to ask. If Jones' mission of repopulation (should he decide to accept it) is to be judged morally responsible *with respect to the predictable level of well-being of those who exist as a result,* it must meet conditions analogous to, though of course more complex than, those involved in an individual act of procreation.

When an individual undertakes to become a parent, she or he is morally obligated—or so I have argued—to do all that can reasonably be done to maximize the odds that the resulting child will have the basic prerequisites for a satisfactory human life, and indeed not to have a child at all if the odds are that it would not. Jones, however, is contemplating the creation of a *large number* of human beings. Hence he must either create them (i.e. launch their development) one at a time, through some rapid and routinized procedure, or else create many of them simultaneously (or perhaps through an expanding chain reaction). It may be that whatever he does he cannot prevent a severely defective infant from coming into existence in, say, one in one thousand cases. Should he, in order to avoid creating these unfortunate individuals, refrain from creating anyone at all?[35]

My answer is that neither the person-affecting view nor a preference for the average over the total-happiness principle requires us to draw this conclusion. A concern for the well-being of the people he brings into existence—*all* of them, and not just the *average* level of happiness—would require, instead, that he take such steps as (1) ensuring the impaired persons as good a life as possible under the circumstances; (2) never ceasing to try to minimize the number of such persons who come into existence, e.g. by preventing the conception of defective individuals where possible; and (3) failing that, aborting defective embryos and fetuses as early as possible in the (artificial) gestation process. It would *not* require, given the great happiness of the great majority of the new people, that he create no one at all in order to create no one who would be unhappy. That requirement would subject Jones to standards of responsibility which we would not think of imposing upon those who procreate in the real world, where there is always *some* possibility that a given couple will produce a child that is in some way impaired, and always a statistical certainty that if *many* people reproduce, even under the best of circumstances, some unhappy human beings will come to exist.

In other words, I suggest that, just as the fact that a given couple *probably* could produce a child who would have a good chance for happiness removes one possible moral obstacle to their becoming parents, so the fact that *most* of the people in Jones' new world would have a good chance of happiness offsets the fact that a few of them would have a lesser chance of happiness, in determining the moral permissibility of his action. In both cases, what moral responsibility requires is that *reasonable* care be taken to ensure the probable well-being of future people, *not* that a degree or a probability of success be demanded which in practice would preclude *ever* bringing new people into existence.

In neither case, however, is the fact that the new persons would (probably, or in most cases) be happy, a positive moral reason for bringing them into existence; it only shows that doing so does not show a lack of concern for *their* well-being, and is therefore not wrong on *that* account. I have not attempted to present a complete account of all the things which should ideally be taken into account in deciding whether, when and how many new people to produce, but they certainly include at least the following:

(1) the rights and interests of presently existing people;
(2) the (average, not total) well-being of the persons we propose to bring into existence;
(3) the effects of the existence of *these* new persons upon *other* future persons, including those in the more distant future; and
(4) the need to try to maximize the well-being of even the *least* well-off of the new people (even where this does not necessarily contribute to the *average* happiness).[36]

I also believe that, other things being equal, we ought to prefer a *longer* human future, with a smaller number of individuals alive at any one time, to a shorter one which contains the same number of individuals at the same average and/or minimal level of happiness. The continuity of the race argues for this, and there are other, e.g. environmental and aesthetic, considerations in its favor. I think that the other factors which I have mentioned are all clearly of moral significance, both in individual procreative decisions and in the shaping of population policies; furthermore, I think that at present all of them point toward the moral necessity of a lower birth rate, in most parts of the world, and in most segments of the population.

Let us turn, therefore, from consideration of the objections to the limitation of population growth, in and of itself, to certain other objections which are raised against some of the means which I have said are necessary to facilitate reductions of the birth rate—i.e. contraception and abortion.

7. Contraception, Abortion, and the Potentiality Principle

Some philosophers, while not necessarily objecting to the goal of population limitation as such, hold beliefs about the moral rights of potential persons which are difficult in practice to reconcile with that goal. I refer to supporters of what has come to be called the potentiality principle.[37] The potentiality principle says that potential persons have a moral right to be permitted to develop into actual persons (i.e. a right to life); or that it is morally wrong, other things being equal, to prevent them from doing so. Depending upon how the term "potential person" is defined, the potentiality principle may be thought to constitute a moral objection to abortion only, or to both abortion and contraception.

A potential person is something more than a merely *possible* person; its existence requires not just that it be empirically possible that a certain (kind of) person will come into existence at some time in the future, but that there be something which exists *now*, and which is capable of *developing* into a person. The definitional issue turns on whether or not conception must have already occurred for there to be a potential person, of the sort which allegedly possesses some right to life. The contemporary English philosopher Richard Hare has argued that there is no reason to deny that "an unfertilized ovum and a sperm which may or may not yet exist in the father's testes"[38] constitute a potential person; after all, the two together *can* develop into a human being (or possibly more than one), given the right circumstances. From this rather broad definition, plus certain other considerations, Hare reaches the surprising conclusion that there is "not only a duty not to abort, but also a duty not to abstain from procreation."[39]

Most defenders of the potentiality principle, however, would deny that there can be said to be a potential person before there is a single, genetically complete organism which is capable of becoming a person. A contemporary American philosopher, Edward Langerak, defends an even narrower definition. He says that

A *potential person* is a being, not yet a person, that will become an actual person in the normal course of its development (for example, a human fetus).[40]

On this definition, ununited sperm/egg pairs are not potential persons, since they do not *normally* develop into persons; they do so only given certain further circumstances, which are statistically extremely rare.[41] We are not, therefore, violating the rights of potential persons whenever we miss an opportunity to procreate.

This narrower definition, however, has its own problems. If only what will become a person *in the normal course of its development* counts as a potential person, then human fetuses which will die or be aborted spontaneously, without artificial medical intervention, are not potential persons. This is a consequence which Langerak is willing to accept, but which I find highly counterintuitive. It would, for instance, require us to say that there are persons alive now who developed from fetuses which were *not* potential persons, which seems absurd.[42] Surely if *any* fetus is to count as a potential person, any fetus which actually develops into a person must so count.

If Langerak nevertheless prefers this very narrow definition it is probably because he realizes that a broader definition, one which counts as a potential person any entity which *could* develop into a person, will cause the potentiality principle to yield some very strange results. Consider, for instance, Michael Tooley's hypothetical example of a serum which, injected into kitten embryos, causes them to develop into persons—not human persons, but self-aware, rational, language-using beings.[43] Would it be seriously wrong to kill a kitten embryo which had accidently been exposed to this serum? Or more wrong than it would have been to kill it before it was so exposed? Would there be a moral obligation to inject as many kitten embryos as possible with the serum, since they would all be capable of becoming persons, with only this minimal human intervention? Only on the narrowest definition can we safely give a negative answer to these questions, if we think that the potentiality principle is true.

But what if the potentiality principle is false? We must ask what reasons there are for believing that potential reasons, in any of the senses of this term which we have discussed, have, *qua* potential persons, a right to life which is significantly stronger than that of living things which are not potential persons. I have argued that we are morally obligated to respect the lives and interests of *future* persons. But this is because they are (will be) real persons, with interests essentially like our own. One may damage the interests of a future person by damaging the fetus from which it develops, but not by aborting (or failing to conceive) a fetus from which a person *might* have developed. In contrast to future persons, merely potential persons—be they unfertilized ova, human embryos or small fetuses—do not have interests of their own, and indeed are not even minimally sentient. Why then should we suppose that they *already* possess the same kinds of moral rights as do persons and other highly sentient beings?

A number of arguments have been proposed to show that potential persons should be accorded at least some of the same moral rights as actual persons (present or future). Hare's is one of the most ingenious. He argues that the Golden Rule (that we should do to others as we wish them to do to us), or rather what he considers a modest extension of it, requires that we treat potential people as having a significant right to life. His proposed extension of the Golden Rule is that we should treat others in ways in which *we are glad we were treated*. Since most of us are glad that our parents met, mated, and brought us into the world, we should consider ourselves morally obligated to treat potential persons in the way that the one(s) which became *us* were treated. Consequently, he concludes, we all have a prima facie obligation not only to have children but to have as many as possible.[44] It is an obligation which can be overridden by other moral considerations, Hare tells us, but nevertheless there is always a prima facie wrong to be rationalized in any decision not to procreate or not to complete a pregnancy.

The shortest response to this argument is that the Golden Rule cannot legitimately be extended in this way. The whole point of that ancient moral principle is that we should respect the interests of other persons, *because* they are persons like ourselves, with the same kinds of interests, the same capacity for suffering, and so on. We should, no doubt (often at least), treat others as we are glad *we* have been treated. But in the relevant sense, *we* were never ununited sperm/egg pairs or tiny embryos; for we are *persons*—conscious, self-motivated beings—and therefore, at the time when the gametes (etc.) *from* which we developed existed, we—the persons *into* which they developed—did not exist. If the various events which resulted in our own conception and birth had never occurred, no wrong would have been done to *us*, since we would never have existed.

Indeed, I think that it makes very little sense to be glad that *we*, the particular persons that we are, were brought into existence. Should I rejoice because my parents timed their procreative efforts in exactly that manner which resulted in *my* conception? If any of an indefinite number of factors had been slightly different, a different child would have been conceived and born, and I would never have existed. But why should I believe it is better for *me* to have existed, rather than any of the other children which my parents might have had? I value my life, but so, in all probability, would they have valued theirs. Had one of them existed instead of me, I would not have lost or been deprived of any of the things I would *now* lose if I lost my life.

If we still tend to feel that it was a remarkably fine thing—for us—that our parents had *us*, rather than other children or no children at all, it is probably either because self-love tends to overpower logic in this case, or because, in one's own case, it is very difficult to avoid some confusion between the possibility of *never having existed* and the possibility of *death or being killed*. Since *death* would be a great evil, we tend to think that *never having existed* would also have been rather bad. But this is an illusion. It would have been irresponsible for my parents to have deliberately had an impaired child or one otherwise predictably unhappy (instead of me), but it would not have inflicted the least bit of harm on *me*. It might even have been a violation of the Golden Rule—but only with respect to *that* child, not with respect to me.

Langerak provides a different argument for considering potential persons, as such, to have a significant right to life. He speaks of the moral rights of persons as moral *values,* and argues that just as we should value mature persons not just for their actual capacities but also for what they have the potential for becoming, so we should value potential persons not just for what they are but for what they can become.[45] If we value excellent leadership, for instance, then we should value those who show the *potential* and not just the *developed capacity* for such leadership; and by analogy if we value persons, and ascribe moral rights to them, then we should also value potential persons, and ascribe at least some of the same rights to them.

This argument turns upon a confusion between two different kinds of value. One is the value which people or potential people may have *for others,* e.g. their predicted ability to contribute to the latter's well-being, in one way or another. The other is the value which persons have *for themselves,* by virtue of their own interests, projects and desires. It is sometimes true that a potential person has (potential) value for others. But it is the second kind of value which is (or should be) the primary basis for the ascription of moral rights. The value that persons have for *themselves* provides a moral basis for according them a full and equal right to life. The values they have for *others* might only justify respecting the lives of *some* persons, or of some much more than the rest. *Potential* persons, on the other hand, have as yet no value for themselves; they are not yet beings with a desire to live, or with interests of their own. And the value that they have for others will often be minimal or clearly negative. In any case, there is no basis for according them moral rights on an equal footing with those of actual persons.

Langerak gives one other argument for believing that potential persons have a right to life. He suggests that the social acceptance of abortion is apt to endanger the respect for human life in general, and that therefore we ought to *confer* upon fetuses a significant right to life, and one which becomes stronger as the fetus becomes more fully developed.[46] I consider the premise of this argument to be empirically implausible; but I do not know how to *prove* that legalized abortion is not apt to cause people to kill their grandparents slightly more frequently, or, as Langerak predicts, to condone infanticide in cases where it is clearly wrong. So let us suppose for the sake of argument that legal abortion *might* have such consequences in some cases. It is still extremely unlikely that these cases would be so numerous or unavoidable as to offset the negative effects, on the lives of present and future persons alike, of *not* having legally available abortion.

Langerak, to be fair, does not think that abortion should *always* be prohibited. He thinks that *early* abortions should be permitted in a variety of circumstances. However, I am much less sanguine than he is about the practical effects of the imposition of legal limitations and preconditions upon the availability of abortions. Granted, every effort should be made to perform necessary abortions earlier rather than later in the pregnancy; and granted it is distressing to think of third trimester abortions being performed for clearly trivial reasons—though I doubt that this actually happens very often, for reasons which should be self-evident. Indeed, it is not entirely unreasonable to "confer" upon late-term fetuses a somewhat greater right to life than can be justified on the basis of their own present interests or degree of sentience. We might do this, and I suspect that we in fact do it, to some extent, in order to protect the rights and sensibilities of existing people.

It should, for instance, concern us that nurses and doctors may be personally traumatized by (and sometimes legally prosecuted for) their role in the performance of late-term abortions.[47] They should certainly have the right to refuse to participate in such procedures, in cases where they judge that the medical indications for it are lacking. But why should they be traumatized if what they are asked to do is not seriously morally wrong? The problem, of course, is that relatively mature fetuses *look* like infants, or like *babies,* to use the more emotionally evocative term; and babies are dear to our hearts, and should be. So it is natural, for most of us, to be disturbed by their destruction, and to want to protect our own sensibilities by protecting them; i.e. by assigning them a right to life stronger than that of a nonhuman being with a comparable level of sentience, and stronger than that of a fertilized ovum or a very small embryo or fetus.

As I have said, this is not an entirely unreasonable suggestion, especially because there are reasons for viewing mature fetuses and infants as already possessing a significant right to life by virtue of their present sentience and mental (or at any rate cerebral) activity. However, if we are to assign them an even stronger right to life than could be justified on these grounds, one based on *our* interests rather than theirs, then we must be very careful to do this in a way which takes into account the rights of those of us who are most directly affected; their most basic interests must not be sacrificed to the sensitivities of distant observers. Legally restricting access to abortion, for poor women, or for *all* women whose pregnancies have passed the first or second trimester, has this result.

I will therefore conclude this section by suggesting to those who urge us to respect the "conferred" rights of potential persons, that the best way to reduce the number of abortions overall, and the number of late-term abortions in particular, is to develop better contraceptives, better access to contraceptives, and *early* abortions, for those of all ages and classes. The *worst* ways are those that increase the number of unwanted births and medically unsafe abortions, and those that subject women to the humiliation of having to prove to legal authorities that they really "need" or "deserve" abortions, on some set of economic, moral, medical, psychiatric or other criteria. These are forms of tyranny, regardless of whether they are practical for the sake of promoting population growth[48] or in the name of the rights of fetuses.

8. The "Contraceptive Morality"

There are other objections to contraception and abortion besides those based on the potentiality principle. One of the most common, and I think one of the cruelest, is the argument that contraceptives and abortion should be forbidden, or at least strongly disapproved of, because they encourage women to be sexually promiscuous. (Christians and political conservatives seem particularly apt to reason in this way.) In the words of the contemporary American philosopher Elizabeth Anscombe,

> Christianity taught that men ought to be as chaste as pagans thought honest women ought to be; the contraceptive morality teaches that women need to be as little chaste as pagans thought men need to be.[49]

As we shall see, there are logical, moral and empirical grounds for thinking this an extremely *weak* objection to the free and legal availability of contraception and abortion. Historically, however, it has played an important role in the reasoning of those who have opposed contraception and abortion, and it continues to play such a role today. The argument about the chastity of women is bound to surface in any public discussion of abortion. Often people ask, "Aren't you encouraging women to have casual sexual intercourse *without accepting the consequences?*" This notion that (only) women should be forced to "accept the consequences" of their sexual behavior is evidently part of the rationale for the Hyde Amendment, which allows federal funds to be used for non-lifesaving abortions only if the woman is pregnant as a result of rape or incest, and therefore (so the reasoning would *appear* to go) did not *voluntarily* engage in any behavior for which she ought to be punished. The effect of this policy—whether deliberate or not—is to treat mandatory motherhood as a way of punishing women for engaging in heterosexual intercourse of their own free will.

This way of viewing the matter generally arises from a number of assumptions, which though common and more or less traditional, are both false and morally pernicious. These include the following:

(1) that sexual activity which is not intended, or not of the right sort, to result in pregnancy and childbirth, is inherently and highly undesirable (e.g. because it is unnatural, immoral, or both), and hence properly punishable;
(2) that it is just to punish only women for such activity, or to punish them far more severely than men, by subjecting them to the fear and often the reality of unwanted pregnancy and motherhood; and
(3) that this method of punishing women will deter women (and perhaps also men) from engaging in nonprocreative sexual activity.

It is clear from the empirical evidence that nonprocreative sexual activity is an almost-universal feature of human behavior, both that which is arguably "natural" and that which is culturally determined. It includes heterosexual intercourse in which one or both partners is infertile (e.g. too young, too old, or in the wrong phase of the ovulation cycle), heterosexual activities of a nonprocreative kind, homesexual activities on the part of both sexes, masturbation, and sexual fantasy. So far as we can tell, these kinds of sexual behavior (except possibly the last one) are as characteristic of our closest biological relatives, the apes and the other primates, as they are of most human societies. This does not show that they are all morally unobjectionable; only that they are highly natural and to some extent irrepressible aspects of human behavior. (Rape may also be highly natural, but that is not an argument for its moral permissibility.)

Is nonprocreative sexual activity, then, natural but morally objectionable on other grounds? *Some* of it certainly is—e.g. rape committed by an infertile male (or female), or against a child or an old person. Rape, of course, is wrong, and seriously so; but it is hard to make a case for saying the same of all voluntary sexual behaviors which are not expected or intended to lead to conception and birth. Each case must be evaluated on its own merits. Solitary (e.g. autoerotic) sexual activities are usually harmless, but not always or necessarily so. Sexual relationships may be carried out with respect for the rights of both parties and with mutual gain; or they may be exploitative, deceitful, sadistic, or otherwise (predictably and unjustly) harmful of one or both parties. It has taken Western civilization two thousand years to relearn (if it ever entirely forgot) what the "pagans" knew, i.e. that not all nonmarital or nonprocreative sex is necessarily bad; it may take us a while longer to realize that not all of it is necessarily good either.

One thing that is clear, however, is that heterosexual intercourse *with* contraception (or abortion, if contraception fails) is often preferable, on moral and practical grounds, to intercourse *without* effective methods of birth control. Whether or not one thinks that it is just to punish women so much more severely than men for nonmarital (and even marital) sexual activities, it is certainly unrealistic to suppose that restricting access to abortion and contraception, at this late date, will significantly alter the amount (though it might, perhaps, alter the *type*) of sexual activity that women and men engage in. What it will do is increase the number of unwanted pregnancies, illegal and/or late-term abortions, unwanted children, and, probably, the number of infanticides and cases of child abuse, divorce, and desertion. In practice, *these* are the consequences one opts for in restricting access to contraception or abortion—not a fantasy world in which all women are "chaste" except when they wish to become pregnant.

9. Summary and Conclusion

I have argued that we have a moral obligation to protect the interests and well-being of those who have not yet been born, but who will be. Neither the present nonexistence of future persons, nor our ignorance of just who they will be, justifies a disregard for the predictable effects of our actions upon their lives. The fact that the very *existence* of future people, as well as how *many* of them there will be, depends upon the actions of persons alive now, shows neither that we can owe them nothing, nor that we owe it to them to bring as many of them into existence as possible. What it shows is that it is not only morally permissible, but essential, that we strive to limit their numbers to whatever extent is necessary to make a satisfactory human existence likely for them.

We are, then, morally obligated to limit our own rate of reproduction. As individuals, we are obligated to be restrained in our procreation,[50] and as a society we are obligated to adopt policies which will promote voluntary reductions in the birth rate, wherever it remains too high. Optimal future population levels, and hence our moral responsibilites with respect to procreation and the formulation of population policies, cannot be determined on the basis of the *total* happiness principle, which might recommend a vastly crowded world in which most people judge their continued existence to be just barely preferable to death. Neither can we be mechanically guided by the *average* happiness principle, which might dictate excessive and unreasonable sacrifices on the part of presently existing persons. It is possible, for instance, that the highest possible average level of, or opportunity for, happiness, say fifty years from now, would be achieved by reducing the world's population to a small fraction of its present size. To do this might require that the majority of people have no children at all; but this might be an excessive sacrifice to expect of them, merely for the sake of giving future persons *as good a chance for happiness as possible*.

On the other hand, if a virtual ban on reproduction, for all but a chosen few, were the only possible way to prevent future generations from existing in a state of extreme misery, then it might, conceivably, be a justifiable sacrifice for us to make. We are not yet faced with that situation; but we should try to make sure that our descendants will not be faced with it either. I have argued that we can best do this by (1) promoting the kinds of social reform which are known to be conducive to a voluntarily lowered birth rate—e.g. economic security for the least advantaged, and the liberation of women—and (2) improving contraceptive techniques and access to contraception and abortion.

To do these things is not to violate the rights of possible or potential persons; for these are not yet beings with a right to life. *Not* to do them, however, would violate the rights of all those future persons who would consequently suffer from poverty and a degraded natural and human environment. If we are misled by the fallacious idea that it is somehow in the interests of future persons to create more and more of them, then we will fail in our most fundamental moral obligations to future generations.

Notes

1. See Jan Narveson, "Future People and Us," *Obligations to Future Generations*, edited by R. I. Sikora and Brian Barry (Temple University Press, Philadelphia, 1978), p. 41.

2. See G. E. M. Anscombe, "Contraception and Chastity" for a philosophical explication and defense of the Roman Catholic Church's opposition to all methods of birth control except total abstinence during the woman's fertile periods (the "rhythm" method). The Catholic

stance against abortion is defended by John T. Noonan, in "An Almost Absolute Value in Human History" (*Biomedical Ethics*, edited by Thomas A. Mappes and Jane S. Zembaty, McGraw-Hill, pp. 413-416, 1981) and "How to Argue About Abortion" (*Contemporary Issues in Bioethics*, edited by Tom Beauchamp and LeRoy Walters, Dickenson, Encino, California, 1978: pp. 210-216).

3. See, for instance, R. M. Hare, "Abortion and the Golden Rule," *Philosophy and Public Affairs*, Vol. 4, No. 3, pp. 201–222; William Anglin, "In Defense of the Potentiality Principle," *Obligations to Future Generations*, pp. 31–37; and R. I. Sikora, "Is It Wrong to Prevent the Existence of Future Generations?," *op. cit.*, pp. 112–166.

4. The Declaration of the 1968 United Nations International Conference on Human Rights illustrates this point of view. It holds that ". . . couples have a basic right to decide freely and responsibly on the number and spacing of their children and a right to adequate education and information in this respect." (*Final Act of the International Conference on Human Rights*, United Nations, New York, 1978, p. 15; quoted by Daniel Callahan in "Ethics and Population Limitation," *Ethics and Population Policy*, p. 25.)

5. Robert McNamara, *Summary Proceedings* of the 1976 Annual Meeting of the World Bank/IFC/IDA, p. 14; quoted by Peter Singer in *Practical Ethics* (Cambridge University Press, 1979), p. 159.

6. See Peter Singer, *Practical Ethics*, p. 160.

7. As quoted by reporter Ann Crittenden, in an article in the *San Francisco Chronicle*, Wednesday, Nov. 26, 1980, p. E–7.

8. Most notably, Garrett Hardin, in 'The Tragedy of the Commons," *Ethics and Population Policy*, pp. 3–18. Hardin argues that because it is in the interest of the individual to have more children than is socially desirable, we must relinquish the freedom to reproduce without limitation, in favor of "mutual coercion mutually agreed upon."

9. Harriet Taylor Mill, "Enfranchisement of Women," *Essays on Sex Equality*, edited by Alice S. Rossi, University of Chicago Press, 1970, p. 103.

10. See Katie Curtin, *Women in China*, Pathfinder Press, New York and Toronto, 1975, pp. 76–81.

11. This suggestion has been made, for instance, by P. R. and A. H. Earlich, in *Population, Resources, Environment*, Freeman, San Francisco, 1970, pp. 321–324. (Quoted by Daniel Callahan, in "Ethics and Population Limitation," p. 38.)

12. Perhaps the most dramatic evidence of such attitudes on the part of (at least certain) medical professionals comes from the classic study done in 1970 by Inge K. Broverman and associates. This study found that a majority of psychiatric clinicians considered the psychologically healthy *man* to be similar to the psychologically healthy *adult*, but different from the psychologically healthy *woman*. A healthy man (or adult), they thought, is competent, independent, assertive, rational, and, in short, stereotypically masculine. A healthy *woman*, on the other hand, was seen as "more submissive, less independent, less adventurous, more easily influenced, less aggressive [and] less competitive"—in short as lacking these highly valued "masculine" traits. ("Sex-Role Stereotypes and Clinical Judgments of Mental Health," by Inge K. Broverman, in *Readings on the Psychology of Women*, edited by Judith M. Bardwick, Harper and Row, New York, 1972; p. 322.)

13. See Michael D. Bayles, "Limits to a Right to Procreate," *Ethics and Population Policy*, pp. 41–55, for a good discussion of the various types of positive and negative economic incentive programs.

14. Of course, those who believe that abortion is a form of murder might reply that any means of preventing abortion is justified, regardless of how unequally its effects are felt. See sections 4, 7, and 8 for arguments against the claim that abortion is morally wrong.

15. See Gregory Kavka, "The Futurity Problem," *Obligations to Future Generations*, pp. 186–203.

16. Kavka, p. 188.

17. See Jan Narveson, "Future People and Us."

18. Joel Feinberg, "The Rights of Animals and Unborn Generations," *Philosophy and Environmental Crisis*, edited by William J. Blackstone, University of Georgia Press, 1974, p. 51.

19. Ibid.

20. See Mary Anne Warren, "On the Moral and Legal Status of Abortion," *Today's Moral Problems*, edited by Richard Wasserstrom, MacMillan, 1975, p. 130.

21. Michael Tooley, "Abortion and Infanticide," in *The Rights and Wrongs of Abortion*, edited by Marshall Cohen, Thomas Nagel, and Thomas Scanlan, Princeton University Press, 1974, p. 59.

22. Some people, and even some philosophers, would deny that they or anyone else has a *self* which is a continuing subject of conscious experiences—though they naturally cannot avoid behaving *as if* they believe that they are such subjects, and thus may be thought in some sense to believe it after all. See David Hume, "Our Idea of Identity," and "Of Personal Identity," selections from the *Treatise of Human Nature*, first published in 1739; in *Personal Identity*, edited by John Perry, University of California Press, 1975, pp. 159–172.

23. Thomas Schwartz, "Obligations to Posterity," *Obligations to Future Generations*, p. 3.

24. Schwartz, p. 6.

25. Schwartz, p. 3.

26. Unless, perhaps, their lives would have been so miserable that nonexistence could be considered preferable, and hence a "benefit."

27. Derek Parfit, "On Doing the Best for Our Children," *Ethics and Population Policy*, pp. 100–101.

28. Narveson, "Future People and Us," p. 49.

29. Parfit, p. 103.

30. Jonathan Bennett, "On Maximizing Happiness," *Obligations to Future Generations*, p. 65.

31. Jan Narveson, "Moral Problems of Population," *Ethics and Population Policy*, p. 71.

32. R. I. Sikora, "Is It Wrong to Prevent the Existence of Future Generations?," *Obligations to Future Generations*, pp. 136–137.

33. Sikora, p. 138.

34. Bennett, p. 66.

35. I am assuming that Jones is not willing to adopt infanticide as a solution. Even if he did the problem might still arise with respect to individuals whose physical defects do not become apparent until still later in their development.

36. This is a version of one of Rawls's principles of justice, which, I am inclined to agree with Rawls, cannot be captured by a strictly utilitarian theory, and certainly not one which treats the average happiness of future persons as the *only* relevant factor in determining our moral responsibilities regarding them. See John Rawls, *A Theory of Justice*, Harvard University Press, 1971, pp. 60–65.

37. See, for instance, R. M. Hare, "Abortion and the Golden Rule," *Philosophy and Public Affairs*, Vol. 4, No. 3, pp. 201–222; William Anglin, "In Defense of the Potentiality Principle," *Obligations to Future Generations*, pp. 31–37; and Edward A. Langerak, "Abortion: Listening to the Middle," *Hastings Center Report*, October 1979, pp. 24–28.

38. Hare, p. 212.

39. Ibid.

40. Langerak, p. 25.

41. See John Noonan, "An Almost Absolute Value in Human History," (*Biomedical Ethics*, edited by Thomas A. Mappes and Jane S. Zembaty, McGraw-Hill, 1981, p. 416).

42. This point was made by David Hoekema, in conversation.

43. Tooley, p. 75.

44. Hare, pp. 211–214.

45. Edward A. Langerak, "Abortion, Potentiality, and Conferred Claims," read at the Eastern Division of the American Philosophical Association, December 1979.

46. Langerak, p. 12.

47. I mean, in particular, procedures in which potentially viable fetuses are deliberately killed or allowed to die.

48. See Hilda Scott, *Does Socialism Liberate Women?* (Beacon Press, Boston, 1974) for an account of the attempts of Eastern European states and the U.S.S.R. to promote population growth by restricting access to contraception and abortion.

49. Anscombe, p. 135.

50. Except, perhaps in special cases. The survivors of groups which have been decimated by genocidal oppression, war or disease may, for instance, rightly feel that they have the right to be as prolific as they choose, in order to replenish their numbers.

Suggested Readings

1. *Having Children: Philosophical and Legal Reflections on Parenthood,* eds. Onora O'Neill and William Ruddick, Oxford University Press, New York, 1979.
2. *Obligations to Future Generations,* eds. R. I. Sikora and Brian Barry, Temple University Press, Philadelphia, 1978.
3. *Philosophy and Environmental Crisis,* ed. William T. Blackstone, University of Georgia Press, Athens, 1974.
4. *The Rights and Wrongs of Abortion,* eds. Marshal Cohen, Thomas Nagel, and Thomas Scanlon, Princeton University Press, 1974.

chapter seven

On the Ethics of the Use of Animals in Science

DALE JAMIESON AND TOM REGAN

As you read this, animals are being killed, burned, radiated, blinded, immobilized and shocked. They are being locked and strapped into the Noble-Collip Drum, tossed about at the rate of 40 revolutions per minute and thrust against the iron projections that line the drum. This procedure crushes bones, destroys tissues, smashes teeth and ruptures internal organs. Right now, somewhere, animals are in isolation, deprived of all social contact, while others are in alien environments, manipulated into cannibalizing members of their own species. It is not just a few animals at issue. In the year 1978 alone, about 200 million animals were used for scientific purposes, about 64 million of these in the United States. This number includes 400,000 dogs, 200,000 cats and 30,000 apes and monkeys.[1] From anyone's point of view, these are disagreeable facts, but some will say they are the concern of scientists only. We who are not scientists cannot get off the hook so easily, however. The use made of animals in science frequently is carried out in the name of improving the quality of human life: to find cures for cancer, heart disease and a thousand other ailments; to develop safe new products for our consumption; and to instruct others in, and to advance our knowledge of, the world in which we live. Because these things are done in our name, ostensibly to help us live better lives, and because these

169

activities frequently are financed by public monies (approximately $5 billion dollars in federal support in the United States for 1980) we cannot in good faith or with good sense avoid confronting the facts about the use of animals in science, and assessing its morality.

In the past this debate has usually been put in terms of being for or against vivisection. But this term, 'vivisection', is ill-suited for our purposes. To vivisect an animal is to dissect it, to cut it, while it is alive. Not all practices that demand our attention involve vivisection. Animals placed in the Noble-Collip drum or those that are radiated or shocked, for example, are not dissected while they are alive. For this reason it would be misleading at best to pose our central question in terms of whether one is for or against vivisection. Our interest lies in assessing the use made of animals in science in general, not just in those cases where they are vivisected.

There are three major areas of science in which animals are routinely used. These are (1) biological and medical education; (2) toxicology testing, where the potential harmful affects for human beings of various chemicals and commercial products are first tested on animals; and (3) original and applied research, including not only research into the causes and treatment of various diseases but also into the basic biochemical nature and behavior of living organisms.[2] All of us are familiar with the use of animals in education from our time spent in laboratory sections in biology, for example, and most of us have an outsider's inkling of what goes on in original and applied research from what we read in the newspapers and are exposed to by the other media. As for the use of animals in toxicity testing, that will become clearer as we proceed, when we discuss various toxicity tests, including the so-called Draize test and the LD-50 test.

It is possible that some people might object to our including all three uses of animals under the general heading of the use of animals in science. In particular, some scientists might have a narrower view of science, according to which only original and applied research counts as "genuine science"; the use of animals in educational contexts or in toxicological testing isn't science, on this view, or not "real" science at any rate. This narrower conception of science is understandable, if science is viewed exclusively in terms of the devising and testing of original hypotheses. The fact remains, however, that it is not by witchcraft or astrology, say, that the acute or chronic toxicity of pesticides, food additives, hair sprays and oven cleaners are determined; it is a matter of applied science. And it is not to turn out persons educated in, say, philology or accounting that lab sections are held in connection with standard courses in biology; it is to educate persons in biological science. So, while there may be a sense in which neither toxicity tests nor instructional labs are "science," there is certainly another sense in which they are a recognized part of those activities carried on by scientists, in their capacity as scientists or as teachers of science, and it is this more general but still proper sense of 'science' that we shall have in mind throughout the pages that follow. Thus, when we inquire into the morality of how animals are used in science or for scientific purposes, we intend to include their use in all three areas—in biological and medical education, in toxicology testing, and in original and applied research—though we shall feel free occasionally to emphasize their use in one area over their use in the others.

Before setting forth our own view regarding the ethics of the use of animals in science, two extreme positions will be characterized and debated. By subjecting their supporting arguments to criticism, we hope to show the need for a more reasonable, less extreme position. We shall call the two positions "The Unlimited Use Position" and "The No Use Position." The former holds that it is permissible to use any animal for any scientific purpose, so long as no human being is wronged. The latter holds that no use of any animal for any scientific purpose is morally permissible. We shall first examine the leading arguments for the Unlimited Use Position.

I.

The first argument that we shall consider is the Cartesian Argument. It is named after the seventeenth century philosopher, René Descartes, who held that animals are mindless machines. Here is the argument.

1. If a practice does not cause pain, then it is morally permissible.
2. Unlimited use of animals for scientific purposes would not cause them any pain.
3. Therefore, the use of any animal for any scientific purpose is morally permissible.

So simple an argument is not without far reaching consequences. The tacit assumption of the Cartesian Argument by the scientists of Descartes' day helped pave the way for the rapid growth of animal experimentation in the seventeenth and eighteenth centuries. The following passage, written by an unknown contempory of Descartes', gives a vivid and unsettling picture of science at that time.

> They [i.e., scientists] administered beatings to dogs with perfect indifference; and made fun of those who pitied the creatures as if they felt pain. They said the animals were clocks; that the cries they emitted when struck, were only the noise of a little spring that had been touched, but that the whole body was without feeling. They nailed poor animals up on boards by their four paws to vivisect them and see the circulation of the blood which was a great subject of controversy.[3]

It is well to remember this passage whenever we doubt that ideas can make a difference. Clearly Descartes' idea that animals are mindless machines profoundly influenced the course of science. The influence of an idea, however, is not a reliable measure of its truth, and we need to ask how reasonable the Cartesian Argument is.

A moment's reflection is enough to show that some crucial qualifications must be added if the Cartesian Argument is to have any plausibility at all. Inflicting pain is not the only way to harm an individual. Suppose, for example, that we were to kill humans painlessly while they are asleep. No one would infer that because such killing would be painless it would therefore be quite all right. But even if the necessary qualifications were introduced, the Cartesian Argument would still remain implausible. The evidence for believing that at least some animals feel pain (and it is only those animals with which we shall be concerned) is virtually the same as the evidence for believing that humans feel pain. Both humans and animals behave in ways that are simply, coherently and consistently explained by supposing that they feel pain. From a physiological point of view, there is no reason to suppose that there are features that are unique to humans that are involved in pain sensations. Veterinary medicine, the law and common-sense all presuppose that some animals feel pain. Though some seem to accept the Cartesian Argument implicitly, it is doubtful that many would try to defend it when it is clearly stated.

The failure of the Cartesian Argument has important implications regarding the moral status of animals. Once we acknowledge the reality of animal consciousness and pain we will be hard pressed indeed to exclude animals from membership in the moral community. Membership in the moral community might be thought of as in some ways analogous to membership in a club, with both qualifications and possible benefits. The key potential benefit of membership is that limits are placed on how others may treat you. For example, as a member, your life and property are protected by moral sanctions. Who belongs to the moral community? Evidently all those individuals who can themselves be treated wrongly qualify as members. But which individuals are these? A variety of answers have been proposed, including the following:

—all and only rational beings;
—all and only autonomous beings (individuals having free will).

It will not be possible to discuss these views in detail.[4] It is sufficient to note their common failing: Infants and severely enfeebled human beings, for example, are neither rational nor autonomous, and yet we treat them wrongly if we cause them significant pain for no good reason. Thus, since we can treat these individuals wrongly, they qualify as members of the moral community; and since they qualify as members of this community despite the fact that they are neither rational nor autonomous, neither rationality nor autonomy are requirements for membership in the moral community.

Still, infants and the enfeebled are human beings, and it might be suggested that membership in the moral community is determined by species membership. In other words, it might be suggested that all and only human beings are members of the moral community. This requirement for membership is also unsatisfactory. To restrict membership in the moral community to those who belong to the "right" species is analogous to the racist's attempt to restrict membership to those who belong to the "right" race, and to the sexist's effort to exclude those of the "wrong" gender.[5] Racism and sexism are today recognized as unacceptable prejudices. Rationally, we recognize that we cannot mark moral boundaries on the basis of such biological differences. Yet this is precisely what those who attempt to restrict membership in the moral community to all and only *Homo Sapiens* are guilty of. They assume that membership in a particular species is the only basis for deciding who does and who does not belong to the moral community. To avoid this prejudice of "speciesism," we must reject this way of setting the boundaries of the moral community, and recognize that when needless pain and suffering are inflicted on infants and enfeebled humans, it is wrong, not because they are members of our species, but because they experience needless pain and suffering. Once this is acknowledged we may then come to see that it must be wrong to cause any individual, human or otherwise, needless pain or suffering. Thus, since many animals are conscious beings who can experience pain, as was argued in response to the Cartesian Argument, we must recognize that we can wrong them by causing them needless pain or suffering. Since they themselves can be wronged, they themselves must be members of the moral community.

The failure of the Cartesian Argument, therefore, does indeed have important implications regarding the moral status of animals. We shall have occasion to remind ourselves later of these implications.

But now let us consider a second argument that might be urged on behalf of the Unlimited Use Position. We shall call this the "Might Makes Right Argument."

1. If a practice is in the interests of the stronger, then it is morally permissible.
2. Humans are stronger than animals.
3. Unlimited use of animals in science would be in the interests of humans.
4. Therefore, the use of any animal for any scientific purpose is morally permissible.

Even if we accept the view that only human interests determine how animals ought to be treated, what premise 3 asserts is false. Sometimes it is not in our interests to allow the use of just any animal for just any scientific purpose. Some animals are members of species that many people care about. Our reasons for caring are sometimes romantic or sentimental. Sometimes they are educational or aesthetic. Increasingly they are prudential. The more we learn about the interrelatedness of life on this planet, the more we recognize that the quality of our lives is inextricably linked to the welfare of other species. Because we care about some animals, we have an interest in how they are treated, and therefore their unlimited use cannot be said to be in the interests of humans. Consider, too, that the first premise, that what is permissible is determined by what is in the interest of the stronger, implies that strong humans do nothing wrong when they pursue their ends by using weaker humans, however badly they might treat them. Thus the Might Makes Right Argument would permit, not just unlimited use of animals, but unlimited use of weak and defenseless humans as well. If we are unwilling to swallow this repugnant conclusion, we must reject this argument. If, on the other hand, we are willing to accept unlimited use of weak and defenseless humans, then most and possibly all animal experimentation and toxicity testing performed in the name of human welfare is unnecessary. However useful animal experimentation or toxicity tests might be in improving the quality of the lives of stronger humans, surely the use of weaker humans would be even more useful. When animals are used, the problem of "extrapolating the data," that is, applying the results to humans, inevitably arises. (We shall have occasion to return to this problem in the pages that follow.) The problem of extrapolation could be overcome, however, if weaker humans instead of animals were used. After all, what could be a better experimental model of a human than another human? But no one, presumably, will seriously argue that weak humans should be exploited in this way. Thus no one will seriously espouse the Might Makes Right Argument.

A third argument, the Soul Argument, overcomes some of these difficulties.

1. Moral constraints only apply to beings who have souls.
2. All humans have souls.
3. No animals have souls.
4. Therefore, moral constraints apply to what may be done to humans but not to what may be done to animals.
5. Therefore, unlimited use of animals for scientific purposes is morally permissible.

One who accepts this argument can use it to avoid the unsavory implications for weaker humans of the Might Makes Right Argument. Since premise 2 states that all humans have souls, it follows that even weak humans have souls; thus the Soul Argument would not permit unlimited use of weak humans by stronger humans. Animals, however, are not protected by morality since they allegedly lack souls. Thus, according to the Soul Argument, morality permits us to use any animal for any scientific reason.

This argument is open to numerous objections. To begin with, the claim that all humans have souls is both vague and difficult to support. What is a soul? How do we know that humans have them but animals don't? On any account, these are not easy questions to answer. Moreover, although the dominant religions of the Western world typically deny that animals have souls, other religions, for example Hinduism and some Native American religions, do attribute souls to animals. Just as there is great controversy concerning the nature of the soul and the very coherence of the concept, so there is controversy about what individuals have souls.

Suppose however, that we were to accept the view that all and only humans have souls. Now, having a soul clearly would make an important difference to an individual's chances for a life beyond the grave. Those lacking a soul will have no chance for a future life. Thus the bodily death of an animal, assuming all animals lack souls, would mark its complete annihilation as a conscious individual. The influential Christian writer, C. S. Lewis, argues that this fact would have the opposite implication from the one drawn in the Soul Argument.[6] If animals have no souls and no possible life beyond the grave, then the pain and suffering that they are made to endure in this life cannot possibly be balanced or overcome by the pleasures and enjoyments of an afterlife. In other words, if animals have no souls there is no possibility that the travails of their earthly existence can be recompensed in a world beyond. Thus the obligation to minimize the pain and suffering of animals during this their only life would seem to be, if anything, increased rather than diminished by their lack of a soul. If this is true, then we shall certainly fail to discharge that obligation if we permit the use of any animal for any scientific purpose. The Soul Argument, rather than providing grounds for the Unlimited Use Position, actually contains the seeds of an argument that can be used to criticize that Position.

A fourth argument for Unlimited Use is the Knowledge Argument.

1. If a practice produces knowledge, then it is morally permissible.
2. Unlimited use of animals for scientific purposes would produce knowledge.
3. Therefore, unlimited use of animals for scientific purposes is morally permissible.

Here we should balk at the first premise. Torturing suspects, spying on citizens, vivisecting cousins, all could produce knowledge, but surely that alone would not make these activities morally all right. Some knowledge is simply not worth the price in pain required to get it, whether those who suffer the pain are humans, as in the activities just listed, or animals, as in the case about to be described.

The Draize Test is a procedure employed by many manufacturers to determine whether proposed new products, most notably new cosmetics, would irritate the eyes of humans.[7] The most recent Federal guidelines for the administration of the Draize Test recommend that a single large volume dose of the test substance be placed in the conjunctival sac in one eye of each of six albino rabbits. The test substance is to remain in the eyes of the rabbits for a week, and observations are to be periodically recorded. The guidelines recommend that in most cases anesthetics should not be used. The rabbits are often immobilized in restraining devices in order to prevent them from clawing at their eyes. At the completion of a week, the irritancy of the test substance is graded on the basis of the degree and severity of the damage in the cornea and iris.

The Draize Test is not a very good test by anyone's standards. It is unreliable and crude. In fact, a 1971 survey of twenty-five laboratories employing the Draize Test concluded that the Draize Test is so unreliable that it ". . . should not be recommended as standard procedures in any new regulation."[8] But even if the Draize Test were a reliable test, the most that we would gain is some knowledge about the properties of some inessential new products. Can anyone really believe that there is a scarcity of cosmetics already on the market? The value of whatever knowledge is provided by the Draize Test is insignificant compared to the cost in animal pain required to obtain it. Indeed, no less a figure than Harold Feinberg, the chairperson of the American Accreditation For the Care of Laboratory Animals Committee, has stated that "the testing of cosmetics is frivolous and should be abolished."[9]

A fifth argument seeks to remedy this deficiency of the Knowledge Argument. Here is the Important Knowledge Argument.

1. If a practice produces important knowledge, then it is morally permissible.

2. Unlimited use of animals for scientific purposes would produce important knowledge.
3. Therefore, unlimited use of animals for scientific purposes is morally permissible.

The Important Knowledge Argument fares no better than the Knowledge Argument. Consider an example. Surely it cannot be denied that it is important to know what substances are carcinogenic in humans. But animal tests for carcinogenicity in humans are often inconclusive. For example, in recent years there has been great controversy over whether one can infer that saccharin or oral conceptives are carcinogenic in humans on the basis of data collected in animal tests. Some have argued that because of the methods used in such research, such an inference cannot be made.[10] Massive doses are administered to rats and mice in these studies over short periods of time; there is no reason to believe that human cancers develop in response to similar conditions. Moreover, unlike humans, rats and mice tend spontaneously to develop a high incidence of tumors. One prominent medical journal remarked with respect to the oral contraceptive controversy:

> It is difficult to see how experiments on strains of animals so exceedingly liable to develop tumors of these various kinds can throw useful light on the carcinogenicity of a compound for man.[11]

If, however, we were to adopt the policy of unlimited use of *humans,* we could conclusively determine which substances are carcinogenic in humans. Moreover, such a policy would be sanctioned by the Important Knowledge Argument, since unlimited toxicology testing and experimentation on humans would unquestionably produce important knowledge. If the production of important knowledge makes a practice permissible, then unlimited testing and experimenting on humans is permissible. But again, this is a repugnant conclusion. If we are unwilling to accept it, we must give up the Important Knowledge Argument. If, on the other hand, we are willing to accept it, then most and possibly all toxicology tests and experiments carried out on animals in the name of human interests are unnecessary, since better models, namely humans, are available.

Finally there is the Freedom Argument. The Freedom Argument does not seek to show directly that unlimited use of animals is permissible. Rather it seeks to show that limitations on a researcher's freedom to use animals are wrong. Here is the argument.

1. Outside limits placed on the scientists's right to freedom of inquiry or academic freedom are not permissible.
2. Any outside restriction placed on the use of animals for scientific purposes would place limits on the scientist's right to freedom of inquiry or academic freedom.
3. Therefore, no outside restrictions on how animals may be used for scientific purposes are morally permissible.

This argument focuses attention away from the value of the goal of science (knowledge or important knowledge) to the value of the freedom to inquire. But though this change is noteworthy, and though this freedom is important and ought to be one among a number of factors considered in the course of examining the ethics of the use of animals in science, it is clear that freedom of inquiry is not the only morally relevant consideration. The right to freedom of inquiry is no more absolute than, say, the right to freedom of speech. There are limits on what can be done by individuals in exercising their rights. To say precisely just what these limits are is difficult; but limits there are. Almost no one would say that the right to freedom of inquiry would sanction some of the things that have been done to humans in the name of science. For example, in the eighteenth century "charity children" were infected with small-pox in experiments conducted by Princess Caroline. Early in the twentieth century condemned criminals in the Philippines were injected with plague bacillus. And as recently as the 1960's, black prisoners in Alabama were left untreated to suffer from syphilis after having been intentionally infected. That there are limitations on what can be done in the name of science is a principle that is enshrined in international agreements, including the Nuremberg Code of 1947 and the World Medical Associa-tion's Declaration of Helsinki drafted in 1961. Since some limits on the right to freedom of inquiry clearly are justified, the unlimited use of animals cannot be defended by appealing to some supposed absolute right to freedom of inquiry. For this reason the Freedom Argument, like the others before it, fails to provide a rational defense of the Unlimited Use Position.[12]

Although we haven't canvassed all possible arguments that might be given in support of the Unlimited Use Position, we have examined those that seem most common. None of these arguments provides any rational support for this Position. It is now time to examine an alternative view.

II.

The No Use Position holds that no use of any animal for any scientific purpose is ever permissible. Is this position rationally defensible? We think not. We propose to argue for this conclusion in ways analogous to the case made against the Unlimited Use Position. We shall characterize some representative arguments for this position, indicating where and why these arguments go wrong.

Before addressing these arguments, it is worth noting that the reasonableness of the No Use Position does not follow from the inadequacy of the Unlimited Use Position, any more than it follows, say, that no men are bald because it is false that all men are. Those who accept the No Use Position may take some comfort in our critique of the Unlimited Use Position, but they cannot infer from that critique that their own position is on the side of the truth.

We shall discuss four arguments for the No Use Position. Here is the Pain Argument.

1. If an action causes pain to another being, then it is not morally permissible.
2. The use of animals for scientific purposes causes animals pain.
3. Therefore, no use of any animal for any scientific purpose is morally permissi-ble.

We should note first that not all scientific uses made of animals cause them pain. For example, some experimental uses of animals involve operant conditioning tech-niques, and most of these do not cause pain at all. Other experiments call for minor modifications in animals' diets or environments. Still others require killing anesthe-tized animals. The Pain Argument does not provide a basis for objecting to any of these uses of animals. Because the Pain Argument cites no morally relevant consid-eration in addition to pain, it cannot provide a thorough-going defense of the No Use Position.

More importantly, the Pain Argument is defective from the outset. Contrary to what the first premise states, it is sometimes permissible to cause pain to others. Dentists cause pain. Surgeons cause pain. Wrestlers, football players, boxers cause pain. But it does not follow that these individuals do something that is not permissi-ble. Granted, the presumption is always against someone's causing pain; neverthe-less, causing pain is not itself sufficient for judging an act impermissible.

Suppose, however, that, unlike the case of dentists, pain is caused againt one's will or without one's informed consent. Does it follow that what we've done is wrong? This is what the Informed Consent Argument alleges. Here is the argument.

1. If an action causes pain to another being without that being's informed consent, then it is not morally permissible.
2. The use of animals for scientific purposes causes animals pain without their informed consent.
3. Therefore, no use of any animal for any scientific purpose is morally permissible.

The second premise is open to the same objections raised against the corresponding premise in the Pain Argument: Not all scientific uses made of animals cause them pain. Thus, one cannot object to every use made of animals on this ground. Besides, animals are not the sort of beings who *can* give or withhold their informed consent. Explanations of what will be done to them in an experiment or test cannot be understood by them, so there is no possibility of "informing" them. Thus, there is no coherent possibility of causing them pain "without their informed consent."

The first premise also falls short of the truth. Suppose that a small child has appendicitis. If not operated on, the condition will worsen and she will die. Scary details omitted, the situation is explained to the child. She will have none of it: "No operation for me," we are told. The operation is performed without the child's consent and causes some amount of pain. Was it wrong to perform the operation? It is preposterous to answer affirmatively. Thus, we have a counterexample to the basic assumption of the Informed Consent Argument, the assumption that it is not permissible to cause others pain without their informed consent.

Still, one might say that there is a difference between hurting others (causing them pain) and harming them (doing something that is detrimental to their welfare). Moreover, it might be suggested that in the example of the child and appendicitis, what we've stumbled upon is the fact that something that hurts might not harm. Accordingly, it might be held that what is always wrong is not causing pain, or causing others pain without their informed consent; rather, what is always wrong is harming others. This suggestion gains additional credence when we observe that even a painless death can be a great harm to a given individual. These considerations suggest another argument. Here is the Harm Argument.

1. If an action harms another being, then it is not morally permissible.
2. The use of animals for scientific purposes harms animals.
3. Therefore, no use of any animal for any scientific purpose is morally permissible.

This argument, like the ones before it, has gaping holes in it. First, it is clear that it will not even serve as a basis for opposing all animal experimentation, since not all animal experimentation harms animals. More fundamentally, it is simply not true that it is always wrong to harm another. Suppose that while walking alone at night, you are attacked and that through luck or skill you repel your assailant who falls beneath your defensive blows, breaks his neck, and is confined to bed from that day forth, completely paralyzed from the neck down. We mince words if we deny that what you did harmed your assailant. Yet we do not say that what you did is therefore wrong. After all, you were innocent; you were just minding your own business. Your assailant, on the other hand, hardly qualifies as innocent. He attacked you. It would surely be an unsatisfactory morality that failed to discriminate between what you as an innocent victim may do in self-defense, and what your attacker can do in offense against your person or your property. Thus despite the initial plausibility of the first premise of the Harm Argument, not all cases of harming another are impermissible.

The difficulties with the Harm Argument suggest a fourth argument, the Innocence Argument.

1. If an action causes harm to an innocent individual, then it is not permissible, no matter what the circumstances.
2. Animals are innocent.
3. The use of animals for scientific purposes harms them.
4. Therefore, no use of any animal for any scientific purpose is morally permissible.

This argument, unlike the Harm Argument, can account for the case of the assailant, since by attacking you the assailant ceases to be innocent, and therefore in harming him you have not wronged him. In this respect if in no other, the Innocence Argument marks a genuine improvement over the Harm Argument. Nevertheless, problems remain. Again, since animals are not always harmed when used for scientific purposes, the Innocence Argument does not provide a foundation for the No Use Position. It could also be argued that animals cannot be viewed as innocent. We shall return to this issue in the following section. The more fundamental question, however, is whether the basic assumption of this argument is correct: Is it always wrong to harm an innocent individual, no matter what the circumstances?

Here we reach a point where philosophical opinion is sharply divided. Some philosophers evidently are prepared to answer this question affirmatively.[13] Others, ourselves included, are not. One way to argue against an affirmative answer to this question is to highlight, by means of more or less far-fetched hypothetical examples, what the implications of an affirmative answer would be. The use of such "thought-experiments" is intended to shed light on the gray areas of our thought by asking how alternative positions would view far-fetched hypothetical cases. The hope is that we may then return to the more complex situations of everyday life with a better understanding of how to reach the best judgment in these cases. So let us construct a thought-experiment, and indicate how it can be used to contest the view that it is always wrong to harm an innocent individual, no matter what the circumstances. (A second thought-experiment will be undertaken near the beginning of Section III.)

Imagine this case.[14] Together with four other friends, you have gone caving (spelunking) along the Pacific coast. The incoming tide catches your group by surprise and you are faced with the necessity of making a quick escape through the last remaining accessible opening to the cave or else all will drown. Unfortunately, the first person to attempt the escape gets wedged in the opening. All efforts to dislodge him, including his own frantic attempts, are unsuccessful. It so happens that one member of your party has brought dynamite along, so that the means exist to widen the opening. However to use the explosive to enlarge the escape route is certain to kill your trapped friend. The situation, then, is this: If the explosive is used, then it is certain that one will die and likely that four will escape unharmed. If the explosive is not used, it is certain that all five will die. All the persons involved are innocent. What ought to be done? Morally speaking, is it permissible to use the dynamite despite the fact that doing so is certain to harm an innocent person?

Those who think it is always wrong to harm an innocent individual, no matter what the circumstances, must say that using the dynamite would be wrong. But how can this be? If the death of one innocent individual is a bad thing, then the death of considerably more than one innocent individual must be that much worse. Accordingly, if it is claimed that you would be doing wrong if you performed an act that brought about the death of one innocent individual *because it is wrong to act in ways that harm an innocent individual,* then it must be a more grievous wrong for you to act in ways that will bring equivalent harm to a greater number of innocent individuals. But if this is so, then we have reason to deny that it is always wrong to harm an innocent individual, *no matter what the circumstances*. What our thought experiment suggests is that it is possible that some circumstances might be so potentially bad that morality will permit us to harm an innocent individual. In the thought-experiment it would be permissible to use the dynamite.

Those who incline toward viewing the prohibition against harming the innocent as absolute, admitting of no exceptions whatever, are not likely to be persuaded to give up this view just by the weight of the argument of the previous paragraphs. The debate will—and should—continue. One point worth making, however, is that those who like ourselves do not view this prohibition as absolute can nevertheless regard it as very serious, just as, for example, one can view the obligation to keep one's promises as a very serious moral requirement without viewing it as absolute. Imagine that you have borrowed a chain saw from a friend, promising to return it whenever he asks for it. Imagine he turns up at your door in a visibly drunken state, accompanied by a bound and gagged companion who has already been severely beaten and is in a state of terror. "I'll have my chainsaw now," he intones. Ought you to return it, under *those* circumstances? The obligation to keep one's promises can be regarded as quite serious without our having to say, yes, by all means, you ought to fetch the chain saw! There are other considerations that bear on the morality of what you ought to do in addition to the fact that you have made a promise. Similarly, the fact that some action will harm an innocent individual is not the only consideration that is relevant to assessing the morality of that action. In saying this we do not mean to suggest that this consideration is not an important one. It is, and we shall attempt to develop its importance more fully in the following section. All that we mean to say is that it is not the only morally relevant consideration.

There would appear to be cases, then, whether they be far-fetched hypothetical ones or ones that might arise in the real world, in which morality permits us to harm an innocent individual. Thus, even in those cases in which animals used for scientific purposes are harmed, and even assuming that they are innocent, it does not follow that how they are used is morally wrong. Like the other arguments reviewed in this section, the Innocence Argument fails to provide an acceptable basis for the No Use Position. Assuming, as we do, that these arguments provide a fair representation of those available to advocates of this position, we conclude that the No Use Position lacks a rationally compelling foundation, either in fact, or in logic, or in morality.

III.

The previous two sections criticized two extreme positions, one favoring, the other opposing, all uses of animals for scientific purposes. In the present section, and in the one that follows, two different arguments will be developed for less extreme positions, positions which though they place severe limitations on when animals may be used in science, do allow for the possibility that some animals may sometimes be used for some purposes, even some that harm them. The argument of the present section takes up where the argument of the last one ended: with the wrongness of harming the innocent. The argument of the next section is based on the different idea of maximizing the balance of good over evil. The differences between the two arguments will be sketched in Section V.

The prohibition against harming innocent individuals is a very serious, but not an absolute, prohibition. Because it is not absolute, it has justified exceptions. The problem is to say under what circumstances an exception is permitted. Perhaps the best way to begin formulating an answer is to again consider the spelunking example. Notice first that in that case we assumed that other alternatives had been exhausted;

for example, every effort had been made to find an alternative route of escape and to dislodge your trapped friend. Second, we assumed that you had very good reason to believe that all would be drowned if the only remaining exit was not widened. Very dreadful consequences—death—would obtain, therefore, for five as compared with one person, if the dynamite was not used. These considerations suggest a modified principle concerning the harming of those who are innocent. We shall call this principle the "Modified Innocence Principle" (MIP), and formulate it in the following way.

(MIP) It is wrong to harm an innocent individual unless it is reasonable to believe that doing so is the only realistic way of avoiding equal harm for many other innocents.[15]

The role of this principle can be illustrated by means of another regrettably not too far-fetched thought-experiment.

Imagine that a terrorist has possession of a well-armed tank and is systematically slaughtering forty-five innocent hostages who he has fastened to a wall.[16] Attempts to negotiate a compromise fail. The man will kill all the hostages if we do nothing. Under the circumstances, there is only one reasonable alternative: Blow up the tank. But there is this complication: The terrorist has strapped a young girl to the tank, and any weapon sufficient to blow up the tank will kill the child. The girl is innocent. Thus to blow up the tank is to harm an innocent, one who herself stands no chance of benefiting from the attack. Ought we to blow up the tank?

MIP would sanction doing so. If, as we argued in the previous section, it is worse that harm befalls many innocent individuals than that an equal harm befall one, then surely it would be worse if all the hostages were killed rather than just the one innocent child. Moreover, we have assumed that other alternatives to the attack have been tried, that they have failed, and that the only realistic way to prevent the slaughter of the remaining hostages is to blow up the tank. Thus MIP should not be understood as sanctioning a policy of "shooting first and asking questions later." It is only *after* other non-violent or less violent alternatives have been exhausted that we are permitted to do what will harm an innocent individual.

Problems remain however. Consider the notion of "equal harm." MIP will not permit harming an innocent just so that others might avoid some minor inconvenience. We cannot, for example, confine innocent vagrants to concentration camps just because we find their appearance aesthetically displeasing. Still, not all harms are equal. It is a matter of degree how much a given harm will detract from an individual's well-being, and problems will arise concerning just how serious a given harm is, or whether two or more different harms are "equal." Moreover, there is also certain to be a problem concerning the number of innocents involved. The thought-experiment involving the terrorist and the tank was a clear case of harming one innocent in order to prevent equal harm to many other innocents. But how many is many? If the only way to avoid the death of two innocents is to kill one, ought we to do this? This question, and others like it, would have to be explored in a comprehensive examination of MIP. We by-pass them now, not because they are unimportant, but because they are less important than another question which cannot be passed over. This concerns the very intelligibility of viewing animals as innocent. The fundamental nature of this issue is clear. If no sense can be made of the idea of the "innocence of animals," then whatever else may be said of MIP, at least this much could be: It simply would be inapplicable to our relations with animals. So let us ask whether sense can be made of the view that animals are innocent.

One argument against the intelligibility of animal innocence is The Moral Agent Argument.

1. Only moral agents can be innocent.
2. Animals are not moral agents.
3. Therefore, animals cannot be innocent.

By "moral agents" is meant individuals who can act from a sense of right and wrong, who can deliberate about what they ought to do, who can act and not merely react, and who thus can be held accountable or responsible for what they do or fail to do. Normal adult human beings are the clearest examples of individuals having the status of moral agents.

The first premise states that only moral agents can be innocent. Why might this be claimed? The most likely explanation is the following. Because moral agents are responsible for their actions, they can be accused of acting wrongly. Individuals who are not moral agents, however, can do no wrong. If a tree falls on someone causing death or injury, it makes no sense to condemn the tree. Since the tree "had no choice," it cannot be faulted. Moral agents can be faulted, however. If a moral agent commits murder, then he has done what is wrong; he is guilty of an offense. Suppose, however, that a moral agent is falsely accused of committing murder; he is not guilty; he is (and here is the crucial word) innocent. Thus it makes perfectly good sense to say that a moral agent is innocent because moral agents can be guilty. It makes no sense to say that a tree is innocent because trees cannot be guilty.

The second premise denies that animals are moral agents. This *seems* true. Granted, we reward and punish animals for their behavior, hoping to incline them towards behaving in ways we prefer and away from those we do not; but it is doubtful that many, if any, animals meet the requirements of moral agency.[17] Thus, if the first premise of the Moral Agent Argument is accepted, and assuming as we shall that the second premise is true, then there would seem to be no way to avoid the conclusion that animals cannot be innocent. If, like trees, they cannot be guilty, then they cannot be innocent either. And if this conclusion cannot be avoided, a conclusive case would have been made against viewing MIP as bearing on the morality of how animals may be treated. Since MIP is concerned with how *innocent* individuals may be treated, it has no bearing on how animals may be treated, if animals cannot be innocent.

But is it true that animals cannot be innocent? The preceding argument at most establishes only that they cannot be innocent in the sense that moral agents can be said to be innocent. Is this the only intelligible sense of 'innocence' that plays a role in our moral thought? The answer is definitely no, if we take our actual practice as our guide. Much of the debate over the morality of abortion, for example, centers on the alleged "innocence of the fetus." If only moral agents can be innocent, then referring to the fetus as "innocent" cannot make sense. The same is true when very young children who are killed or maimed are referred to as "innocent victims." Since they are not moral agents, it ought to be senseless to refer to them in this way. But in actual practice we do speak this way, which suggests that the concept of innocence is not restricted in its application to moral agents only, but can be meaningfully applied to those individuals who are *moral patients*.[18] These are those individuals who, though they are not moral agents and thus can do no wrong, can be the *undeserving recipients* of wrongs done to them by others. That is, they can *be* wronged, even though they can *do* no wrong. Children *are* the innocent victims of war, in this sense, not because they can be falsely accused of some wrongdoing, but because they can be made to suffer undeserved harm, in this case, undeserved harm done to them by those who make war.

A question arises regarding what individuals qualify as moral patients. Our answer hearkens back to our earlier discussion of the moral community. An individual qualifies as a member of that community, we claimed, if it is possible for others to wrong her directly. Thus moral agents qualify, but so do moral patients. Young children, the aged and helpless, the mentally enfeebled and the emotionally deranged of all ages, qualify as members of the moral community if it is possible to wrong them. In order to avoid the prejudice of speciesism we must also recognize that all those *animals* who can be harmed must likewise be recognized as members of the moral community, not because they can do what is wrong, but because, as moral patients, they can suffer wrongs.

An argument has been offered for the intelligibility of the idea of animal innocence. This is a controversial subject, and we shall return to it again at the beginning of the following section. If we assume for the moment that animals can be innocent in a morally relevant way, then we may also assume that MIP does apply to how we may treat them, and thus develop the implications of its applicability to the use of animals in science by means of the following argument, the Modified Innocence Argument.

1. It is wrong to harm the innocent unless we have very good reason to believe that this is the only realistic way to prevent equal harm for many other innocents.
2. Animals are innocent.
3. Therefore, it is not permissible to harm them unless the conditions set forth in premise (1) are satisfied.
4. At least a great deal of the use of animals in science harmful to them fails to meet the conditions set forth in premise (1).
5. Therefore, at least a great deal of this use is wrong.

The first and second premises already have been addressed. The conclusion drawn in step three follows from steps one and two. The step that remains to be examined is the fourth one, and it is to the task of defending it that we shall now turn.

As a minimal condition, MIP requires that it be reasonable to believe that the harming of an innocent will prevent equal harm to many other innocents. Apart from the issue of experimentation, it is clear that not all uses of animals in science harmful to them satisfy this requirement. For example, very many animals are harmed for instructional purposes in school and laboratory settings and in science fairs. The fulfillment of these purposes cannot reasonably be viewed as an essential step leading to the prevention of equal harms for many other innocents.[19] As for experimentation, it is clear that there are many cases in which animals are harmed to obtain trivial bits of knowledge. For example, recently the Canadian Department of Indian Affairs and Northern Development spent $80,000 to determine the effect of oil spills on polar bears.[20] The procedure involved immersing three polar bears in a container of crude oil and water. One polar bear died after licking oil from her fur for 12 hours. A second polar bear was killed for "humane reasons" after suffering intense pain from kidney failure. The third survived after suffering from severe infection that was caused by injections that the bear was given through her oil-stained skin by vetinarians who were attempting to treat her for the kidney and liver damage that was caused by her immersion in oil. The Canadian government, with the cooperation of the American government, is now planning to conduct similar experiments on dolphins.

The polar bear experiment is not an isolated incident. There is a growing body of literature that documents the triviality of much that routinely passes for "original scientific research."[21] The situation in toxicology testing is regrettably similar, as the following test illustrates.

The standard measure of the toxicity of a substance (i.e., the accepted measure of the degree to which a given substance is poisonous to humans) is its median lethal dose. The median lethal dose, or the LD_{50} as it is called, is defined as the amount of a substance needed to kill 50% of the test animals to which it is administered. The

United States Government requires that the LD_{50} be determined for each new substance bound for the market. The substances in question are not just exotic life-saving drugs, but include such ordinary products as the latest household detergent, shoe polish, oven cleaner, deodorants and soda pop. There are at least two reasons for believing that these tests, which cause great harm to the test animals, will not prevent equal harm to many other innocents. First, many of the substances for which the LD_{50} is obtained already are known to be relatively non-toxic. As a result, enormous quantities of these substances must be forcibly fed or otherwise administered to the test animals in order to cause 50% fatalities. In such cases it is often very clear long before 50% of the test animals have died, that the substance poses no serious threat to human beings. To put the point baldly: Determining the toxicity of substances which are never likely to harm anyone except the test animals to whom they are initially administered, is blatantly impermissible, given MIP. There is no good reason to believe that these tests *will* prevent equal harm to many other innocents.

But secondly, the data obtained in LD_{50} tests often are just not reliable. There are a number of reasons why. (1) It is not always possible to extrapolate toxicity data from animals to humans. As an expert in the field has noted, "(t)here are countless known examples of . . . species differences."[22] Penicillin is highly toxic to guinea pigs but not to humans, while strychnine is highly poisonous to humans but not to guinea pigs. Dinitrophonol will not cause cataracts in most laboratory animals but will in humans, and morphine, which is an effective sedative for humans, has the exact opposite effect on cats. (More will be said about the problem of extrapolation in the next section.) (2) LD_{50} tests are not performed in a uniform way. Differences in the test animals' Strain, sex, age, ambient and nutritional condition, and so forth, often result in the reporting of different LD_{50}'s for the same substance. Studies of four household chemicals conducted in six different laboratories produced toxicity data that were inconsistent, not just with respect to the absolute toxicity of the four substances but with respect to their relative toxicity as well.[23] Though this is perhaps an extreme case, the phenomenon is not uncommon, and serves to illustrate why a test like the LD_{50} fails to comply with MIP: We simply do not have good reason to believe that the harm done to the test animals will prevent equal harm to many other innocents.

MIP also requires that other realistic alternatives be exhausted before it is permissible to harm an innocent individual. This requirement does make a difference. If, prior to attempted negotiations with the terrorist, for example, we blew up the tank, we would be morally culpable. We would have resorted to violence, knowing this would harm the innocent child, without having first determined whether we could have acted to prevent harm being done to *all* the innocents. So let us ask whether all scientific uses of animals harmful to them is undertaken only after other realistic alternatives have been tried.

Unfortunately, the answer is no: a great deal of the use made of animals in science clearly fails to satisfy this requirement, though of course we cannot say exactly how much, anymore than we can say exactly how much water there is in the Pacific. What we can say is that the amount in each case is *a lot*. "But there are no alternatives," it is often said. This is an answer that we shall examine more fully shortly. Sometimes, however, there *are* well established alternatives to the use of animals. These alternatives include tissue and cell cultures, mathematical modeling, chemical analysis, mechanical models, clinical examination and epidemological surveys.[24] In cases where there are established, scientifically viable alternatives to using animals and other innocent individuals who can be hurt or harmed (e.g., humans), MIP requires that these alternatives be employed and not the innocents.

However, it remains true that sometimes, in some cases, there are no known alternatives that have been proven to be scientifically reliable. What does MIP imply about these cases? Here we must take note of an important disanalogy between the scientific enterprise and our thought-experiments. Those experiments presented us with crisis situations in which the alternatives are clearly defined, in which neither time nor circumstances allow for the investigation of new options, and in which we could not reasonably be expected to have done anything before the crisis developed so that we might have another realistic option at our disposal. (There is nothing we could reasonably be expected to do today, for example, to increase the options that would be available to us in the extremely unlikely event that we should find ourselves in the predicament we imagined in the spelunking example). There is, however, a great deal that science can begin to do today and could have done in the past in an effort to explore alternatives to the use of animals for scientific purposes. Time and circumstances *do* allow for the scientific investigation of such alternatives; indeed, it is part of the very essence of the scientific enterprise to search for new ways to approach old (and emerging) problems. The longer the life-sciences, including psychology,[25] are delayed in making a conscientious effort to search for alternatives, the greater the wrong, given MIP, since an insufficient commitment in this regard itself offends against the spirit of MIP. To harm the innocent is so *serious* a moral matter that we must do all that we can reasonably be expected to do so that we can avoid causing this harm. If the life-sciences, through lack of will, funding, or both, fail to do all that can reasonably be expected of them in this regard, then we have no reason to assume that the use made of animals in science is justified "because there are no available alternatives." On the contrary, we have reason to deny the moral propriety of such use. To put this same point differently: Since we are justified in believing that it is wrong to harm the innocent unless we can be shown that it isn't, we are justified in regarding the harm caused to animals in science as unjustified unless we can be shown that all that reasonably could be done has been done to avoid causing it. If we cannot be shown that these efforts have been made, then we are right to regard their use as wrong, given MIP.

Viewed from this perspective, *at least most* harmful use of animals in science ought to be regarded as morally unjustified. The "search for alternatives" has been a largely token effort, one that has not been given a priority anywhere approaching that required by MIP. But this is not the fault only of those involved in the life-sciences. As a society we have not seriously thought about the moral status of animals. We have failed to recognize that animals are members of the moral community, or we have minimized the importance of their membership. As a result, we have not funded the search for alternatives sufficiently. Since (as it is well said) "research goes where the money is," the investigation of alternatives has not prospered.

Those involved in the life-sciences are not entirely free of responsibility however. Though they do not control the flow of money from public and private sources, their voice is not without its influence. Moreover, the voices of scientists carry more weight in determining what research finds funding than do the voices of ordinary citizens, or even the voices of those active in the humane movement. A demand on the part of scientists that the search for alternatives be given the priority MIP requires is essential, if this search is to have any chance of receiving the funding that acceptance of MIP would require.

We may conclude the present section, then, as follows. About much use of animals in science that harms them, it is false to suppose that it will prevent equal harm befalling many other innocents. About some harmful use that might prevent such harm, it is false to suppose that these uses are known to be the only realistic way to achieve such results. And about most use of animals that causes them harm, it is false to suppose that as a society we have made the conscientious effort to search for alternatives that the MIP requires. Thus, if MIP should guide our behavior with respect to animals, we cannot avoid concluding that *at least most* of the uses made of animals in science that harms them is not morally permissible—is morally wrong.

IV.

The argument of the previous section relied heavily on the idea that animals are innocent. The attempt to undermine this idea by means of the Moral Agent Argument was considered and found wanting. There are other ways to contest this idea, however. The Rights Argument is one.

1. Only those individuals who have rights can be innocent.
2. Animals cannot have rights.
3. Therefore, animals cannot be innocent.

A defense of the first premise might proceed along the following lines. To speak of individuals as innocent assumes that they can suffer *undeserved* harm. But undeserved harm must be harm that is unjust or unfair, and what is unjust or unfair is what violates an individual's rights. Thus, only those individuals who have rights can be the recipients of undeserved harm. As for the second premise, not very long ago it was assumed to be so obvious as not to require any supporting argument at all. Recently, however, the idea of animal rights has been debated, and there is a steadily growing body of literature, in an expanding number of prestigious professional journals from scientific and humanistic disciplines, devoted to the reflective assessment of this idea.[26] It will not be possible to review this debate on the present occasion. We mention it only in order to indicate how the idea of the innocence of animals is relevant to the more widely discussed idea of animal rights. A thorough examination of the former idea would have to include a thorough examination of the latter one as well.

It is possible to approach the question of the ethics of animal use in science from a perspective that does not place fundamental importance on innocence and the allied idea of rights. Utilitarianism is one such perspective. It is a view that has attracted many able thinkers, and represents today, in the English speaking world at least, the primary alternative to views of morality that place central importance on individual rights. Moreover, utilitarianism's most influential advocates, from Jeremy Bentham (1748–1832) and John Stuart Mill (1806–1873) to the contemporary Australian philosopher Peter Singer, have explicitly recognized the membership of animals in the moral community. It will be instructive, therefore, to sketch the utilitarian position in general and to mark its implications for the use of animals for scientific purposes in particular.

Utilitarianism is the view that we ought to act so as to bring about the greatest possible balance of good over evil for everyone affected. Utilitarianism is thus not a selfish doctrine; it does not prescribe that each individual is to act so as to maximize his or her own self-interest. For the utilitarian, your neighbor's good counts the same as yours; in Bentham's words, "Each to count for one, no one for more than one." In trying to decide what ought to be done, therefore, we must consider the interests of everyone involved, being certain to count equal interests equally. The point of view required by utilitarianism is uncompromisingly impartial; we are not allowed to favor our own interests, or those of our friends, or say, White-Anglo-Saxon-Protestant's, over the like interests of others. It is, in the words of the nineteenth century utilitarian Henry Sidgwick, "the point of view of the universe." For the utilitarian, the ideas of the innocence and the rights of individuals are not independent considerations to be used in determining what ought to be done. They have a role only if they bear on the determination of what the best consequences would be. Utilitarianism recommends a "forward-looking" morality. Results are the only things that matter in the determination of right and wrong.

Utilitarians have disagreed over many points, including the nature of the good consequences they seek and the evil ones they seek to avoid. Classical utilitarians, including Bentham and Mill, viewed goodness as pleasure and evil as pain. Some recent utilitarians understand goodness as the satisfaction of an individual's preferences.[27] On either view, many animals must find a place in the utilitarian calculation of the best consequences, if, following these thinkers, we agree that many animals can experience what is pleasant or painful, or have preferences. For the sake of simplicity, in what follows we shall think of good consequences (utility) as pleasure, and bad consequences (disutility) as pain.

Bentham, in an oft-quoted and justly famous passage, declares the relevance of the pain of animals in the following way.

> The French have already discovered that the blackness of the skin is no reason why a human being should be abandoned without redress to the caprice of a tormentor. It may come one day to be recognized, that the number of the legs, the villosity of the skin, or the termination of the *os sacrum,* are reasons equally insufficient for abandoning a sensitive being to the same fate . . . (T)he question is not, Can they *reason?* nor, Can they *talk?* but, Can they *suffer?*[28]

If we assume, as we have throughout, that the animals of which we speak can suffer, how might a utilitarian such as Bentham argue against their use for scientific purposes? Clearly no utilitarian would accept the principal assumption of the Pain Argument; the assumption that it is *always* wrong to cause another pain. The permissibility of causing pain, like the permissibility of performing any other act, must depend for the utilitarian on the utility of doing it, and since it could be true in any given case that we will bring about the best consequences for everyone involved by an act that causes pain to some individual(s), the utilitarian will not accept the prohibition against causing pain as absolute (as impermissible at all times, no matter what the consequences).

It remains true, nevertheless, that utilitarians will regard causing pain as a negative feature of an act. Any action which causes pain and fails to bring about a greater amount of pleasure will be ruled out by the utilitarian as morally wrong, except when every other alternative action would bring about an even greater balance of pain over pleasure. Thus one way of formulating the Utilitarian Argument against the use of animals in science is the following.

1. Acts are not morally permissible if they cause pain to some individuals and yet fail to bring about the best possible consequences for everyone involved.
2. A great deal of the scientific use of animals causes them pain and fails to bring about the best possible consequences.
3. Therefore, a great deal of this use is not morally permissible.

There are many reasons for accepting the second premise of this argument. Even in the case of animal based experimentation or research, much is redundant, and is carried on well beyond the threshold needed for replication. Experimental studies of shock are a good example. As early as 1946 a survey of the literature indicated that over 800 papers had been published on experimental studies of shock. These studies induced shock by various means, including: tournequets, hammer-blows, rotations in the Noble-Collip drum, gunshot wounds, strangulation, intestinal loops, burning and freezing. By 1954 a survey article reported that although "animal investigations in the field of traumatic shock have yielded diversified and often contradictory results," the investigators looked forward to "future experimentation in this field."[29] In 1974 researchers still described their work as "preliminary." Presumably such work will continue as long as someone is willing to fund it.

There is no question but that much animal experimentation, like the research on shock described in the previous paragraph, continues from habit, convenience, desire for professional advancement and so forth. Dr. Roger Ulrich, one of the leading researchers in aggression studies, has performed experiments on rats that involve blinding, mutilation and castration, as well as the administration of electric shock and bursts of intense noise. Recently, in a letter to the American Psychological Association's *Monitor,* he wrote:

> Initially my research was prompted by the desire to understand and help solve the problem of human aggression but I later discovered that the results of my work did not seem to justify its continuance. Instead I began to wonder if perhaps financial rewards, professional prestige, the opportunity to travel, etc., were the maintaining factors.[30]

Other experiments are performed in order to confirm hypotheses that almost everyone already knows are true. The experiments on polar bears discussed in the previous section are an obvious example. As one Vancouver newspaper editorialized:

> The experts wanted to determine the effects of oil spills on the polar bears. Apparently no children of, say, 12 years of age were on hand to give them a pretty good idea.[31]

Moreover, similar experiments had been conducted in Canada on seals only five years before. To the surprise of no one except possibly the researchers, most of the seals died after being immersed in oil.

Other experiments are performed in order to falsify hypotheses that almost everyone knows are false. Here is the voice of David Hubel of Harvard Medical School reporting one such case.

> A few years ago the notion was advanced that memories might be recorded in the form of large molecules, with the information encoded in a sequence of smaller molecules, as genetic information is encoded in DNA. Few people familiar with the highly patterned specificity of connections in the brain took the idea seriously, and yet much time was consumed in many laboratories teaching animals tasks, grinding up their brains and either finding differences in the brain chemistry of the trained animals or finding "statistically significant" improvement in the ability of other animals, into which extracts of the trained animals' brains were injected, to learn the same tasks. The fad has died out. . . .[32]

Many animal experiments are rendered useless by the unreliability of the data obtained. Experimental results have been found to vary depending on the time of day that the experiment was performed, the appearance of the researcher, the temperature of the room and other equally subtle factors. It is almost impossible to control such complex background variables.[33] Moreover, even when the data are reliable with respect to the test animals, the problem of extrapolating the results to humans remains severe. As two prominent researchers from the Institute of Experimental Pathology and Toxicology of the Albany Medical College have written:

> At the present time . . . the legitimate question can still be asked, for we do not have the answer: "How can we be sure that the extrapolation of animal data to man is accurate?"[34]

After noting substantive difficulties in extrapolating data, the authors conclude:

> To be sure, these data may have little or no relevance to man, but they are the best basis for prediction of hazard to man that we have at the present time. . . . Unfortunately, Alexander Pope's remark of many years ago, "The proper study of mankind is man" is still true. Various committees of the World Health Organization and of the National Academy of Sciences are in general agreement with this statement.[35]

In another paper, one of the co-authors goes so far as to advance the proposal that routinely using animals as test or experimental models is premature at best.

> Species differences in metabolism is one of the primary reasons why projection of animal data to man is not always possible. Differences in the metabolic pathways and the rate of detoxification are observed among the animal species and between animals and man. That is why early trial in man, to learn something of the metabolic rate and pathway in man, as compared to animals, is recommended before long-term animal studies are initiated.[36]

The extrapolation problem is so severe, then, that at least one prominent toxicologist has advocated human studies *before* long-term animal studies! This suggestion, of course, raises ethical issues of its own. But one must certainly wonder why and how animal tests would be necessary at all in a situation in which a substance had already been administered to humans.

The utilitarian argument could go even futher. John Cairns, Director of the Imperial Cancer Research Fund's Mill Hill Laboratory in London, has pointed out that during the last 150 years in the Western world, there has been an enormous increase in life expectancy.[37] He notes that this increase in life expectancy began before the advent of "what we would call medical science" and argues that it is primarily due to better nutrition and hygiene rather than to the development of exotic new drugs and surgical procedures. He goes on to say that the chance of dying of cancer in the United States has not altered appreciably in the last 35 years, in spite of intense research activity. Claims to the contrary are based on statistical gimmicks: Since 'cure' is defined as survival five years after diagnosis, the earlier a cancer is diagnosed the greater the likelihood of cure, even if the course of the disease and the time of death are unaffected in any way. In commenting on the eradication of infectious diseases, Cairns claims:

> It is significant, however, that what is often thought of as one of the accomplishments of sophisticated medical science was, in large part, the product of some fairly simple improvements in public health. In the end, history may well repeat itself and the same prove to be true for cancer.[38]

Cairns is not the only prominent figure in the scientific establishment to have made such an argument. Perhaps it goes too far, but it does suggest how thorough-going a utilitarian critique of animal experimentation, or the use of animals in toxicology experiments or in education, can be. If most of our use of animals in these activities are largely irrelevant to producing longer and pleasanter lives, then there is no justification for using animals in ways that cause them pain.

But it is not just the unreliability and redundancy of the data that utilitarians will contest. They can also object to the *kind* of animal used for scientific purposes. Rocks cannot feel pleasure or pain. Only conscious beings can. Nevertheless, there are great differences among conscious beings regarding the degree or level of their consciousness. Some conscious beings have a conception of their own identity, a self-concept: they can make plans for the future, regret the past, and envision their own bodily death. Beings that lack a concept of self might experience something like pleasure, but they cannot anticipate future pleasure, nor regret those pleasures they have missed in the past. It is for this reason that we think of some beings as having more complex, richer and "higher" states of consciousness than other conscious beings. Beings with a sense of self are utility "hot spots," so to speak. Because they have the kind of consciousness they do, they can experience richer, fuller pleasures and pains, and because of this we should take special care to maximize their pleasures and minimize their pains. That would seem to be a winning strategy for bringing about the best consequences.

Where, precisely, we draw the line between animals who do, and those who do not, have a concept of self is unclear. Probably there is no *precise* line to be drawn. That problem is not what demands our attention just now. The point to notice is that utilitarianism will not allow the use of animals having higher levels of consciousness, even if their use would bring about a net balance of good over evil, if these same (or better) results could be obtained by using animals of less highly developed consciousness. Wherever possible, that is, utilitarianism requires that science deal with the most rudimentary forms of conscious life *and* as few of these as possible, or, most preferable by far, with non-conscious beings, living or otherwise. Since there is ample evidence that most chimpanzees, for example, have a sense of self,[39] and growing evidence that some species of Cetaceans do,[40] the case for regarding these animals as having higher consciousness is increasingly reinforced and the utilitarian grounds for cautioning against the use of these animals for scientific purposes is correspondingly strengthened. It is exceedingly doubtful that the 30,000 primates used for scientific purposes in America in 1978 were used justifiably, given the Utilitarian Argument.

There is welcome evidence that contemporary scientists, unlike Descartes' contemporaries, are becoming increasingly sensitive to the issues discussed in the previous paragraph. Talk of "the Three R's" is in the air. The goal of research, it is said, is replacement, reduction and refinement. Commenting on these ideas, D. H. Smyth writes that "Replacement (means) the substitution of insentient material for conscious living higher animals. Reduction (means) reduction in the number of animals used to obtain information of given amount and precision. Refinement (means) any decrease in the incidence or severity of inhumane procedure (i.e., pain or suffering) applied to those animals which still have to be used."[41] These are goals that both utilitarians and supporters of the Modified Innocence Principle can endorse. But both positions can be used to press the case for justification of the use of animals in science at a deeper level. The question is, how can any use of any animal for any scientific purpose be justified? To be told that, whenever possible, we ought to replace, reduce or refine, does not address this question. Built into the Three R's is the assumption that the use of animals in science sometimes *is* justified, and it is precisely this question that must be addressed rather than begged. Utilitarianism provides us with one way of answering it, the Modified Innocence Principle provides us with another; but the Three R's provides us with no answer at all.

Perhaps it will be replied that the goal of refinement gets at the heart of the matter. "Only that suffering that is absolutely necessary for the scientific integrity of an experiment or test is allowed," it may be said. Suppose this is true. Does it follow that, judged on utilitarian grounds, the animal's use is permissible? It does not. The larger question is whether *the experiment, test, or other use of the animal is itself justified*. Only if it is can the pain involved be justified. Until the issue of the moral justifiability of the animal's use is addressed, therefore, the justification of the animal's pain, even if the pain is "kept to a minimum," remains in doubt.[42]

In summary, the principle of utility demands that stringent requirements be met before we can be justified in using any animal for any scientific purpose that causes it pain. It must be shown that a proposed use will promote the utilitarian objective of bringing about the greatest possible balance of good over evil for everyone involved. If it does not, then, as premise 2 of the Utilitarian Argument asserts, the procedure is morally wrong. There is ample reason to believe that at least a great deal of the use of animals in science does not satisfy this requirement. Thus, if utility be our guide, there is strong reason to condemn much of the current use made of animals in science.

V.

In the two preceding sections we sketched two moral perspectives that converge on the same general conclusion: At least much of the scientific use made of animals is morally wrong and ought to be stopped. Despite their agreement in a broad range of cases however, the Principle of Utility and the Modified Innocence Principle (MIP) support conflicting judgments in some cases.

Recall that MIP will allow harming an innocent only if we have very good reason to believe that this is the only realistic way to prevent equivalent harm to many other innocents. MIP does not sanction harming innocents so that others may reap positive goods (e.g., pleasures); it is limited to the prevention or elimination of harms or evils (e.g., pain). Thus, in principle, MIP will not allow, say, contests between a few innocent Christians and hungry lions so that great amounts of otherwise unobtainable pleasure might be enjoyed by large numbers of Roman spectators. MIP does not permit evil (the harming of innocents) so that good may come. In principle, Utilitarianism could allow this. Classical utilitarianism is aggregative in nature: it is the *total* of goods and evils, for *all* the individuals involved, that matters. Theoretically, then, it is possible that achieving the optimal balance of good over evil in any given case will necessitate harming the innocent. The point can be illustrated abstractly by imagining that we face a choice between two alternatives, A_1 which will harm an innocent individual and A_2 which will not. A utilitarian, we may assume, will assign some disutility, some minus-score, to the harm caused in A_1. Suppose this is -20. Suppose further, however, that A_1 would bring about much better consequences for others than A_2; suppose that the difference is a magnitude of 100 to 1, A_1 yielding benefits that total $+1000$, A_2 yielding only $+10$. A greater balance of good over evil would result if we did A_1 than if we did A_2. Utilitarians, therefore, must choose the former alternative, but not those who accept MIP: they must favor the latter alternative (A_2).

The Principles of Utility and that of Modified Innocence do differ in theory, therefore, despite their agreement in many practical cases. Which principle ought we to accept? That is far too large an issue to be decided here, but it is pursued in considerable depth in some of the other essays in the present volume.[43] It is enough to realize that utilitarianism theoretically could allow more use of animals in science that harms the animals than MIP allows. Whether or not this difference is a sign of the moral superiority or inferiority of utilitarianism in comparison to MIP, at least this much is clear: there is a difference.

VI.

Some general points should be kept in mind as we conclude. First, given either the Principle of Utility or MIP, to harm an animal is in need of moral defense; both principles view the harming of an individual as *presumptively* wrong, as something that is wrong unless it can be shown that it isn't. Given either principle, therefore, the burden of proof must always be on those who cause harm to animals in scientific settings. Unless these persons can show that what they do is morally permissible, we are entitled to believe that it is not. This burden, obvious as it may seem, has not always been recognized. Too often it has been "those who speak for the animals" who have been called upon to shoulder the burden of proof. But it is not the critics, it is the advocates of animal use in science who should bear it. This fundamental point must never be lost sight of in the debate over the ethics of the use of animals in science.

Second, the kind of knowledge (one might better say "wisdom") sometimes required to determine the permissibility of using an animal, especially in experiments in basic research, clearly is not the exclusive property of any particular profession, let alone any particular branch of science. For that reason we should draw upon the expertise of many people, from many fields, to review experimental proposals before they are funded. It is very important that these decisions not be left just to those who have a professional interest in their outcome. Not very long ago in this country experiments were performed on humans with impunity. Today we have recognized the merits of the idea that decisions about the permissibility of research that might harm human subjects must be made on a case by case basis, involving the best judgment of persons from diverse areas of expertise; we wouldn't dream of leaving these decisions entirely in the hands of those doing the research. Because animals cannot, except by prejudice, be excluded from the moral community, it is reason, not "mere sentiment," that calls for similar procedural safeguards for their use in science generally and in scientific experimentation in particular. It is not enough, even if it is a salutary development, that principles for the care and maintenance of laboratory animals are in place,[44] though even here one should raise questions about how conscientiously these principles are enforced. How often, for example, has a scientific establishment been found in violation of these principles? And how impartial are those in whose hands the business of enforcement rests? One need not prejudge the answers to these questions by insisting upon the propriety of asking them.

At this point someone will accuse us of being "anti-scientific" or, more soberly, perhaps it will be argued that instituting procedural safeguards of the kind we recommend, in which research proposals are considered case by case by a panel of experts from diverse fields, would "rein in science," thus having a chilling effect on important research. The "anti-science" accusation will be answered in this essay's final paragraph. As for the "chilling effect" argument, it is true that adopting the kind of procedural safeguards we recommend *would* place limits on what scientists would be permitted to do. These safeguards would thus restrict the scientists's "freedom to inquire." The right to inquire, however, as was argued earlier, is not absolute; one may not do anything one pleases in the name of this right; it can and should be limited by other, weightier moral concerns. It is no longer possible in this country, for example, to infect poor Black males in Alabama with syphillis and to record the development of the disease when left untreated. This *is* a restriction on science, but one which ought to be viewed as welcome and appropriate. An unfortunate consequence of instituting and effectively enforcing procedural safeguards for the use of animals in science, it is true, is that research proposals would have to be screened by another, interdisciplinary committee, requiring that yet another set of forms be filled out and so forth. Both the bureaucracy and the red tape are almost certain to increase if our call for safeguards is heeded. Researchers may see "Big Brother" at work, and descry, in the words of a leader in brain transplant research, Robert J. White, "the ever-present danger of government control of biological research through the limitation of animal availability and experimental design."[45] But the inconvenience "red-tape" causes would seem to be a comparatively small price to pay to insure that scientific practice meets the demands of morality. The life-sciences are not physics, and the costs that must be borne in the conduct of biological and psychological research cannot be measured merely in dollars and cents.

In reply it may be objected that the kind of safeguards we propose would be impracticable, and, in any event, would cost too much to implement. Neither objection is well-founded. In July of 1977 some initial procedural safeguards for experimental animals were put into place in Sweden. It has been noted that simply by establishing ethics committees to review research proposals, research designs have been improved; and these designs often require the use of fewer animals than was formerly the rule.[46] In addition, greater use is being made of animals with less highly developed conscious lives, animals which, not surprisingly, are cheaper to procure and maintain; and the employment of less harmful procedures is growing. It has been reported that the Swedish approach has proven satisfactory to many, both in the scientific and in the animal welfare communities. The "Swedish experiment" suggests that it is possible to develop a framework that is practical and financially sound, a framework which, though not a panacea, does go some way toward protecting the interests of animals while at the same time nurturing our interest in the growth and maintenance of science.

Two final points. First, nothing that we have said should be taken as condemning the motives, intentions or character of those engaged in scientific research. We are not saying that these people are nasty, vicious, cruel, dehumanized, heartless, depraved, pitiless, evil people. No one who uses animals in science has been accused of being, in White's terminology, a "monster-scientist, perpetrator of abominable crimes."[47] Neither are we saying that "all scientists" are on an ego-trip, motivated to do their work only to pump out another publication, to be used to secure yet another grant, to be parlayed into yet a bigger name, yet another promotion, yet another raise, and so forth and so forth. These accusations may have powerful rhetorical force in some quarters, but they have no place, and have found none, here, in a reflective assessment of the ethics of the use of animals in science. Our concern throughout has been to assess the ethics of *what* scientists do, not *why* they do it. The point that must be recognized is that people can do what is wrong even though they have the best motives, the best intentions, even though they are "the nicest people." The question of the moral status of animal use in science thus is not to be decided by discovering the motives or intentions of those who do it *or* of those who criticize it. The sooner all the parties to the debate realize this, the better.[48]

Lastly, there is the idea of alternatives again. The search for alternatives to using animals in science is only in its infancy. Many scientists tend to scorn the idea and to believe that the number and utility of alternatives are very limited. One would have thought that recent developments would have put this attitude to rest. To cite just one encouraging example, a promising new bacterial test for carcinogens has been developed by Professor Bruce Ames at the University of California. Whereas animal tests for carcinogenicity typically take two to three years and cost in excess of $150,000, the Ames' test takes two to three days, uses no animals, and costs just a few hundred dollars.[49] Ames himself stops short of claiming that his test is 100% accurate, and he does not rule out the present need to use animals as an ancillary part of research into carcinogens. Yet his test does much to suggest the potential benefits to be realized from the search for alternatives, both in terms of the savings in animal pain and in dollars and cents. Those skeptical of "alternatives" ("impossible" it may be said) may hold their ground, but we should not be discouraged. Yesterday's "impossibilities" are today's commonplaces. We must press on despite the skeptics, acting to insure that adequate funds become available to those qualified to search for alternatives. The call to intensify the search is not "antiscientific." In fact, it is just the opposite. It is a call to scientists to use their skill, knowledge and ingenuity to progress toward our common aspirations: a more humane approach to the practice of science. It is a call to *do* science, not to abandon it. The commitment to search for alternatives should be viewed as an index both of our moral *and* our scientific progress.[50]

Notes

1. For documentation and additional information see J. Diner, *Physical and Mental Suffering of Experimental Animals* (Washington: Animal Welfare Institute, 1979); and R. Ryder, *Victims of Science* (London: Davis-Poynter, 1975).

2. These three areas are identified and discussed more fully by Andrew N. Rowan in his *Alternatives to Laboratory Animals: Definition and Discussion* (Washington: The Institute for the Study of Animal Problems, 1980).

3. As quoted in L. Rosenfield, *From Animal Machine to Beast Machine* (New York: Octagon Books, 1968) p. 54.

4. These views are discussed more fully in Tom Regan, "The Moral Basis of Vegetarianism," *Canadian Journal of Philosophy* (1975), pp. 181–214. Reprinted in Tom Regan, *All That Dwell Therein: Animal Rights and Environmental Ethics* (Berkeley: University of California Press, 1982).

5. Richard Ryder was the first to argue in this way in *op. cit.*

6. C. S. Lewis, "Vivisection" in *Undeceptions* (London: Geoffrey Blass, 1971).

7. In January 1981 Revlon, Inc. the world's largest cosmetics' manufacturer, announced that it had awarded Rockefeller University $750,000 to research and develop an alternative to the Draize test. The company also granted $25,000 to establish a trust, the purpose of which is to fund further research into alternatives. Thus other cosmetic companies can join Revlon's pioneering move—(this is the first time a commercial firm has funded the search for alternatives to the use of live animals for testing)—by the simple expedient of contributing to the trust. The political realities being what they are, chances are good that Revlon's efforts will soon be imitated by other firms in the cosmetics' industry. Revlon's actions were prompted by a uncommonly well organized campaign, involving more than four hundred separate animal welfare related organizations, conducted over a two year period. Through meetings with representatives of Revlon, through the media, through petitions to the Congress, through letter writing campaigns, and through protest marches and rallies, the Coalition to Stop the Draize Rabbit Blinding Tests, Inc. helped to persuade Revlon to take its revolutionary step. The Coalition's success gives a clear demonstration of what can be done on behalf of animals and what must be done to succeed. When the money required to seek alternatives is on hand, there will be no lack of persons willing to do it.

8. M. Weil and R. Scala, "A Study of Intra- and Inter- Laboratory Variability in the Results of Rabbit Eye and Skin and Irritation Tests," *Toxicology and Applied Pharmacology* 19 (1971), pp. 271–360.

9. Dr. Feinberg made this claim while serving on a panel discussion on animal experimentation, sponsored by the Anti-Cruelty Society of Chicago, in October 1980.

10. Some of these issues are explored in a rather extreme way in S. Epstein, *The Politics of Cancer* (Garden City: Anchor Press/Doubleday, 1979).

11. *British Medical Journal,* October 28, 1972, p. 190. We have taken this example as well as several others from Deborah Mayo's unpublished paper, "Against a Scientific Justification of Animal Experiments."

12. Recently even many scientists have become concerned about the possibilities inherent in certain kinds of research. The interested reader should see the essays collected in the following volumes: G. Holton and R. Morison (eds.), *Limits of Scientific Inquiry* (New York: W. W. Norton and Co., 1978); K. Wulff (ed.), *Regulation of Scientific Inquiry: Social Concerns with Research,* American Association for the Advancement of Science Selected Symposium no. 37 (Boulder, CO: Westview Press, 1979); J. Richards (ed.), *Recombinant DNA: Science, Ethics and Politics* (New York: Academic Press, 1978); and D. Jackson and S. Stich (eds.), *The Recombinant DNA Debate* (Englewood Cliffs, NJ: Prentice-Hall 1979).

13. Baruch Brody is apparently one such philosopher. See his *Abortion and the Sanctity of Life: A Philosophical View* (Cambridge: The MIT Press, 1974).

14. The example is given by the contemporary American philosopher, Richard Brandt in his essay "A Moral Principle About Killing," in Marvin Kohl, ed., *Beneficent Euthanasia* (Buffalo: Prometheus Books, 1972). The philosophical propriety of using more or less unusual hypothetical examples in assessing moral principles is critically discussed by the contemporary English philosopher G.E.M. Anscombe in her "Modern Moral Philosophy," *Philosophy,* 33 (1958), reprinted in Judith J. Thomson and Gerald Dworkin, eds., *Ethics* (New York: Harper & Row, 1968).

15. MIP would probably have to be reformulated to account for a range of cases (e.g., "innocent threats") with which we are not primarily concerned in this paper. Insane persons can kill just as surely as sane ones and, though they are innocent, morality surely allows us to defend ourselves against their threatening attacks.

16. Here we develop an example introduced by Robert Nozick in Chapter 3 of his *Anarchy, State and Utopia* (New York: Basic Books, 1979).

17. The possibility that certain species of animals have a morality of their own, based on mutual sympathy, is explored and defended by James Rachels in "Do Animals Have a Right to Liberty?", Tom Regan and Peter Singer, eds., *Animal Rights and Human Obligations* (Englewood Cliffs: Prentice-Hall, 1976).

18. For further comments on this term, see G. J. Warnock in his *The Object of Morality* (New York: Methuen, 1971).

19. For a fuller discussion of these issues, see Heather McGiffin and Nancie Brownley, eds., *Animals in Education: The Use of Animals in High School Biology Classes and Science Fairs* (Washington: Institute for the Study of Animal Problems, 1980).

20. The results have not been published in a professional journal. But see the reports published in the Vancouver, B.C. newspapers (*The Province and The Vancouver Sun*) on March 28, 1980 and April 8, 1980. This case and the relevant documentation were brought to our attention by David Rinehart of the *Greenpeace Examiner.*

21. See again, the works by Diner and Ryder referred to in Footnote 1, as well as Peter Singer, *Animal Liberation* (New York: Avon Books, 1975).

22. R. Levine, *Pharmacology: Drug Actions and Reactions* (New York: Little, Brown, 1978).

23. These studies are reported in R. Loosli, "Duplicate Testing and Reproducibility," in Regamey, Hennessen, Ikic and Ungar, *International Symposium on Laboratory Medicine* (Basel: S. Karger, 1967).

24. These methods are reviewed in, for example, Rowan, *op. cit.,* and Ryder, *op. cit.*

25. For a critical assessment of the use made of animals in psychological research, see Alan Bowd, "Ethical Reservations About Psychological Research with Animals," *The Psychological Record.*

26. See 'A Select Bibliography on Animal Rights and Human Obligations," *Inquiry,* Vol Nos. 1–2, 1978.

27. For example, R. M. Hare in "Ethical Theory and Utilitarianism," in H. D. Lewis (ed.), *Contemporary British Philosophy* 4 (London: Allen and Unwin, 1976); and P. Singer, *Practical Ethics* (Cambridge: Cambridge University Press, 1980).

28. Jeremy Bentham, *The Principles of Moral and Legislation* (1789) Chapter 17, Section 1; reprinted in T. Regan and P. Singer (eds.), *Animal Rights and Human Obligations, op. cit.*

29. S. Rosenthal and R. Milliean, *Pharmacological Review* 6 (1954), p. 489. See also Peter Singer, *Animal Liberation, op. cit.*

30. *Monitor,* March, 1978, p. 16. The view that science develops mainly through habit, convenience, desire for prestige and so forth is one that has gained currency in contemporary philosophy of science. See, for example, T. Kuhn, *The Structure of Scientific Revolutions,* Second Edition (Chicago: University of Chicago Press, 1970); Paul Feyerabend, *Against Method* (London: New Left Books, 1975); and L. Laudan, *Progress and Its Problems* (Berkeley: University of California Press, 1977).

31. *The Vancouver Sun,* March 28, 1978.

32. David Hubel, "The Brain," *Scientific American* 241 (1979), p. 53.

33. The literature concerning such difficulties has been proliferating. See, for example. H. Magalhaes (ed.), *Environmental Variables in Animal Experimentation* (New Jersey: Associated University Presses, Inc., 1974).

34. F. Coulston and D. Serrone, "The Comparative Approach to the Role of Nonhuman Primates in Evaluation of Drug Toxicity in Man: A Review," *Annals of the New York Academy of Sciences* 162 (1969), p. 682.

35. *Ibid.,* pp. 682–683.

36. F. Coulston, "Benefits and Risks Involved in the Development of Modern Pharmaceutical Products," presented in Bonn and in Luxemburg in September, 1980.

37. J. Cairns, *Cancer: Science and Society* (San Francisco: W. H. Freeman and Co., 1978).

38. *Ibid.,* p. 7.

39. On chimpanzees, see G. Gallup, "Self-Recognition in Primates," *American Psychologist* 32 (1977), 329–338.

40. On Cetaceans, see the essays collected in K. Norris (ed.), *Whales, Dolphins, and Porpoises* (Berkeley: University of California Press, 1966) and J. McIntyre (ed.), *Mind in the Waters* (New York: Charles Scribners' Son, 1974).

41. D. H. Smyth, *Alternatives to Animal Experiments* (London: Scholar Press, 1978) p. 14.

42. For further comments on the ambiguity of "unnecessary suffering," see Tom Regan, "Cruelty, Kindness and Unnecessary Suffering," *Philosophy,* Vol. 55, No. 214, 1980.

43. See, in particular, the essays "Utilitarianism," "Justice and Equality," and "Rights."

44. These federal regulations are part of The Animal Welfare Act. The physical facilities in which animals used in science are housed and the attention given to some of their basic needs (food, water) have improved as a result of these regulations. Not all animals are covered by the Act, however, rats and mice being notable exceptions; and the regulations apply to, and thus are enforcable only in the case of, federally supported programs.

45. R. J. White, "Antivivisection: The Reluctant Hydra," *The American Scholar,* vol. 40, no. 3 (Summer 1971); reprinted in Tom Regan and Peter Singer (eds.), *Animal Rights and Human Obligations, op. cit.*

46. For a discussion of the Swedish experiment, see M. Ross, "The Ethics of Animal Experimentation: Control in Practice," *Australian Psychologist* 13 (1978).

47. *op. cit.,* p. 166.

48. Some of these matters are discussed in Tom Regan, "Cruelty, Kindness, and Unnecessary Suffering," *op. cit.*

49. See "Bacterial Tests for Potential Carcinogens," *Scientific American* 241 (1979).

50. We wish to thank Barbara Orlans and Andrew Rowan for helpful comments on an earlier draft of this essay. Professor Jamieson's work on this project was assisted by a grant from the University Awards Committee of the State University of New York, while Professor Regan's was assisted by a grant from the National Endowment for the Humanities. It is a pleasure to express our gratitude in a public way to these respective agencies.

Suggested Readings

J. Diner, *Physical and Mental Suffering of Experimental Animals* (Washington; The Animal Welfare Institute, 1978).

G. Holton and R. Morrison, eds., *The Limits of Scientific Inquiry* (New York: W. W. Norton and Co., 1978).

T. Regan and P. Singer, eds., *Animal Rights and Human Obligations* (Englewood Cliffs: Prentice-Hall, 1976).

A. Rowan, *Alternatives to Laboratory Animals: Definition and Discussion* (Washington: The Institute for the Study of Animal Problems, 1980).

R. Ryder, *Victims of Science* (London: Davis-Poynter, 1975).

H. Salt, *Animals' Rights in Relation to Social Progress* (Clark's Summit, Pa.: Society for Animal Rights, 1980).

P. Singer, *Animal Liberation* (New York: Avon Books, 1975).

D. Smyth, *Alternatives to Animal Experiments* (London: The Scholar Press, 1978).

J. Vyvyan, *The Dark Face of Science* (Levittown, NY: Transatlantic Arts, 1972).

chapter eight

Individual Rights

LAWRENCE C. BECKER

There are four crucial issues in an adequate philosophical examination of individual rights: the *definition* of various types of rights; the *justfication* of them; the *scope* of them (that is, who can have them); and the *place* of rights—their importance relative to other sorts of considerations—in moral argument. I shall deal with each of these issues. My purpose is to bring out the central problems in each case and to give some indication of the direction of current philosophical work on it.

The Place of Rights

Moral arguments produce a bewildering array of claims and counter-claims. Amnesty International says that everyone has a right not to be tortured. The torturers say that the benefits they want outweigh the costs to the victims, and that they (the torturers) have an obligation to carry out the orders of their superiors. But what kind of human being could do the things that Amnesty International describes? Could anyone you admire systematically, maliciously, and in cold blood administer crippling beatings day after day, electric shocks to the genitals, starvation diets, and the like? Not likely—because we have standards of character and conduct that we expect people to live up to no matter how serious the consequences. That is why the rugby players whose plane crashed in the Andes were right to cannibalize their dead to avoid starvation, but would not have been right to kill others in order to survive. And so it goes. Duties are pitted against desires, rights against consequences, ideals against practicality, social welfare against individual welfare, cost-benefit analysis against obligations.

Rights are just one of the many sorts of considerations that go into moral arguments. But rights have a special prominence in popular rhetoric, in political debate, in legal argument, and in moral philosophy. The most poignant claims of oppressed people are put in terms of rights to freedom and equality. Counterclaims from people in power are put in terms of rights to liberty and property. Pro- anti-abortion battles are waged over the right to life and a woman's right to control her body. All sorts of political action groups form around rights: civil rights, women's rights, prisoners' rights, children's rights, gay rights, the rights of the handicapped. The list is long and familiar.

What is not so familiar is the difficulty of getting a satisfactory account of the *place* of rights in moral arguments. Consider property rights. If I own some land, I have a bundle of rights with respect to it. But what rights? And how are they related to other important considerations? Suppose, due to a drought, my land now contains the only source of water for hundreds of miles. Do I have the right to withhold that water from my neighbors, or from travellers? Do I have the right to sell it at an exhorbitant price? Do I have the right to sell it at all? Perhaps life-threatening emergencies override my rights. (Or perhaps those in need have rights to life that override my property rights.) And what about zoning? Suppose I want to develop my land, but my neighbors think a development would lessen the value of their own property, disturb their peace and quiet, and generally degrade the quality of their environment. Should I have the right, because I own the land, to do what I choose? Or should the interests, desires and welfare of my neighbors prevent me? These questions illustrate the problem of establishing the proper place of rights in moral argument. Are rights the most important kind of moral considerations? Or just one of many? Do rights automatically take priority over everything else? Or must they always be balanced against other factors?

Here is an instructive conceit—instructive, that is, if you can study it with a straight face. The basic metaphor comes from the contemporary legal theorist Ronald Dworkin,[1] but he had the good taste not to elaborate it.

Think of a card game called Moral Argument. The cards—sometimes called "considerations"—are divided into four suits: Rights, Consequences, Ideals, and Desires. (In real moral arguments, of course, the considerations are more numerous and divided somewhat differently. There is normally a place for Needs, for example, as well as for Duties, Social Goals, Social Welfare, and so on. But this is a simplified game.)

In this game, Rights is the most powerful suit, analogous to Spades in an ordinary deck of playing cards. Consequences, Ideals, and Desires follow in descending order.

Each suit is double, however. Each positive consideration—Ace, King, Queen, and so on—is matched by a negative one in the same suit. So there is a $+10$ of Desires, but also a -10. Each suit thus has 26 cards, and there are 104 in the full deck.

Moral Argument is a four-handed game. There is no bidding. The players merely "make arguments" (tricks) by laying down considerations (cards) in turn. The Dealer leads, and positive and negative considerations are played in turn. (If the Dealer plays a negative, West must play a positive, North must respond with a negative, and East ends the argument with a positive consideration.)

The object of the game is to take arguments (take tricks) by either nullifying or besting the considerations already on the table. You nullify a 3 with the other 3 óf the same suit, for example. You best a 3 with a 4 or better of the same suit—or with a 3 or better of a more powerful suit. (Remember that the weakest suit is Desires, followed up the scale by Ideals, Consequences, and Rights.)

Here is a sample of play. Dealer leads with a small negative Desire—say a -4. West nullifies it with a $+4$ of the same suit. North bests both of those considerations with a $+4$ of the same suit. North bests both of those considerations with a -10 Ideal, and East takes the argument with a $+10$ Consequence. Simple game.

Now imagine that there are two radically different ways of playing Moral Argument. The standard "weak" game is the one I just described. It is played by most competitors. But certain hard-nosed tournament players favor a "strong" game in which one or more of the suits can be trump. And there are disputes about this, too. Hedonists make Desires trump. Utilitarians favor Consequences. And Intuitionists play a rather messy game in which any one of the suits—or none at all—may be trump depending on the circumstances in which the game is being played.

The toughest game of all is played by a few hardy Rights Theorists. (Detractors call this version Social Suicide.) In this game Rights are always trump. They take any argument constructed from considerations of Consequences, Ideals, and Desires. In such a game the following scenario is common: Dealer leads with a positive ideal—not a particularly high one, perhaps. Something like "Write good letters to your lover." West counters with a big negative desire: "I hate writing letters." North bests both of those with a big consequence: "What would the world be like if everyone were so selfish?" And then East takes the argument with the lowest right in the deck: "I don't have to if I don't want to." Not a game for the faint of heart.

The metaphor points to the problem of deciding how important rights are going to be in moral argument. And the different versions of the game correspond roughly to the various logical possibilities.

It is unlikely that anyone actually favors the strict "Rights are trump" rule, even though some writers occasionally speak as though they do. Dworkin says:

> Individual rights are political trumps . . . Individuals have rights, when, for some reason, a collective goal is not a sufficient justification for denying them what they wish.[2]

Harvard philosopher Robert Nozick opens his book this way:

> Individuals have rights, and there are things no person or group may do to them (without violating their rights). So strong and far-reaching are these rights that they raise the question of what, if anything, the state and its officials may do. How much room do individual rights leave for the state?[3]

Alan Gewirth, a philosopher at the University of Chicago, says:

> Whatever else may be demanded of moral rules and principles, they cannot be held to fulfill even their minimal point if they do not require that persons be protected in their rights . . .[4]

And Harvard law professor Charles Fried, says that "the violation of a right is always wrong."[5]

But in fact all of these writers would reject the view that just any right must be honored regardless of the consequences. If I have a right to the last bit of sugar in the vicinity (because I just bought it, though the shopkeeper has not yet handed it over), and it is suddenly needed to save the life of a diabetic who has collapsed on the floor next to me, does my right to the sugar trump her desperate need for it? No serious rights theorist would say so. Most acknowledge that rights can be overridden in emergencies—at least those rights that are not essential for one's health or survival. Furthermore, even basic rights may conflict to produce difficult cases. Nozick raises the case of the "innocent shield"—an innocent person used as a shield by an attacker. May you kill the shield to save your life?[6] It is unclear.

The fact is, however, that most rights are thought of as having built-in exceptions. John Locke, for example, in Chapter V of his *Second Treatise of Government*, argued that people were entitled to property rights in whatever they acquired through their labor—but only if they left as much and as good for others. Current discussions of Locke's "labor theory" of property rights agree that this qualification is necessary.[7] And yet another qualification is introduced by those who divide rights into strong or basic ones (such as rights to life and well-being) and weak or non-basic ones, and then hold that only the basic ones are trumps. Some of what Dworkin says can be understood this way.[8]

In any case, most rights theorists take a position roughly equivalent to the standard game—the game in which rights are merely the most powerful considerations in moral arguments rather than trumps. The Ace of Rights beats any other Ace, but the 2 of Rights doesn't.

ALTERNATIVES

Even this position gets strong opposition, however. Some people want to think of rights simply as rules of thumb which place the burden of proof on anyone who wants to go against them.[9] Such a conception of rights amounts to this: If I want to do something and you don't want me to do it, so far we have a standoff. But if I have a right to do it, there is no standoff. Unless you come forward with a good argument against my plan, I may disregard your wishes and go ahead. On this view, rights amount to something more than ordinary moral considerations, but not very much more.

We leave rights theory altogether if we hold that rights are actually subordinate to other considerations. This corresponds to playing the Moral Argument game with Consequences, or Ideals, or even Desires on top. And if we play the "messy" version—letting intuitions decide when to treat Rights as trump and when to treat some other suit (or none) as trump, we have also abandoned rights theory.

The choice we make about the place of rights in moral argument is a crucial one. Our political system differs from Great Britian's on this issue. They do not have a bill of rights which is immune from repeal through the ordinary legislative process. We do. And the Western liberal democracies generally differ from revolutionary socialist regimes on the importance of individual rights. The philosophical basis for this important choice ultimately depends on the definitions of various types of rights, and on the sorts of justification we can give for them.

Types of Rights

What is a right? Everyone agrees that there is no simple answer to that question because there are so many radically different types of rights. The word 'right' is multiply ambiguous.

One important thing to get straight from the outset is the difference between the specialized and the unspecialized use of the term 'right.' In the unspecialized use, "I have a right to do it" may mean no more than "I am justified in doing it." A right in this sense is not a separate sort of moral consideration at all. It is simply any sort of consideration that is sufficient to justify a course of action. But here we are concerned with the other category—the specialized use of "right"—in which "I have a right to do it" means "I have a special sort of moral claim to do it." But what "special sort"? Again, there isn't just one.

CLAIM-RIGHTS, LIBERTIES, POWERS AND IMMUNITIES

Wesley Hohfeld, an American legal theorist working in the early part of this century, distinguished four sorts,[10] and his distinctions are enormously useful. The idea is to think about what is on "the other side" of a right. If *you* have a right of some sort, what does that mean for *my* situation?

Claim-rights. One thing it might mean is that I have a duty to you. If you have a right not to be tortured, that means I have a duty not to do it. If you have a right to get pay for your work, your employer has a duty to pay for it. When rights correlate with duties in this way they are called claims, or claim-rights, or sometimes rights in the strict sense.

Liberties. But sometimes there is not a duty on the other side. Sometimes there is just a kind of moral or legal vacuum. If you have a right to run in the race, that doesn't mean that the other runners have a duty to let you win. It simply means that they have no claim-right to the victory—no claim-right that you not win. Such rights are called liberties, or liberty-rights, or (less accurately) privileges. The United States Supreme Court has made it clear that a woman's legal right to an abortion is at present a liberty-right, not a claim-right. Women are simply at liberty to have abortions; no particular person has a duty to perform them, and states have no duty to pay for them.

Powers. A third sort of right is a power. If you have the right to make a will, that means that you have the power to change some of the rights and duties of those around you. You can make me your executor, for example, which imposes duties on me. Or, as I would much prefer, you can make me your beneficiary. When you have a power, or power-right, people on the other side of it have a liability. They are, in effect, at your mercy.

Immunities. A fourth sort of right is an immunity. The other side of this is a disability or lack of power. If you have the right to remain silent, then I lack the power-right to make you speak.

Schematically, Hohfeld's distinctions look like this:

CLAIM RIGHTS	LIBERTIES	POWERS	IMMUNITIES
↑	↑	↑	↑
correlate with	correlate with	correlate with	correlate with
↓	↓	↓	↓
DUTIES	"NO-RIGHTS"	LIABILITIES	DISABILITIES

Careful attention to these distinctions is important. Rights are often compounds of two or more types, but until the elements of the compound have been identified, it is hard to make much progress in a moral argument about it.

Consider, for example, how you would deal with the following argument: "All rights, if they are genuine legal rights, have to be enforceable. If they are enforceable, that means the law can require people to respect them. If people are required to respect them, then duties are being imposed. So it is just a fraud to say in one breath that women have the right to have abortions and in the next breath to say that no one has a duty to provide or perform abortions. Either women have the right or they don't. If they do, then we have the duty to provide them.''

There are several mistakes in this argument, but the fundamental one is its failure to see that the law might enforce (with appropriate duties) Hohfeldian "no-rights," liabilities and disabilities. The law might make sure, for example, that no one interferes with doctors who decide to perform abortions or women who decide to have them. The law might insist that hospitals permit staff doctors to schedule abortions in just the same way they schedule other elective surgery. The liberty right to an abortion, then, would be buttressed by a duty on the part of hosptials not to put obstacles in the way. Doctors and their patients would then have correlative claim-rights against their hospitals, but those claim-rights would be for the enforcement of liberties.

NEGATIVE AND POSITIVE, GENERAL AND SPECIAL RIGHTS

Just two other distinctions are of crucial importance here. (For the moment I shall leave aside "natural," "conventional," "moral" and "legal" rights because those categories have to do with how a right is justified. Similarly, "human" rights, "women's" rights and so forth refer to scope—to those who are in the class of right-holders.)

One distinction is between *negative* and *positive rights*. Negative rights are rights to be free from interference. Criminal law defines many of these rights by imposing duties of restraint on people. We have duties to refrain from murder, mayhem, rape, pillage, and theft, and others have the corresponding negative rights against us. Positive rights, on the other hand, are rights to assistance of some sort. Rights to food, to health care, and to an equal share of the world's resources would be positive rights. One of the most fundamental disagreements in political theory is between advocates of the minimal or "nightwatchman" state (who hold that the government has no business enforcing any [non-contractual] positive rights at all) and advocates of the welfare state (who insist that the government must enforce some positive rights).

The other important distinction is between general and special rights. In law, general rights are sometimes referred to as rights *in rem*—rights "against the world." Special rights are rights *in personam*—rights "against (specific) persons." My right not to be murdered is a general one; I have that right "against" everyone—against the world. But my right to compensation for my work is a special one. It comes from a special relationship between me and my employer. This distinction brings out the importance of identifying who is on the other side of a right. Until that is settled, it is hard to get very far with a moral argument about the right.

GETTING A GENERAL DEFINITION

Now with all that said, are we any closer to a general answer to the question of what a right is? Is there a general answer? Not a very useful one, I think. The various types of rights are different enough so that anything true of them all will be very general indeed. Wittgenstein liked to use the example of the problem of defining the concept of a game. There are so many different kinds of games that it is hard to find any interesting feature common to them all. Some are played alone (solitaire), and others are not. Some are played to win, and others are not (Spin the Bottle). Some are played just for fun; others are serious business for professionals. Some have fixed rules; others (like impromptu children's games) do not. And so on. Rights are a bit like that.

Even so, rights have a few common elements which are important. One is that rights are more than just norms, or expectations, or standards of conduct. They are rules which define the boundaries of what is "owed" to a specified group of people (the right holders) by another group (the right respecters). Consider the statement, "When Americans greet strangers, they typically smile and shake hands." Imagine this being given as a piece of advice to foreigners. Would it state a rule defining what is "owed" to strangers by Americans? No. It would merely define a general practice, or expectation. The statement, "Keep your promises," however, is quite different. It does state a rule defining what is owed. And the people who are owed—that is, the promises—are often said to have a right to what was promised.

This feature of rights accounts for two other general characteristics. One has to do with gratitude and indebtedness. When you respect my rights, you haven't done me a favor. I don't "owe" you anything for it—not even gratitude. (Though civility is not out of place.) The contemporary American philosopher Joel Feinberg has explicated this aspect of rights very well.[11] The other characteristic is that rights are supposed to be enforceable in a way that mere ideals or desires are not. If I simply want you to do something for me and you do not, that is too bad for me. Depending on the circumstance, it might not be good of you to refuse, but if all I have on my side is the fact that I want your help, I do not have any business twisting your arm for it. If I have a right to your help, however, and you refuse it, some sort of arm-twisting is presumably in order. I say some sort because of course the extent of it depends on the sort of right involved. If the right is a moral but not a legal one, verbal demands are frequently as far as one can go. But the general principle is important: If I have a right to it I can justifiably take steps to extract it from you if you fail to hand it over.

If rights are to be enforceable, however, they must be specific. They must indicate *who* has the right against whom, what the *content* of the right is, and what *kind of enforcement* is appropriate. Some claims of right are criticized on just this ground. What could "Everyone has a right to an education" mean? If it means that everyone has a right to go to school, then we can readily understand how it could be enforced. If it means more than that (say, for example, that the state has a duty to see to it that everyone actually learns calculus), could it be enforced at all? If it cannot be enforced, is it really a "right"?

Finally, there is *compensation*. The violation of rights—unlike other moral considerations—always at least raises a presumption that the victims should be compensated. If our desires conflict, and mine must be sacrificed, I am just unfortunate. But if my rights conflict with your desires, and for some reason my rights must (or just are) sacrificed, I am presumably "owed" something. Often this takes the form of compensation for my loss. Sometimes it merely means that I am owed an apology. But always, when rights are involved, a violation leaves unfinished business.

So to summarize: Rights are rules that define what is owed to some (the right holders) by others. Rights may be demanded and enforced. They are therefore part of our system of permissions and requirements.

Beyond that, because rights are so various, there is not much else one can usefully say about their general nature.

The Justification of Rights

Even so, the common elements I have described are enough by themselves to pose special problems for justification. Rights are very stringent moral considerations—regardless of whether they are trumps. And if they are treated as trumps, the justification problem is even more difficult. There is no generally agreed upon general justification at present—not even a generally agreed upon strategy. What we have instead are some commonsense convictions buttressed with a variety of more or less unsatisfactory arguments.

The commonsense convictions are these: Individual human beings (and other sorts of beings who are relevantly similar to them) are not simply replaceable parts of the universal machine. Each one of us has an importance, a worth, a "dignity" that makes it wrong for others to abuse us or use us, against our will, without a very strong moral justification. We are justified in demanding such respect; it is owed to us. And if we don't get it, we are justified in using coercion to get it. In this sense at least we have rights—and they are "natural" rights because they are justified independently of any special agreement or contract we have made, or any special form of government we live under, or any special role or status we have in society. These "natural" rights include at least all the standard negative ones found in the criminal law of every country: e.g., rights to be free from murder, battery, assault, and so forth. Whether they also include other negative rights—such as the right not to give self-incriminating testimony—is a disputed point. Whether they include some positive rights as well—rights, say, to a decent standard of living—is also disputed.

What is not disputed—at the level of commonsense—is the conviction that we also have a welter of "conventional" rights—rights that come from government guarantees, contracts we have made, and special roles we occupy. The problem of justification is a double one: to examine the arguments for both natural and conventional rights.

The general strategies for a reasoned justification are fairly limited in number. I shall not consider, here, the various religious positions, and the relativistic view that whatever is believed in a given society is 'moral' for members of that society. I am only concerned here with the problem of whether we can construct a secular, reasoned justification for rights. The leading candidates are utilitarian, contractarian, rationalist, and intuitionist lines of argument. But I shall also discuss the possibility of deriving natural rights from the prior existence of conventional ones, and the possibility that being a "person" is by itself a sufficient condition for having rights.

THE UTILITY OF RIGHTS

The most obvious approach to justification is to point out the usefulness, or "utility", of rights. Utilitarians tend to think that in a perfect world, people would decide what to do by considering the consequences of every act—balancing the pros and cons for everyone involved and doing what is best, on balance, for everyone. Crudely put, the principle would be: Figure out, in each case, what would produce the greatest good for the greatest number (i.e., what would maximize aggregate welfare), and then do it. This is called *act-utilitarianism*.

The problem is that in the real world we cannot operate that way. We not only don't have the time for such case-by-case analysis (sometimes decisions have to be made instantly), but we usually lack the information necessary for figuring out what all the consequences will be. On the other hand, we do know, from human history as a whole, that certain *kinds* of acts usually turn out to have more bad consequences than good ones. Murder, torture, rape, theft, and so on are examples. The obvious solution is to identify the sorts of acts that are usually bad on balance. Next, for each type of act, identify the unusual circumstances in which it is likely to be good (the murder of a Hitler, perhaps). Then write a rule about every type of act. Example: Thou shalt not murder (except for Hitler). The thought is that if we live by these rules, we will maximize welfare in the long run because we will make fewer errors than we would if we were to try to calculate the consequences in each case. If that is so, then everyone should live by the rules—even when the rules are onerous, inconvenient, costly, and seem to lead to bad rather than good consequences in a particular case. This is *rule-utilitarianism*.

The way rights get into this picture is that some of these utilitarian rules will impose duties on us—duties that correlate with claim-rights. Other rules will define liberties, and powers, and immunities. Some of these rules will apply only to special circumstances (in marriage, for example). They will define conventional rights. Others—the ones about murder, perhaps—will apply across the board and define "natural" rights. The strength of the rules—whether rights are trumps or not—will also depend on utility. Does it usually turn out for the best when a given right is treated as a trump? What about compensation? What about enforcement? The rule-utilitarian will calculate the consequences of all these factors for each right and work out a full definition of the right.

As a strategy for justifying rights, however, rule-utilitarianism has one glaring difficulty. (This is quite apart from the well-known general difficulties of utilitarianism: e.g., What reason do I have for maximizing aggregate welfare rather than merely my own? What is aggregate welfare? A total of some sort? An average? What is individual welfare and how is it measured? And so on.)

The problem is this: Every rule (defining a right) has exceptions. And exceptions are added to or subtracted from the rules on the basis of our experience with the consequences. So the rules are in flux. (It may be permissible to murder a Hitler, but what about an Idi Amin?) Whenever we act in terms of a rule, then, we have to decide if our situation either constitutes a new exception or falls under one of the old ones. At that point we are (almost?) back to calculating the consequences of every act directly. All rules have the form "Do x—unless it would be better if you didn't"! Not much of a rule. And "the right not to be tortured unless it would be better (for social welfare) if you were," is not much of a right, either! This is just another way of playing Moral Argument with Consequences as trump.

Whether this difficulty is decisive against utilitarian justifications for rights is disputed. At least one leading authority on utilitarianism doesn't think so.[12] But the problem noted certainly complicates matters in a way that requires extensive discussion. The focus of that discussion will be whether the rule-utilitarian can ever justify a right which trumps the consequences of the act under consideration. Are rights only convenient rules of thumb to be abandoned whenever we have the time, intelligence and information needed to calculate the consequences in a particular case? Or can we show that there are at least some important cases in which, despite the consequences for that case, we should nonetheless follow the rule?

All the plausible defenses of rule utilitarianism of which I am aware rely heavily at this point on evidence of human foibles. It is said that people in general simply cannot be trusted to calculate the consequences. Further, even when they can be, even when those who might be trusted to do it try to do it, the rest of us get so jumpy and angry and suspicious that the resulting social instability is not worth the price. How many act-utilitarians would you trust to run the country? Better to put up with the occasional irrationality of adherence to a relatively fixed but well-considered rule.

Rebuttals to this response raise the problem of "secret" violations of the rules. If the problem is social stability, then as long as people continue to trust you—to think you take rights seriously—that is all that matters. The maintenance of stability is essentially an image problem, to be solved by secrecy, deceit, or a public relations expert. But is it really all right to abandon the rules as long as you can maintain social stability? Is murder and torture for the common good justifiable in such a case? The argument is far from finished.

RIGHTS AS PART OF THE SOCIAL CONTRACT

Social contract theory seems a promising alternative. Its controlling idea is agreement, and it uses agreement to solve the problems of political authority and justice. What gives government its authority? The consent of the governed, say social contract theorists. If people consent to a particular form of government and set of laws—if they promise to obey—then they have an obligation to obey. They "give" the government its authority. Similarly, if people agree to a decision in advance, that decision is a fair one—a "just" one. True, its consequences may turn out to be bad. (People make mistakes, and only hindsight is twenty-twenty . . .) But no one who agreed to it can complain of having been "used" or treated unfairly in the decision-making itself.

So perhaps when it comes to deciding what the basic structure of society should be, we should use social agreement or consent as the test—rather than social utility. (After all, the parties to the social contract will probably do their best to calculate the consequences anyway, as the basis for deciding what to consent to.)

Problems arise immediately. An actual, explicit contract is out of the question as the basis for any large, ongoing society. Even if one could start from scratch and get all the adults to agree, what would be the justification for holding children, immigrants, and succeeding generations to the agreement? What if they were to demand a renegotiation on the grounds that they were not part of the original process? If actual, explicit agreement is the test, won't every social contract have to be renegotiated for every new member? Further, actual consent is a slippery notion. There are the problems of tacit consent. (If I live quietly in a society, accepting the benefits of its laws, have I consented to them? Am I obligated to obey them?) And there are the problems of symbolic consent. (Do I have to take an oath, or can I just throw my hat in the air and shout for joy?)

Most serious of all, there are the problems of non-voluntary and uninformed agreement. Consent can be manipulated. People who are ignorant of the consequences for themselves, or who are impulsive, or careless, or under pressure, often make bad bargains. And sometimes the options are so limited that the "agreement" is a farce. (If a man puts a gun to my head and makes me an offer I can't refuse, is the "agreement" I make a just one?)

Problems such as these prompt a revision of social contract theory: the move from the idea of an *actual* contract to the idea of a *hypothetical* one. In hypothetical social contract theory, the test of justice is whether people *would* agree to a given proposal, *if* they were fully rational, fully informed, fully free to choose, and equal in power. Under those conditions we could trust any agreements people make. Since those conditions are ideal rather than real, however, we have to "imagine" what agreements people would make. The problem now becomes *how* to imagine what the agreements would be. What would it be like to be an "ideal" social contractor? What would such a person choose?

Harvard philosopher John Rawls has proposed an answer.[13] Imagine, he says, that the parties to such a hypothetical social contract must reach agreement from behind a "veil of ignorance." Each person is ignorant of his or her sex, age, race, social status, education, talents, religion, and conception of what is good in life. People behind the veil of ignorance only know general things about the world: how many males there are; what the social status of various races is; what slavery is; the possible forms of government; how many people like pornography and ice cream and wilderness areas; and so forth. Under those conditions, Rawls says, people could not manipulate the rules to their personal advantage. They would have to choose rules they could live with no matter what their particular situation turned out to be. The procedure is analogous to giving one child the knife to cut the cupcake, and the other child first choice of the pieces. The result is going to be fair.

The way rights get into the picture is straightforward. If I must pick the rules which define the basic institutions of the society I am to live in—*without knowing* whether I am male or female, black or white, rich or poor, a member of a despised minority or an honored elite—then I am going to want some built-in safeguards. And I *may* want those safeguards in the form of rights—especially negative rights against murder, torture, theft, and the like. I may also want some (positive) rights to guarantee a minimal level of well-being.

I emphasize the phrase "I *may* want . . . rights," for this is just the sticky point. The act of imagination we are asked to perform here is very difficult. It is hard to say just what people would choose from behind the veil of ignorance. Some critics have contended that the principle of utility, rather than a set of rules, is the safeguard that would be chosen.[14] Their argument runs along the following lines:

We know that respecting rights is expensive—not only in money but in time, lost opportunities, social turmoil, and so on. (Think of the cost of a fair trial for Robert Kennedy's assassin. Think of the cost of respecting the rights of the former Shah of Iran.) Further, we know that sometimes these costs can overwhelm a social order. Some third world nations argue, for example, that they are too fragile to be able to afford the luxury of what we call a right to a free press. We ourselves suspend many individual rights during national emergencies. (An example is the internment of Japanese-Americans during World War II.) Rawls acknowledges this and explicitly says that his arguments for rights apply only to stable, developed nations.

But even so, is it clear that people would choose rights over consequences from behind the veil of ignorance? Suppose the rational social contractors argued in this way: We want a society which maximizes aggregate (or average) welfare. To have such a society, we will have to arrange the laws so that they maintain a significant level of peace and order. That means that most of the people will have to be kept reasonably happy (or at least well away from the rebellion point). To do that, we will have to have rules which provide a sense of security and stability to most people. Perhaps we will need rules which give everyone that sense most of the time, and most people that sense all of the time. But would we really choose (from behind the veil) to bear the cost of adopting rules which guarantee individual rights as trumps? Wouldn't we thereby lose many opportunities to maintain or improve the general welfare? (If we had denied the Shah's "right" to enter the U. S. for medical treatment, we would have saved ourselves, the hostages, and probably even the Iranians great losses.) There are many such situations—cases in which honoring the rights of a single individual is quite costly. Yet the probability that any one of us will be such an individual is quite small—perhaps one in a million. So wouldn't a rational contractor take the risk and opt for a society in which the basic principle was respect for utility rather than respect for rights?

Rawls says no. He argues that people behind the veil of ignorance would adopt a very low-risk stategy. They would, he thinks, adopt a so-called "maximin" strategy—one in which they *minimized the maximum* damage that could be done to them if things went very wrong. Rawls' critics object the he simply has arbitrarily *defined* contractors into this risk-avoiding position. The issue is far from settled. The use of social contract theory to justify rights remains problematic.

RATIONALISTIC ARGUMENTS

A strikingly different strategy is employed by people who attempt to derive rights from the nature of moral agency itself. A *moral agent* is someone who is capable of the sort of actions that we are willing to praise or blame, morally. An amoeba moves, but we don't blame it for what it does. Some humans also escape moral and legal responsibility for their actions—through diminished capacity or insanity. Why is this? What makes someone a moral agent?

A full answer to that question is a large task, but here we only have to pay attention to one important feature of moral agents: they are "rational"—at least in the very weak sense that they have a conception of what is good for them and strive to get it. Another way of saying this is to say that moral agents are purposive; their acts (at least some of them) are goal-directed. Nevermind for the moment that agents have radically different goals, and that some agents are very active in pursuit of their goals while others are rather passive. Nevermind that some agents are selfish while others are not. We are for the moment only concerned with this one "formal" or "contextual" feature of agency: purposiveness. What does it mean for rights?

Alan Gewirth has recently argued[15] that *every* moral agent is forced to claim, on pain of self-contradiction, that *all* moral agents have equal rights to freedom and well-being. This conclusion does not say directly that moral agents "have" rights; it only says that they must claim that they do. But Gewirth says that much is enough.

In outline, his argument goes this way. First he notes that, by definition, agents regard their own purposes as good. Not necessarily as "morally good," but good enough to strive for. A consequence of this, Gewirth says, is that agents must regard the things necessary to purposive action *per se* as "necessary goods"—that is, as goods that they "must" have to carry out their purposes. These necessary goods are certain minimal levels of freedom and well-being.

The next step is to make the transition from necessary goods to rights. Every agent must make the following claim, as we have already seen: "My freedom and well-being are necessary goods." This claim is, Gewirth says, equivalent to "I must have freedom and well-being." And that claim is tantamount to claiming rights to freedom and well-being for oneself.

The final step is to show that because agents lay claim to rights for themselves on this basis, they are logically committed to holding that all other agents have the same rights. The reason is simple. Being a purposive agent is a sufficient condition for claiming rights in one's own case. It therefore follows that it must be a sufficient condition in every other similar case—that is, for every other purposive agent. Thus all moral agents—merely by virtue of their nature as rational, purposive creatures—must hold that all such agents have rights to freedom and well-being.

There are at least two problems with this approach, however. One is the proposition that the goods necessary for my purposive activity are "normatively necessary goods." The other is the contention that "my freedom and well-being are necessary goods" entails the assertion "I have rights to freedom and well-being." Gewirth has arguments for these moves, of course, and is aware of the objections to them, but some critics remain unconvinced.[16]

One objection is this: All that is entailed by the assertion "x is a necessary good for me" is that it is also a necessary good for me that others let me have x. And how is that tantamount to the claim that I have a right to x? This sort of objection can be pressed against all rationalistic arguments (e.g., Kant's, Hegel's, Gewirth's). How is it that the necessities, or interests, or claims, or demands, or actions of agents give rise to rights? It is easy to see how they give rise to principles about what is good (for the agent, and by extension, for any agent). It is not so easy to see how they give rise to rights. Until this issue is settled in a way that is generally agreed to be satisfactory, rationalistic arguments for rights will remain as problematic as the others.

RIGHTS AND PERSONS

Less overtly rationalistic arguments about the relation between "personhood" and rights have also been offered. Their thought is that there must be something about simply being a person—some property of personhood—which generates rights.[17] In my judgment these attempts do not fare very well—at least when distinguished from strictly utilitarian, contractarian, or rationalistic ones (above) or intuitionistic ones. But they are worth considering.

These arguments begin with descriptions (sometimes value-loaded ones). Persons are sharply distinguished from "things." Persons think, feel, hope, care, plan, and strive. Persons do not just live; they have *lives*. Persons (even the worst of them) have a worth, a dignity, an intrinsic value which must be respected. Persons, simply by their nature, "have a claim" on our feelings and our conduct. To "use" persons as "things" is to *de*-personalize them—to deny the *fact* of their personhood. Besides: People—our handiest examples of personhood—actively demand our respect. In a very real sense, to fail to demand at least minimal respect is to fail to be a "fully human" individual. (Think of the kind of passivity, servility, and loss of self-esteen that we call "dehumanizing.") So isn't the recognition of human rights just a logical consequence of the recognition of someone as a person? (Note the similarity to Gewirth's general strategy.)

The problem, however, is again the connection between the "facts" about persons and the very special sort of moral consideration that rights are. No characteristic of persons—or combination of characteristics—seems sufficient to generate rights by itself. People make claims, but so what? They surely don't have rights to everything they claim. So which claims are valid ones? We need a separate argument—from utility, perhaps, or from contract, or from necessity a la Gewirth—to answer that question. Similarly for other properties of person. People have interests, projects, desires, feelings, fears, expectations, needs, and hopes. They have worth and dignity. But none of these things is sufficient to generate rights. My "worth" may entail that you should admire me, respect me, and value me. But how does it entail that I have a "right" of some sort against you? I have interests, but merely having an interest in something doesn't get me a right to it. Far from being sufficient for rights, it is not even clear that interests, desires, and so on are necessary for rights. If they are, then we cannot ascribe rights to the permanently comatose, and perhaps not even to very young infants.[18] Such consequences are unacceptable to many.

A more modest line may be taken, however. The idea is to construct rebuttable presumptions in favor of rights out of the typical characteristics of persons. This approach begins with the recognition that a part of the behavior typical of persons amounts to claiming rights for themselves. This is just a fact. The question is, Do we have any good reason for thinking such claims are unjustifiable? If they are not unjustifiable, and people do in fact make them, then what reasoned objection can there be to honoring them? The burden of proof is on the sceptic.[19]

Of course the claims that come "naturally" or "necessarily" out of personhood should probably be distinguished from ephemeral ones (but why?). And conflicts among claims must be resolved. (What if ten people claim the right to kill me against my will? Is my claim to a right to life a "good reason" against the presumptive validity of theirs? Why? Why aren't their claims good reasons against the presumptive validity of mine? Or do all eleven claims have to be balanced against one another? If so, is there a standoff? Or do ten outweigh one?) These problems threaten to overwhelm even this more modest approach.

THE ARGUMENT FROM CONVENTIONAL RIGHTS

Oxford philosopher of law H. L. A. Hart has proposed a radically different line of argument.[20] In outline, it is this:

We know that there are all sorts of special rights—rights created by promises and permissions, for example. If I promise you something (in a way we recognize as binding), then you gain a right to the thing. If you give me permission to enter your house, I gain the right to do it. But how? How can a permission or a promise change people's liberties in this way? Hart argues that only on the assumption that people have a general right to be free from interference from others can we make sense of the right-creating character of promises and permissions. If I have a general right to do as I please (within the limits imposed by everyone else's similar right), then I can give up part of it by granting you a liberty you didn't otherwise have. So the recognition of special rights implies the recognition of a general right to liberty.

This is an important and instructive line of argument. But like the others, it is vulnerable to objections. One is that it simply avoids altogether the crucial question of the justification of special rights. We know that people believe they have such rights and they act as though they do. But what reason is there for thinking such arrangements are good ones? Why shouldn't people simply calculate the consequences in each case and do what maximizes social (or personal) welfare? We have seen how difficult it is to give a utilitarian or contractarian answer to that question. Yet until it is answered, the derivation of general rights from special ones cannot get started. The second objection is simply that (apparently) only a right to liberty (construed fairly narrowly) can be derived in this way. This leaves unanswered a great many questions about rights.

INTUITIONIST ARGUMENTS

Yet rights remain a prominent feature of the moral landscape. People just do draw lines beyond which they will not go. They request, want, hope, strive, and negotiate, but they also demand, insist, and refuse. Whether these rebellion points and demand points are explicitly expressed in the language of rights or not, they are equivalent to claims of right whether or not these claims are justified, the behavior persists.

Some theorists have decided to turn this situation to their advantage by treating rights as basic, or axiomatic features of morality. The argument goes this way.

A moral judgment is made, and reasons are offered for it. Then more reasons are given to prove the first set of reasons, and still more to prove the second set, and so on. Eventually, if we are to avoid an endless regress of reason-giving, we must bring this process to a stop. All arguments must end somewhere.

But where? What moral principles can we accept without justification—in the way that we accept the axioms of deductive logic, or indeed the very process of reason giving itself? It is true that we cannot give reasons to justify reasoning, because that is circular. Giving the reasons presupposes the legitimacy of the process of reason giving itself—the very thing we are trying to prove. And it is equally true that nothing can be said (or needs to be said?) in defense of the law of identity: "For all x, x is x." If you can't just "see" it, there is nothing that can be said to "justify" or "prove" it to you. At most we can simply give examples, redescribe case after case, and try out different verbal formulas. ("All right. If you don't get the 'For all x' business, try this: Everything is what it is. Get it now?")

Perhaps rights are equally fundamental in morality. Perhaps they are stopping points for arguments—axioms or laws we simply must accept without justification. Perhaps if you can't just "see" that people have certain rights, nothing can be said to prove it to you. Perhaps the most we can do is simply try to get you to see it by giving examples, redescribing case after case, and trying out different verbal formulas.[21]

In fact, moral arguments often proceed this way. Each side to the abortion controversy has its own descriptions. Are we talking about a fetus or a baby? In the uterus or the womb? Of a pregnant woman or a mother? Are we preventing a human life or taking one? The descriptions are designed to bring us to "see' the reality. The only difficulty is, we disagree about what "the" reality is in many of these moral cases. Should murderers be seen as victims of bad socialization? If so, blame and hatred of them are out of place.

This is both the strength and the weakness of intuitionist approaches to rights theory. Arguments certainly must stop somewhere. But can rights possibly be such stopping places? Aren't there radical disagreements among moral agents about what rights people have? And don't those disagreements weaken the intuitionist position?

The short answer is that there *are* radical disagreements which weaken the intuitionist position. It is no accident that where intuitionists have the most success is with negative rights—rights to freedom from interference.[22] Virtually everyone "sees" the rights to be free from murder, rape, torture, beatings, fraud and theft. But with positive rights—rights to active help from others—intuitions are in complete disarray. Some people see no such rights; others see them very clearly. Arguments back and forth on this matter often amount to little more than "trading intuitions."

And even in the case of negative rights, intuitions differ. Does wartime killing constitute murder? When is killing in self-defense justifiable? May we ever sacrifice the lives of a few to save the lives of many? What constitutes rape? If a man has a "reasonable" but mistaken belief that the woman consented, when she in fact did not, is he guilty of rape? What about an unreasonable belief? What if his belief in her consent was reasonable but in fact he just didn't care whether she consented or not? And what about theft? Is it permissible to steal if no one is hurt by it? (Think of taking a towel from a Holiday Inn.) And who has these rights to be free from murder and pain? Only human beings? Why not chimpanzees? And cows? (Shouldn't we all become vegetarians?)

People's intuitions on rights turn out to differ so much—on the details of negative rights and the very existence of positive ones—that intuitionism fares no better than the other justifications. This fact, combined with the difficulty of distinguishing intuitions on these matters from arbitrary cultural conditioning, makes intuitionistic arguments *for rights* very weak.

I emphasize the phrase "for rights". Intuitions about rights are just not as cross-culturally stable as intuitions about the fundamentals of logic. Aristotle, after all, saw nothing wrong with certain forms of slavery and the subjugation of women. But the fundamental formal principles of his deductive logic coincide with ours. Thus to reject intuitionist arguments for rights is not to reject them across the board—even in other areas of morality. Perhaps, for example, the ultimate support for the utilitarian principle comes from intuition.

TWO SPECIAL PROBLEMS

I want to conclude this section on the justification of rights by mentioning two special problems of current interest. One is positive rights. The other is inalienable rights.

Positive Rights. It is hard to overestimate the importance of the debate over the existence of positive rights. If a right to well-being exists—even to a minimal level of well-being—then very significant changes in the distribution of wealth and the use of the world's resources are required. Thus one of the battlelines between political left wing and political right wing is drawn here. To say that people have a legal claim-right to a minimum wage, a right to health care, and a right to food, clothing, and shelter is to align oneself with advocates of the welfare state. To deny that people have such rights (to say instead, for example, that the affluent should give charity to the needy) is to align oneself with libertarians.

Libertarians argue[23] that negative rights are clearly justifiable and fundamental. Positive ones, on the other hand, are questionable. The utility of guaranteeing respect for positive rights is disputed by free market theorists. (Is the welfare state efficient? What does it do to human initiative and incentive?) Intuitions conflict wildly about them. And people wonder whether rational contractors would choose to have them. Furthermore, positive rights (necessarily) violate negative ones, meaning that no coherent system of positive and negative rights is possible. After all, positive rights often require taking things (money, time, property) from the "haves" and giving them to the "have nots". How can you do this without violating negative rights if the "haves" are unwilling to give up what they have? And at the very least, my positive rights always limit your negative ones. If the negative ones are not in doubt, and the positive ones are in fact disputed, the positive ones should go.

Welfare rights theorists reply[24] that every plausible basis for rights requires both positive and negative rights. The right to freedom is worthless unless people have the ability to exercise that freedom. Well-being, no less than freedom, is a good that is necessary for carrying out one's purposes. So any coherent system of rights, it is argued, will include both positive and negative ones. Conflicts between the two sorts of rights are no more of a problem than conflicts between negative rights. After all, my right to liberty is limited by yours: I violate yours if I use mine to tie you to the chair for my amusement. So why can't my rights to liberty and property also be limited by your rights to well-being?

This issue is hotly debated and deeply divisive, politically. It is also very important—in personal moral life and public policy as well as moral philosophy.

Inalienable Rights. The question of alienability is equally important. Are there any rights that I can, through my own choices, give up or forfeit? Does a murderer forfeit her right to life by taking the life of another? Does a terrorist forfeit his right not to be tortured for information about the bomb he has planted in a public hospital? Does a woman who voluntarily consents to an unequal marriage give up her right to equality with her husband? Can people (morally) sell themselves into slavery?

Arguments about alienability are ultimately tied to the justification one offers for rights. If Gewirth is correct, for example, that every rational agent must claim equal rights to freedom and well-being for every such agent, then selling oneself into slavery may involve a contradiction.[25] A contract theorist might argue that selling oneself into (unconditional) slavery is not an agreement one could actually keep. At some point one would rebel, indicating that a rule permitting such slavery is not one that contractors could "really" agree to. Nozick, who takes voluntary agreements to be the very paradigm of just ones, thinks that a truly free society would permit people to sell themselves.[26] In any case it is clear that the issue is of fundamental significance.

The Scope of Rights

To conclude this survey of the philosophical issues in rights theory, I want to make a few brief remarks on the question of the scope of rights. Do animals have rights? Do fetuses? The permanently comatose? Do children have the same basic rights as adults? Do inanimate objects (ecosystems, historic buildings, art objects) have rights? These are important questions for both law and morality. Decisions on vegetarianism and animal experimentation, abortion, euthanasia, child care, and environmental law hang on the answers.

It might be thought that the answers have to come from the strategy chosen for justifying rights. After all, if one uses a social contract justification, presumably rights would go only to those agents chosen by rational contractors. Rationalistic arguments justify rights only for (rational) moral agents—and perhaps those who, in the normal course of maturation, will become rational agents. The answers of utilitarian and intuitionist approaches are not so obvious, but at least their general methods for arriving at answers are clear.

This is too quick, however. There is another important source of rights—an indirect one—which a primary focus on rights theory often overlooks. I refer to the fact that rights can be derived by first establishing the existence of their "other sides"—their correlative duties, no-rights, liabilities and disabilities. If people have duties to animals, fetuses, the comatose, the environment, and so on, it may be inferred that these rights have derivative claim-rights against us. (After all, it is not necessary to be able to make a claim to have claim-rights. Infants cannot make claims. People who are stuporously drunk can't either. That doesn't mean they have no claim-rights.)

The major problem here is showing that the duties we have are *to* the animals (or trees, or whatever) rather than simply *about* them. If I promise you (much against my desires) to be nice to your friends, my promise is *about* your friends, but *to* you. I owe the duty to *you*. And you are the one who has the claim-right against me. Similarly, if my duty to protect the environment is really a duty to keep the planet habitable for my fellow human beings, then it is a duty *about* but not *to* the environment. The environment, for that reason, has no derivative claim-rights as a consequence of my duty.

There has been some sharp dispute on this issue,[27] and the focal point is the concept of a beneficiary. If an entity can be the beneficiary of a duty (as opposed simply to being the object of it, or to being affected by it), then it seems clear that the duty could, in principle, be "to" that entity. (It still might not be, of course. Presumably your friends are possible beneficiaries, dullards though they are. Yet my duty is to you.)

The question is, What is the range of possible beneficiaries? Can a tree be benefitted? Some say no—that only those entities that have "interest," "projects," or "can suffer pain and feel pleasure" can be benefitted in the sense required. (Note that this position tilts toward granting derivative rights to some animals but denies them to insensate creatures.) Other people say yes—that any (living?) entity can be said to "have a good" and therefore be capable of being benefitted. We know that water, sunlight, and nutrients are good for poison ivy—even though no humans may want it around. It can be benefitted, even though it is not aware of what is good for it. This situation, after all, is not so different from our own. We are not always aware of what is in our best interests. The notion of "best interests" is constructed not only by referring to our conscious projects, desires, fears, and so on but by thinking about the sort of creatures we are and the things that are "good for us." Can't the same be done for trees? If so, they can be the beneficiaries of our duties, and the holders of derivative rights. In that case the scope of rights would be vastly expanded.

The outcome of this debate is still in doubt, but its importance is not. Given the prominence we currently give to rights in arguments about public policy, it is inevitable that the battles over our treatment of animals, our practices with regard to abortion and euthanasia, our treatment of children, and our concern for the environment will be stated in terms of rights. To make sense of them, let alone to make progress on them, we will have to make progress on all of these philosophical issues concerning rights.

Conclusions

After a recital of inconclusive arguments, incomplete analyses, and seemingly intractable problems such as we have just been through, some readers make a series of inexcusable errors: They assume that philosophers have made no significant headway on these issues. (After all, aren't we still going over the same ground Plato and Aristotle covered?) They assume that philosophers are not likely to make headway on these issues in the future. (After all, haven't we just seen that all the current theories are seriously flawed?) They assume that every flawed theory is equal to every other, and in fact equal to no theory at all. And so they conclude that all these issues are just "matters of faith or opinion" after all—and that philosophy is at bottom irrelevant to them. Nothing could be further from the truth.

Progress in philosophy is analogous to counting. You approach the "end" as a limit. When you have counted to ten thousand, you are in one sense no closer to the end of the series of integers than when you started. (There is still an infinite number of integers left to count.) But you are a lot farther from the beginning. Ten thousand is a bigger number than ten.

Progress in philosophy is something like that. In one sense we never get to the end—we never dispose of the basic questions. And so we will always be covering the same ground. But that doesn't mean we make no progress. Work that builds on previous work—whether by refining it, rejecting it, or incorporating it into a new position—increases our sophistication in handling these fundamental issues. We owe it to ourselves—and to others—to take these moral issues seriously enough to get this increased sophistication—if for no other reason than to help us avoid the errors of blind adherence to a dubious or incoherent principle.

It would be a mistake to suppose, however, that all we have achieved in moral philosophy is negative results—the ruling out of dozens of theories as incoherent or inconclusive. We have also learned a great deal about the nature of the problems. Without that knowledge, very little progress can be made. Every theory and every analysis sketched in this essay will richly repay further study: It will teach you more about the nature of the problems.

Further study will also narrow the range of seemingly intractable disagreements. When you find, for example, that theorists who reject rights are not really rejecting the need for protecting individuals in some way against the tyranny of the stronger, but only objecting to a particular way of doing it, things don't look so bleak. When you can locate the disagreement between libertarians and welfare theorists over negative and positive rights, you've taken a significant step toward handling it. This essay has taken a few such steps. The point reached is nowhere near the end. But thanks to the hard work of the philosophers we have surveyed, it is also a long way from the beginning.

Notes

1. Ronald Dworkin, *Taking Rights Seriously* (Cambridge, Harvard U. Press, 1977) p. xi.
2. *Ibid.*
3. Robert Nozick, *Anarchy, State and Utopia* (New York, Basic Books, 1974) p. ix.

4. Alan Gewirth, *Reason and Morality* (Chicago, University of Chicago, Press, 1978).

5. Charles Fried, *Right and Wrong* (Cambridge, Harvard U. Press, 1978), p. 108.

6. Nozick, pp. 34–35.

7. See Nozick, pp. 178–182, and Lawrence C. Becker, *Property Rights: Philosophic Foundations* (Boston, Routledge, 1977) Chapter Four. This chapter is reprinted in Virginia Held (ed.) *Property, Profits and Economic Justice* (Belmont, CA., Wadsworth, 1980) pp.60–83.

8. Dworkin,p. 191.

9. See R. G. Frey, *Rights and Interest* (Oxford, Oxford University Press, 1980).

10. W. N. Hohfeld, *Fundamental Legal Conceptions* (New Haven, Yale University Press, 1919).

11. Joel Feinberg, "The Nature and Value of Rights," *Journal of Value Inquiry* 4 (1970): 243–257. The relevant portion is reprinted in David Lyons (ed.) *Rights* (Belmont, CA., Wadsworth, 1979) pp. 78–91.

12. David Lyons, "Human Rights and the General Welfare," *Philosophy & Public Affairs* 6 (1977): 113–129, and his "Mill's Theory of Justice" in A. I. Goldman and J. Kim (eds.), *Values and Morals* (Dordrecht, Reidel, 1978), pp. 1–20.

13. John Rawls, *A Theory of Justice* (Cambridge, Harvard, 1971).

14. See some of the criticism in Norman Daniels (ed.), *Reading Rawls* (New York, Basic Books, n.d.) especially the article by H. L. A. Hart.

15. Gewirth, *Reason and Morality*.

16. See the review of *Reason and Morality* by Henry Veatch in *Ethics* 89 (1979): 401–414.

17. See Charles Fried, *Right and Wrong,* and (perhaps) A. I. Melden, *Rights and Persons* (Berkeley, U. of California Press, 1977).

18. See Michael Tooley, "Abortion and Infanticide," *Philosophy & Public Affairs* 2 (1972): 37–65, amended and expanded in M. Cohen (ed.) *The Rights and Wrongs of Abortion* (Princeton, Princeton U. Press, 1974) pp. 52–84.

19. I develop such an argument, for obligations, in my book *On Justifying Moral Judgments* (New York, Humanities Press, 1973).

20. H. L. A. Hart, "Are There Any Natural Rights?" *Philosophical Review 64 (1955): 175–191. Reprinted in David Lyons (ed.) Rights,* pp. 14–25.

21. William Gass has argued this point in "The Case of the Obliging Stranger," *Philosophical Review* 66 (1957): 193–204. See also A. I. Melden, *Rights and Persons,* pp. 185–206.

22. Nozick's book is an example. So is Judith Jarvis Thomson's work on rights—e.g., "Self-Defense and Rights," *The Lindley Lecture* (Lawrence, University of Kansas Press, 1976).

23. For an example, see Roger Pilon, "Ordering Rights Consistently," 13 *Georgia Law Review* 1171–1196 (1980).

24. See Samuel Sheffler, "Natural Rights, Equality and the Minimal State," *Canadian Journal of Philosophy* 6 (1976): 59–

25. Gewirth, pp. 264–266.

26. Nozick, p. 331.

27. Hart, "Are There any Natural Rights?" cited above; David Lyons, "Rights, Claimants and Beneficiaries" *American Philosophical Quarterly,* 6 (1969): 173–185; Joel Feinberg, "The Rights of Animals and Unborn Generations" in W. Blackstone (ed.) *Philosophy and Environmental Crisis* (Athens, U. of Georgia Press, 1974); and Lawrence C. Becker, "Three Types of Rights" 13 *Georgia Law Review* 1197–1220.

Suggested Readings

BOOKS:

(1) Becker, Lawrence C., *Property Rights: Philosophic Foundations* (Boston, Routledge & Kegan Paul, 1977).

(2) Dworkin, Ronald, *Taking Rights Seriously* (Cambridge, Harvard University Press, 1977).

(3) Frey, Raymond, *Rights and Interests* (Oxford, Oxford University Press, 1980).

(4) Gewirth, Alan, *Reason and Morality* (Chicago, University of Chicago Press, 1978).

(5) Lyons, David (ed.) *Rights* (Belmont, CA, Wadsworth, 1979).

(6) Meldin, A. I., *Rights and Persons* (Berkeley, University of California Press, 1977).

ARTICLES

(7) Symposium on Rights, 13 *Georgia Law Review* (1980).

(8) Feinberg, Joel, "The Nature and Value of Rights," *Journal of Value Inquiry* 4 (1970): 243–257.

(9) Feinberg, Joel, "The Rights of Animals and Unborn Generations" in William Blackstone (ed.) *Philosophy and Environmental Crisis* (Athens, University of Georgia Press, 1974).

(10) Hart, H. L. A., "Are There Any Natural Rights?" *Philosophical Review* 64 (1955): 175–191.

(11) Martin, Rex and James W. Nickel, "A Bibliography on the Nature and Foundations of Rights, 1947–1977," *Political Theory* 6 (1978): 395–415.

(12) Martin, Rex and James W. Nickel, "Recent Work on the Concept of Rights," *American Philosophical Quarterly* 17 (1980): 165–180.

chapter nine

_____

Utilitarianism

DAN W. BROCK

Consider several examples of actions that you would likely have little difficulty deciding are either right or wrong, and how you might naturally come to that decision.

Case 1. You have made a promise to a friend that you would meet her later that evening to return a book that she needs to study for an exam the next morning. On the way to meet the friend, you come across an automobile accident in which someone has been seriously injured. Knowing that you will be unable to return the book to your friend in time for her to use it before the exam, you nevertheless take the injured person to the hospital.

   Why is this the right action? A natural account would be that the bad effects of your action, the disappointed expectations and perhaps worse performance on the exam of your friend, are less important than the good effects of your action, securing medical care for the accident victim.

Case 2. You are a physician in a medical emergency in which three persons, in order to survive, need medicine which is in scarce supply. One of the three, Smith, requires all of the available supply of the medicine to survive, while the other two, Brown and Black, will both survive if each receives one-half the available supply. You give the medicine to Brown and Black, and thereby save them, knowing that as a result Smith will die.

Why is this the right action? Once again, a natural account would be that though it is certainly bad for Smith to die, morality requires us to consider the consequences for all affected by our actions, and it is better to save the lives of two persons than of one person, when one cannot save all three.

Case 3. You are a legislator considering whether some wilderness land should be opened to oil exploration. How would you go about making the morally best decision? A natural way to proceed would be to try to assess the costs and benefits of each alternative, e.g. the likelihood of increased supply and lower prices of oil, the amount of loss of recreational use if the land is developed, and so forth. You then support the alternative that promises the greater balance of benefits over costs for all affected.

Case 4. Out for a December afternoon's walk along a lake, you come upon a young boy who has fallen into the lake, apparently cannot swim, and is desperately calling for help. You realize that you could jump in and save him with no significant risk to yourself, but the water would be very cold and your new clothes would be ruined. You pass on, pretending to yourself that you didn't hear him.

Why would doing this be clearly and seriously wrong? Though the boy was a perfect stranger, the obvious point would seem to be that you could have prevented a great harm to the boy, at only a small cost or inconvenience to yourself, and so the consequences of saving the boy would be far better than those of your failing to do so.

In each of these cases, and in many more that we might cite, it seems natural to think that whether an action is right or wrong depends on what its consequences will be for all affected by it.

Utilitarianism, the subject of this Chapter, takes this very common and plausible way of thinking about moral questions and decisions, this approach to morality deeply rooted in our ordinary moral experience, and systematizes it in a formal moral theory. Utilitarianism, more precisely, is the moral theory that actions are morally right just in case they produce at least as good consequences as any alternative action open to a person, morally wrong if they do not. Sometimes utilitarianism is construed more narrowly so as already to presuppose a specific account of what are good consequences, e.g. human happiness. Then the theory could be called a happiness maximization theory. However, we shall leave open at the outset what is the proper theory of moral value or the good, i.e. what *are* good consequences, and so construe utilitarianism as a general *consequentialist* moral theory. It holds that the consequences, and only the consequences, of actions are relevant to their moral evaluation. This is a highly abstract characterization of utilitarianism, however, and in the first section of this essay we shall have to see just how it is to be filled out in order to come to understand better what the theory is, and how it differs from alternative moral theories. In the second section we shall examine some of the principal arguments and considerations that can be offered in support of utilitarianism. Finally, in the third section we shall consider some of the major kinds of objections that have been brought against utilitarianism. This will help us to understand better the nature of a utilitarian moral theory, and on what points it differs from its principal competitors, as well as fill out our evaluation of its acceptability.

I. *The Formulation of Utilitarianism*

We must now elaborate just what the utilitarian principle means. The utilitarian principle can be stated as follows:

UP: An action is morally right if and only if it produces at least as much utility as any alternative action available to the agent, morally wrong if it does not.

For completeness, we can add that if two or more actions produce the same amount of utility, but more than any other possible alternative action, the principle implies that it is morally indifferent which is performed and either would be morally right. In addition, the production of utility is to be construed broadly so as to include the prevention of disutility (e.g. unhappiness). The utilitarian is interested in maximizing the overall quantity of utility, and this can occur through producing utility or preventing disutility. The utilitarian principle thus covers cases where all alternatives are bad—that is will produce some net disutility—and requires one to act so as to minimize evil by choosing the lesser evil.

Notice first that the principle is to be understood *normatively,* not *descriptively.* It does not purport to describe the basis on which a person or group of persons as a matter of fact morally evaluate actions, though of course it may well turn out to be a correct description of at least some people's moral views. Rather, it is offered as the correct standard for moral appraisal of actions, as the standard we ought to adopt and use in such appraisals. In Sections II and III we shall evaluate whether there is good reason to believe that utilitarianism is the correct or most acceptable moral theory, the principle that we *should* use in making moral judgments; for now, the point is only that it is offered as the correct or best standard for moral evaluation.

Notice second that it is at once both an individual or personal, as well as social and political ethic. It provides a standard by which any individual can morally evaluate any action he is considering performing. But at the same time it provides a standard by which social, political, and legal institutions can be morally evaluated, viz. the extent to which they promote utility or good consequences, say the happiness of those affected by them. Proposals for social change, and for the reform of laws and social and political institutions, for example laws and social institutions governing many of the moral issues taken up in other chapters of this book such as paternalism, homosexuality, reverse discrimination, and so forth, can be evaluated by the utilitarian principle. Since we are interested in and make moral evaluations at both the individual and social levels, any complete moral theory should be capable of being applied at both levels.

We shall consider the concept of utility or account of good consequences shortly, but it might seem that whatever account we adopt, we nevertheless can never know what all the consequences of any action we have performed or are considering performing will be, and so can never know whether any given action is or was morally right or wrong. But we do know that some actions are right and wrong, the critic of utilitarianism may urge, and so utilitarianism cannot be the correct moral theory. We need a distinction here between what might be called *subjective* and *objective* consequence versions of utilitarianism. On the *objective version,* actions are to be evaluated by the consequences they in fact have, both in the near and distant future, whether or not those consequences were foreseen or foreseeable by the person performing the action. On the *subjective version,* actions are to be evaluated by the consequences that were foreseen, or could reasonably have been foreseen, by the person performing the action. Now clearly on the subjective consequence version, it is not the case that we can never know whether an action is or was right or wrong; this difficulty for utilitarianism could then be avoided by adopting the subjective consequence version. There is, nevertheless, a serious problem with that version. It implies the unwelcome result that an action that turns out to have disastrous consequences is morally right so long as those consequences were unforeseen and unforeseeable by the person performing it. Among issues considered in this book, DNA research and nuclear power provide the most obvious possible examples. Yet there is a clear sense in which an action that turns out to have disastrous consequences was not the best alternative, was not the action that ought to have been performed. We shall, therefore, adopt here the objective consequence version in what follows as the criterion of right action, though we must then note two points. First, it remains that at the time of deliberation and decision, the most a person can do is to estimate the expected consequences of alternative actions attaching probabilities to various possible consequences. What the utilitarian principle requires is that the agent then act so as to maximize expected utility. Second, it follows that sometimes a person may be blameworthy for doing what turns out to be objectively right and praiseworthy for doing what turns out to be objectively wrong, in each case because the agent did not foresee and could not reasonably have foreseen that the consequences would turn out as they did. The most a utilitarian can require is that a person act on the best reasonably available estimate of the consequences of possible alternative actions. So *right action* is the action that in fact has the best consequences, while a wrongful act is one which fails to bring about the best consequences. We shall still have to see whether consequences can be measured in the manner utilitarianism requires, but it is at least not obvious that the theory fails at the outset simply because we can never be certain what all the consequences of any action will be.

Now still leaving open the proper conception of utility or good consequences, we need to consider *whose* utility is to count. Assume for the moment that utility is equivalent to happiness. Then on the utilitarian view actions are to be evaluated according to the happiness they produce for anyone affected by them. Happiness is happiness, no matter whose it is, and utilitarian morality requires that any person's happiness is to count equally with any other person's; differences are only of degree or amount, and no person's or group's happiness counts for more than another's just because it is that particular person's or group's. This view is to be contrasted with the theory of practical reasoning usually called *rational* (or ethical) *egoism* according to which each person ought to act so as to maximize only his/her own happiness or interests, and need not be concerned with the interests of other persons, except insofar as doing so indirectly promotes his/her own interests. It is in making the happiness of each person count the same that utilitarianism satisfies a condition of impartiality or equality commonly considered essential to morality.

A further clarification needed in the meaning of the utilitarian principle is whether in maximizing utility, again let us assume that to be happiness, we are to produce the greatest *total* amount of happiness (i.e. the sum of happiness of all individuals) or the greatest *average,* happiness per person. So long as the actions under consideration have no effect on the number of persons who will exist, each formulation will yield the same appraisal of alternative actions and policies. But since many policy issues will have some effect on population size, e.g. tax deductions for dependent children, and welfare programs, as well as policies undertaken for the explicit purpose of affecting population size, e.g. abortion and sterilization, population effects cannot be ignored. Total utilitarianism has the following difficulty. Suppose, as seems in fact possible, that we could undertake rapidly to expand the population. While the increased burden on food supplies, etc. might well substantially reduce the average per capita happiness, the happiness of the additional persons created could well surpass the decrease in the happiness of already existing persons. Total utilitarianism requires that we increase population up to the point where the overall total happiness of the new larger population no longer increases due to the size of the decreases in average happiness. But that seems consistent with population policies that would substantially reduce the level of happiness of everyone. Average utilitarianism avoids some but not all of these difficulties. It will not require increases in population that would bring the happiness of each present and future person down to a low level and so reduce the average happiness, but it would require population increases that raise average happiness by sacrificing the happiness of all present persons for the high average happiness of future persons. It is unclear why presently existing persons should accept theories with either of these implications. Average utilitarianism also has the implausible implication that it is morally wrong to have children if their prospects for happiness while tolerably good are merely slightly below average.

In order to meet some problems of this sort, we might say that utilitarianism should not be construed so as to require creating new persons merely because doing so would increase the average *or* total happiness. The underlying point of utilitarianism, it could be argued, is that given that people exist, it is better that they be happy than unhappy; utilitarianism requires making people happy, not making happy people. But the view that utilitarianism is only concerned with increases or decreases in existing persons' utility seems incompatible with another plausible view that it is wrong to create a person knowing that he will have an intolerable life filled with misery and suffering. Why should we ignore the happiness resulting from creating happy persons, while counting the unhappiness resulting from creating unhappy persons? Whether this and other complexities can be resolved and a plausible utilitarian population policy developed is uncertain. But it should be emphasized that utilitarians clearly do count effects on the happiness of future persons who will in fact exist whatever we do, so there is no dispute about whether not yet existing persons, e.g. future generations, can ever count in the moral calculus.

One other point about whose utility is to count should be mentioned here. On some moral views, only human beings, but not other creatures, e.g. animals, count in the moral calculus. This is not so on the utilitarian theory. For convenience, we said earlier that the utilitarian counts effects on the happiness of all persons, but the more precise formulation is commonly in terms of effects on all *sentient creatures*. In what senses animals are happy and unhappy may be controversial, so to make the point clearest suppose that utility is taken to be pleasure and the absence of pain. It is relatively non-controversial that at least many kinds of animals can and do experience pain and suffering. But if so, then a utilitarian is committed in the moral evaluation of actions to taking account of the pain that will be caused to animals as well as to humans, and to counting pain caused to animals equally with pain caused to humans, except insofar as they differ in amount. Utilitarianism thus requires expanding our moral horizons beyond human beings, a demand which may well have radical implications for, among other things, the ways in which animals are used in medical experimentation and raised for food. All this is not to say that utilitarians consider animals to be moral agents, i.e. capable of deliberating and deciding what it is morally right to do, and acting on the basis of that decision. Utilitarians agree with other moral theorists that they are not.

THE CONCEPT OF UTILITY

We must now consider what account of utility, value, or good consequences utilitarians employ. What is it that utilitarians urge us to maximize by our actions? As noted earlier, we have been construing utilitarianism as a general consequentialist moral theory, leaving open what good consequences are taken to be. This makes utilitarianism equivalent to what is commonly called a *teleological* moral theory according to which the moral rightness and wrongness of any action is determined solely by the value of the consequences of that action. So-called *deontological* moral theories deny that moral rightness is *solely* a function of consequences, and claim that some kinds of actions may be right or wrong independently of the consequences they produce. We shall consider the deontologist's claim in Section III, but for now the point is that utilitarianism broadly construed is compatible with virtually any account of what are good consequences. Nevertheless, for the theory to have specific content and to serve in guiding and evaluating action, some particular account of what consequences are valuable or good must be adopted. Specifically, we need an account of what has *intrinsic value,* that is what is valuable apart from its consequences or relations to other things. Situations or things may be valuable or good instrumentally, as productive of intrinsic value, though not themselves intrinsically valuable; for example, though money is often pursued, it is commonly considered not to be intrinsically valuable, but only instrumentally valuable for the ways it can lead to what does have intrinsic value, say happiness. While instrumental value is not to be neglected, it is clearly intrinsic value that is fundamental in a theory of value or good consequences, and with which we shall be concerned below.

What are the principal candidates for a theory of value or good consequences? We shall mention here four: 1) happiness; 2) the satisfaction of desires or preferences; 3) the promotion of interests or welfare; and 4) a final account which it is difficult aptly to name but which is associated with what is commonly called "ideal utilitarianism." Early utilitarians like Jeremy Bentham (1748–1832) and J. S. Mill (1806–1873) argued on some occasions that what had intrinsic value and so should be maximized in our actions was only pleasure and the avoidance of pain. However, they usually made clear that they were construing pleasure and displeasure broadly so as to include not merely such pleasures as arise from eating or sexual activity, but also activities generally that are enjoyed for their own sake such as a game of tennis or reading a book. Because the concepts of pleasure and pain are often construed more narrowly, we shall consider as the first conception of value the happiness conception, one which is naturally construed to include all activities enjoyed for their own sakes. The concept of happiness is a complex one, but its core for our purposes is that for persons to be happy is for them to be undergoing a conscious experience that they like or enjoy for its own sake. One important feature of the happiness conception of value is that while persons can be mistaken about whether some activity will make them happy, it is generally thought that one cannot be mistaken about whether one is enjoying an experience or activity at the time one undergoes it. On the happiness conception then, it is conscious experience enjoyed for its own sake that has intrinsic value, and each person is in a privileged position for determining what they enjoy or what makes them happy.

The most common alternative conception of value among utilitarians to the pleasure or happiness conception is the desire or preference satisfaction conception, sometimes called "preference utilitarianism." On this conception, what has intrinsic value or is a good consequence of an action is the satisfaction of some person's desire or preference. How does this differ from the happiness conception? We can note here two ways. First, sometimes people value things such as honesty, making their own choices, serving God's will, and so forth, without believing that they will be made happy by them, and even if they will be, not solely *for the reason* that such things will make them happy. The preference conception reflects such values in a way that the happiness conception seems not to, and so more fully reflects the utilitarian's concern with the preferences that people in fact have for states of affairs other than being happy. Second, happiness and desire satisfaction versions of utilitarianism may have substantially different implications on some important moral questions. For example, happiness utilitarianism seems to imply that it is right to kill persons whose expected future prospects for happiness are, on the average version below average, or on the total version negative, assuming that killing them will not affect others' happiness. This is an implication that virtually any utilitarian will seek to avoid. Desire satisfaction utilitarianism does avoid it, since a person with prospects for an unhappy life may nevertheless have a strong desire to live and so should not be killed.

A third alternative conception of value is the promotion of human interests or welfare. The most significant difference between this conception and both the happiness and desire conceptions is that what is in a person's interests or promotes his welfare need not solely depend on what he happens now to want or enjoy. Human interests or welfare have a content that is commonly not thought to be determined solely by a person's wants or enjoyments. Good health, a minimum level of nutrition, education, and so forth, are in a person's interests, for his welfare, and this can be true whether or not one happens to want them or enjoy them. The interest or welfare conception thus gives a theory of value that makes possible a critical evaluation of a particular person's actual desires or enjoyments. Precisely what critical evaluation is made possible will depend on the particular theory of human interests or welfare, sometimes formulated as a theory of human nature, that underlies this conception. We cannot attempt to develop any such theory here, nor to determine whether it is truly independent of or must ultimately be based on happiness or desire satisfaction, but we can at least point out one of the more important issues at stake in deciding which conception of value to adopt.

A person's desires and preferences are the product of biological needs and the socialization process by which he or she is inducted into a society, state, and various social groups. They are importantly determined by and will tend to reflect and reinforce the existing social arrangements, power and authority relations, and expectations in one's environment. Consequently, utilitarianism formulated so as to require maximal satisfaction of preferences as they exist, in turn serves to reinforce the existing social structure; it will have a significant conservative bias. For example, a racist or sexist society may foster racist or sexist preferences in its members, and preference utilitarianism seems committed then to seeking the satisfaction of these preferences. The interest or welfare conception, with its appeal to some normative theory of human nature, avoids this commitment to the status quo and the preferences fostered there, and so provides utilitarianism, especially as applied at the social and political level, with potentially greater critical force in the evaluation of existing social structures and practices. But the plausibility of this conception depends directly both on the strength of the underlying theory of human interests or welfare, and as well on avoiding the objectionable implications of the view that some people know what is good for other persons better than those other person themselves do. Totalitarian political regimes have often claimed to know better than their subjects what is "best" for them in order to try to justify imposing oppressive policies on an unwilling populace.

Finally, we shall mention the conception of value or good consequences associated with ideal utilitarianism. Two common objections to utilitarianism, as we shall see in Section III, are that a) it ignores the distribution of utility among different persons, and b) that it cannot account for the wrongness of an act, for example, of promise-breaking, independent of the consequences of that particular act. A utilitarian who is sympathetic to such objections could respond by revising his conception of value or good consequences to accommodate them. For example, he redefines utility as determined not merely by the amount of happiness, but by the distribution of happiness as well, and assigns some disutility to the state of affairs that a promise has been broken, disutility in addition to the disutility of the consequences of breaking that promise. Doing so will seriously complicate his theory of value, but it will allow him to accept and accommodate within his theory virtually all of the standard sorts of moral objections made to utilitarianism. To *any* consideration to which the critic argues utilitarianism fails to give proper moral weight, ideal utilitarianism can assign just that weight in its theory of value. However, it does so at the cost of transforming the theory in its substantive content into one of its non-consequentialist or non-utilitarian competitors; this "ideal utilitarianism" remains utilitarian in form only, since actions are now sometimes evaluated independently of their consequences. Since the important issue for moral philosophy concerns just what is the most acceptable moral theory, and not whether it is still called utilitarianism, we shall assume that utility or good consequences are defined in one of the first three ways considered above; this will fix the content of utilitarianism and in turn enable comparison of it with its principal competing alternatives. We now shall consider briefly whether utility can be measured, and if so, how.

THE MEASUREMENT OF UTILITY

There are two aspects of the problem of the measurement of utility, for each of which utilitarians must give a satisfactory account. The theoretical aspect is to show how it is at least in principle possible, that is logically and conceptually possible, to make the required measurements of utility. If such measurements are in principle impossible, then the utilitarian principle is useless and not even a possible standard of moral appraisal. The practical aspect is to show, given that measurement of utility makes theoretical sense, how we can in practical decision-making at least make approximations of the measurement required. If no practical approximation is possible, utilitarianism could neither be an account of how anyone does in fact reason on moral questions nor a criterion that anyone might adopt in practical contexts for moral evaluation of actions and social policies. We shall not be able to do more than indicate the nature of the measurement problem, and suggest the direction of one possible line of solution; the issues and work on this problem are far more complex and technical than our discussion will indicate.

What is the theoretical problem of the measurement of utility? Since nearly all actions or social policies that we would recognize as raising a significant moral issue will affect more than one person, what utilitarianism requires is that we be able to measure the effects for the happiness or desires of all affected by the action. There are two distinct parts of the problem. Suppose, to take a simple case, that I am deciding whether to take a vacation at the seashore or in the mountains. First, I must determine which alternative I want most, or which will make me happiest. But then I must count in the desires or happiness of the other members of my family who will accompany me as well. There seems no difficulty, at least in principle, with my determining which alternative I want most or expect to make me happiest, and if all members of my family have the same preference, there is no problem. But if we do not all agree, then the problem is how the desires or happiness of different persons are to be combined. This is the *interpersonal aggregation* part of the measurement problem. If we are trying to maximize the happiness or desire satisfaction of the entire family, we cannot merely vote and go where the majority prefers, because doing so will ignore differences between family members in the *intensity* of their preferences for the seashore or mountains, or differences in the extent to which one or the other choice will affect the happiness of each. Some may be just a bit happier in the mountains, but would enjoy the seashore nearly as much, while others may be miserable in the mountains but enjoy the seashore immensely; merely voting will not do if we want our choice to maximize the happiness of the whole family. It would seem that what we require is a measure of units of happiness or desire strength (what is sometimes called a *cardinal measure* of utility), one which also employs the same units for each different person, allowing one person's utility to be added to or subtracted from another's (what is sometimes called the *interpersonal comparison* of utility), so that we can measure the overall effect of an action on the group. This would be what Bentham called a "felicific calculus," somewhat as follows:

	Change in level of Happiness	
	Seashore	*Mountains*
Husband	+ 12	+ 15
Wife	+ 25	− 15
Son	− 8	+ 20
Daughter	+ 10	+ 10
Total	+ 39	+ 30

As a matter of fact, we do not have any such calculus. The question though, at the theoretical or conceptual level, is not whether we do, but whether we could have such a calculus. Many writers in utility theory and many economists believe that such a calculus is in principle impossible. We shall consider one argument for this view in a moment, but we should not lose sight of the fact that we continually make judgments in daily life that we believe to be sensible and to be at least rough and ready approximations to what our imaginary calculus yielded above concerning the sea-shore and the mountains.

Probably the most influential reason for the belief that interpersonal comparisons of utility are in principle impossible is the assumption that what has utility, for example happiness or desire satisfaction, is a private mental state, accessible only to the person experiencing it, and for the existence of which individual introspection is the only possible evidence. There is no way for me to measure my satisfaction against yours, it is claimed, for while I am directly aware of my mental states, and in particular my satisfaction, no one else can have access to my mental states, and vice versa for you and your mental states.

Critics challenge this argument by observing that it leads to a radical and dubious skepticism about the existence of "other minds" and whether other people have any mental states at all. It would imply that I have no more reason for believing that other human beings are conscious and experience feelings and sensations as I do, than that they are complex robots lacking consciousness entirely. That is a form of skepticism that goes far beyond mere doubts about interpersonal utility comparisons. More-over, it would seem that we do have various sorts of evidence about other people's level of happiness or desire satisfaction. Very generally, there are various biological, physiological, and behavioral correlates to level of happiness or desire satisfaction; for example, verbally expressed attitudes, level of biological need satisfaction, willingness to expend time and resources, and so forth. And these appear to be interpersonal correlates as well, ones which would allow bridging the interpersonal hurdle in the aggregation of utility. This is not to say that we have anything as precise as the calculations supposed above concerning the mountains and seashore, but it is to suggest that we may not be in principle barred from sensible interpersonal comparisons of happiness or desire strength. And if we turn to what has been called above the practical aspect of the problem of utility measurement, these same biologi-cal, physiological, and behavioral correlates seems to be just what we appeal to in the practical approximations to a felicific calculus we attempt in daily life.

It should be emphasized that utility formulated as happiness is different from utility as desire satisfaction, as well as from other conceptions, and that there are specific difficulties and details of the measurement problem unique to each particular conception of utility. Nevertheless, we suggest the provisional conclusion that the measurement problem does not constitute an insuperable objection to utilitarianism. It is also worth adding that since nearly all other alternative moral theories also take effects on happiness or desire satisfaction to be one (though, unlike utilitarianism, not the only) relevant consideration in the moral evaluation of actions, they too are faced with giving an account of how interpersonal comparisons of utility are sensible. Were this in fact an insuperable difficulty, it would bring down most moral theories, and not just utilitarianism.

ACT UTILITARIANISM, RULE UTILITARIANISM AND UTILITARIAN GENERALIZATION

Until now, we have been assuming that utilitarians morally evaluate any particular *action* by assessing what the consequences of *it* will be in comparison with those of *its* alternatives; this view is called *act utilitarianism* (AU). However, many normative objections to utilitarianism, as we shall see in Section III, take the form that utilitarianism so applied countenances the performance of acts many persons believe to be wrong, such as punishing innocent persons, cheating on taxes and breaking promises, if utility will be maximized in that particular instance by doing so. More-over, since people's capacities of judgment are highly fallible, each person deciding each case on its own utilitarian merits would likely produce disastrous results, and would also undermine the coordination and predictability that social and legal rules provide; for example, if I am to loan you money, I want to know that you accept the principle that debts must be repaid whether or not repaying happens to maximize utility. As a result of difficulties like these many utilitarians have adopted some form of *rule utilitarianism* (RU) according to which a) particular actions are to be evaluated by their conformance to moral, social, or legal rules, and b) only the rules are evaluated by the utilitarian standard. An alternative to either AU or RU is *utilitarian generalization* (UG) according to which a particular action is to be evaluated not by *its* consequences, but by the consequences of *everyone* performing acts of a similar kind.

A bewildering variety of versions of rule utilitarianism and utilitarian generalization have been developed, and we can only illustrate them with a few of the most prominent versions. However, before doing so, we need first to consider two sorts of rules that the act utilitarian can endorse without abandoning AU in favor of RU. The first is what has been called rules of thumb or decision-making guides. The act utilitarian is committed to the utilitarian principle as the correct standard for the moral evaluation of actions, as what we might call the *standard of moral rightness*. But this does not commit him to endorse it as well as the proper guide or rule to follow in the *actual process of making moral decisions*. Rather, he can support whatever decision-making procedure will in fact lead to the best decisions and actions as evaluated by the utilitarian standard of rightness, i.e. whatever procedure will lead to results maximizing utility. Thus, because we often lack sufficient time and informa-tion, are biased in favor of our own interests, etc. the act utilitarian goal of always acting so as to maximize utility may be better served in the long run by adopting certain more specific rules as guides to decision and action, rather than appealing directly to the principle of utility each time we act. Perhaps most important here is the common human propensity to rationalize and delude ourselves into thinking *we* need not follow some burdensome moral requirement like keeping a promise or commitment because in this case the best consequences will be produced by violat-ing it, that is, into thinking that we can justifiably make an exception for ourselves. It may be best in the long run to adopt the rule of thumb, "keep your promises," and only attempt to calculate the consequences of keeping as opposed to breaking a particular promise when there is good reason to believe that keeping it would have *very much* worse consequences than breaking it. However, even if the utilitarian adopts rules of thumb such as "do not lie" or "keep your promises," they are merely rules of thumb, and need not be followed when in a particular case we have good reason to believe that, all things considered, utility will be best promoted by violating them. And so they will be of no help against objections that utilitarianism wrongly sanctions actions of particular sorts, for example the deliberate punishment of an innocent person, just in case doing so will in fact maximize utility.

Act utilitarians are not, however, restricted to viewing all social and moral rules as rules of thumb. While allowing that an agent ought to decide how to act by appeal to the utilitarian standard, they can nevertheless consistently support the adoption of social practices and legal rules that do not allow direct appeal to the utilitarian principle in particular cases. These practices and rules may also punish particular actions that do in fact maximize utility. This may seem paradoxical since act utilitarians are then in the position of forbidding and punishing acts that they grant were right. An example will help make the point clear. Consider an act utilitarian legislator deciding whether laws requiring payment of one's debts should allow as an excuse justifying non-payment that in the case at hand utility was maximized by the non-payment. As already noted, critics of act utilitarianism would here point out that agents would frequently be mistaken in attempts to identify exceptions to the requirement of repayment justifiable on utilitarian grounds. Moreover, there are substantial benefits in being able to predict how an individual will act without having to know whether he expects his action to maximize utility. But considerations of these sorts will provide a legislator with sound act utilitarian reasons for supporting laws requiring debt repayment that do not permit the legal defense that non-payment in the case at hand maximized utility. The legislator is seeking to discourage a class of actions (non-payment of debts) *most but not all of which* are, on utilitarian grounds, wrong, and where it is not feasible to identify and discourage only those acts in the class that are in fact wrong. AU holds, at the same time, that citizens should obey such laws if, and only if, doing so in the instance at hand will maximize utility. There will, therefore, be some actions which on AU grounds justifiably break such laws (because utility is maximized in those cases by doing so) that the law, nevertheless, rightly on AU grounds, forbids and punishes. This argument is of a quite general sort and has a great many possible applications—with regard to the issues covered in this book, the reader might consider how it could apply to the paternalistic use of involuntary commitment of non-dangerous mentally ill persons on grounds that they will benefit from the treatment then afforded. It thus seems that act utilitarians can consistently support seemingly non-utilitarian social and legal institutions, without thereby abandoning AU.

We shall now turn to a consideration of specific versions of rule utilitarianism and utilitarian generalization, but before doing so, it may be helpful to stress first three questions central to the assessment of any form of RU or UG: first, does it in fact diverge in its normative implications for specific moral issues from AU?; second, if it does so diverge, does it do so in ways favorable to the rule or generalized as opposed to the act version, and in ways that help meet or avoid the standard normative objections to AU?; third, are versions of rule or generalized utilitarianism which require conformance to rules even in cases when doing so will fail to maximize utility consistent with the fundamental utilitarian proposal that morality requires us to act so as to maximize utility?

Let us now consider one form of rule utilitarianism:

RU: An act is right if and only if it conforms to a set of rules the general acceptance of which in the agent's society would maximize utility.

RU has the two-level structure noted above, and so might seem to prevent the justifiction of particular acts of promise-breaking, deliberate punishment of innocent persons, etc. merely because there would be a small gain in utility in a particular instance from doing so. Notice that if we were to substitute "strict conformance to" for "general acceptance of" in the formulation of RU, RU and AU would be extensionally equivalent, that is, RU would never yield a moral evaluation of any action different than AU. That is because the rule that would maximize utility if *everyone, always* successfully conformed to it is just the act utilitarian standard. However, since there can be "general acceptance" of a set of moral rules in a society without everyone accepting them, and since a single individual can accept a set of rules and yet on occasion fail to conform to them, the set of rules picked out by RU need not necessarily be equivalent to the act utilitarian standard. Moreover, because of the sorts of reasons already mentioned that justify act utilitarians supporting non-utilitarian rules, as well as considerations such as the limits on the complexity of rules real persons can learn and follow, the set of rules that could be learned and generally accepted by most people, as RU requires, may well turn out to be different than the act utilitarian standard.

We can only mention two difficulties here in developing and defending RU. First, since it is a crucial feature of RU that rules are to be evaluated for their utility production in a particular society, we need a way of identifying the society of which the agent is a member, and it is by no means clear how to do this. For example, is the society that a person is a member of identical with their nation state, some narrower group like an ethnic group to which they belong, or a group broader than their nation state? Can a person be a member of more than one society? Defenders of RU need to provide a definite and plausible answer to this problem of societal identification. In general, it is a difficulty of RU that it is unclear precisely what calculations are necessary for the determination of utility maximizing rules, much less what the outcome of such calculations would be. Second, there is a problem concerning non-utility maximizing practices in the agent's society. For example, it may be that rules quite different from those in fact governing the institution of marriage in our own society would, if generally accepted, produce a utility maximizing institution of marriage. Yet it seems a mistake to make the rightness of action that takes place within the institution of marriage as it in fact exists in a given society depend on rules for marriage that may nowhere exist, ones which, indeed, may never have been fully thought out. We can add to these two difficulties that a proponent of RU must still provide an answer to the third question we posed earlier for all rule utilitarians: why should a utilitarian follow RU in the case at hand if doing so will fail to maximize utility? None of this is to say that some version of RU may not prove to be a preferable alternative to AU, but difficulties such as these must be met before that will be shown to be so. In further evaluating RU, the reader might attempt to work out what the implications of it or another version of rule utilitarianism would be for some of the substantive moral issues discussed in other chapters of this book, and whether those implications are more acceptable than those of AU.

The other alternative to AU that we shall consider here is what has been called *utilitarian generalization:*

UG: An act is right if and only if the consequences of everyone's performing an act of the same kind would produce at least as much utility as everyone's performing any alternative action.

It should be clear how UG seems to help the utilitarian with many of the normative objections to his theory. For example, while the consequences of *one* person's cheating on his taxes might be such as to maximize overall utility (he could use the money in a worthwhile way and the government would never miss it), the consequences of *everyone's* doing so would be disastrous because the tax system financing valuable government services would break down; therefore, it seems that such tax cheating could be right according to AU, but wrong according to UG, and that UG and not AU provides the acceptable result. But on closer examination, it is doubtful whether AU and UG do in fact diverge.

The crucial question is how acts are determined to be of the "the same kind" for purposes of assessing the consequences of everyone performing them, and in particular the relevance of what other persons are doing. Actions would seem to be "the same kind" for a utilitarian just in case there are no differences in the properties of each that affect the utility they each produce. But then two acts of tax cheating, one of which contributes to the breakdown of the tax system because it is performed in circumstances in which many others are also cheating, and the other of which has no discernible effect on the tax system because it is performed in circumstances in which few others are cheating, are not, from a utilitarian perspective, acts of "the same kind." Everyone, in the sense of all tax-paying citizens, could not perform an act of this latter sort, because if they did the acts would thereby be of the former sort. The point is that the *circumstances* in which the acts are performed, and in particular the extent to which others are cheating, can make two acts of cheating have different effects on general utility. While both acts are acts of cheating, they are not from a utilitarian perspective acts of the same kind, because they differ in their utility-producing properties. So the person who is considering cheating when *his* doing so will have no bad effects on the tax system because few others are also cheating, will conclude that if everyone cheated when *their* doing so would have no effect on the tax system, then no more than a few could cheat and, hence, the results would not be bad. But that result of UG is the same that AU has for cheating when few others will cheat, and so one's own cheating will have no bad effects. On the other hand, if one is considering cheating when enough others are cheating so that one's doing so will contribute to the breakdown of the tax system, then *his* cheating will have bad consequences and on AU be wrong. But on UG, if everyone who could cheat did cheat in *those* circumstances, then nearly everyone would cheat and the consequences would also be bad; here too, AU and UG do not diverge. So it has seemed to most that AU and UG are extensionally equivalent in virtually all cases in which they were thought to diverge, and that UG does *not* in fact possess the advantage it seems at first to have over AU.

There is one response open to the generalization theorist which should be mentioned here. He might argue that even if few enough others will in fact cheat so as to have no discernible effect on the tax system, cheating is still wrong because if, contrary to fact, everyone else did cheat the consequences would be disastrous, and so it is wrong for anyone to do so. On this interpretation, the generalization theorist makes the relevant test of moral rightness what the consequences would be if everyone who could cheated, regardless of whether those others will in fact do so. This will make the generalization test non-equivalent to AU, and it will as well yield results on cases of the tax cheating sort closer to most people's considered moral views. This view, however, does not appear to be an interpretation of the generalization test that a consistent utilitarian may adopt because it explicitly ignores features of the actual circumstances in which acts are performed that affect the utility those acts produce. Rather, this version of the generalization test is more likely justified by appeal to the notion of fairness—it is unfair not to do one's part in supporting the tax system (and in cooperative activities generally) from which one benefits, whether or not failing to do one's part by cheating might in a particular case maximize utility. And, as I shall argue in Section III, the requirement of fairness is a moral requirement independent of and not fully accounted for by the utilitarian principle.

Because of the difficulties in developing consistently utilitarian versions of rule utilitarianism or utilitarian generalization whose practical implications are clear and are more plausible than those of AU we shall assume in what follows, unless it is indicated to the contrary, that utilitarianism is understood in its act version.

II. *Arguments for Utilitarianism*

Now that we have a clearer idea what the utilitarian moral theory is, we need to consider how it is to be evaluated. How are we to decide whether it is an acceptable theory? Any full answer to this question would be controversial and would take us into a host of complexities that cannot be considered here. But we can distinguish three different sorts of defenses that have commonly been offered of utilitarianism, often in response to what its critics have considered its major difficulties. The first sort of defense is a conceptual one, a response to the objection that the theory cannot be formulated so as to yield determinate results, and so to serve as a guide to decision-making, on all moral questions. We have already discussed what is probably the most frequently cited instance of this sort of objection, viz. that it is not possible, either in principle or in practice, to make the measurements of utility, and in particular the interpersonal comparisons of utility, that the theory requires. We have considered objections of this sort in our discussion of how the theory is to be given precise content, and while some such objections do represent real difficulties, we have seen that it is not unreasonable to believe that the utilitarian may be able to meet them. The remaining two kinds of defenses of utilitarianism both assume that these conceptual problems can be solved and that the theory can be given precise and determinate content, and then proceed to provide a defense of its normative content.

The first sort of normative defense I shall call the considered moral judgment test. Probably the most frequent objection to utilitarianism is that it has implications for specific moral questions that are morally unacceptable; e.g. it permits the deliberate punishment of innocent persons. That is, when we compare what utilitarianism tells us is morally right on particular moral questions with what on reflection and after consideration we believe is right on those same questions, there is a sharp and unacceptable conflict. In Section III, we will examine a number of objections of this sort to determine what the utilitarian's response is, and the extent to which the putative conflicts with our considered moral judgments do indeed exist. But nearly all utilitarians have been unwilling to rely completely on the test of how well their theory fits the considered moral judgments of persons. Early utilitarians like Bentham and J. S. Mill were social and political reformers, and proposed utilitarianism as a moral theory to contribute to and justify the reform of common moral views of their day. This is no less true of utilitarians today. So while some fit with our considered moral judgments is accepted by utilitarians as necessary to the adequacy of their theory, there is no agreement about how much fit, and in what places, is necessary. The other sort of normative defense involves providing arguments directly in support of the utilitarian principle, and independent of the extent to which it fits our considered moral judgments. If this can be done, then we may be justified in at least some cases in abandoning our moral convictions where they conflict with utilitarianism. So before going on to consider how well utilitarianism fits our considered moral judgments, we shall examine how the general utilitarian principle can be supported and defended. We shall consider several such arguments here, though of course there are others.

First, the utilitarian principle can be shown to follow from a plausible account of the moral point of view. This account is sometimes called the *ideal observer* view. What is it to consider a question, say what the proper level of welfare benefits should be, from the moral point of view? If you and others about whose happiness you care are not now, and are not likely to be, on welfare then on self-interested grounds you would perhaps want the benefit level set very low. But judging from the moral point of view requires going beyond mere self-interest in order to satisfy some condition of impartiality; from the moral point of view each person (or sentient creature) is to count for one and no person more than one, as Bentham once put it. But given that each person is to count equally, we still need to know how each is to count, which consequences or considerations, as they effect any person, are relevant from the moral point of view? Here, it seems plausible to say that the welfare, happiness, or desire satisfaction of each person is to count; that is what we are concerned with when we judge from the moral point of view. Finally, we want such judgments to be rational in the sense that they are not made in conditions that lead to mistakes, conditions such as being rushed, being made under emotional stress, being based on false information, and so forth, and rational in the sense that they count effects on both present and future happiness.

To consider questions from this version of the moral point of view is to take the position of a *rational, impartial,* and *benevolent* spectator or observer. How will such a spectator judge? He will approve of actions to the extent that they in fact promote the welfare, both now and in the future, of all affected by them. We can think of him as merging or conflating all actual individuals into one super-individual, and then approving of actions that maximize the happiness of that super-individual. But this just is to judge according to the utilitarian principle. (It is worth noting that this conception of the moral point of view, in ignoring the differences between persons, ignores both the distribution of utility between different persons as well as the number of persons that exist. It therefore supports total and not average utilitarianism.) So the utilitarian principle is the standard entailed by a highly plausible account of the moral point of view, and whatever strength this account of the moral point of view has is transferred to the utilitarian principle.

A second, related argument attempts to show that utilitarianism is the favored candidate for a principle of rational social choice, drawing upon a relatively non-controversial assumption of decision theory, as well as everyday decision making. Scholars of decision theory commonly assume that *rational individual choice* requires a person to choose so as to maximize his expected welfare, happiness, or desire satisfaction, i.e. his utility, over time. Individual choice, so far as it is rational, eliminates any mistakes that produce an avoidable sacrifice of the chooser's utility, and is not subject to the particular irrationality of imprudence. By imprudence, we here mean the ignoring or discounting of effects on one's future welfare, just because they are future and not present effects, and apart from considerations of the uncertainty of the future effects. Foregoing a great and certain benefit tomorrow for a very small gain today is a paradigm case of irrationality; for example, it is irrational to lose a long sought opportunity to attend medical school merely because filing your application by the deadline prevents you from spending the day at the beach. The principle of rational individual choice then requires that we be impartial between our present and future happiness (after all, it is our future) and to maximize total happiness over our entire life. But morality is not merely a matter of maximizing one's own happiness with no concern for the happiness of others, and so a moral principle will have to be a principle of rational *social,* not merely individual, choice. But the natural way to arrive at that would seem to be to extend the temporal impartiality over different parts of a single individual's life of the principle of rational individual choice, to an impartiality over all present and future persons as well. The principle of rational social choice then states that actions are preferred that maximize over time the welfare of all persons affected by them. But once again, this is the utilitarian principle, derived now from widely accepted notions of individual and social choice.

A somewhat different way of looking at essentially the same point is to notice how non-controversial is the assumption that if doing something will promote one's own interest, then that is a reason for doing it. Almost no one denies that self-interest is a reason for action; this is most obvious if you simply consider your own case, and that your own interests serve as reasons for you to act, and also, what is different, motivate you to act. But likewise, almost no one denies that morality is different from and goes beyond mere self-interest; morality is impartial or universal, and takes account of the interests of everyone. But morality would then seem naturally to require the impartial promotion of the interests of all, and this is the utilitarian position.

Utilitarianism, as the examples with which we began this chapter served to indicate, gives expression to a very natural and plausible general way of thinking about morality. In a nutshell, what could be more natural than that morality is about, or requires, promoting the good. And what is a more natural view of the good than the welfare, happiness, or desire satisfaction of all persons. This is not really an argument for utilitarianism, though it does show utilitarianism to embody a very common conception of morality. We can, however, turn it into a burden of proof or burden of justification argument directed against any alternative non-utilitarian morality. Since the utilitarian principle states that an action is morally right just in case it produces at least as much utility as any alternative action open to an agent, then to be a different theory any alternative to utilitarianism must hold that it is sometimes right to act in ways that either produce preventable human unhappiness, or fail to produce as much happiness as might have been produced. If happiness is a good, as most non-utilitarians are inclined to grant, then both these features of non-utilitarian theories would seem to stand in need of explanation and defense. Otherwise, for example, following moral rules such as "do not lie" or "keep your promises" when doing so will not maximize happiness seems, as the contemporary Australian utilitarian J. J. C. Smart has put it, a form of superstitious rule-worship.

Finally, there is one other consideration that we shall mention here which, while not in itself an argument for utilitarianism, does constitute a significant advantage of it in comparison with most alternative moral theories. Utilitarianism is both a simple and fully determinate or complete moral theory. Both these features stem from its character as a theory requiring maximization of a single variable. While the necessary empirical calculations of consequences for evaluating actions will be very complex in most instances, the theory is *simple* in the sense that we only calculate the effects of an action for a single variable, say happiness, and then maximize for that variable. It is fully *determinate* in that it is in principle possible to determine for any action whether it can be expected to produce at least as much happiness as any alternative action open to its agent. If it will, it is morally right; if not, it is wrong. Often, as noted earlier, we will be uncertain regarding what an action's consequences will be, and so we can only make assessments of expected utility discounted for probabilities, but the principle nevertheless gives us a decision criterion applicable in *every* case. The principle applies to any action, and makes that action's rightness or wrongness, given the principle, an empirical question depending on its consequences for utility. It is by making the moral evaluation of action empirically settleable in this way that the theory is fully determinate. There is in principle a correct answer to the moral assessment of any possible action.

This is an especial virtue when utilitarianism is compared with the major competing moral theories. A common feature of nearly all non-utilitarian theories is that they make a *plurality* of different properties of actions relevant to their moral assessment. For example, lying, promise-breaking, injuring and causing pain, are all considered by many persons to be wrong; but it may sometimes be necessary to lie or break a promise in order to avoid injuring or causing pain. We are then faced with a case of moral conflict and what might be called "the priority problem"; which moral consideration or duty is more important, and what, all things considered, ought we to do? The more complex the non-utilitarian theory, the more difficult the priority problem is likely to be. Utilitarianism, in virtue of being a single variable, maximizing theory, does not face the priority problem. The nature and importance of the priority problem will become clearer when we consider some of the sorts of objections that are commonly directed against utilitarianism, but suffice it to say for now that this problem has proved to be particularly intractable; it has proved to be extraordinarily difficult to formulate any plausible priority rules, rankings, or weightings for different moral considerations, rights, or duties that provide satisfactory resolutions of all such possible cases of moral conflict. But to the extent that we lack such priority rules, then in situations of moral conflict like those cited above, which after all are just the hard moral problems for which a moral theory should provide some guidance, the non-utilitarian theory fails to provide any guidance and we are thrown back without help to our moral intuitions. We might then say that these non-utilitarian theories are only partial theories, and to make matters worse, are incomplete at just the crucial and controversial places. It is for this reason that its fully determinate character is often thought to be a substantial virtue of utilitarianism.

III. Objections to Utilitarianism

In this final section we shall consider some of the principal normative or moral objections that have been brought against utilitarianism. We shall not attempt to determine which if any objections are conclusive against the theory, but only to bring out where the main points of dispute between utilitarians and their critics lie. It should be emphasized as well that any full assessment of utilitarianism requires not merely the formulation and evaluation of it, but the elaboration and assessment of alternative moral theories as well. That, of course, is not possible here, but only then would we be in a position to determine how utilitarianism fares in comparison with its principal competitors. Before taking up specific objections, two general forms of such objections should be noted. First, since the objections we will be considering in this section are moral objections, they will have the general form that utilitarianism has implications for specific moral issues that are in unacceptable conflict with our considered moral views on those issues. We called this, in the last section, the considered moral judgment test, and noted that virtually all utilitarians accept it as at least a partial test of the acceptability of their theory. Consequently, one defense of utilitarianism against such objections takes the general form of attempting to show that utilitarianism correctly applied does not in fact have implications incompatible with our considered moral views. The issue here then might be characterized as, does utilitarianism get the correct results on moral questions? But supposing that it does, we still need to ask whether it gets those results for the right reasons or in the right way. For example, is it wrong to perform involuntary euthanasia because doing so turns out not to maximize utility, or simply because doing so would violate the right not to be killed? The point is that persons do not merely have beliefs that particular sorts of actions are right or wrong, but they have beliefs as well about *why* they are right or wrong, about the *reasons* that make them right or wrong. If utilitarianism is an acceptable moral theory it should not merely be able to produce the right results on specific moral questions, but it should correctly represent as well the reasoning that in fact supports persons' judgments on those issues.

JUSTICE AND FAIRNESS

The most important traditional objection to utilitarianism is that it conflicts with requirements of justice. This objection, however, in fact encompasses more than one difficulty, and we shall concentrate first on the issue of distributive justice. Since there is no consensus among non-utilitarians about the correct theory of distributive justice, there is no agreement about the precise nature of this difficulty for utilitarianism, but in general it is that while utilitarianism requires action that maximizes the *amount* (average or total) of utility, morality requires a just or fair *distribution* of utility between different individuals. Utilitarians are indifferent to how utility is distributed among different persons, except insofar as how it is distributed affects the total or average amount of utility produced. That implication was clear in the utilitarian account of the moral point of view noted in Section II, according to which the impartial spectator could merge all actual individuals into one super-individual and then approve of actions according to how much utility they produce for that super-individual. Let us consider two examples of this distributional objection, and of how the utilitarian might respond. First, consider the distribution of income in a society. This is a very complex moral issue, but part of many persons' beliefs about just distributions are views such as the following: "no one should have great luxuries while others are starving," "there should be minimum income floors below which no one should be allowed to fall," and so forth. Implicit in many such views is that there is some, though not absolute, independent moral weight to a principle of equality in distribution. Some such commitment to equality underlies the well-known distributive principle advanced by the contemporary Harvard philosopher John Rawls to the effect that inequalities in social and economic advantages are only justified to the extent that they maximize the expectations of the worst-off group in society. The point is that there are losses or sacrifices to disadvantaged groups that cannot be justified by even greater gains to better off groups; while perhaps utility maximizing, such distributions would be unjust or unfair.

In assessing the utilitarian's response to such objections, it is important to distinguish between the distribution of utility, e.g. happiness, and of the means to utility, e.g. income. Utilitarians argue that the morally preferred distribution is the one that maximizes total utility, not total income. That allows the utilitarian to make a *prima facie* case for equality in income distribution. This case is based on the declining marginal utility of money; that is, a given increment of money or annual income, say $1,000, will produce more utility for a person whose income is $10,000 than for one whose income is $100,000. Give this, and other things being equal, we will maximize the utility of a given sum of money by distributing it equally, and so there is a *prima facie* case to be made on utilitarian grounds for equality in the distribution of income. Of course, the utilitarian will nevertheless permit inequalities in income that serve as *incentives* for bringing forth greater efforts in people, that promote capital accumulation, and that in general increase the total income available for distribution. There may be a utilitarian case for income floors below which no one is permitted to fall because of the very high utility produced by satisfying basic needs, with inequalities permitted in incomes above the floors that increase total income and in turn total utility. This is a vastly oversimplified account of a very complex issue, but it is perhaps enough to suggest that utilitarians may be able to accommodate the seemingly non-utilitarian beliefs about distribution cited above, more specifically that there is a place for an at least limited principle of equality within a utilitarian distributive framework, and finally that a utilitarian distribution of income may be closer to many persons' considered moral views than might at first be supposed.

It should be emphasized, however, that the distributive objection to utilitarianism is not limited only to the distribution of income. Consider another example of that objection, one which appeals to the notion of fairness. In the not very distant past in the United States there was a selective service system with mandatory military service, but with exemptions granted to persons in jobs and professions considered especially important to the "national interest"—here substitute, especially conducive to the general utility. That system was criticized as unfair on the grounds that since everyone generally benefitted from having available a system of national defense, it was unfair to exempt some from having to do their part in producing that benefit, specifically from bearing the substantial burden of two years of involuntary service in the armed forces, often at great risk and cost to themselves. Critics argued that even if the exemption system did serve the national interest or general utility, fairness required that all who were able to serve should bear an equal risk of having to serve. Given that fewer were needed than could serve, it was argued that a lottery system to select from all able to serve would fairly distribute the burden, and such a system did eventually replace the deferment system. This is an example, and it is only one example of a very general sort of argument with many other applications, of how fairness and utility maximization can conflict in the design of social practices, and in the way they distribute benefits and burdens. It seems doubtful whether the utilitarian can fully account for the moral requirement of fairness, and so it may be necessary for him to reject claims of fairness when they conflict with utility maximization.

It is worth adding that utilitarianism diverges from some prominent though less egalitarian theories of distribution, as well as from more egalitarian theories such as Rawls'. Underlying many persons views about income distribution and property rights is some form of labor theory of property, a theory that builds on intuitions like, "I made it, its mine." John Locke defended a theory of this sort in the seventeenth century, and Robert Nozick is a recent prominent defender of such a view. On Nozick's view, what is important is who did what—moral claims to property are *historically* based; they are founded on principles of just *acquisition, transfer,* and *rectification,* and *whatever* distribution happens to come about in accordance with such principles is just. The utilitarian account of just distribution, on the other hand, focuses on the pattern of distribution at any point in time, and whether the pattern is utility maximizing; it does not matter who has what except in so far as that affects total utility. But this does not give people, according to the historical theorist, what they deserve or are entitled to; it does not accord with the notion of justice as rendering to each his due.

The place of considerations of desert are more prominent still in objections to utilitarian accounts of *retributive justice,* specifically, utilitarian theories of punishment. Once again, the crux of the disagreement lies in the relevance of forward versus backward looking considerations. The fines and imprisonments inflicted on convicted criminals create a disutility for them, in addition to the cost and disutility to society of maintaining a criminal justice system. Utilitarians must find some compensating benefits from such a system if it is to be morally justified, and the good consequences they commonly note from criminal punishment are the forward looking or future benefits of deterring others from committing similar offenses, and protection of society from, as well as reform of, the criminal while he is imprisoned. In the absence of any such future benefits, a utilitarian ought to view punishment as morally unjustified. Retributive theories of punishment, on the other hand, make backward-looking considerations, in particular the criminal's past wrong action, necessary for a full account of the justification of punishment. Only the past responsible and wrongful act of the criminal explains why he deserves punishment, as well as why innocent persons do not deserve to be punished. A fair or just system of punishment, the retributive theorist urges, constrains the promotion of the desirable ends of deterrence, reform, and protection by the requirement that punishment be deserved. It is a common criticism of utilitarianism that it implies that the deliberate punishment of an innocent person could be morally justified. For example, when the authorities do not know who has committed a particularly ghastly crime, they might only be able to stop riots or acts of private vengence against the group believed responsible by framing and punishing an innocent member of that group. The prominence of this objection to utilitarianism lies not in any belief that such circumstances often occur, but in the clear focus it seems to bring to the relevance of backward-looking considerations of desert.

We can also use this example to illustrate common moves made by utilitarians and their critics in consideration of moral objections generally. The utilitarian will point out that the authorities could rarely if ever reasonably believe that such deliberate punishment of an innocent person was their best alternative (e.g. they could protect those against whom the riots are directed), especially when account is taken of the *indirect effects* of the act (e.g. the disrespect for law created if the frame-up comes out, the precedent that would be set leading to future abuses, etc.). The critic will respond that even taking into account all such considerations, it is still possible, however unlikely and uncommon, that the authorities could reasonably believe that framing the innocent person was the best utilitarian alternative; nevertheless, he argues, such punishment of an innocent person would still be wrong. The utilitarian is likely at this point to respond that if we have carefully considered all the consequences of the frame-up, and it still clearly is the alternative maximizing utility, then it is not obvious that the utilitarian is mistaken in permitting it. There is a certain force to this utilitarian response, for unless we simply insist that the deliberate punishment of an innocent person must *always* be wrong (and that claim would certainly need support), then once the case has been carefully specified it *is* no longer so clear that punishment of the innocent person, though certainly to be regreted, is not morally permissible, and indeed obligatory. In general, the utilitarian's strategy is to show that once we have carefully and realistically specified the putative moral counter-example to his view, it no longer is so clear that his theory implies the wrong result, or that the putative counterexample really is a counterexample.

One final response of the critic may be noted. He may grant that as fully specified, it is uncertain whether the innocent person ought to be punished, but hold that the utilitarian treatment of the case remains defective because it neglects the independent moral principle at stake in the case and which would be violated by the punishment, a principle requiring that punishment, to be fair or just, must be deserved. Even if that principle is not absolute, the requirement it expresses is morally important and non-utilitarian—it is not based merely on its usefulness in promoting utility. The reader may find the general structure suggested here in the debate between utilitarians and their critics over the force of this moral objection repeated in consideration of other moral objections raised to utilitarianism; in those cases too, it will be important not only to carefully and realistically specify the particular case so as fairly to assess its force against utilitarianism, but to determine the general non-utilitarian principle(s) on which the objection implicitly rests.

MORAL RIGHTS

Often objections to utilitarianism are framed in terms of moral rights—some actions which would maximize utility are nevertheless wrong, the critic urges, because they would violate someone's rights. What actions are objected to on these grounds will depend on what rights people have; rights commonly appealed to include rights to privacy or liberty, to life or not to be killed, not to have serious physical harm inflicted on one, to equality of opportunity, and so forth. Moral rights are generally not claimed to be absolute (that is, never permissibly violated) but rather to be *prima facie,* that is, rights which can sometimes be justifiably overridden by other moral considerations. However, the feature that has provided rights such an important place in disputes about utilitarianism is that the mere fact that violating, rather than respecting, a right would produce some increase in utility is not sufficient to justify a right's violation. Insofar as individual rights are, in part, rights against the government, they are designed to place limits on the way in which the government may carry out policies and programs that promote the national interest or the general welfare. Since we can insist on our rights, waive them, forfeit them, and so forth, they are a moral instrument that places control in the rightholder over the area of behavior that the right protects. For example, if I have a right to liberty that includes the liberty to decide whom I will marry or what kind of career I will pursue, that right permits me to decide about spouse and career as I see fit, at least within certain limits, and does not require that I decide in the way that will maximize utility.

Individual rights in fact have two distinct functions that it is useful to distinguish. The first is to give the rightholder some protection against his interests being overridden by the greater interests or needs of others. For example, many Americans possess or could acquire skills that they could almost certainly put to use in underdeveloped areas of the world in ways that would produce more utility than does the use they in fact make of their abilities; consider physicians, engineers, agricultural economists, and so forth. If there is a right to personal liberty that includes choosing which profession you will enter, and where you will practice it, that right rests the decision with you; hence, it is not obligatory that you choose as the greater needs and interests of others would dictate. The other function of rights arises when only the interests or utility of the rightholder will be affected by his action. Here, rights give the rightholder an entitlement to decide how he will act within the confines of the right, and protect him from paternalistic, utility-maximizing interference from others, even when his choice may be foolish and fail best to promote his own good. In each case, then, theories that give important place to moral rights will generally place an important value on respect for individual autonomy, on leaving an individual free, at least within significant limits, to order his life as he sees fit. The ultimate force of objections to utilitarianism based on its conflict with moral rights depends on the plausibility of the theory of rights from which those objections are made. Rights are discussed elsewhere in this volume, and we cannot attempt to develop and defend a theory of rights here, but can only note the importance commonly accorded such objections to utilitarianism.

Associated with the objection based on moral rights, in fact at times formulated as such an objection, is the criticism that there are certain kinds of actions that are wrong in themselves, and apart from the consequences they happen on a particular occasion to produce; common examples are promise-breaking or lying. The claim is not that the consequences of a particular act of promise-breaking or lying are not relevant to their overall moral assessment, but rather that their consequences are only part of what is relevant to such assessment. Promise-breaking or lying violates, as it is sometimes put, a moral injunction requiring respect for persons or governing relations between persons as moral agents that is not founded solely on a utilitarian calculus. It is in order to isolate acts of these sorts (from which no bad consequences will arise) that cases are developed such as secret promises to a person on his death-bed, the later breaking of which will cause no disappointed expectations in the recipient of the promise. The related objection is that the promisor still has some moral reason to perform as promised, *even though* better consequences might be produced by breaking the promise. We shall not pursue here the assessment of objections such as this, but the reader may find it helpful to look for the dialectical structure noted above in the discussion of the punishment of the innocent objection.

HOW CONSEQUENCES ARE PRODUCED, AND BY WHOM

We turn now to a different kind of objection, one that grants that consequences are relevant for moral assessment, but adds that how, and by whom, those consequences are brought about is relevant as well. Consider two cases. In the first, you decide to take a vacation instead of contributing to famine relief, knowing that as a result some unknown person in a distant land will die of starvation. In the second, you send such a starving person poisoned food in order to bring about his death. The morally significant consequence appears to be the same in each case, someone dies, and yet many persons would judge the second act to be more seriously wrong than the first. One issue between utilitarians and their critics is whether there is any morally significant difference between two actions such as these, again once they are more fully and realistically spelled out. If we remain convinced that there is, then the next question is what makes them morally different. What is the relevant distinction between them, and is it a distinction of which utilitarians can consistently take account? Even among non-utilitarians who agree that there is a moral difference between cases of this sort, there is no agreement as to just what the relevant difference is. Some have argued that in the first, the death is merely a *foreseen but unintended consequence* of what you do, while in the second the death is the *intended result* of your action; on this position, part of the "doctrine of double effect," there is a stronger moral prohibition of intentionally bringing about harms, than there is of causing a harm which is a foreseen but unintended consequence of what one does. Others have argued that *negative duties,* here a duty not to kill, are more stringent morally than *positive duties,* here a duty to save. Still others have thought there is a morally relevant difference between *acts,* here killing, and *omissions,* here failing to save, or between *causing* harm and *failing to prevent* harm. A defense of the moral significance of any of these seemingly non-utilitarian distinctions would require testing them against our considered moral judgments over a wide array of different cases in which they would be relevant and so would make some moral difference. Moreover, we would want to see as well whether the distinctions could be integrated into a coherent and consistent non-utilitarian moral theory that more adequately accounted for our considered moral judgments.

A related objection to utilitarianism is that we each have a special responsibility for what we deliberately do, one which is different from and stronger than our responsibility for preventing the wrongful acts of others, even if the bad consequences might be similar in either case. For example, suppose a terrorist threatens to kill several innocent victims unless you execute another innocent person against whom he has an unfounded grudge. It is sometimes argued that, even apart from worries about the bad precedent set by giving in to such threats, it would be wrong to give in to the threat because you would then be responsible for the death of the person that you kill, while if you refuse it is the terrorist and not you that would be responsible for the resulting deaths; refusing to give in to his threat is necessary to maintain your own moral integrity. Utilitarians can respond that if there are really no other alternatives, and no other relevant consequences to the two alternatives besides the number of deaths resulting in each, then it is only a confused and self-indulgent moral squeamishness, an attempt not to dirty one's own hands, that underlies the refusal to kill one in order to save more.

SUPEREROGATORY ACTIONS

We can consider one final objection to utilitarianism here. This is that it is too demanding, requires too much of persons, and in particular confuses what is morally required or obligatory with what, though praiseworthy, goes beyond the call of duty. Utilitarianism morally *requires*, makes it a moral *duty*, always to act in the manner that will produce the most utility possible. Suppose a hiker comes across a small child being viciously attacked by a dangerous wild animal. The child will likely be killed if he does not intervene, but there is a substantial risk of serious injury or death to the hiker if he attempts to do so. Without hesitation, he rushes to the aid of the child and succeeds in rescuing it. In many such cases of heroism, it is reasonable to assume that the act of intervening maximized expected utility in comparison with available alternatives, though at very grave risk or sacrifice to the heroic intervenor. We usually regard persons who perform such heroic acts as worthy of our moral admiration; their heroic acts go beyond what is morally required of a person. Utilitarianism, on the other, would make the act morally required, and a failure of the hiker to risk his own life to save the child morally wrong or forbidden, and worthy of moral condemnation. So it seems that utilitarianism fails to account for the class of acts commonly considered good or praiseworthy to do, but not morally required or obligatory, frequently labelled "supererogatory acts."

Another example may bring the difficulty closer to home. Much of the income of the average middle-class (or better off) American is spent on goods and services relatively inefficient in the production of utility in comparison with donating that money to, for example, organizations such as Oxfam or Care devoted to aiding victims of famine and poverty. Utilitarianism seems to require us to reduce our living standards drastically by donating our income towards such ends up to the point that the hardship to us and others we provide care for outweighs the gain in suffering prevented by further donations. A person who does provide this much aid to others at this much sacrifice to himself again may certainly be worthy of our admiration and respect since he evidences an uncommon concern for the needs of others. But on reflection, are we prepared to accept that doing so is morally required or obligatory, and the failure to do so morally wrong, a blameworthy moral failure? Here again, there appears to be a sharp conflict between the implications of utilitarianism and the considered moral views of most people. There are several possible responses open to the utilitarian; we shall only mention three here, and leave the reader to consider how they might be elaborated and defended. First, he can argue that in cases like aiding the victims of famine, the considered moral judgment that doing so is not obligatory is defective and ought to be revised. Second, he might attempt to incorporate within his theory a general distinction between the *morally best* action and that which is *morally obligatory*, and argue that it is only a failure to carry out one's obligations that is wrong and that justifies moral blame. Finally, he might argue that such actions are not considered morally obligatory and blameworthy only because, human nature being what it is, most people simply are unable to perform actions which involve great sacrifices of their own interests for the benefit of others.

All of the difficulties for utilitarianism that we have considered have only been sketched in barest outline. A far more detailed development of the objections, as well as of the responses open to a utilitarian, would be necessary for a fair assessment of the ultimate strength of such objections. There are in addition other objections that have figured prominently in the ongoing debate over utilitarianism that we have not had space to mention here. So there is further philosophical work left for the reader in order to reach a well-grounded conclusion about the overall acceptability of utilitarianism. What we have attempted is to fill out our consideration of utilitarianism by selecting objections to it that are of a rather general and far-reaching nature, ones which are often taken to be central or fundamental objections, and which further illuminate the theory of utilitarianism and how it differs from its competitors.

Suggested Readings

Michael Bayles (ed.), *Contemporary Utilitarianism*. Garden City, NY: Anchor Books, 1968.

Richard Brandt, *A Theory of the Good and the Right*. Oxford: Oxford University Press, 1979.

Dan W. Brock, "Recent Work in Utilitarianism," *American Philosophical Quarterly* (10) 1973, pp. 241–276.

D. H. Hodgson, *Consequences of Utilitarianism*. Oxford: Oxford University Press, 1967.

David Lyons, *The Forms and Limits of Utilitarianism*. Oxford: Oxford University Press, 1965.

Harlan Miller and William Williams (eds.), *The Limits of Utilitarianism*. Minneapolis: University of Minnesota Press, 1981.

J. S. Mill, *Utilitarianism*. many editions.

Jan Narveson, *Morality and Utility*. Baltimore, Maryland. The Johns Hopkins Press, 1967.

New Essays on John Stuart Mill and Utilitarianism, *Canadian Journal of Philosophy,* Supplementary Volume V, 1979.

Donald H. Regan, *Utilitarianism and Co-operation*. Oxford: Oxford University Press, 1980.

Rolf Sartorius, *Individual Conduct and Social Norms*. Encino, Calif.: Dickenson Publishing, 1975.

Henry Sidgwick, *The Methods of Ethics*. New York: Dover Publications, 1966. Reprint of 1907 edition.

Peter Singer, *Practical Ethics*. Cambridge: Cambridge University Press, 1979.

J. J. C. Smart and Bernard Williams, *Utilitarianism: For and Against*. Cambridge: Cambridge University Press, 1973.

chapter ten

Justice and Equality

DAVID A. J. RICHARDS

Since the earliest philosophical reflection on the concept of justice and its place in political and social discourse, justice has been supposed to involve or implicate the idea of equality; and, this view of the concept has, despite dramatic shifts in the substantive interpretation of what equality is or should be, remained a perennial constant of serious self-conscious discourse and debate about justice. In this essay, I try to explain the formal idea of justice which appears to unite all serious philosophical reflection on the idea, and then to focus on two levels of disagreement about how the underlying idea of equality should be interpreted—first, the level of common-sense criteria (like need, merit, rights, or the like), and second, the level of fundamental moral principles (utilitarianism, Kantian mutual respect, and the like). Finally, I turn to the implications of these philosophical disagreements for the understanding of various substantive controversies over issues of justice, for example, distributive justice of basic goods and resources, the liberal priority of free speech and personal autonomy, and the retributive justice of punishment.

I. The Formal Concept of Justice

Questions about justice are marked by a characteristic mode of moral criticism of acts, persons, and institutions. We speak or think, for example, of an unfairness in earned income, as between the wages paid a man and woman, when we query the appropriateness of the ground for the wage disparity; or we discuss an injustice in criminal sentencing, as between a convicted white and black, when we find that the difference in treatment appears to lack a relevant kind of justification. Such cases raise issues of justice because we appear not to be treating wage earners or convicted criminals alike. We evaluate such cases in terms of a *formal* concept (what Aristotle called treating like cases alike or giving each man his due)[1] and a *substantive* theory (in terms of which we determine the material standards of being alike or due). The formal aspect of justice is philosophically uncontroversial: it unites, as we shall see, classical political and moral theorists as disparate as Aristotle, Hume and Kant, who deploy the formal concept in terms of radically antagonistic substantive theories. Indeed, it is possible to deny that there can be any such reasonable substantive theory (on the ground, for example, that substantive questions of morality are irreducibly subjective and incapable of rational discussion), and still affirm the formal concept of justice, denying not that justice is treating like cases alike, but that each person's opinion of what makes cases alike is as good as any other's.[2] Thus, the formal concept of justice transcends not only diverse substantive moral theories, but also diverse objective and subjective theories of what morality is.

The formal concept of justice rests on the idea of equality, for cases are judged to be alike or treatment regarded as due relative to some standard which specifies that cases are alike or that conduct is due. Accordingly, the interest in a philosophical view of justice is not its formulation of the formal concept, but its conception of the substantive theory of equality in terms of which issues of justice are properly adjudicated.

II. The Criteria of Justice

There are two levels at which philosophical theories of substantive equality are pitched: first, the lower-order standards of common sense reasoning in terms of which cases are judged alike or certain treatment due; second, more fundamental philosophical principles of ultimate morality in terms of which such common sense judgments are claimed to be explicable. Let us first discuss the lower-order standards, or what we shall call the common sense criteria of justice.

When people of practical wisdom and affairs address complex political, social, or economic issues in terms of open-ended deliberation regarding the just course of policy or conduct, they often deliberate in terms of a number of disparate common sense considerations. In a discussion of our example of wage disparities between men and women, several kinds of considerations would characteristically be given weight: for example, customary or conventional standards of pay in a certain industry or business may be accorded some deliberative weight; or levels of effort expended and output delivered may constitute important work-based criteria of merit which would be consulted; or levels of need, understood as forms of basic human interest without which severe injury, privation, and even death may occur, would also be consulted as grounds for claims.[3] Or, in a discussion of the retributive justice of a sentencing policy that allows disparities in sentencing between persons of different races, a number of distinct criteria would be given weight. For example, general conceptions of the gravity of the wrongful act (murder is more grave than a petty larceny) and the culpability of the actor (intentional acts are more culpable than acts of ordinary inadvertent negligence) are retributive considerations which should set limits of proportionality applied alike to all morally similar acts and offenders. Also relevant are general deterrence considerations concerning what level of sanction would be more likely to deter people in general from comparable wrongdoing, and specific deterrence considerations regarding what form of punishment would be likely to deter the offender himself from repeating the act. The legitimate concern for protection would consider the imminent dangerousness of the offender as a ground for whether or how long he or she might be isolated; and the aim of reform would fix punishment in terms of the likelihood that she or he might thus come to reform the character that led to the wrongdoing.[4]

These examples of the criteria of justice indicate the complexity of interpreting justice in terms of such criteria, viz., in distributive justice, treating like cases alike or giving each her due relative to rights, or deserts, or needs, or—in retributive justice—relative to wrongdoing or culpability, or general or specific deterrence, or protection, or reform. The complexity is of two kinds, each of which introduces deep uncertainty into discussions of justice pitched at the level of common sense criteria.

First, the *interpretation* of each of the criteria is itself extremely controversial. In discussions of distributive justice, for example, conservative theories interpret rights completely in terms of customary or conventional expectations[5] (thus, the wage differentials between men and women, if customary, might be fair), and tend to regard any more expansive conception of human or natural rights (regarding, for example, the right of women to be treated with dignity as persons) as nonsense, and, worse than nonsense, dangerous;[6] the idea of deserts as a criterion for special reward, is sometimes interpreted in terms of a mixture of talent, effort, and good fortune, whereas other interpretations which reward only purely voluntary, non-fortuitous conduct, argue that only effort can, morally, be given significant weight;[7] and, the interpretation of needs ranges from pedestrian definitions in terms of shelter and adequate diet, to complex moral ideals of unalienated "species man."[8] In discussions of retributive justice, considerable controversy rages over the substantive content of the moral values that retributive justice enforces, and whether and in what way these values are a necessary or sufficient condition of just punishment;[9] people debate how general deterrence is to be measured and assessed (is, for example, the proper method that of the marginal deterrence comparison of the increment in deterrence any form of penalty affords, and should, accordingly, certainty of punishment be accorded much greater deterrent weight than severity of punishment?);[10] the difficulties of measuring dangerousness for purposes of protection are enormous;[11] and, modern thought about criminal justice debates the soundness of interpreting reform in terms of an open-ended therapeutic paternalism (curing the person for her or his own good) which is, in fact, empirically baseless and morally abusive, at the expense of the earlier and sounder view of reform as moral atonement.[12]

Second, the *relative weight* of each of the criteria, in a balanced assessment of the justice of distribution or punishment, is even more controversial. Indeed, some substantive theories of both distributive and retributive justice are marked by their wholesale repudiation of certain of the criteria of justice, and their exclusive focus on one or another of the other criteria. Spencer's theory of social justice, for example, focusses on deserts, and repudiates needs;[13] whereas Kropotkin's identifies needs as the only sound ground for distribution, and rejects deserts as immoral.[14] Someone committed to the pattern of justice expressed by the modern welfare state clearly gives some weight to rights, deserts, and needs; but, both the interpretation and relative weighting of each varies widely.[15] For example, two people both committed to the welfare state pattern may, nonetheless, disagree over whether rights should be conventional expectations or should be associated with substantive claims (for example, rights to employment); the former may be committed to welfare (satisfying needs), but not to full employment, whereas the latter may regard full employment as a moral right, and welfare as a residual category of no central social importance.[16] Similarly, some contemporary forms of retributivism give decisive weight to the *lex talionis* idea of an eye for an eye, fairly administered, and give no weight, for example, to the lack of marginal deterrence evidence for the death penalty, arguing that death simply is the appropriate penalty for certain wrongs.[17] Other forms of contemporary retributivism deny that wrongdoing is ever a sufficient condition of either punishment or its form, and give decisive weight to general deterrence evidence (for them, the death penalty is immoral, and should be unconstitutional);[18] some exponents of this view completely repudiate paternalistic therapeutic reform as a just ground of criminal incarceration.[19]

In view of both these complexities of interpretation and weighting, the analysis of justice in terms of the common sense criteria clarifies rather than rationally resolves the nature of disagreement about issues of substantive justice. We are told that formal justice, understood as treating like cases alike or giving each her due, can be interpreted in terms of common sense criteria of likeness or dueness (rights, or deserts, or needs), but we find, on examination, that these criteria are extremely controversial, both in the interpretation and relative weighting of each of them.

There are three natural positions to take to this degree of philosophical indeterminacy. First, if one believes that moral questions are incapable of reasonable discussion, the fact of such ranges of interpretation and weighting will only reenforce one's general moral position. Second, if one finds, as many contemporary philosophers do,[20] such moral subjectivism indefensible, one may regard such indeterminacy as not reflective of moral subjectivism, but of the plurality of ultimate values;[21] the role of philosophical examination, on this view, is to advance critical discourse about these ultimate values and their trade-offs; in fact, on such critical examination, many of these superficial disagreements can be resolved, either by careful analysis of conceptual confusion or by getting the facts right. Third, one may agree with the moral pluralists about the capacity of philosophy to clarify critical discourse even at the level of common sense criteria, but also urge the need for a more fundamental philosophical perspective of moral impartiality from which these disagreements may be reasonably assessed.[22] Perhaps we may find that no single moral principle, which we might articulate from such a perspective, can do justice to the plurality of moral values previously identified, in which case we will have to rest content with the approach of the moral pluralists. But it is a mark of the philosophical naturalness, indeed inevitability, of this higher-order inquiry, that moral pluralists, invariably, take their position only *after* they have found no way of doing justice to their intuitive judgments from this higher-order perspective.

Having identified a number of questions that lay before us, let us turn to an examination of the competing ethical theories which purport to tell us what substantive justice is.

III. Philosophical Principles of Justice

Three leading philosophical theories of the higher-order kind dominate the classical and contemporary literature: *perfectionism, utilitarianism,* and *contractarian natural rights.* Each theory affords a different interpretation of the idea of equality in terms of which justice, understood in terms of treating like cases alike or giving each her due, is interpreted; in consequence, each theory has significantly different practical implications. The substantive contrast is, as we shall see, most dramatic between perfectionism and the common egalitarian perspective that unites utilitarianism and contractarian natural rights.

For convenience, we may classify basic moral theories as *teleological* and *deontological.* Teleological moral conceptions define the nature of what makes acts or institutions substantively right, or persons morally virtuous, in terms of their tendency to produce the maximum total or aggregate amount of good over evil, where the good and its opposite may be defined either hedonistically (pleasure vs. pain) or in a non-hedonistic way, e.g., in terms of certain ideal values or disvalues (e.g., knowledge vs. ignorance). Deontological moral theories are defined, in part, negatively: they do not define the right or moral virtue in terms of maximizing the good in the teleological way. Perfectionism and utilitarianism are both teleological moral theories; contractarian natural rights theory is deontological.

A. PERFECTIONISM

Perfectionism, a substantive moral theory of equality classically stated in Aristotle[23] and more recently found in Nietzsche,[24] dramatically brings out how an interpretation of equality, in terms of which the formal concept of justice is given material content, may mandate radically unequal forms of treatment. The perfectionist moral principle is the teleological one that the right-making characteristic of acts, and institutions and the good-making characteristic of persons is their tendency to maximize the aggregate display of the ideal goods of intellectual and artistic excellence, heroic exploits, magnificent works and performances. Accordingly, the perfectionist theory of substantive equality is that persons are alike or cases similar to the extent that the persons or cases involve the same display of admirable excellences of talent; two novelists or composers of equal excellence should, thus, receive the same moral status and consideration. But, the converse proposition would also be true: not only that two artists or thinkers of excellence are morally unequal to the extent one may be graded more admirable than the other, but that anyone lacking such excellences would be radically unequal, indeed lack any independent moral worth.

When we wed this substantive moral conception of equality to the formal concept of justice, rather striking inequalities of treatment are just. Since many persons lack the capacity for excellence of the defined kinds, whole classes of people will have no independent moral claim on resources or power, or, will have moral weight only to the extent that their existence or work makes possible the flourishing of the only class of persons (those of excellence) who have moral worth. The practical political consequence, in the views of both Aristotle and Nietzsche, is a purported moral justification for slavery, political aristocracy, and caste systems, to the extent that such institutions reflect these moral distinctions;[25] those who lack the capacity for excellence are relegated to positions where they serve the needs of those who alone have independent moral worth, by supplying, for example, the kind of manual labor and material goods which enable the talented to have the leisure and freedom to engage in the only task of moral worth, and, without distraction, cultivate their capacities for excellence. Again in both Aristotle and Nietzsche, this conception is viewed as justifying the subjection of women.[26] Since women are assumed to lack the capacity for such excellence, it would be just to relegate them to the subordinate role of wife or mother where they may perform their only legitimate moral function, nurture and support of men capable of excellence.

One natural objection to these expressly drawn consequences of the perfectionist theory of justice in Aristotle and Nietzsche is that the judgments of natural capacity, on which such theories rest, are unreasonably made. The judgment that women, for example, lack natural capacities for the required excellences cannot be sustained as an empirical proposition; to the extent that it ever could have been reasonably supposed to be true (for example, by a philosopher of Aristotle's stature), such views rested on a self-fulfilling prophesy which, having trammelled women's opportunities for self-realization unnaturally, then inferred judgments of natural capacity from the results of such unjust treatment.[27] However, this form of objection, while valid, is not an objection of principle: it objects only to the ways in which Aristotle and Nietzsche applied their perfectionist principles, to their lack of concern for some kind of fair opportunity to acquire the specified excellences, not to the idea that such capacities for excellences are, wherever found, the sound measure of moral equality.

Correspondingly, the objection that Aristotle and Nietzsche's conceptions of the relevant excellences are too narrow would leave unquestioned their fundamental principle. Perhaps less aesthetic or intellectual or courageous excellences will be supposed to have some proper place among the ideal goods to be maximized; or some weighting will be suggested giving some weight to plebeian excellences like ordinary craftmanship at basic tasks of work and a greater weight to rarer forms of cultural accomplishment. While such conceptions of other ideal ends of hierarchies among ends might mitigate some of the more striking inequalities that Aristotle and Nietzsche justify, they would still express a perfectionist moral principle.

A more profound objection to perfectionism is that its definition of equality is, in principle, wrong, that our talents are the result of a morally fortuitous lottery and so are not a satisfactory foundation for moral equality. Certainly there has been no more profound shift in moral conception within Western philosophical thought than the shift from the kind of perfectionism, which pervades ancient Greek philosophy, to the kind of egalitarian conception of human equality associated with both utilitarianism and contractarian natural rights. Both utilitarian and natural rights theory rest on the same fundamental moral idea of equality, treating persons as equals. Although they give, as we shall see, variant interpretations to this idea, they both repudiate *the perfectionist conception that moral worth can be identified with the display of creative or heroic excellences;* treating persons as equals encompasses all persons— the talented and untalented, the excellent as well as the mediocre and the below mediocre. Indeed, after the democratic political revolutions following the Enlightenment, this general egalitarian conception of equality has become so fundamental that any serious perfectionist challenge to it, as that of Nietzsche, naturally takes the form of an attack on morality itself.[28] In order to understand how this can be so, we must turn to the philosophical analysis of the moral imperative to treat persons as equals, and inquire why utilitarian and natural rights theories regard it as fundamental and thus repudiate perfectionism.

B. TREATING PERSONS AS EQUALS

The idea of treating persons as equals is a way of expressing the most general features of the concept of ethics or moral right: in evaluating our conduct ethically, we inquire whether our conduct treats persons in the way we would ourselves, so situated, want to be treated. The underlying idea appears to be one of equality: since we are all equal as persons, conduct—to be regarded as ethical—must express this equality, the benchmark of common humanity in terms of which we can sensibly make such judgments. Clearly, the substantive moral conception of equality here is not a merely formal one: certain conceptions of equality are not only ruled out (for example, perfectionism), but made the subject of moral criticism (for example, racial or gender stereotypes).

In order to interpret the substantive content of treating persons as equals, we require a theory of the person in terms of which equal treatment can be interpreted. The distinctive character of utilitarianism and contractarian natural rights emerges in the different ways they meet this task.

1. Utilitarianism. Utilitarianism, in the form classically defended by Bentham,[29] John Stuart Mill,[30] and Henry Sidgwick,[31] defines the ultimate principle of morality in terms of the teleological conception of maximizing the aggregate of pleasure over pain of all sentient creatures. The appeal of this theory is twofold. First, it affords a natural interpretation of treating persons as equals, for all pleasures and pains are impartially registered by the utilitarian calculus, no matter who experiences such pleasures or pains (whatever race or gender or nationality) and no matter in what things or activities one experiences pleasure or pain. The theory thus explains the immorality of perfectionism, which focuses only on a narrow range of pleasures to the exclusion of all others, and other familiar forms of prejudice (racism, for example, fails to give proper weight to the pleasures and pains of racial minorities); and the theory also broadly expresses liberal tolerance for diverse conceptions of the good, for all things in which persons take pleasure are of weight, no matter what the sources of the pleasure. Second, utilitarianism explains, in a lucid and elegant way, how judgments of moral right and wrong can be tied to concrete facts in the world: namely, acts and institutions are right if they can be shown to have a tendency to maximize aggregate pleasure in the required way. Utilitarianism thus appeals to empiricist sympathies (e.g., the cost-benefits), for it is easily wedded to ongoing empirical inquiry into how forms of social, economic, or political institution operate and what types of reform would better meet the utilitarian standard.

The utilitarian theory of justice interprets formal justice in terms of counting equal pleasures and pains equally: Anyone's pleasure or pain must be given the same weight as the like pleasure or pain of anyone else, no matter who these individuals happen to be, be they prince or pauper, man or woman, black or white. Thus does utilitarianism require equality in treatment. However, on questions of distributive and retributive justice, utilitarianism is completely aggregative: the sole question is which pattern of distribution or retribution will, over all, result in the greatest aggregate of pleasure over pain. This principle may be consistent with great inequality in the distribution of resources (some may have a superabundance of resources, and others very little) if such inequality results in a greater aggregate (the aggregate of pleasure over pain over-all is greater with the more unequal distribution than it would be if the distribution were more equal). Traditionally, utilitarian theories of economic distribution have argued that certain empirical assumptions about the world make it unlikely that gross inequality will be thus required.[32] These assumptions include the fact that persons have similar capacities for pleasure and pain (sometimes called similar "utility functions"), so that no person's greater sensibility in experiencing more pleasure from certain resources would require that more such resources be given that person (since more pleasure over all will be secured); in addition, these assumptions include *diminishing marginal utility*: that, as more resources are given a person, the pleasure in them diminishes, so that greater pleasure over all is secured by giving the resource to another who lacks the resource (since that person will secure more pleasure than the person who already has the resource). Given these assumptions, a more equal distribution of resources will, other things being equal, tend to maximize the aggregate of pleasure in the required way. We will inquire further into the validity of this argument when we investigate the implications of different philosophical theories for concrete controversies over justice. For now, we should, however, observe a striking fact about the form of the argument: it attempts to express intuitive ideas about the constraints that justice or human rights place on the pursuit of aggregative conceptions of the public good within a theory which is itself completely aggregative.

Both classical and contemporary critics of utilitarianism pose a more fundamental objection:[33] the appeal of utilitarianism rests, in part, on its providing a plausible moral interpretation of the basic imperative of treating persons as equals (in terms, for example, of its universalistic concern for the pleasure or pain of all and its studied neutrality about the objects of pleasure), but this appeal is ill-founded and deceptive. It suggests that utilitarianism expresses basic respect for the person, but, it is alleged, utilitarianism has no concern for the *person* at all. *Utilitarianism does not treat persons as equals; it treats pleasures as equal.* Hence, the utilitarian principle fundamentally confuses two morally distinct cases: first, the case in which a person, in order to better realize his or her long term interests, *chooses* present privation (for example, the discipline of education); and second, the case in which a community *imposes* privation on one person in order better to maximize the aggregate of pleasure of all persons over all. The first case is unobjectionable: persons have the right to choose to forego current pleasures in order better to realize their long term goals. But, the second, inter-personal case is objectionable. Society is not obviously justified in imposing sacrifices on individuals to promote an increase in aggregate pleasure. Utilitarianism confuses the two cases because it focuses obsessionally on pleasure and the aggregation thereof. Pleasures and pains are viewed as impersonal facts, abstracted from the life of the person who gives them meaning and significance. These impersonal facts are then added, subtracted, multiplied, and divided until we find the requisite aggregate of the relevant facts; no imposition of sacrifice on the individual person can, in principle, be ruled out, and no claim (including the claim to basic rights such as the right to life itself) can be accorded ultimate respect, for the sacrifice and denial of the claim may alone secure the greatest aggregate of utility.

Utilitarians respond to such objections in two ways. First, some utilitarians, like Bentham, simply embrace such consequences: ideals of human and natural rights are nonsense, and, worse than nonsense, dangerous; they encourage the resolution of ethical problems by appeals to arbitrarily vague and speculative moral values (e.g., natural rights), in the place of the kind of scientific and calculative mangerial planning by experts that utilitarianism requires.[34] Hence, appeals to individual rights, personal dignity, or ideals of equal distribution have no decisive weight unless they can be squared with the utilitarian principle. Utilitarians, like Bentham and others, are correct to point out that the importance of moral philosophy to living is that, at least sometimes, such critical moral reflection leads one to *revise* one's preanalytic beliefs on the ground that they reflect prejudice or inconsistency; for them, beliefs that there are intrinsic moral constraints on the pursuit of aggregate utility are of this kind. Second, less doctrinaire utilitarians do not reject these common sense judgments wholesale, but suitably reinterpret the utilitarian principle to attempt to accommodate them. The most notable example of this move, one which prefigures later utilitarians in this connection,[35] is John Stuart Mill's abandonment of Bentham's equal weighting of all pleasures and pains in favor of a greater weighting to be given to certain kinds of pleasures and pains, namely, pleasures experienced in the realization of, and pains in the frustration of, certain capacities of higher intelligence, craftsmanship, and personal independence.[36] Mill's idea appears to be that since a rational person, properly informed and fully reflective, would give such pleasures and pains a much higher weight than others, the aggregative utilitarian principle would reflect such greater weights; such higher pleasures, no matter where located, should be treated alike, but treated differently from the lower pleasures which, in general, should be less aggressively pursued. Mill's reformulation of the utilitarian interpretation of treating pleasures alike does not answer the general objection that utilitarians fail to treat persons as equals, for, again, it is pleasures, not persons, which are here to be treated alike. But it does narrow the gap between Bentham's doctrinaire utilitarianism and common sense judgments about the importance of equality and rights. For Mill supposes that, taking into account the greater weight of the higher pleasures and other facts about the need for simple rules of conduct not easily abused by prejudice and irrationality, many common sense moral judgments about uncompromisable human rights and claims to equality could be given a utilitarian justification.[37] Indeed, Mill argues, expressly in contrast to Bentham, that ideas of moral and human rights play a proper and important role in political discourse.[38] We shall have occasion to return to Mill's arguments in this connection when we examine political controversies over free speech and autonomy.

2. *Contractarian natural rights*. We may call theories of natural rights contractarian in the sense that, implicitly or explicitly, they express a normative conception of the inviolability of each person through the contractarian requirement, in some form or others, that each person, concerned to preserve their interests in rational independence, must *consent* to the relevant principles of justice or political right. Like utilitarianism, contractarian natural rights starts from the basic moral imperative, treating persons as equals. But, in contrast to the teleological and aggregative conception that utilitarianism has of the imperative (roughly, the pleasures and pains of all persons—possibly all sentient creatures—are morally relevant and count in the utilitarian calculus), contractarian natural rights focuses the interpretation of equality on the person and bases its interpretation on a theory of the moral status of persons. This theory was classically stated by Immanuel Kant in terms of his conception of rational autonomy.[39] On this view, the fundamental fact of ethics is the person, the entity who has natural capacities self-critically to evaluate, order, and revise the ends of his or her life on the basis of arguments or evidence to which, as a free and rational being, the individual reasonably assents. Kant characterizes beings with these natural capacities as possessing sovereignty in the kingdom of ends, determining what their ends shall be: each person has a kind of ultimate moral independence in establishing his or her system of ends, and revising them in accord with the dictates of his or her rational judgment, in a fully and freely self-reflective manner. It is important to see that Kant's focus on personhood (as opposed to the utilitarian concentration on pleasure and pain) provides a different interpretation of two features also given significance by utilitarianism: first, natural rights theory is broadly universalistic: any creature with the natural capacities of personhood possesses human rights (irrespective of race, gender, religious affiliation, or the like); and second, respect for rational autonomy leaves up to the person the definition of her or his rational good, and thus requires respect for quite diverse conceptions of personal good. Since both theories express these two features, both utilitarianism and contractarian natural rights share a broad common moral grounds (both take treating persons as equals as fundamental), in contrast to perfectionism with its denial of moral weight to the untalented, which both theories repudiate.

The striking difference between utilitarianism and natural rights derives from the aggregative interpretation of treating persons as equals which utilitarianism involves and the non-aggregative character of the natural rights interpretation. For contractarian natural rights, treating persons as equals must be interpreted in terms of the theory of rational autonomy, the capacity of persons to be sovereigns in the kingdom of ends. From this perspective, the pursuit of pleasure or the avoidance of pain have no ultimate or fundamental or basic moral significance; their significance, to the extent they have one, depends on the evaluative weight that persons give them in their lives, weightings which appear to be enormously diverse, certainly not invariably in terms of the good of pleasure or the evil of pain, as utilitarianism, simplistically, supposes.[40] For contractarian natural rights, the morally ultimate unit is the person; from this perspective, the deep mistake of the utilitarian interpretation of treating persons as equals is to fail to take personhood seriously, by dissolving it into simpler ingredients (pleasure, pain), which have no comparable moral significance. Thus, it permits, indeed requires, the sacrifice of the well-being of individual persons for the sake of maximizing aggregate utility. In contrast, the contractarian interpretation of treating persons as equals insists on the necessity of respect for the equal capacity of persons to evaluate, order, and control their own lives. Since respect for this equal capacity is morally fundamental, a central implication is that the person's reasonable demands for integrity, and the goods that make such integrity possible, must be guaranteed *prior* to any pursuit of the aggregate public good.[41] We may think of these demands as rationally desired *goods, which persons with autonomy would want whatever else they choose reasonably to pursue.* Such goods would include forms of action and forebearance by other individuals (not injurying, rendering mutual aid) irrespective of institutional relations to one another, and the goods made possible by co-operative social life (food, work, education, income, and the like).[42] The autonomy-based interpretation of treating persons as equals would thus place a high premium on institutional arrangements (e.g., educational and employment opportunities, taxation, penal institutions) which cultivate, on fair terms to all, the capacities for independent and self-critical rational evaluation which are at the foundation of personhood.

The consequence of this person-centered normative conception, with its focus on the demands of person, on fair terms, for respect and dignity, is clearly a theory of justice with a much more egalitarian thrust than the utilitarian aggregative conception. This consequence has been dramatically drawn by John Rawls in his formulation of a contractarian model to express the ideas here sketched.

Rawl's basic analytic model is a kind of ideal contract:[43] acceptable moral principles are those that perfectly rational persons each motivated to preserve his or her higher-order interests in rational independence, in a hypothetical "original position" of equal liberty, would agree to as the ultimate standards of conduct that are applicable at large.[44] Persons in the original position are thought of as ignorant of any knowledge of their specific situations, values, or identities, but as possessing all knowledge of general empirical facts, capable of interpersonal validation, and as holding reasonable beliefs. Since Rawls desires to employ the thought experiment of the original position to ascertain the basic principles of *justice* (hence, to formulate and defend a theory of justice), he stipulates that the contractors must make choices in circumstances where there are *conflicting claims* to a *limited supply* of certain general goods; hence, they must choose principles to decide how these conflicting claims must be resolved.[45]

The original position presents a problem of rational choice under uncertainty. Rational people in the original position have no way of predicting the probability that they will end up in any specific role or situation in life. If a contractor agrees to principles which permit deprivations of liberty and property rights and later discovers that he occupies a severely disadvantaged position, he will, by definition, have no just complaint about such deprivations, even if they render his life prospects meager and bitterly servile. To avoid such consequences, the rational strategy in choosing the basic principles of justice would be the conservative or "maximin" strategy:[46] one would choose that alternative, or that principle, whose worst outcome is *better than* the worst outcome of any other alternative. Hence, even if a person were born into the worst possible situation, e.g., into a poor family and with serious birth defects, she would still be better off than she would be in a society governed by other principles. Hence, the best worst result is secured: the minimum is maximized.

The choice of which fundamental principles of justice to adopt requires consideration of the weight to be assigned to general goods by the contractors in the original position. "General goods" are those things or conditions that are typically the objects of rational choices or desires as the necessary means to a variety of personal goals.[47] It is natural to classify forms of liberty as general goods. Liberty for one person, A, to do X requires the absence of external constraints, constraints either to do or not to do X. The existence of various rights and liberties is necessary for a person to pursue his particular ends, whatever they may be. Liberties of thought and expression (freedom of speech, the press, religion, association), civil rights (impartial administration of civil and criminal law in defense of property and person), political rights (the right to vote and participate in political constitutions), and freedom of physical, economic, and social movement are fundamental in this respect. Similarly, it is natural to include as well the existence of opportunities, property, and wealth as basic distributive goods.[48]

The importance of these general goods derives in substantial part from the fact that they are a means to the promotion of self-respect, self-esteen, and personal autonomy.[49] Autonomy, in this sense, is the capacity of persons to plan and shape their lives in accordance with evidence and arguments to which, as rational and free beings, they personally assent. The competent exercise of such capacities in the pursuit of one's life plan forms the basis of self-respect,[50] and in their absence one is liable to suffer from despair, apathy, and cynicism. Thus, persons in the original position, each concerned to create favorable conditions for the successful pursuit of his life plan, but ignorant of the particulars of his position in the resulting social order, would agree to regulate access to general goods so as to maximize the possibility that every member of society will be able to achieve self-respect.

An important feature of this contractarian approach to identifying just principles of social interaction (e.g., the just distribution of general goods) is the assumption that the contractors operate behind a *veil of ignorance*: they are ignorant of the specific interests, preferences, advantages, or disadvantages which they may possess as members of the society whose guiding moral principles they, as contractors, are to determine. This assumption assures that the principles decided on in the original position will be neutral as between divergent visions of the good life, for the ignorance of specific individuating traits deprives the contractors of any basis for illegitimately distorting their decisions in favor of their own vision. Such neutrality or impartiality, a fundamental feature of the idea of political right, ensures to members of a just society the right to choose their own lives as free and rational beings.[51]

In such ways, contractarian theory embodies the Kantian idea of autonomy because the principles would rationally be agreed to by persons who are necessarily impartial and in a position of equal liberty (there is no basis to secure advantages by threats). Further, the Kantian idea of equality is expressed by the fact that the contractors would make their choice under a veil of ignorance whereby they do not know their specific identities, thus depriving them of any way of taking account of any fortuitous features of themselves other than their equal personhood.

In the context of an advanced industrial state, Rawls argues that the maximin strategy would require the contractors to give special weight to the liberties above enumerated over the general goods of wealth and status. Because political and other liberties are among the fundamental factors that shape a person's capacity to become a fully rational being and to enjoy the life of such a being, the rational contractors could not, consistently with the maximin strategy of rational choice, agree to any set of principles except on guaranteeing that these liberties are distributed equally to all. Use of the maximin strategy in choosing principles relating to these liberties, then, tends to eliminate the possibility of a class disadvantaged with respect to liberty; the highest lowest condition is equality of liberty for all persons.

By contrast, given that a certain minimum level of property and income is guaranteed, the rational interest in property and income is not as fundamental as the interest in these liberties. Assuming the greatest amount of equal liberty for all and some measure of fair opportunity is secured, inequalities in property and income above the minimum are permissible only if there are countervailing advantages. A relatively poor person, with full liberty and basic opportunity, may be better off in a system that allows inequalities in the distribution of wealth than in a system that requires strict equality of wealth; the consequences of allowing unequal wealth (for example, incentive effects on encouraging persons to work more than they would under equal shares) may so increase the aggregate GNP that the worse off person has a higher amount of wealth though a lower relative share than he would under equality (equal shares of a much smaller pie would yield a lower actual wealth to the worst off person).

The general consequence of such reasoning, setting a few details aside, is a structure of principles which we may schematically[52] summarize as follows:

> *The principle of equal liberty*. Basic social institutions are to be so arranged so that every person is guaranteed the greatest equal liberty and opportunity compatible with a like liberty and opportunity for all.
> *The difference principle*. Inequalities in the distribution by institutions of general goods like income, wealth, and status are to be allowed only if they are required to advance the interests of all persons more than strict, equality would and they advance the interests of the least advantaged persons as much as possible.

Rawls puts these principles in lexicographic order:[53] the difference principle applies *only when* the first principle is satisfied. Since the equal liberty principle has priority over the difference principle, at least in the circumstances of an advance industrial society, no inequality in the distribution of the liberties can be justified in order to secure economic advantages.

Rawls' formulation of a contractarian model of justice does not, of course, exhaust the alternative ways in which one may express the underlying Kantian conception on which his theory rests,[54] and some of these alternative conceptions may disagree, to varying extents,[55] with certain of Rawls' substantive principles (notably, the difference principle). However, all such conceptions agree with the priority that Rawls gives the principle of equal liberty over other considerations, and follow his pioneering construction in urging the overriding importance of inviolable moral constraints, ones expressive of respect for persons rather than utilitarian aggregation; indeed, all such theories are expressly anti-utilitarian.

IV. Substantive Applications

We entered into the foregoing discussion of alternative accounts of justice in response to the persistent conflicts discovered in the common sense criteria of justice. Our hope was that a philosophical examination of the leading ethical theories (perfectionism, utilitarianism, contractarian natural rights) would afford a useful perspective from which we could clarify both the interpretation and weighting of the common sense criteria. We cannot here discuss in detail how these perspectives would clarify all the current controversies over political, social, and economic justice. Accordingly, we shall limit discussion here to a brief and schematic discussion of three such areas of controversy: (1) the distribution of basic goods and resources, (2) the liberal priority of free speech and the right of personal autonomy, and (3) retributive justice issues in sentencing policy. We focus here on utilitarianism and contractarian natural rights, since they constitute the most serious contemporary contenders for basic moral perspective. We have already made a number of objections to utilitarianism, and shall continue to do so in the following discussion.

Nonetheless, all moral theories are counterintuitive in some respects, and thus a theory like utilitarianism, so seriously defended by many thoughtful and humane people, deserves further examination in spite of apparent deficiencies. On balance, we want a kind of critical comparison among available moral theories, comparing strengths and weaknesses. Thus, we harness together the discussion of utilitarian and contractarian natural rights to facilitate such a critical comparison for the reader.

(1) THE JUSTICE OF DISTRIBUTING GOODS AND RESOURCES

We saw earlier that the common sense criteria for a just distribution of goods and resources included such criteria as rights, deserts, and needs, and that these criteria were subject to different interpretations and weightings. From the perspective of our foregoing discussion of utilitarianism and contractarian natural rights, we can see that each perspective would afford a different conception of the proper place of these factors in a just distribution.

For utilitarianism, the ultimate moral principal is that we must maximize the aggregate of pleasure over pain for all sentient beings. Accordingly, the common sense criteria of rights, deserts, and needs would have a place and weight in moral deliberation given by utilitarian aggregation. Rights, understood as conventional or customary expectations, would have some proper role, since the stability of expectations is an important utilitarian good, one enabling people to plan and not subjecting people to the pain of frustrated expectations. Desert criteria would have weight in terms of utilitarian aims since providing incentives encourages people to work harder and produce more, thus resulting in a larger utilitarian aggregate over all. Needs, being forms of basic interests whose frustration leads to privation and harm, would clearly have some place in a utilitarian calculus of maximizing pleasure and minimizing pain.

For utilitarianism, the relative weighting of these criteria would depend on complex assessments of matters of fact regarding the role of customary expectations, the importance of incentives, and the incidence of needs unmet in other ways; utilitarians, who disagree (as they often have done) about these factual questions, may also disagree about the implications of utilitarianism for a proper weighting of these criteria. Utilitarians of stature thus range from conservative defenders of natural hierarchy (David Hume),[56] to reformist defenders of managerial intelligence (Bentham),[57] to profound liberal democrats with socialist tendencies (John Stuart Mill).[58]

Utilitarian economists have claimed, as we earlier saw, that the utilitarian principle, in view of assumptions about similar utility functions and diminishing marginal utility, has a tendency to sanction equal distribution of goods and resources.[59] But this claim is quite controversial: neither of its supporting assumptions appear to be well established. As an empirical matter, persons may have very different capacities to experience pleasure and pain; further, we often reasonably believe that one person's highly cultivated hedonistic sensibility and another's exquisite refinements of displeasure and frustration are much greater than other persons' more stolid and apathetic emotional life. Surely, we *should* ignore such differences in considering basic distributive questions, but this moral intuition should not distort the facts, as utilitarianism here appears to do. Further, the assumption of diminishing marginal utility is *often* factually false: persons obsessed with social position and status may experience psychological gains in an incremental increase of their wealth which may far exceed the gains experienced by a poor person were that increment transferred. Such facts *should* make no difference in the justice of redistributing wealth from the wealthier to the poorer person, but this moral point should not blind us to the facts.

When we put aside the dubious assumptions of similar utility functions and diminishing marginal utility, we can see that the utilitarian conception of distributive justice tends to have no natural tendency to equalize at all; rather it focuses on maximizing aggregates (for example, size of GNP).[60] There is some concern with relieving needs on the utilitarian view, but this concern would be tempered by interest in incentive effects: probably, a utilitarian should believe only in the most minimal forms of welfare payments, payments structured in some way either to encourage or manipulate the poor into productive work.[61] Incentive arguments would have a central place in so far as desert-based arguments could be shown to encourage work toward a larger GNP; and, rights-based arguments of customary expectation would have considerable weight both directly to prevent frustration and, indirectly, to provide a stable and reliable environment for productive work and business activity.

In contrast, the contractarian theory of justice appears, at least in Rawls' formulation of it, to be quite clearly egalitarian in its broad implications for the distribution of goods and resources. The main principle here would be the difference principle according to which inequalities in income and wealth are justified *only* if such inequalities are necessary to elicit performance which, in fact, makes the worst off class better off than it would be with an equal or more equal distribution. In short, the benchmark of distributive justice is equality or near equality and the position of the worst off class; if an unequal distribution results in a better lot for the worst off class, then the unequal distribution is more just than the equal. This conception, clearly, has an equalizing *tendency,* since inequality is suspect unless it can meet the stringent requirements of the difference principle; inequalities, to be just, must have the prescribed consequence of making the worst off better off.[62]

The common sense criteria of justice, considerations of rights, desert, and need, would have a place in the contractarian view; however, both the interpretation and weight of each of them would be different than under utilitarianism. Rights, under contractarian thought, would not only be customary expectations, but also legitimate affirmative claims to the goods required by the difference principle, which, on some interpretations of notions of autonomous dignity and self-respect, might include not only rights to work, but to working environments which insure that work is meaningful and allow scope for personal self-realization.[63] Desert criteria would be interpreted in terms of the incentive effects required by the difference principle, but these incentive effects must not simply lead to a greater aggregate (as the utilitarian theory of justice requires) but must be shown to work out to make the worst off better off. Finally, the focus of the difference principle on the worst off would clearly place enormous weight on the satisfaction of needs.

Both the utilitarian and contractarian conceptions of justice would not only explain some features of our pre-analytic common sense criteria of just distribution, but would also lead us to reflect on our interpretation and weighting of these criteria. The importance of philosophical reflection, focused on utilitarianism or contractarian natural rights, is precisely this: it enables us not only to understand the deeper moral foundations of what we believe, but also stimulates self-critical reflection leading to refinement of our beliefs and convictions. For example, the difference principle in the contractarian conception requires that a different weight be given to the concept of desert than some persons pre-analytically suppose, for the difference principle not only expresses the common sense judgment that greater income is "deserved" if it attaches to a job which requires more or harder work, but it requires, contrary to some Americans' common sense on these matters, that the greater income is necessary to elicit the work in question and must work out as the difference principle requires (making the worst off better off). Now, it is no conclusive objection to a moral theory that it departs from common sense in this way, if it supplies a reasonable moral criticism of the state of common sense.[64] Here, Rawls would appear to argue that the kind of weight that common sense gives to "desert" reflects an unexamined and indefensible conception of natural property rights in one's talents and their exercise, when, in fact, one's talents are, from the perspective of Kantian personhood, a morally fortuitous feature of one's self which must, accordingly, be subordinated to the deeper demands of equal respect for autonomy. Since the difference principle is alleged to reflect such equal respect, the common sense view, on examination, appears to be itself condemned by this principle.

(2) THE PRIORITY OF LIBERTY: OF FREE SPEECH AND PERSONAL AUTONOMY

A central issue of political justice in contemporary society is the priority given to individual liberty in constitutional democracy, in particular, the preeminence of free speech values among political values and the growing force of the right to personal autonomy in our law, both in the form of the constitutional right to privacy[65] and in legal reforms decriminalizing various "victimless" crimes, notably, consensual homosexuality.[66]

Now, as we have seen, both utilitarianism and contractarian natural rights accept the view that persons may define their good in diverse ways: utilitarianism in its idea that all pleasures and pains are equal, contractarian natural rights in its conception of rational autonomy. Both conceptions have been supposed to explicate the priority of liberty in constitutional democracy, but they do so in differing ways and with varying success.

As an initial matter, utilitarianism appears to give no natural expression to the idea of rights of liberty; Bentham, for example, regarded such ideas as nonsense and dangerous,[67] and clearly believed that the preferable type of social rule would be governance by a managerial elite enlightened by the utilitarian principle. As noted, John Stuart Mill modified Bentham's conception of the equality of all pleasures and pains in order to give greater weight to the experience of pleasure in, and pain in the frustration of, certain activities of higher-order intelligence and personal independence.[68] In his remarkable *On Liberty*, Mill assumes such a utilitarian weighting and deploys it in the defense both of the priority of free speech over other political values and an articulation of the right of personal autonomy, prohibiting interference with any person if the person's conduct does not harm others.[69]

Mill's arguments in *On Liberty* are powerful and cogent, but it is difficult to square them with a consistent utilitarian view. In his defense of free speech, for example, Mill argues for free speech on the grounds (1) that only such freedom will secure greater truth, (2) that the truth is better winnowed from the false, and (3) that truths are held with greater tenacity because arrived at by an independent mind.[70] The former two arguments are utilitarian, and, as such, controversial: why must, for example, total freedom of speech be guaranteed to insure a greater quantity of truth? Surely, if the production of truth is our aim, this aim might be just as well, and perhaps better, produced, if free speech were limited to a small class of highly educated experts.[71] Mill's third argument is not utilitarian at all, for he extends it not only to truths but to things clearly false, arguing that the independence of mind thus facilitated by free speech is a good in itself. Indeed, it is, but it is not necessarily a utilitarian good. Why, for a consistent utilitarian, should tenaciously held falsities, even if independently arrived at, have any utilitarian weight, when such falsities may lead to irrational pursuit of ends, and thus to the spread of pain and frustration, the utilitarian evils? Mill assumes, at this point, fundamental moral values of autonomous personhood, ones which are, in fact, non-utilitarian. Why should Mill have shifted to these values in his defense of the priority of liberty?

Contractarian natural rights theory makes clear why one might shift in precisely this way. The autonomy-based interpretation of treating persons as equals, which contractarian theory expresses, gives fundamental normative weight to the cultivation of self-critical rationality and independence of mind, the basis of developed personhood.[72] Accordingly, persons in Rawls' original position naturally agree to the principle of greatest equal liberty, which guarantees freedom of thought and speech, which is prior to other considerations of justice.[73]

In the same way, the autonomy-based interpretation of treating persons as equals brings out the moral basis of Mill's argument for a right of personal autonomy. His argument cannot be that protecting certain persons' choices from majoritarian prejudice and bigotry is justified on utilitarian grounds, for the greatest happiness of the greatest number would be secured by allowing the majority to work its collective will. Surely, the pain of self-doubt and ambivalence about one's majoritarian way of life that genuine toleration for minority ways of life calls for are genuine utilitarian evils, and cannot be denied, as Mill's argument requires, appropriate utilitarian weight. A majoritarian political theory like utilitarianism cannot account for the principles of individual rights and toleration, principles to which Mill's argument here intuitively appeals; indeed, utilitarianism appears clearly unable to give proper weight to the value of independence which both free speech and the right of personal autonomy rest on. In order to understand these arguments, we must interpret them not in utilitarian terms, but in terms of the conception that public morality may only criminalize or condemn conduct when the conduct violates principles which are required by the autonomy-based interpretation of treating persons as equals. When majoritarian attitudes overreach their proper moral scope, as in, for example, the criminalization or condemnation of consensual adult homosexuality,[74] those attitudes are justly condemned on the basis of the right to personal autonomy which protects personal dignity from such overreaching.[75]

(3) RETRIBUTIVE JUSTICE: OF SENTENCING

We saw earlier that the common sense criteria of retributive justice in the sentencing of criminals included such criteria as proportional gravity of the act and the culpability of the offender, general and specific deterrence, protection, and reform. The utilitarian and contractarian conceptions present quite different analyses of how these criteria are to be interpreted and weighed.

The utilitarian conception of retributive justice, or justice in punishment, is dictated by its basic idea of the equality of pleasures and pains before the utilitarian calculus. Since punishment is, by definition, a form of inflicting pain, it registers negatively on the utilitarian calculus, and must, to be justified, yield some balance of pleasure sufficient to maximize aggregate pleasure over all. Accordingly, utilitarians have traditionally criticized strong retributive theories of punishment, ones which suppose moral wrongdoing per se to be both a sufficient condition of punishment and of the form of the punishment (for example, the lex talionis, of the death penalty for murder, and the like).[76] Such punishment would, for a utilitarian, be clearly wrong: the punishment is inflicted without any evidence that the pain inflicted yields a surplus of pleasure and, hence, maximizes the aggregate. The classical utilitarian approach to punishment, as in Bentham, was to criticize such strong retributive ideas as irrational, and to focus, instead, on considerations of general deterrence and reform, with subsidiary concerns for specific deterrence and protection.[77] Evidence that a certain level of penal sanction would have general deterrent effects on others tempted to commit a comparable crime was, for Bentham, a part of the needed utilitarian evidence that inflicting pain by punishment would yield a surplus of pleasure on balance (here, some, who would otherwise inflict injury and pain on others, will not—because of the general deterrent effects of the sanction). The requirement that such evidence be given was used by Bentham to criticize sharply the severity of English penalties and to emphasize that certainty of punishment might secure more general deterrence with far less severe penalties—all to the better satisfaction of the utilitarian principle.[78] In addition, Bentham was an early philosophical sponsor of the prison (in the form of his "Panopticon"), in which considerations of reform were to play a predominant role.[79] Such arguments for the central role of reform led naturally to the approval on utilitarian grounds of paternalistic considerations of manipulating (or reforming) the criminal for his or her own good, which found expression in the institutional role of discretion (the instrument of the supervision of reform) in sentencing, probation and parole policy.[80] Since a main concern is to reform the criminal, it follows that periods of incarceration must be varied as is necessary to bring about the desired reform.

Bentham clearly believed that the role of general deterrence in the utilitarian theory of criminal justice adequately explained and justified intuitive principles of just punishment, ones requiring that punishment be inflicted only on those guilty of some clearly defined wrong who had the capacity and fair opportunity and mental state to have done otherwise.[81] Bentham argued that since general deterrence requires that infliction of a sanction have a tendency to deter others from comparable wrongdoing, these requirements of just punishment are justified because they advance this aim by ensuring that criminals could have been deterred by the punishment. But, this, as H. L. A. Hart has eloquently observed,[82] is a rather striking *non sequitur,* (an unwarranted inference): from the fact that certain actual criminals could not have been capable of being deterred if they lacked certain capacities, opportunities, and mental states, Bentham infers that people in general could not be deterred without these requirements. But this is clearly not so. Suppose crimes were made strict liability offenses, meaning that performing an act suffices for liability and that no incapacity or absence of intent, knowledge, or negligence would avoid liability. General deterrence might be increased by such strict liability: whereas before strict liability persons might have an incentive to commit the crime in the hope of avoiding liability on the basis of a colorable excuse of mistake and the like, now they have no such incentive. So Bentham's general deterrence argument cannot explain these intuitive conceptions of just punishment; yet these ideas of fairness in punishment seem deeply reasonable. Certainly, in the *criminal* law, strict liability is unjust even though it might better secure general deterrence. Classical utilitarianism seems unable to explain these reasonable judgments.

In addition, Bentham's explanation for the role of proportionality in just sentencing will not do. Bentham argues, on general deterrence grounds, that more serious crimes are given more severe penalties to increase deterrence.[83] But consider two cases: in the first, a wealthy person robs $1,000 "for kicks"; in the other, a poor person, to save his children from malnutrition, robs $1,000. On Bentham's marginal deterrence theory, the poorer person should clearly receive the more severe sentence, since a much greater threat would be required to deter him from the crime than the wealthy person. But clearly, such a more severe sentence would be unjust: the poor man is not as culpable as the rich man, and the sentences should reflect this moral fact.[84]

In contrast, contemporary formulations of contractarian natural rights theory appear better able to do justice to these considered judgments. First, the autonomy-based interpretation of treating persons as equals yields a conception of ethical principles of obligation and duty (for example, not inflicting harms, mutual aid, and the like) and how conflicts among them are, in general, to be resolved; and these principles are alone those to be enforced through the criminal law.[85] Second, the enforcement of these principles through the criminal law is expressly made the subject of principles of just punishment, which establish the moral constraints on the just distribution of criminal sanctions required by the contractarian conception.[86] These principles would include a form of the principle of greatest equal liberty, which requires that persons, before they are justly made the subject of criminal sanctions, must be secured—consistent with their rational autonomy—a greatest liberty, capacity, and opportunity to avoid such sanctions consistent with the same for all other persons.[87] In addition, a principle of proportionality would require that sanctions, consistent with the gravity of underlying wrongs and the culpability reflected in the equal liberty principle, should reflect these gradations.[88]

Such principles would explain the constraints of just punishment and proportionality which classical utilitariansim is unable to explicate. The equal liberty principle imposes the basic requirement of fairness that no person be used as a general deterrent example to others unless he or she can be regarded as having the fair capacity, opportunity, and mental state to have done otherwise. In this way, consistent with the autonomy-based interpretation of treating persons as equals, people are guaranteed basic respect for their autonomy in planning their lives; they are subject to criminal sanctions only when they have undertaken conduct fairly subject to such penalties. These requirements of personal culpability, as conditions of just punishment, combined with the principle of proportionality, elucidate why the gradation of punishments, consistent with gravity of offense and culpability of offender, also acts as a constraint on the pursuit of general deterrence and other aims.[89]

These considerations bear upon an important area of contemporary controversy over criminal sentencing in the United States, viz., the attack on discretion in sentencing, probation, and parole, a policy which results in a pattern of highly erratic sentences within the same jurisdiction and among different jurisdictions.[90] The emphasis on discretion is, as we have seen, the natural product of utilitarian reform, which tended to criticize retributive considerations at all levels and focus, alternatively, on therapeutic reform. The underlying model is, of course, medical: just as a patient is released when cured, criminals should be correspondingly released when reformed.[91] The goal of reform here is under current attack for two reasons: first, prisons do not reform, so that emphasis on this policy is irrational and misplaced;[92] second, the role of discretion here is unjust, failing to reflect the basic requirement of justice that punishments reflect the underlying gravity of offenses and culpability of offenders.[93] The erratic patterns of sentences, allowed by emphasis on reform, have no consistent principle and fail, relative to standards of offenses of equal gravity and offenders of equal culpability, to treat like cases alike.

The attack on policies aimed at reform is, obviously, supported by the contractarian conception of just punishment here sketched. The role of discretion in sentencing should be governed by articulate standards rooted in consistent application of the underlying principles of justice in punishment.[94]

Nothing in this argument calls for more severe sentences. Indeed, the contractarian conception supports, within the constraints of the principles of just punishment, the central role that general deterrence should play in determining sanctions.[95] Indeed, to the extent that general deterrence is better secured by *more certain* than by *more severe* sentences, length of sentences should be reduced and certainty of punishment increased. The present argument for more determinacy and consistency in sentencing, thus, could be implemented in the context of much less severe sentences: the point is not to increase sentences, which are already too severe, but to insure that sentences, whatever they are (and they should be shorter), are more consistently applied and should reflect underlying moral principles on which criminal justice, to be worthy of its name, properly rests.

V. Conclusion

We began this essay with two examples of alleged injustice: disparities in wages for men and women, and different sentences for convicted criminals of different races. Our discussion had brought out the kinds of complex claims that such allegations implicitly make. The claim that women are unjustly paid less than men appeals to relevant criteria of justice in wages and assumes that no relevant difference underlies the gender-based discrimination in wages; accordingly, such discrimination is unjust. Similarly, injustices in sentencing appear when no relevant ground for different treatment (whether gravity of act, culpability of offender, general or specific deterrence, reform, etc.) can explain sentencing disparities: whites with the same culpability and same gravity of offense in circumstances otherwise relevantly similar receive a certain penalty (for example, death) much less often than blacks. Accordingly, we identify an injustice and we seek ways to rectify it, including, perhaps, the abolition of the death penalty itself. In both cases, the absence of any ground or relevant difference, when it becomes systematic and perhaps institutional in character, leads us to speak and think of larger injustices which may explain such unfairness, for example, the moral evil of sexism or of racism; and we regard the attack on such unjust prejudices, for example, desegregation in basic schooling, as a more fundamental way to rectify such injustices.

The structure of our argument has been to set out the concept of formal justice (treating like cases alike) and to investigate the two kinds of ways in which substantive equality is specified: first, in terms of common sense criteria; second, in terms of explicitly articulated and defended principles of morality. We have shown that contemporary moral discourse focuses on the imperative of treating persons as equals, and have attempted to show how different interpretations of the imperative have substantive policy implications. The conclusion is an invitation to further philosophical investigation, a task which may both clarify and invite reconsideration of our initial convictions, and which may carry us into the deeper self-criticism of underlying emotional attitudes (racism, sexism)—their psychology, their history, their cultural and social supports—and how to reduce their force as root causes of injustice in personal, social, political, and economic life. The social and personal stakes are large, for in such inquiries we can relearn what Socrates taught: that philosophy may heal the divisions of the soul, uniting in a critical passion our intelligence and our hunger for justice.

Notes

1. See Aristotle, *Nicomachean Ethics* 1131a10-1131a24, at pp. 118–120, Martin Ostwald trans. (The Library of Liberal Arts: Indianapolis-New York, 1962).

2. See, e.g., Ch. Perelman, *The Idea of Justice and the Problem of Argument*, John Petrie trans. (The Humanities Press: New York 1963).

3. For a useful exploration of these common sense criteria, see David Miller, *Social Justice* (Clarendon Press: Oxford 1976) at pp. 52–153.

4. See, in general, David A. J. Richards, *The Moral Criticism of Law* (Dickenson-Wadsworth: Encino, Calif., 1977) at pp. 229–259.

5. See, for example, David Miller's discussion of Hume, supra note 3–1, at 157–179

6. See, e.g., Jeremy Bentham, *Anarchical Fallacies*, in *The Works of Jeremy Bentham*, Book II, John Bowring ed. (Edinburgh, 1843).

7. See David Miller, supra note 3–1, at 83–121. For the claim that justice should only reward voluntary effort, not natural ability alone, see Henry Sidgwick, *The Principles of Political Economy* (Macmillan: London, 1883), at pp. 505–06, 531.

8. For some discussion of this concept, see Karl Marx, *Economic and Philosophical Manuscripts*, in *Karl Marx: Early Writings*, T. B. Bottomore trans. (C. A. Watts: London, 1963) at pp. 126–134

9. See, e.g., David A. J. Richards, supra note 3–2, at 230–235.

10. For one defense of this claim, see *Id.* at 244–245

11. See, e.g., Andrew Von Hirsch, "Prediction of Criminal Conduct and Preventive Confinement of Convicted Persons", *Buffalo Law Review,* Vol., 21 (1972), pp. 717–58. See also Norval Morris, *The Future of Imprisonment* (University of Chicago Press: Chicago, 1974) at pp. 28–57

12. For powerful statements of this position, see Andrew Von Hirsch, *Doing Justice* (Hill and Wang: New York, 1976); Norval Morris, *The Future of Imprisonment*, supra note 4–7.

13. For useful discussion, See David Miller, supra note 3–1, at 180–208.

14. For useful discussion, see *Id.* at pp. 209–244.

15. For attempted sociological explanation of such judgmental differences, see *Id.* at pp. 253–335.

16. Cf. James W. Nickel, "Is There a Human Right to Employment?", *The Philosophical Forum*, Vol. X (1978–79), at pp. 149–170

17. See, e.g., Walter Berns, *For Capital Punishment* Basic Books: New York, 1979).

18. See David A. J. Richards, supra note 3–2, at pp. 229–59. Cf. David A. J. Richards, "Human Rights and the Moral Foundations of the Substantive Criminal Law", *Georgia Law Review* 13 (1979), 1395–1446, at pp. 1442–1445.

19. See the works by Von Hirsch and Norval Morris at note 5–1, supra.

20. For a cogent statement of the arguments against subjectivism, see Richard B. Brandt, *Ethical Theory* (Prentice-Hall: Englewood Cliffs, N. J., 1959), at pp. 203–239, 271–293.

21. See, e.g., Brian Barry, *Political Argument* (Routledge & Kegan Paul: London, 1965); see also David Miller, supra note 3–1.

22. For a clear form of this kind of argument, see John Stuart Mill, *Utilitarianism*, Oskar Piest ed. (The Library of Liberal Arts: Indianapolis-New York, 1957), at 52–79.

23. The whole of Aristotle's *Nicomachean Ethics* is an attempt to describe the excellences which morality requires us to maximize; but, see, especially Book 10 for a characterization of the special weight Aristotle gave to the human excellence of theoretical wisdom.

24. For perhaps the clearest statement by Nietzsche of this principle, and a clear recognition of its implications, see *Twilight of the Idols*, in *The Portable Nietzsche*, Walter Kaufmann trans. (Viking: New York, 1954), at p. 534.

25. On slavery, see Aristotle, *Politics*, Book I, chapters 3–7, Ernest Barker trans. (Oxford University Press: New York, 1962); and Nietzsche, *Beyond Good and Evil*, Helen Zimmern trans. (T. N. Foulis: Edinburgh and London, 1907), at pp. 189, 196, and *The Antichrist*, in *The Portable Nietzsche*, supra note 8–2, at p. 639; on caste systems, see Nietzsche, *The Antichrist*, at pp. 644 ff.; on aristocracies, see Aristotle, *Politics*, Book III.

26. For Aristotle on women, see *Politics*, supra note 9–1, Book I, chapter 12; for Nietzsche's critique of feminist movements from the point of view of "the military and aristocratic spirit", see *Beyond Good and Evil,* supra note 9–1 at p. 188.

27. For the classic critique of this form of mistake, see John Stuart Mill, *The Subjection of Women*, in J. S. Mill and H. T. Mill, *Essays on Sex Equality*, A. S. Rossi, ed. (University of Chicago Press: Chicago, 1970) at pp. 125–156.

28. For a statement of this view of Nietzsche, see G. J. Warnock, *Contemporary Moral Philosophy* (St. Martin's Press: New York, 1967), at pp. 50–51. See, in general, G. J. Warnock, *The Object of Morality* (Methuen: London, 1971).

29. See, e.g., Jeremy Bentham, *Principles of Morals and Legislation* (Hafner Library: New York, 1948).

30. See J. S. Mill, supra note 7–1.

31. Henry Sidgwick, *The Methods of Ethics* (Macmillan: London 1963) (seventh edition).

32. The classic statement is A. C. Pigou, *The Economics of Welfare* (Macmillan: London, 1920). Cf. Henry Sidgwick, supra note 4–3, Book III.

33. For a classical statement, see Richard Price, *A Review of the Principal Questions in Morals* (Clarendon Press: Oxford, 1948)(originally published, 1758) at p. 160; for a recent contemporary statement, see H. L. A. Hart, "Between Utility and Rights", in *The Idea of Freedom*, A. Ryan ed. (Oxford University Press: Oxford, 1979), at pp. 77–80.

34. See Bentham, supra note 4–2.

35. For recent utilitarians who importantly incorporate Millian ideas of autonomy or per-

sonhood, see Jonathan Glover, *Causing Death and Saving Lives* (Penguin: Harmondsworth, 1977); Peter Singer, *Practical Ethics* (Cambridge University Press: Cambridge, 1979).

36. See J. S. Mill, supra note 7–1 at 9–33.

37. *Id.* at 52–79

38. See *Id.* See also John Stuart Mill, *On Liberty*, Alburey Castell ed. (Appleton-Century-Crofts: New York, 1947).

39. See, in general, Immanuel Kant, *Foundations of the Metaphysics of Morals,* Lewis White Beck trans. (The Library of Liberal Arts: New York 1959). For Kant's invocation of a contractarian metaphor to express his ideas, see I. Kant, "Concerning the Common Saying: This May Be True in Theory, But Does Not Apply in Practice", in *Society, Law, and Morality* 159–72 (F. Olafson ed. 1961).

40. For some, pleasure, as such, is unworthy of pursuit, and forms of pain may be embraced as the test of one's mettle or ideals. Such total abnegation is, sureley, no less common than its utilitarian opposite. Most persons are, of course, moderately in between these extremes: sometimes finding pleasure worthy of pursuit, sometimes not; sometimes avoiding pain, sometimes embracing it.

41. Cf. John Rawls, *A Theory of Justice* (Harvard University Press: Cambridge, Mass., 1971)

42. For general forms of argument for comprehensive moral principles regulating such goods, see David A. J. Richards, *A Theory of Reasons for Action* (Clarendon Press: Oxford, 1971) and Alan Gewirth, *Reason and Morality* (University of Chicago Press: Chicago, 1978).

43. See, in general, John Rawls, supra note 18–1; see also David A. J. Richards, supra note 18–2, at 75–91.

44. See John Rawls, supra note 18–1, at 11–22

45. On the circumstances of justice see *Id.* at 126–130.

46. *Id.* at 150–61.

47. *Id.* at 407–16.

48. See David A. J. Richards, "Equal Opportunity and School Financing: Towards a Moral Theory of Constitutional Adjudication", *University of Chicago Law Review* 41 (1973) 32, at pp. 41–49.

49. See John Rawls, supra note 18–1, at 433, 440–46.

50. See David A. J. Richards, supra note 18–2, at 257, 265–68; R. W. White, *Ego and Reality in Psychoanalytic Theory* (International Universities Prss: New York, 1963).

51. Cf. Ronald Dworkin, *Liberalism,* in Stuart Hampshire, *Public and Private Morality* (Cambridge University Press: Cambridge, 1978) at 113–43.

52. I adapt this formulation from Richards, supra note 18–1, at 121, focussing on the priority of the liberties to wealth for purposes of simplicity of exposition. The treatment of opportunity issues, thus, is not here focussed on; and questions of capacity distribution are put aside. For Rawls' more complex formulation, see John Rawls, supra note 18–1, at 302–03.

53. See, e.g., *Id.* at 243–51.

54. Two plausible alternative conceptions are those of equal concern and respect, and universalizability. For the former, see Ronald Dworkin, *Taking Rights Seriously* (Harvard University Press: Cambridge, Mass., 1978), at 150 ("Justice and Rights", ch. 6). For the latter, see Alan Gewirth, supra note 18–2.

55. For the most striking criticism by a theorist who works in this anti-utilitarian tradition of any form of redistribution (absent compensation for prior wrongs), see Robert Nozick, *Anarchy, State, and Utopia* (Basic Books: New York, 1974). For express criticism of the difference principle, see *Id.* at 183–231. Alan Gewirth, in contrast, disagrees with the difference principle, but argues for moral rights to minimum welfare funded out of redistributive taxation. See Alan Gewirth, supra note 18–2, at 312–327.

56. For a useful characterization of Hume's position, see David Miller, supra note 3–1, at 157–179.

57. See Bentham, supra note 11–1

58. For Mill's liberalism, see *On Liberty,* supra note 15–4; for Mill's socialist leanings, see John Stuart Mill, "Chapters on Socialism", in *Essays on Economics and Society* (University of Toronto Press: Toronto, 1967); and, "On the Probable Futurity of the Labouring Classes", Book IV, chapter vii, *Principles of Political Economy with Some of their Applications of Social Philosophy* (University of Toronto Press: Toronto, 1965). I have learned much about Mill's views on economic issues from Adina Schwartz's unpublished doctoral dissertation, *John Stuart Mill: A Problem for Social Philosophy,* The Rockefeller University, New York 1976.

59. See sources at note 12–1, supra.

262 David A. J. Richards

60. The idea being that a larger GNP is, *per se,* a more just society, no matter how the distributive shares are allocated.

61. For Bentham's views along these lines, see Elie Halevy, *The Growth of Philosophic Radicalism,* Mary Morris trans. (Beacon Press: Boston 1960) at pp. 232–234.

62. See John Rawls, supra note 18–1, at 100–108.

63. See, e.g., Kai Nielsen, "Class and Justice", in John Arthur and William H. Shaw, *Justice and Economic Distribution* (Prentice-Hall: Englewood Cliffs, N.J., 1978) at 225–245

64. For Rawls' related idea of reflective equilibrium, see John Rawls, supra note 18–1, at 17–22.

65. The constitutional right to privacy has been invoked by the Supreme Court of the United States in declaring unconstitutional laws prohibiting the use or sale of contraceptives, or of abortion services. For the contraception cases, see *Carey v. Population Servs. Int'l,* 431 U.S. 678 (1977); *Eisenstadt v. Baird,* 405 U.S. 438 (1972); *Griswold v. Connecticut,* 381 U.S. 479 (1965). The leading abortion case is *Roe v. Wade,* 410 U.S. 113 (1973).

66. The Supreme Court recently upheld the refusal to extend the constitutional right to privacy to consensual adult homosexuality. *Doe v. Commonwealth's Attorney for Richmond,* 425 U.S. 901 (1976), *aff'g mem.,* 403 F. Supp. 1199 (E.D. Va. 1975) (three-judge court). However, there has been a gradual movement toward decriminalization of consensual sodomy by legislative repeal. As of 1976, at least 18 states had decriminalized sodomy. See Rizzo, "The Constitutionality of Sodomy Statutes", 45 *Fordham L. Rev.* 553, 570 n.93 (1976). A more recent overview indicates that 21 states have decriminalized. See Rivera, "Our Straight-Laced Judges: The Legal Position of Homosexual Persons in the United States", 30 *Hastings L. J.* 799, 950–51 (1979).

67. See Bentham, supra note 4–2.

68. See Mill, supra note 7–1, at 9–33

69. See J. S. Mill, *On Liberty,* supra note 15–4

70. See *Id.* 15–54.

71. Or, if the scope of free speech protection were sharply limited to certain kinds of statements likely to stimulate the discovery of truth.

72. For a further development of this interpretation, see David A. J. Richards, "Human Rights and Moral Ideals: An Essay on the Moral Theory of Liberalism", *Social Theory and Practice* 5 (1980) at 461–488.

73. See John Rawls, supra note 18–1, at 195–257

74. See David A. J. Richards, "Unnatural Acts and the Constitutional Right to Privacy: a Moral Theory", *Fordham Law Review* 45 (1977) at 1281–1348; also, "Sexual Autonomy and the Constitutional Right to Privacy: A Case Study in Human Rights and the Unwritten Constitution", *Hastings Law Journal* 30 (1979) at 957–1018.

75. See the works cited at note 31–1, supra. See also David A. J. Richards, "Commercial Sex and the Rights of the Person: a Moral Argument for the Decriminalization of Prostitution", *University of Pennsylvania Law Review* 127 (1979) at 1195–1287.

76. The most notable philosophical exponent of this position was Kant. For criticism of Kant's position from a contemporary contractarian natural rights perspective, see Richards, supra note 3–2, at 229–259.

77. See, in general, Bentham, supra note 11–1.

78. See Elie Halevy, supra note 26–2, at 71–73.

79. See, for a general discussion of some interest, Michel Foucault, *Discipline and Punish* Alan Sheridan trans. (Vintage: New York 1979) at 195–228.

80. For a useful historical discussion of the growth of discretion in American practice, see David J. Rothman, *Conscience and Convenience* (Little, Brown: Boston, 1980).

81. For discussion of Bentham's argument, see H. L. A. Hart, *Punishment and Responsibility* (Oxford University Press: New York, 1968) at 17–24

82. See *Id.*

83. Jeremy Bentham, *Principles of Penal Law,* Pt. II, Bk. 1, c. 6, in 1 *Bentham's Works,* J. Bowring ed. (Edinburgh: 1843).

84. See J. F. Stephen, *Law, Equality, Fraternity,* R. J. White ed. (Cambridge University Press: Cambridge, 1967), at 152–54.

85. For further discussion, see David A. J. Richards, "Human Rights", supra note 6–1, at 1414–1416

86. See *Id.* at 1416–1420

87. *Id.* at 1417–18

88. *Id.* at 1418
89. *Id.*at 1430–34, 1442–45
90. For statements of this criticism, see Marvin E. Frankel, *Criminal Sentences* (Hill and Wang: New York 1973); also works by Von Hirsch and Morris at note 5–1, supra.
91. Cf. David J. Rothman, supra note 32–4, 74–75, 124–25, 144, 253, 282, 385–86, 419–20. For express use of the hospital analogy for prisons, see *Id.* 124, 386–87.
92. See, especially, Norval Morris, supra note 4–7, 28–57.
93. See, especially, Von Hirsch, supra note 5–1.
94. See Von Hirsch, supra note 5–1.
95. See Richards, "Human Rights", supra note 6–1, at 1418–19, 1442–45. See also Richards, supra note 3–2, at 229–259.

Suggested Readings

(1) Aristotle, *Nicomachean Ethics* (M. Ostwald Trans.) Liberal Arts: New York 1962, BK. V.
(2) Barry, Brian, *Political Argument*. Routledge & Kegan Paul: London 1965.
(3) Hare, R. M., *Freedom and Reason*. Clarendon Press: Oxford 1963.
(4) Hume, David, *A Treatise of Human Nature*, L. A. Selby-Bigge ed., Clarendon Press: Oxford 1964, BK. III.
(5) Kant, Immanuel, *Foundations of the Metaphysics of Morals* (L. W. Beck Trans.) Liberal Arts Press: New York 1959.
(6) Mill, J. S., *Utilitarianism* Liberal Arts: New York 1957.
(7) Miller, David, *Social Justice* Clarendon Press: Oxford 1976
(8) Perelman, Chaim, *The Idea of Justice and the Problem of Argument* Humanities Press: New York 1963.
(9) Plato, *The Republic* (H. D. P. Lee Trans.)Penguin: Harmondsworth, Middlesex 1955.
(10) Rawls, John, *A Theory of Justice* Harvard University Press: Cambridge, 1971.
(11) Richards, David A. J., *The Moral Criticism of Law* Dickenson-Wadsworth: Encino, California 1977.
(12) Williams, Bernard, "The Idea of Equality", in *Problems of the Self* Cambridge at the University Press 1973 at 230–279.

chapter eleven

Capitalism, Socialism and Justice

KAI NIELSEN

I

There is, understandably, a not inconsiderable amount of argument about justice under capitalism and socialism as well as much argument about what principles of justice, if any, would characterize these socio-economic systems. When we reflect on capitalist and socialist societies, when we think about fundamental alternatives in our social world, we want to gain, if we can, a sense of which societies, particularly under optimal conditions, would be the juster societies and which would answer most fully to the needs and legitimate aspirations of human beings. However, before we can even begin to approach these questions, we should say something about what capitalism and socialism are.

I shall characterize capitalism and socialism in their 'pure' forms and then contrast them with what some regard as perversions and others simply as mutations of these pure forms. These perversions/mutations are State capitalism, on the one hand, and State socialism, on the other. There is a strong tendency on the part of both many socialists and some capitalists to regard these Statist forms as not being 'genuine socialism' or 'genuine capitalism'.

I shall not here make any such stipulations, though I am inclined to view with sympathy, as my argument will make clear, the view that State socialism is a flawed version of socialism. It is perhaps unavoidable under certain circumstances, but it still is a long way from the idea or (if you will) the ideal of a socialist society.

A common view of the difference between capitalism and socialism simply equates capitalism with the private ownership of capital and socialism with the public or State ownership of capital. The basic distinction is drawn in terms of the legal ownership of the means or instruments of production. It is, however, a mistake to characterize either capitalism or socialism solely in terms of legal relations of ownership. We also need to take note of forms of effective control and power, as well as different class formations and different conceptions of democracy. Capitalism is a system in which a class of owners (the capitalists), typically a numerically very small class, owns and controls most of the means of production and buys the labour power—where that labour power is a commodity—of workers. These workers (the proletariat) typically are the greater majority of the people in the society. The capitalists use the proletariat's labour power to produce wealth, i.e. to produce profits and accumulate capital, which in turn is owned and controlled by the capitalist. Capitalism is thus a system of wage labour with private ownership and control of the means of production, and, as a consequence, a capitalist society is a class society divided into two principal classes—classes that Marxists regard as antagonistic classes—the capitalist class, which owns and controls the major means of production and buys labour power, and the working class (the proletariat), which either owns no means of production or very little and sells its labour power to the capitalist for wages.

A socialist society by contrast is a society in which all ablebodied people are, except during periods of childhood and retirement, workers. In its pure form it is, no more than capitalism, a state ownership and control of the means of production. It is rather a form of social ownership and control of the means of production. This means that the workers collectively have effective control of their own workplaces. This further requires that a socialist society be a worker's democracy which in turn means that it will, unlike a capitalist society, which is at best a political democracy, also be an economic and industrial democracy, with workers, in the form of worker's councils and the like, owning and controlling their own means of production and workplace and deciding, in consultation and cooperation with other workers, who similarly own and control their means of production and workplace, what is to be produced, how much is to be produced, what is to be done with what is to be produced and what the working hours and conditions are to be.

Such a society will be decentralized with participatory control for the individuals, though the various working units will also be centrally coordinated by democratically elected and recallable worker's representatives from the various working units. The inequalities of wealth, power and control characteristic of all capitalist societies (pure and impure) could not obtain in a socialist society of the pure and paradigmatic form I have just described. In a socialist society the needs of everyone are considered alike and the ultimate community unit is all of humankind.

A socialist society would be a society in which every able-bodied adult person would be required to work—he who does not work does not eat—and labour contribution would be according to ability. But the wage relation would be abolished—no one would or could sell their labour power as a commodity, for there would be no one to buy it—and the workers would be in cooperative control of their own instruments of production in a society in which the cleavage between physical and mental labour would gradually be overcome, through the all around development of human beings. It must be borne in mind, however, that the construction of a socialist society takes time and that I am, in the above description, describing socialism in a very developed form after the springs of social wealth flow freely and the capitalist mentality is a thing of the past.

It is important to recognize that we probably do not have anywhere at the present time any very good exemplars of either capitalism or socialism in its pure form. The plain reality is that in extant industrial societies (though in varying degrees and in somewhat different kinds) we have State capitalism and State socialism, the perversions or mutations of the pure forms. In advanced capitalist countries, such as West Germany, Sweden, and France, we have State capitalism in fairly developed forms with what is called a 'mixed economy'. What makes such societies State capitalist societies is not essentially that there are some State owned branches of production, but that the State has taken on the responsibility of regulating and managing the entire economy. *Laissez faire* capitalism is a thing of the past (if indeed it ever existed in anything like a pure form then). However, unlike a socialist society, even a State socialist society, the State owned production sectors in State capitalist countries still, like the private sectors of the economy, produce to maximize profit and capital accumulation. The crucial thing that distinguishes them from the pure forms of capitalism is State regulation of the economy, including, of course, the private sector as well as the public sector. It is this that makes it appropriate to refer to such societies as *State* capitalist societies. All the major capitalist countries are now, though in degrees that vary somewhat, State capitalist societies.

However, it is also the case that the Soviet Union, the Eastern European countries in economic union with the Soviet Union, China and Cuba are all—again in varying degrees—State socialist societies. In these countries we have (again in varying degrees) stratified, bureaucratic, hierarchical societies "in which the maximization of material goods production—subject to the constraint of preserving hierarchical control—is a primary objective."[1] The State apparatus, with its few leaders, is at the pinnacle of such bureaucratic hierarchies. It is they, in the name of the workers, and not the workers themselves, who exert the principal control over the economy.

Even in their impure forms, there are still important differences between State capitalism and State socialism. Unlike State capitalist societies, in State socialist societies there is no way to inherit ownership and control of the means of production. Moreover, "state socialist societies have gone much further toward equalizing the distribution of essential goods and services such as food, housing, medical care, and transportation."[2] The underlying rationale of socialist production is the satisfaction of the needs of everyone in the community with an interest in capital accumulation only being instrumental to that end. (In the case of nascent socialist societies such as the Soviet Union and China, societies starting from a very weak industrial base, that instrumental value can be very great indeed, for plainly without a sound industrial base needs cannot be adequately met and in some instances cannot be met at all.) *In this respect* a State socialist society is no different from any other socialist society. But crucial differences remain. In particular, Non-Statist socialist societies are participatory and democratic forms of socialism in which State bureaucracies and social and economic hierarchies managing the society have been eliminated. We have in a socialist society of the pure form a society of self-governing and self-managing workers with directly chosen representatives subject to recall and replacement. Socialism should not be confused with State ownership, as perhaps it is in the Soviet Union, or with the labour reformism and welfare policies of even the most progressive social democracies (Sweden, Iceland and Denmark), as some in capitalist countries have a tendency to do. What is central to socialism is the common or social ownership and control of the means of production in a society in which everyone is a worker. The ownership and control is vested in these workers, working together fraternally and cooperatively.

II

The four socio-economic systems previously discussed (1) capitalism (*laissez faire*, competitive capitalism), (2) State capitalism, (3) State socialism and (4) socialism may be viewed as models both for how industrial societies *can* be organized and for how they *ought* to be organized. State capitalism and State socialism—both in various forms and degrees—are not only models; they are also social realities. *Laissez faire* capitalism and socialism (participatory socialism if you will) remain at present only ideals: conceptions of what some people think a just or a truly human society would be like.

What I would like to do now is to articulate, particularly where they have strong philosophical representation, what some of those alternative conceptions and accounts of justice are when they are matched with these four distinct systems for organizing society, beginning with *laissez faire* capitalism, especially as this view is defended by this century's leading philosophical spokesman for libertarianism, Robert Nozick.

For libertarians individual liberty is the cardinal moral conception. It can never be sacrificed or traded off or even be diminished to attain a greater equality or even to attain a more extensive overall system of secure basic liberties. It is, for libertarians, the highest value in the firmament of values.

Liberty for libertarians is negative liberty. They would indeed be happy, as an initial rough characterization, with J.S. Mill's conception of liberty as that of a person having the right, free from interference, to pursue what that person takes to be her own good in her own way as long as her actions do not interfere with the similar liberties of others. In a free society, we must not be interfered with in the doing of what we want to do as long as we do not violate the rights of others. To be free is to be able to choose your own life plans according to your own lights and to be free from governmental and other institutional interference or regulation.

The conception of justice that goes with that libertarian stress on freedom—a conception defended most elaborately by Robert Nozick—claims that justice exists to protect an individual's liberty. Given this conception, it is taken by libertarians to be an evident corollary that whatever economic arrangements we freely consent to are thereby just, if they do not involve fraud, deceit or the appropriation of something already justly appropriated or acquired.[3] Contrary to orthodox liberal assumptions— Welfare State capitalist assumptions—there is no particular *pattern of distribution* that justice requires. And since there is no pattern of distribution that justice requires, it cannot be the case, unless it can be shown that extensive rectifications of past injustices are in order, that justice demands extensive economic redistribution.

Not only do libertarians conceive of liberty negatively as the right to choose as one will, free from interference, they also, in stressing, as they do, individual rights, stress negative rights. Indeed it is very likely that 'negative rights' for a libertarian is redundant. They are the only kind of genuine rights except for contractually acquired. There are things we have a right to do and have, if we can do them or get them, where we, in these activities, are not to be interfered with by others. There are boundaries between people that just *must* not be crossed.

The rights that people have that must not be transgressed are *negative rights* because they require, vis-á-vis the person having the rights, others to refrain from interfering with the person exercising those rights. But they do not require others to do anything for that person. They are *only* morally required not to interfere with the exercise of those rights. They are not required to do anything positive for the rights-bearer which will in anyway help him to exercise those rights.

The central thing to see is that there are negative rights that all human beings have that can never, according to such an account, justly or rightly be overridden. But no one is obliged or in anyway morally required to do anything for anyone, unless they have agreed to do so or they have already harmed that person and must rectify a past violation of rights. Even when the society has the industrial and technical capacity to do so, there is no obligation at all to provide people with material goods they might urgently need or with health care or with education or with meaningful, satisfying or even gainful work. There is no obligation in any circumstances (where there has been no violation of rights) to meet even the most basic subsistence needs of other persons, even when it is not difficult for the agent to whom a plea for aid is directed to do so. The appropriate way to view human beings, on a libertarian account, is as autonomous and responsible individuals capable of fending for themselves. We must, of course, not harm them but we need not help them no matter how dire their straights unless we are responsible for their being in such straights. What is to be done, according to libertarians, is to create a social environment in which human beings are left to fashion their own lives free from the interference of others. We neither need a big daddy nor a big brother and we have a right to be free from any such paternalistic interference with our lives. It is evident enough that libertarianism is a radical individualism.

It is a deeply embedded libertarian belief that *only* by an acknowledgment of this near absolute right to negative liberty, to choose without interference how one is to live one's life, and what social arrangements one will make, can the distinctiveness or separateness of individuals as persons be respected. Such a conception, when translated into a social theory, involves a rejection of anything like the Welfare State and involves either a rejection of state authority altogether, and the acceptance of *individualistic* anarchism, or the commitment to the accepting as legitimate a minimal, night watchman state. It involves endorsing the minimal state and rejecting the legitimacy of any more extensive state control or state functions. The State, for example, has no right to tax us and to take that money—money in reality stolen from us—and use it for its redistributive schemes, no matter how benevolent they may be. This remains the case even when the redistributive schemes are enlightened and humane and would relieve considerable misery. The States' legitimate functions are limited to protecting the negative rights of its citizens. That is to say, it is to protect them from theft, fraud, violence, coercion and the like. But it has no right to get into the redistribution business. It can and should play a night watchman role but it is not to play a paternalistic role.

It is called the minimal state because its authority is so severely restricted and it is called the night watchman state because of the minimal legitimate functions it has.

Libertarians are also committed to a parallel economic doctrine, namely *laissez-faire* capitalism. Just as they reject the Welfare State and defend a minimal State, they reject contemporary corporate or State capitalism and defend *laissez-faire* (free market, competitive) capitalism. To disturb the free market, on their view, is to tread on liberty and to redistribute wealth through taxation is to engage in coercive practices which in effect utilize forced labour. It is, on the libertarian view, quite incompatible with justice to do anything like that.

There is, as the above indicates, an unequivocal commitment to an utterly free market economic system on the part of libertarians. A genuine respect for liberty will, when thought through, generate, on their view, a moral commitment to the priority of liberty. But then we cannot rightly prevent capitalist acts between consenting adults. Moreover, it is precisely a genuinely free market capitalist economy which will best sustain, at least in industrial societies, the priority of liberty. So, if to will the end is to will the necessary means to the end, then such a commitment to liberty requires, they believe, an acceptance of a free market economic system.

In speaking of the market I am talking about the buying and selling of goods—the exchange of products and the buying and selling of labour power. In a *laissez-faire* economic system, there can be no overall social planning—no five-year plan. Rather individual initiative, decision and choice shape the content of production and distribution of economic goods. Individuals and enterprises must be free to exchange as they please without either governmental restriction or assistance. (This is, of course, very unlike existing forms of capitalism.) It is a core claim of libertarians that—as far as industrial societies are concerned—only a social system with such a competitive capitalism can be thoroughly just.

Laissez-faire capitalism, unlike contemporary State capitalism—the capitalism we are familiar with—will respect our just entitlements and will not violate our freedom by forced redistributive schemes—schemes, like transfers through taxation, which, if adopted, cannot but lead to a diminishing of liberty and an overriding of the negative rights and liberties of people. Moreover, if this market system were really adopted, libertarians claim, it would also enhance the productive efficiency of capitalism. Free of government restrictions on the market, the capitalist system would flourish so that the springs of social wealth would at last flow forth freely. The distribution of benefits and burdens will not, of course, be equal, or indeed result in any preferred pattern, but free market initiative will produce such abundance that wealth will in fact be spread to all. Socialism's promise of need satisfaction, libertarians claim, can be met without its violation of rights and liberty. There will be a genuine trickle down. The capitalist will be free in such a system to make a very good profit indeed. But, in a fierce but fair competitive system, he will, if he is going to survive, proceed in an optimally efficient and productive manner. Such efficiency provides the mechanism to unlock the springs of social wealth. It will, under a free market system, flow so fully that the fact that some will be comparatively worse off than others will be amply compensated for by the fact that the worse off in such a market will still be better off than they would be under any other social system. Such a *laissez-faire* capitalist system encourages innovation and development, ensures efficiency and, at the same time, protects, what is, morally speaking, most fundamental, namely individual liberty.

Libertarians also argue that the *laissez-faire* market system is more flexible and more responsive to consumer demands than any rival system. In such a system customers can get what they want. So people are not only free to work on what they wish and work for whom they wish, they can in the free market get more readily what they want. This kind of 'economic democracy' squares very well, libertarians claim, with their general and pervasive commitment to the priority of liberty and to individual rights. More people more of the time can do whatever it is they want to do. What could be better?

III

Robert Nozick in the middle sections of his *Anarchy, State and Utopia* develops, as a further specification of this libertarian social theory, a distinctive *entitlement* theory of justice. What this means can be explained as follows.

Justice, for Nozick, as for libertarians generally, is a backward looking virtue concerned with who, because of his past acts, is entitled to what. It is not, for him, a forward looking virtue concerned with what distributive or redistributive patterns to achieve or to maintain.[4] Instead, an entitlement theory is concerned most fundamentally with (1) justice in original acquisition, (2) justice in transfer, as in a voluntary exchange from a just original acquisition, and (3), where some injustice in acquisition or transfer has already taken place, justice in rectification. In determining what is just, it is almost always crucial to ascertain what happened in the past: how some state of affairs came about. This is why Nozick calls the entitlement theory an historical theory. Whether a certain distribution of benefits and burdens is just does not depend *at all* on what the actual pattern of distribution is but on how the pattern came about. *Any* pattern of holdings is just, if the distributive pattern results from just original acquisitions and just transfers, or, where in the past some violation in the justice of original acquisition has occurred or something like fraud in transfer has occurred, rectification is required and the pattern meets those requirements.

Our common talk—at least common in roughly liberal circles—of 'distributive justice' is not, on Nozick's view, ideologically neutral. It gives us a skewed picture of what justice is. If we are held captive by that theory, we will, when we think of what is just or unjust, operate with a picture something like that of an adult in a position of authority seeking to make a fair division of a pie to children. But in our social life there is no authority, no central distribution centre, which is "entitled to control all the resources" and decide "how they are to be doled out" in what this authority takes to be a fair way. We should reject such paternalistic political images. The morally appropriate picture is one of a society in which each person gets what he gets from his own efforts or from others who give to him these things in exchange or as a gift. "In a free society, diverse persons control different resources, and new holdings arise out of the voluntary exchanges and actions of persons. There is no more a distributing of shares along some pre-determined pattern than there is a distributing of mates in a society in which persons choose whom they shall marry. The total result is the product of many individual decisions which the different individuals involved are entitled to make."[5] There is no overall governing principle here. *Justice just is these various entitlements*. It is not some preferred distributive pattern, either egalitarian or otherwise. "The complete principle of distributive justice would say simply that a distribution is just if everyone is entitled to the holdings they possess under the distribution."[6]

For such an account one plain and very central question is *how do we*, if indeed we can at all, *identify a just original acquisition?*

In trying to specify a principle of justice in original acquisition, Nozick turns to John Locke's theory of acquisition and his conception of property rights. Nozick finds all sorts of difficulties in it. Some of them seem to me to be genuine while others seem laboured. Yet he accepts what he regards as the core of Locke's account here, though he does have his own special interpretation of it.[7] My interest is not whether it is a correct description of Locke but with whether it is an adequate specification of justice in initial acquisition.

This Lockean account of justice in initial acquisition gives us an account of when we came to have a property right in some unowned object. *We gain a property right in such an object, we are entitled to such an object, when (a) we mix our labour with it and (b) when there is "enough and as good left in common for others."* (B is called *Locke's proviso*.) If (a) and (b) obtain we have justly acquired it. We are now entitled to it; it is now a holding of ours and, as something which is ours, we are entitled to do with it what we like as long as we do not harm others in doing so. Thus, if I find a stick in an unowned forest and I fashion it into a spear (thus mixing my labour with it), it is thereby mine, if there are enough other sticks of similar quality lying around for others to use. I now own it and can do with it what I will, short of harming others with it by, for example, running them through.

Mixing one's labour with something previously unowned is a *necessary* but not a *sufficient* condition for coming to own such an object in an original just acquisition. We do not automatically get full ownership over something if "the stock of unowned objects that might be improved is limited. When this condition obtains, it is crucial to ask whether the appropriation of the unowned object worsens the situation of others."[8] The Lockean proviso that there be "enough and as good left in common for others" is "meant to ensure that the situation of others is not worsened."[9] This, for Nozick, understandably enough, is an utterly crucial condition. Yet it is subject to at least two readings and only on one of those two readings can it be utilized by Nozick in a way that would make sense of his account.

On the first reading of 'being made worse off by another's appropriation' (the one Nozick does not intend) one loses one's chance to improve one's situation by that appropriation. Suppose I am in the truffle selling business and there is an unowned stand of forest with lots of truffles. Pierre appropriates it before me and I lose my chance for a new source of comparatively cheap truffles. This is one way I may be made worse off by another's appropriation. I have simply lost an opportunity to improve my situation. On the second reading of 'being made worse off by another's appropriation' (the one Nozick does intend) one is made worse off because after the appropriation one is no longer able to use freely what one previously could. Considering the base line from where one started, one is now worse off.

The first way of taking the Lockean proviso seems too strong. An acquisition which violates it does not seem plainly unfair or, in many instances, otherwise morally questionable. Indeed, if the Lockean proviso were read in that strong way, it would make just acquisition almost impossible. Thus the second way seems to be more appropriate.

Taking that second understanding of 'being made worse off', we should now ask whether the situation of persons being unable to appropriate, because there are no more accessible and useful unowned objects, is worsened, by a system allowing appropriation and permanent property? Nozick thinks not because he believes that the social product is increased by putting the means of production in the hands of those who can use it most efficiently.

Nozick is trying to show us that even in situations where there are no more accessible and unowned objects, the *intent* behind Locke's proviso of "enough and as good left" is not violated. It is not violated because the situation of the non-owners is not worsened, for, with the capitalist system—the system emerging out of these acquisitions—people, even without ownership, are not worse off than they were before in the important sense that they are still free to do as much as they were previously able to do before the question of such acquisition arose. Moreover, with the increase of the social product, their general material condition is not worsened but improved.

What we are not justified in doing by any original acquisition, either with or without any combination of transfers, is to bring about a situation where the person, making the acquisition or the transfer, "violates the proviso by making the siutation of others worse *than their base line situation*".[10] A person cannot "appropriate the only water hole in a desert and charge what he will. Nor may he charge what he will, if he possesses one, and "unfortunately it happens that all the water holes in the desert dry up, except for his."[11] Similarly, an owner's "property right in the only island in the area does not allow him to order a castaway from a shipwreck off his island as a trespasser."[12] All these violate the Lockean proviso. But a "medical researcher who synthesizes a new substance that effectively treats a certain disease and who refuses to sell except on his terms does not worsen the situation of others by depriving them of whatever he has appropriated."[13] He has a right, not to be overridden, to refuse to sell it.

Nozick believes that a competitive capitalist socio-economic system will not sanction actions which violate the Lockean proviso. "The free operation of a market system will not actually run afoul of the Lockean proviso . . . ."[14] This being so, there will be no justification for state action in the acquisition of property and the like. We do not need a State with powers greater than the minimal state.

IV

Nozick's conception of how we determine whether original acquisitions are just is subject to an array of criticisms, criticisms which reflect back on his entitlement theory generally and on the very foundations of libertarianism.

For Nozick an acquisition is a just acquisition of an unowned object only if it doesn't make people worse off than they were before the acquisition. Suppose we have a system of property relations that bring about a state of affairs S in which many people remain miserable and are worked very hard at very low wages, but still are not worse off, everything considered, than they were prior to the institution of those property relations. However, the situation is one in which another state of affairs S' could be brought about in which there is generally much less misery and exploitation. But to bring about S' requires some overriding of that system of private property, i.e. those just initial acquisitions. It requires, that is, the end of a system of private property rights in the *means of production* and the institution of a social ownership and control of the means of production. Even if this new situation S' would provide better work at a better pay scale and be a situation in which there was far less misery than in S, still, on Nozick's account, we should stick with S and take property rights as inalienable and absolute as long as the Lockean proviso is met. Such a judgment conflicts in a radical way with my considered judgments. It seems to me just wrong, indeed evil, to stick with inalienable *property* rights in such a situation: a situation where by sanctioning them we ensure far more misery than would otherwise obtain. Nozick, no doubt, would reply that here I am simply invoking an 'end-state principle' of a roughly utilitarian sort. I would reply that whatever we should say *in general* about utilitarian reasoning it is morally arbitrary not to so reason here. We have a duty to prevent misery where we reasonably can. To treat some *property* rights, particularly property rights in the means of production, as inalienable when by overriding them great suffering for many people can be alleviated is, morally speaking, monstrous.[15]

An actual example might help make vivid the moral point I am trying to make. The *Latifundia* system of land tenure and property ownership in Latin America sustains and legally protects a highly inefficient system of agriculture where, conservatively speaking, 1% of all farm families control at least one-half of all farm land.[16] Millions of landless peasants live in circumstances of misery and degradation. Even if they are not worse off than they were before such property acquisitions were made and even if the initial acquisitions were just, to treat such property rights as inalienable in such circumstances is through and through evil. It may be important, as Nozick stresses again and again, to consider, where justice is at issue, how the holdings came about. But that cannot be the whole story. Even if the holdings came about justly it may be unjust and indeed deeply evil to persist in claiming those holdings.

To see what is involved in such a judgment consider the case of the medical researcher who effectively synthesizes a new substance which will effectively cure cancer. Nozick rightly remarks that if he refuses to sell it except on his own terms, he does not violate the Lockean proviso, even if he does sell it at such a high price that few can purchase it and many will die from cancer who otherwise would not if they had had the drug. Nozick says that if the researcher so acts he has done nothing wrong. He can do what he likes with his property as long as he doesn't use it in such a way that he harms others. By so acting, he doesn't harm others, though he admittedly doesn't help them, for without the new drug they would have died anyway. They are no worse off than they otherwise would be if he hadn't made the invention. So by making the invention, by acquiring that particular bit of property, he hasn't done them any harm. I say such behaviour on the part of the researcher is morally monstrous. To have a drug that will save lives and prevent extensive misery and yet to withhold it from those who need it is simply vile. In such a situation there are moral obligations to provide *mutual aid* and to relieve suffering; if the researcher is not willing to make the drug available, property which he owns or not, he should be forced to do so by the State or by social pressure.

Nozick would respond that such state intervention would be too destructive of human freedom to be morally acceptable. But why should this be so if we interfere with freedom in *such cases*? Why should we think this would start a slippery slope that would lead to our interfering with freedom all over the place? There are no good grounds for believing that that will be the upshot of overriding property rights in such a circumstance.

There is also a distinct lack of realism in Nozick's account. He gives us what in effect is an inapplicable model. For any of the property relations that now actually obtain, we do not know, or even have any reasonable grounds for believing, that they were acquired by an original just acquisition meeting anything like the Lockean proviso. What we do know is that, if we go back far enough, there were plenty of unowned objects around that could have been initially acquired under conditions that would meet the Lockean proviso. At one time there must have been more than enough to go around and as good in kind or nearly so. But what the original transfers were like we do not know. It is, of course, *logically* possible that they could have been just transfers but it is far more likely that plunder, the use of violence, force, and deceit were there from the very beginning. In many cases it surely must be the case that we can hardly properly speak of anything like a contractual transfer, but just of marauders seizing other people's holdings. We do not know what these human transactions were like; there are no reasonable grounds for believing that the present holdings of people are on Nozick's criteria just and legitimate holdings. Nozick does not claim that we can tell this about our actual holdings. He frankly throws up his hands at this problem, but this shows that his model is inapplicable to the real world. It is a model which is utterly useless in determining what our actual entitlements are. In an important sense his 'historical theory' is very unhistorical.

V

This hard-hearted doctrine which would deny that there are duties to mutual aid or duties of beneficence and which conceptualizes things as if there were only one form of wrong doing, namely the violation of rights, does rest on a foundation of sorts or at least has a rationale. Nozick believes that if in deciding what we *must* do—what morality requires of us—we count the consequences in terms of human happiness or the misery resulting from the working of his system of individual rights, it will not infrequently *require* some persons to contribute to the assistance of others, but this, Nozick maintains, violates their moral autonomy and commits the fundamental utilitarian error of not having regard for the separateness of persons. It fails to acknowledge the inviolability of persons. It is on this insistence on the moral centrality of a regard for the separateness of persons that this rights-based theory has its foundations. On consequentialist conceptions, as kindly as they may seem, people are violated and sacrificed for others. And this, to return my compliment, is itself morally monstrous.

However, as H.L.A. Hart has pointed out, Nozick engages in some rather hysterical hyperbole here.[17] It is plainly violating the integrity of a person to kill him, to take one of his vital organs, to force him to marry another person against his will, to silence him in his expression of his convictions, but it is altogether another thing again to tax a very rich peron's income to save others from great suffering or to require that a person's invention (say a cure for cancer) be publicly available where its availability would relieve great suffering and save lives. Taking your vital organs without your permission just does make you a resource for others, taking some of your very great income to meet very basic needs of others is not so treating you. Such redistributive measures do not sacrifice people, violate their integrity or treat them as means only.

Nozick is surely right in stressing the deep moral import of individuals being able to shape their own lives, in being free to carve out a meaningful life for themselves. But in a capitalist system—or at least in a system of unrestricted capitalism—it is only a very privileged or lucky few who can do so. The rights and liberties that Nozick takes to be morally required are a very restrictive list. We have an inviolable right not to be interfered with in certain determinate ways. That is, others must abstain from murdering us, assaulting us, stealing from us, breaching contracts with us and the like. These rights are what have been called *negative* rights and they require abstension from certain things on the part of others. But to limit rights to negative rights is an arbitrary move. Why should people not have a right to have their basic needs met (health needs, needs for security and decent housing, needs for meaningful work and for education) where these needs can be met? It is simply morally arbitrary (to put it minimally) to claim that a person has an absolute, permanent, exclusive, inheritable and unmodifiable right to own and control productive property (say a factory) and to deny, in a society of reasonable affluence, that a person has any right at all to an education, to health care and to be protected from starvation. It is meaningless to talk of the protection of an individual's right to a meaningful life which he shapes himself while denying him the right to the necessary means to live such a life. Under the system of unrestricted capitalism Nozick favors, most people, through no fault of their own, would find it quite impossible to live the meaningful life that Nozick takes to be essential to a human life. To will such a life is to will the necessary means to it. Among these necessary means are certain material and social conditions and opportunities that libertarians claim that society—that is individuals acting collectively—are under no moral constraint to provide. This turns the familiar libertarian description of a 'free society' into a cruel joke. To think of a system of unrestricted capitalism as a 'free society' is to have a very impoverished conception of a free society.

VI

Nozick is a trenchant critic of egalitarianism of both a Welfare State sort and a socialist sort. To press home his point, and make it vividly concrete, he develops his Wilt Chamberlain parable, a parable many, on first reading at least, find quite compelling.

Nozick asks us to suppose we are living in an egalitarian society operating under an egalitarian principle of justice—a principle which specifies that a certain patterned end-result is to obtain. Suppose Wilt Chamberlain lives in that society as well as many avid basketball fans who are very keen on seeing Wilt play. Suppose further he signs the following contract with a professional basketball team. In each home game twenty-five cents added to the price of each ticket will go to him. The season starts and the home fans cheerfully attend the games quite willing to pay the extra twenty-five cents to see Wilt play basketball. During the course of the season Wilt gains a very considerable additional income—say 250,000 dollars—upsetting the previously egalitarian income patterns in our egalitarian society. But isn't he plainly entitled to the extra income? He freely contracted for it, he worked for it, and the fans freely and happily paid the extra twenty-five cents to see him play. It was their money, on a previously equal distribution, to do with what they wanted to as long as they did not so use it as to harm others. In this instance, they simply disposed of their resources as they wanted to and people who didn't go to the games cannot complain that any injustice has been done to them, for they still have what they were entitled to (their rightful 'shares') under the egalitarian distributional pattern. To keep an egalitarian pattern would, Nozick claims, be too destructive of individual liberty. We must, in the name of liberty and a respect for people's rights and moral integrity, reject patterned end-state principles of justice. (An end-state distributional principle is a principle which maintains that the justice of a distribution depends on certain structural features of the situation it depicts, such as its utility or the degree of equality which results from acting in accordance with it. Where a principle of justice is an end-state principle which specifies that holdings are to vary along with some natural dimension or some combination of natural dimensions, it is also called a patterned principle by Nozick.)

VII

This argument of Nozick's has been, I believe, refuted by G. A. Cohen and in the course of his refutation Cohen also makes plain how a socialist society would not undermine liberty in the way Nozick fears.[18]

I shall set out and examine some of the core portions of Cohen's argument. He first points out that the Chamberlain parable, as Nozick presents it, seems morally innocuous. What could be wrong, we ask ourselves, with the fans so financially compensating Chamberlain? They get to see him play, which is what they want, and he gets some more money, which is what he wants. And he doesn't get it by stealing from them or by defrauding them or coercing them or exploiting them, for they voluntarily transfer some of their holdings to him to get what they want. This respects both their freedom and his freedom. If the initial situation is just, which *ex hypothesis* it is, the resulting situation of just transfers must also be just. If we have respect for liberty and believe that justice requires liberty, we will not view it as morally right to require (by some deliberate social policy) a redistribution so as to return to the *initial status quo* before Chamberlain made his wad. It seems morally arbitrary to require such a redistribution.

Cohen argues that actually it is not and that there is a rationale for such a redistribution that respecters of liberty should acknowledge. The reason why we should limit the amount that Wilt Chamberlain, or any individual should have a right to hold, is to prevent them or their heirs from acquiring through such holdings an unacceptable amount of power and control over others. Through their enhanced wealth, which will tend to go on accumulating (the rich tend to get richer), they will gain power, in a previously egalitarian society, the possession of which tends to undermine the liberty of others. Because of this accrual of power to the rich, the non-rich have rather less control over their lives than they otherwise would have.[19] Even if, as in this case, the Wilt Chamberlain types come to hold what they hold in a morally innocuous way, the effects of their coming to have these holdings, whatever their intentions, are going to be anything but innocuous. It is slightly hysterical to get worried about Wilt Chamberlain *per se* but the effect of a number of people so acquiring holdings in that way is to create a situation in which there will be a large power differential between this class of people and others. And this will translate into a differential in their respective liberty, one which is plainly harmful to democracy. If we prize moral autonomy we will not favor such situations. In short, what Cohen shows is that the Chamberlain transaction is not, as Nozick presents it, beneficial or even harmless to everyone with an interest in it. Quite to the contrary, "it threatens to generate a situation in which some have unacceptable amounts of power over others".[20] Indeed it is very likely to worsen the situation of many people.

Once Chamberlain has received the "payments he is in a very special position of power in what was previously an egalitarian society".[21] Socialists will be wary of such transactions because they can see the potentially destructive effects of them on both liberty and equality in an egalitarian society. The socialist's reluctance here is not grounded in envy of Wilt Chamberlain's getting such a wad. The socialist's worry is about the potential for undermining an egalitarian society (a republic of equals), where people are genuinely equals and can control their own political and social destinies, free from the coercive control of power hierarchies who gain control of the society. In an egalitarian society, at last free from class division and domination, the socialist sees a wedge being entered, which, if allowed to widen, will once more set the society on the road to class division and domination. The resistance of socialists to *such* freedoms flows from their commitment to a society where, for all of us, there will be no master above us or servants under us, a society where we will be free and equal moral persons living together in fraternity and solidarity. Seeing the Chamberlain case as morally innocuous fails to take into consideration the corrupting effects of such precedents on such a society.

It is also false to say, as Nozick does, that third parties, people who are not party to the transaction, have not been affected. Nozick points out, rightly enough, that these people still have "their legitimate shares; their shares are not changed".[22] But they still have been affected in an important sense, for "a person's effective share depends on what he can do with what he has, and that depends not only on how much he has but on what others have and on how what others have is distributed".[23] If it is distributed equally among them, or roughly equally, he will often be better placed than if some have especially large shares. Third parties, including the as yet unborn, therefore, have an interest against the making of the contract in the Chamberlain parable. This relevant interest is ignored in Nozick's depiction of the voluntary agreement between Chamberlain and the fans.

Nozick seems to take as absolute, or nearly so, the fans' entitlement to dispose of their resources (in this instance their money) as they deem fit, as long as they do not harm others. But why should this right be so absolute? Their rights would be violated only if they are taken to be absolute. But why not take all rights as *prima facie* and as defeasible? They can be overridden without being violated, if certain conditions obtain. Nozick has not shown that any restrictions which would forbid the Chamberlain transaction must be unjustified. Although it might turn out that sanctioning *that* transaction will not be particularly harmful, if we do so in that case, we must sanction such transactions in relevantly similar cases. But if we do allow such arrangements it is likely that they will generate an inordinate power and consequent control in the hands of a few. With that power we have at least the very real possibility of the control of the many by the few with the big holdings. This is something that is repeatedly neglected in bourgeois apologetics.[24] And Nozick indeed utterly neglects it. But it is a potent source of harm to many human beings.

Nozick is prepared to bite the bullet by accepting what many would take to be *a reductio* argument against his position. As we have seen, we are not justified, according to Nozick, in taxing millionaires, where they have justly acquired their millions, to finance a milk subsidy for undernourished children of indigent families. (We are assuming here, what we probably can never actually ascertain, namely, that the millions were justly acquired.) By so taxing these millionaires we would, Nozick would have it, be violating their rights. And Nozick will not accept the argument, previously made, that we are justified in doing this because by doing it "the effective liberty of the children would be greatly enhanced at little expense to the millionaire's freedom". Nozick cannot accept that, since he does not try to *maximize* freedom, but "forbids any act which restricts freedom".[25] We cannot justifiably override the liberty of an individual in order to strengthen the entire system of liberty.

We cannot interfere with the millionaires' liberties in order to maximize liberty in the world, because that would, according to Nozick, be treating the millionaire as a means. We must always treat persons as ends and never merely as means. But there is no good reason to believe that the millionaire is being treated merely or only as a means. His person remains inviolable. It is just that, in terms of the respect we have for other persons, i.e. the lives of those undernourished children, one of his *prima facie* rights, namely the right to do with his *property* what he likes, is being limited in a determinate and limited circumstance. This does not show that he is being treated merely as a means or that his person is not being held as inviolable. If we take away some of the millionaires' property through taxation we have not thereby treated him as a means only. It is not at all like taking one of his kidneys without his permission. We do not violate him as a person or take his interests to be of no account.

Nozick has not *justified* an appeal to certain rights as being absolute. Given that Nozick has failed in that task, socialists plainly "need not apologize for being willing to restrict freedom in order to expand it".[26] Generally, libertarians wish to take their stand here and argue that they are the protectors of individual rights and liberty with a conception of society which, if it were to be exemplified in modern industrial societies, would have to be exemplified in competitive capitalist societies.

I have been concerned to show that this is not true. We cannot equate such a capitalist society with a free society. It would further some freedoms and severely restrict others.[27] It would maximize the freedom of the market place for those who are the great owners of capital. It would further strengthen the control the big capitalists have on society and further undermine the freedom of most people.[28] It would give economic freedom to the privileged few while weakening generally the structures of freedom in the society. It legitimizes selfishness and makes a virtue of callousness in human relations.[29]

VIII

Nozickian libertarianism is not the only moral defense of *laissez faire* capitalism, but it is the strongest and most philosophically sophisticated. If my arguments in the last two sections have been near to the mark, we have good reason to believe that capitalism in its pure form has little claim to being a socio-economic system which protects liberty or makes justice a reality. It should not be our ideal of a legitimate society.

State Capitalism, particularly the Welfare State Capitalism defended by contemporary liberals and social democrats, has a different conception of the just society, as we have seen and as we shall see more fully in what follows. Our next question is whether, as Welfare State liberals believe, but socialist critics deny, a Welfare State capitalist society would be as just or juster than a non-Statist socialist system. We shall explore this question by concentrating on *A Theory of Justice*, the seminal work by Nozick's colleague at Harvard, John Rawls.

IX

I shall begin by examining some of the core arguments between Rawls and his socialist critics in an attempt to see if we can get a grip on whether, under conditions of material abundance, ideal but still achievable forms of socialism are, or are not, juster social systems than ideal but still achievable forms of Welfare State capitalism.

I shall first simply state fundamental liberal principles of justice and fundamental socialist principles of justice—and then turn to commentary on them. The liberal principles are in Rawls's formulation and the socialist principles are my own.

Liberal Principles of Justice: Justice as Fairness
(1) Each person is to have an equal right to the most extensive total system of equal basic liberties compatible with a similar system of liberty for all.
(2) Social and economic inequalities are to be arranged so that they are both:
    (a) to the greatest benefit of the least advantaged consistent with the just savings principle, and
    (b) attached to offices and positions open to all under conditions of fair equality of opportunity.

Socialist Principles of Justice: Justice as Equality
(1) Each person is to have an equal right to the most extensive total system of equal basic liberties and opportunities (including equal opportunities for meaningful work, for self-determination and political and economic participation) compatible with a like treatment of all. (This principle gives expression to a commitment to attain and/or sustain equal moral autonomy and equal self-respect.)
(2) After provisions are made for common social (community) values, for capital overhead to preserve the society's productive capacity, allowances are made for differing unmanipulated needs and preferences, and due weight is given to the just entitlements of individuals, the income and wealth (the common stock of means) is to be so divided that each person will have a right to an equal share. The necessary burdens requisite to enhance human well-being are also to be equally shared, subject, of course, to limitations by differing abilities and differing situations (natural environment not class position).[30]

I have put Rawls's principles and my socialist principles cheek to jowl for ease of comparison. I shall now consider the comparative merits of these respective principles. (These principles, of course, need to be related, as the argument unfolds, to their characteristic theories.) In this way we can get before us some of the case for and against liberal justice and socialist justice.[31]

Both the Liberal Principles and the Socialist Principles (as I shall refer to them henceforth) build on what is, in societies such as ours, the pervasive and deep conviction that there is a link between fairness and equality and a belief in the importance of liberty.

The first principle of Liberal Justice (Rawls's first principle), *the equal liberty principle*, and a key part of his second principle, *the difference principle*, i.e. social and economic inequalities are to be arranged so that they are to the greatest benefit of the least advantaged, are very attractive and very plausible sounding principles indeed. They seem to encapsulate the essence of liberal justice.[32]

The equal liberty principle can be seen as a principle which directs us to try to bring into existence a society where everyone can do what he or she likes, where each can, as fully as possible, satisfy his or her desires, subject only to the restriction that doing what they like be compatible with everyone's being able to do what he or she likes. In other words, people can do what they like except where doing that undermines a like liberty for others, i.e., prevents others from being able to do what they like. In fine, liberty can only justifiably be restricted, when the restriction of some particular liberty or liberties would be necessary, to protect the most extensive system possible of equal liberties. It is Rawls's belief that liberty can be sacrificed, in circumstances of relative affluence, *only* to ensure or protect a still greater liberty *for all*.

There are certain qualifications that we should make to this claim, but it remains, all the same, an attractive ideal. Would we not, if we reflect carefully on the matter, want a world in which each and every person could do, to the fullest extent possible, whatever it is they want—where everyone could most fully realize their aims and ideals, achieve their hopes, live their lives as they really wish to, subject only to the restriction, that their so living be compatible with a like condition of life for their fellow human beings? This is surely a very attractive conception.

Secondly—and here is where the *difference* principle comes into play—if there must be some inequalities, as apparently there must, what fairer or better arrangement could be devised than an arrangement in which the inequalities are justified *when, and only when,* the positions of relative advantage can be fairly competed for and the resultant inequalities benefit everyone, or, where they cannot benefit everyone, or where we cannot ascertain that they benefit everyone, they benefit, more than any alternative arrangement, the most disadvantaged stratum of society? What could be *fairer,* where we must allow some inequalities, than to allow inequalities only when they, more than any other arrangement, are to the advantage of the most disadvantaged? It is bad enough that some people have to be disadvantaged; it is still worse when they do *not* get the maximal advantages that could go with their being in that disadvantaged position. The humane and just thing to do is to try to ensure that the inequalities that exist will be such that they mitigate, as much as possible, the situation of the most disadvantaged. This is Rawls's essential reasoning about the *difference* principle. It surely seems humane and reasonable and it is a core ideal of liberal egalitarianism.

Someone arguing for the Socialist Principles could very well begin their critique of the Liberal Principles by starting with the *difference* principle, namely with the claim that inequalities are just, or at least are justified, only if they maximally benefit the worst off under the constraints articulated by Rawls. For it could be the case, as Rawls allows, that the Liberal Principles are in force, that they actually are being correctly applied, and that we would, if we reasoned in accordance with them, still be committed to accepting as *just* a not inconsiderable disparity in total life prospects between children of entrepreneurs and the professional class, on the one hand, and children of unskilled labourers or people on welfare, on the other, even when those children are equally talented, equally energetic and the like.

This seems manifestly unjust. It is unfair that one child's life prospects are such that, when he starts out in life, it is close to inevitable that he will end up working (if he has any work at all) all his life in a factory, a mine or the like, while another child's life prospects are such that it makes it almsot inevitable that he will enter the professional or entrepreneurial strata of society. Such disparities in life prospects are basically unfair or unjust, unless they are unalterable or the costs of their cure are worse than the grave ills they perpetuate. Given that such disparities in total life prospects are such plain ills *and* that they do not appear to be unalterable, the burden of proof is surely on the defender of the capitalist order to show that they cannot be altered or that the costs of breaking down these disparities are too high.

The liberal Rawlsian response is that they are necessary evils that we have to live with, even in affluent societies, to avoid still greater evils. It is, such liberals would plausibly argue, bad enough that such inequalities in total life prospects must exist, but it is still worse, by narrowing them, to make the children of unskilled workers still worse off. It is, everything considered, juster and more decent, to accept these not inconsiderable disparities in life and apply the *difference* principle, accepting only such reductions in these disparities as are sanctioned by the *difference* principle.

If we start, as defenders of both the Liberal Principles and the Socialist Principles insist, with the deep underlying commitment that in the design of institutions all people are to have *a right to equal concern and respect,* and if we believe that liberation from class society is possible, we will not be satisfied with the *difference* principle, even when it is surrounded by Rawls's safeguards, for, where such differences in whole life prospects obtain, there will be differences in power and control in society riding with these differences in life prospects. Differences, recall, sanctioned by the *difference* principle. These in turn will make it impossible for the most disadvantaged effectively to exercise anything like fully equal citizenship and this in turn will undermine their standing on a footing of equal liberty with the more advantaged, e.g. the capitalists and the professional elite. Moreover, much work in capitalist society is degrading and undermining of human autonomy, and, where the worker sees her condition with any clarity, undermining of self-respect. This could be lessened in capitalist society but not obliterated, for in the capitalist production process workers are simply told to carry out certain tasks. In that very important area of their lives, they lack autonomy. They work for a salary and do what they are told; they, generally, have no alternative, except the even more degrading alternative of going on the dole.

Where this is seen by people subjected to alienated labour, there is a tendency to suffer a loss of self-respect, a loss not certain to be made good by abiding by Rawls' *difference* principle. Contrary to Rawls, then, it is arguable that in a society of material abundance the most disadvantaged would, where fully informed and rational, choose, the second Socialist Principle rather than the *difference* principle, if they prize the good of self-respect and autonomy as much as Rawls believes they would and should. They would prefer, under these circumstances, a somewhat lesser income (lesser material wealth) if this would enable them to have a greater control over their own lives—a fuller realization of liberty and the good of self-respect. They would not and should not accept the differences in power and control acceptable under the *difference* principle.

It is not envy or irrationality that leads to such a Socialist insistence on levelling, but a commitment to the fullest achievement possible of equal liberty, i.e. equal control for each person over the design of his life.

A socialist belief is that this cannot be attained in class society with its inevitable differences in power and control in society. State capitalist societies, committed to Liberal Principles, can ameliorate this condition and they are an advance over *laissez faire* capitalism with its commitment to libertarianism. But in class society—any class society—equal citizenship, equal liberty and equal opportunity cannot be attained. Thus, if they are otherwise obtainable, a capitalist society (even a Social Democratically oriented Liberal Welfare State Capitalism) cannot be a fully just society. It is the claim of socialism that there are such alternatives: that there is a liberation, or at least the reasonable hope of liberation, from class society.

Rawls would respond—and most liberals would follow him here—that liberation from class society is impossible because classes are inevitable. To believe in the possibility of such a liberation is to be held captive to a Marxist myth. Classes are rooted in our very human situation. Old classes will come and go but class society will remain.

So a core dispute between liberals and socialists is not fundamentally over justice or morality at all, but over a matter of political sociology: over whether classes are or are not inevitable. Are they? I think to answer that we need first to carry out some disambiguation of what we are asking. We first must distinguish *class* and *strata*.

When we speak of social stratification we are speaking of the differential ranking of individuals in a society. Such a ranking implies a ranking of higher and lower in terms of prestige and authority. Caste systems and the traditional systems of Estates are extreme cases. (I speak here of the Three Estates in France: Nobles, Clergy, Citizens and (up to 1866) in Sweden of the Four Estates: Nobles, Clergy, Citizens and

Peasants.) Having such strata involves accepting as binding some commonly accepted norms of the society with the stratification (the differential *ranking*) in
question. Classes, by contrast, are not defined (except often for convenience) in
terms of legal barriers, let alone religious ones, but principally in economic terms in
relation to the means of production, of who has the effective control of industry, land
and labour power.[33]

Must any society have some social stratification? The usual answer is Yes, but
even if that is so, why couldn't it be minimal or at least much less than we now have?
Even if some social stratification is unavoidable, it does not follow that there must be
society-wide norms whose enforcement discriminates between various people in
certain social positions such that a person in one social position is disadvantaged in
his or her whole life prospects, as is the case of the child of the unskilled labourer. At
the very least, it has not been shown that this situation of disadvantage is inescap-
able.[34]

Must any society have classes? Probably not. It certainly seems at least possible
that there could be social ownership and control of the means of production. Workers
could run and control their own places of work. They could, while remaining
workers, also engage in whatever training and education is necessary to gain the
knowledge and skills to run complex operations. We could have an *industrial democracy* in which there would be no authoritarian work orientation. That, by itself,
would do a lot to get rid of classes, for there would, in that circumstance, be no group
of people who own and control the means of production and another distinct group
who, without such ownership and control, sell their labour power and work for a
wage.

Is such a thing possible in a complex industry? I think it is plainly possible to run
factories, even large factories, with workers' councils. Workers discuss together all
aspects of the factory operation and carry through workers' self-management.
Overall policy is decided democratically and those people in positions of authority
are there because they have been elected by workers. It is vital that they can be
recalled by workers and, with a firm system of rotation, people, who for a time are in
positions of authority, remain workers themselves.

Still, might not a group of mandarins arise from amongst the most skilled workers?
And might not their position very easily, indeed perhaps quite unintentionally,
become such that both their whole life prospects, and in turn the whole life prospects
of their children, would be very different indeed from the life prospects of the less
skilled workers and their children?

If industrial democracy were actually in place and if there were utterly free and
good education (including higher education) designed in part to counter the effects of
such inequalities in the education of the children's parents, it is not evident that such
a group of skilled experts would have to become such controlling, prestigious and
privileged mandarins. And it is even less evident that their positions of prestige
would have to be passed on over generations.

Some might say that it very well may be *possible* to have a classless society but that
such a society would be *undesirable* since it would involve too much State interference in people's lives. The costs of equality, they will claim, are just too high. When
we speak, as I did above, of job rotation to break down the social stratification that
constantly threatens to develop into classes or controlling elites, who are the 'we' to
do this, if it isn't the State, i.e. a few individuals with a monopoly of power in the
society? And would not doing this then involve an intolerable amount of interference
in people's lives? Again we are back to some of the worries of the libertarians.

It is not at all evident to me that workers of the future—workers who are much
more educated and politically aware than workers today—could not, and would not,
see that it was in their collective self-interest *not* to allow such stratifications to

continue and that they would act to overcome them and to prevent their re-emergence. Moreover, I do not see why there very well might not, with the educational institutions and what we now call the mass media on the side of social equality, be a considerable and increasingly stable consensus, rooted in what is plainly in the self-interest of the workers, to keep a condition of classlessness and not allow a re-emergence of a social stratification that might very well lead again to something very like class society. It seems to me a not unrealistic expectation to believe that consensus would be stable so that there would not be that constant interference, or indeed even frequent interference, with the lives of people to maintain that equality that is the bugbear of libertarians. At least this is not an unreasonable hope, though it is, of course, a hope which, if we come to live through the proper testing conditions, experience might come to shatter.

X

I bring this essay to its final section with the frustrated awareness that the dialectic of the argument is not nearly at an end in the great debate between liberalism and socialism. That is hardly surprising in that it is the most important moral and social issue of our time. As religion once did, it divides and touches our deepest hopes for ourselves and for our children. The issue will be fought out in the next few decades in a long and complicated and many leveled struggle. Given the complexity of what is involved here, it is hardly to be wondered that there are myriads of issues crying for discussion that I have not even touched on. Indeed, even for the two issues I shall discuss in this last section, there are many loose ends which must remain.

(1) In comparing the Liberal Principles and the Socialist Principles, I have argued that the socialist second principle ought to be accepted rather than the *difference* principle, but I have said nothing in favour of the first principle, either to distinguish it from the first liberal principle or to show why, as both the liberal formulation and the socialist formulation do, such stress should be placed on the attainment and protection of equal liberty and moral autonomy.

It is crucial first to recognize that neither Rawls nor I even try to articulate eternal principles of justice to be accepted in all historical epochs and circumstances. Our equal liberty principles, for example, only have application in conditions of moderate scarcity or relative abundance. Brecht's 'Eats first, morality afterwards' should never be forgotten.

It is also the case that the liberal first principle and the socialist first principle are very alike in that they call for the widest possible system of equal liberty, though the socialist principle makes more explicit what is involved. It is not basic differences over whether to accept something like an equal liberty principle that divide liberals and socialists.

However, there are people (some utilitarians among them) who would not accept the equal liberty principle. Why, they would ask, even in situations of abundance, give such weight to liberty, to self-determination, and to something as obscure and airy-fairy as the good of self-respect? Why care so much about equal citizenship, equal autonomy, and the good of self-respect? The answer, I believe, lies in recognizing that the value of moral autonomy and the good of self-respect are rooted in deeply felt considered judgments and beliefs abut what it is to live a human life. It is tied up, I believe, with our deepest hopes about ourselves and about what it would be to live a life with integrity.

The need to have some control over one's own existence, to be able to direct and orient one's own life according to a conception chosen by oneself from alternatives that seem meaningful to one, is a very powerful and persistent need indeed and becomes more powerful the more securely one's basic subsistence needs are met and the more leisured one is from endless backbreaking toil. That in barest outline is why the attainment and protection of equal liberty and autonomy are so important.

(2) I have argued for socialism over *laissez faire* capitalism. But suppose I am wrong and socialism is not a reasonable non-fanciful possibility and our actual choices are only between State capitalism and State socialism. Then is it not reasonable to believe that, not State capitalism *sans phrase,* but Liberal Welfare State capitalism is a juster and better social system than *any form* of State socialism? Isn't Sweden clearly a better society to live in than Cuba?

It is not unreasonable to be skeptical about whether the aims of socialism are attainable. If it is not reasonable to believe that they are, should we opt for the reformist aims of social democracy or State socialism?

Now, in view of the Liberal Principles and Socialist Principles of justice I have articulated, we readily can see that even the best forms of State capitalism and State socialism are flawed in terms of liberty, the good of self-respect, equal citizenship, equality and industrial democracy, and that they both are hierarchical, bureaucratic societies with elites and with paternalistic control.

However, unlike some actual State capitalist and State socialist societies, there is no reason at all why possible forms of each could not be political democracies, have respect for rights and civil liberties and be societies of plenty. Assuming this much, what grounds, if any, in terms of justice and morality, do we have for choosing one of these social systems over the other? Three reasons can be given for choosing State socialism. First, State socialism is committed to maximally, and equally, satisfy needs and to foster capital accumulations as instrumental only to that. State capitalism, by contrast, has no such underlying rationale. Second, State capitalism rests on its class structure. State socialism will indeed produce elites, but a) its belief system cannot justify their existence, except as temporary expedients, and b) the elites lack the clear structural means of the capitalist class for intragenerationally passing on their privileges. Third, since socialists are committed to attaining classlessness and to taking the standpoint of labour, there are strong grounds, in terms of social legitimization in the socialist belief system, to push for a greater equality and for the expansion of liberty.

There is, of course, much more to be said on this topic. There are normative points and normative-cum-factual points to be made on both sides; but, in the above arguments, we still have reason, where the choice is so narrowed, to prefer State socialism in its *best forms* to State capitalism in its best forms.

However, the core of my defense has been of socialism and not of State socialism. Conventional wisdom—a very ideologically convenient conventional wisdom—identifies commitment to it with a belief in a Marxist fairy tale, a possibly pleasant dream but not something which could come to have a real social exemplification. It is, we are given to understand, the secular equivalent of pie-in-the-sky-by-and-by, for those who cannot bear to look at social reality straight in the face, but who can no longer accept Jewish or Christian fairy tales. I have not tried to show that socialism is on the historical agenda, let alone that it is inevitable. But I have tried to provide some reason for believing that the popular 'political realism' and cultural pessimism are forms of ideological posturing *and* that socialism remains a *reasonable possibility.* If it is such a possibility, then I think that close reflection on justice and morality will give a person of humane sentiments and a reasonable grasp of the relevant facts good grounds indeed to struggle to make that possibility a reality.

Notes

1. Richard C. Edwards, Michael Reich and Thomas E. Weisskopf (eds.) *The Capitalist System,* (Second Edition), (Prentice Hall, Inc.: Englewood Cliffs, New Jersey, 1978), p. xii.

This is an excellent source for the political, economic, sociological, and other empirical issues essential for understanding the issues argued in this essay.

2. *Ibid.*, p. xiii.

3. That this economic doctrine is actually such a corollary of liberty is powerfully challenged by G. A. Cohen in his "Capitalism, Freedom and the Proletariat" in *The Idea of Freedom*, Alan Ryan (ed.) (Oxford University Press: Oxford, 1979), pp. 9–25 and by John Exdell, "Liberty, Equality and Capitalism", *Canadian Journal of Philosophy*, (1981).

4. Robert Nozick argues this is the middle section of *Anarchy, State and Utopia* (Basic Books Inc.: New York, 1974) and it has been argued by Antony Flew in "Equality *or* Justice", *Midwest Studies in Philosophy*, Vol. III (1978), pp. 176–194 and "A Theory of Social Justice" in *Contemporary British Philosophy*, H. D. Lewis (ed.) (Humanities Press: New York, 1976), pp. 69–85. I have criticized such accounts in my "Impediments to Radical Egalitarianism", *American Philosophical Quarterly*, (1981) and my "A Rationale for Egalitarianism", *Social Research*, (1981).

5. Nozick, *op. cit.*, pp. 150–1.

6. *Ibid.*, pp. 152–3.

7. Virginia Held, "John Locke on Robert Nozick", *Social Research*, Vol. 43 (1976) pp. 169–195 and Shadia Drury, "Robert Nozick and the Right to Property" in *Theories of Property*, Anthony Parel and Thomas Flanagan (eds.), (Waterloo, Ontario: Wilfred Laurier University Press, 1979), pp. 361–379. Among other things, these authors, in their perceptive criticisms of Nozick, show how far he departs here from Locke. Filmer is his genuine antecedent.

8. Nozick, *op. cit.*, pp. 175–6.

9. *Ibid.*

10. *Ibid.* H. L. A. Hart points out that the base line situation Nozick assumes is the 'state of nature', but, aside from not having any very clear conception of what this is, no reason is given for taking such a low base line. H. L. A. Hart, "Between Utility and Rights" in *The Idea of Freedom*.

11. Nozick, *op. cit.*, pp. 179–180.

12. *Ibid.*, pp. 180–181.

13. *Ibid.*

14. *Ibid.*

15. George Kateb, "The Night Watchman State", *The American Scholar* (1977), pp. 816–825.

16. Ernest Feder, "Latifundia and Agricultural Labour in Latin America" in *Peasants and Peasant Societies* in Teodor Shanin (ed.) (Penguin Books Ltd., 1971: Harmondworth, Middlesex, England, 1971) p. 83.

17. Hart, *op. cit.*

18. G. A. Cohen, "Robert Nozick and Wilt Chamberlain: How Patterns Preserve Liberty" in *Justice and Economic Distribution*, J. Arthur and W. H. Shaw, eds. (Englewood Cliffs, N.J.: Prentice-Hall, 1978) pp. 246–262. See also his essay cited in footnote 3.

19. Cohen, "Robert Nozick and Wilt Chamberlain: How Patterns Preserve Liberty", p. 251.

20. *Ibid.*

21. *Ibid.*

22. Nozick, *op. cit.*, pp. 160–1.

23. *Ibid.*

24. Cohen, "Robert Nozick and Wilt Chamberlain: How Patterns Preserve Liberty," p. 253.

25. Nozick, *op. cit.* See Cohen, as well, "Robert Nozick and Wilt Chamberlain: How Patterns Preserve Liberty", p. 256.

26. Cohen, "Robert Nozick and Wilt Chamberlain: How Patterns Preserve Liberty", p. 257.

27. Cohen, "Capitalism, Freedom and the Proletariat".

28. Martin J. Sklar, "Liberty and Equality and Socialism", *Socialist Revolution*, Vol. 7 No. 4 (July-August, 1977), pp. 92–104.

29. Boris Frankel, "Review Symposium of Anarchy, State and Utopia", *Theory and Society*, Vol. 3 (1976), pp. 443–449.

30. It might be thought that there is a qualifying element in my second principle of socialist justice that gives everything away to the libertarian. Things are to be divided equally *only after due weight is given to the just entitlements of individuals*. What more could Nozick ask for? But the catch here is on the reading to be given to 'due weight'. As my discussion of the principle makes clear, as well as my discussion of Nozick's principles of justice, entitlements cannot be legitimately insisted on in situations where insisting on them would cause great harm and suffering or in an undermining of human liberty, e.g. one cannot rightly hold on to one's patent

rights and let thousands die as a result of hanging on to them, and one cannot hold on to productive property where having that property gives one power over the lives of others such that whole life prospects of people are radically unequal. Thus, 'due weight' is accorded one's entitlements by recognizing that to have an entitlement to something is to have a *prima facie* right to it and that we have a *prima facie* obligation not to interfere with the exercising of that right. Such a recognition is giving 'due weight'. However, in order to maintain patterns which preserve liberty, we will occasionally be required to override a particular entitlement, just as we will also disallow some entitlements (e.g. no one is allowed privately to own productive property) in order to maintain patterns which preserve liberty. This is consistent with insisting that we can never rightly ignore the claims of entitlement.

31. Kai Nielsen "Class and Justice" in *Justice and Economic Distribution* and "Radical Egalitarian Justice: Justice as Equality" *Social Theory and Practice*, Vol. 5 No. 2 (1979).

32. Stuart Hampshire, "What Is The Just Society?", *The New York Review of Books*, Vol. 18 No 3 (February 24, 1972), pp. 34–39.

33. G. A. Cohen, *Karl Marx's Theory of History: A Defense*, (Clarendon Press: Oxford, 1978), pp. 73–77, 207–215 and Chapter VIII.

34. Steven Lukes, *Essays in Social Theory*, (The Macmillan Press Ltd. London, 1977), Chapter 5.

Suggested Readings

BOOKS

1. Richard C. Edwards, Michael Reich and Thomas E. Weisskopf (eds.), *The Capitalist System*, (Prentice-Hall, Inc.: Englewood Cliffs, New Jersey, 1978).
2. Samuel Bowles and Herbert Gintis, *Schooling in Capitalist America*, (Basic Books, Inc.: New York, 1976).
3. Harry Braverman, *Labor and Monopoly Capital*, (Monthly Review Press: New York, 1974).
4. Robert Nozick, *Anarchy, State and Utopia*, (Basic Books Inc.: New York, 1974).
5. Jeffrey Paul (ed.), *Reading Nozick*, (Rowman and Littlefield: Totowa, New Jersey, 1981).
6. John Arthur and William Shaw (eds.), *Justice and Economic Distribution*, (Prentice-Hall Inc.: Englewood Cliffs, New Jersey, 1978).
7. James Sterba (ed.), *Justice: Alternative Political Perspectives*, (Wadsworth Publishing Company: Belmont, California, 1980).
8. F. A. Hayek, *The Constitution of Liberty*, (Henry Regnery Company, Chicago, 1960).
9. Milton Friedman, *Capitalism and Freedom*, (The University of Chicago Press: Chicago, 1958).
10. John Rawls, *A Theory of Justice*, (Harvard University Press: Cambridge, Massachusetts, 1971).
11. Norman Daniels (ed.), *Reading Rawls*, (Basic Books: New York, 1974).
12. Kai Nielsen and Roger Shiner (eds.), *New Essays on Contract Theory*, (Canadian Association for Publishing in Philosophy: Guelph, Ontario, 1977).
13. Robert Paul Wolff, *Understanding Rawls*, (Princeton University Press: Princeton, New Jersey, 1977).
14. Milton Fisk, *Ethics and Society: A Marxist Interpretation of Value*, (The Harvester Press Ltd.: Brighton, Sussex, 1980).
15. Kai Nielsen and Steven Patten (eds.), *Marx and Moral Philosophy*, (Canadian Association for Publishing in Philosophy: Guelph, Ontario, 1981).
16. Marshall Cohen *et. al.* (eds.), *Marx, Justice and History*, (Princeton, University Press: Princeton, New Jersey, 1980).
17. Stanley Moore, *The Choice Between Socialism and Communism*, (Harvard University Press: Cambridge, Massachusetts, 1980).
18. Allen Wood, *Karl Marx*, (Routledge & Kegan Paul, London, 1981).
19. David Schweickart, *Capitalism or Worker Control? An Ethical and Economic Appraisal*, (Praeger: New York, 1980).
20. Steven Lukes, *Essays in Social Theory*, (The Macmillan Press Ltd.: London, 1977).
21. Allen Buchanan, *Marx and Justice* (Rowman and Littlefield: Totowa, New Jersey, 1982).

ARTICLES

1. Ronald Dworkin, "Liberalism", in Stuart Hampshire (ed.), *Public and Private Morality,* (Cambridge University Press, 1978).
2. G. A. Cohen, "Capitalism, Freedom and the Proletariat", in Alan Ryan (ed.), *The Idea of Freedom,* (Oxford University Press: Oxford, 1979).
3. Allen Gilbert, "Equality and Social Theory in Rawls' Theory of Justice", *The Occasional Review,* (Autumn, 1978).
4. David Schweickart, "Should Rawls be a Socialist?", *Social Theory and Practice,* Vol. 5, No. 1, (Fall, 1978).
5. Barry Clark and Herbert Gintis, "Rawlsian Justice and Economic Systems", *Philosophy and Public Affairs,* Vol. 7, No. 4, (Summer, 1978).
6. Herbert Gintis, "Communication and Politics: Marxism and the 'Problem' of Liberal Democracy", *Socialist Review,* No. 50–1, (March-June, 1980).
7. Michael Teitelman, "On the Theory of the Practice of the Theory of Justice", *Journal of Chinese Philosophy,* Vol. 5, (1978).
8. Robert Amdur, "Rawls' Theory of Justice—Domestic and International Perspectives", *World Politics,* Vol. 29 (April, 1977).
9. David Gauthier, "The Social Contract as Ideology", *Philosophy and Public Affairs,* Vol. 6, No. 2 (Winter, 1977).
10. David Gauthier, "Justice and Natural Endowment: Toward a Critique of Rawls' Ideological Framework", *Social Theory and Practice,* Vol. 3, No. 1 (Spring, 1974).
11. John Gray, "On Liberty, Liberalism and Essential Contestability", *British Journal of Political Science,* Vol. 8, Part 4 (October, 1978).
12. John Exdell, "Liberty, Equality and Capitalism", *Canadian Journal of Philosophy,* (1981).
13. Allen Gilbert, "Historical Theory and the Structure of Moral Argument in Marx", *Political Theory,* (1981).
14. Virginia Held, "John Locke on Robert Nozick", *Social Research,* Vol. 43, (1976).
15. John D. Hudson, "Nozick, Libertarianism and Rights", *Arizona Law Review,* Vol. 19, No. 1 (1977).
16. H. L. A. Hart, "Between Utility and Rights", Alan Ryan (ed.), *The Idea of Freedom,* (Oxford University Press: Oxford, 1979).
17. Martin J. Sklar, "Liberty and Equality and Socialism", *Socialist Revolution,* Vol. 7, No. 4 (1977).
18. Andrew Collier, "On the Production of Moral Ideology", *Radical Philosophy 9,* (Winter, 1974).
19. Anthony Skillen, "Marxism and Morality", *Radical Philosophy 8,* (Summer, 1974).
20. Peter Binns, "Anti-Moralism", *Radical Philosophy 10,* (Spring, 1975).
21. Gary Young, "Justice and Capitalist Production", *Canadian Journal of Philosophy,* Vol. VIII, No. 3 (September, 1978).
22. Allen Buchanan, "Exploitation, Alienation and Injustice", *Canadian Journal of Philosophy,* Vol. IX, No. 1, (March, 1979).
23. Richard J. Arneson, "What's Wrong with Exploitation?", *Ethics,* Vol. 21, No. 2, (January, 1981).
24. George Lichtheim, "What Socialism Is and Is Not", *The New York Review of Books,* Vol. XIV, (April 9, 1970).
25. Kai Nielsen, "Justice and Ideology: Justice as Ideology", *Windsor Yearbook of Access to Justice,* Vol. 1, No. 1 (1981).
26. Kai Nielsen, "Impediments to Radical Egalitarianism",' *American Philosophical Quarterly,* (1981).
27. Kai Nielsen, "A Rationale For Egalitarianism", *Social Research,* (1981).
28. Kai Nielsen, "Radical Egalitarian Justice: Justice as Equality", *Social Theory and Practice,* Vol. 5, No. 2, (1979).
29. Hilliard Aronovitch, "Marxian Morality", *Canadian Journal of Philosophy* Vol. X, No. 3 (September, 1980).
30. G. A. Cohen, "Freedom, Justice & Capitalism," *New Left Review,* No. 126, (March-April, 1981).
31. Richard W. Miller, "Rights and Reality," *The Philosophical Review,* Vol. XC, No. 3 (July 1981).
32. Ronald Dworkin, "What is Equality?" *Philosophy & Public Affairs,* Vol. 10 (1981).
33. Richard Norman, "Does Equality Destroy Liberty", in Keith Graham (ed.), *New Perspectives in Political Philosophy* (Cambridge University Press, 1982).

chapter twelve

International Human Rights

HUGO ADAM BEDAU

I

§1. INTRODUCTION.

The idea of human rights, popularized throughout the world during the past generation, is not new. Its origins are as old as medieval European moral and political
theory, and the idea was firmly established during the 17th century by Hugo Grotius
(1583–1645), the Dutch legal theorist, and John Locke (1632–1704), the English
philosopher. Their influence—and that of their contemporaries and successors,
especially in the English-speaking world—has been so great that the history of our
legal and political institutions, as well as of our ordinary moral thinking, is unintelligible apart from the doctrines about human rights they forged. Thus we tend to take
human rights for granted in a way that falsifies and disguises their true nature.
Common though human rights (or, at least, talk about them) may be for us today, in
many parts of the world even now they are unknown. Moreover, it is easy to
conceive of societies with otherwise well developed moral ideas in which no place is
accorded to human rights. In fact, describing such societies in some detail is one of
the best ways to understand what a human right is and why they are important.

§2. A SOCIETY WITHOUT RIGHTS.

Consider first a society of persons exactly like us, except that their entire moral code
consists of the Biblical ten commandments: Thou shalt honor thy father and mother,

thou shalt not kill, etc. (See Exodus 20:3–17 for the full list). Let us assume that everyone in this society (henceforth, Society I) is familiar with these rules, accepts them, and knows that everyone else does. Each of these rules in effect consists of a specific command (Do this!) or specific prohibition (Don't do that!). It follows that the members of Society I view everyone's conduct as governed by a set of ten explicit and exceptionless moral rules of categorical significance; since they come from God, they rest on the highest authority. It also follows that everyone in Society I has clear notions of right and wrong: The right thing to do is to obey the rule, the wrong thing is to transgress it; anything not covered by a rule is morally indifferent. Given a few additional assumptions, such a set of rules turns ethical decision-making into a wholly determinate enterprise. From this fact alone we can see, in case we had not noticed, that the moral thinking of persons in Society I is very different from ours.

Chief among the relevant things that are absent from the moral thinking of this society is any conception of persons as creatures with *rights*. Morality, under the acknowledged rules, requires everyone to honor his and her parents, for example; but the idea that the parents have a *right* to the respect of their children is missing. Likewise, morality requires that persons not murder anyone, and that it is morally wrong to do so; but there is no implication that murder is *a wrong,* that it *injures* the victim (that is, not only inflicts harm but does an injustice), or that it *violates the rights* of the victim. Again, morality in this society requires that personal property be respected (cf. the 8th and 9th commandments); but there is no reason to think that this is because property-owners have *rights* in their property. In short, in conceiving of Society I, we are presented with the idea of a society that has a morality, but not a morality that involves a conception of anyone's having any rights. This enables us to see the difference between a conception of morality that contrasts right and wrong conduct, and a more particular moral conception in which having (one or more) rights is contrasted with not having (a or any) rights.

§3. RIGHTS WITHOUT HUMAN RIGHTS.

Now let us consider a second society (hereinafter, Society II) like the first one, but with an important new feature. In Society II persons are understood to have rights, but only under certain conditions; as a consequence, given any right, some persons will have it and others (perhaps most others) will lack it. For instance, employees can claim rights against their employers, and vice versa; but no one else has those rights. Property owners can point to their rights as they prohibit use of their land by trespassers; but those without property have no such rights. If you and I make an agreement in Society II, then each of us has certain rights under it (you, perhaps, to a certain sum of money from me, and I to a certain performance on your part). But no one else has such rights, unless they are also parties to a similar agreement. We could even imagine in addition that Society II includes a caste structure, according to which members of any given caste claim rights of deference and authority over the members of every lower class; members of the lowest caste would thus have no caste-rights or claims based on caste-rights against anyone else.

In Society II, therefore, a vast array of human relations—economic, social, legal, political—are governed from the moral point of view by the rights that one person can claim against another. Even the Do's and Don'ts generated by the basic commandments that Society I and II both accept might be explained in Society II by reference to the rights of persons. Thus, the commandment against theft could be explained in Society II (but not in Society I) by reference to the way theft violates the property-owner's rights to his property.

The distinctive thing about these rights, however, is that in every case they arise out of *special* circumstances, such as particular transactions between individual persons (buying, marrying, contracting, etc.) or particular social relationships in which given persons stand to one another (caste, family, employment, etc.). Accordingly, the rights any person holds are subject to loss as a consequence of a change in status, such as divorce, disinheritance, or demotion. No rights in Society II are immune or invulnerable to changing social and institutional relationships. Persons who lack or lose the status cannot acquire or keep the rights in question.

Understandably, rights such as these have been called "special" rights.[1] If the theory of human rights is correct, not all rights are special. There are some rights— not in Society II, however, as we have seen—that are held by *all* persons regardless of their status or other socio-economic contingencies. How this can be so, and what these rights are, are questions to which we will shortly turn.

§4. THE PREFERABILITY OF LIFE IN A SOCIETY WITH HUMAN RIGHTS

It seems natural to suggest that a society that lacks rights is morally inferior to a society that has rights, that is, that has a conception of rights, acknowledges that persons have rights, and seeks to enforce valid claims of rights. Similarly, it seems natural to suggest that a society that has only special rights and thus lacks any conception of human rights is morally inferior to a society that has such a conception, acknowledges that persons have human rights, and enforces claims made properly on that basis. It is easy to see why one might take such views about the way in which granting a role for rights enhances a society's moral tone. This is especially plain when the moral quality of a society is seen and evaluated from the perspective of any individual in it, taken at random.

With a right, a person has a basis for claiming deference to his own will—non-interference by others, protection for his interests, certain benefits to which he is entitled, and remedy when these entitlements are violated or ignored. His right is a moral shield against others who would thwart his interests, and a moral sword with which he can carve out a fair share of whatever it is to which he has the right. This is equally true whether we are speaking of a special right or a basic human right. But if all rights are special, and none is a human right as such, then it is possible for some persons (the ones who have no or only a few special rights) to be bereft of this shield and this sword in their dealings with neighbors, associates, and strangers. Thus it seems reasonable, other things being equal, to prefer to live in a society that acknowledges *some* rights rather than in a society that acknowledges none: You might be fortunate enough to be one of the persons who acquires one or more of these rights. By the same token, it seems preferable to be a member of a society that acknowledges *human* rights rather than of a society that acknowledges only special rights: No matter how badly circumstances might treat you during the course of your life, you would never be without the status and protection afforded by those rights. As one philosopher has remarked, "one ought to be able to claim as entitlements [that is, as human rights] those minimal things without which it is impossible to develop one's capabilities and to live a life as a human being."[2]

A critic of the doctrine of human rights could validly raise two objections to the foregoing that tarnish, even if they do not completely mar, the initial lustre on the position being defended here. First, it could be argued that it matters little to the victim of neglect, misfortune, and the violence of others that he can complain of his rights being violated or neglected, since in all such cases he could complain equally rigorously that he suffers grave harms of various sorts. That is, he can adequately characterize his misery and discomfort in moral terms without having to invoke any appeal to his *rights*. Furthermore, the objection might continue, preference for a society that takes human rights seriously must depend to a considerable extent on *what* rights are claimed, acknowledged, and enforced. Rights would look must less attractive to even their most ardent advocates if children could claim them against their parents, but never the reverse; or if trees and stones had rights but persons and other living creatures didn't; or if each of us had a right to step on cracks in the sidewalk but none of us had any right to own property.

These two objections must both be conceded in principle; but they do not establish anything very troublesome for the theorist of human rights. The second objection can be blunted by pointing out that there is no likelihood of our ever encountering a society in which such a bizarre pattern of rights exists. The reason is that rights are intimately connected with claims *persons* can make, claims that derive from or presuppose both the capacity to *act* and the consciousness of *interests* in need of protection and implementation. Stones, trees, and young children (as opposed to their parents) do not satisfy these conditions. The first objection is misleading, since it remains true that the point of human rights talk is not to accomplish something that no other kind of moral talk can do. Its purpose is to help depict human relationships in a distinctive way, not solely or primarily because certain benefits accrue to us that way, but because the alternative pictures of our condition and circumstances, those that deny or ignore our rights, seem shallow and false.

II

§5. THE ELEMENTS OF A THEORY OF HUMAN RIGHTS

Human rights, like other moral concepts, do not grow on trees, so they cannot be harvested and scrutinized for their fine structure by any of the means known to empirical (behavioral or physical) science. They are creatures of ethical theories, and so it is to ethical theories that we must look if we are to understand what human rights are. As we have seen, it is possible to conceive of societies in which no one has any rights (§2), as well as of societies in which no one has any human rights (§3). Yet in both types of society, as we have also seen, persons could evaluate their conduct by reference to the moral concepts and rules they do acknowledge. It follows that there must be moral theories—however primitive and inadequate they may be—that make no reference to, have no use for, human rights. Such theories lack the concept of a human right; they do not admit of the characterization of any moral status or relation between persons in its terms. This suggests that it is important (at least for moral philosophers) to ask what an ethical theory would be like that did include a prominent role for human rights. In particular, what would the human rights portion of an ethical theory have to be like if the theory were to make intelligible and persuasive the moral claims in terms of human rights that those who accepted this theory would want to make? Conversely, given a doctrine of human rights, what sort of ethical theory is needed to explain and rationalize such a doctrine?

It is fairly clear that a theory of human rights would have to include many things, and at a minimum the following: (a) a conception of human rights, including an account of what it is for something to be a human right as distinct from some other kind of right; (b) an exhaustive list of particular human rights, or at least a criterion by means of which we can determine whether any given substantive claim of human rights is genuine, spurious, or borderline; (c) a taxonomy of types or categories into which human rights can be sorted; (d) an account of how these rights arise, where they come from, the factors that shape their content and structure; (e) a specification of the role human rights play in the overall moral theory of which they are a part, e.g., how our rights are related to our moral principles, obligations, and responsibilities;

(f) an account of why some rights are more basic or fundamental than others, so that priorities among human rights can be established and the relative gravity of their neglect or violation evaluated; (g) the legal and political institutions that must be created and maintained if these rights are to be effective and secure in the lives of those who have them.

This is a tall order, and it is doubtful whether there is any theory of human rights presently available that meets all these requirements. What follows, therefore, can be expected to supply these desiderata in only a provisional manner.

§6. WHAT HUMAN RIGHTS DO WE HAVE?

Let us start in the middle of things by considering what human rights we have. Lists of such rights abound; one of the briefest and certainly the most familiar is the one in our own Declaration of Independence (1776): "life, liberty, and the pursuit of happiness." Another list, more elaborate, somewhat less familiar, and far more important to us now—unlike the Declaration it is part of the fundamental law of the land—is the Bill of Rights (1789), the first ten amendments to the federal constitution.* In less than five hundred words, the Bill of Rights enumerates thirty or so activities and conditions, each of which is prohibited (because it would violate the rights of persons) or is to be allowed to anyone desiring it (because it is within the rights of persons). Thanks to later amendments, notably the fourteenth (1867), and to judicial interpretation by the Supreme Court, these rights (albeit originally addressed to Congress in particular and by implication to the federal government exclusively) apply to all "persons" anywhere in the United States, citizen or not, and state governments as well must respect them. Thus they amount to *human* rights recognized by *national* constitutional law.

Another list, much longer, better known elsewhere in the world, and far more recent, but lacking the status of domestic constitutional law in any nation,† is the United Nations' Declaration of Human Rights (1948), a product of the early years of the UN's General Assembly and developed by an international Commission of scholars and experts from many fields. Divided into thirty articles, this manifesto is perhaps the best list of international human rights currently available. All of the problems involved in developing an adequate theory of human rights can be illustrated by reference to the over seventy rights cited in this Declaration. Whatever may turn out to be, on examination, the obscure or questionable features of this Declaration, (see below, part V), it must be regarded as the triumphant product of several centuries of political, legal, and moral inquiry into the basic elements of what the Preamble to the Declaration rights calls "the dignity and worth of the human person."

Philosophers, however, at least in recent years, have been much less generous in identifying human rights than the writers of constitutions and manifestos have been. Some years ago, the English legal philosopher H. L. A. Hart defended the view that there is only one basic human right, "the equal right of all men to be free."[4] More recently, the American philosopher, A. I. Melden has agreed there is only one basic human right, but he characterized it as "the right [of persons] to conduct their own

---

*There are, of course, other federal constitutional rights besides those in the Bill of Rights, but they need not be considered here.
†The status of the Declaration in international law is a complicated matter, and it might be argued that the more recent Covenants (on Economic, Social, and Cultural Rights; on Civil and Political Rights; on the Elimination of All Forms of Racial Discrimination) adopted by the General Assembly, are now of more significance because of the mere handful of "third-world" countries that voted in 1948 on the Declaration.[3]

292   Hugo Adam Bedau

affairs in the pursuit of their interests.''⁵ John Rawls, in his important philosophical treatise, *A Theory of Justice* (1971), proposed no human rights at all, although it has been argued that at the basis of his entire theory there lies one such tacit right, viz. the right of all persons "to equal concern and respect in the design and administration of the political institutions that govern them."⁶

§7. *PHILOSOPHERS VS. POLITICIANS ON HUMAN RIGHTS*

Why have philosophers been so stingy when writers of constitutions and manifestos (let us call them politicians) have been so generous in the number and variety of human rights they have recognized? There are three explanations, and each sheds some light on the answer. The first possibility is simply that one of the two positions is wrong. Either the philosophers are wrong for failing to recognize more than one human right (their theories are deficient, they have overlooked good arguments for more human rights, etc.); or the politicians are wrong in describing so many different things as human rights (the fact that in a manifesto or a constitution you don't have to give any argument for what you include, much less any consistent and persuasive set of reasons, helps conceal this from the authors of such documents as well as from their audiences).

A second possibility is that neither position is in error, because the more fully developed lists of human rights prepared by politicians can in fact be derived from the germinal human right that philosophers have identified. The chief purpose of the philosopher has been to find a formulation of a really basic human right that is clearly implied by sound premises, whereas the chief purpose of political writers has been to help the common man, lawyers, courts, and legislatures to see the general limits and responsibility of government. Accordingly, the two purposes dictate different strategies and a different characterization of human rights, but no inconsistencies.

There is something to be said for each of these explanations; but neither provides the full answer. The first reason may be more correct than we might like to admit, since it is very doubtful that we could derive the full list of human rights cited in the UN Declaration or even in the Bill of Rights from the central and solitary human right identified by Hart, Melden, or Rawls. Several further assumptions, which these philosophers would be unlikely to grant, would be required. If the longer political lists cannot be derived from the shorter philosophical lists, then it is distinctly possible that each list is inadequate as it stands.

But there is a third possibility, and it is likely to appear more convincing the more we study it. Both politicians and philosophers may be correct after all, with the apparent inconsistency between their lists explained away by the fact that philosophers have in mind, if only tacitly, a much more restricted conception of what counts as a human right than do those who draft and popularize manifestos and constitutions. In a word, the philosopher typically thinks of the human right that he acknowledges in his moral theory in a different way. He regards it as *absolute*, inalienable, unforfeitable, and unwaivable. Below (§16), we shall examine these standard epithets more closely, and show how human rights as we find them in, say, the UN Declaration, cannot be conceived to have these traits. If we want to avail ourselves of this third possibility, we must allow that the terms, 'human right,' 'basic right,' 'natural right,' are somewhat ambiguous, and that what philosophers have come to mean by them is not identical with what other writers have meant by them. This would hardly be an unprecedented discovery; we know we cannot infer that different writers always mean the same thing when they use the same words. At any rate, this third possibility, which would allow us more nearly to reconcile the views in our context of philosophers with those of non-philosophers, deserves serious consideration.

This is not to deny that there are genuine disagreements among philosophers, and between philosophical doctrines and political documents, over exactly what our human rights are. But explanations that draw attention to different purposes (and even different meanings) may go most of the way toward accounting for the discrepancies in the number of human rights supplied by philosophers as opposed to those cited by more popular (political, legal) writers.

§8. ARE THERE TYPES OF HUMAN RIGHTS?

Rights, including human rights, are not all of one type; it is useful to see how they are alike and unlike, lest we be caught too firmly in the grip of some one kind of right and, unawares, take it to be the basis for interpreting the logic of all human rights. If one glances over lists of human rights, such as those cited earlier (§6), one will discover three main categories.

One group is typified by the First Amendment right of Americans, to the effect that "Congress shall make no law . . . abridging the freedom of . . . the press," and by the provision of Article 15 (1) in the UN Declaration that "No one shall be arbitrarily deprived of his nationality . . ." In both cases, the language quoted is intended to express a limitation on the authority of government to do things that interfere with the *liberty* or freedom of the person to do as he or she wishes (viz., worship, publish). The implication in each case is that governments are to be deprived of this authority because otherwise they would interfere with persons in ways that would violate their basic rights.

A second group of rights is typified by the Fifteenth Amendment to the federal constitution, declaring "the right of citizens . . . to vote shall not be denied or abridged . . . on account of race," and the more encompassing language of Article 21 (1) of the UN Declaration: "Everyone has the right to take part in the government of his country." In both cases, what is asserted or implied is that persons shall not be excluded from the political decision-making process in their own countries; they have the right *to participate* in a certain activity, viz., self-government.

A third group of rights is typified by the Sixth Amendment provision that "In all criminal prosecutions, the accused shall enjoy the right to a speedy and public trial," and by Article 25 (1) of the UN Declaration, which says that "Everyone has the right to a standard of living adequate for the health and well being of himself and of his family . . ." This type of right is intended to guarantee the creation and maintenance of certain *institutions* in terms of which a wide range of human affairs (viz., criminal justice, the economy) are to be managed.

The three types of rights illustrated above (there may be others; these three are not meant to be either an exhaustive or an exclusive taxonomy) are often called, respectively, civil liberties, civil rights, and welfare or socio-economic rights. Any theory of human rights is likely to have some rights of each of these types. Some philosophers have argued that civil liberties are "negative" rights, and that as such they are the more basic.[7] Others have suggested that the history of human rights indicate a rough progression that starts with a people and its government recognizing first the civil liberties, then the civil rights, and finally the socio-economic rights.[8] These are interesting claims, but we must ignore them here. Suffice it to say that if human rights are adequately illustrated by such documents as the Bill of Rights and the UN Declaration, then not all human rights have the same central purpose or aim. Rather, they arise out of and are addressed to different kinds of considerations, and so require different types of institutions and enforcement procedures under law if they are to be secured.

§9. THE IMPORTANCE OF TYPES OF HUMAN RIGHTS

How significant is the distinction among the three types of rights illustrated above? This question raises two others—the degree to which a society can acknowledge one sort of right without also acknowledging rights of the other two sorts, and whether a right's being of one type rather than another tells us something about its importance.

Suppose a person said to you each of the following things: (a)'Leave me alone to do as I please; I'm not harming anyone.' (b) 'Give me a voice in determining how and what you decide you are going to do in all those things you do that affect me.' (c) 'Arrange the distribution of the resources at your disposal so that if I want some of them, there will be some for me to have. ' The differences among these three remarks are roughly equivalent to the differences, respectively, among the three types of rights outlined in §8. It is clear that under most interpretations it is possible to comply with (a) without also complying with (b) and (c); (b) and (c) are similarly independent of each other and of (a). But it is also clear that someone with power over another is not always likely to grant either (a) or (c) even if the other person demands them; therefore (b) seems more important than either (a) or (c), since it may underlie the willingness to respond in a manner that conforms to (a) and (c). Yet, one might also argue, unless the request (c) is granted first, there may be little or no opportunity for someone who wants to request either (a) or (b) to do so; so (c) looks the most important. And it is not difficult to think of a similar argument that would elevate (a) over both (b) and (c). In short, although it is possible to distinguish the meaning of the remarks (a), (b), and (c) from each other, and to conceive of a world in which one, but not the other two, was generally complied with, empirically-speaking there is good reason to believe that compliance with each is tied to compliance with the other two.

The application of this reasoning to our initial question above is straightforward. A society that ignores civil liberties (cf. the point of remark (a) above) is in fact likely to violate the civil rights of its members (cf. (b)) and flout as well the human rights persons have to institutions that provide essential services (cf. (c)). For this reason, it is undesirable to make too much of the conceptual distinctions among the types of human rights discussed here.

A shorter answer will have to suffice for the second question. If rights can be ordered by their relative importance at all, it is not clear why this ranking should be done by reference to their type. (To advert to the example above, with the three types of requests, is there any reason to believe that a request of type (a) is always more important or more fundamental than a request of type (b) or type (c), or vice versa?) It is far more likely that a ranking of relative importance will have to be done by reference to the *content* of the right, the kind of thing or activity that the right protects. Thinkers who write within the western liberal tradition tend to attach most importance to civil liberties and least importance to welfare rights. But if such a ranking is correct, it is not likely to derive from the fact that these rights are of different types, but rather from the fact that some of the rights concern things that are more basic than what the other rights concern, in the obvious way that the right not to be tortured is more basic than the right to belong to a political party, and the right to enough to eat more basic than the right to free public education.

§10. WHERE DOES ONE HUMAN RIGHT END AND ANOTHER BEGIN?

Individuating human rights, so that each can be given explicit formulation exclusive of others, is something more easily imagined than accomplished. The problem can be illustrated by examining the classic *right to life*. Every theory of human rights and every manifesto in which human rights have been asserted mentions this right. But in what does it consist, exactly? What is the right to life a right *to*? or *from*?

For Thomas Jefferson, one commentator asserted, it was "the right not to be deprived of life."[9] If so, then it appears the right to life could be exhaustively specified in terms of the moral and legal wrongfulness of murder. On this view, our right to life is what lies behind our conviction that murder is a crime; but that is all. During the past century, however, other thinkers have offered very different views: "the right to be let alone," "the right to a minimum subsistence," "the right to work"—each has been said to be part of or implied by our basic right to life.[10] One is tempted to say that the right to life has proved to be a portmanteau concept, in the sense that a large set of what appear to be more specific rights can be packed into it, and that these more specific rights bear on a wide range of conditions under which human life may be prevented, terminated, preserved, or fulfilled. Thus, what began as a single right, abstractly stated (the right to life), ends up as a dozen or more rights, with the somewhat paradoxical result that a right to *one* thing, "life," is indistinguishable from a host of more specific rights to *many different* things.

There are several ways to cope with this apparent paradox and proliferation. One way, of course, is to insist that anyone who thinks that the right to minimum subsistence is *part* of the right to life, is simply wrong. The right to life is one thing, the right to work and to have minimal subsistence are different things altogether; the latter are neither implied by nor parts of the former. (Some would press this line of objection even further and deny that the latter are human rights at all, but we may ignore this here.) A second line of argument is that the talk about certain rights being implied by or being part of the right to life is simply a product of confusion, a confusion that arises out of the truth that the right to life is *presupposed* by having the right to work or to minimum subsistence. A person (so this argument goes) could not have or claim the right to work unless he already had the right to life (just as he could not claim the right to work unless he were already alive). Thus, some rights (R_2) presuppose other rights (R_1), though there is no reason in this for going on to say that when R_2 presupposes R_1, it must be because R_2 is part of R_1, or because R_1 implies R_2. Yet a third argument here might concede that the original claim of implication (if not of inclusion) is correct: If a person has the right to life, then he has the right to whatever means are in fact necessary to exercise that right. Since work and minimal subsistence are necessary to the exercise of the right to live, the right to life implies work and minimal subsistence as matters of right.

What is common to all three of these very different positions is that the right to life is taken to be conceptually distinguishable from all these other rights, whatever its relation (empirical or conceptual) to them may be. To make good on this assumption certain criteria are needed for determining when verbally or conceptually distinguishable entities (call them 'R_1' and 'R_2') are such that one (R_1) presupposes the other (R_2) but not the converse, implies the other, is part of the other, is a necessary condition of the other, or is wholly distinct from the other. Notice that this, like so much else we encounter in this discussion, is a problem of rights theories generally; it is not peculiar to theories of *human* rights. Anything less than a full-scale theory of rights, human and otherwise, is not likely to be able to provide such criteria.

What has been illustrated here with the right to life can be replicated with any of the classic "natural" rights, such as the right to liberty, security of person, and property. Does it matter? Should it count as a defect in a theory of human rights if the theory does not give an explicit, exhaustive, and exclusive list of all and only the human rights we have? One might argue that it doesn't, because there is no one fixed standpoint from which to view what our rights are, and so no reason to expect a theory of human rights to generate a canonical list, on the model of a tidy set of axioms which together are complete, independent, and consistent. What is needed is a working criterion of human rights, something that will enable us to tell in any given case whether or not a certain pattern of conduct, or a certain kind of act, is within one's human rights, or is a violation of someone's human rights. Exactly *which* right it is, or violates, and whether it is a part of or implied by a given right, are not by themselves very important questions; the answers in any case will turn on which of several possible ways one might choose to formulate the issues. Whether the right to life includes a right to breathe, or implies such a right, or whether it includes or implies breathing but no right to breathe, or whether we have equally basic rights to live and to breathe, are questions that turn on what is the most useful way to see the distinctions and connections in the fabric of human life and in socio-economic relations.

§11. HUMAN RIGHTS AND DUTIES

Philosophically, one of the most challenging issues concerning the nature of human rights is how they are related to *duties,* and in particular whether every human right in fact can be "reduced" to one or more duties of other persons. The issue can be illustrated by reference to a classic divergence of position between Hobbes and Bentham.

Thomas Hobbes (1588–1679) took the position that everyone has exactly one "natural" right, viz., the right to do whatever the person judges to be conducive to his life and well-being. He also held that anyone could acquire special rights under certain conditions. He drew attention to the way in which contracting with another person could create a pair of rights at the same time that it created a pair of duties. Thus, when you and I agree in writing that for a certain sum from me, you will build a garage for my house by a certain date, you acquire the right from me to that sum and impose on yourself the duty to build the garage by the date. Concurrently, I impose on myself the duty to pay you the sum and acquire from you the right to have the garage built by the date specified. In such a case, the rights and duties are inseparably correlated; I cannot have the right unless you have the duty, and vice versa. In fact, my right and your duty are the same thing seen from opposite sides. But this is not true of my "natural" right. There is no duty on anyone anywhere (in Hobbes's theory, not even a duty of non-interference with me) that coordinates with my right. So, on Hobbes's view, even if there is one type of right (special rights) that is unintelligible apart from a duty, there is another type of right—our "natural" right—that isn't. Exactly the same view is held by H. L. A. Hart; all persons, he argues, have a natural right of freedom to which no duties are correlated; it is this right, he says, that lies at the basis of all economic competition.[11]

Jeremy Bentham (1748–1832) attacked the doctrine of "natural" rights with many weapons, one of which was that there is "no right without a correspondent obligation."[12] "It is by imposing obligations," as he put it elsewhere in his writings, "that rights are established or granted."[13] If this is true of human rights, then it must be possible to express everything contained in that idea in terms of obligations or duties on others, in which case there is no reason we should even mention, much less stress, human *rights,* except to look at situations from the standpoint of possible or actual victims, or of potential beneficiaries, of these duties. We would do as well or better to look at things from the standpoint of possible or actual violators, and speak exclusively of human *duties* and the importance of performing them, because the duties come first.*

*In this connection, it is interesting to note that the one contemporary philosopher who devotes attention to developing a list of "natural duties" happens also to be a philosopher who neglects any role for human rights in his theory: John Rawls (recall, however, §6). See his *Theory of Justice* (1971), §19.

Most philosophers, however, do not take a position as extreme as Bentham's. Instead, they insist only that with every right, special or human, there is one or more duties "correlated" with it. (If a duty D merely correlates with a right R, then it is unreasonable to regard D as more basic than R just as it would be silly to try to reduce my being tall to your being short: either we have both or neither.) Thus, in his recent extensive discussion of *Basic Rights,* Henry Shue insists that every basic human right has "correlated" with it three types of duties: Duties to *avoid* depriving a person of his rights, duties to *protect* persons from such deprivations by others, and duties to *aid* the victims of past deprivations.[14] This emphasis on duties is meant to avoid leaving the defense of human rights in a vacuum, bereft of any moral significance for the specific conduct of others. But the duties are not intended to explain or generate the rights; if anything, the rights are supposed to explain and generate the duties—though one might also say that the two are strictly inseparable.

We have, then, four distinct possible positions: (i) There are human rights to which no duties of anyone are correlated; (ii) there are human rights that generate duties on others; (iii) there are human rights, and there are human duties, each as fundamental or basic as the other; (iv) human rights are but the shadows cast by human duties, which come first and remain the fundamental entities.

Which of these views, or which combination, is the best way to develop a theory of human rights has yet to be resolved.

III

Let us now try to state in a more systematic way what it is that makes a right a *human* right, rather than some other kind of right, or some other kind of moral concept altogether. There is a minimum of four major factors that must be examined closely.

§12. HUMAN RIGHTS AS MORAL RIGHTS

First, human rights are unquestionably *moral* rights. This means not so much that there is another species of rights, the immoral or amoral ones, but that there are certain principles or norms, warranted from the moral point of view, which underlie human rights. Persons have the human rights they do because these rights are entailed by certain moral principles or norms. Having a human right, therefore, is not anything that can be established merely by asserting or claiming something as a human right, nor are the human rights you and I have a matter of taste or opinion. They are a matter of what is entailed by an adequate moral theory.

In addition, the fact that human rights are moral rights allows them to be contrasted with *legal* rights. Unlike legal rights, human rights do not evaporate or come into being as a direct consequence of changes in positive law, whether common-law, statutory, or constitutional. No legislature or court, dictator or junta can modify my human rights or add or subtract from them. All that the law can do is recognize or ignore these rights; all that governments can do is honor or violate them. Because human rights are moral rights, a government's failure to enforce them under law does not constitute evidence that its citizens do not have these rights; such a failure of enforcement would indicate that persons probably do not have these rights as legal rights. (A legal right without legal guarantees and legal remedies for its violation is a very strange thing, indeed.) Because human rights are moral rights, governments and legal systems ought to recognize and accord these rights to all persons.

§13. HUMAN RIGHTS AS UNIVERSAL RIGHTS

Second, human rights are *universal* rights; this much is evident from the very title of the UN Declaration. It was also plain to earlier writers, such as Sir William Blackstone (1723–1780), the great authority on English law; he spoke of "the rights of persons," admirably protected (so he thought) by English criminal law, as "the rights of all mankind."[15] Special rights, as we have seen (recall §2), are confined to persons who bear a certain title, hold a certain status, or are party to a special transaction. Human rights, by contrast, belong to all members of the species regardless of the natural and socio-economic factors that divide them. Differences in sex, age, race, color, wealth, intelligence, talent, etc., are no bar to having human rights. No right could count as a human right if the question could arise whether a given human being has it. However much egalitarianism—the ideal of human equality—may seem of dubious validity or be on the defensive, every theory of human rights is tacitly committed to a doctrine of equal rights: There are no two human beings such that one could have more or better human rights than the other (though, of course, one might have them better protected than the other).

One of the classic objections to human rights stems directly from this egalitarianism or universality. Bentham argued "in regard to most rights, it is true that what is every man's right is no man's right."[16] His point seemed to be that if I have a right to a given piece of land, and if the doctrine of equal rights entails that you have an equal right to the same land, then either we share rights in the land (and so neither of us has an exclusive right in it) or our claims of right will lead only to conflict and confusion. But this is the result of a deliberately perverse interpretation by Bentham of the concept of equal human rights, and of a special kind of example. If 'equal rights' means you and I have an *equal right to* do, say, or have something, then in most cases there will be no paradox at all. If I have the right to vote, and you do, too, each of us can have the *same* right as the other without any paradox. The same is true with most of our equal rights; either we can take turns in exercising them (as in exercising the right to speak from a given platform) or we can exercise them concurrently and without conflict (as in exercising the right to vote or to worship). However, if 'equal rights' means you and I have a *right to equal* shares, or to the very same thing, then paradox may well result (as it would in the property example above). But there is little reason ever to interpret the claim of equal rights so that it yields this paradox.

§14. WHO HAS HUMAN RIGHTS?

Some questions of interpretation do arise at another point, however. Are human rights to be thought of as possessed by all and only *persons, human beings,* or *human persons*? On the first alternative, some animals ("smart" chimpanzees, for instance), androids, and non-human "intelligences" from outer space—if there are any—might turn out to have human rights. On the last alternative, human fetuses and severely retarded adults might lack human rights. On the middle alternative neither of these results is likely to occur, and so it is the least controversial way to resolve the problem. The concept of human rights was not designed to embrace non-human persons, and it was clearly intended to exclude infra-human beings, such as animals. The nonviable human fetus is the most troubling real-life (as distinct from science fiction) type of borderline case, because each of us was once one. Suffice it to say here that it is very doubtful whether any light can be shed on the abortion controversy by appealing to the concept of human rights, and the right to life in particular. This right was never designed to deal with the abortion issue, and is unlikely to persuade any defender of abortion to change her convictions.

§15. WHY DO HUMAN BEINGS HAVE HUMAN RIGHTS?

What it is about all and only human beings that makes it true that we all have the same complement of rights is not easy to say, and philosophers have defended very different answers. Three centuries ago, during the hey-day of the "natural" rights philosophy, the explanation would have been formulated in terms of man's *essence*. Even if this were an acceptable answer, it is incomplete: one wants to know what it is about man's essence that gives rise to rights. Some philosophers such as Jacques Maritain (1933–1973), have pointed directly to God—His will and creation of man— as the answer. Others have tried to identify in a more empirical manner the distinctive features of man's essence that are relevant to the possession and exercise of rights. Thus, the *capacity to feel pain*—no doubt an important fact about human beings—is often cited as the relevant factor; certainly, there is no doubt that protecting human rights will reduce the duration, intensity, and frequency with which people are in pain. But this factor cannot be decisive because it is shared with the whole of the animal kingdom (and in fact this has led some philosophers to argue that non-human animals, too, have rights). A more distinctive trait of humanity and the one traditionally associated with man's essence is *rationality*. Yet the standards of minimal rationality are not clear, and insofar as they are it is doubtful whether all and only human beings meet them; it is certain that no human being meets them during the whole of a lifetime. Philosophers inspired by the Kantian moral tradition are likely to cite the *autonomy* of persons, the distinctive capacity of persons to deliberate, choose, and act as self-ruling agents. But this, too, looks both overly broad and disappointingly narrow once it is carefully scrutinized. As for the ultimate court of appeal—the *intrinsic worth* of all persons—this simply begs the entire question. It is not, of course, that we are better advised to think of persons as lacking intrinsic worth. It is rather that there seems little point in trying to explain our human rights in this way, since our alleged intrinsic worth is hardly less in need of explanation itself. Why not stop one step earlier, and take human rights as self-explanatory and self-generating?

A different view of the matter would be to regard any doctrine of human rights as an expression of, and thus rooted in, a general moral conception of human life. In this conception, no human beings are excluded from its scope, and there are no special or unique features of human beings to be cited as *the* point of origin or ground for human rights. "Instead of looking for a basis for human rights, we need to see more clearly and in its rich and complex detail just what it is for persons to have the rights they have as human beings. It is here that all explanations come to an end." [17]

§16. HUMAN RIGHTS AS UNCONDITIONAL RIGHTS

Third, human rights are said to be *unconditional* rights. They arise, as we have seen, out of our "nature," as human beings, rather than out of anything special, local, transitory, or contingent. Traditional "natural" rights theories characterized the unconditional status of human rights by various epithets, still current today, such as "inalienable," "indefeasible," "imprescriptible," and "absolute." Each of these attributes leaves problems in its wake, however, and it is worth seeing why.

According to the philosophers of the 17th and 18th centuries, a right is inalienable if and only if the right-holder either cannot or morally ought not to transfer it, by gift, sale, or deed, to another, so that what began as A's right to do *x* (or to decide whether or not to do *x*) becomes B's right to do *x* (or to make A do *x* if B so desires). The classic example of an inalienable right is the right to liberty. In a day when slavery was common, the doctrine that the right to liberty was inalienable was a potentially revolutionary idea (cf. §20 below). However, given the two tests of inalienability above, it is easy to see only that liberty satisfies at most one of them. Liberty can be alienated—a person can, in fact, do what it takes to enslave himself to another, voluntarily; so the most that can be claimed is that it would be morally wrong to do so. Today, most of us would agree with this judgment; we would disagree, if at all, only over *why* it would be morally wrong to enslave oneself. (To explain this by appeal to the human right of liberty would be circular, of course, since it is the unconditional feature of this right that we are trying to explain by reference to its alleged inalienability!)

The reason earlier rights theorists had for holding that it was morally wrong to alienate one's liberty was that God had put men under a duty which would be violated if they chose to enslave themselves, or allowed themselves to be enslaved by others. Today, anyone would be quick to see that such a defense of inalienable rights depends on a religious metaphysics that seriously weakens the probative value of the argument. If we subtract it, however, we are left with only those cases of inalienable rights that rest on the (logical and physical) impossibility of alienation. But are there any such rights? It is doubtful whether any of our most important rights, including life, liberty, and bodily security, are impossible to alienate. So describing human rights as inalienable is likely either to be false, or to require a severe narrowing of the range of rights that count as human, or to be a not very helpful way of saying that these rights ought not to be alienated.

Similar problems arise when human rights are described as "imprescriptible." The French Declaration of the Rights of Man and Citizen (1789), a rallying point of the French Revolution, proclaimed the rights therein cited as "imprescriptible." Bentham, one of the Declaration's severest critics, gleefully pointed out that this epithet creates a dilemma for those who embrace it. If it means that a right *cannot* be abrogated, suspended, repudiated, or ignored by government, then this is "rhetorical nonsense." Any government in fact *can* (and most of them do even today) abrogate, suspend, repudiate, or ignore rights at sometime or another. So such rights can be prescripted; therefore, they are not imprescriptible. If, however, it means that a right *ought not* to be abrogated, then it all depends on what the right is a right to, and what the social consequences will be over time from acknowledging this right in law. By this criterion Bentham had what he regarded as conclusive reasons for the view that nothing cited as a right in the Declaration of '89 ought to be described as "imprescriptible." Exactly the same dilemma awaits the claim that human rights are "indefeasible," i.e., that nothing can or ought to defeat or override them. The details of Bentham's argument need not trouble us here, for they are not very convincing except to other positivistic utilitarians. But the general form of his objection does suggest that the theory of human rights is not illuminated by trying to explain why human rights are unconditional by reference to their "imprescriptible" or "indefeasible" nature.

§17. ARE ANY HUMAN RIGHTS ABSOLUTE?

Another tempting but even more troublesome epithet is "absolute." To say that a human right is absolute is to say that there are no conditions under which it could be morally right for other persons intentionally to refuse to act on, honor, support, prevent interference with or the neglect of, the exercise of this right by someone who wants to exercise it. This seems to be too strong, for several different reasons.

One is that it is difficult to conceive of two or more absolute human rights. Certainly, the dozens of rights listed in the UN Declaration cannot all be absolute, because we have no assurance that they won't lead to conflicts with each other. There is no guarantee in describing what I do or have as something protected by one of my human rights that it cannot possibly conflict with something you do or have that can be described in the same way. The more human rights we acknowledge, the greater the likelihood that at least under some conditions such a conflict might arise. Think, for example, of the possible conflict of rights that occurs in the case of the pregnant woman who wants an abortion: she claims an "absolute" human right to do with her body as she wishes, but this conflicts with the "absolute" human right of the fetus—if fetuses do have human rights (recall §13)—to live.

Second, even if we look at a human right that is often thought, above all others, to have a claim to be absolute—the right of bodily security that torture violates—we can think of a morally acceptable exception. Suppose someone has constructed and cleverly hidden a "doomsday" machine, and set it to go off in a few hours, unless we do what he says. What he says is that we must let him torture ten people chosen at random. Would we refuse to torture *him,* if we could, for the sole purpose of extracting an account of where his machine was hidden and, if possible, of how to defuse it in time? If we did proceed to torture him, would we acknowledge that we had deliberately violated an *absolute* right of his? If we did, what compensation or remedy would we think it proper for us to provide for this deliberate violation?

Third, the practice of punishment seems to pose an insurmountable problem. By definition, a punishment is the sort of thing that deprives a person of one or more of his rights. Thus, imprisonment deprives a person of his liberty, and being justly sentenced to prison as punishment deprives a person of his right to liberty for the period of his sentence. If, therefore, punishment is ever justified, and if we have a human right to liberty—as we are assured on every side that we do—then there must be conditions under which the punished person cannot appeal to his human rights to nullify the legitimacy of the treatment he is undergoing. His right to liberty can not be an absolute human right. The traditional theory of "natural" rights would cope with this argument (as it would with the previous one) by appealing to the concept of *forfeiture* of rights. A person who violates another's rights is said to forfeit his own. Whatever merits this move may have, it is an odd way to defend the idea of human rights as absolute. It seems much more plausible to infer that if a right can be forfeited, then it was not absolute in the first place. Rather, it was contingent or *prima facie,* that is, a right that should be honored and protected by those in a position to violate or neglect it, provided that no other countervailing and superior moral consideration indicates otherwise. Disarming the "doomsday" machine and punishing the guilty are just such superior moral considerations.

Human rights are also inseparably connected with the idea that there must be "due process of law"—fair and equal treatment under the laws and legal institutions of the country—before anyone can be rightfully deprived of his human rights. And so one might seize on this idea as a way of trying to capture the unconditional nature of human rights. The problem here, however, is that *any* right, special or human, seems deserving of protection against all violations except those authorized by due process of law. At least, this is how the United States' Constitution has been applied to the rights of persons subject to its authority.

§18. CAN HUMAN RIGHTS BE WAIVED?

If human rights are unconditional, then it might seem that a person could not waive or properly neglect, much less refuse to exercise, such a right. One waives her rights when she chooses not to act upon or within it; in 1980, all but a handful of adults in the United States waived the right to run for public office, and nearly half of them waived the right to vote in the presidential election. Unlike the alienation of a right, waiving a right permits the right-holder to act on it at another time. Waiver is thus not another form of divestiture or relinquishment. It is also not a form of violation, or toleration in the face of violation, as when a land-owner does not protest a trespasser on his land.

Some philosophers have strongly denied that human rights can be waived, or, if they can be, that they ever ought to be. It has been claimed, for example, that to waive one's human rights would be to tolerate a suspension of "one's status as a person."[18] Let us concede that human rights are crucial to one's status as a person. If, however, you have (as the UN Declaration insists you do) a human right to emigrate, and yet you choose *not* to emigrate, then it seems that your choice should be regarded as a waiver of your human right.* Yet why, by this waiver, should you be said to have suspended or in any way jeopardized your status as a person? Of course, if the only human right you have (as H. L. A. Hart argued; recall §6) is the right to be free (and if this is not a portmanteau right, in the manner suggested in §10), then perhaps you *cannot* waive this right (for to do so would be to exercise it after all!); and if I could waive it I *would* alter my "status as a person." Thus it appears that much turns not on what a waiver of rights is, but on what our human rights are.

§19. HUMAN RIGHTS, GOVERNMENTS, AND OTHER PERSONS

Finally, whereas special rights are aimed at or addressed to specific persons (an employee's rights are aimed at or addressed to his employer, since it is the employer who can violate them), human rights are addressed to or aimed at *all* persons and especially at all governments. Unlike special rights, which not everyone can violate, a person's human rights are such that anyone could have one or more of these rights violated at any time by any or all of a large number of persons, and especially by one's own (local or national) government. Where whole groups or classes of persons are involved as victims of rights-violations, as they often are when human rights are violated,† it is not so much this or that individual human being who should be regarded as addressed by the claim of right. It is governments, especially the governments of the persons whose rights are being violated, and in particular the officials of those governments who are the persons in the best position to investigate and verify the violation, and (if anybody can) to remedy and prevent it in the future. They are the ones who, intentionally or negligently, have failed in their duties toward those whose rights are being violated.

IV

Scepticism over human rights flourishes for several reasons. One is that there is no standard or agreed-upon analysis of the concept of a human right. Another is that the standard current list of these rights in the UN Declaration is vulnerable to several troubling criticisms.‡ A third is that any theory of human rights confronts the

---

*Should I be said to have exercised my right to emigrate, after all, when I choose *not* to emigrate? It is true that in general if one has the right (but no duty) to do something, then one can "exercise the right" not to do it. Here, 'the right' refers to the right to *choose* what to do. But choosing not to emigrate is not a special form of choosing to emigrate, and for that reason is not a form of exercising the right to emigrate.

†This does not imply that groups, races, or nationalities have human rights as such. Human rights are a distinctly individuating concept, so that from the fact that a human right of every person in a definable (racial or national) group is being violated, it does not follow that any right of the group is being violated. This is not to deny that groups may have rights; but only to say that if they do, they are not individual rights, as human rights are.

‡Among them, these: (i) Some of the rights turn out to be duties, e.g., "elementary education shall be compulsory" (Article 26 (1)); (ii) some are virtual tautologies, e.g., "No one may be compelled to belong to an association" (Article 20 (2)); (iii) some of the rights are either frivolous if taken literally or must be trivialized if they are to be made universal, e.g., "everyone has the right to . . . periodic holidays with pay" (Article 24); (iv) some seem to be so insignificant that it is unclear why they are regarded as human rights at all, e.g., the right to

standard objections posed by moral relativism, subjectivism, and nihilism. It is not possible here to remove all these difficulties, but there are some that are worthy of review because of the way they shed light on several practical aspects of the idea of international human rights.

§20. HUMAN RIGHTS AS REVOLUTIONARY AND ANARCHIC

Two centuries ago, two leading English thinkers, Edmund Burke (1729–1797), one of Parliament's most reflective conservative members, and Bentham, the utilitarian law reformer, attacked, each in his own way, the French Declaration of the Rights of Man, on the ground that the very idea of "natural" rights of man was anarchic and revolutionary. As Burke put it, "abstract principles of natural right . . . were the most idle, because the most useless and the most dangerous to resort to. They superceded society, and broke asunder all those bonds which had formed the happiness of mankind for ages."[20] Bentham denounced the same Declaration in language even more alarming. Appeals to the natural rights of man, he claimed, do nothing but "sow the seeds of anarchy broad-cast . . . What, then, was their object in declaring the existence of imprescriptible rights . . . ? This and no other—to excite and keep up a spirit of resistance to all laws . . . "[21] As there is little or nothing peculiar to the language of the French Declaration, in contrast to other human rights manifestos, to warrant such objections—they are as applicable to the "natural" rights asserted by Locke and Jefferson—it behooves the defender of human rights to assess the merit of the Burke-Bentham criticism.

To some extent it must be conceded that appeals to human rights were and still are revolutionary in their intention. The aim has always been to revolutionize human relations, social, economic, and political, by bringing into play a new way to conceive of social justice, one founded not on class or racial divisions but on a recognition of equal rights. So much is evident to any reader of Tom Paine's epochal book, *The Rights of Man* (1791), or of Mary Wollstonecraft's less well known but nevertheless classic *Vindications of the Rights of Woman* (1792). Insofar as those with political or economic power do not acknowledge equal rights to the weak and the poor, there is no doubt that the appeal to human rights will appear, and will be, revolutionary in its ultimate intention. (The England of Burke and Bentham was, if anything, a model of a society riven by class antagonisms, unearned privileges, dismal prospects for vast numbers amid great prosperity and wealth for others.) The revolutionary potential for human rights in our day in many parts of the world is equally evident. But to describe the ultimate intention in this way is not to condemn it, unless it can be shown that *any* revolution in human affairs aimed to achieve a recognition under law of equal human rights is morally wrong. Whether any such argument could be sound may be safely doubted. So, this point must be granted to the Burkes and the Benthams, but not with the results they implied.

Whether, however, there is an anarchic—chaotic and destructive—effect of the appeal to human rights, as Burke and Bentham alleged, is far less clear. If it can be argued that the ideological foundation of the United States Constitution was expressed in the appeal in the Declaration of Independence to the "natural and unalienable rights of life, liberty, and pursuit of happiness," then the subsequent

copyright in Article 27 (2). It is even doubtful whether the General Assembly that proclaimed the UN Declaration understood what a human right is. On the one hand it described these rights as a "standard of achievement," which makes them more like "ideals, purposes or aspirations than . . . rights."[19] On the other hand it allowed that "the general welfare" (Article 29 (2)) may limit any or all of these rights, in which case human rights are incapable of serving as a protection for the individual against policies that would sacrifice him for the common good, public interest, or "general welfare."

relative stability of this nation for two centuries suggests there is nothing inherently anarchic about "natural" or human rights or in the attempt to found a stable government upon such a foundation.

§21. HUMAN RIGHTS AS A MODE OF CULTURAL IMPERIALISM

One of the chief objections in recent decades to the idea of human rights is that it is a culture-bound doctrine, so that its propagation elsewhere is just another form of Western imperialism, and an especially embarrassing one because of the moral pretensions essential to any doctrine of human rights. Sometimes this objection points to the peculiarly central role that European thinkers (Grotius, Hobbes, Locke, Rousseau, Kant) have had in the development of human rights doctrines. On other occasions, the focus is on the origins of the theory in Judeo-Christian religious and theological convictions that are not shared by Buddhists or Moslems. In yet other forms, this criticism emerges from Marxists, according to whom all doctrines of human rights are supposedly the products of existing bourgeoise society and incapable of transcending its limits. Several replies are in order to this complex objection.

First, we must distinguish between criticizing the *concept* of a human right, and criticizing any given *list* of human rights. Undoubtedly, lists of human rights reflect the socio-cultural consciousness of the societies that formulate them. It is hardly surprising that in four centuries of thought about human rights, what our rights are has undergone change. But the idea that human beings as such have rights—the central conception of any theory, doctrine, or list of human rights—is much less prone to revision; it could even be argued that this conception has undergone very little change in the centuries since it first gained prominence.

Second, we must distinguish between the *origins* of a doctrine or idea, including the theories and beliefs of those thinkers in whom the conception first was popularized, and the *merits* of the arguments that can be advanced on behalf of a doctrine embodying the idea. Of course the arguments advanced by Grotius, Locke, and others centuries ago connected their beliefs in God and liberal individualism with the human rights they defended. Anything else is unimaginable. But that does not imply that there are not other and better viewpoints from which to defend the same central notion.

Third, we must distinguish between the *claims* that human beings have human rights, especially when addressed to peoples and governments in those areas of the world where these rights seem to be ignored or violated, and the *methods* used at any given time by the friends of human rights to get them implemented (see also below, §23). The claims may well be true and significant, even if the methods are ineffective or too closely linked with unmistakable signs of genuine imperialism. In principle, there is as much and as little that is imperialistic about shared beliefs in human rights as there is in shared beliefs about vaccination, double-entry bookkeeping, and romanized alphabets.

Fourth, there is impressive evidence, and has been for several decades, of what might be called the human rights traditions in non-Western cultures. Most Westerners are unfamiliar with the literature in which these traditions are expressed. For example, Buddhist and Hindu advocates of human rights are not unknown, even if the prevailing socio-economic ideology of the typical Asian Buddhist or Hindu is not identical with that of the typical Western Christian or Jew.

Finally, even though it is true that Marx argued that the human rights of his day were nothing but "bourgeoise rights,"[22] and therefore were to be distrusted by workers and the proletariat, subsequent Marxist theory need not be interpreted as incompatible with the very conception of a human right. At least, any number of professing Marxist thinkers in recent decades have thought it possible to explain and defend human rights. Indeed, some have even gone so far as to imply that only their Marxist Socialism provides a basis for the socio-economic or welfare rights so prominent in all modern discussions of human rights. The fact that the U.S.S.R., for example, has a long record of human rights violations and of unwillingness to enforce the human rights privisions of the Helsinki Accord (1975) is more the fault of the Soviet government than of contemporary Marxist theory. One might also take a stronger line of reply, and argue that insofar as Marxist theory really is incompatible with any conception, list or doctrine, of human rights, then that is a mark against Marxism; it is not a defect in the idea of human rights.

§22. SOCIAL COSTS AND HUMAN RIGHTS

Perhaps the argument most frequently heard, if not in the United States, then in the "third world," where the need for human rights is the most acute and their violation chronic, is that the social and economic costs for human rights are too great to pay. Either, it is claimed, these societies can submit to the social discipline to make "a great leap forward" economically, from which all will benefit; or they can honor human rights, which will lead to dispersal of political power, and thus a reduced rate of economic development. The friends of human rights are thus challenged with the ultimate irony: Yield to the blandishments and protests of the ideology of human rights, and everyone will be worse off!

One cannot help but notice that this argument seems to rest primarily on a straightforward *empirical* claim. Those who advance this argument appear not to question the importance of human rights, much less the very concept. What they challenge is the actual feasibility, given the social realities of their own nation, of implementing human rights for all their peoples at the present time except at terrific cost to understandable material aspirations. It is largely a question of empirical economics whether such constraints in fact exist; perhaps they do and perhaps they don't. But it is not only economics that are at issue. One wants to know how much such an argument is influenced by tacit beliefs about the legitimacy of the current pattern of the distribution of wealth and of future transfers of wealth from the Haves in the society to the Have-nots. If it is believed that starving the poor and destroying labor unions are necessary conditions of achieving economic growth, then one must wonder who it is that is supposed to profit from the economic growth if and when it eventually takes place. Why should the poor, whether employed or not, be sacrificed by a national policy that projects economic growth only at their expense? Is everyone going to share in both the costs of rapid industrialization and in the eventual benefits, or not?

Thus, what begins as an apparently purely empirical question—is it necessary to ignore human rights in order to achieve a more rapid rate of economic growth?—turns out to involve deeper questions about social justice. The whole argument in fact may be a travesty because it really rests on nothing more than the selfishness of the well-off and their indifference to the welfare of their poorer countrymen. It is impossible to justify suppression or neglect of human rights, on the ground that it is the best thing to do, if all that this is supposed to accomplish is greater wealth for the classes who are already the most powerful and wealthy.

§23. HUMAN RIGHTS VIOLATIONS IN OTHER COUNTRIES

Finally, there is the argument that it is foolish and morally wrong for persons in one country to complain about alleged human rights violations in another country. Foolish, because the complainers are in no position to verify that such violations exist; and even if they can, the violations will not cease merely because international do-gooders complain of them. Morally wrong, because if the complaints go beyond protest to involve intervention to bring the violations to an end, that would be tantamount to letting the complainers make themselves the self-appointed guardians of human rights in other countries, when the truth is that they probably have less than a perfect record of honoring such rights at home. Criticisms in this vein during the late 1970s were more than once provoked by the way in which human rights concerns were introduced into foreign policy discussions during the administration of President Carter.

The verification of human rights violations (again, where the UN Declaration is taken as the point of reference for what these rights are) does pose problems, but they are not insuperable. Documentation of such violations is readily available, and is presented at frequent intervals, both by private organizations, such as Amnesty International, and also by the U.S. State Department in its reports (required by law) to the Congress. Of course, there may be disputed or borderline cases where allegations of human rights violations cannot be conclusively verified. But there is no reason why these cases should cause all protests to cease, for there are plenty of other cases where the evidence is quite clear that the offending government has made efforts to conceal the evidence of its own conduct in violating the rights of its citizens.

Whether violations of human rights in country A will cease because citizens of or government spokesmen in country B protest, is a complex empirical question. True, if such protests are rare and infrequent, or issued against a background of hypocritical or cynical denial of the same kind of rights-violations at home, their effect is likely to be slight. But if they are prominent and sustained, issued in concert by several nations against the offenders, and if the rights-violations that are protested against are grievous and manifest, then there is evidence that such protests can have useful effect. Even if no such effect was achieved yesterday, perhaps it will be tomorrow. Failure in these matters is no more a reason to cease preventive and remedial efforts than it is anywhere else in human affairs.

As for the argument concerning intervention, it is basically misconceived. First, it is very easy in many cases for country B to go beyond mere protest of human rights violations in country A without acting in any way that qualifies as "intervention in the domestic affairs of another nation." It can withdraw its ambassadors, impound country A's assets in its banks, withhold payments of debts to country A, request the UN to send an inspection team to country A, and so forth. Second, nation A cannot plead immunity or impunity to attempts by nation B to bring to an end human rights violations in A against A's own citizens. No government obtains the right to torture or starve persons merely by confining these crimes to its own citizens, any more than parents have the right to beat their own children or a husband to abuse his wife—just so long as the violence is kept within the family. Whether armed intervention, or the threat thereof, by one nation into the affairs of another would in fact prove to be an effective way to stop human rights violations is, it must be admitted, very doubtful. Too often aggressive nations have attempted to mask their invasions of a neighbor on this pretext (Germany did it when it invaded Poland in 1939, and the U.S.S.R. did it when it invaded Afghanistan in 1980). The issue, then, is not the right to intervene, but the effectiveness and the costs of doing so. To judge by the unblemished record of nations to refuse to intervene on this ground (except, as noted above, when it can serve as a pretext for disreputable ambitions), there is little reason to worry over foolhardy misadventures of this sort. If anything, it is the silence and apparent indifference of most nations to the violations of human rights by their neighbors, allies, and trading partners that should give all persons pause.

Notes

1. H. L. A. Hart, "Are There Any Natural Rights?", *The Philosophical Review*, 64 (1955), pp. 175–192, at p. 183.
2. Richard Wasserstrom, "Rights, Human Rights, and Racial Discrimination," *The Journal of Philosophy*, 61 (1964), pp. 628–640, at p. 636.
3. For the text of the covenants, see Ian Brownlie, ed., *Basic Documents on Human Rights*, Oxford, Clarendon Press, 1971, or Walter Laqueur and Barry Rubin, eds., *The Human Rights Reader*, New York, New American Library, 1979.
4. Hart, *op. cit.*, p. 175.
5. A. I. Melden, *Rights and Persons*, Berkeley and Los Angeles, University of California Press, 1977, p. 166.
6. Ronald Dworkin, *Taking Rights Seriously*, Cambridge, Mass., Harvard University Press, 1977, p. 180.
7. Charles Fried, *Right and Wrong*, Cambridge, Mass., Harvard University Press, 1978, p. 110.
8. Richard P. Claude, ed., *Comparative Human Rights*, Baltimore and London, The Johns Hopkins University Press, 1976, pp. 41f.
9. A. Delafield Smith, *The Right to Life*, Chapel Hill, N.C., University of North Carolina Press, 1955, p. 12.
10. See H. A. Bedau, "The Right to Life," *The Monist*, 52 (1968), pp. 550–572, at p. 550f.
11. Hart, *op. cit.*, p. 179.
12. Jeremy Bentham, "Anarchical Fallacies," excerpted in A. I. Melden, ed., *Human Rights*, Belmont, California, Wadsworth Publishing Co., 1970, pp. 28–39, at p. 36.
13. Quoted in David Lyons, "Rights, Claimants, and Beneficiaries," *American Philosophical Quarterly*, 6 (1969), pp. 173–185, at p. 173.
14. Henry Shue, *Basic Rights: Subsistence, Affluence, and U.S. Foreign Policy*, Princeton, N.J., Princeton University Press, 1980, p. 52.
15. William Blackstone, *Commentaries on the Laws of England*, I (1765), p. 129.
16. Bentham, *op. cit.*, p. 34.
17. Melden, *op. cit.*, p. 200.
18. *Ibid.*, p. 167.
19. Christopher R. Hill, ed., *Rights and Wrongs; Some Essays on Human Rights*, Baltimore, Penguin Books, 1969, p. 24.
20. Quoted in Peter J. Stanlis, *Edmund Burke and the Natural Law*, Ann Arbor, Michigan, The University of Michigan Press, 1958, pp. 129f.
21. Bentham, *op. cit.*, pp. 31, 32f.
22. Karl Marx, "Critique of the Gotha Program," in Lewis S. Feuer, ed., *Basic Writings on Politics and Philosophy: Karl Marx and Friedrich Engels*, Garden City, N.Y., Doubleday & Co., 1959, pp. 112–132, at p. 118.

Suggested Readings

§1   For the early history of human rights, see Richard Tuck, *Natural Rights Theories: Their Origin and Development*, Cambridge University Press, 1979. Human rights, it has been said, is the older doctrine of "natural" rights minus its metaethics; see A. I. Melden and W. K. Frankena, "Symposium: The Concept of Universal Human Rights," in *Science, Language, and Human Rights*, Philadelphia, University of Pennsylvania Press, 1952, pp. 167–207, at p. 193.

§6   On the Declaration of Independence, see Morton White, *The Philosophy of the American Revolution*, New York, Oxford University Press, 1978, especially chapters 4–6. On the Bill of Rights, see Richard L. Perry and John C. Cooper, eds., *Sources of Our Liberties*, New York, American Bar Foundation 1959; on the U.N. Declaration, see U.N.E.S.C.O., ed., *Human Rights*, New York, Columbia University Press, 1949, and Maurice Cranston, *What Are Human Rights?* New York, Taplinger Co., 1973.

§8–9   The idea of types of human rights and their importance has been discussed from various perspectives by H. A. Bedau, Charles R. Beitz, Thomas M. Scanlon and Henry Shue, in their essays in Peter G. Brown and Douglas MacLean, eds., *Human Rights and U.S. Foreign Policy*, Lexington, Mass., Lexington Books, 1979.

§10   On the right to life, see H. A. Bedau, "The Right to Life," *The Monist*, 52 (1968), pp. 550–572, and George P. Fletcher, "The Right to Life," *The Monist* 63 (1980), pp. 135–155.

§11   On the correlation of rights and duties, see David Braybrooke, "The Firm But Untidy Correlativity of Rights and Obligations," *Canadian Journal of Philosophy*, 1 (1972), pp. 351–363.

§12   For a general survey of the recent literature on rights and human rights, see Rex Martin and James W. Nickel, "Recent Work on the Concept of Rights," *American Philosophical Quarterly*, 17 (1980), pp. 165–180; and J. Roland Pennock, "Rights, Natural Rights, and Human Rights—A General View," in J. R. Pennock and J. W. Chapman, eds., *Human Rights: Nomos XXIII*, New York, N.Y. University Press, 1981, pp. 1–28.

§14   On the right to life of the fetus, and the conflict of rights between a human fetus and its pregnant mother, see Judith Jarvis Thomson, "A Defense of Abortion," *Philosophy and Public Affairs*, 1 (1971), pp. 47–66. On animals, see Tom Regan and Peter Singer, eds., *Animal Rights and Human Obligations*, Englewood Cliffs, N.J., Prentice-Hall, 1976.

§15   For the views of Jacques Maritain, see his *The Rights of Man and Natural Law*, London, Geoffrey Bles, 1944.

§16   The best discussion of the idea of "inalienable" rights is in White, *op. cit.*, pp. 195–213.

§17   For a defense of several "absolute" human rights, see John Finnis, *Natural Law and Natural Rights*, Oxford, Clarendon Press, 1980, pp. 223–226. A good criticism of the doctrine of forfeiture is to be found in Fletcher, *op. cit.*

§20   On socialist conceptions of human rights, see Maria Hirszowicz, "The Marxist Approach," *International Social Science Journal*, 17 (1966), pp. 11–21; and Istvan Kovacs et al., *Socialist Concept of Human Rights*, Budapest, Akademiai Kaido, 1966. For non-western sources of human rights, see U.N.E.S.C.O., *op. cit.*, Robert M. MacIver, ed., *Great Expressions of Human Rights*, New York, Harper Bros., 1950; Jeanne Hersch, ed., *Birthright of Man*, New York, UNIPUB Inc., 1969; and Romila Thapar, "The Hindu and Buddhist Traditions," *International Social Science Journal*, 18 (1966), pp. 31–40.

§§21–22   On various practical and foreign policy aspects of international human rights, see Brown and MacLean, *op. cit.*; Henry Shue, *Basic Rights: Subsistence, Affluence, and U.S. Foreign Policy*, Princeton, N.J., Princeton University Press, 1980; and Donald P. Kommers and Gilburt D. Loescher, eds., *Human Rights and American Foreign Policy*, Notre Dame, Indiana, University of Notre Dame Press, 1979. On the actual status of human rights in various countries currently allied with the United States, see the series of documents published by the Committee on International Relations, U.S. House of Representatives, e.g., "Human Rights Conditions in Selected Countries and the U.S. Response," 95th Congress, 2nd Session, July 25, 1978.

About the Authors

DONALD VANDEVEER is a native of Baltimore, Maryland. He received a Ph.D. in philosophy from the University of Chicago in 1968 and taught at the University of Illinois (Urbana) in 1969. Since then he has taught at North Carolina State University, where he is currently Professor of Philosophy. His published essays are in the fields of moral and political philosophy, and biomedical ethics. With the support of a grant from the National Endowment for the Humanities he is currently writing a book on paternalism.

JOSEPH MARGOLIS is at present Professor of Philosophy, Temple University. He has taught widely in the United States and Canada for the past thirty years. He has authored more than a dozen volumes, including *Psychotherapy and Morality* (1966), *Values and Conduct* (1971), *Negativities. The Limits of Life* (1975). His most recent books are *Persons and Minds* (1978) and *Art and Philosophy* (1980).

LOUIS I. KATZNER was born and raised in Baltimore, Maryland. He graduated from Brown University and received his Ph.D. from the University of Michigan. He has published a number of articles on reverse discrimination, the ethics of biomedical research and the theory of justice. He has also developed the unique Master of Arts Program in Applied Philosophy at Bowling Green State University.

STEPHEN P. STICH is a native of New York City. A graduate of the University of Pennsylvania, he received his Ph.D. from Princeton University in 1968. He taught for a dozen years at the University of Michigan in Ann Arbor, and is currently a member of the Department of Philosophy and the Committee on the History and Philosophy of Science at the University of Maryland. He is editor of *Innate Ideas* and *The Recombinant DNA Debate*.

RICHARD ROUTLEY, originally from New Zealand, but a person without a country, is a somewhat itinerant philosopher who is paid for pursuing his intellectual interests by the Australian National University. He has published well over a hundred papers mainly on nonclassical logics and semantics, on metaphysics, and on environmental philosophy and environmental topics. Recent books include *Exploring Meinong's Jungle and Beyond* and *Environmental Philosophy*. He is strongly interested, in a way that integrates theory and practice, in environmental problems and social alternatives. It may be of interest to the readers of the essay on nuclear power to note that Richard and Val Routley live in a home without electricity.

VAL ROUTLEY finds that a good deal of her time is taken up with the practical activities of a rural subsistence lifestyle (working on buildings, growing food, looking after animals, and so on). She is also an active environmentalist, having worked mainly on the issues of nuclear power and of Australian forestry. She is (co-) author of *The Fight for the Forests* (3 editions, ANU) and of papers on environmental subjects and in most areas of philosophy, including environmental philosophy.

MARY ANNE WARREN received her Ph.D. from U.C. Berkeley in 1975, and currently teaches philosophy at San Francisco State. She has published articles on abortion, affirmative action, the feminist concept of androgyny, and other topics, and an encyclopedia, *The Nature of Woman* (Edgepress, 1980).

DALE JAMIESON was born in Iowa in 1947. He grew up in California and was educated mainly at San Francisco State University and the University of North Carolina, spending some time at the Universities of California and London as well. Since 1980 he has taught at the University of Colorado where he is associated with the Center for the Study of Values and Social Policy. He is the editor of *Philosophy Looks at Film,* and co-editor of *Art: Now.*

TOM REGAN is Professor of Philosophy at North Carolina State University, where he has twice been named Outstanding Teacher and, in 1977, was named Alumni Distinguished Professor. Born and raised in Pittsburgh, Pennsylvania, he received his undergraduate training in philosophy at Thiel College and was awarded an M.A. and Ph.D. in philosophy from the University of Virginia. He is the author of *Understanding Philosophy,* co-editor (with Peter Singer) of *Animal Rights and Human Obligations,* and editor of *Matters of Life and Death.* A collection of his lectures and essays *(All That Dwell Therein: Essays on Animal Rights and Environmental Ethics)* has just been published.

LAWRENCE C. BECKER was born in Lincoln, Nebraska, in 1939. He graduated from Midland College, received his Ph.D. from the University of Chicago, and has done post-doctroal study at Oxford and Harvard. Since 1965, he has taught at Hollins College, where he is professor of philosophy. He is the author of *On Justifying Moral Judgments* (1973), and *Property Rights: Philosophic Foundations* (1977).

DAN W. BROCK was born in Mineola, New York in 1937. He graduated in economics from Cornell University, and received his Ph.D. in philosophy from Columbia University in 1970. He joined the Brown University philosophy department in 1969, where he is now Professor of Philosophy, and has been a Visiting Professor at the University of Michigan. He is serving as the Staff Philosopher on the President's Commission for the Study of Ethical Problems in Medicine and Biomedical and Behavioral Research during the 1981-82 academic year.

DAVID A. J. RICHARDS was born in East Orange, New Jersey, in 1944. He received his undergraduate degree from Harvard College, his law degree from Harvard Law School, and his doctorate of philosophy from Oxford University. He has practiced law in New York and taught philosophy as visiting associate professor of philosophy at Barnard College, Columbia University, and is currently professor of law at New York University, where he teaches constitutional law, criminal law, and jurisprudence. His publications include *A Theory of Reasons for Action* (1971) and *The Moral Criticism of Law* (1977).

KAI NIELSEN, born in 1926, is Professor of Philosophy at the University of Calgary. He has taught at Hamilton College, Amherst College, The State University of New York at Binghamton, Rhodes University, The University of Ottawa, The Graduate Center of the City University of New York, Brooklyn College and New York University. In 1981-1982 he will be Visiting Senior Scholar at the Hastings Center. Dr. Nielsen is an editor of *The Canadian Journal of Philosophy.* He has written *Reason and Practice* (1971), *Contemporary Critiques of Religion* (1971), *Ethics Without God* (1973) and *Scepticism* (1973).

HUGO ADAM BEDAU was born in Portland, Oregon, in 1926. He served two years in the Naval Reserve (1944-1946) and graduated summa cum laude from the University of Redlands in 1949. His Ph.D. is from Harvard University (1961) and he has taught at Dartmouth College, Princeton University, and Reed College. Since 1966, he has been at Tufts University, where he is now Austin Fletcher Professor of Philosophy. He is the author of *The Courts, The Constitution, and Capital Punishment,* editor of *Justice and Equality* and *Civil Disobedience,* and coauthor, with Edwin Schur, of *Victimless Crimes.*